Ultimate Azure AI Services for Gen AI Solutions

Build Advanced Gen AI Solutions with Azure OpenAI, LangChain and Vector Databases to Enhance Efficiency, and Revolutionize Enterprise Operations

Shanthababu Pandian

www.orangeava.com

First Published: May 2025

Published By: Orange Education Pvt Ltd, AVA®

Address: 9, Daryaganj, Delhi, 110002, India

275 New North Road Islington Suite 1314 London,
N1 7AA, United Kingdom

ISBN (PBK): 978-93-48107-46-6
ISBN (E-BOOK): 978-93-48107-31-2

Scan the QR code to explore our entire catalogue

www.orangeava.com

Dedicated To

My Beloved Grandma:

Late Smt. Sornammal Subramanian

About the Author

With over 23 years of IT experience, Shanthababu Pandian is a seasoned tech executive specializing in data science, generative AI, machine learning, and artificial intelligence. He holds three master's degrees (M.Tech, MBA, and M.S.), a bachelor's degree in Electronics and Communication Engineering, a postgraduate degree in AI & ML from the University of Texas, and a certification in Data Science from IIT Guwahati. He is currently pursuing a PhD in AI at Anna University, Chennai.

Shanthababu has extensive experience in data engineering, analytics, and developing AI-driven solutions. He has successfully delivered projects for clients in the healthcare, financial, and retail sectors across the US and the UK. He is a master at implementing governance frameworks into place, directing agile, cross-functional teams, and creating AI-powered products.

He is a well-known thought leader who has presented more than 50 national and international lectures and authored more than 100 books and articles. He has also reviewed more than 75 technical publications in the areas of programming, data, artificial intelligence, and the cloud. He continues to motivate the next generation of AI and data specialists by serving as a mentor and counselor to IT institutions.

About the Technical Reviewers

S.Ponmalar is an academician with over 25 years of field and domain experience in Information and Communication Engineering, specializing in areas such as optical communication, Networks, Machine Learning, and Computer vision. She has obtained her Doctoral degree in Information and Communcation Engineering from Anna University and is a recognized supervisor, guiding many PG and PhD scholars. She has published over 30 research papers in many reputed Journals and Conferences. Her interest in upgrading with recent trends and technology has obligated her to read and review articles and books from various publishers.

Tanay Agrawal is a seasoned Deep Learning Researcher with over eight years of experience in AI and machine learning, having made significant contributions across multiple startups. He began his journey by working on an AutoML platform at MateLabs, enabling efficient and accessible machine learning model creation. Tanay then joined Curl HG, where he played a pivotal role in building SARA, an advanced Information Extraction Engine for energy trading sector. Following the company's acquisition, he transitioned to Xplorazzi as an AI Researcher, focusing on retail technology, including automated checkout kiosks and retail surveillance solutions.

As the author of the book *Hyperparameter Optimization in Machine Learning*, Tanay has shared his expertise through talks at esteemed conferences such as PyData London, PyData Delhi, and PyCon India.

In his entrepreneurial journey, Tanay co-founded TryonLabs.ai, where he developed a diffusion-based virtual try-on technology for garments. This technology, once open-sourced, has since become a foundational model that is widely adopted in the industry. Under his leadership, TryonLabs delivered AI-driven solutions to over 120 D2C fashion brands globally.

Currently, Tanay serves as the CTO of Videoit, a company he co-founded to transform the e-commerce experience for D2C brands. Videoit is building a suite of AI applications to bridge the gap between ad clicks and conversions. Tanay continues to innovate at the intersection of AI, retail, and consumer technology, driving an impact on a global scale.

Preface

The rapid evolution of **Generative AI (Gen AI)** is transforming industries, redefining how we interact with technology, and opening new possibilities for innovation. This book is a comprehensive guide tailored for learners at all levels–whether you are a beginner eager to explore Gen AI, a professional seeking to upskill, or an expert looking to enhance existing ML systems. By focusing on **Azure OpenAI Services**, **Azure AI technologies**, and practical implementation, this resource equips readers with the tools and knowledge to navigate the dynamic landscape of AI-driven solutions.

The content bridges theoretical understanding and real-world application, diving deep into **Large Language Models (LLMs)**, **vector databases**, **embedding techniques**, and **prompt engineering**. Special emphasis has been placed on the Azure ecosystem, covering essential components such as **Azure Storage**, **Search Services**, **OpenAI Studio**, and **Prompt Flow**. Each chapter is designed to provide hands-on insights into building scalable, cost-effective, and responsible AI solutions using **Python programming** and **Azure tools**. Whether you are developing AI models, optimizing data systems, or implementing cutting-edge applications, this book ensures a seamless learning experience.

This book aims to inspire confidence and creativity in applying Gen AI concepts across industries by including real-world examples, detailed workflows, and actionable strategies. You will embark on the fascinating world of Generative AI and Azure, unlocking the potential to transform ideas into impactful solutions.

Chapter 1. Introduction to Generative AI: This chapter explores the evolution of AI with a focus on transformer architectures, distinguishing Generative AI (Gen AI) from classical AI and ML. It examines the core characteristics of Gen AI, including its ability to transform text, images, and videos, and explains why generative models are referred to as Large Language Models (LLMs). The chapter discusses the theories behind these models, such as neural networks and training methodologies, highlighting how they produce human-like content. Practical examples, including code snippets, are provided to deepen understanding. The chapter concludes by addressing the ethical considerations and security challenges of Gen AI, emphasizing its importance and applications across industries.

Chapter 2. Exploring LLMs and Its Capabilities: This chapter explores the foundations of Large Language Models (LLMs), focusing on their key components and functionality. It delves into embedding layers, transformer blocks, multi-head self-attention mechanisms, feed-forward neural networks, positional encoding, and decoders. The chapter also explains output layers, loss functions, attention masks, and fine-tuning layers, unravelling how these elements work together. Finally, it highlights the critical role of fine-tuning in optimizing LLMs for specific tasks.

Chapter 3. Vector Database and Embedding Techniques: This chapter explores the mechanisms of vector databases, including indexing, querying, and so on. It provides an analogy to simplify their concepts, and delves into underlying theories, similarity measures, and working mechanisms. The chapter also covers categories of vector databases, the concept of serverless vector databases, and popular options such as Pinecone, Faiss, and Chroma. Practical steps with code examples are included for working with Pinecone and Faiss, providing hands-on insights into their functionality.

Chapter 4. Prompt Engineering and Its Significance: This chapter delves into prompt engineering, its significance in Generative AI, and the components and categories of prompts. It explores techniques such as N-shot prompting, Chain-of-Thought (CoT) prompting, Directional Stimulus Prompting (DSP), React prompting, and Multimodal CoT prompting. The chapter covers how to craft, evaluate, refine, and scale prompts for optimal model performance. Practical examples include Q&A, text summarization, chatbot responses, and document classification. Additionally, it provides the best practices and guidelines for crafting effective prompts to build strategic AI models.

Chapter 5. Azure Storage for Azure OpenAI Implementations: This chapter explores Azure Storage and Integration strategies and Azure Search Services for enhancing Azure OpenAI implementations. It discusses how Azure Blob Storage and Azure Data Lake Storage (ADLS) support unstructured data storage, enabling seamless access for AI applications' training, inference, and processing tasks. The chapter also examines scalable, secure, and high-availability storage solutions, along with architectural designs and best practices for Azure OpenAI integration. Strategies to improve data retrieval, storage efficiency, and search functionality are also covered.

Chapter 6. Azure AI Search Services for Azure OpenAI Implementations: This chapter explores Azure AI Search Services, highlighting their significance and core components, including indexes, indexers, and data sources. It provides a detailed guide on implementing Azure Search and building solutions using these services. The chapter examines mechanisms for indexing and organizing data stored in Azure Storage, emphasizing scalability and performance for handling large data volumes and user queries. Best practices for ensuring fast, responsive search experiences in AI applications are also covered.

Chapter 7. Getting Started with Generative AI Using Azure OpenAI Services: This chapter provides an in-depth overview of Azure OpenAI Services and their practical applications. It explores Azure OpenAI Studio, including the Playground, Chat, and Assistant features, and guides you through setting up prompts, configuration parameters, and data integration. The chapter covers the OpenAI deployment process, building and fine-tuning models, and leveraging endpoints for custom solutions. It also delves into Azure OpenAI integration with LangChain, content moderation, version handling, and deployment scalability. Additionally, you will learn to build AI apps using public and private data, deploy web applications, and integrate AI solutions with MS Teams and other tools.

Chapter 8. Advanced Azure AI Studio–I: This chapter introduces Azure AI Studio as a transformative platform for Generative AI development, empowering developers to build, test, and deploy AI solutions confidently. It explores models, capabilities, responsible AI practices, and prompt orchestration through features such as prompt flow. The chapter highlights how Azure AI Studio enables the creation of custom AI products, integration of pre-built services, and tools for prompt evaluation. It also addresses content safety, privacy, security, and compliance, equipping developers with ethical and responsible AI practices to navigate the complexities of Generative AI effectively.

Chapter 9. Advanced Azure AI Studio–II: This chapter explores Azure AI Speech, Language, and Vision Studios, showcasing their capabilities for easily creating custom projects and models. It covers both no-code and code-based approaches using client libraries and REST APIs. You will learn to utilize Speech Studio for text-to-speech solutions and Language Studio for processing textual data. The chapter also delves into Azure AI Vision, offering innovative features such as image analysis, text extraction via OCR, and facial recognition. Focusing on responsible AI practices, it demonstrates how to integrate vision capabilities into applications without requiring machine learning expertise.

Chapter 10. Generative AI Use Cases for Industries–I: This chapter explores the diverse use cases of Generative AI across industries and its transformative impact on business development, user benefits, and quality of life. It highlights AI's role in healthcare, including medical report analysis, drug discovery, personalized medicine, and patient care. Applications in finance, such as fraud detection, financial forecasting, and customer service, are examined, along with its use in entertainment for generating music, art, and virtual influencers. The chapter also delves into Industry 4.0 applications in manufacturing, precision agriculture, and food processing. Finally, it discusses ethical considerations, security challenges, and the broader implications of Generative AI in these fields.

Chapter 11. Gen AI Implementation Use Case with Azure OpenAI–II: This chapter explores how Azure OpenAI solutions drive business growth and innovation across industries. It highlights applications in telehealth, analyzing call center data to improve patient experiences, and manufacturing, where it automates processes and predicts equipment failures. In banking and financial services, Azure OpenAI enhances advisor support, while in education, it streamlines workflows and supports learning implementations. The chapter showcases how these solutions elevate operational efficiency and provide strategic advantages for businesses.

Get a Free eBook

We hope you are enjoying your recently purchased book! Your feedback is incredibly valuable to us, and to all other readers looking for great books.

If you found this book helpful or enjoyable, we would truly appreciate it, if you could take a moment to leave a short review with a 5 star rating on Amazon. It helps us grow, and lets other readers discover our books.

As a thank you, we would love to send you a free digital copy of this book, and a **30%** discount code on your next cart value on our official websites:

www.orangeava.com

www.orangeava.in (For Indian Subcontinent)

☑ **Here's how:**

Leave a review for the book on Amazon.

Take a screenshot of your review, and send an email to **info@orangeava.com** (it can be just the confirmation screen).

Once, we receive your screenshot, we will send you the digital file, within 24 hours.

Thank you so much for your support – it means a lot to us!

Downloading the code bundles and colored images

Please follow the links or scan the QR codes to download the ***Code Bundles and Images*** of the book:

https://github.com/ava-orange-education/Ultimate-Azure-AI-Services-for-Gen-AI-Solutions

The code bundles and images of the book are also hosted on ***https://rebrand.ly/e17824***

In case there's an update to the code, it will be updated on the existing GitHub repository.

Errata

We take immense pride in our work at **Orange Education Pvt Ltd,** and follow best practices to ensure the accuracy of our content to provide an indulging reading experience to our subscribers. Our readers are our mirrors, and we use their inputs to reflect and improve upon human errors, if any, that may have occurred during the publishing processes involved. To let us maintain the quality and help us reach out to any readers who might be having difficulties due to any unforeseen errors, please write to us at :

errata@orangeava.com

Your support, suggestions, and feedback are highly appreciated.

DID YOU KNOW

Did you know that Orange Education Pvt Ltd offers eBook versions of every book published, with PDF and ePub files available? You can upgrade to the eBook version at **www.orangeava.com** and as a print book customer, you are entitled to a discount on the eBook copy. Get in touch with us at: **info@orangeava.com** for more details.

At **www.orangeava.com**, you can also read a collection of free technical articles, sign up for a range of free newsletters, and receive exclusive discounts and offers on Print Books and eBooks.

PIRACY

If you come across any illegal copies of our works in any form on the internet, we would be grateful if you would provide us with the location address or website name. Please contact us at **info@orangeava.com** with a link to the material.

ARE YOU INTERESTED IN AUTHORING WITH US?

If there is a topic that you have expertise in, and you are interested in either writing or contributing to a book, please write to us at **business@orangeava.com**. We are on a journey to help developers and tech professionals to gain insights on the present technological advancements and innovations happening across the globe and build a community that believes Knowledge is best acquired by sharing and learning with others. Please reach out to us to learn what our audience demands and how you can be part of this educational reform. We also welcome ideas from tech experts and help them build learning and development content for their domains.

REVIEWS

Please leave a review. Once you have read and used this book, why not leave a review on the site that you purchased it from? Potential readers can then see and use your unbiased opinion to make purchase decisions. We at Orange Education would love to know what you think about our products, and our authors can learn from your feedback. Thank you!

For more information about Orange Education, please visit **www.orangeava.com**.

Table of Contents

CHAPTER 1
Introduction to Generative AI

Introduction

This chapter will discuss Generative AI and the evolution of Artificial Intelligence (AI) as well as transformer architecture backgrounds. It will then discuss how Gen AI differs from classical AI and ML. The core of Generative AI and its characteristics transformed text, images, and video processing using Gen AI. We should remember that not all Gen AI models are Large Language Models (LLMs), but all LLMs are a type of Gen AI. Moreover, LLMs specifically refine how we generate and interact with the given textual data. The theories and rules behind these models and how they relate to neural networks, training approaches and text generation are equivalent to human-like content. Why do industries require Gen AI, and what are the significant benefits along with Gen AI ethics and high-level security aspects of this technology?

Structure

In this chapter, we will discuss the following topics:

- Introduction to Generative AI
- Evolution of Gen AI
- Generative AI and its Characteristics
- Gen AI Transformer Architecture
- How Gen AI Differs from Classical AI and ML
- How Industries Get Benefits out of Generative AI
- Gen AI Ethics and High-Level Security

Introduction to Generative AI

In recent years, Generative AI has become the buzzword in this busy world. Every industry and every commoner talks about AI in all forms. In this book, Generative AI, or, shortly, Gen AI, will be discussed at a very detailed level, and experiments will be conducted to build the Gen AI application using various tools and technologies.

Definition of Gen AI – A simple one-line answer is as follows:

"The application will generate new information for you from your input."

We cannot treat all this information as simple and take it lightly. It is compelling and insightful and provides solutions for various problem statements and decision-making purposes for numerous industries' specific challenges in multiple aspects. This is the main reason all industries are focusing on building their own Gen AI tools and integrating multiple AI tools to accomplish their needs and necessities.

It does not matter what input format you use; simultaneously, you can generate your desired output format. We will discuss the input and output type and format in detail in the upcoming chapters and how technologies are helping to achieve this. *Figure 1.1* shows the simple block diagram of the Gen AI System.

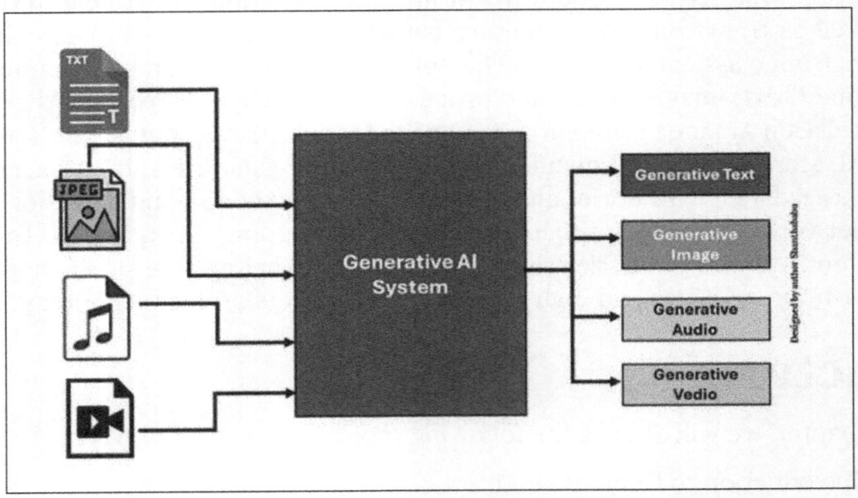

Figure 1.1: *Simple Block Diagram of Gen AI*

Technically, we can define Gen AI as a branch of "*Artificial Intelligence*" that involves using specific algorithms and larger models to create new and original content from input. This category can generate content that is not replicated or copied from the original input data and shares the relevant characteristics. Undoubtedly, the end product is entirely new and relevant to business aspects.

Characteristics of Gen AI Involving LLMs:

The characteristics of Gen AI involving LLMs are as follows:

- Gen AI has non-deterministic outputs and creates new and original content based on the business point of view.

- This involves a complex training mechanism to generate synthetic data for various business perspectives.
- It consists of the massive number of Neural Networks involved internally to generate accurate data for analysis.
- It adds more creative elements to generate precise content to attain the expectations.
- Ultimately, it helps to generate additional training data to support unbalanced situations.

Benefits of LLMs:

- We can build very creative and innovative products for business solutions.
- We can enhance the customer experience journey from past collections of data to strengthen customer bonding.
- We can construct high-time and cost-effective products from vast quantities of data.
- We can customize the products to be highly scalable to achieve the results.
- We can ease the process of data analysis with less effort by using tools and technologies.
- We can also automate the task behind the screen with practical solutions, and reduce manual interventions.

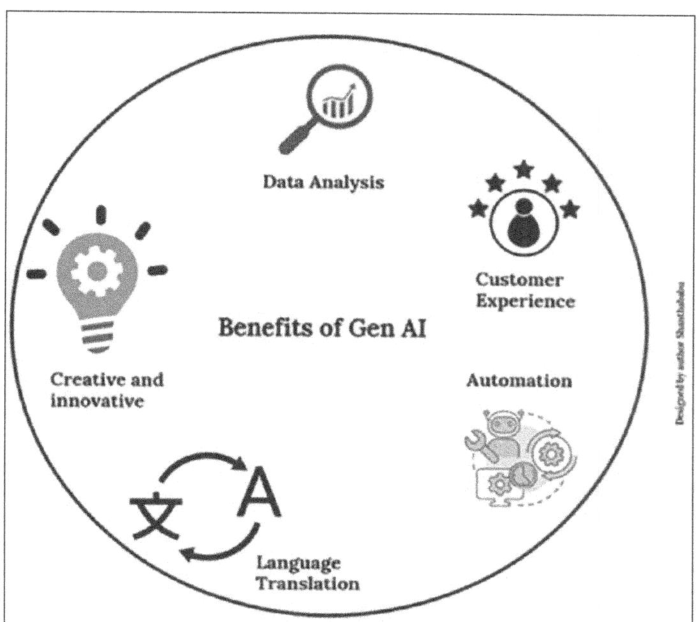

Figure 1.2: *Benefits of Gen AI*

Evolution of Gen AI

The popularity of Gen AI has been around for decades, but its actual breakthrough in the industry is subsequent to the introduction of ChatGPT in the market. The main objective is to generate the content, whether text, image, audio, or video. Gen AI is an exceptionally revolutionary technology that brings abundant benefits to businesses irrespective of any domain.

The Evolution of Gen AI started in the 1950s and has had a long journey with significant milestones.

1952–Love Letter: British computer scientist Christopher Strachey built a software program to generate Love Letter text. It was considered one of the earliest examples of creativity and natural language generated by TEXT.

1965-66–First Chatbot: During 1965-66, Joseph Weizenbaum, a computer scientist at the MIT Artificial Intelligence Laboratory, built the first chatbot application. It was called ELIZA. It was designed to simulate a discussion with a Rogerian psychotherapist using the concepts behind pattern-matching approaches and scripted-based responses.

This chatbot is a pioneer for pre-programmed responses based on those inputs. It paves the way for natural language processing, human-computer interaction, future chatbots, and conversational agent developments.

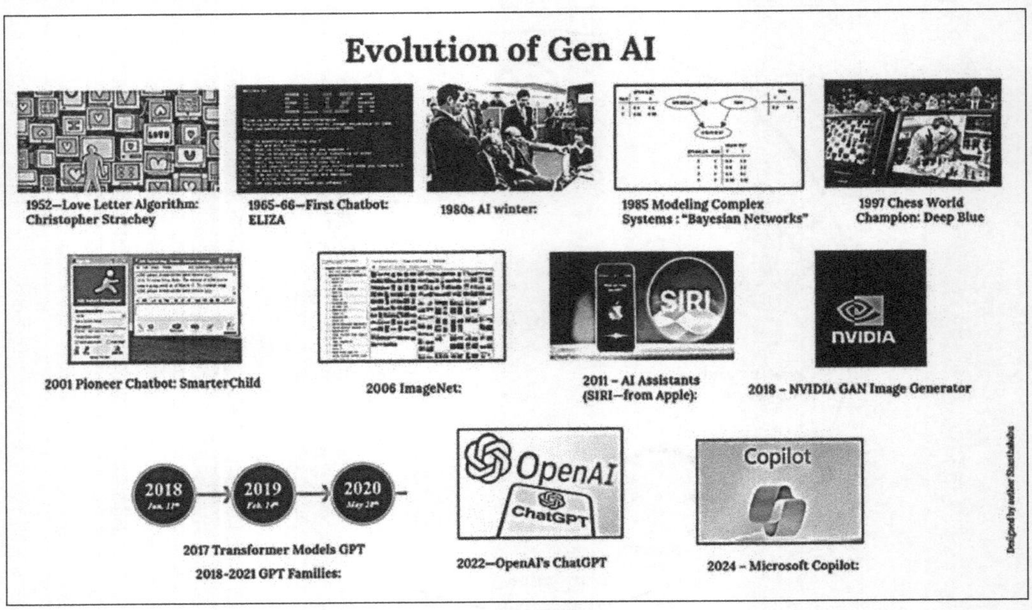

Figure 1.3: *Evolution of Gen AI*

1980s AI Winter: In AI history, there was a slowdown in this technology during the 1980s. During this period, action was taken to reduce funding and interest in AI research and development, and typically, in other fields, hype, disappointment, and critique occurred in the AI domain, resulting in funding cuts. However, work continued in the area of neural networks.

1985 Modeling Complex Systems: During this period, Judea Pearl, a computational scientist and a great philosopher, introduced typical mathematical-based ***"Bayesian Networks"*** that seeded for the complex system modeling in the Generative AI era.

1997 Chess World Champion: The famous IBM chess computer "Deep Blue" defeated the chess world champion Garry Kasparov. This is the best evidence of AI's decision-making strategy and the event that unlocks the potential of Generative AI.

2001 Pioneer Chatbot: In 2001, Active Buddy developed the "**SmarterChild**" chatbot version of the Generative AI application and launched it on AOL's (American Online) Instant Messaging (AIM) platform. One of the pioneering CHATBOTS extensively used by most consumers, the product was designed to provide information regarding entertainment and services to major AIM users.

2006 ImageNet: Dr. Fei-Fei Li at Stanford University invented the "ImageNet" product, which utilizes a larger volume of visual databases to train the computer vision algorithm for object detection and recognition, which involves a more significant contribution of Deep Learning and AI.

2011 – AI Assistants (SIRI–from Apple): In 2011, Apple introduced the AI Assistants (SIRI). It revolutionized voice-based assistance and was the first product that came into public hands as a highly convenient and practical device for houses. It supports various aspects of assistance, such as Boss meeting reminders, voice recognition communication, and integrating and controlling other devices based on the command.

2017 Transformer Models: Open AI organization released a Generative Pre-Trained Transformer (GPT-1) language model that helps to generate the text based on the given input prompt.

2018 – NVIDIA GAN Image Generator: The breakthrough of NVIDIA's AI image generator is a landmark in the AI art creation environment. It introduces the StyleGAN architecture, which can generate highly creative, realistic, customizable images based on needs. Due of its compact size, training time, and excellent operation, all these abilities are set to transform the way we use Generative AI.

2018-2021 GPT Families: During this period, the extension of transmission models (GTP-3 and 4) expanded further along with the massive parameters inputs and generated creative human-like text and images at different levels and incomparable height of the technology expansion in AI space.

2022–OpenAI's ChatGPT: After the introduction of ChatGPT, Gen AI utilization increased enormously since its capabilities include unlivable content creation, precise answers, and more interaction with humans. Nowadays, everyone has an account in ChatGPT.

2024 – Microsoft Copilot: As we know, Microsoft is always unique in technology adoption, no exception in this Gen AI; they introduced the Copilot by integrating ChatGPT with Microsoft 365, which is a significant milestone and brings excellent features for many business use cases. This is a major release from Microsoft's Azure OpenAI Studio with unique features to build highly intelligent tools and technologies for many industries' innovative solutions. Indeed, we are going to cover most of them in this book.

Note:

Evolution of Gen AI

1952–*Love Letter: Christopher Strachey, a British Computer Scientist.*

1965-66–*First Chatbot: During 1965-66, Joseph Weizenbaum, a computer scientist, built the first chatbot application.*

1980s- AI *winter: In AI history, there was a slowdown in AI technology.*

1985- *Modeling Complex Systems: During this period, Judea Pearl, a computational scientist, and great philosopher, introduced typical mathematical-based systems.*

1997- *Chess World Champion: The famous IBM chess computer "Deep Blue" defeated the chess world champion Garry Kasparov.*

2001- *Pioneer Chatbot: In 2001, Active Buddy developed the "SmarterChild" chatbot version on AOL's (American Online) Instant Messaging (AIM) platform.*

2006- *ImageNet: Dr. Fei-Fei Li at Stanford University invented the "ImageNet" product, a computer vision algorithm for object detection and recognition.*

2011– AI Assistants (SIRI–*from Apple*)*: In 2011, Apple introduced the AI Assistants (SIRI).*

2017-22- *Transformer Models: GPT Families and OpenAI's ChatGPT.*

2024– *Microsoft Copilot: As we know, Microsoft is always unique in technology adoption.*

Gen AI - Transformer Architecture

Transformer Architecture Overview:

One of the Generative AI models is the **Transformer-Based Model**, which primarily adopts neural network techniques and natural language processing methodologies, such as text generation, sentiment analysis, question-and-answer, text summarization, and language translation.

In simple terms, the transformer architecture works as a Football team in which the players have the connection and thought process of passing the ball from one side of the court to the target to hit the ball inside the goalpost. This is a very high collaborative effort incurred process.

Since these transformer models are built from the deep neural network-based mathematical model, their structure and function replicate the human brain system, which consists of multiple layers of neurons. So, each neuron can receive various input data, perform a powerful mathematical computation internally with the data, and process the influential output.

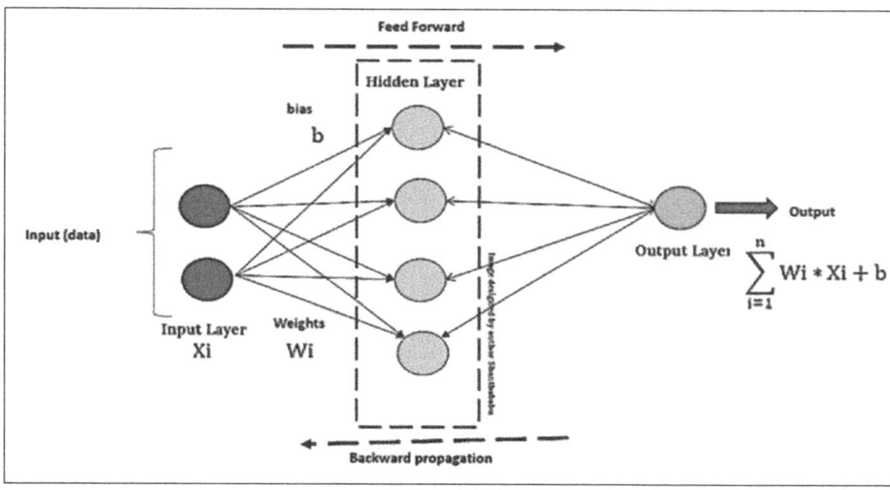

***Figure 1.4**: Neural Network*

The transformer model is highly capable of generating high-quality text in various contexts based on the demand and requirements. This model uses a **SELF-ATTENTION MECHANISM,** a distinctive feature that captures long-range dependencies and is more effective than traditional Deep Learning and NLP models.

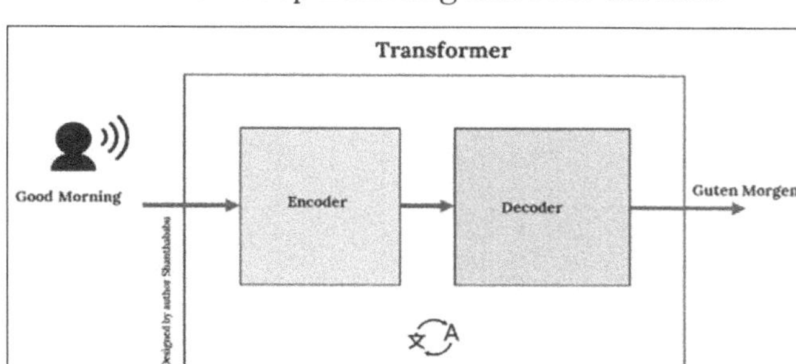

***Figure 1.5**: Simple Language Translation Transformer Representation*

Components of Transformer Architecture

Let us discuss the components of Transformer Architecture:

At a very high level, this architecture uses two major pilers: **Encoder** and **Decoder.**

- **ENCODER:** It takes the input feed, extracts context, and then the meanings from the data, which it passes onto the decoder.
- **DECODER:** It is responsible for converting the input into several sequences from the encoder's feed. These embeddings are processed by the SELF-ATTENTION technique. The decoder's architecture is similar to the encoder and produces the generative output.
- **SELF-ATTENTION:** Self-attention is an important process stage. In this stage, it captures the significance of each word and the relationships between them. This is typically how humans experience understanding what verbs, nouns, and adjectives are. Nouns are when we speak and write and the thought process of how each word relates to every other word in a sentence.

The rest of the components are Input and Output.

- **INPUT:** This is just an input for the system.
- **OUTPUT:** The output is the sequence generated by the transformer.

Let us think big. *Figure* 1.6 shows the Transformer Architecture (Universal Picture). There is nothing new we cannot add here.

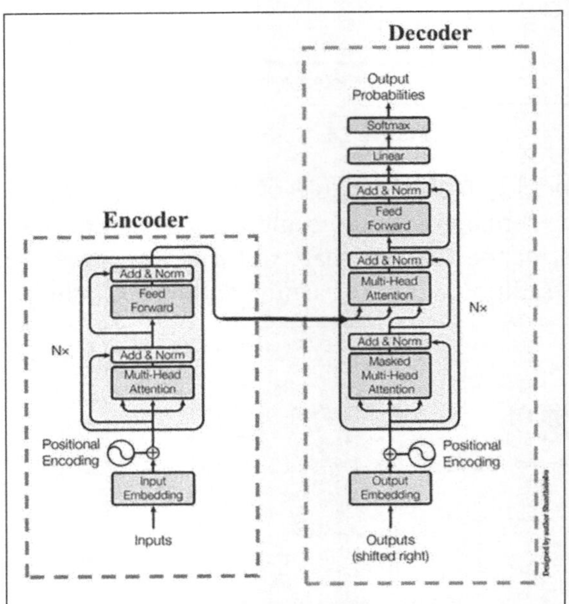

***Figure 1.6**: Transformer Architecture (Universal Picture)*

As we understood from the earlier explanation, the "***Transformer Architecture***" follows an **ENCODER-DECODER** structure and does not depend on the model, such as the Recurrence and Convolutions, to generate an output.

The left part is **ENCODER,** and the right part is **DECODER.**

ENCODER

The Encoder consists of N identical layers. Each layer contains a MULTI-HEAD ATTENTION LAYER and a FEED FORWARD NEURAL NETWORK as a fully connected set of blocks. The output of each layer is used as an input to the subsequent layer with the same dimensionality. The block count depends on the value of x. If x=8, there are N8 blocks and layers inside the encoder at the left part of the encoder.

As per the mechanism, the **ENCODER** maps a set of inputs as sequences, and continuous inputs are representations. They undergo the Nx block and layer with x times the "Addition and Normalization" process, which is then fed into a DECODER; refer to *Figure 1.6*.

Before getting into the encoder, let us understand what **Input Embedding** and **Positional Encoding** are.

Even the AI system cannot understand the word(s) directly, so we have to convert them into numbers prior to feeding them into the system; the mechanism of this conversion should be implemented in sensible ways to build an input sequence into the system.

This process is called **Input-Embedding**, the first component in the encoder's block. You will see it in *Figure 1.6*, in which the input is transformed into sensible numbers, constructed in multidimensional vector space, and fed into Multi-Head Attention (MHA) later than positioning them with the help of the positional encoding process. Let us discuss the following steps:

Step 1: We have to organize the input sentence into a comma-separated list of the words.

Step 2: Add two additional tokens to indicate the start and end of the sentence.

Step 3: Follow the vocabulary list, and have to map each vocabulary with a unique number; this is the so-called indexing.

Step 4: As per the standards, we have to normalize all these words as **One Hot Encoding** to build the high-dimensional vector base. The process of converting each word into these high-dimensional vectors is called **Input Embedding** or **Token Embedding**.

Step 5: The Transformer works differently from LSTM, where the input is fed into the system parallelly. This means the order of the sentence might be lost. Technically, adding additional information of the same dimension as the input vector to represent the sequence of the words in the sentence, which is called **Positional Encoding**.

So, finally, the combination of input embedding and positional encoding vectors will be fed into Multi-Head Attention (MHA).

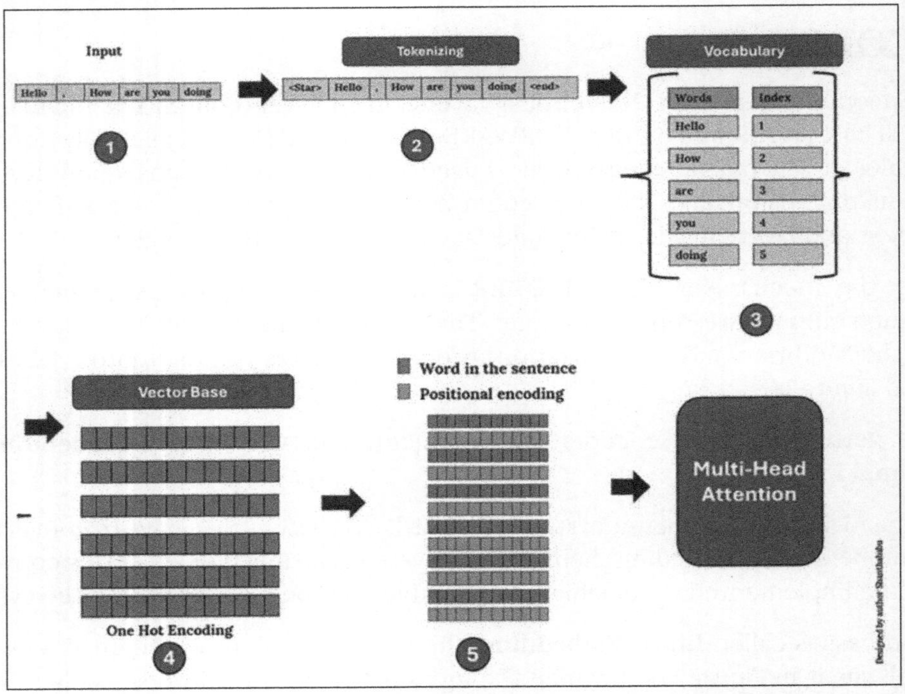

***Figure 1.7**: Input and Positional Embedding in Transformer Architecture*

The Positional Encoding Layer is a Matrix, because: The positional encoding scheme in transformer architecture has each position versus index mapped to a vector. Therefore, the output of the positional encoding layer is a matrix.

Let us do a little deep dive into the **Single and Multi-Head Attention layers.**

As we can see, the attention layers are in the encoder and decoder, which are part of the transformer architecture.

Stage 1: Tokenization and Embeddings: This is the pre-stage in the attrition layer building; at this stage, the given input text has been tokenized, and the embedding of each word in the input query, as shown in *Figure* 1.8.

Stage 2: Vectorization: In this stage of the attention layer, which consists of three neural networks, each word produces three output vectors, such as Queries, Keys, and Values. This process takes place for each word in the given input query.

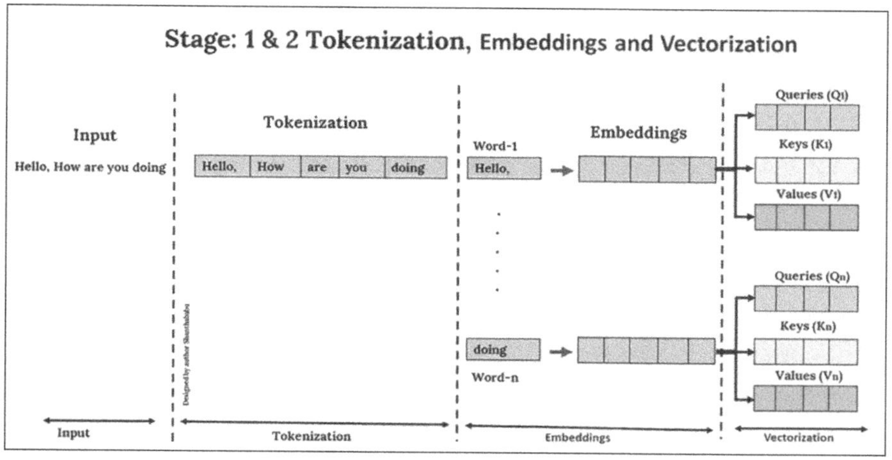

Figure 1.8: *Stage 1 and 2 Attention - Tokenization, Embeddings, and Vectorization*

Stage 3: Calculating the Word's Score: In this stage, the score of each word is calculated by multiplying Q and K. The process starts with the dot product of the first word's Vector Query (Q) and all the Vectors of K of the input.

This process will confirm the similarity measure of each product of Q and K.

The exercises will start the dot product between the first word of the query (Q1) and all keys (K1...Kn) in the input sentence, which are used to produce the scores.

If the Q and K vectors are aligned and have meaningful values, their dot product will produce a significant value as an outcome.

If the Q and K vectors are close to orthogonal, then the result of the dot-product will approach zero.

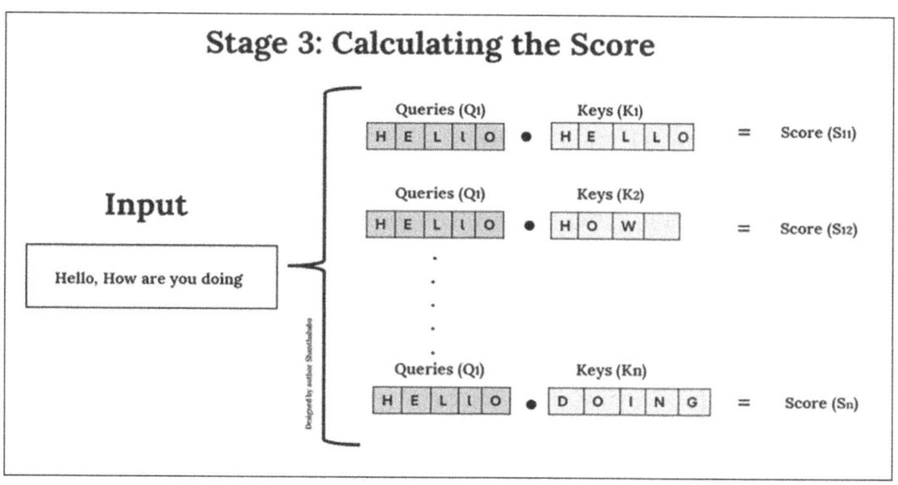

Figure 1.9: *Stage 3: Attention – Calculating the Score*

Stage 4: Calculating Scaled Value Vectors: In this stage, the Values (V) are scaled up using the scores derived from Stage 3. The resulting scaled value vectors are summarized as a final step, building the attention vector for each word from the input.

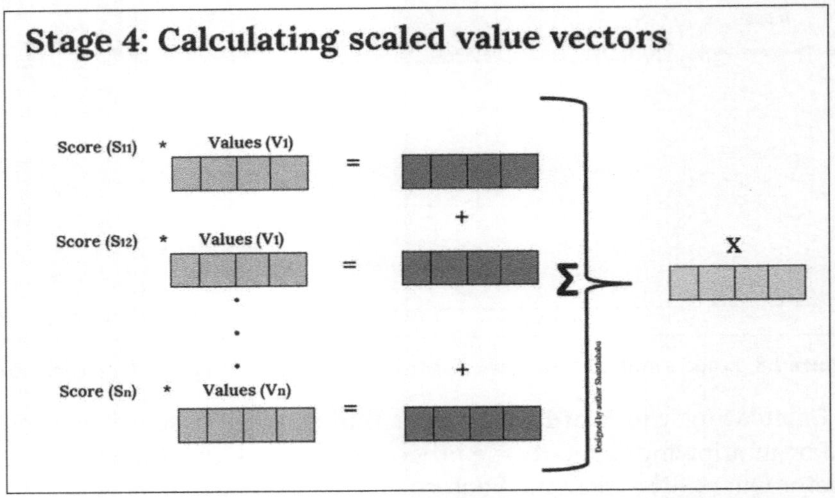

Figure 1.10: *Stage 4: Attention – Calculating Scaled Value Vectors*

This X vector is the attention vector for Query 1. We have to do this exercise for every query for the given input and build Xn vectors; the resulting vectors are the attention layer's outputs.

Each resulting vector, Xn, depends on the Query (Qn) for that word and also depends on the Keys (Kn) and Values (Vn) of all the words in the input text. The overall outcome makes the attention powerful in the form of sequential tasks and able to embed it into the context of the entire input representation.

So far, we have discussed the Single-Head Attention (SHA) layer. Let us get in touch with the Multi-Head Attention (MHA) layer. This is an expansion of **SHA** that allows faster computation.

As we know, in Single-Head Attention, the embedding vectors for each word are 512 dimensional. In Multi-Head Attention, the **Query, Key,** and **Value** vectors are equally split into **8 Heads**, which means **Q** and **K** have **64-dimensional vectors**. Finally, this will be multiplied by **V (8 heads),** and the attention layer will be applied to each head using the same method we explored in SHA. Then, each head is concatenated together to form (64*6=512) 512-dimensional attention vectors as the resulting attention vectors, as shown in *Figure 1.11*:

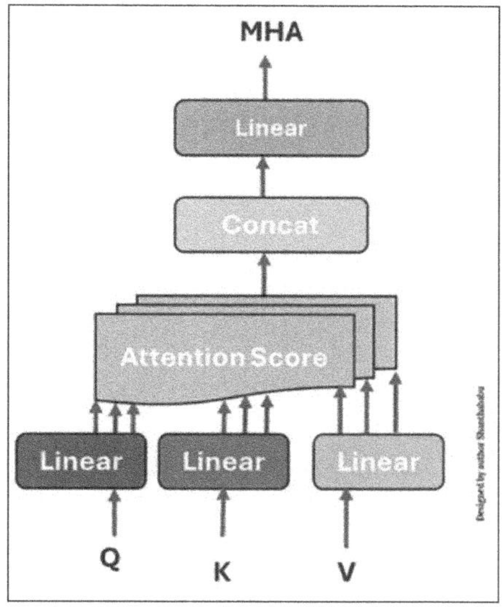

***Figure 1.11**: Attention* – MHA

The encoder represents encodings and produces embeddings from each query using the attention mechanism; the decoder works in the other route and generates the output text. Let us discuss this quickly.

DECODER

The **DECODER part** receives the encoder's output succeeding a set of processes we discussed. Functionally, the decoder is similar to the encoder. It also consists of a stack of Nx layers x=6; the architecture has six matching layers, each composed of three sets of sublayers. The sublayers are classified as follows for better understanding:

- Decoder Self-Attention
- Encoder-Decoder Attention
- Position-wise Feed-Forward Networks

These sublayers employ a residual connection around them, followed by layer normalization.

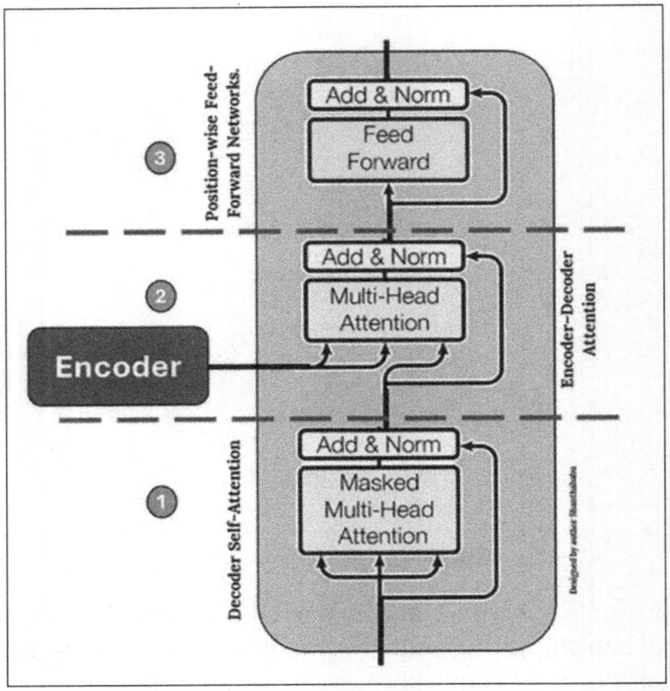

Figure 1.12: *DECODER and its Layers*

Decoder Self-Attention (First Sublayer):

This decoder self-attention is the first sublayer that receives the preceding output of the decoder, enriches the output with the positional information, and implements Multi-Head Self-Attention (MHA/MHSA) over it by introducing suppressing the matrix mask over the values produced by the matrices scaled multiplication.

As we discussed earlier, the encoder is designed to handle all words in the input sequence despite their position in the input order. Still, the decoder is designed to attend only to the previous words. This is the main difference between an encoder and a decoder.

Hence, the prediction for a word at position depends on the words previous to the input sequence. Please refer to *Figure* 1.12 – indicated by 1.

Encoder-Decoder Attention (Second Sublayer):

This encoder-decoder attention is the second sublayer that receives multi-head mechanism input/queries from the decoder side from the previous decoder's output (the first sublayer's output) along with the keys(K) and values(V) from the encoder's output (the left side of the architecture diagram). This layer is also MHA. In this layer, the decoder attends to all the words in the input sequence concerning the MHSA mechanism, similar to layer one in the encoder.

Please refer to *Figure 1.12* – indicated by 2.

Position-wise Feed-Forward Networks (Third Sublayer):

This position-wise feed-forward network layer is the third and final layer in the decoder. It is similar to the one implemented in the second sublayer of the encoder. Along with the three sub-layers, the decoder has residual connections, followed by a normalization layer. Please refer to *Figure 1.12* – indicated by 3.

Linear and Softmax Layer:

This layer sits outside the encoder and decoder blocks and is the final layer in this architecture. The output vector from the decoder undergoes a linear transformation in this layer. There, the output changes the dimension of the vector size 512 into the size of the vocabulary. The Softmax layer further converts the vector into ~10,000 probabilities. Basically, the Softmax function is used to create a probability distribution that reveals the likelihood of each token in the sequence.

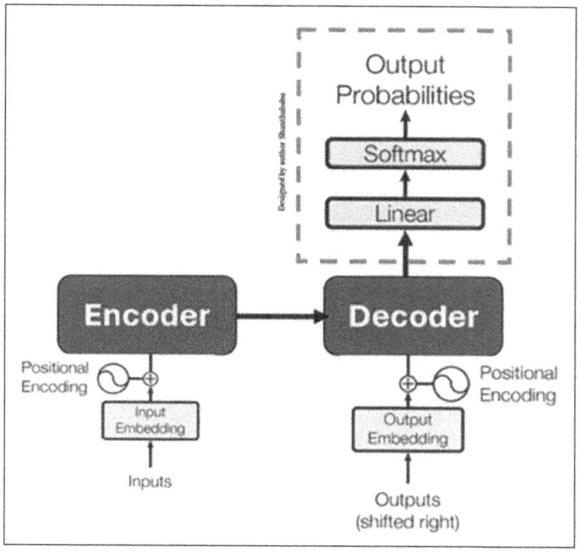

Figure 1.13: *Linear and Softmax Layer*

Note: *Transformers have a simple architecture consisting of an encoder and a decoder. In the encoder, the model first takes the input text and translates it as vectors, which use attention. The decoder works in the opposite direction and goes from the vectorized transformation into the sentence of the entire word. The output could be in any language.*

The concept of self-attention is essential in this transformer's architecture. Self-attention captures the input of a sentence and understands the meaning of each word and the relationships between them. This process is very similar to the human understanding of verbs and nouns, how adjectives relate to nouns, and how words are associated with every other word in the input sentence.

Gen AI versus Classical AIML

AIML is a collection of technologies under one roof, such as Data Science, Machine Learning, Deep Learning, NLP, and Computer Vision. All these technologies utilize a specific dataset and format depending on the technology used. The output includes numeric text, images, and video. The output is mainly statistical-based, but in the case of Gen AI, it is completely independent of the input format, outputs a hundred percent new data, and is highly creative.

Machine Learning (ML)

As we know, **"Machine learning"** is a subset of artificial intelligence that uses various algorithms to analyze the data, insights of the data taken for analyses, and make predictions as well as informed decisions based on the nature of the data.

ML has the following algorithms and is designed to learn and improve from training datasets, using relevant statistical techniques to identify patterns, insights, and relationships between them.

- **Supervised Learning:**
    - **Regression**
        - Linear Regression
        - Decision Tree Regression
        - Random Forest
        - KNN Model
        - Support Vector Machines (SVMs)
    - **Classification**
        - Logistic Regression
        - Naive Bayes Classifier
        - Decision Tree
        - Random Forests
        - Support Vector Machines
        - K-Nearest Neighbor
        - K-Means Clustering
- **Unsupervised Learning:**
    - **Clustering**
        - K-Means Clustering
        - K-Nearest Neighbor (KNN)

- Hierarchal Clustering
- Anomaly Detection
- Neural Networks
- Principle Component Analysis (PCA)
- Apriori Algorithm

We are not going to explore each algorithm in the following list since it is out of the scope of this book, but we will undoubtedly discuss Gen AI and ML's futures, benefits, pros, and cons.

Certainly, ML can continue updating and improving its capability to make accurate predictions and classification problems. As the volume of data grows and large datasets slow down, the difficulty of handling ML solutions increases. ML algorithms are difficult to train, time-consuming, and expensive.

Challenges with Interpretability:

ML Deep learning algorithms are incredibly complex in certain scenarios that are complex and challenging to interpret. This lack of clarity can prevent businesses from understanding how to make decisions and challenge them to build trust in ML systems. This is critical in the healthcare, banking, and finance industries, where decisions are high risk.

Costs and Resources Incurred:

It requires significant investment in technology, infrastructure, data acquisition, cleaning, preparation costs, and specialized and expert development and training.

Data Quality:

The accuracy and reliability of the ML model depends on data quality. The data should be complete and balanced for accurate predictions and decisions. Otherwise, this would require high maintenance costs and effort for data cleansing, validation, and monitoring.

Data Security and Privacy:

Data collection raises data security and privacy concerns. Businesses are responsible for ensuring that this challenge is handled sensibly by the customer data. Incidents such as data breaches and unauthorized access to customer-sensitive information are significant drawbacks of ML implementation.

Generative AI

Generative AI, or Gen AI in short, is a branch of AI that uses specifics to generate new content that mimics the data fed and trained on. The fundamental concept of Gen AI is to learn patterns and relationships in a given data (structured and unstructured) to create exclusively new text, summary, images, audio, and video as responses based on the underlying patterns in the input data.

As we understood from our earlier topics, the mechanics of Gen AI are powered by neural networks. These networks help analyze data to discover patterns and generate new, highly creative, and innovative content based on our requirements. This Gen AI technology utilizes several learning methods during training, including semi-supervised learning and unsupervised techniques.

Two major Gen AI models are available: **Generative Adversarial Networks (GANs)** and **Transformers**.

GANs are best at creating visual and multimedia data. Transformer-based models, such as GPT and its family, specialize in generating text. They can understand the context of available public and private data. On the other hand, ML always relies on ML-specific algorithms. They allow the processing of large volumes of data collected from various sources based on the use cases, followed by learning the patterns and classification from the data and what is trained on.

Because of intelligence techniques such as Generative Adversarial Networks (GANs), Variational Autoencoders (VAEs), and Transformers, GenAI has become a possible solution provided space and enables models to develop rich thoughtful large datasets and produce extraordinary and genuine synthetic content based on the business needs. It opens up endless possibilities for several industries.

Multiple Gen AI tools are available and ready for business purposes.

Let us discuss the commonly available Gen AI tools. They have various powerful features and have emerged for different purposes in several industries.

- **ChatGPT:** ChatGPT is an extensive language model chatbot developed by OpenAI. It is predominantly used for natural language understanding and generating text, summaries, images, and more, mainly for tasks such as customized chatbot tools, content creation, and language translation. It largely depends on the use cases.
- **Gemini/Google Bard:** Gemini, formerly known as Bard, is a Gen AI chatbot developed by Google. This tool can also understand human language and simulate a conversation with users. It analyzes a user request and then works to identify the input's intention. Initially, it was an experimental AI chatbot tool. It is designed for research, report generation, educational material creation, and writing coding tasks.
- **Copilot/Bing Chat:** This is a Microsoft product formerly called Bing. You can ask any complex questions, and you can get comprehensive answers as well as summarized information. It is also a conversational AI language model focusing on information retrieval, task automation, and content creation.

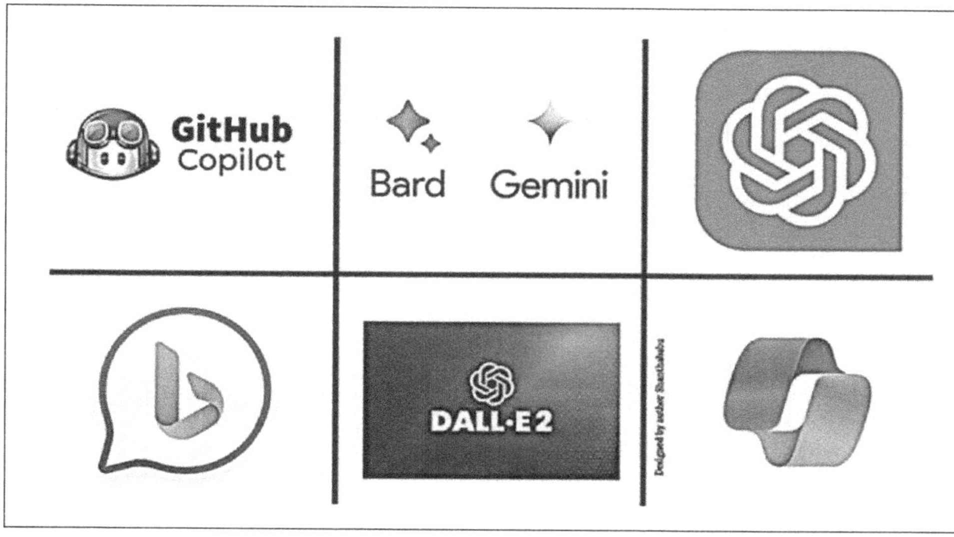

***Figure 1.14**: Leading Gen AI Tools in the Market*

- **GitHub Copilot:** GitHub Copilot differs from the earlier mentioned tools and is a specialized tool for code completion developed using **GitHub** and **OpenAI** technology. Its primary objective is to assist users in autocompleting code for multiple IDEs, such as Visual Studio Code, Visual Studio, JetBrains, and more. Ultimately, it helps the developer with code assistance, enhancing code writing efficiency, reducing errors, and learning new programming languages.
- **DALL-E 2:** DALL-E 2 is a recent advanced state-of-the-art AI tool for creative image generation on the OpenAI platform. It is more potent than DALL-E. Using neural network techniques, it can produce exceptionally realistic and comprehensive pictures based on textual description as input. It can generate many more images for specific inputs and edit the existing images with additional parameters.

The former-discussed AI tools help to reshape operations and consumer interactions across many industries, and many more advanced AI tools are evolving based on different use cases based on business demands irrespective of domains,

Let us deep dive into Gen AI and compare ML now:

Learning Experience (Gen AI and ML):

Gen AI models learn from data distribution and targeting to generate new data (text, summary, images, audio, and video) that recalls the input training data. The models are obtained and extracted from the input data, and new, innovative, creative instances are created from what they have learned.

In contrast, ML models are focused on learning patterns and classifications, followed by making predictions or classifications based on input data. Basically, this is focused on finding relationships and correlations within the data to make accurate predictions and patterns based on the requirements.

Data Usage/Utilization (Gen AI and ML):

Gen AI models typically require a large amount of data that accurately reflects the underlying data distribution. Without any questions, if we have more varied data, the model can capture the complexity and diversity of the actual data and produce the output. On the other hand, ML can also work with less data, which might lead to accuracy.

In both cases, insufficient or biased data can lead to poor generalization and generate unrealistic outputs. So, the dataset has to stratify the demand to produce the expected output.

Scope of Output (Gen AI and ML):

The critical distinction between ML and Gen AI lies in generating output capability. Gen AI models can create new data, such as text, summary, images, audio, and video, that are unconventional and resemble the outlines and styles they have learned from the input data. At the same time, ML algorithms make predictions or classifications based on available data in the given dataset.

In some situations, Gen AI can produce unrealistic or unreasonable outputs due to its confidence in learned patterns and the nature of the model; this is called "Hallucinations." However, it can be controlled using techniques we will learn later in this book.

ML algorithms, on the other hand, are more focused on making precise predictions and classifications based on datasets.

Gen AI's Drawbacks

Of course, every technology and methodology has disadvantages. We will explore some of Gen AI's key drawbacks, including:

- **Amount of Data:** One major disadvantage of Gen AI is the requirement for large amounts of data, which, too, compromises quality. Otherwise, the generated outputs may be deprived of stability and semantic meaning, making them inappropriate for targeted tasks.
- **Data Quality:** Of course, data quality is a critical factor in AIML and Gen AI; there is no question about this. The impact will be reflected during the Gen AI training stage, even though extensive datasets will be needed to learn the pattern and build the solution.
- **Lack of Accuracy:** Gen AI models usually struggle with maintaining consistency,

accuracy, and semantic coherence in their outputs. This limitation makes Gen AI less suitable for tasks that expect precise output and adherence to rules in the following domains: document generation in legal, financial, real estate, and research.

Because of the nature of Gen AI, it overcomes the drawbacks discussed in ML earlier.

Let us understand the key differences between ML and Gen AI:

Factors/Parameters	**ML**	**Gen AI**
Core	Learn from data	Learn from data
Objective	Focused on data analysis to find patterns and make accurate predictions and classifications.	Focused on creating new data (text, summary, images, audio, and video) extracted from the input data.
Techniques Applied to the Data	Depending on the use case and whether it is supervised or unsupervised.	Gen AI mainly uses techniques such as GANs, VAEs, and Transformers, which involve twofold learning. • How to review the data • How to Generate the data
Model Outputs	Predictions, classifications, and inferences based on the use case and nature of the data learned relationships.	It generates completely new resources based on the requirements, such as text, summary, images, audio, and video.
Performance Metrics	Based on the model, predictive accuracy metrics such as: • MSE, RMSE, R-squared • Confusion matrix • ROC curve and AUC score • Cross-validation	Realism • Coherence • Diversity

***Table 1.1**: ML versus Gen AI*

Foundation Models

With respect to Gen AI, many open-source "FOUNDATION MODELS" are available in the market, including large-scale, adaptable AI models, which can reshape your enterprise AI scope and bring huge business benefits. At the same time, there are risks and factors such as biases and security impacts.

These foundation models will form the basis of generative AI's future across the enterprise. The current buzzword around Gen AI is that **Large Language models (LLMs)** fall into this foundation model category.

The foundation models work with multiple data types, such as semi-structured, structured, and unstructured data. Because of this, businesses can make new associations across data types and increase the range of tasks that AI can use to provide solutions.

Large Language Model (LLM)

An LLM is an advanced generative artificial intelligence algorithm that applies typical neural network techniques with many parameters to process the desired output. It can understand any human language and any input text format.

LLMs are highly efficient in capturing complex entity relationships in the given input.

LLMs are capable of generating text using syntactics and semantics of the data from any language.

Ultimately, it helps to build conversational AI applications such as RAG, Text, Summary, Chat-bots, Image generation, Building coding, and so on.

Top LLMs are:

- GPT-4
- LLAMA 2
- ChatGPT
- FALCON
- Mistral 7B

In the former list, the GPT (Generative Pre-trained Transformer) is the most potent and popular LLM model; it has its own history, as we discussed in the earlier topic of this chapter (Evolution of Gen AI 2018-2021 GPT Families).

- 2018 GPT-1 – 117 million parameters and 985 million words
- 2019 GPT-2 – 1.5 billion parameters
- 2020 GPT-3 – 15 billion parameters. Chat GPT is also based on this model
- 2023 GPT-4 – Trillions of parameters

Many use cases influence Gen AI. Let us discuss a few common use cases here:

- **Text Generation:** Generally, this use case is used to generate stories and scripts in the form of text-based content that could be utilized in research, official, and social media perspectives.
- **Question Answering (Q and A Chatbot):** This use case has a higher potential than others. It helps to generate the most relevant answer(s) based on input

questions to help any size of organization, institution, and government clarify, explore, or understand the vast document collection for various initiatives.

- **Text Summarization**: In most scenarios, the organization, institution, or government entity needs a concise summary of a massive volume of documents to help explain a policy or process document based on the demand. Data would be available in public or private.

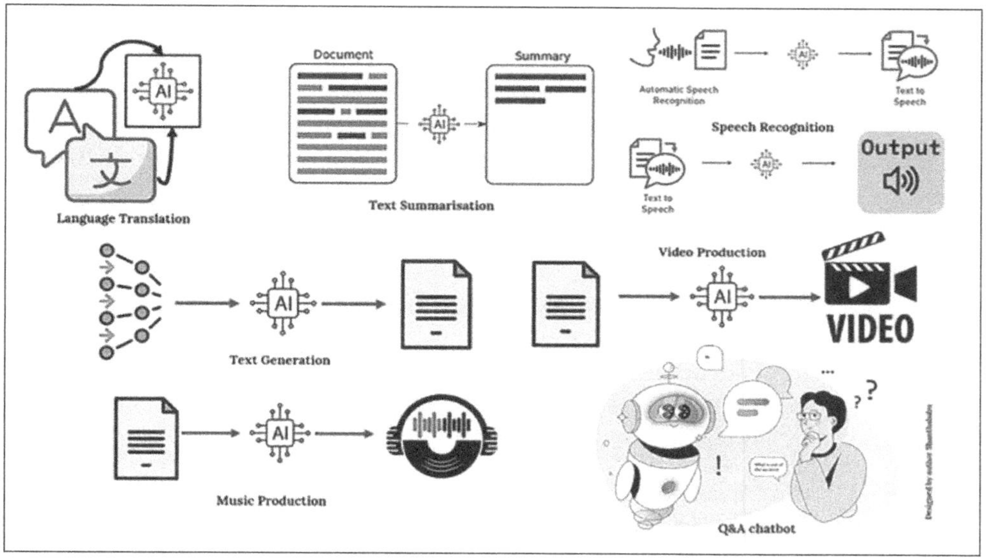

Figure: 1.15: *Gen AI – High-Level Use Cases*

- **Language Translation**: This use case helps translate between languages. It is another high-potential use case next to text generation and Q and A, especially for helping a non-English speaker interact with a critical government service, law forum, legal document translation, and more.
- **Speech Recognition:** This use case helps translate from one language to another using audio. It can process the audio. It would be any of the following conversions: audio-to-audio, text-to-audio, and audio-to-text. This helps many domains based on their needs.
- **Music–Video Production:** This is a typically entertained specific use case for general purpose. It helps create new music or videos based on precise input content to produce the output in the required format. A musician or social media creator can utilize this feature and build content with practical and quality outputs in less time.

How Industries Get Benefits out of Gen AI

In general, all new technology benefits various industries to gain their market. Gen AI is no exception in its new journey. From an industry-specific point of view, there are huge lists. Let us take a look at the vital industries as follows:

- **Financial Functions:** As we know, Gen AI helps produce content, generate ideas, and provide a Q and A perspective. Specific to financial functions, the contribution of Gen AI is enormous. Majorly written tasks include contracts, drafting responses for investor communications, reviewing general ledger entries, financial scenario generation, automated financial report generation, extracting business strategic insights, and supplementing a credit review.
- **Demand Forecasting:** GenAI is an emerging transformative force in the current scenario and can provide real-time data insights and demand forecasting. This can help update forecasting models dynamically from previous market cycles quickly based on customer feedback, product reviews, market competition across different websites, access to market cannibalization, product loyalty on the customer side, and more. Using all this information, Gen AI can make real-time amendments to an organization's marketing strategies and help it gain a competitive advantage.

  GenAI uses unconventional forecasting models to derive demand sensing and forecasting from various data, such as consumer sentiment, price changes, demographics, seasons, and climate.
- **Healthcare Diagnosis and Prediction:** Gen AI has rapidly become a significant factor in the healthcare industry. However, experts must understand how to use all technology to support and avoid the risks inherent in applying it to patient care. Multiple use cases across healthcare in different segments exist. At the same time, Gen AI brings about some clear uncertainties and risks. Alongside this, it promises to increase efficiency and quality as well as create new value for the healthcare domain, some of which are as follows:
  - Support real-time patient monitoring and building reports
  - Accelerating the drug discovery and development process
  - Improve clinical trial planning and execution
  - Building sophisticated medical imaging and analysis
  - Medical research and prediction of pandemic readiness

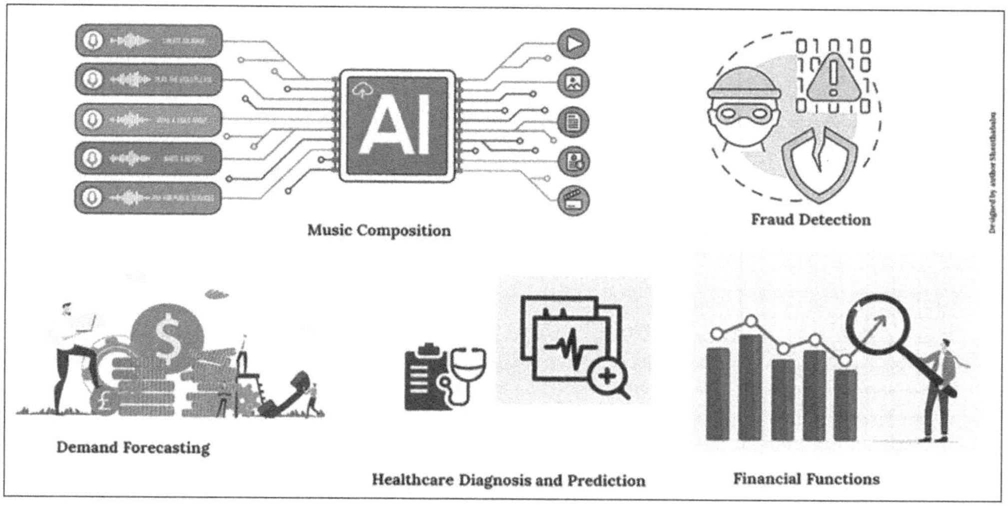

***Figure 1.16**: Gen AI – Industry Benefits*

- **Fraud Detection:** Gen AI for fraud detection is transforming risk decision-making. It offers dynamic, evolving solutions that address the challenges and obstacles in the existing approaches using classical AI solutions. Gen AI is thereby transforming the landscape of fraud detection with new energy.
    - It has the ability of near real-time analysis to capture fraudulent transactions and context-aware analysis capabilities, helping a lot in fraud detection.
    - Gen AI has excellent adaptive learning from historical and real-time data to detect fraud.
    - High predictive capabilities, customization of the output, and reducing huge manual oversight are more attractive features of Gen AI.
    - It is an excellent way to support synthetic data generation aspects, enhance privacy preservation, and ensure balancing the imbalanced datasets for further analysis.
- **Music Composition:** Gen AI is highly innovative and creative in producing new data, summaries, and images, and it is also capable of producing excellent music. It efficiently generates new chimes, measures, trills, and whole songs.

    Of course, this technology can potentially transform how music is created, using some samples to produce new and novel work. Two main approaches are used here.

    Using an algorithm on a large music dataset as a sample so that the algorithm can learn the patterns and structures of music ultimately generates new music that closely resembles the training data provided.

    They are inducing arbitrary sequences of notes and exploring the various musical combinations.

Across various industries, many Gen AI use cases have emerged in recent days for automating and simplifying workflows, which are effective time-intensive processes for knowledge workers, such as art and design, content creation, fashion design, legal firms, automating engineering and data processes, and supporting language translation services.

Gen AI Ethics and High-Level Security

Gen AI technology is becoming more advanced nowadays, and many ethical issues are associated with its implementation. On the other hand, it simulates human intelligence and decision-making. This brings many risks, including those to human safety.

Alongside the data requirements for Gen AI implementation, we need a massive volume of data to train the model, so that there might be changes and threats in addressing customers' and patients' privacy and security concerns. If we collected the data with poor quality or synthesis, the results would be dangerous, and practically, we could not go for productization versions.

So, Gen AI ethics came into the picture to answer the preceding challenges. It consists of principles and guidelines for designing, developing, testing, and deploying products for how end users can use Gen AI safely in their day-to-day lives, and get the maximum benefits without any fear.

All these sets of principles and guidelines are bundled into Gen AI ethics policy packs; this is needed to ensure that the organization, development team, staff, and stakeholders follow ethical AI guidelines to minimize risks and, at the same time, focus on improving the lives of all human beings without any risk threats.

All industries must consider the issues listed down while handling Gen AI ethics appropriately:

Ethical Considerations Factors

Listed down are the key ethical considerations for building any Gen AI product:

- **Justice:** Justification from the perspective of Gen AI, without any discrimination such as group, community, race, gender, or economic status.
- **Confidentiality:** Gen AI products must ensure the protection of individual data and information.
- **Safety:** It must protect against unauthorized access and manipulation of sensitive data.
- **Accountability:** Showing who is accountable for the behavior and resolution provided by the Gen AI product.
- **Clarity:** Explain how the Gen AI product operates, including data considerations,

the choice of algorithms, how the model was trained, and the justification of the product's decision.

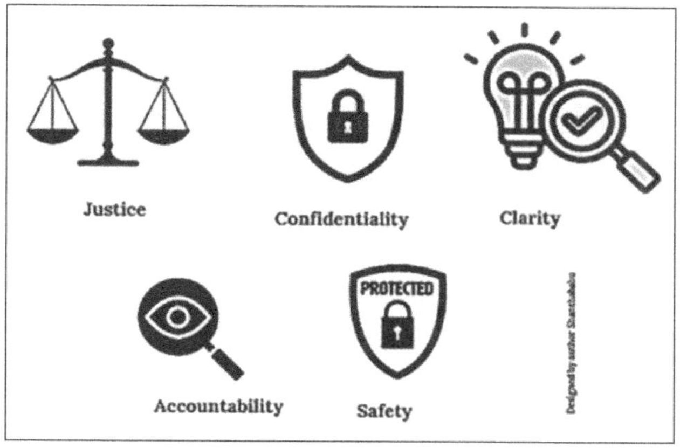

Figure 1.17: *Gen AI – Ethical Considerations Factors*

Let us focus on a few scenarios of ethically protecting Gen AI products, starting with:

Copyright and Legal Coverage:

Concerning Gen AI, the input for the model would be in any format; here, most of the feed is in the form of documents, text, and data from various internet sources. Building a model with internal data will not have issues concerning copyright and legal questions since all the documents and text are verified in advance of sharing for model training. If public data is used, then the Gen AI tool creates text, summary, and images that can create a problem, specifically while handling banking and financial-customer data, pharmaceutical-drug formula, legal forum-clients and case details, and hospital and patient treatment details. So, questions about reputation and security might arise from the respective organizations. Hence, Gen AI product companies must look to validate the output of the models and get advice from SMEs and legal teams to provide approvals on copyright challenges, IP, and privacy concerns.

Safer and Unharmful Content:

Gen AI systems can create content based on the input text, summary, image, and more, and based on the prompt instructions; the outcome from the systems can generate enormous throughput and much-improved content, but they can also be used for harm, but we could not do this intentionally or unintentionally. Still, in some cases, Gen AI-generated emails sent to external organizations or government entities from the company's system in offensive language or unnecessarily harmful messages to the leadership team, customers, and employees will create significant issues. While handling this requirement, we must ensure that the content meets the company's ethical outlook and realize the reputation of individuals and organizations.

Disclosure of Sensitive Information:

Gen AI tools can make an organization more democratic, supporting a system and making it more accessible. The composition of democratization and accessibility, disclosing sensitive information about patient and consumer interests, is unintentionally exposed to the outside world. The outcome of unintentional occurrences could breach the patient, and customer trustworthiness could carry legal implications. So when we build Gen AI products, we get clear guidelines from the governance body and aligned communication across all pillars and approvals–emphasizing the responsibilities of safeguarding sensitive information and protecting personal data.

Employee New Roles and Opportunities:

As we know, Gen AI can perform many more daily tasks than knowledge workers, including writing, content creation, build summarization, and data analysis. Automation has always replaced workers in an ongoing situation, right from the many industry revolutions in history. So, Gen AI is not exceptional in this case.

The ethical responses included preparing the workforce for Gen AI-specific jobs and roles such as Gen AI engineers, Prompt engineers, and specialized test engineers. This impacts organizational design and hierarchy. This system indeed prepares the organization for a new growth path.

Along with the aforementioned ethical actions, Gen AI is responsible for the provenance of data and privacy destruction, the explainability and interpretability of the Gen AI product, and the strengthening of the existing biases in the system.

Conclusion

In this chapter, we introduced Gen AI and Transformer Architecture. We studied each component and its role in this architecture, along with a clear pictorial representation. We explored how this architecture primarily adopts neural network techniques and natural language processing methodologies, such as text generation, sentiment analysis, question-and-answer, text summarization, and language translation

We explored very detailed walkthroughs of both technologies along with factors influencing them, such as challenges with interpretability, cost and resources, data quality, data security, and privacy. We covered the comparisons and drawbacks of Gen AI and touched upon the commonly available Gen AI tools, their features, and their tenacities for several industries' needs: ChatGPT, Gemini, Copilot, GitHub Copilot, and Dall-E 2. We explored how industries benefit from Gen AI in a very detailed fashion in the areas of financial functions, demand forecasting, healthcare diagnosis and prediction, fraud detection, and music composition.

In the next chapter, we will discuss LLMs and their capabilities in detail, provide an overview of the essential components of LLMs and architecture, and explain how models work.

CHAPTER 2
Exploring LLMs and Its Capabilities

Introduction

In the previous chapter, we delved into Gen AI, its unique traits, and the advantages it brings. We then took a closer look at the evolution of Gen AI and examined its Transformer Architecture as well as its key elements: the ENCODER, DECODER, SELF-ATTENTION, INPUT, and OUTPUT. We also compared Gen AI to traditional AI and ML, highlighting the former's limitations. To illustrate the real-world impact of Gen AI, we provided classic industry examples and discussed the ethical implications of its use in high-level security.

Now, let us dive into the fascinating world of LLMs. We will explore what LLMs are, their networks, and the key components that make them tick. We will take a detailed look at the primary components of LLMs, such as embedding layers, transformer blocks, multi-head self-attention mechanisms, feedforward neural networks, positional encoding, and decoders. We will also unravel the mysteries of output layers, loss functions, and fine-tuning layers, as well as explain the concept of attention masks. Finally, we will discuss the importance of fine-tuning and its role in optimizing performance.

Structure

In this chapter, we will discuss the following topics:

- Overview of Large Language Models (LLMs)
    - Exploring Available LLMs in the Market
- Types of Large Language Models (LLMs)
- Applications of Large Language Model (LLM)
- Working Principles of Large Language Models
    - LLMs: Architecture and its Essential Components
        - Transformer Blocks
        - Embedding Layers

        - Positional Encoding
        - Encoder
        - Multi-Head-Self-Attention Mechanisms
        - Feedforward Neural Networks
        - Decoder
- Fine-Tuning in LLM and its Importance
    - Fine-Tuning Process of LLMs and their Types
    - Fine-Tuning Benefits
    - Output Layers, Loss Functions, and Fine-Tuning Layers
    - Domain Adaptation Methodology
    - When to Opt for Fine-Tuning
- Advantages of Large Language Models
    - Challenges in Large Language Models (LLMs)

Overview of Large Language Models (LLM)

Large language models are typical AI systems designed to process and analyze substantial amounts of data and then process required information as a desired output in response to user strategic prompting techniques.

Without any skepticism, these types of AI systems are trained on gigantic volumes of data sets using advanced ML algorithms to learn the patterns among the dataset irrespective of the data structure, which means any data format.

LLM is a neural network family with trillions of parameters trained on enormous amounts of data using supervised learning and multiple layers of an algorithm. These models can perform a wide variety of tasks, from simple text generation to drug design and legal advisory documents.

In recent years, LLMs have become increasingly important in various applications and products across different use cases.

Large Language Models (LLMs)

An LLM is an AI algorithm that applies typical neural network techniques with numerous parameters to process and understand human languages or text as input. It uses self-supervised learning techniques to generate text, translation, summary writing, creative image generation from texts, developing codes, and creating chat-bot applications (RAG and Q and A). Classic examples of such LLMs are GPT, Chat, BERT, LaMDA, and so on.

LLM is purely based on deep learning methodologies, and these models are highly efficient in capturing complex entity relationships in the given input. The input could be text, summary, structured, or unstructured, and the output would be text, summary, image, audio, and video. The text uses the syntactic and semantics of any language.

Exploring Available LLMs in the Market

Let us discuss common LLMs in the market, such as GPT-4o, T5, and BERT. These models showcase outstanding capabilities, including language understanding and generation, and open up new possibilities in various domains. Google, OpenAI, Meta, and others introduced all these LLMs for their specific tasks.

- **Bidirectional Encoder Representations from Transformers (BERT):** Google introduced it based on the transformer architecture and follows the deep learning model technique. This means every output element is connected to another input element, and the weightings between the two elements are dynamically calculated based on their connections. Moreover, the framework was trained using text from Wikipedia data.
- **Robustly Optimized BERT Pretraining Approach (RoBERTa):** This model is an improvised performance of the BERT transformer architecture, which Facebook AI Research develops.
- **Generative Pre-trained Transformer 4- (GPT-4o):** This is the latest product from OpenAI that came into the market in 2023. This model is much different from the earlier version; it can consider input in not only text but also images and also shows impressive performance. The maximum input length was increased to 32,768 tokens, which is an additional benefit of the model. This model is not open source and is accessible through API only. This means you have to pay to access the model for your needs.
- **ChatGPT 3.5 and 4:** ChatGPT has two versions. 3.5 (Free Tier) is free to access, and 4.0 (20 USD per month) is paid. The earlier version supported a text-only model owned by OpenAI. It can take input from around 20 billion parameters. ChatGPT is a sibling model for InstructGPT. This means that it was designed specifically to receive prompts and provide very detailed responses in the form of paragraphs, bullet points, and classified formats for user benefit.
- **LLaMA 2:** LLaMa is Meta's open-source product. It has various sizes, from 7B to 70B parameters, and offers two model variants, 1 and 2, respectively.

  LLaMa Chat (or LLaMA 1) is a general-purpose model similar to the GPT family, capable of tasks such as Q and A, generating text, and language translation.

  Code LLaMa (or LLaMa 2) is the best fit for challenging tasks, such as reasoning, coding, and proficiency tests. It utilizes the reinforcement learning methodology from human feedback and can handle 2.2 trillion tokens.

  The models are open source, so they are free for research purposes and commercial purposes. Both models have performance capabilities for fine-tuning scripts.

- **FALCON:** This was developed by Technology Innovation Institute. It has various ranges of parameter capabilities, such as 180B, 40B, 7.5B, and 1.3B. Based on its xxB, it has powerful performance, which varies in aspects of linguistic accuracy, versatility, and efficiency. On the other hand, it has the following issues: complete data dependency and concerns about ethical facets.
- **Language Model for Dialogue Applications (LaMDA):** This Google model can handle 173 billion parameters and is trained explicitly on dialogue. LaMDA is specifically designed to excel in dialogue-based interactions, allowing it to engage in more natural and contextually rich conversations with users.

  The model's potential use cases vary, ranging from customer service-based chatbots to supporting personal assistants. Google's earlier chatbot version was called Meena, and the conversational service is much more powerful and renamed into BARD.
- **Pathways Language Model (PaLM):** This model is also developed by Google. It can handle 540 billion parameters. Basically, this was designed to build and handle many different tasks and learn new ones more quickly than other models. It is capable of performing hundreds of language-related tasks and has achieved state-of-the-art performance. Its extraordinary feature is that it generates explanations for scenarios requiring multiple complex logical steps, such as explaining how to solve problems.

As discussed, the various LLMs are text generation models, such as GPT, that can generate consistent and grammatically precise text in different languages and formats.

LLMs aim to predict the next character, word, or sentence based on the previous ones in a running sequence. In this sense, language modeling encodes the rules and structures of a language in a way that a machine can understand.

LLMs can capture the structure of human language in terms of grammar, syntax, and semantics. These features help the model create content, translate languages, summarize, and perform text-editing tasks, including spelling correction.

Types of Large Language Models (LLMs)

We have discussed commonly available LLMs in the market, which can be broadly classified into three types:

- Pre-training models
- Fine-tuning models

- Multimodal models
- **Pre-Training Models:** LLMs are initially pre-trained on a massive amount of data from the internet, which is a vast amount of public data. During pre-training, the model can analyze the context and learn to predict the next word in a sentence with the help of surrounding words. This capability helps the model learn grammar, reasoning, and facts.

  Commonly available models, such as the GPT family, are trained on vast amounts of data. During the training, they learn a wide range of languages, their patterns, and structures.

  They are used as a starting point, and this will involve further training and fine-tuning for specific tasks along with a small amount of data.
- **Fine-Tuning Models**: After pre-training, the model undergoes fine-tuning on more specific tasks and a considerable size of the dataset. Fine-tuning is an additional process to enhance the model's performance. Basically, the set of parameters is updated on a new data set. It can be translation, summarization, sentiment analyses, and Q and A.

  These models are often used in leading industrial-specific applications, where task-specific language models are essential to use cases.

  Models such as BERT and RoBERTa are pre-trained on a large dataset and then fine-tuned on a small set of data for a specific task perspective. Fine-tuned models are highly effective and qualified for tasks such as text classification, sentiment analysis, and Q and A chat.
- **Multimodal Models**: The models are focused on a single type of data. However, this multimodal model is much more capable than the other models. It can understand and process the details from multiple modalities and handle text, images, audio, and videos.

  Moreover, this model utilizes the multimodal neural network, which effectively enhances overall performance. Combining visual and textual indicators has enhanced the understanding of data. It can handle uncertain situations better than unimodal models.

  These models can understand the relationships between images and text, allowing them to generate text descriptions of images or even generate images from textual descriptions.

  Models such as DALL-E 1, DALL-E 2, and CLIP combine text with other data types, such as images or video, to create more innovative and robust language models.

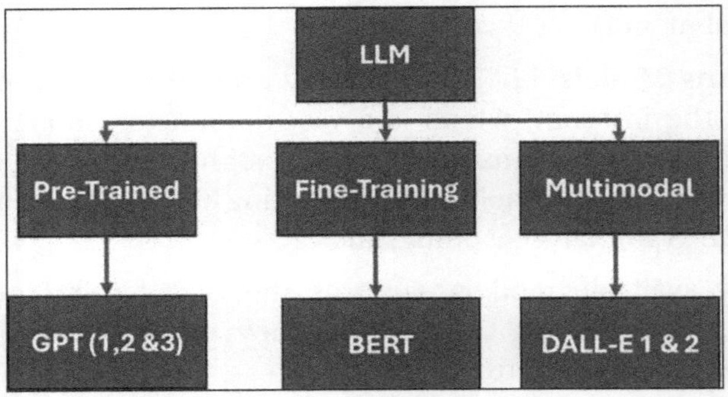

***Figure 2.1**: Types of Large Language Models (LLMs)*

Applications of Large Language Model (LLM)

LLMs have a wide range of applications in specific domains; there are no limitations. Let us explore some notable applications.

- **Content Generation**: LLMs can enable automated content generation for research papers, advertisements, and articles related to product marketing, technical and non-technical blog posts, new product descriptions and benefits, workflows and procedures, and social media marketing and captions.
- **Language Translation**: LLMs can provide accurate and more confident translations across different languages based on the demand for Language X into Y. This ability allows them to support global-level languages, ease communication, and advance multilingual collaboration views. Specifically, government document translations for board support and legal aspects to build a smooth relationship between countries and ease border security and developments.
- **Chatbots and Virtual Assistants**: LLMs are potent conversational agents. This allows businesses to provide customer support, handle issues and inquiries about products, and assist end-users, ultimately reducing the need for human assistance and improving customer experience in a timely manner and on a highly flexible timeline. They can also close queries and issues quickly.
- **Text Summarization**: One of the great features of LLMs is that they can extract essential information from massive textbooks and generate concise summaries. This capability results in quick and fast news generation, aggregation, research analysis, and document analysis as well as processing.
- **Q and A:** The best use case for LLMs is Q and A. They are really capable of understanding the context of the questions and getting precise answers, which is valuable for building Q and A systems and retrieval applications across many industries.

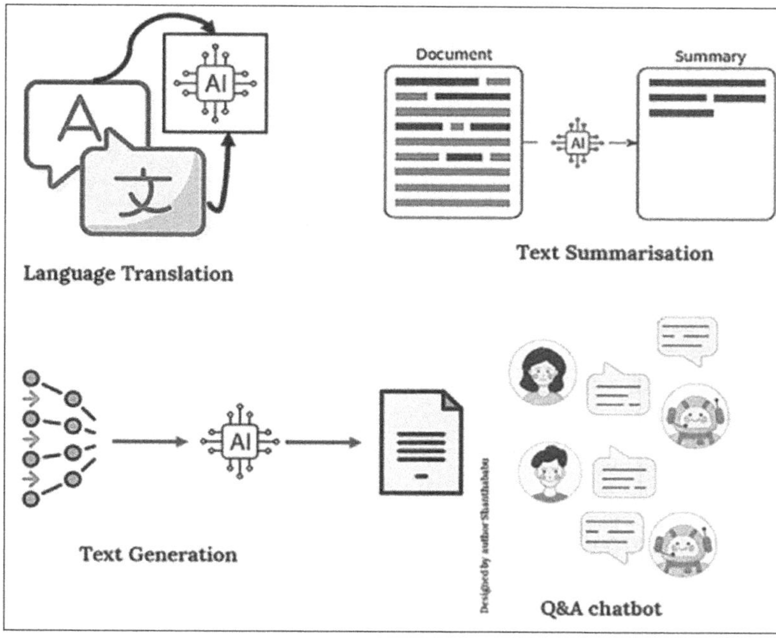

Figure 2.2*: Large Language Model (LLM): Applications*

Working Principles of Large Language Models

In simple terms, "*The LLMs work on neural network architectures and deep learning principles to process and understand tasks.*"

All these models are trained on a huge volume of data using self-supervised learning techniques, understanding the patterns and relationships among the training data during the training.

From an architectural point of view, Transformer-based LLM Model architecture consists of multiple layers, including **feed-forward layers, embedding layers, and attention layers**.

Of course, they employ attention mechanisms, such as self and multi-attention.

The architecture of LLM is the same as the transformer architecture, which we have discussed in *Chapter 1, Introduction to Generative AI*.

Here, let us discuss the architecture of LLM from a high-level perspective without replicating.

The following factors determine LLM's architecture:

- Objectives of the model design
- Computational resources

- Types of Language Processing tasks

Transformer-based LLM models typically follow a general architecture that includes the following components:

- Input Layers
- Input Embeddings
- Positional Encoding
- Encoder Layers
    - Self/Multi Head-Attention Mechanism
    - Feed-Forward Neural Network
    - Normalization Layer
- Decoder Layers
    - Multi-Head Attention
    - Feed-Forward Neural Network
    - Normalization Layer
- Linear and Softmax
- Output Probabilities
- Output Layers

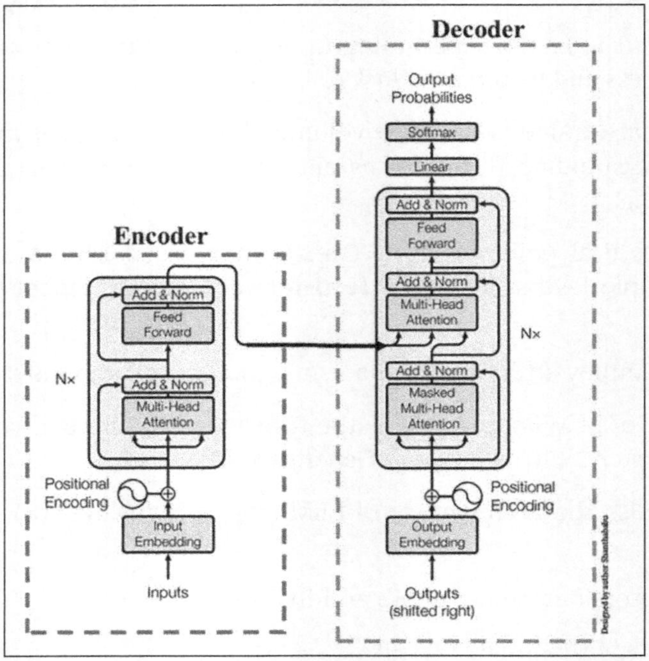

***Figure 2.3**: Transformer-based LLM Architecture (Universal Picture)*

- **Input Layer:** This is just an input for the system.
- **Output Layer**: The output is the sequence generated by the transformer.
- **Input Embeddings:** In this architecture, the input is not considered as word(s) directly; each word will be converted into numbers before it is fed into the system. The mechanism of this conversion process is to build an input sequence into the system, called "***Input embedding***."

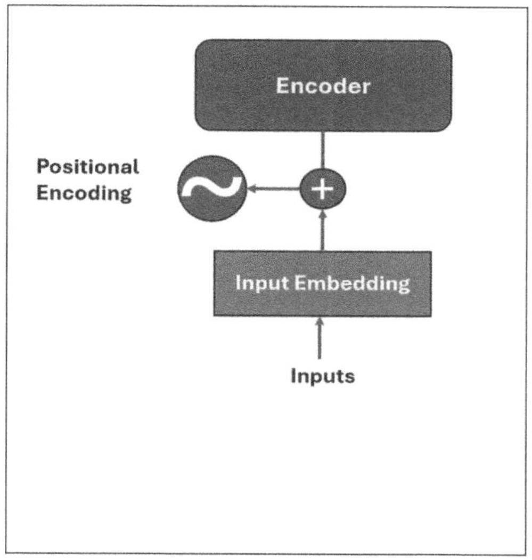

Figure 2.4: *Transformer-Input Embedding and Positional Encoding*

- **Positional Encoding:** Positional encoding is the process of adding additional information to the input embeddings. The positions of the tokens are additional details because the transformers do not encode their order, unlike how LSTM functions. This enables the model to process the tokens while considering their sequential input order.

  Based on a neural network technique, the encoder analyzes the input text and creates hidden states that protect the context and meaning of text data.
- **Encoder:** The encoder layers comprise the transformer architecture's core. It consists of multiple layers and fundamental sub-components of each layer, such as:
  - Self-Attention/Multi-Head mechanism
  - Feed-forward Neural Network

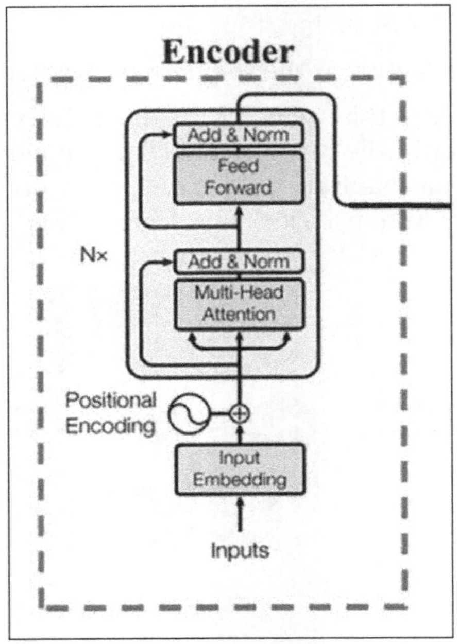

***Figure* 2.5:** *Transformer-Encoder Layer*

- **Self-Attention Mechanism:** This is a key mechanism used in transformer architecture. It allows the model to pay attention to different parts of input sequences when processing each element, count the significance of other tokens in the input sequence, and consider the dependencies and relationships between different tokens in a context-aware methodology, enabling each token to learn to understand all the surrounding tokens.

The masked MHA layer masks some tokens randomly to make this system learn situations.

For example, consider the following input sentence:

Hello, how are you doing?

If we have just reached the word **how**, the input of the encoder could be as follows:

Hello, how <masked sequence>

Self-Attention will run dot-products between word vectors and determine the most substantial relationships in the given input sequence of the word and all the other words, as represented in *Figure* 2.6. This attention mechanism will work out well and provide a more significant relationship between the given input sequence of words, resulting in better outcomes. If x=8, then there are N8 blocks and layers inside the encoder; the transformer model runs eight attention mechanisms in parallel to speed up the overall calculations. This process is named **"Multi-Head Attention (MHA)."**

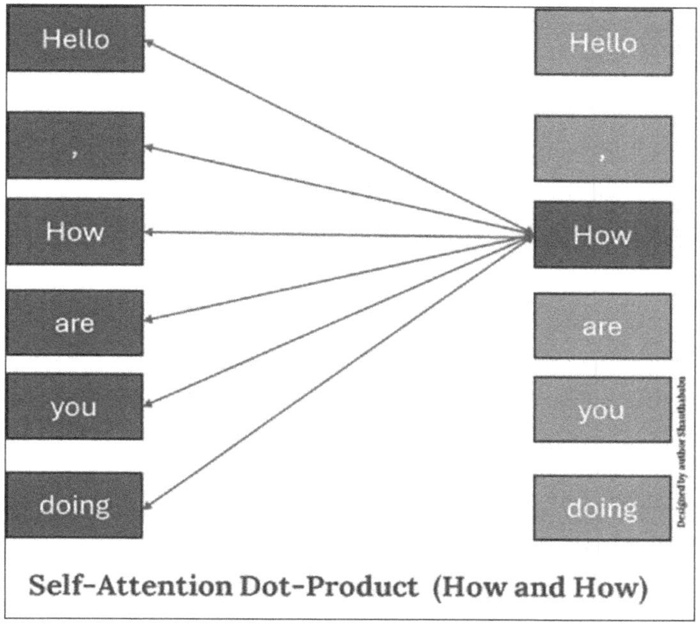

Figure 2.6: *Self-Attention - Including Itself ("How" and "How")*

- **Feed-Forward Neural Network:** FNN fully connects layers with non-linear activation functions, enabling the model to capture complex relationships between tokens. This layer is applied to each token individually after the previous step, such as the self-attention step.

  FNN are nodes and do not form loops. They are also known as multi-layer neural networks. As the name implies, all information is only passed forward. During data flow operations, the input nodes receive data, which travels through hidden layers, and exit through the output nodes, similar to deep learning concepts.

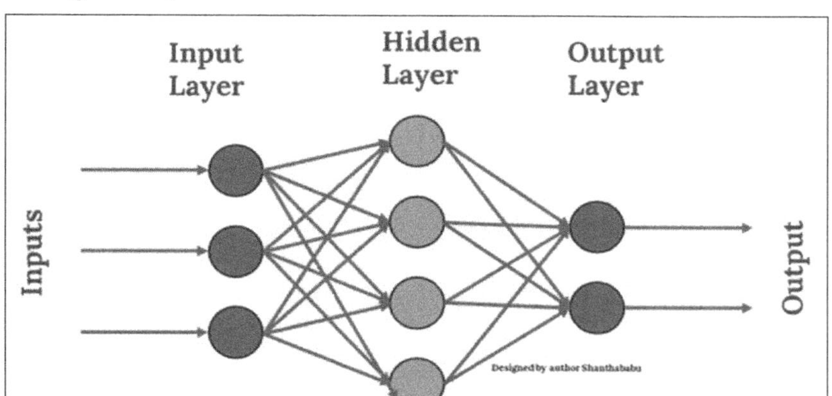

Figure 2.7: *Feed-Forward Neural Network*

- **Decoder Layers**: This layer consists of the following components and the encoder's input:
    - o Multi-Head Attention
    - o Encoder-Decoder Attention
    - o Linear Normalization and Softmax Layer
    - o Output Layers

It enables autoregressive generation, where the model can generate sequential outputs by attending to the previously generated tokens.

- **Multi-Head Attention:** In this component, self-attention is performed concurrently with uniquely learned attention weights. This enables the model to capture different types of relationships and concurrently attend to various parts of the input sequence.
- **Encoder-Decoder Attention:** This encoder-decoder attention is the second sublayer that receives the multi-head mechanism input/queries from the decoder side from the previous decoder's output (the first sublayer's output) along with the keys (K) and values (V) from the encoder's output (the left side of the architecture diagram). This layer is also MHA. In this layer, the decoder attends to all the words in the input sequence concerning the MHSA mechanism, similar to layer one in the encoder.

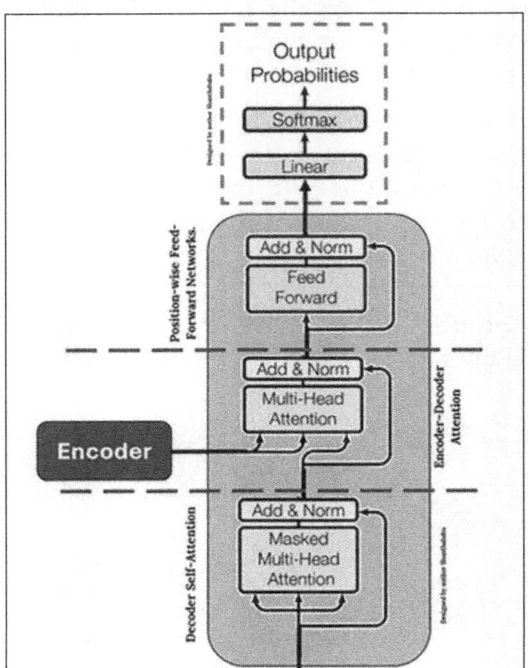

Figure 2.8: *Decoder Layer*

- **Layer Normalization:** This layer came into action after each sub-component in the transformer architecture at the decoders block. It helps the learning process, steadily improves the model's capacity, and generalizes across different inputs.
- **SoftMax:** SoftMax activation is generally used to generate a probability distribution over the next token feed.
- **Output Layers:** This can vary depending on the specific task.

Factors Influencing LLM Architecture Functions: We have discussed the layers and elements of LLM architecture. Even though the components function with their own roles and responsibilities, the following factors would influence the architecture's overall functions.

- Input interpretations
- Model size
- Parameter count
- Self-Attention mechanisms
- Objectives of the training
- Efficiency of the computation
- Encoding, decoding, and output generation

Note: *Types of Large Language Models (LLMs) include pre-training, fine-tuning, and multimodal models.*

Large Language Model (LLM)-Applications: Content Generation, Language Translation, Chatbots and Virtual Assistants, Text Summarization, and Q and A.

The following factors determine the LLM's architecture, objective of the model design, computational resources, and type of language processing tasks.

Transformer-based LLM models typically follow a general architecture that includes input layers, encoder layers, decoder layers, and output layers.

Controlled Output of LLMs and their Significance

The quality of the LLM output is always discussed in the context of "**HALLUCINATIONS.**" Uncontrolled output can lead to incorrect content, potentially misleading the end user and, in some situations, to threats, unsecured privacy concerns, and harmful results.

We can observe the LLM hallucination index, choose the appropriate temperature to achieve quality and reasonable output from the LLM, and correct it depending on many factors. Of course, considerable costs are incurred during the controlled output, and if a weaker LLM is used for costing purposes, it leads to serious consequences while dealing with critical decision-making. Therefore, we must control the occurrence of hallucinations and confirm that information generated using LLM is truthful, relevant, and consistent.

We can adopt the following techniques to control and enhance the LLM's output. In the following chapters, we will discuss all these techniques in detail.

- Embeddings and text chunks
- Vector and Index optimization
- Building memorization and caching
- Adapting parallel processing
- Monitoring, logging, and profiling

Fine-Tuning Process of LLM and their Types

Fine-tuning is a process for the pre-trained model, which has already been trained and learned patterns and features on a large dataset and needs to be tuned further on a smaller dataset and domain-specific task.

Any model requires fine-tuning before entering the production environment. The fine-tuning process typically involves feeding the task-specific data to the model, where we have to adjust its parameters throughout the forward-back propagation. The major objective is to minimize the loss function, which measures the difference between the actual facts of the dataset and the model's predictions; ultimately, this process updates the model's parameters based on the requirements and makes it more aligned with the specialized task we are targeting.

The pre-trained model is a transfer learning method in which a pre-trained model is trained on a large dataset and adapted to work for a precise task. However, for fine-tuning, the dataset required for the entire process is much smaller compared to the pre-training model.

The fine-tuning process allows developers to customize pre-trained language models for dedicated tasks.

Types of Fine-Tuning

Various approaches to Fine-Tuning LLMs are available; let us explore them. We should remember that not all methods for fine-tuning LLMs are created equally. Each technique serves its unique purpose based on different applications and scopes. In some scenarios, you aim to adapt a model for a new task.

At a high level, there are two methods for fine-tuning:

- Primary fine-tuning
    - Feature extraction, Feature-based, or Repurposing
    - Full fine-tuning I and II
- Potential fine-tuning
    - Supervised fine-tuning
    - Instruction fine-tuning

Feature Extraction, Feature-based, or Repurposing: This is one of the primary approaches, as the name implies, that uses a pre-trained LLM, which is treated as a feature extractor component, and transforms the input text into a fixed-sized array list. Additionally, a separate classifier network has to be applied to predict the text's class in terms of probability. The classifier's weight continues changing during the training, making it resource-friendly. In this method, the model, having been trained on a sizable amount of data, has already learned the substantial features that can be repurposed for the specific task, and so it is also known as "**Repurposing or Feature-based.**" It offers a cost-effective way to fine-tune LLMs, but potentially less effective. Please note that only the final layers will be adjusted for fine-tuning purposes.

Full Fine-Tuning: This is another primary approach to fine-tuning LLMs. Here, the entire model has to be trained on task-specific data; this means all the model layers are adjusted during the training process. As per the process, we allow the entire model to learn from the task-specific dataset; this can lead to a more insightful adaptation to the specific task and potentially perform better than the feature extraction method. The downside is that it requires more computational resources and time consumption when compared to the feature extraction tuning method.

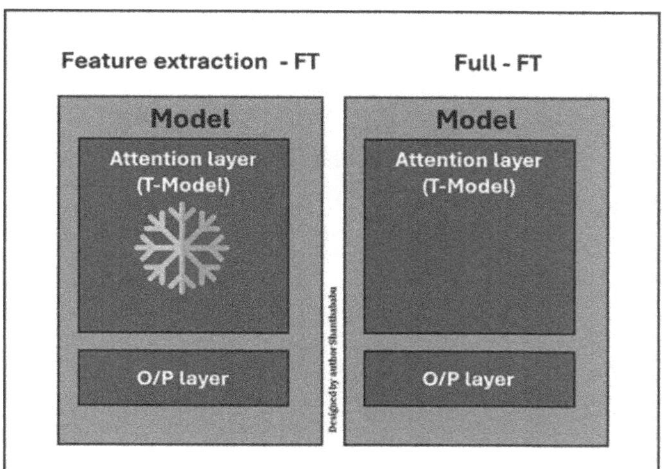

***Figure 2.9**: Fine - Tuning (Feature Extraction and Full FT)*

The full fine-tuning method is further classified into two types: Full fine-tuning I and Full fine-tuning II.

Full Fine-Tuning I: In this method, a dense layer is added during training to enhance the performance of pre-trained LLM. The weights of the newly added layers are adjusted, and the weights of the pre-trained LLM layer are frozen during the training. Performance-wise, it shows marginally better performance than the feature-based method.

Full Fine-Tuning II: In this method, the entire model is unfrozen during training, and all the model weights are kept updated, where new features overwrite old knowledge and lead to catastrophic forgetting in the model. This model delivers superior results and is more resource-intensive.

Supervised Fine-Tuning: As we know, the supervised model is well-trained with labeled data and will be trained further on a task-specific basis. Since the model is naturally supervised and the dataset has input-output pairs, the model can learn to map inputs to matching outputs using this tuning method.

Functionally, in this method, the pre-trained LLMs are trained for specific downstream tasks using labeled and validated input and output data combinations. During the training, the model's weights are adjusted based on the gradient factors derived from the task-specific loss, which represents the difference between the LLM's predictions and the base truth of labeled data.

The supervised fine-tuning method also learns task-specific patterns and nuances present in the labeled input and the output data.

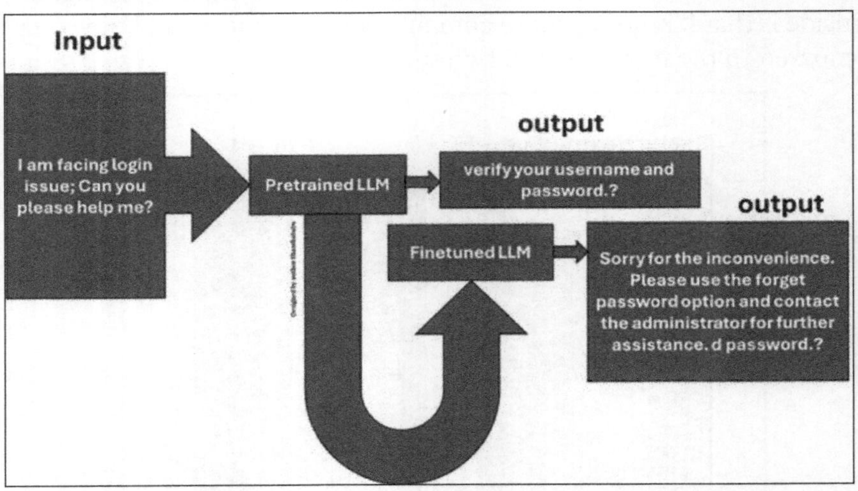

Figure 2.10: *Fine - Tuning (Supervised Fine-Tuning)*

The supervised fine-tuning method is further classified into the following types based on the tuning approach.

The most common are:

- **Basic Hyperparameter Tuning:** This is a straightforward approach that manually adjusts the model's key hyperparameters specific to an algorithm until reaching the desired performance, such as the batch size, epochs length, and learning rate.
- **Multi-Task Learning:** This method fine-tunes the model for multiple related tasks concurrently. The goal is to influence cohesion and variation across the list of tasks considered during the training and is expected to improve the model's performance.
- **Few-Shot Learning:** In this method, the model is exposed to a few classical tasks in terms of "shots" in the idea of models to understand the new task. This method helps the models to learn, enable, and adapt to a new task with considerable data. Basically, we will try to utilize the vast knowledge from the earlier training and use it for new tasks to reduce expenses.

Instruction Fine-Tuning: This method is something special; even though the huge amount of data trains the models, it cannot respond to specific modes of prompts. In such situations, the instruction fine-tuning method is applicable to change the behavior and response of the model, in which the input and output are augmented with given instructions in the prompt template with multiple options. This exercise will enable the models to generalize more quickly to new tasks using an instruction-tuned-based method.

Terminology Closer to LLM During Training

Multiple terminologies are emerging regarding LLMs, and the following terms are recommended. It is essential to know the theory behind them and understand the concepts.

- **Loss Function:** This is the ratio of the predicted output and the actual output as inputs, computed as a numerical value representing the error. The objective is to minimize this error factor by adjusting the model's parameters through an optimization process. LLMs utilize cross-entropy as a loss function during training to measure the difference between the predicted and the actual probability distribution factors observed in the training.

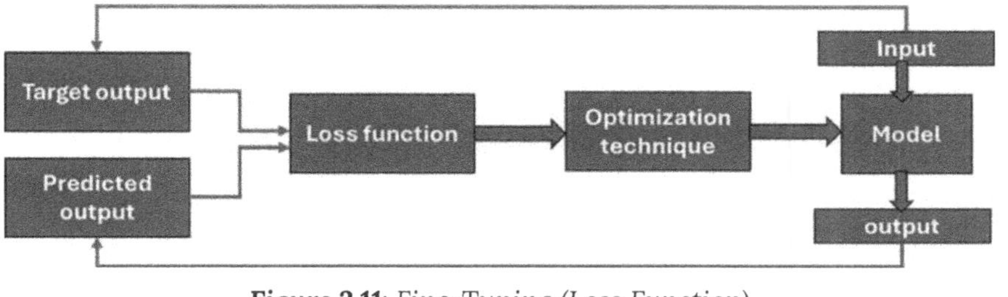

Figure 2.11: *Fine-Tuning (Loss Function)*

- **Domain Adaptation:** In the AIML domain, many techniques exist to adapt and improve the performance of a model in which annotation-related details play a major role. This exercise is called domain adaptation, and it enhances this capability by using the knowledge learned from another related domain with adequate labeled data.

  The domain adaptation technique helps by exposing the common hidden factors across the source and target domain data and reducing the marginal and conditional mismatches in the observation of the feature space between domains.
- **Source Domain:** This data was analyzed and distributed in the frame on which the model is trained using labeled data.
- **Target Domain:** The model has been pre-trained on a different domain to perform a similar task.

Let us say samples are collected from two different but similar domains.

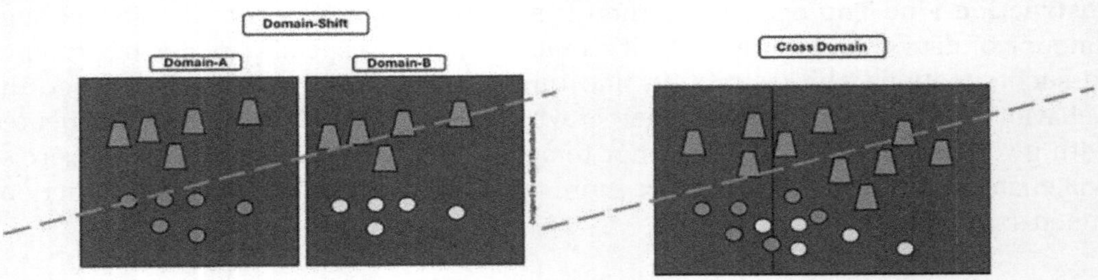

Figure 2.12: *Domain Adaptation (Shift and Cross)*

LLMs need to adopt a specific domain to satisfy the needs of a particular task and improve the model's accuracy.

There are different techniques that help adapt an LLM for a domain-specific task:

- **Prompt Tuning:** Feeding the appropriate instructions to the LLM and generating the desired output text. We will discuss this in detail in the upcoming chapters.
- **Retrieval-Augmented Generation (RAG):** In some scenarios, the feed content to the prompt might be too large, and the prompt could not accommodate it. In this case, the retriever step can be added as an additional step. In this step, the relevant content is retrieved to augment the context of the prompt to an LLM.
- **Supervised Fine-Tuning (SFT):** Please refer to the earlier details in this chapter.

  Note:

  a. *Loss Function: This is the ratio of the predicted output and the actual output as inputs, computed as a numerical value representing the error.*

b. *This exercise is called domain adaptation, and it enhances this capability by using knowledge learned from another related domain with adequate labeled data.*

When to Opt for Fine-Tuning

We always have to justify our actions, so let us review some crucial and industry-specific scenarios when considering fine-tuning.

- **Data Availability and Limitations:** We need to understand one thing: fine-tuning is particularly favorable when you have limited labeled data for your domain-specific task. We cannot expect to train the model from scratch in the pharmaceutical, healthcare, and legal domains. We cannot go for a larger dataset for various reasons, such as data privacy, security, and so on. So, instead of training a model from scratch, we could leverage the knowledge of pre-trained models and adapt it to our domain-specific tasks using a smaller dataset to train effectively.
- **Resources and Time:** As we know, deep learning models require very high computational resources and time. In addition to a pre-trained model, additional fine-tuning provides a more efficient model. If we avoid the initial training and follow the fine-tuning process, we will find a solution faster. These approaches will help the pharma industry, specifically during drug design.
- **Transfer Learning:** The fine-tuning process is a critical component of transfer learning, especially whenever a pre-trained model's knowledge is transferred to a new and specific task for demand. To avoid training a model from scratch, we can pre-train and fine-tune it. These kinds of processes are generally adopted for a larger volume of image analysis in the healthcare and medical device industries to diagnose disease.
- **Data Security and Compliance**: Data is always a sensitive entity, irrespective of any domain. So, while working with sensitive data, we cannot leave or leak information and follow up on security and compliance concerns. Under these conditions, we might need to fine-tune our model to secure data with highly secure infrastructure and policies in place. This activity would ensure that the model never leaves the data and controlled environment, and would follow up on governance. The following domains are highly recommended: banking, finance, legal, government policies, and insurance.

Fine-Tuning Benefits

Fine-tuning is an additional process to enhance the model's performance. After pre-training, the model must undergo fine-tuning on tasks that are more specific to the dataset, which is considerable in size. During this process, there are multiple benefits; let us focus on a few of them here.

- **Improved Performance:** Since the model learns the new data for a specific task, it automatically increases the overall performance and output stability.
- **Domain Knowledge Enrichment**: This process allows the model to adapt to the specifics of a domain and its related domain-specific vocabulary. It helps the model to generate text, summaries, and other outputs in domains such as law, finance, real estate, and medical.
- **Model Efficiency:** By adapting a pre-trained process for a specific task along with a set of data, the model avoids training needs, which saves the computational cost very effectively.
- **Generalization:** Due to this process, the model would generalize and exhibit better performance on relevant training data and bring out patterns and insights present in the data.

Once the models are fine-tuned, they gain the following capabilities and build the following tools or products for domain-specific use. Indeed, this would enhance many more competencies than the earlier version.

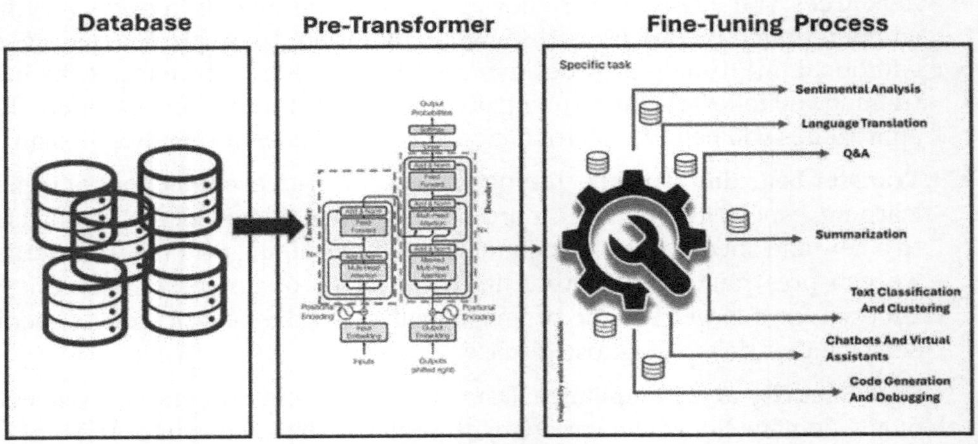

***Figure 2.13**: Fine-Tuning the Models*

Advantages of Large Language Models

Overall, LLMs represent a significant advancement in NLP and Gen AI technology. They offer unparalleled performance, flexibility, and scalability across a wide range of applications and domains, along with their challenges. However, computational costs and ethical considerations are major drawbacks. Even though industries are building systems with high computational speeds and excellent ethical considerations, the advantages must be tapped into for industry-specific use cases to carefully specify how we can interact with and understand natural language.

- **Improved Performance:** LLMs have demonstrated the state-of-the-art performance on a wide range of tasks, including text generation, text classification, language translation, text summarization, Q and A, and much more. Depending on their size and scale, they capture complex patterns and semantic relationships among the input text, leading to more accurate, contextually relevant, and required outputs.
- **Versatility:** LLMs are versatile and can be fine-tuned for specific tasks with relatively minimal additional training data. This flexibility makes them suitable for a wide range of applications across different industries, including healthcare, finance, education, customer service, and more.
- **Zero-Shot and Few-Shot**: LLMs are capable of zero-shot and few-shot learning, which means that they can perform tasks without explicitly being trained on examples of that specific task. This capability enables them to generalize across different tasks and domains, which makes them adaptable to new and unseen scenarios with minimal guidance.
- **Language Understanding**: LLMs have a strong understanding of natural language semantics, syntax, and context, allowing them to generate coherent, contextually relevant responses back to the system. This enables natural and engaging user interactions in conversational systems, chatbots, and virtual assistants.

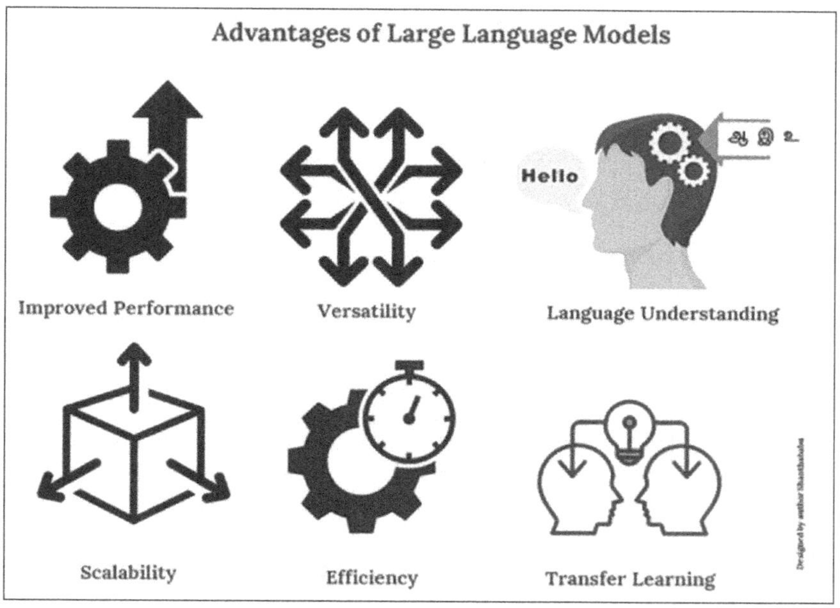

Figure 2.14: *Advantages of Large Language Models*

- **Scalability:** LLMs can scale to accommodate vast amounts of data and parameters, which is why they need vast amounts of data. This enables them to capture various phonological nuances and handle diverse languages as well as domains. It also ensures that they can continue improving performance as more data becomes available for training and tests.

- **Efficiency:** Despite their size, LLMs can be deployed efficiently using modern hardware accelerators, such as Graphics Processing Units (GPUs) and Tensor Processing Units (TPUs), in a cloud environment. This allows them to process large volumes of text data and generate responses in real-time or near real-time, making them practical for various real-world applications.
- **Transfer Learning:** LLMs are pre-trained on massive datasets, which enables them to capture a vast amount of general language, patterns, and knowledge from various sources of text data. This pre-trained knowledge can be transferred to downstream tasks with fine-tuning, reducing the need for extensive task-specific training and helping the development of innovative Gen AI applications.

Challenges in Large Language Models (LLMs)

So far, we have discussed the exponential abilities of the LLMs in terms of current trends and future technology as part of AI-powered applications across industries. On the other hand, LLMs also consist of challenges and drawbacks.

What are those challenges? Yes, they are end-to-end, right from Gen AI tools' design, development, and deployment, which also come with significant challenges–and not stopping there, beyond that, such as privacy, security, and ethics issues.

Here are some of the key challenges associated with LLMs:

- **Resource Intensiveness**: As we know, LLMs require huge amounts of data for training and fine-tuning; significantly, they require massive computational resources with high power, such as GPUs or TPUs and, of course, a large-scale dataset. This sets a barrier to the entry of smaller organizations that want to get into this journey, and even researchers, who used to have limited access to such resources for their research purposes due to cost and sponsors.
- **Prejudice and Fairness**: LLMs can inadvertently amplify the biases in the given training data, leading to unexpectedly biased outputs with hallucinations. Addressing these issues is a complex challenge, and the volume of the data is not analyzed well, such as in machine learning or data science programs. Because these technologies require careful curation of analysis and training data as well as the development of bias detection and mitigation techniques earlier in the process, we can also follow those steps in Gen AI.
- **Ethical Use:** This is a significant concern across all industries because LLMs

have the potential to generate harmful or misleading content due to their nature, which includes high fabrication, hate speech, irrelevant content, deepfakes, and so on. Ensuring the ethical use of LLMs involves implementing security and privacy aspects, such as content restraint, fact-checking, impact assessments, and responsible deployment in practices.

- **Privacy Concerns:** This is closer to ethical implications. LLMs may be trained on sensitive or private data that accidentally reveals confidential information through generated outputs publicly. Protecting user privacy and data security is essential to the code of ethics, so appropriate governance must be in place to control all these elements.
- **Strength of Interpretability**: LLMs are robust, but their output might be sensitive and threaten data privacy, even if the impact is small due to input or adversarial attacks. It is our response that by enhancing the robustness of LLMs and improving their interpretability, much ongoing research is in place, focusing on increasing trust and reliability in AI systems.

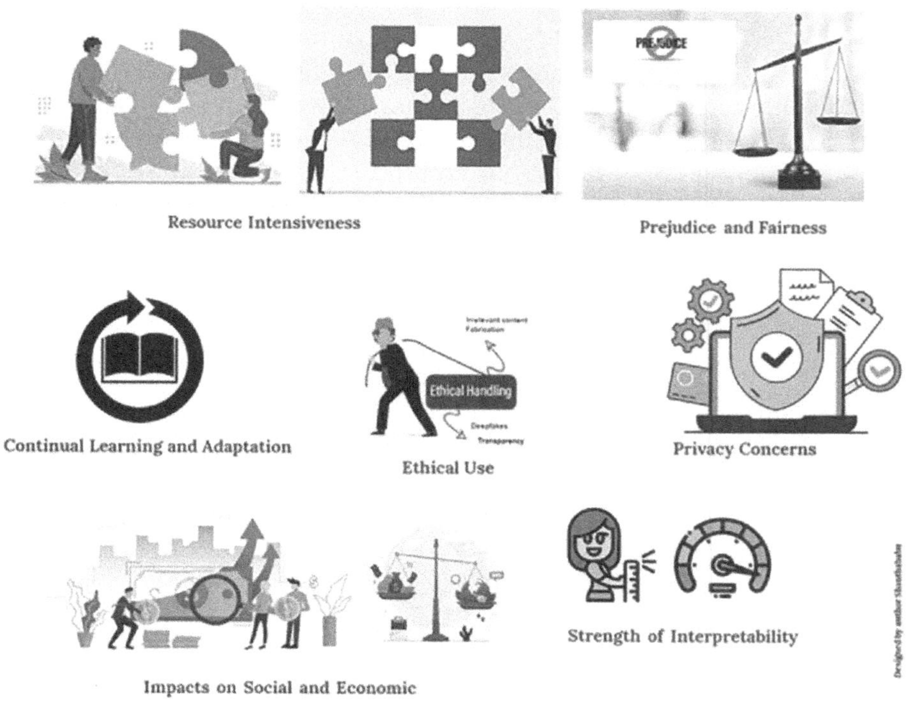

***Figure 2.15**: Challenges in Large Language Models (LLMs)*

- **Continual Learning and Continual Adaptation (CL and CA)**: LLMs typically undergo daily pre-training on large datasets, the volume of which is increasing exponentially, either publicly available or private data (in-house), followed by fine-tuning on domain-specific data. Enabling LLMs to learn and adapt to new information without devastating and, at the same time, continual learning is also a challenging area with implications for real-time applications.

- **Impacts on Social and Economic Factors**: The adoption of LLMs could impact social and economic factors, including job shifts, transformations in the labor pool, and movements in power dynamics. Of course, serious market policies and stronger stakeholder engagement should be implemented to address all these impacts.

Collaboration will be required across all disciplines without questions or arguments, including data collection, AI research and development, aligning with ethics, building policy packages, and grooming domain-specific expertise to guide the entire portfolio.

By responding to and aggressively easing all these challenges, we can tackle LLMs' significant transformative potential, minimize potential risks, and maximize societal benefits.

Conclusion

In this chapter, we understood the Large Language Models (LLMs), detailing their definition and functionality. LLMs leverage neural network techniques with numerous parameters to process and understand human languages, enabling tasks such as text generation, translation, summarization, creative image generation from text, and coding development for various applications. We also explored various types of LLMs along with their specific applications in content generation, virtual assistants, text summarization, and language translation.

We delved into the architecture and components of LLMs, providing a comprehensive understanding of their working principles. Additionally, we examined the significance of controlled outputs and detailed the fine-tuning processes. Benefits such as enhanced performance, efficiency, and generalization were contrasted with challenges, including resource intensiveness, bias, ethical considerations, privacy, interpretability, continual learning, and socio-economic impacts.

In the next chapter, we will shift our focus to vector databases, exploring their mechanisms, distinguishing characteristics, and theoretical foundations. Topics will include types of similarity measures, operational mechanisms, and a review of prominent vector databases such as Pinecone, Faiss, Chroma, and Azure Search, providing an analogy-driven understanding of their role in modern data systems.

Chapter 3
Vector Database and Embedding Techniques

Introduction

In the previous chapter, we explored LLMs, their key components, and the available LLMs in the market–GPT, Chat, BERT, LaMDA, and others. We understood the types of Large Language Models (LLMs), their applications, working principles, and the general architecture. We explored the advantages and challenges of Large Language Models, and related them with industry-specific examples. We also went through the varied aspects of fine-tuning.

This chapter will explore vector database mechanisms, including indexing, querying, and other features. It will also discuss the differences between vector databases and traditional database systems, as well as the characteristics of vector databases. It will present an analogy to understand vector databases, delve into its theories, similarity measures, and its working mechanism. The chapter will explore the different categories within the vector database, understand what serverless vector databases are and their scope, as well as learn about the multiple vector databases available in the market, including Pinecone, Faiss, and Chroma. Detailed steps with code will be provided for working with the Pinecone and FAISS vector databases.

Structure

In this chapter, we will discuss the following topics:

- Defining a Vector Database
  - Need for Vector Database
  - Characteristics of Vector Databases
  - Vector Database versus Traditional Database
- Embeddings and Techniques
- Working Mechanism of a Vector Database

- Serverless Vector Databases
- Vector Embedding and DB-Specific Use Cases
- Semantic and Similarity Search
    - Types of Similarity Measures
- Analogy to Understand Vector Databases
    - Classification of Vector Databases
    - Popular Vector Databases on the Market
    - Working with Pinecone and FAISS Vector Database

Defining a Vector Database

A vector database is one of the new generations of database management systems. It can store data as fixed-length lists of numbers or high-dimensional vectors and implement approximate nearest-neighbor algorithms. Because of this feature, it can search the database with a query and retrieve the closest matching data from the database records stored in the vector database.

It is in the form of high-dimensional mathematical representations, such as features or attributes. In the current scenario, this is explicitly designed to accelerate artificial intelligence application development and simplify the operationalization of AI-powered applications and their workload requirements. It helps remembering inputs using semantic and similarity searches, perform high-computational and powered searches, and make recommendations for various use cases concerning Gen AI in trends across all industries. It can be used predominantly for similarity and multi-modal searches, large language models, and so on.

The vectors are generated by applying a selected form of transformation or embedding function to raw data, such as structured and unstructured data types, including text, images, audio, and video. The LLM framework provides various methods to build the embedding based on the requirements. All these embedding functions can be based on multiple methods, in which word embeddings play a vital role in Gen AI-based use cases.

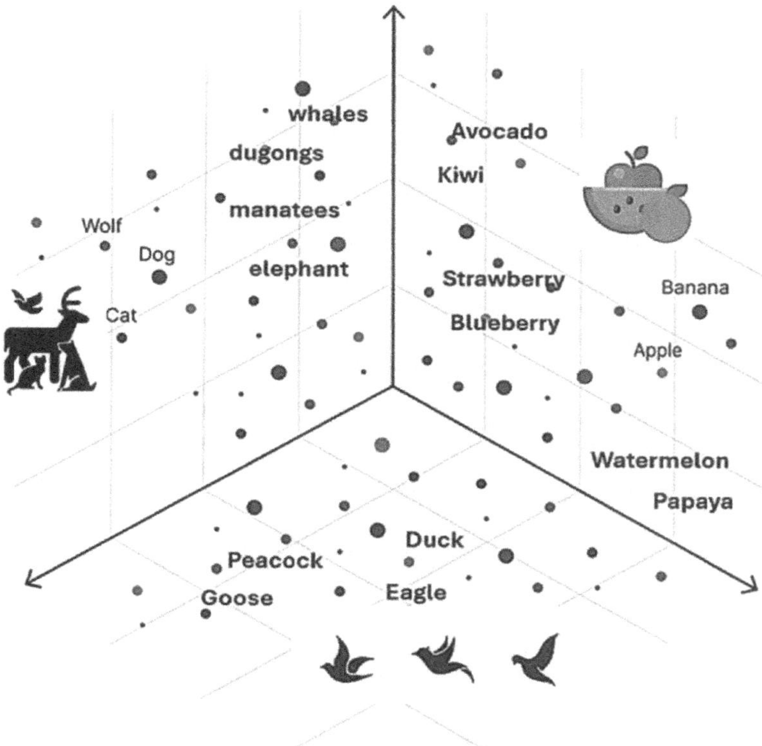

Figure 3.1: *Vector Database (Dimensional Vector Space)*

Need for a Vector Database

You might ask why a new database form suddenly appeared in the database world. This section will help you understand the importance of vector databases and why they are unavoidable when dealing with a massive volume of data in multidimensional space.

Traditional databases are typically designed for well-structured data with high integrity between columns and rows in terms of relationships. Of course, we need this setup to build concrete database models to handle enterprise-level applications.

The need for vector databases emerged when we started storing and dealing with semi-structured and unstructured data types, such as images, audio, and video for specific use cases at industry-level problem statements and high utilization of social media platforms.

Handling data in terms of vector data representation is extremely resource-intensive. However, vector data representation can be highly scalable, searchable, extendable, and dimensional, making it well-suited for Gen AI-specific products and applications.

Characteristics of Vector Databases

- It is capable and compact enough to store data in all formats (text, images, video, and so on).
- It adapts embedding techniques and has highly indexed features.
- It offers a complete solution for complex and vast volumes of datasets.
- It organizes the dataset through high-dimensional vectors with high retrieval speed.
- Each dimension in the vector space corresponds to a specific feature or attribute of the data it represents in the storage.
- It enables advanced analytics and insights by leveraging vector-based representations much faster than traditional databases.
- It offers flexible schema designs to accommodate varying vector dimensions and different types, such as sparse and dense vectors.
- It empowers applications such as content recommendation, anomaly detection, semantic search, and personalized user experiences.
- It is optimized for real-time or near-real-time query processing. It can quickly retrieve similar vectors and perform similarity searches on large datasets.
- It is suitable for applications requiring low-latency responses due to its features.

Vector Database versus Traditional Database

As we know how the traditional databases work, let us explore how a vector database differs from traditional database systems. It is primarily related to its design, capabilities, assessment methodology, storage format, and so on.

Foundational Data Model:

Traditional databases are table-based structures with defined rows and columns as well as well-organized database systems. A traditional database model enforces a predefined schema and ensures data integrity between tables by primary and foreign key relationships as well as concrete constraints.

Conversely, vector databases depart from the relational model and incorporate multidimensional vectors to store and manage the data. This feature system allows for a more flexible description of complex relationships between data, encompassing all types of data such as text, summaries, images, audio, and video. It supports unstructured or semi-structured vector data, representing each entity as a numerical vector (for example, embeddings and feature vectors).

Storage and Retrieval Efficiency:

As we are familiar with traditional database systems and their tabular structure, we may need help handling data efficiently while building longer query and retrieval times, increased storage, and computational requirements.

The storage and retrieval efficiency in the vector database is improved by efficiently storing multidimensional arrays, while features such as similarity search enhance the storage and retrieval efficiency.

Traditional databases are typically designed to scale vertically by adding more resources to a single server. However, vector databases are often built with horizontal scalability, allowing them to distribute data across multiple nodes in a cluster for parallel processing and improved performance, even for complex queries.

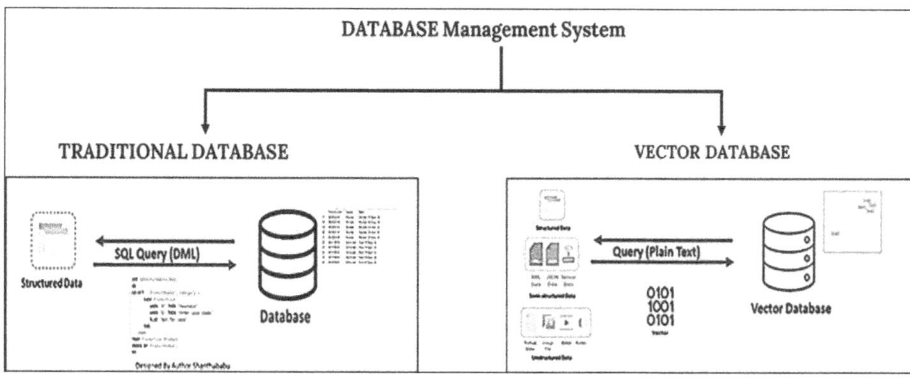

Figure 3.2: *Traditional Database versus Vector Database*

Query Processing:

In both systems, query processing and its outcome play a significant role. As we have experienced, traditional databases are highly constructed using relational database management concepts.

Traditional databases are notable for their ability to ensure data consistency and integrity. However, for large-scale, high-dimensional data, there may be better choices, as complex queries are required to find the most similar records in a database with millions of records and high computational speed.

Ultimately, relational queries involve very composite joins, a combination of multiple aggregation functions, and critical business-specific filters. Monitoring query performance and optimization is always challenging for developers.

Vector databases store data in a high-dimensional format. They focus on vector-oriented operations such as calculating distances, finding nearest neighbors, and performing vector-based computations such as dot product and cosine similarity methodology.

Here, the query involves simple text in English; there is no need to worry about building queries using joins, aggregation functions, and data filtering. All of these are taken care of by the vector database itself.

Moreover, vector databases can also process unstructured or semi-structured data such as images, audio, video, and text (JSON, XML), which relational databases cannot.

Comparison of Vector and Traditional Databases

We have discussed how vector databases differ from traditional databases in terms of operational aspects. Let us discuss them here in terms of functional elements.

- **Database/Collection:** In traditional databases, the database is a collection of tables, but in vector databases, it is a collection.

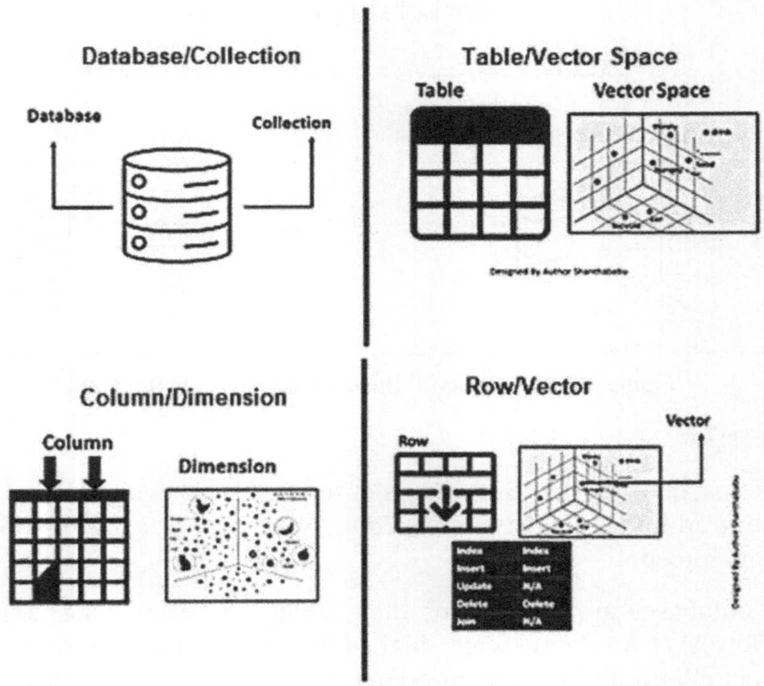

Figure 3.3: *Traditional Database versus Vector Database (Functional)*

- **Table/Vector Space:** In traditional databases, tables are collections of entities with rigid constraints, such as primary and foreign keys and other limitations. However, in vector databases, the space is a multidimensional vector space.
- **Column/Dimension:** In traditional databases, columns, attributes, features, and well-defined type and length are related to other tables as RDBMS concepts. But in the vector database, it is called a dimension (n-dimensions).

- **Row/Vectors:** In traditional databases, the row is the information stored in the table, but in the vector database, information is stored in the form of an embedding vector, which is mathematically represented in the vector space as numerical values, irrespective of the data stored in the vector database.

Embeddings and Techniques

Let us understand how vector databases store data and the logic behind embedding techniques. In vector databases, data is stored using vector embeddings, demonstrating objects in a multidimensional space.

Each object is assigned to a vector point that captures various characteristics of that object and converts them into numerical vector values. It is done in a compressed format that captures their characteristics during the embedding process. When searching (querying) the data, it uses these embeddings to efficiently retrieve very similar and appropriate objects based on their positions in the multidimensional vector space, according to the requirements of the query.

The simple mechanism behind this is that similar objects are assigned to some vector space and have vectors closer to each other in the vector space. In contrast, dissimilar objects have vectors that are apart. This results in clusters in the vector space, which can be represented visually or mathematically to identify relationships or patterns among the data. This is represented in *Figure* 3.4.

This capability enables vector databases to perform fast retrieval and high-similarity search operations, with excellent features such as CRUD operations, metadata management, horizontal scaling, and serverless operations.

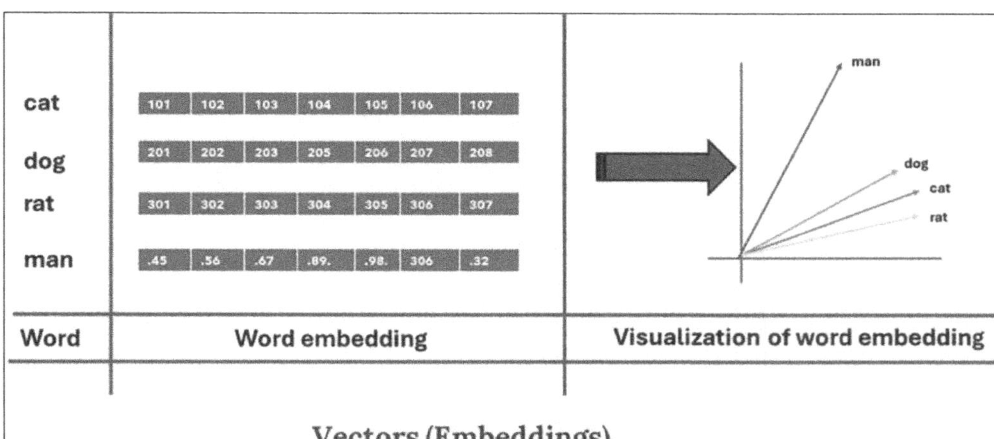

***Figure* 3.4**: *Vector Embedding and Visualization*

Gen AI-based applications are demanding and rely on vector embedding techniques because they carry semantic information in the features. This allows LLMs and frameworks to gain an understanding of the data and maintain long-term memory that they can adopt when implementing complex tasks on massive volumes of data stored in the vector database.

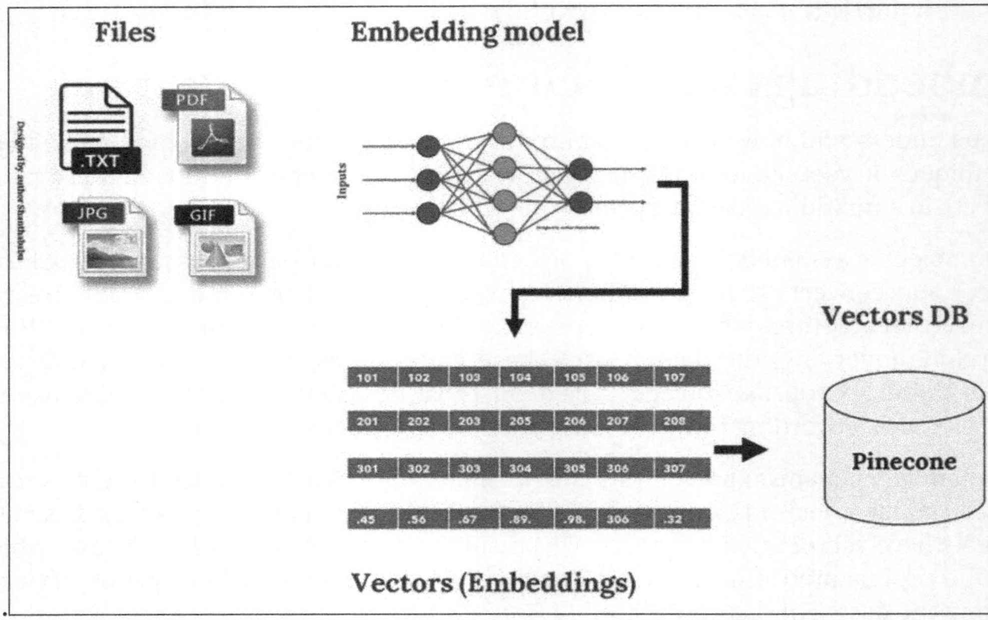

Figure 3.5: *Vector Embedding and Storage in a Database*

Working Mechanism of a Vector Database

The vector database helps the entire Gen AI application enhance performance at different levels. The working mechanism is simple and consists of the following components:

- Input Query
- Embedded Modeling Building
- Similarity Search Operations
- Output Generation and Response
- Chain of Queries

Input Query: This occurs when the user inputs a question or query into the Gen AI application, which could be a chatbot or agent.

Embedded Modeling Building: As mentioned earlier, the inputs are converted into a compact numerical representation and stored in a database with high-dimensional space. This process is called **vector embedding**.

Similarity Search Operations: The input vector embedding is compared with other embeddings stored in the database, and similarity search measures are executed to identify closely related embeddings based on the content available in the database.

Output Generation and Response: After the appropriate search, closely matching data is retrieved from the database, and a response in the form of embeddings is generated back to our query/questions as output for the application. This response contains relevant information linked to the recognized embeddings in the given vector space.

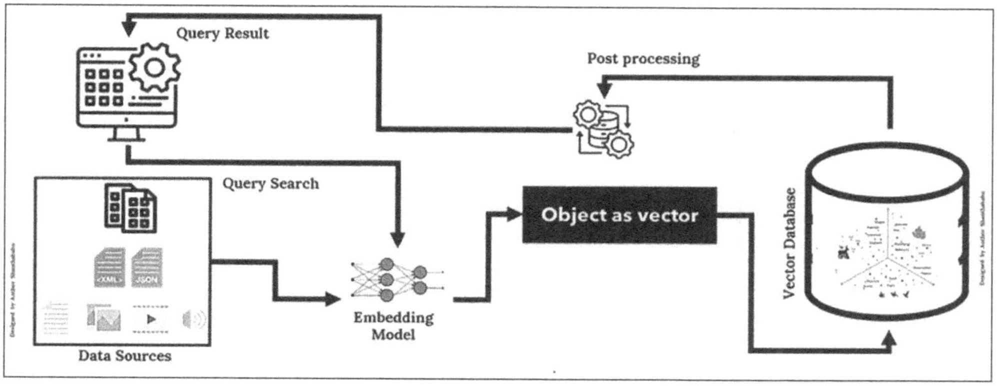

Figure 3.6: *Vector Database (Working Mechanism)*

Chain of Queries: The output generates and responds to the application, keeping the answer in cache memory for the following questions and forming the sequential chain operations.

In simple terms, the working mechanism consists of the following steps:

1. Vector databases first convert data into embedding vectors.
2. Embedding vectors store them in vector databases.
3. Configuration of indexing based on the required dimensions.
4. Input text by interacting with the embedding vector.
5. Internally, it searches for the nearest neighbor in the vector database.
6. Use the index to retrieve the relevant results.
7. The retrieved data would be fine-tuned, formatted, and shared for action in the next feed.

Serverless Vector Databases

We could call the vector database the "Next Generation" of databases, with more advanced architectures to handle fast retrieval, semantic and similarity search,

CRUD operations, filtering metadata for specific scenarios, and horizontal scaling to enhance performance. Typically, they fall into serverless categories. Moreover, this comparatively cost-effective storage and high computing power support highly complex AI-based applications dealing with complex data.

Traditional database architecture, where we manage and monitor servers and infrastructure, is highly challenging and expensive. However, vector databases are becoming serverless, away from the underlying infrastructure and maintenance. This allows us to focus on data and AI applications without the need for database server management.

Serverless vector databases combine significant benefits, such as the capabilities of serverless computing and vector database features. They differ from traditional databases in that they eliminate the need for server management, allow resources to scale up and down, and handle infrastructure on a regular basis.

In simple terms, Serverless Vector Databases have the following benefits:

- **High Scalability:** It can automatically scale the resources up and down based on the demand.
- **Workload**: It supports and allows AI applications to handle dynamic workloads without manual interference.
- **Effortless**: No worries about managing servers or infrastructure; the team can focus on other critical tasks.
- **Cost-Effectiveness**: It eliminates infrastructure investment and maintenance costs.

Vector Embedding and DB-Specific Use Cases

The vector database is a high-potential source and instrumental for Gen AI implementation; this vector embedding feature helps us perform multiple tasks irrespective of domains and industries.

Let us explore a few of them.

- **Information Retrieval Generation (RAG):** Vector embedding and database contributions to information retrieval are significant tasks in RAG-based applications. These powerful techniques influence search engine operations phenomenally, exponentially extending demand and fulfilling requirements.
- **Similarity Search Operations:** Since the vector database is a high-dimensional indexed system, the indexing and indexer are well-organized within the vector database architecture itself. This feature helps us find the similarities between different occurrences in the vector data more quickly and efficiently than in a traditional system.

- **Classification and Clustering:** We know that classification and clustering use cases play a role. These are significant problem statements for Machine Learning and Data Science-specific tasks, and we also have dedicated algorithms. Additionally, vector embedding techniques help classify and cluster use cases precisely and with well-enhanced approaches due to index, similarity, and retrieval features. This allows us to train and build machine learning algorithm models to group and classify datasets and provide solutions.
- **Recommendation Systems**: As we know, recommendation systems are a classic use case in many NLP and Advanced NLP solutions across various industries, specifically in retail, sales, and marketing. To accomplish all these requirements, vector databases and their architectures already have many features, such as index, indexer, and similarity, which lead to exponentially accurate recommendation systems that relate products, items, descriptions, and more.
- **Sentiment Analysis:** This type of analysis is prevalent and in high demand in retail and marketing industries to assess a product or item among critical customers. Based on the response, the manufacturer would enhance the product quality and features in the next release, or the product might be recalled to satisfy the customer. This embedding model helps us categorize and derive sentiment solutions efficiently.

Many applications require vector databases and embedding techniques to enhance Gen AI product performance; we will discuss those in the coming chapters with detailed steps.

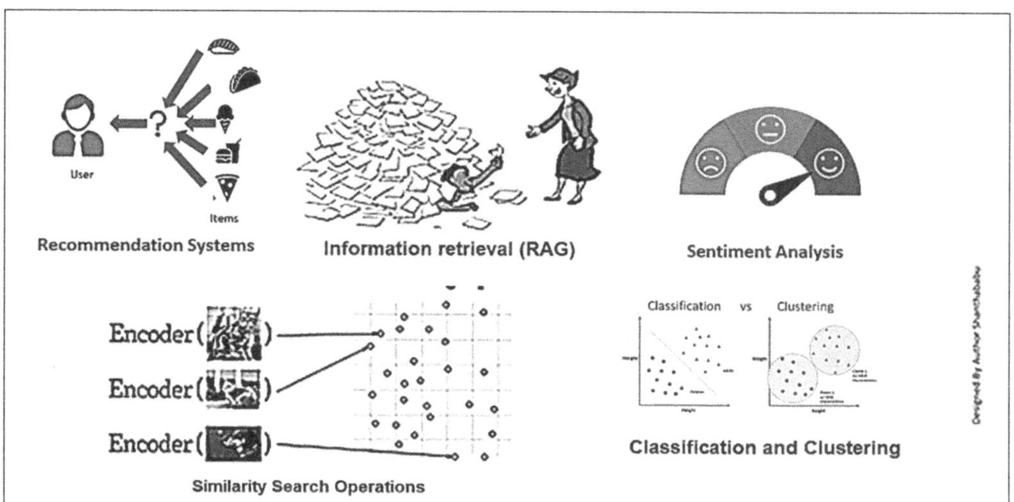

Figure 3.7: *Vector Embedding and DB-Specific Use Cases*

Semantic and Similarity Search

Vector databases' unique features include semantic and similarity search. These two features simplify life and reduce the burden of complex query building in production development, ultimately replacing complex SQL queries.

Semantic Search: This is basically semantic search-based technology. During the operation, this technology helps search for keywords using eloquent conversation practices. This means it interprets the meaning of words and phrases, and the results will return the content that matches the sense of an input query. It also carefully avoids not matching content with the input query. It can understand words from the input query's intent and the end user's search context. It improves the quality of search results by understanding natural languages accurately and focusing on the context of purpose. This search predominantly helps with text generation and summarizing application purposes.

The following figure shows the Semantic Search for Input Query: Vitamins A and C-based fruits.

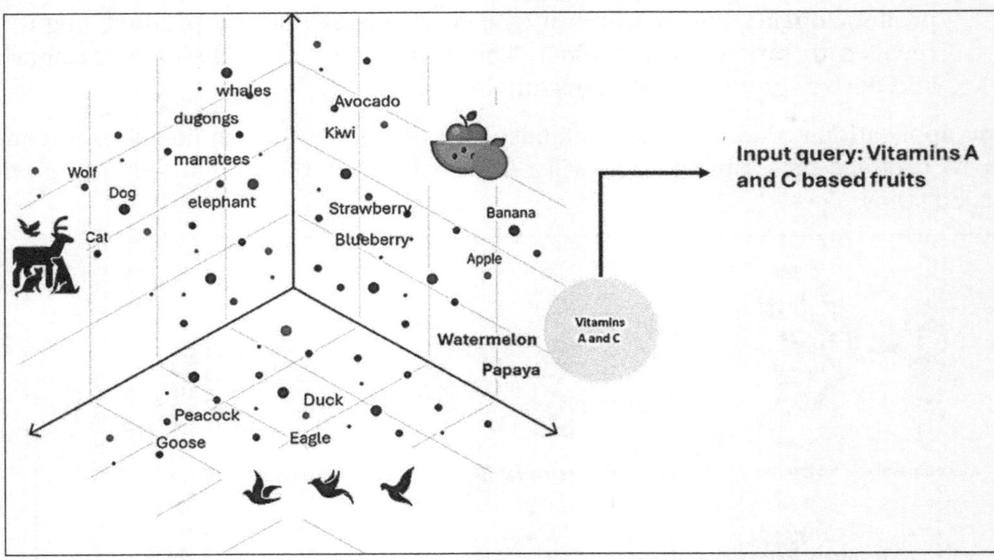

Figure 3.8: *Semantic Search: Input Query: Find Vitamins A and C-Based Fruits*

Similarity Search: This is a critical feature of vector databases that helps us discover the closeness of two vectors and assess how they resemble each other. This specific feature enables us to find similarities and generate the expected context as text or a summary. It allows us to identify similarities in images, audio, and video files.

Understanding the similarities between vectors enables us to extract the similarity between the data objects stored in the vector database. This process helps us understand patterns and insights and leads to decisions for specific use cases and product perspectives.

The mechanism of similarity search is not keyword-based. Instead, it goes with the meaning in the multidimensional vector space.

It uses the "**Hierarchical Navigable Small World (HNSW)**" graph indexes for vector similarity search operations. This is a highly acceptable technology with fast search speeds and quick recall, ultimately exhibiting excellent performance.

When user queries are received through the application interface as input, they are cascaded into the database's vector space. Prior to this, the input query is also converted into a query vector to align with the vector database. This enhances the search and retrieval speed. Additionally, it enables the database to understand what is expected from the user's query and response.

Generally, the vector search starts at the top layer of the HNSW index, and the search operations gradually move on, narrowing down to the closely related vector space. Internally, it builds the graph representation to ease the search operations. This space contains the most relevant data points for our results or the required response back to the system.

The algorithm helps us to identify or locate the area of the right graph position, which contains the vectors closest to the input query.

Internally, it compares the query vectors to all the other data points in the vector space, using "distance" and a concept called **SIMILARITY** for the outside world to estimate how close they are. After finding the best match between the user's input query and the stored vector embedding data in the vector database, the LLM helps us generate the appropriate response as text, summary, or new documents specific to requirements back to the application. This process further trains the LLM over time and improves its capabilities.

We will briefly discuss the various metrics similarity search operations used to determine the distance between the vector spaces, such as Euclidean distance, Dot Product, and Cosine similarity.

Figure 3.9 illustrates the Similarity Search for Input Query: Find fruits with higher water content. Input query: Animal with four legs and one tail, able to brake, and domestic animal in the multidimensional vector space.

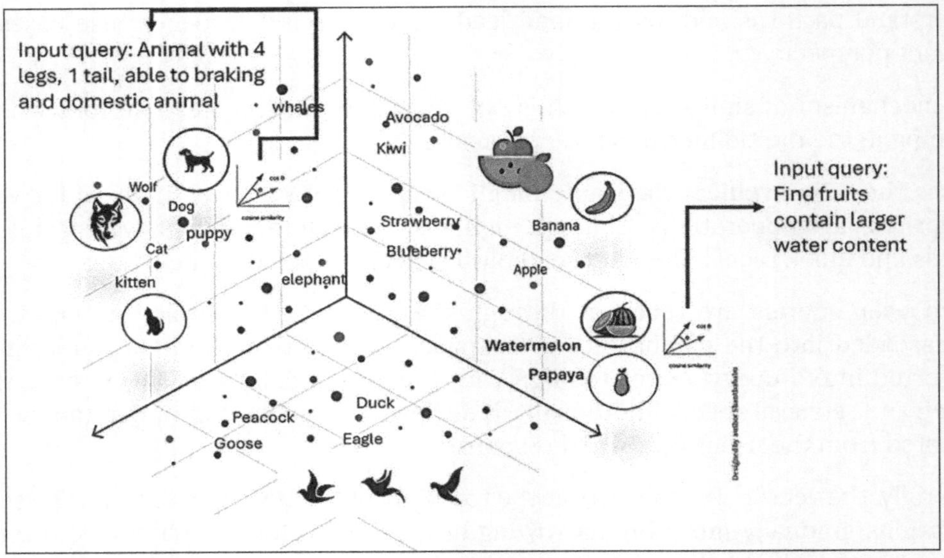

Figure 3.9: *Similarity Search*

Types of Similarity Measures

Fundamentally, these measures are mathematical in nature. These measuring methods form the basis of how a vector database compares the closeness of vector space and identifies the most relevant data points as results for the given input query. Different methods are used, and each method depends on the nature of the data, such as Euclidean Distance, Dot Product, and Cosine Similarity.

Euclidean Distance: In the vector space, this measures the straight-line distance between two vectors, such as A and B. The range spans from 0 to infinity.

- If it is **0**, then the two vectors are identical;
- If it is ∞, both vectors are dissimilar for larger values.

Dot Product: This method discusses the alignment of two vectors' positions and offers different possibilities of alignment, such as in the same direction, opposite directions, or perpendicular to each other.

It ranges from -∞ to ∞.

- **Positive value represents** vectors that point in the same direction.
- **0 value** represents orthogonal vectors.
- **Negative value represents** vectors that point in opposite directions.

Cosine Similarity: It measures the similarity of two vectors using the angle between them. In this measure, the angle is only considered for the similarity calculation.

It ranges from -1 to 1:

- 1 represents identical vectors.
- 0 represents orthogonal vectors.
- -1 represents vectors that are entirely opposed.

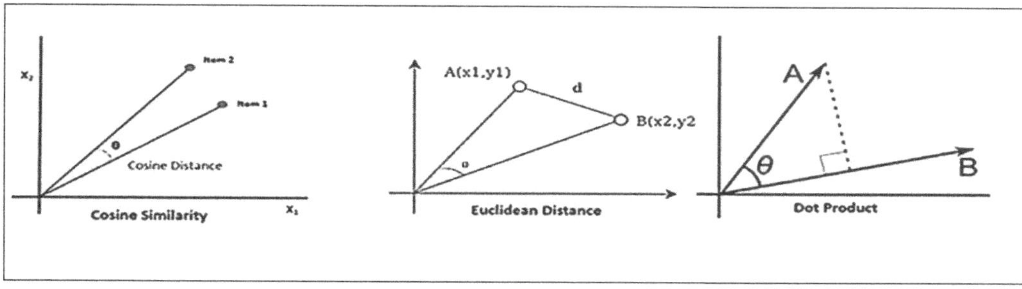

Figure 3.10: *Types of Similarity Measures*

Analogy to Understand Vector Database

To understand better, we can consider examples such as libraries, department stores, vegetable shops, and so on.

In the library, the books are arranged based on age group, literature, drama, poetry, math, science, history, and languages.

In the department store, the products are arranged based on their categories, physical and chemical nature, purposes, manufacturer's specifics, customer usages, and quantity bases–such as rice, wheat, oil, soap, and snacks. They are further divided into multiple sub-categories.

In the vegetable shop, the vegetables, such as potatoes, tomatoes, brinjals, onions, and beans, are arranged.

You can imagine all these analogies and the purpose of arranging them appropriately for easy access and to get things done faster and more accurately from specific places.

In the same fashion, the data is automatically arranged congruently based on content that has the same similarity. Let us consider the preceding analogies for vector databases, similar to organizing books/products/vegetables on shelves based on their characteristics. In similar conduct, data is automatically arranged in the vector database space within the given dimension, while searching internally in the vector database by applying the search mechanism, relevant data is brought back to the model. The model can articulate the content and pass it on as application output. Otherwise, it will display a message such as 'Not Available' or 'Unavailable,' and the LLM will communicate appropriate statements back to the system.

***Figure 3.11:** Analogy to Understand Vector Database*

Classification of Vector Databases

As the demand for vector databases is increasing exponentially, various organizations are building their own vector database products to support and enhance their market stability. Some are new to the market, while others are adding new vector database capabilities to their existing products.

- Pure Vector Databases
- Text Search Databases
- Vector-Capable NoSQL Databases
- Vector-Capable SQL Databases
- Vector Libraries

Pure Vector Databases: This category is designed to effectively store and supervise vector embeddings and metadata. Architecturally, it is intended to separate the derived embeddings from the data source. Examples: **Pinecone and Chroma.**

Text Search Databases: This category is famous for its full-text search and rich documents. The search index is a dedicated data structure that supports efficient and fast textual data searching. **Example: Elasticsearch and Solr.**

Vector-Capable NoSQL Databases: This category is very new to the market and small. It has not been utilized and tested for real-time purposes, so its performance is lower than that of other vector databases. **Examples: MongoDB and Azure Cosmos DB.**

Vector-Capable SQL Databases: This category is comparatively small and typically based on the relational database model. It supports vector search with similarity searches such as dot-product, cosine, and Euclidean distance. **Examples: SingleStoreDB and pgvector**.

Vector Libraries: This category is a dynamic vector representation model that uses multiple templates. It enables us to perform a vector similarity search using the "ANN algorithm," and the implementation is more accessible than in another category.

Examples: Facebook Faiss, Google ScaNN, and Spotify Annoy.

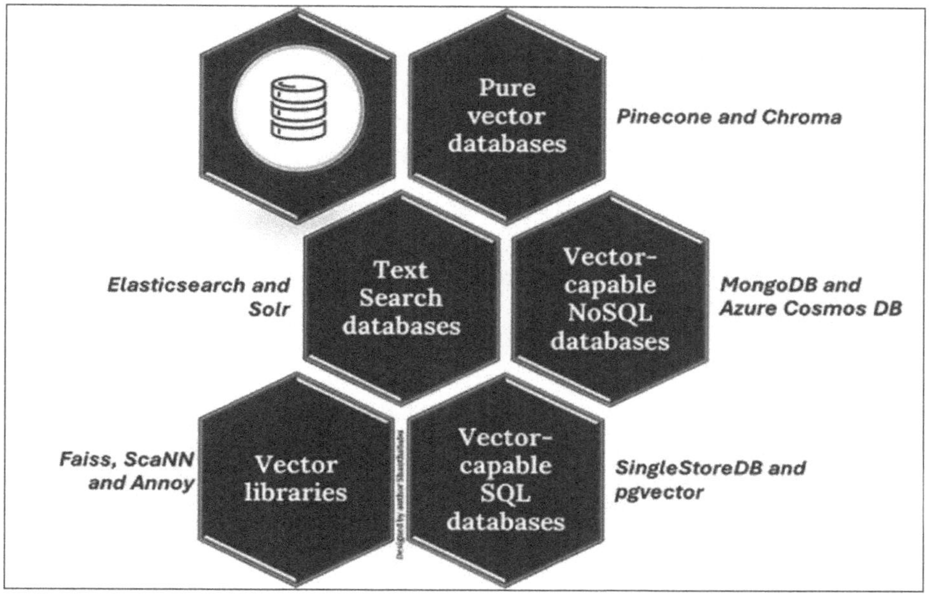

Figure 3.12: *Classification of Vector Databases*

Popular Vector Databases in the Market

As demand increases, the industry introduces several popular vector databases into the market. Based on market demand, let us discuss the best leading vector databases available and choices from a Gen AI application development perspective.

All these databases and their libraries provide very specialized features, performance, and optimizations for handling vector data efficiently by enabling various tasks, such as search engine operations, namely semantic, similarity, classification, and clustering systems at different values of scales.

Besides the following, other vector databases are available in the market:

- Pinecone
- Faiss
- Chroma
- MongoDB Atlas
- Elasticsearch
- Pgvector
- Apache Cassandra
- OpenSearch

Let us discuss the top five here:

Pinecone: This is a managed, cloud-native vector database, not open-source. We can connect to the database through the API from the code itself; no infrastructure is required. It can process the data promptly, with high indexing and filtering expertise. It supports high-quality consequence responses, securing fast and accurate results across a wide range of search operation requests from the applications.

Gen AI and AI developers can build AI solutions without any infrastructure, maintenance, monitoring, and more. This is an easily configurable pay-as-you-go model, ideal for individual users' purposes or smaller projects.

Additionally, it has features such as classification, rank tracking, and duplicate detection.

Faiss: This was developed by the Facebook AI Research team. It is an open-source and dense-vector similarity search pattern using a set of vectors, and it offers a "Dot Product" vector comparison mechanism. This includes high-performance vector searches, exceptionally fast search speeds, and clustering library models. It is also highly efficient at handling CPU and GPU computations for large-scale data. However, the major drawback is that it only allows offline index add/deletion updates.

Chroma: This open-source vector database facilitates data storage and retrieval as well as employs semantic search operations on text data. It has rich features such as queries, filtering, density estimates, and building visualization.

It helps the LLM application perform enhanced NLP operations and significantly reduces hallucinations while generating text, summaries, facts, and more.

It also specializes in generating visualization and discovery from high-dimensional vector space. Using native interfaces, raw data points are transformed into visuals and patterns.

MongoDB Atlas: This fully multi-cloud-managed data platform has an extensive array and vector search facilities, such as text or vocabulary. It can handle various workloads, such as transactional and search operations. It has high availability, data durability, high archival, and backup features.

It has a specialized vector index and independent scaling ability that is automatically synchronized with the database and easily configurable without additional infrastructure to perform the operations.

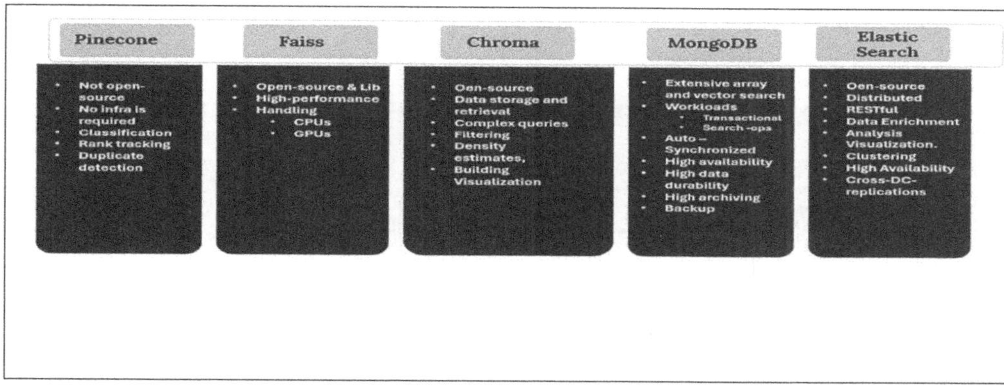

Figure 3.13: *Comparison of Popular Vector Databases*

Elasticsearch: This open-source vector database facilitates distributed and RESTful analytics capabilities. It is part of the "Elastic Stack," which includes open-source tools for various activities such as data collection and storage, data enrichment, analysis, and visualization.

It has excellent features, including clustering, high availability, cross-datacenter-specific replications, fast searching, fine-tuning, and complex analytics assessments. It can also expand horizontally. This will help identify errors to keep clusters highly secure and accessible for LLM applications.

Working with Pinecone Vector Database

Let us discuss how to work with the Pinecone vector database using simple steps to create a vector database through a browser-based interface. By referring to the API key, we can connect it using Python code.

Step 1:

https://www.pinecone.io/solutions/semantic/

New user sign-up. Click on "`Sign Up Free`."

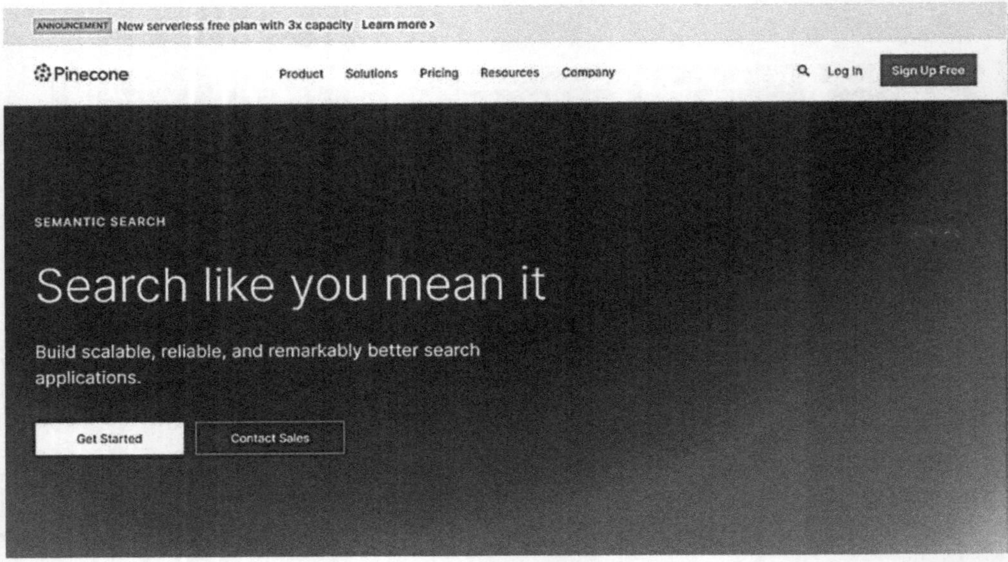

Figure 3.14: *Pinecone Main Page*

Step 2: Select Google/GitHub/Microsoft login or use Pincone-based login.

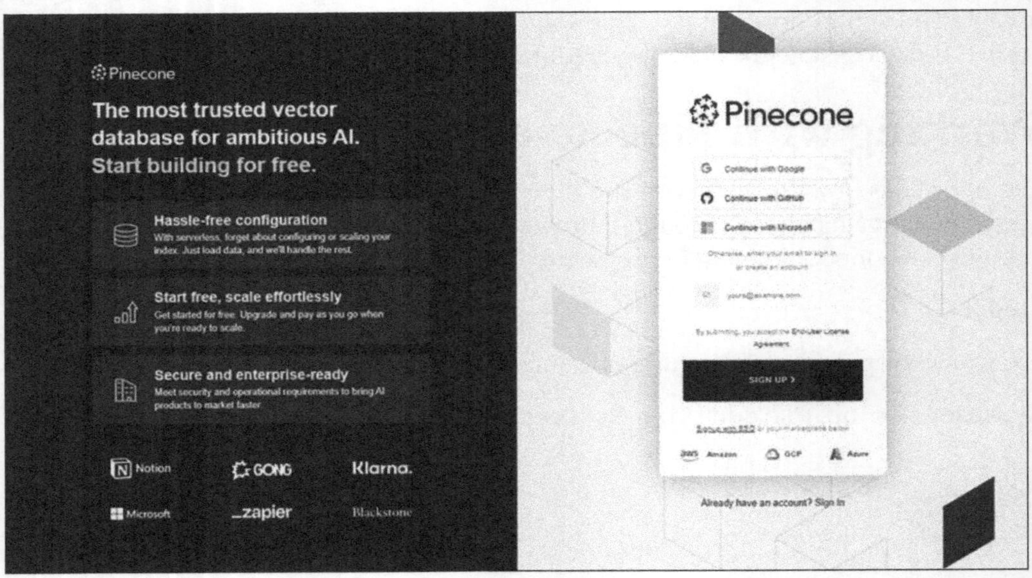

Figure 3.15: *Pinecone Login Page*

Once you successfully log in, you will be placed on the starter package by default. If you want to enhance your utilization, you can go with Standard or Enterprise; it will be charged based on the features, capacity, and support.

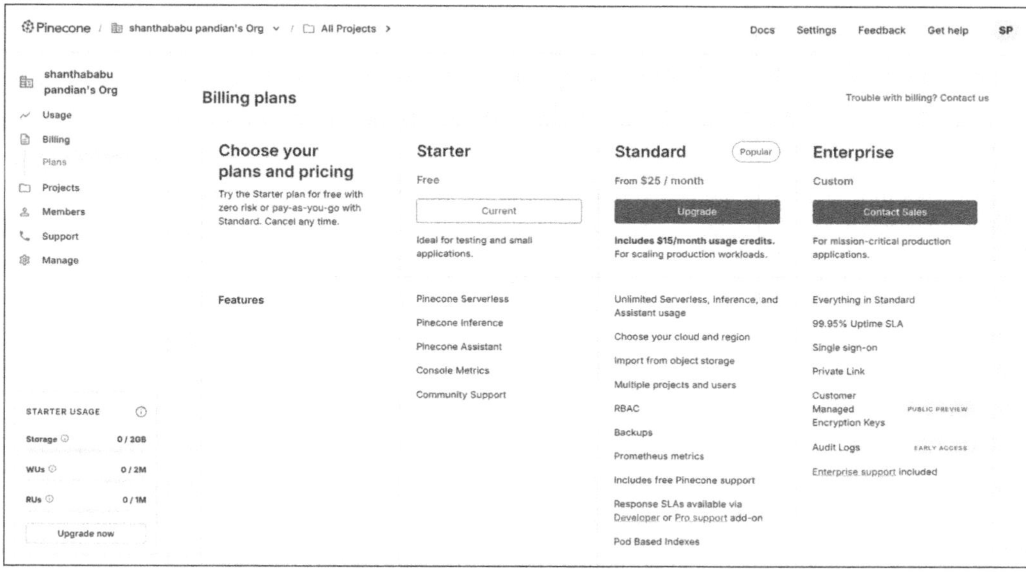

Figure 3.16: *Pinecone Billing Page*

After a successful login, the application will take you to the index page.

Step 3: Click the "**`Create Index`**" button to create a new index.

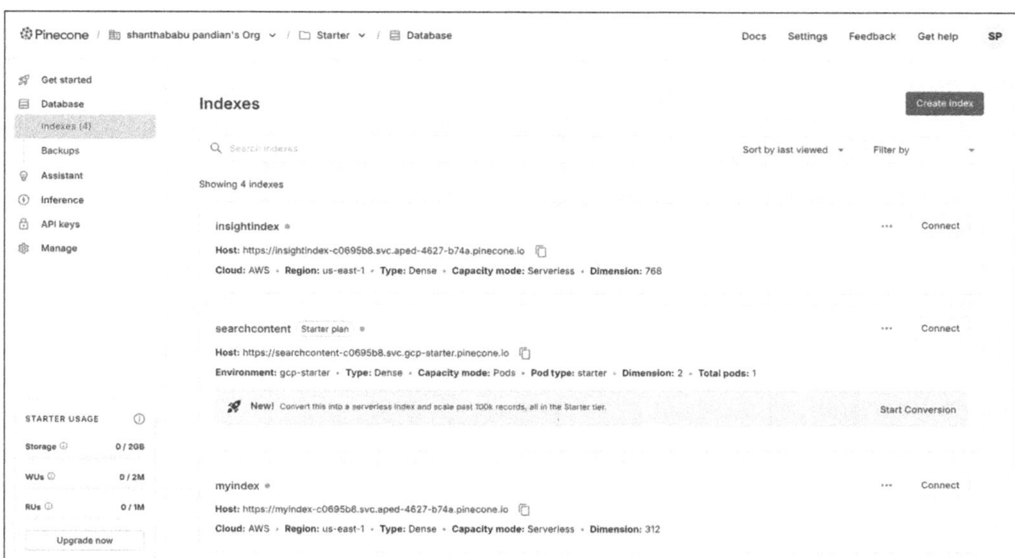

Figure 3.17: *Pinecone Index Creation Page*

Step 4: Enter the name of the index.

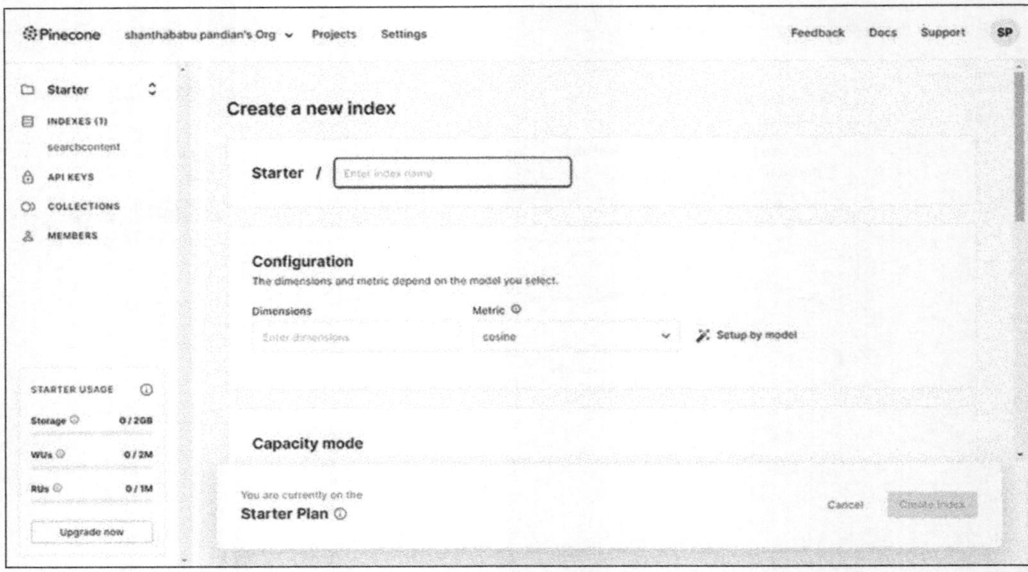

Figure 3.18: *Pinecone Index Configuration Page-I*

Step 5: Enter the dimensions and **`Metric`** (from the drop-down list box); your index is ready. You can select the **`REGION`** (Example: us-east-1).

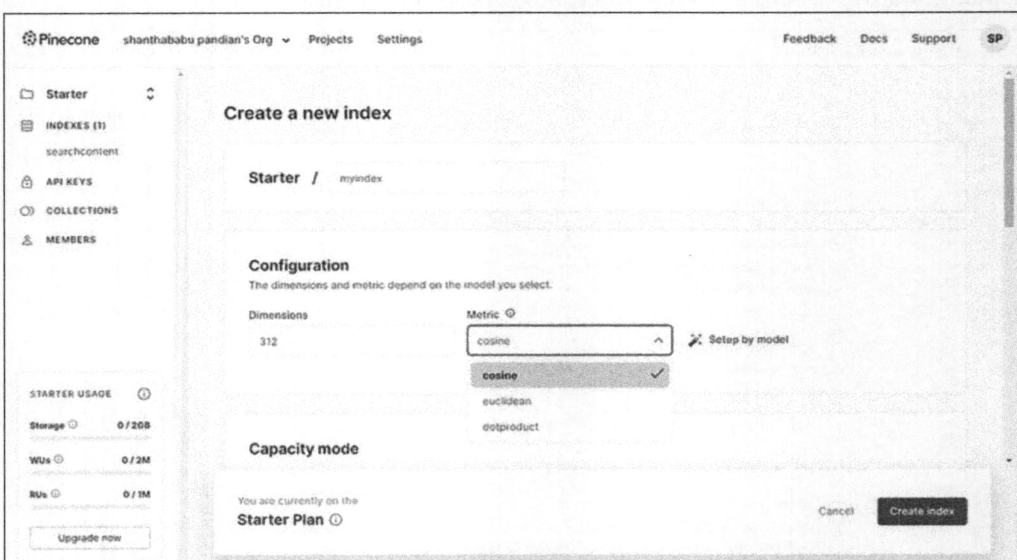

Figure 3.19: *Pinecone Index Configuration Page-II*

Step 6: Create API Key; click the "**`Create API Key`**" button.

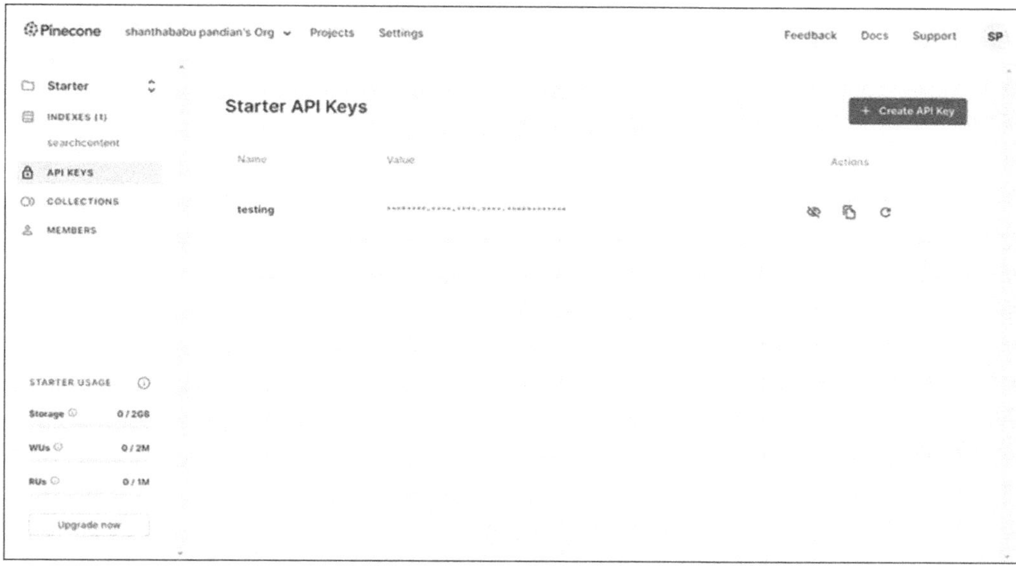

Figure 3.20: *Pinecone API Key Configuration Page-I*

Step 7: You will see a small pop-up screen asking you to enter the API key name and fill in the information.

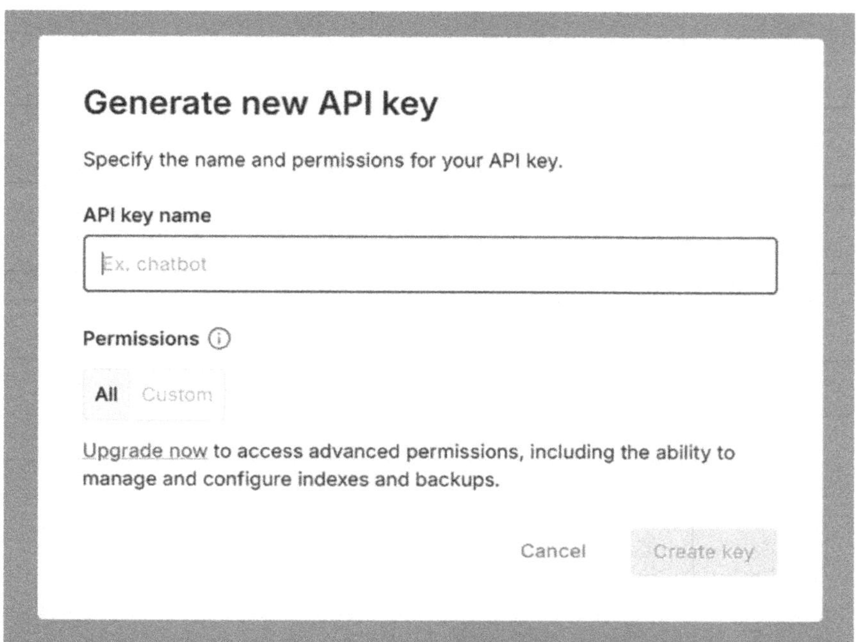

Figure 3.21: *Pinecone API Key Configuration Page-II*

It should be in lowercase, and you can include numerals as well.

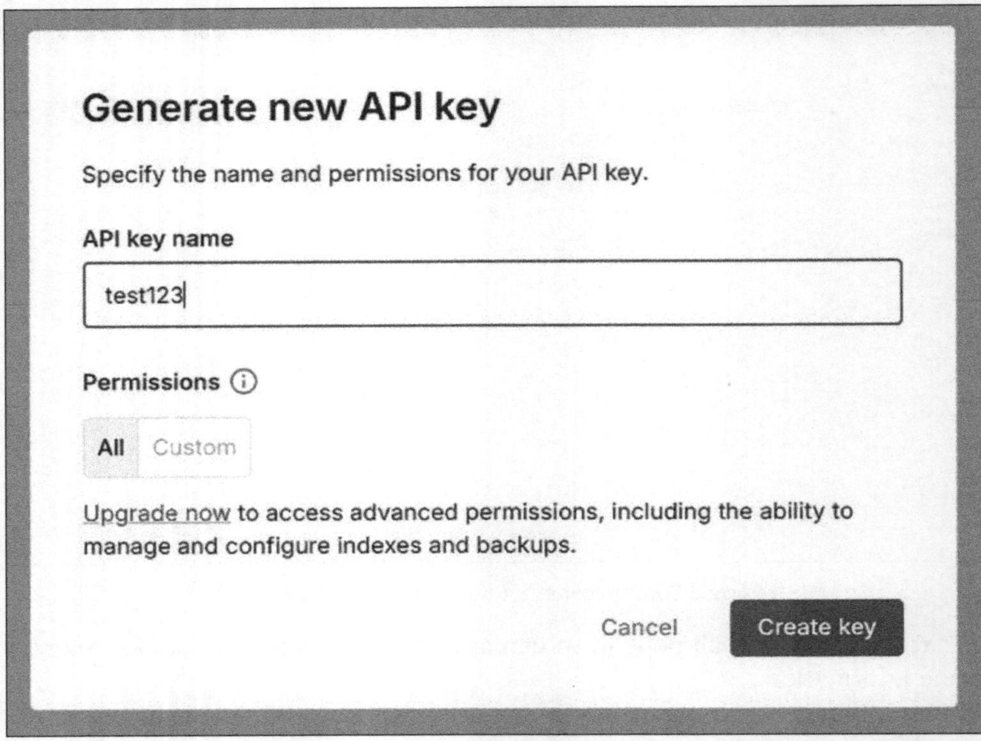

Figure 3.22: *Pinecone API Key Configuration Page-III*

Once it is done, your new API key will appear on the list. Near the API key, you will see four icons, each representing an individual purpose.

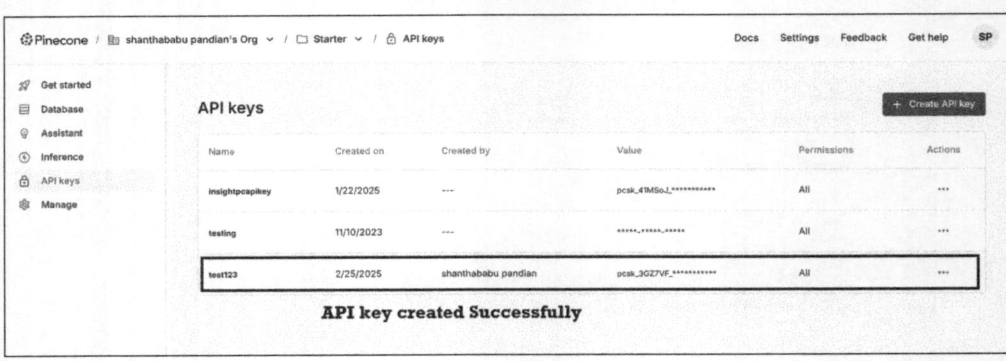

Figure 3.23: *Pinecone API Key List Page*

Step 8: If you want to delete the API key, click on the `Delete` icon, which is the leftmost icon. A popup screen will appear to confirm the deletion by entering the same key.

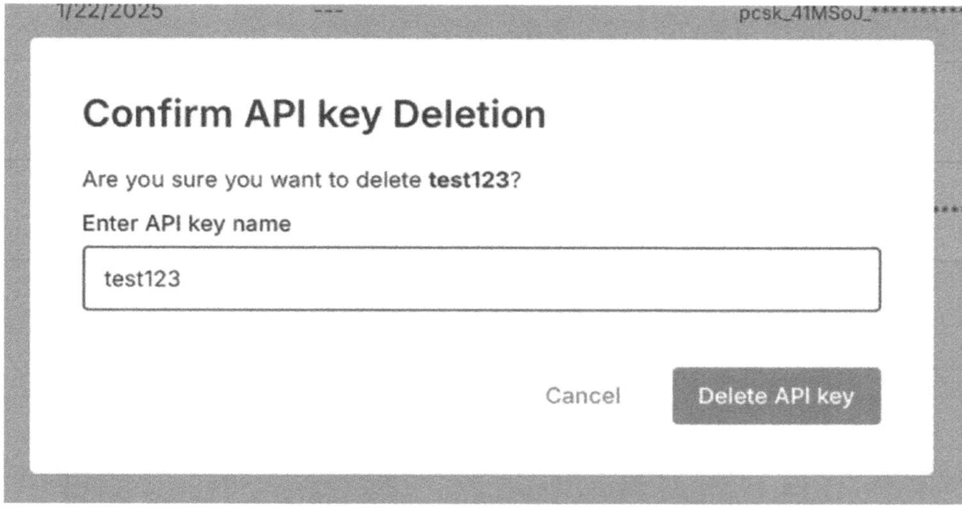

Figure 3.24: *Pinecone API Key Deleting Process*

If you want to explore more, you can visit the document page.

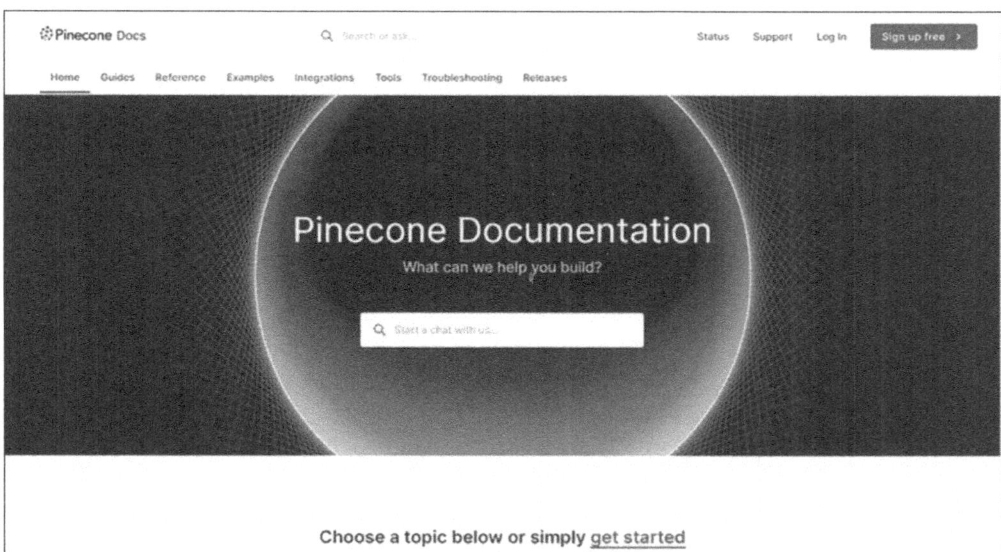

Figure 3.25: *Pinecone Documentation Page*

So far, we have discussed creating the vector database index and providing dimensions, API Keys, and settings for the Pinecone web application. Let us use a simple code snippet to access the document through the vector database by passing a query (Prompt) to get a response. Remember, this is not open-source.

Technical Requirements:

- OpenAI: https://platform.openai.com/docs/overview
    - Requirements: You must create an account to get the Open API Key if you haven't already created one.
- Colab : https://colab.research.google.com/
- Pinecone: https://www.pinecone.io/solutions/semantic/
    - Create API Keys, indexes, and environments.
- Langchain framework
- Google Drive: Create a folder and upload the document required for our exercises to ask Q&A (RAG).
- Install the required Python libraries for this implementation.

Install the following libraries:

```
print("**************************************")
print("Libraries are installed successfully. ")
print("**************************************")
!pip install langchain
!pip install openai
!pip install PyPDF2
!pip install pinecone-client
```

Output

```
************************************
Libraries have been installed successfully.
************************************
```

Ready to code for simple vector database implementation using Pinecone, OpenAI, and Langchain.

```
# Mount your drive to access the files from Google Drive.
from google.colab import drive
drive.mount('/content/drive/')
```

Output

```
Mounted at /content/drive/
```

```
print("**************************************")
print("Libraries are imported successfully. ")
print("**************************************")
import os
from PyPDF2 import PdfReader
from langchain.embeddings.openai import OpenAIEmbeddings
```

```
from langchain.text_splitter import CharacterTextSplitter
from langchain.text_splitter import RecursiveCharacterTextSplitter
from langchain.llms import OpenAI
from langchain.vectorstores import Pinecone
from langchain.document_loaders import TextLoader
from langchain.chains.question_answering import load_qa_chain
from langchain.llms import OpenAI
```

Output

```
***********************************
Libraries are imported successfully.
***********************************
```

```
print("*************************************************")
print("Environment variables are created successfully. ")
print("*************************************************")

# Creating environment variables.
os.environ["OPENAI_API_KEY"] = "XXXXXXXXXXXXXXXXXXXXXXXXXXXXXXXXXXXXX"
os.environ["PINECONE_API_KEY"] = "xxxxxxxxxxxxxxxxxxxxxxxxxxxxxxxxxx"
PINECONE_API_KEY = os.environ.get('PINECONE_API_KEY',
xxxxxxxxxxxxxxxxxxx')
PINECONE_API_ENV = os.environ.get('PINECONE_API_ENV', 'gcp-starter')
```

Output

```
Environment variables are created successfully
```

```
# llm is ready with minimal temperature.
llm = OpenAI(OpenAI=api_keys, temperature=0.1)


# Initialize pinecone
import pinecone
pinecone.init(
    api_key=PINECONE_API_KEY,  # find at app.pinecone.io
    environment=PINECONE_API_ENV  # next to the api key in the console
)

index_name = "abcdefg" # put the name of your pinecone index here

# Provide the path of pdf files.
pdfreader = PdfReader(filepath)

Loop through the file pages and get the content.
```

```
from typing_extensions import Concatenate
# Read text from pdf.
raw_text = ''
for i, page in enumerate(pdfreader.pages):
    content = page.extract_text()
    if content:
        raw_text += content

Print the content

raw_text
```

Output

```
'Machine Learning Engineering  \non AWS\nBuild, scale, and secure machine learning systems and MLOps \npipelines in production\nJoshua Arvin La
ngineering on AWS\nCopyright © 2022 Packt Publishing\nAll rights reserved . No part of this book may be reproduced, stored in a retrieval syste
y means, without the prior written permission of the publisher, except in the case \nof brief quotations embedded in critical articles or revie
reparation of this book to ensure the accuracy of the information \npresented. However, the information contained in this book is sold without
either the author, nor Packt Publishing or its dealers and distributors, will be held liable \nfor any damages caused or alleged to have been c
k.\nPackt Publishing has endeavored to provide trademark information about all of the ...'
```

Figure 3.26: *Sample Document Output from the Object*

```
# We need to split the text using Character Text Split.

text_splitter = CharacterTextSplitter(
    separator = "\n",
    chunk_size = 800,
    chunk_overlap  = 200,
    length_function = len,
)
texts = text_splitter.split_text(raw_text)


# Find the length of the overall text.
len(texts)
```

Output

1286

```
# Creating embeddings of objects from OpenAI.
embeddings = OpenAIEmbeddings()

# Connecting embedding object and text object along with Pinecone index.
print("*************************")
print("Pinecone object is ready.")
print("*************************")
vectordb = Pinecone.from_texts(texts,embeddings,index_name="demoindex")
```

Output

```
Pinecone objects are ready.

# Create a retriever object to query the vector database.
retriever = vectordb.as_retriever(score_threshold = 0.3)

chain = load_qa_chain(OpenAI(), chain_type="stuff")

query = "Who is the author?"
docs = vectordb.similarity_search(query, k=3)
chain.run(input_documents=docs, question=query)
```

Output

```
John Alan

docs = vectordb.similarity_search("What is age of the author")
chain.run(input_documents=docs, question=query)
```

Output

```
The name of the book is not given in the context provided.
(The age of the author is not mentioned in the book)
```

Combining Multiple Chains Using simple Sequential Chain

```
from langchain.chains import LLMChain
master_template=PromptTemplate(input_variables=['Technical require-
ments'],template="Please tell me about {Technical requirements}")
level_1_chain=LLMChain(llm=llm,prompt=master_template)

References_template=PromptTemplate(input_variables=['Further reading'],-
template="Suggest me some References and further reading {Further read-
ing}")
level_2_chain=LLMChain(llm=llm,prompt=References_template)
from langchain.chains import SimpleSequentialChain
comb_chain=SimpleSequentialChain(chains=[level_1_chain,level_2_chain])
comb_chain.run("Deep Learning Containers")
```

Output

```
'\n\nReferences:\n\n1. Grogan, P. (2020). Deep Learning Containers: What They Are and How to Use Them. Retrieved from https://t
-are-and-how-to-use-them-3c8d1d7bac84\n\n2. KubeFlow. (2020). Deep Learning Containers. Retrieved from https://www.kubeflow.org
S., & Liu, Y. (2020). A Comprehensive Guide to Deep Learning Containers. Retrieved from https://towardsdatascience.com/a-compre
\n4. Zaremba, M., & Wawrzyniak, M. (2020). Deep Learning Containers. Retrieved from https://www.michalzaremba.pl/deep-learning-
earning Container? Retrieved'
```

Figure 3.27: *Sample Document Output from Pinecone Vector Database Object*

Working with the FAISS Vector Database

The FAISS vector database is much simpler than Pinecone. It is an open-source library model.

Install, import, and create the relevant objects so we can start working with the data.

Technical Requirements:

- OpenAI: https://platform.openai.com/docs/overview
  - Requirements: You must create an account to get the Open API Key, if you haven't already created one.
- Colab : https://colab.research.google.com/
- Langchain framework
- Google Drive: Create a folder and upload the document required for our exercises to ask Q&A (RAG).
- Install the required Python libraries for this implementation.

Install the following libraries:

```
print("************************************")
print("Libraries are installed successfully. ")
print("************************************")
!pip install langchain
!pip install openai
!pip install PyPDF2
!pip install faiss-cpu
!pip install tiktoken
!pip install load_dotenv
```

Output

```
************************************
Libraries have been installed successfully.
************************************
```

Ready to code for simple vector database implementation using Faiss, OpenAI, and Langchain.

```
# Mount your drive to access the files from Google Drive.
from google.colab import drive
drive.mount('/content/drive/')
```

Output

```
Mounted at /content/drive/
```

```
print("**************************************")
print("Libraries are imported successfully. ")
print("**************************************")
from dotenv import load_dotenv
import os
from PyPDF2 import PdfReader
from langchain.text_splitter import CharacterTextSplitter
from langchain.embeddings.openai import OpenAIEmbeddings
from langchain import FAISS
from langchain.chains.question_answering import load_qa_chain
from langchain.llms import OpenAI
from langchain.callbacks import get_openai_callback
load_dotenv()
```

Output

```
************************************
Libraries are imported successfully.
************************************
```

```
print("*************************************************")
print("Environment variables are created successfully. ")
print("*************************************************")
```

Output

```
Environment variables are created successfully.

# llm is ready with minimal temperature.
llm = OpenAI(OpenAI=api_keys, temperature=0.1)


# Provide the path of pdf files.
pdfreader = PdfReader("file path")
# Load the data
data = pdfreader

Loop through the file pages and get the content.

from typing_extensions import Concatenate
# Read text from pdf.
raw_text = ''
for i, page in enumerate(pdfreader.pages):
    content = page.extract_text()
```

```
    if content:
        raw_text += content
```

Print the content

```
raw_text
```

Output

```
'Cell Biology  \nThe interior of human cells is divided into the  nucleus  and the  cytoplasm . The nucleus is a \nspherical or oval -shap
ytoplasm is the region outside \nthe nucleus that contains cell organelles and  cytosol , or cytoplasmic solution. Intracellular fluid \ni
de the organelles and the cell nucleus . \n \nCells Every living organism is made up of one or more cells. Cells are the basic units of li
independent life and show all the characteristics of a living thing. Figures \n1.1 and 1.2 show examples of plant cells vi ewed under the
n be clearly seen when the cell is mounted in water. An Elodea leaf cell, for example, is seen to \npossess a cell wall and several green
not so obvious ca n \noften be shown up more clearly by the addition of dyes called s…'
```

Figure 3.28: *Sample Document Output from Object*

```
# We need to split the text using Character Text Split.

text_splitter = CharacterTextSplitter(
    separator = "\n",
    chunk_size = 800,
    chunk_overlap  = 200,
    length_function = len,
)

chunks = text_splitter.split_text(raw_text)


# Creating embeddings of objects from OpenAI.
embeddings = OpenAIEmbeddings()


# Connecting embedding object and text object along with FAISS index.
print("*************************")
print("FAISS object is ready.")
print("*************************")
vectordb = FAISS.from_texts(chunks, embeddings)
```

Output

The FAISS objective is ready.

```
# Create a retriever object to query the vector database.
retriever = vectordb.as_retriever(score_threshold = 0.3)

chain = load_qa_chain(OpenAI(), chain_type="stuff")

query = "What is Cell Biology?"
```

```
docs = knowledgeBase.similarity_search(query, k=3)
chain.run(input_documents=docs, question=query)
```

Output

```
Cell Biology is the study of cells and their structures, functions, and processes.
It focuses on the organization and properties of cells, as well as how they interact with their surroundings.
```

Figure 3.29: *Output from FAISS Vector Database Object-Sample Query-I*

```
query = "What is Diffusion?"
docs = knowledgeBase.similarity_search(query)
chain.run(input_documents=docs, question=query)
```

Output

```
Diffusion is the movement of molecules from an area of high concentration to an area of low
concentration until the concentration becomes equal.
It is a passive process that does not require energy and is important
for the exchange of substances in cells,
such as oxygen and carbon dioxide, and in multicellular organisms for
the movement of respiratory gases and dissolved food.
The cell membrane plays a role in controlling the passage of
substances during diffusion.
```

Figure 3.30: *Output from FAISS Vector Database Object-Sample Query-II*

```
query = "Explain Sterile Petri dish"
docs = knowledgeBase.similarity_search(query)
chain.run(input_documents=docs, question=query)
```

Output

```
A sterile Petri dish is a container used in microbiology to culture microorganisms.
It is commonly referred to as a plate and can be made of either plastic or glass.
Glass Petri dishes can be sterilized in an autoclave,
while plastic Petri dishes are already sterilized during their manufacture.
This ensures that no unwanted microbes are present in the dish,
creating a sterile environment for the growth of specific microorganisms.
```

Figure 3.31: *Output from FAISS Vector Database Object-Sample Query-III*

Conclusion

In this chapter, we discussed the definition of a vector database and its role as part of the new generation of database management systems. We explored how it stores data with fixed-length lists of numbers and high-dimensional vectors, its need for dealing with multiple file formats, how all these are helping with specific use cases at industry-level problem statements, and how social media platforms are utilizing them. We discussed the characteristics of vector databases precisely with classical evidence followed by exploring the differences between vector databases and traditional databases in terms of design, capabilities, assessing methodology, storing format, and more.

We understood the functional differences between the vector and traditional databases by comparing them across different aspects. We gained insight into the working mechanism of vector databases with neat diagrams illustrating their components that help to build Gen AI applications, such as input queries, embedded modeling building, similarity search operations, output generation and response, and chain of queries. We also understood how vector databases act as serverless vector databases and their advantages.

We have reviewed significant vector embeddings and DB-specific use cases, such as information retrieval (RAG), similarity search operations, classification and clustering, recommendation systems, and sentiment analysis.

Using a classic example, we exclusively discussed and experimented with working with the Pinecone vector database and the FAISS vector database.

In the next chapter, we will explore prompt engineering and its importance in Generative AI, components prompts, and their categories. We will discuss various prompt engineering techniques and how to generate knowledge prompting.

Chapter 4
Prompt Engineering and Its Significance

Introduction

In the previous chapter, we explored the definition and significance of vector databases as part of the new generation of database management systems. We discussed how, particularly for Gen AI products and applications, vector data representation is resource-intensive yet incredibly scalable, searchable, expandable, and dimensional. With an emphasis on the function of embeddings in vector databases, we examined the design, capabilities, evaluation techniques, and storage formats of vector databases in comparison to standard databases. Additionally, we looked at well-known vector databases like Pinecone, Faiss, and Chroma and included comprehensive instructions along with code for using Pinecone and FAISS.

This chapter will explore prompt engineering and its importance in Generative AI, component prompts, and categories. We will discuss various prompt engineering techniques such as N-shot prompting, Chain-of-Thought (CoT) prompting, Directional Stimulus Prompting (DSP), React prompting, Multimodal CoT prompting, Graph prompting, and how to generate knowledge prompting. Understanding the problem, how to craft the initial prompt, evaluating the model's response, iterating and refining the prompt, testing the prompt on different models, and scaling the prompt performance. We will explore the prompt engineering aspects through examples such as Q and A, text summarization, chatbot responses, document classification, and named entity recognition, along with the best practices and guidelines for writing prompts while building strategic models.

Structure

In this chapter, we will discuss the following topics:

- Prompt Engineering and Significance in Gen AI
- Components and Elements of Prompt

- Instructions, Context, Input and Output Data, and More
- Role Prompting
  - Professional, Expert, Fictional Roles, and More
  - Effectiveness of Role Prompting Techniques
  - Role Prompt's Flip Side
  - Prompting: Voice Specific
- Prompt Engineering Techniques
  - Single and Multiple Prompt
  - Best Practices for Building Effective Prompts

Prompt Engineering and Significance in Gen AI

Let us understand prompt engineering first, then discuss its significance in Gen AI.

We can describe prompt engineering in various ways.

Prompt engineering is the process of designing and improving the input prompt(s) for LLMs and instructing the vector database to get the desired outputs for Gen AI, which could be chatbots, agents, and so on.

Although Gen AI's objective is to replicate human thoughts and feelings, it needs accurate guidance and directions to produce high-quality and relevant output for the given task. So, in prompt engineering aspects, we must select the correct role and formats of output, including words, sentences, phrases, and indications to the LLMs to generate the appropriate and desired output for the selected fields or domains. This helps Gen AI products to interact more meaningfully with users. Of course, every prompt engineer must apply their creative and innovative thoughts through trial and error by creating rational input text pools to operate an application's Gen AI effectively.

Prompt engineering involves a single and/or set of prompts, which are simple instructions and examples using any language to steer LLMs in their behavior in the environment. This allows us to align the LLMs' output with the user's objectives without the model being retrained expensively.

Effective design-engineered prompts can make LLMs suitable for a comprehensive variety of tasks for which they were initially trained.

In simple terms, prompts act as instructions to demonstrate LLM, using vector database details and providing the desired input-output mapping. This is an alternative to fine-tuning.

Before getting into Prompt Engineering, let us recap LLMs, which have a neural network learning ability-based architecture pattern that helps analyze the prompt. Internally, multiple components help the application build the right content. (Please refer to *Chapter 1, Introduction to Generative* AI.)

The first component focuses on the most appropriate words for the context based on its abilities, finding the most relevant word for the given context or prompt.

The next component helps the system remember the order of the words and ensures that the prompt makes sense of the right context. Following this, it generates an appropriate and logical list of words for the set of lines by probabilistically combining the words to meet the expectation of context for the given prompt.

In summary, an LLM's unique brain architecture helps it pay attention to the following factors: the right words, the order of remembrance, and probabilities of assignments to the next words in the context.

LLMs have proven to be a remarkable advancement in understanding and generating tasks specific to Natural Language Processing (NLP).

Significance of Prompt Engineering

So far, we have discussed and understood facts about prompt engineering. Prompt engineers bridge the gap between Gen AI product users and LLMs. They identify scripts and templates your users can customize and complete to receive the best results from the language models. These engineers conduct experiments using diverse inputs to construct a prompt library that application developers can utilize in different situations.

Prompt engineering helps make AI applications more efficient and effective. Application developers typically include open-ended user input within a prompt before sending it to the AI model.

For instance, think about AI chatbots. Users might type an incomplete issue such as, "Where to buy a shirt?" Internally, the application's code incorporates an engineered prompt saying, "You function as a sales assistant for a clothing company." A user from Alabama is asking you where they can purchase a shirt. Provide the three closest store locations with a shirt in stock." The chatbot then generates more relevant and accurate information.

Components and Elements of Prompt

Regarding prompt engineering, prompts consist of the following major components or elements, each with its own importance, such as instructions, context, input data, and output data.

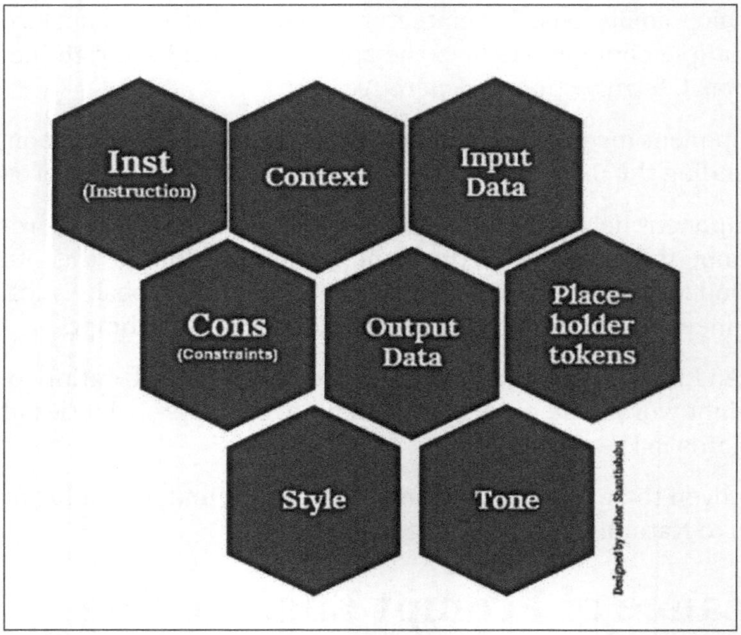

***Figure 4.1**: Elements of Prompt*

- **Instructions**: This is a major element that helps with specific tasks or sets of instructions that the model wants to perform precisely during the operations. If there is any unclarity in this instruction, the overall system will react differently and send unexpected or unwanted output back to the user. This instruction describes the requirements, objectives, and format of input and output for the specific task. Focus on the point where it explicitly explains the task requirements for the model.

  Here is an example:

  ```
  Summarize Sachin Tendulkar's achievements from the following
  passage clearly in five-point sentences.
  ```

- **Context**: Context is a supporting element that can help steer the LLM to produce better responses by focusing on certain logical guidance. The desired context is input as an example, and the desirable output will be obtained. It provides distinct illustrations of how different contexts are inputs and how they should map to outputs.

  Here is an example:

  ```
  In the context of the major achievements of Sachin Tendulkar,
  provide a concise
  summary of the main findings from the given input.
  ```

- **Input Data**: The input (query, prompt, or question) that we are interested in finding a response for; it can be a set of questions or statements. This is the input data and the actual content feed for the model, and we have to make sure that the input data is relevant to the given instructions. The objective is for the input to be intended to generate the required response based on instructions and context.

  Here is an example:

  ```
  Sachin Tendulkar is a cricket icon known as the "God of Cricket."
  He holds the record for the highest run-scorer in Test and ODI
  cricket, with 100 international centuries. Tendulkar's 24-year
  career was marked by exceptional batting skills, versatility, and
  numerous contributions to Indian cricket, including a pivotal
  role in winning the 2011 ICC Cricket World Cup. Off the field, his
  humility and dedication have made him a respected figure, and his
  legacy continues to inspire cricketers worldwide.
  ```

- **Output Data:** Based on the instructions, context, and input data, when this was executed in the OpenAI playground within the system panel, the following answer was obtained:

  ```
  1. Sachin Tendulkar is known as the "God of Cricket" and holds the
  record for the highest run-scorer in Test and ODI cricket with 100
  international centuries.
  2. Over his 24-year career, he showcased exceptional batting
  skills and versatility, impacting Indian cricket.
  3. Tendulkar played a significant role in India's 2011 ICC Cricket
  World Cup victory.
  4. His humility and dedication off the field have earned him respect
  worldwide, making him a revered figure in the cricketing community.
  5. Sachin Tendulkar's legacy continues to inspire cricketers
  globally, solidifying his status as one of the sport's all-time
  greats.
  ```

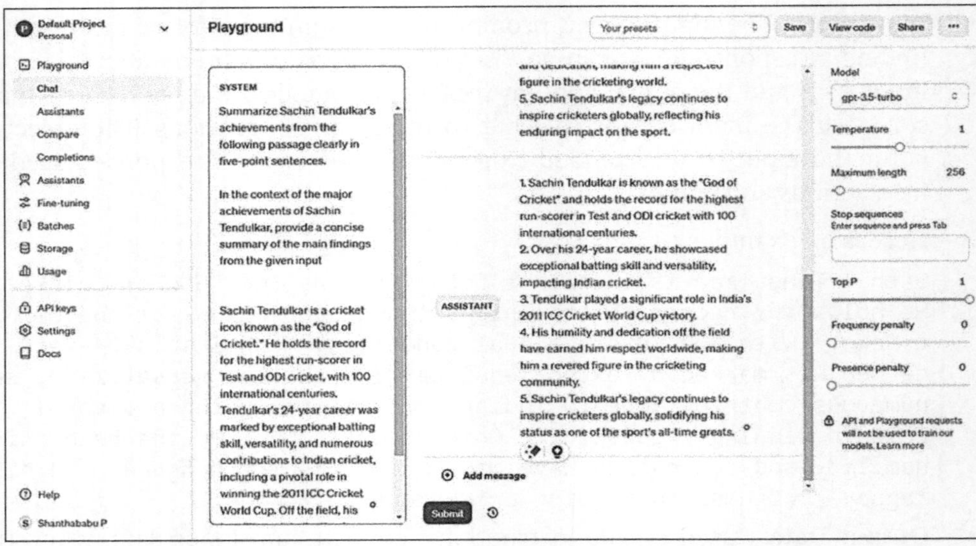

Figure 4.2: *Prompt Elements in the OpenAI Playground*

Output Indicator: This represents the format and type of the output with a specific indicator. This means that the sentiment is an indicator of expected output, and based on the input text, the output would be neutral, negative, or positive.

`Instructions: Classify the text as neutral, negative, or positive.`

Here is an example:

System Input

Input: `The food in the restaurant is good.`

Output indicator: Sentiment:

Figure 4.3 shows the output through an assistant as "`Positive`."

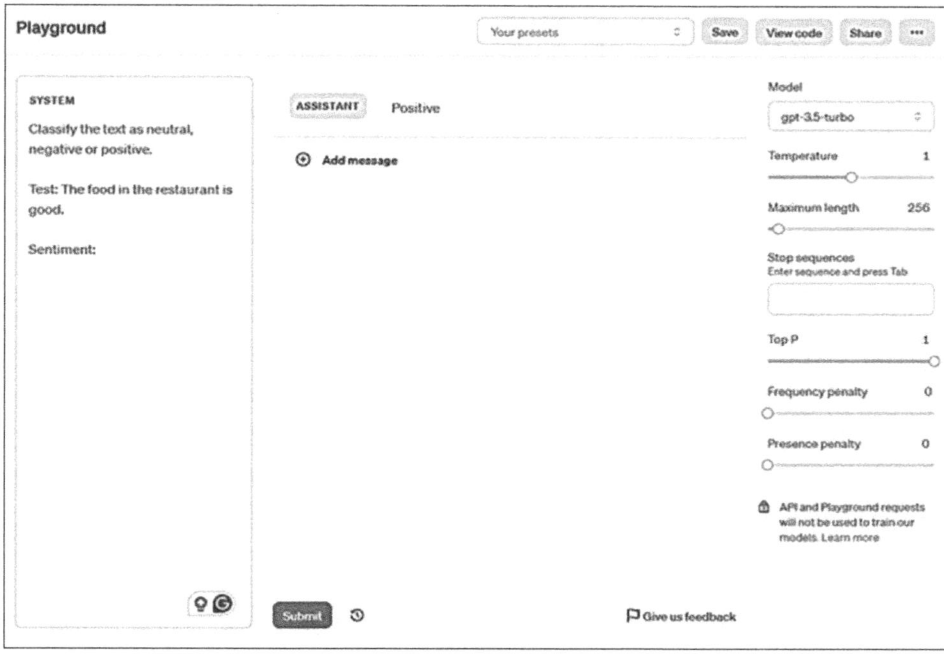

Figure 4.3: *Prompt Elements with Output Indicator (Sentiment)*

Placeholder Tokens: The placeholder token element is a powerful way to design your prompt engineering, and it helps us manage the output format and structure it properly. It supports multiple output generations. We use placeholder tokens as variable inputs for the prompt input and to indicate that the LLM should insert its response into the generated text from the dataset residing in the vector database.

Here is an example:

System Input

Imagine you are visiting a **`[Country]`** for a business trip. You have **`[Number_of_Days]`** days to participate in the tech event. What kind of visas and other papers would you need? Provide a brief description of each and explain. Given the output in point and priority-based.

Placeholder tokens are **`[Country]`** and **`[Number_of_Days]`**

Output

```
To visit New York, USA, for a business trip to participate in a techno
event for five days, you would typically need the following visas and
documents:

  1. Business Visa:
     - A Business Visa is necessary to enter the USA for business pur-
```

```
poses, including attending meetings, conferences, or trade shows.
- You will need to apply for a Business Visa (B1 Visa) at the
U.S. Embassy or Consulate in your home country.
- The visa application may require documentation such as a letter
of invitation from the tech event organizers, proof of accommoda-
tion, flight itinerary, and proof of sufficient funds.

2. Electronic System for Travel Authorization (ESTA):
- ESTA is required for citizens of countries under the Visa Waiv-
er Program (VWP) who are traveling to the USA for short business
trips or tourism.
- You need to apply for an ESTA at least 72 hours before your de-
parture to the USA.
- ESTA grants you authorization to travel to the USA without a
visa for stays up to 90 days.

3. Invitation Letter:
 - An invitation letter from the tech event organizers in New York
can be helpful in supporting your visa application and explaining
the purpose of your visit.
- The invitation letter should detail the event dates.
```

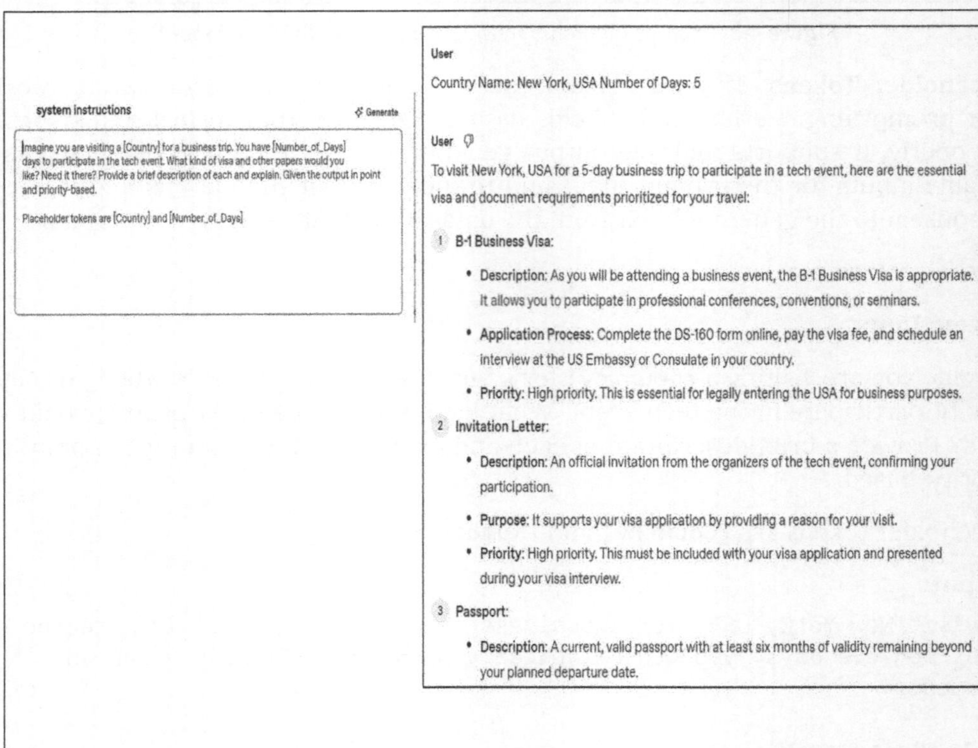

Figure 4.4: *Prompt Elements with Placeholder Tokens*

Sample 2: Prompt elements with placeholder tokens such as country (for instance, France), city (for instance, Paris), and number of days (for instance, 10).

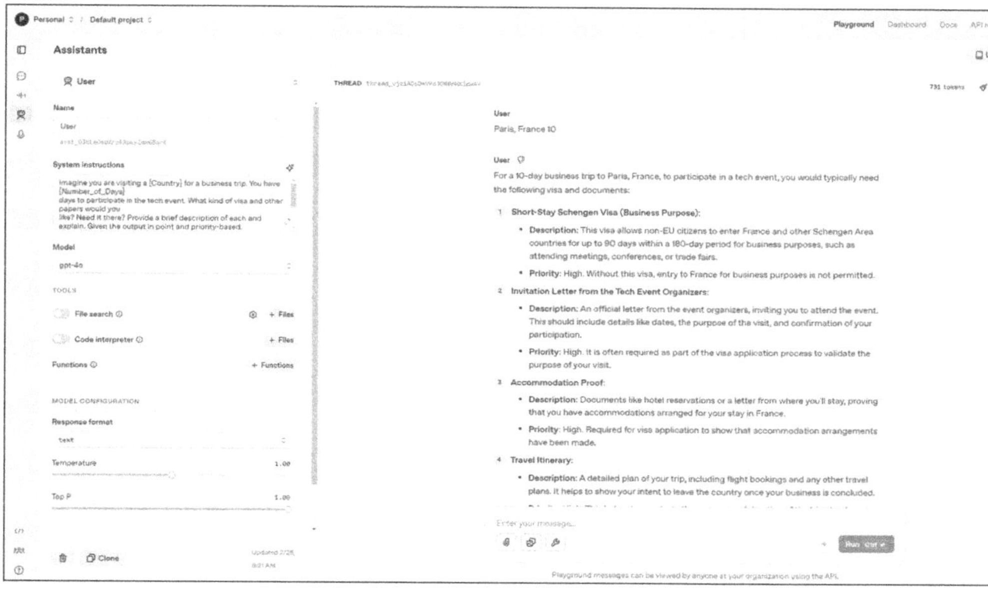

Figure 4.5: *Prompt Elements with Placeholder Tokens (Countries: Paris, France, and 10 days)*

Constraints: This element imposes specific constraints on the LLM response to ensure that it meets specific requirements and guidelines, and prevents awkward content to maintain ethics. The required constraints must be explicitly or implicitly expressed within the prompt by carefully creating the description and context.

Here is an example,

System input

Compose a **short 8-line** poem about Gen AI and its impact on industry with an AXAA rhyme scheme.

Constraints: **short 8-line**

Output

```
Gen AI, a force in the industry's fray,

Revolutionizing with each passing day,
Tech advancements lead the way,
Bringing efficiency, come what may.

Automation and machine learning in play,
Boosting productivity with a seamless array,
```

```
Future of work, brighter display,
Gen AI, here to stay.
```

System input

```
Compose a short 8-line poem about the city of London with an AABB rhyme scheme.
```

Constraints: **short 8-line**

```
In London town, the red buses race
Past palaces and landmarks of grace
The Thames flows steady, a silent guide
Through streets where history can't hide

From Big Ben's chime to the Tower's keep
In its heart, old stories sleep
London, a city alive and grand
Where the past and present hand in hand
```

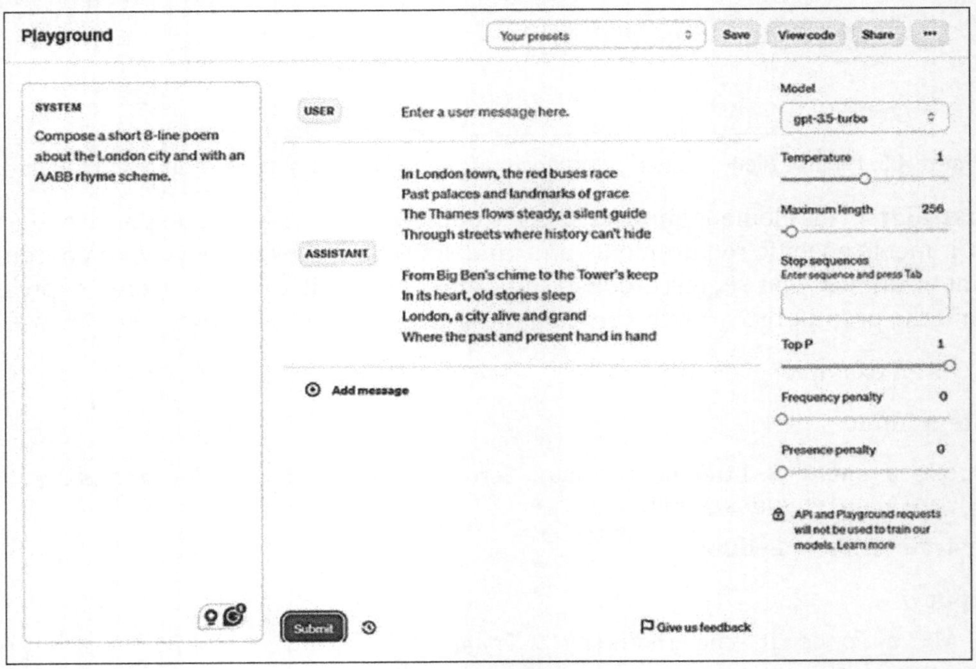

Figure 4.6: *Prompt Elements with Constraints*

Tone and Style: Provide a certain tone and style to the input prompt to modulate the model response based on the business requirements. Since the prompt is in simple English language, we can provide the desired tone specific to the business requirements, such as conversational, formal, assertive, authoritative, optimistic, casual, animated, influential, fun tone, or more.

Based on everyone's understanding, the preceding tone is a parameter of the prompt, and it helps us generate outputs that align with the intended purpose and audience.

System input

System input with `<tone>/<style>`

System input

```
Write 50 words about a brand-new Laptop. Use 20 years of salesman tone.
```

Input

```
XYZ Laptop
```

Assistance

```
Introducing the XYZ Laptop, the latest innovation in portable computing!
With blazing-fast speeds, an ultra-crisp 4K display, and a sleek, light-
weight design, this powerhouse is perfect for both work and play. Expe-
rience unparalleled performances and stay ahead of the curve. Don't miss
out-upgrade to the XYZ Laptop today!
```

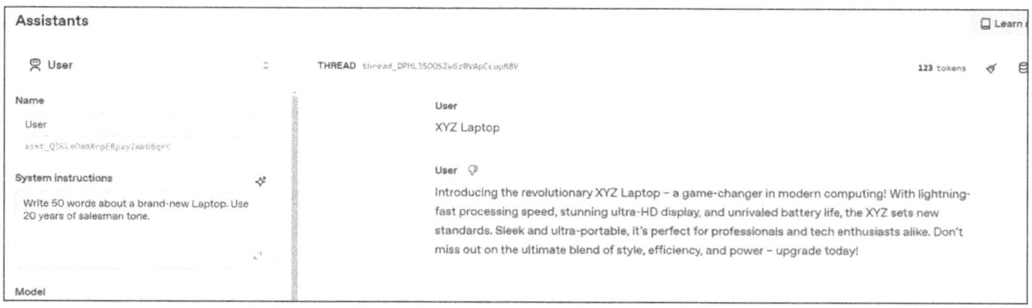

Figure 4.7*: Prompt Elements with <tone= salesmen tone>*

System input

```
Write 50 words about a brand-new Laptop. Use a fun tone.
```

Input

```
XYZ Laptop
```

Assistance

```
Meet the XYZ Laptop—a sleek, electrifying gadget that's ready to zap
your daily grind into a fun escapade! With juice that lasts all day and
speeds faster than your cat chasing a laser, it's your ultimate sidekick
for adventures both pixelated and real. Get ready to zip-zap-zoom! 🚀💻
```

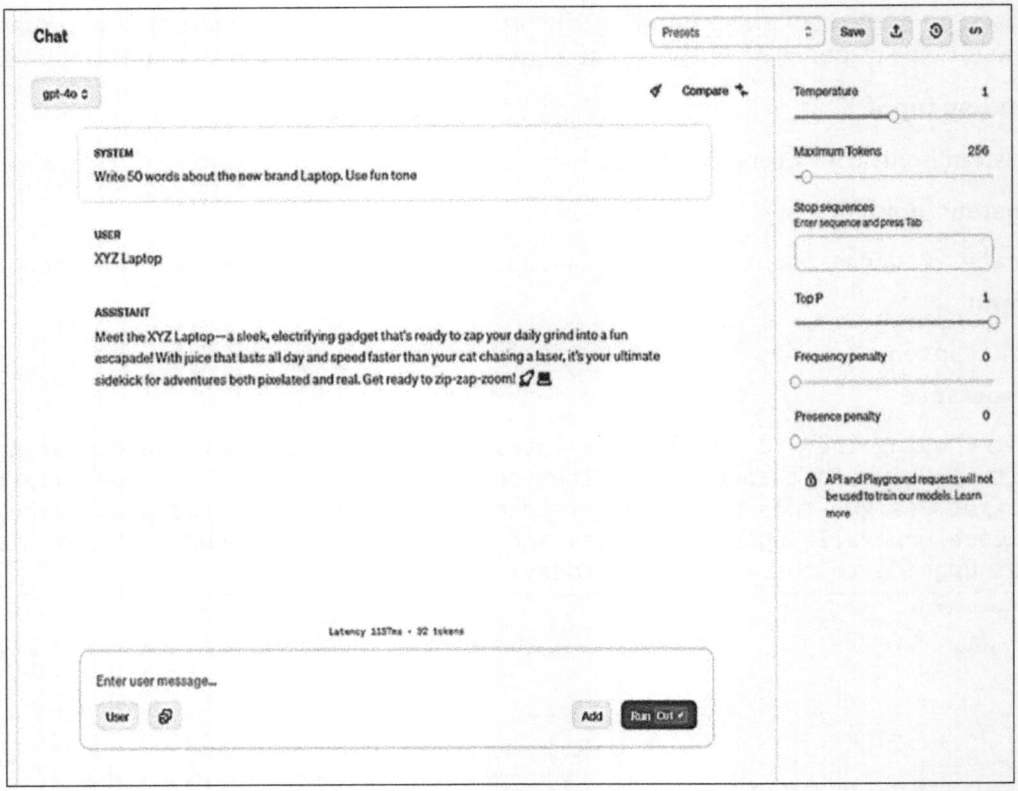

Figure 4.8: *Prompt Elements with <tone= fun tone>*

Role Prompting

While designing prompt engineering, we can provide the specific "Role" or "Persona," which explicitly defines the system's role as acting like that persona, guiding the LLM, and generating contextually appropriate, accurate, and relevant responses based on the nature of the role given in the prompt along with the input. This method of prompting plays a major role between the user and the model, helping us create a more participatory and interactive experience as well as achieve higher-quality results.

With the input prompt, we could specify the answer from the relevant field SMEs in that domain by specifying the field, such as medicine, engineering, law, sales executive, magician, and so on. The objective of this approach would help us prompt more specific and informed responses from the LLMs. This approach can also inspire models to provide more detailed and nuanced output, illustrating their broad pre-trained knowledge from the domain expert perspective.

Role prompting can take several forms based on the requirements and scenario.

- **Professional:**
    - Professor
    - Doctor
    - Engineer
    - Lawyers
- **Expert Roles:**
    - Marketing Analyst
    - Sales Executive
    - Stock Exchange Analyst
    - Sports Analyst
- **Fictional Roles:**
    - Magician
    - Story Writer
    - Artist
- **Guiding Roles:**
    - Travel Advisor
    - History Narrator
    - Educational Advisor
- **Collaborative Roles:**
    - Customer Service Representative
    - Reviewer (Movies, Products, and more)
    - Communications Specialist

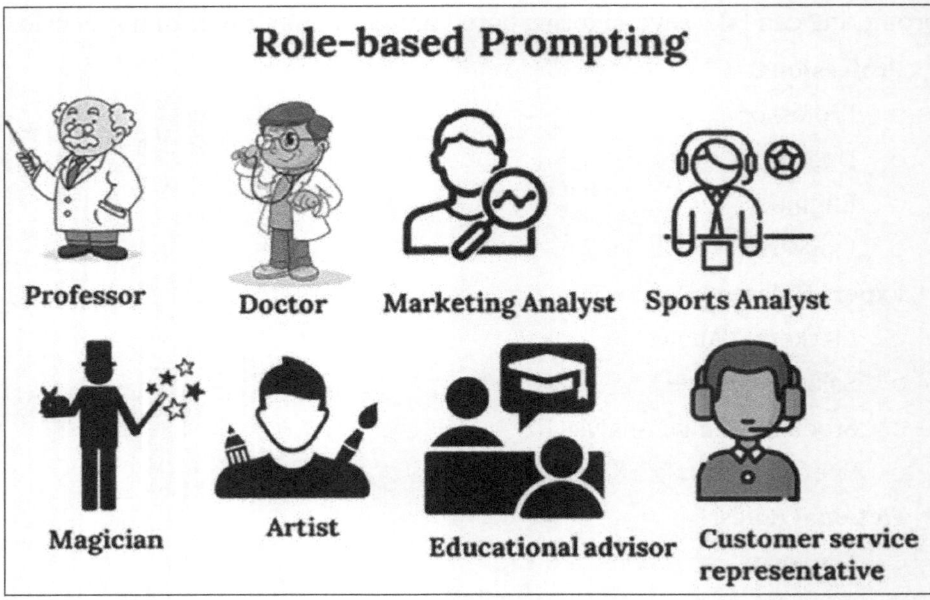

Figure 4.9: *Role Prompting Characters*

Let us explore a few roles along with the domains.

Role: Physics Professor

Topic: Atomic Physics

```
You are a physics professor who specializes in atomic physics. Please
provide an introduction to "Atomic Physics" using narrative techniques
that are easy to understand for college juniors.
```

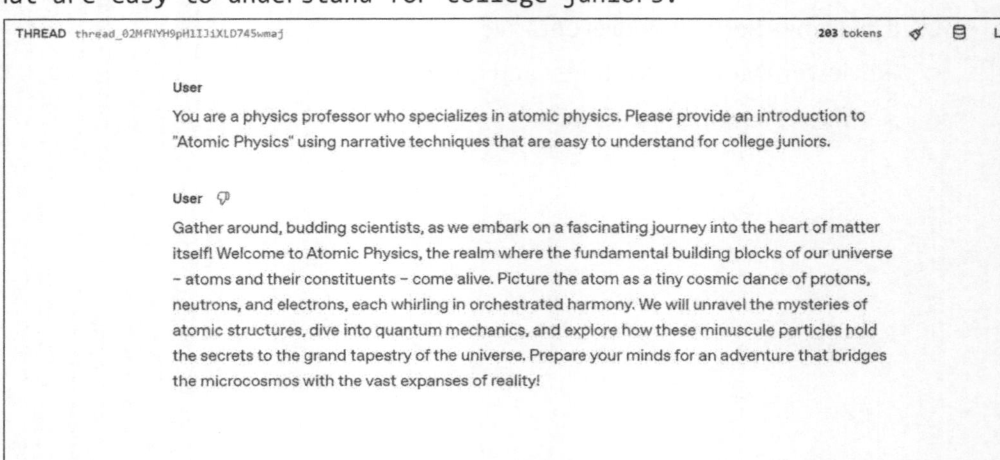

Figure 4.10: *Role Prompt (Role: Physics Professor, Topic: Atomic Physics)*

Role: Educational Adviser

Topic: Advice for higher secondary schooling completed students

```
You are an educational adviser who has specialized in this field for more than twenty years. Please advise students who have just completed their higher secondary and are pursuing their university courses.
```

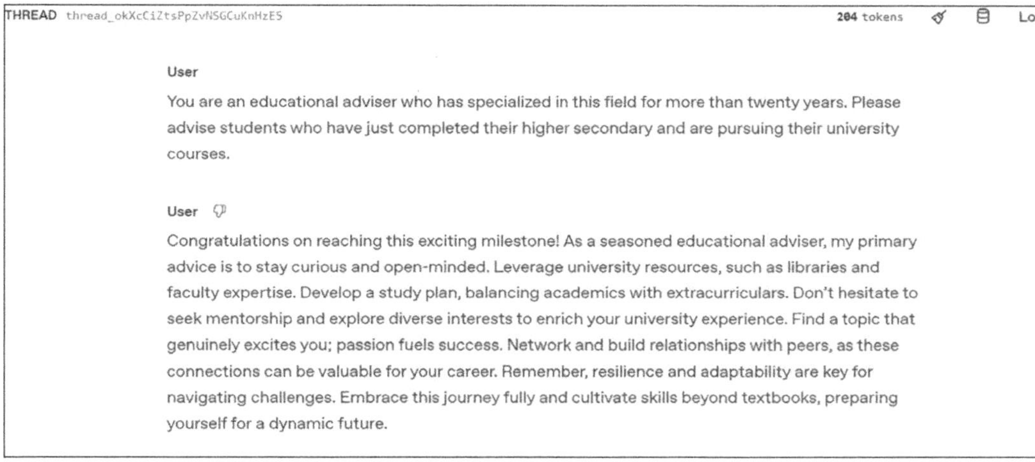

Figure 4.11: *Role Prompt (Role: Educational, Advisor Topic: Students)*

Role: Customer Service Representative

Topic: New product launch email

```
You are a customer service representative. Draft a short email to the client to purchase the new product launch along with short benefits and costs.
```

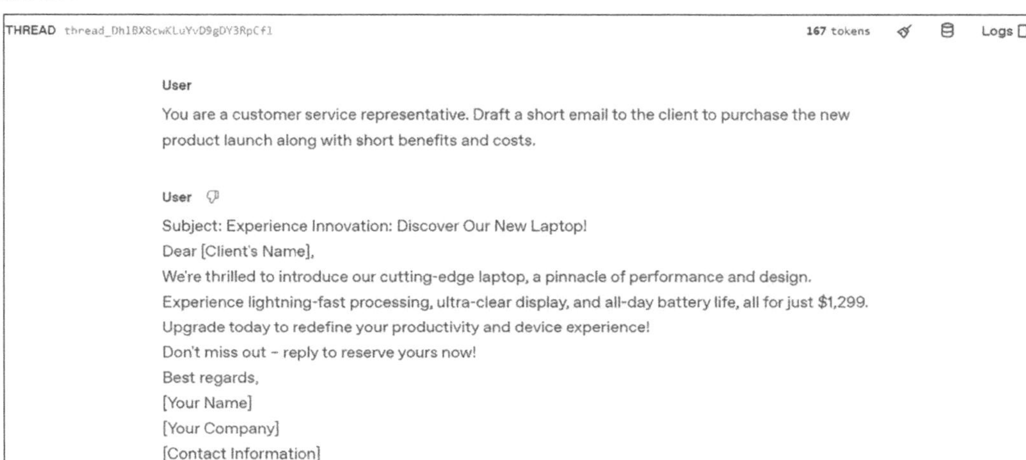

Figure 4.12: *Role Prompt (Role: Customer Service Representative Topic: New Product Launch Email)*

Effectiveness of Role Prompting Techniques:

The effectiveness of role prompting techniques is explored through the following methods:

- **Confidence in Adaptability:** It clarifies and distinguishes the role and enhances the model's ability to understand and adjust to the given situation based on the requirements. The appropriate and well-defined role would help the LLM generate the desired response from the users. Prompting this role would help generate informative and promising output with LLMs. It enables a more efficient framework and interactions with LLMs as well as helps us build a wide range of applications specific to various domains.
- **Enhanced Relevance and Contextuality:** We understand that the role prompts us to generate responses that are more relevant and tailored to specific contexts or scenarios. For instance, when the AI model is prompted to act as a "*customer service representative*," it can provide more accurate and concerning support for the end user, and sometimes it improves user engagement by adopting a given role. Eventually, the AI model can engage with users more effectively and create a more interactive and entrancing experience.
- **Coherence and Consistency**: Coherence and Consistency are major aspects of any tool and technology. This role prompting can ensure that the AI model maintains a consistent tone and style throughout the interaction with the end user, which is particularly important in professional or formal contexts to manage both features.
- **Appropriate Guidance:** This approach provides scenario-specific guidance, allowing the AI to follow predefined guidelines and protocols appropriate for the given role and scenario. This feature leads to more coherent and logical responses.
- **Facilitation of Complex Tasks:** We must build super-specialized assistance when designing AI-based assistance products. Hence, we need to provide role-prompting approaches with respective roles specific to the task. Since the tool has to answer all these tasks that require domain-specific knowledge, such as scientists, doctors, reviewers, teachers, technical support engineers, or legal advice, role prompting can direct the AI model to use relevant terminology and frameworks, enhancing the quality of assistance in the best ways. Role prompts can be used in training simulations where the AI model can act as a specific character and help end users practice and develop their skills in controlled environments.
- **End-User Satisfaction and Trust**: When we define a role prompting appropriately, the model works closely with the given prompt and generates trustworthy and satisfactory output. Users often appreciate the role prompting

can achieve by simulating human-like understanding and responses back to the user. This approach helps them feel personalized and contextually aware.

Role Prompt's Flip Side

Following are the various ways to approach the flip side of the role prompt:

- **Restrictive Responses:** Constraints while providing the role prompt would limit the creative scope. Thus, the model's ability could be limited, as it may focus narrowly on the role's perspective and provide few creative solutions because it typically adheres too strictly to the assigned role in the prompt.
- **Reliability:** In some cases, role prompting may not be reliable for complete results. LLM's output mostly depends on external factors, such as base data quality, training data, and generalized knowledge.
- **Ethics and Concerns:** If we are not clear and explicitly define the role of the specific requirements, the output might go against the ethics and biasing concerns; this approach is just an additional feature in prompt engineering. Of course, we can keep our questions straightforward, provided we are able to generate a pleasing response from the LLMs.

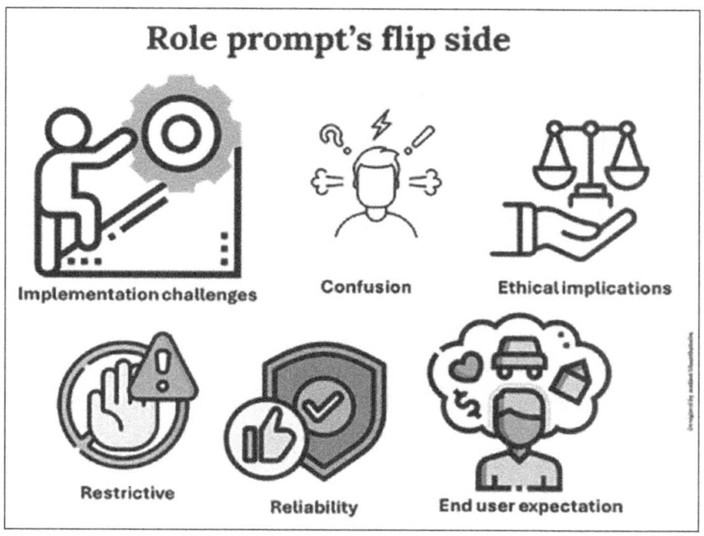

Figure 4.13: *Role Prompt's Flip Side*

- **End User Expectations:** It might mislead the authorities. End users might attribute excessive authority to the role and its recommendations, which can sometimes lead to overconfidence in its responses without proper verification and validation with real SMEs or Expert reviews or opinions.
- **Overconfidence or Confusion:** If we provide a role prompt that is too specific, the end user might not fully understand the generated output from the LLMs

with respect to the situation or scenario given to the AI model. Ultimately, the responses will reduce the effectiveness of the interaction with the model.

- **Ethical Implications:** Assigning roles, prompting, and involving sensitive topics or personalities can raise ethical concerns as part of industry concerns, particularly if the AI is perceived to be speaking on behalf of real individuals or groups. So, we must be careful while handling this approach.
- **Implementation Challenges:** Sometimes, design role prompting might be complicated and challenging to maintain. So, creating effective role prompts requires a careful design approach and additional tuning to ensure that the AI behaves as intended without going off track from the objective of the AI product. Continuously monitoring and updating role prompts activity as well as adapting to new information and contexts can be highly resource-intensive.

Prompting: Voice Specific

As discussed, we can develop the prompt using various tones and styles and tailor it to the desired voice so that LLMs can generate content that aligns with the voice owner, such as inspirational, motivational, professional, friendly, or humorous. This approach helps us further enhance the value and effectiveness of AI-generated content by reflecting the brand's unique communication style.

USER

You're the businessman's voice.
A few lines of the importance of the women's education

ASSISTANT

Certainly. Here are a few lines on the importance of women's education from a business perspective:

"Investing in women's education is not just a social imperative; it's a strategic business decision. An educated female workforce drives innovation, enhances problem-solving, and boosts overall company performance. Women's education broadens the talent pool, bringing diverse perspectives that are critical for competitive advantage. Moreover, empowering women through education leads to more robust economies, greater consumer spending, and improved family well-being, all of which create a thriving market for businesses to grow. It's clear: supporting women's education is a win-win for both society and the bottom line."

Figure 4.14: *Prompting with Voice Specific*

Prompt Engineering Techniques

So far, we have discussed the elements, components, and effectiveness of prompt engineering. To ensure a clear understanding, prompt engineering is an art that helps us create precise input requests for LLMs and leads us to an envisioned output from the model that matches the expectations and objectives.

Prompt engineering is broadly classified into single or multiple modes of prompt operation, and involves enhancing AI systems to generate exceptional text, summaries, images, audio, and videos based on our requirements and intellectual inputs using high-quality prompts.

Single Prompt Techniques: As the name implies, these prompt techniques direct you to solve your task in a single prompt. The following list of prompts falls under this category:

- Zero-Shot
- Few-Shot
- Chain-of-Thought (CoT)
- Program Aided Language

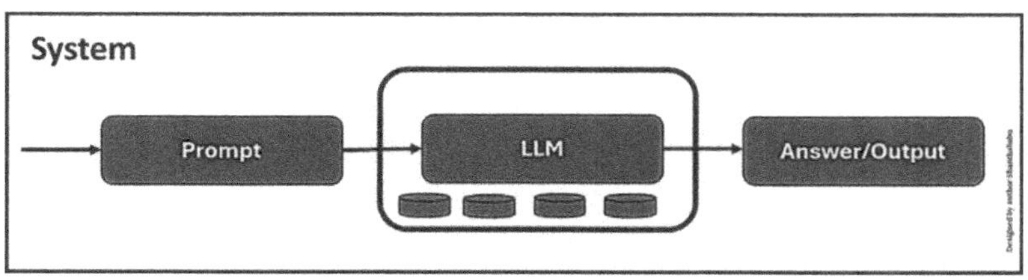

***Figure 4.15**: Single Prompt Techniques*

Zero-Shot Prompting: This technique is the simplest. It uses natural language instructions, helps create the output without training data, and extracts the output from the existing knowledge and data relationships by the mechanism of encoding the parameters. Internally, it retrieves the content based on the question and its understanding of the related context in the available data while training.

Sample:

```
Classify the text as neutral, positive, or negative
```

Sentiment:

Input (s):

```
The food in the restaurant is good.
The food in the restaurant is okay.
The food in the restaurant is not that great.
```

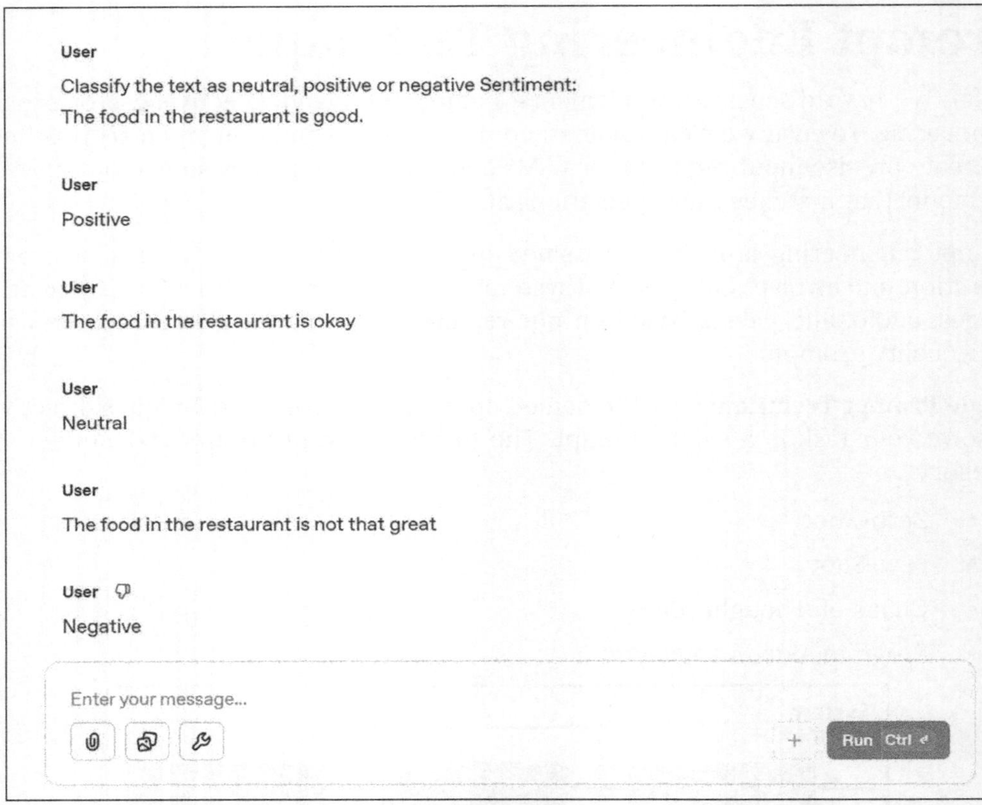

***Figure 4.16**: Zero Prompting*

Few-Shot Prompting: This technique is somewhat special. It involves providing guidance on the language model with examples. It generates more relevant responses, especially for the model to learn from the given prompt and steer the desired output. The model performs better than zero prompt techniques. However, this technique is not suitable for complicated requirements.

Sample:

```
The food in the restaurant is good //Positive
The food in the restaurant is okay //Negative
The food in the restaurant is not that much great //Neutral
```

Input (s):

```
The movie is good to watch.
The music is not that much great.
BGM is not good in the movie.
```

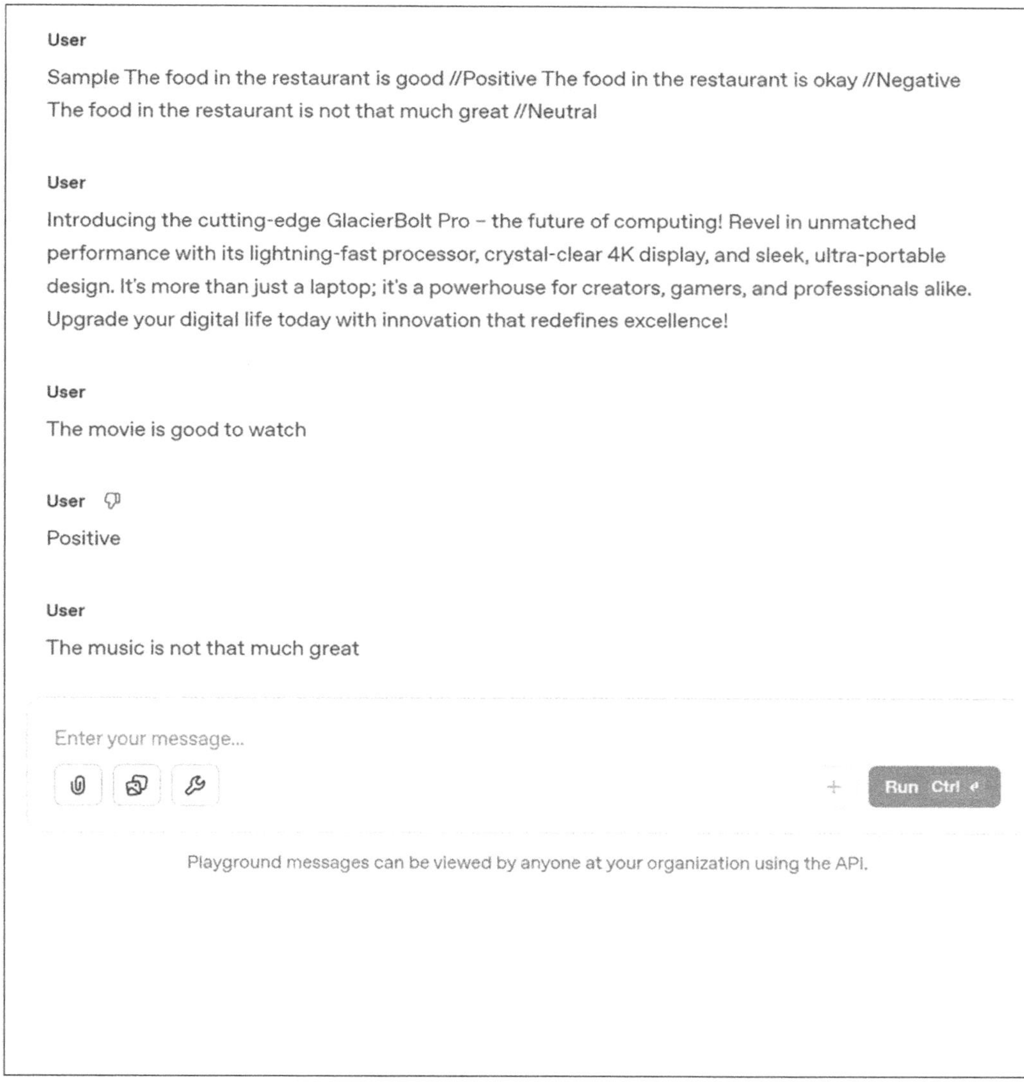

Figure 4.17: *Few-Shot Prompting*

Direct Prompting: This technique will provide the question and answer directly as a sample for input to generate the output in a Q and A pattern.

Input:

```
Question: Who was the captain of India for the 1983 World Cup?
Answer: Kapil Dev

Question: Who was the maximum run-taker from India during the 1983 World
Cup?
Answer: Kapil Dev
```

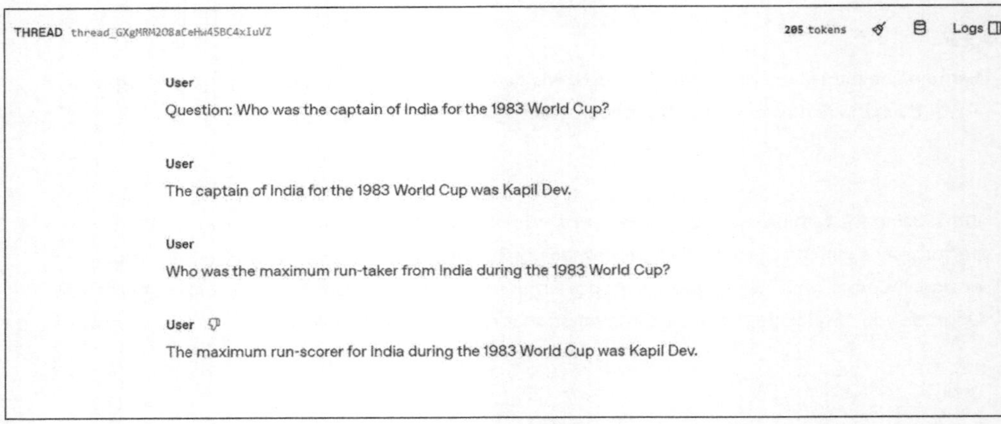

Figure 4.18: *Direct Prompting*

Chain-of-Thought Prompting (CoT): In this technique, complex questions or problem statements are broken down into smaller parts. This enables the model to think of problems like how humans approach solving a problem. It means that the question is broken into smaller segments, allowing the model to analyze the problem more deeply and thoroughly and provide more accurate answers.

System

```
Q: Shantha has Rs. 5000. He purchased two shirts, each Rs. 750, and two
pants, Rs. 1000, and he spent Rs. 350 for dinner. How much balance does
he have?
A: Shantha has Rs. 5000. He purchased 2 shirts, each 750 Rs. 2*750,
shirts = Rs. 1500, pants 1000*2=2000, dinner=350, total expenses=
1500+2000+350
The balance amount in hand =5000-3850=1150
```

Input

```
Babu spent 150, 200, and 350 on breakfast, lunch, and dinner, respec-
tively. He has 100 left over. How much does he carry with him for the
day?
```

Assistant

```
To find out how much Babu carried with him for the day, we need to add up
the total amount he spent and his remaining balance.
- Breakfast: Rs. 150
- Lunch: Rs. 200
- Dinner: Rs. 350
- Remaining balance: Rs. 100
Total amount spent: 150 + 200 + 350 = Rs. 700
Adding the remaining balance: 700 + 100 = Rs. 800
So, Babu carried Rs. 800 with him for the day.
```

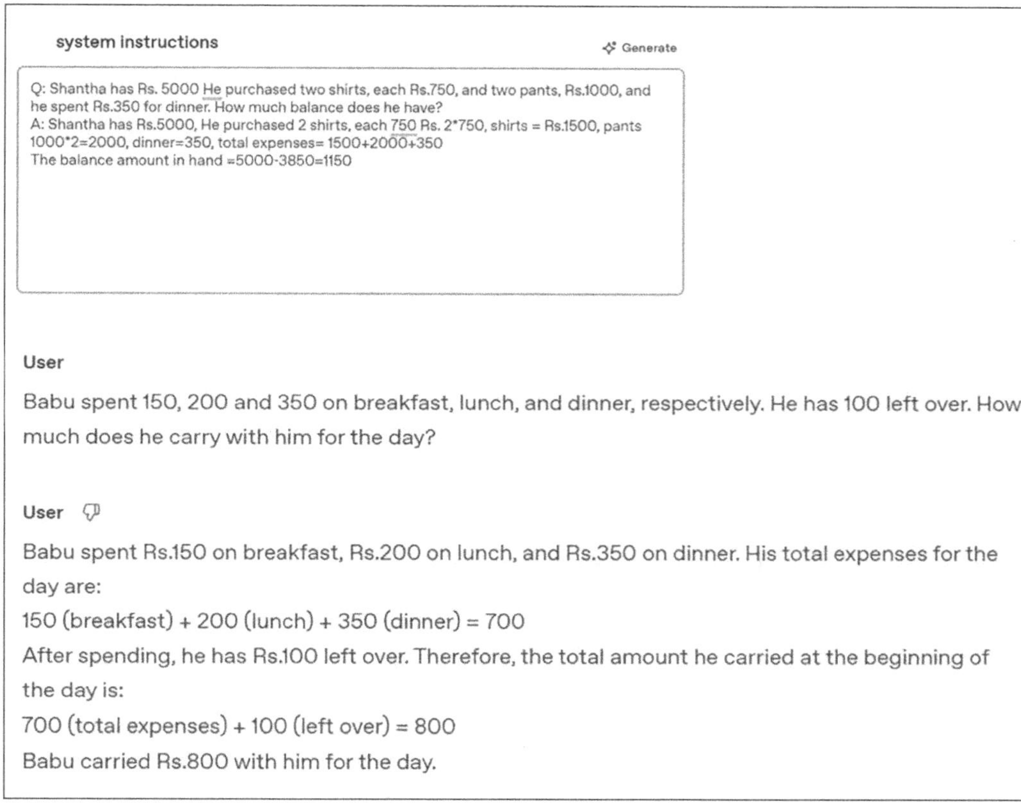

Figure 4.19: *Chain-of-Thought Prompting*

Furthermore, to improve the CoT, there is a technique called "**Self-Consistency**," which is a highly decoding strategy applied to more complex reasoning problem statements. The process involves sampling from a distinct set of reasoning paths and selecting the most prominent answer. This approach is the typical way where humans break a larger problem into a chain of sub-tasks and finally put them together. Internally, the sub-task's output will be the sub-sequence task's input.

This approach simply hits a model with the same given prompt multiple times and proceeds with the results, either ***Important*** or ***Not Important***, based on the voting of the majority declared as the final answer. This comes under the "Multiple Prompt Techniques" series.

Input

```
Hello Shanthababu,
Thank you for shopping with us. We'd like to let you know that SP
Publishers has received your order and is preparing it for shipment.
Your estimated delivery date is indicated as follows. If you would like
to view the status of your order or make any changes to it, please visit
Your Orders on Amazon.in.
Classify the preceding email as IMPORTANT or NOT IMPORTANT as it relates
to this online order. Let's think step by step.
```

Assistance

```
To determine whether the email is IMPORTANT or NOT IMPORTANT in relation
to the online order, let's go through the details step-by-step:
1. **Sender Information**: The email is from the company or service
provider (SP Publishers via Amazon.in) from whom the order was placed.
2. **Order Confirmation**: This email confirms that SP Publishers has
received the order and is processing it.
3. **Shipment Information**: This email provides information regarding
the preparation of the shipment.
4. **Estimated Delivery Date**: The email indicates the estimated
delivery date.
5. **Actions Available**: The email suggests how to check the order
status or make any changes, by visiting "Your Orders" on Amazon.in
Consider these points:
- The email confirms that the order has been received and is being
processed, which is essential information for the customer.
- The system provides details about the shipment, including an estimated
delivery date.
- It gives the customer options to check the status or make changes,
which might be necessary if there are any issues or sudden changes.
Given these important points of information, the email is highly
relevant to the order and its status.
Therefore, the classification of the email can be determined as:
**IMPORTANT**
```

User

To determine if the preceding email should be classified as IMPORTANT or NOT IMPORTANT, let's analyze the content step by step:

1. **Sender and Purpose**: The email is from a retailer, in this case, presumably an acknowledgment from Amazon or a vendor via Amazon regarding an order that Shanthababu placed. Because it concerns an order, it directly pertains to a financial transaction and a product or service that Shanthababu purchased.
2. **Content**:
    - **Order Confirmation**: The email confirms that the order has been received. This is crucial for any buyer to ensure that the transaction was successful.
    - **Shipment Preparation**: It mentions that the order is being prepared for shipment, which pertains to the progress of the delivery process.
    - **Estimated Delivery Date**: Providing an estimated delivery date is crucial for planning purposes, especially if the recipient needs the item by a certain time.
    - **Order Tracking and Changes:** The option to view order status or make changes provides flexibility in managing the order.
3. **Implications of Ignoring**: If this email is ignored or not seen as essential, Shanthababu might miss critical updates about the order, such as delays, changes, or issues that need addressing.

Based on these observations, this email directly impacts Shanthababu's awareness and management of his order. Notifications regarding purchases, deliveries, and order management are generally considered important to the buyer because they involve time, money, and personal or business needs.

Figure 4.20: *Self-Consistency Prompting*

Program-Aided Language Models (PAL)

The PAL prompting approach is an extended version of CoT, with an additional explanation as a natural language in the prompt.

System

```
Shantha has Rs. 5000. He purchased two shirts, each Rs. 750, and two
pants, Rs. 1000,  and he spent Rs. 350 for dinner. Thus, his balance is
Rs. 5000.
A: Shantha's purchase and dinner expenses details
shirts= 750*2=1500
pants=1000*2=2000
dinner=350
total =shirts+pants+dinner
```

Input

```
Babu has Rs. 8000. He purchased five shirts, each Rs. 750, and three
pairs of pants, Rs. 1000. What is Babu's total expenditure, and how
much balance does he have?
```

Assistant

Now, let us calculate Babu's total expenditure and his remaining balance step by step.

```
1. **Total expenditure on shirts:**
- Price of one shirt = Rs. 750
- Number of shirts = 5
- Total expenditure on shirts = 750 * 5 = Rs. 3750

2. **Total expenditure on pants:**
- Price of one pair of pants =Rs. 1000
- Number of pairs of pants = 3
- Total expenditure on pants = 1000 * 3 = Rs. 3000


3. **Total expenditure:**
- Total expenditure on shirts + Total expenditure on pants.
- Total expenditure = Rs. 3750+ Rs.3000= Rs, 6750

4. **Remaining balance:**
- Initial amount = Rs,8000
- Total expenditure = Rs. 6750
- Remaining balance = 8000 - 6750 = Rs. 1250

Babu's total expenditure is Rs. 6750, and his remaining balance is Rs.
1250.
```

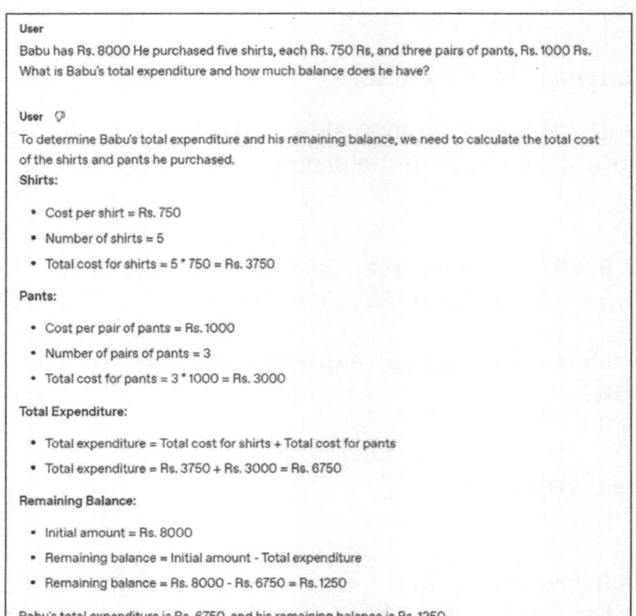
User

Babu has Rs. 8000 He purchased five shirts, each Rs. 750 Rs, and three pairs of pants, Rs. 1000 Rs. What is Babu's total expenditure and how much balance does he have?

User

To determine Babu's total expenditure and his remaining balance, we need to calculate the total cost of the shirts and pants he purchased.

Shirts:

- Cost per shirt = Rs. 750
- Number of shirts = 5
- Total cost for shirts = 5 * 750 = Rs. 3750

Pants:

- Cost per pair of pants = Rs. 1000
- Number of pairs of pants = 3
- Total cost for pants = 3 * 1000 = Rs. 3000

Total Expenditure:

- Total expenditure = Total cost for shirts + Total cost for pants
- Total expenditure = Rs. 3750 + Rs. 3000 = Rs. 6750

Remaining Balance:

- Initial amount = Rs. 8000
- Remaining balance = Initial amount - Total expenditure
- Remaining balance = Rs. 8000 - Rs. 6750 = Rs. 1250

Babu's total expenditure is Rs. 6750, and his remaining balance is Rs. 1250.

Figure 4.21: *Program-Aided Language Models Prompting*

Multiple Prompt Techniques: Groups of prompts are used for different strategies that are applied to the LLM, and combined results will be driven from the model.

- Self-Ask Prompting
- Directional Stimulus Prompting (DSP)
- Generated Knowledge Prompting (GKP)
- Chain-of-Table Prompting
- Tree of Thoughts (ToT)
- Least to Most Prompting
- ReAct Prompting

Self-Ask Prompting: This approach is an advancement from Direct, Self-Consistency Chain-of-Thought prompt techniques, in which the reasonings are explicitly defined with follow-up mode, so that the LLM is able to break the question into smaller chunks and follow-ups to understand the question with high clarity and give the precise answers. In each follow-up, the LLM will give intermediate answers, and once it reaches the logical ending, it will provide the final answer. Since there are a bunch of questions and follow-ups, this approach is called self-asking prompting.

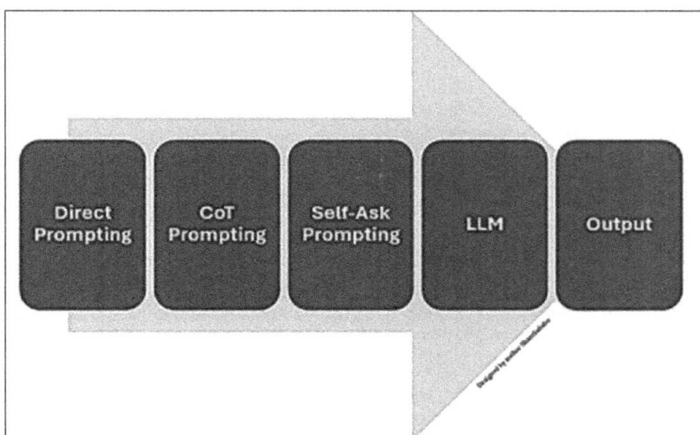

Figure 4.22: *Self-Ask Prompting Workflow*

Input

```
Question: Who are the openers? Sachin and Ganguly opened the innings.
Are you following up on the questions needed here? Yes
Follow up: The total score is 375. How much did Sachin score?
Intermediate answer: Sachin scored 145, which included a total score of
375.
Follow up: what are the extras?
Intermediate answer: Extra score of 25
Follow up: How many Ganguly scored?
```

```
Intermediate answer: Ganguly's score of 205
So, the final answer is Ganguly's score of 205, Sachin's score of 145,
and an extra 25.
Question: Ganguly scored 45, and Sachin also opened the innings along
with Ganguly. The total score is 105, of which 15 is extra; how much was
the Sachin score? Did both batsmen score equally or not?
Are you following up on the questions needed here? Yes
```

Output

```
Follow up: The total score is 105. How much did Sachin score?
Intermediate answer: Removing the extras (15), the combined runs scored
by Sachin and Ganguly are 105 - 15 = 90.
Follow up: How many Ganguly scored?
Intermediate answer: Ganguly scored 45.
Follow up: How much did Sachin score?
Intermediate answer: Sachin's score can be calculated by subtracting
Ganguly's score from the combined runs. Sachin scored 90 - 45 = 45.
So, the final answer is Sachin scored 45, Ganguly scored 45, and there
were 15 extras.
Both batsmen scored equally.
```

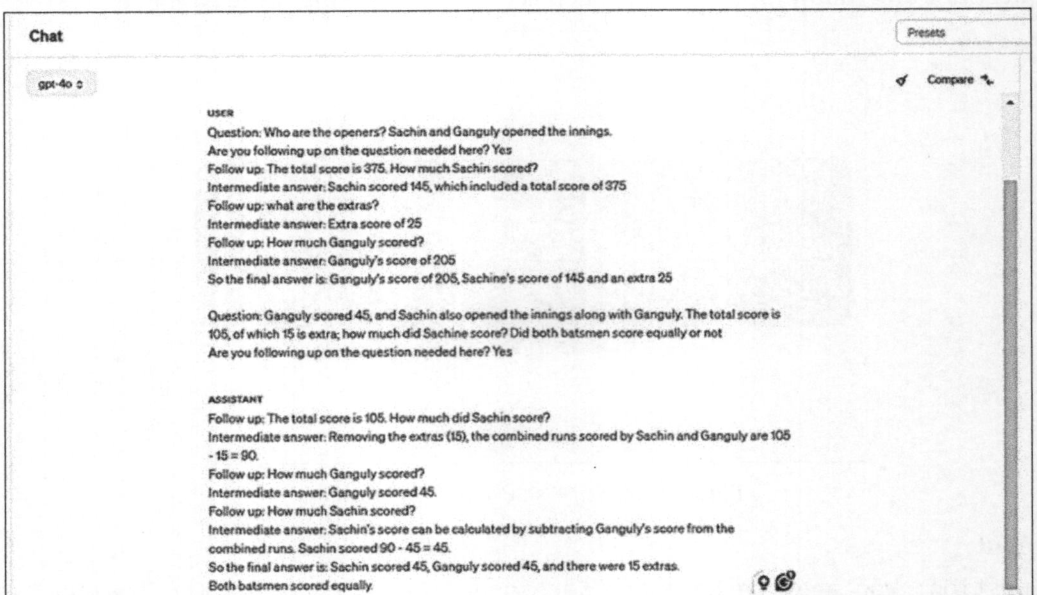

Figure 4.23: *Self-Ask Prompting*

So far, we have discussed Single Prompt Techniques. Let us now delve into Multiple Prompt Techniques.

Directional Stimulus Prompting (DSP): This technique provides the LLM with specific hints, inputs, and appropriate directions for building constructive output as a summary. It is a part of the "Multiple Prompt Techniques" series.

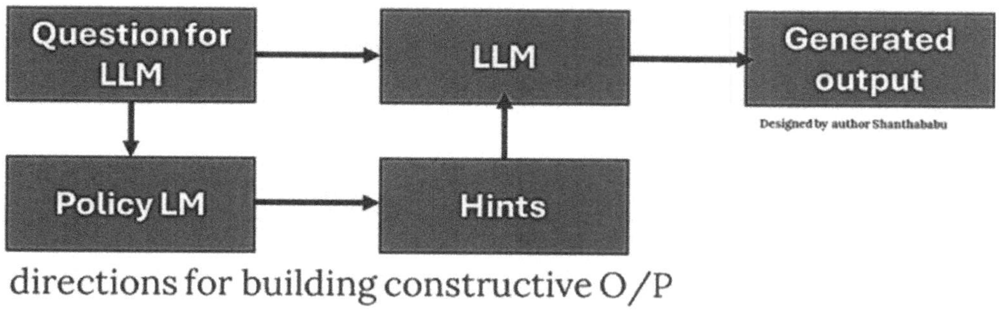

***Figure 4.24**: Directional Stimulus Prompting Workflow*

Input

```
Write a poem on sunrise in 4 lines
Hint: Yellow, Bird, Milkman, Tea Shop, Vitamin D
```

Output

```
Golden rays kiss the earth, the sky alive in yellow,
Birds chime in a morning song, each note sweet and mellow.
The milkman hums his route, delivers on daybreak's promise,
The tea shop brews warmth and joy, Vitamin D's gentle solace.
```

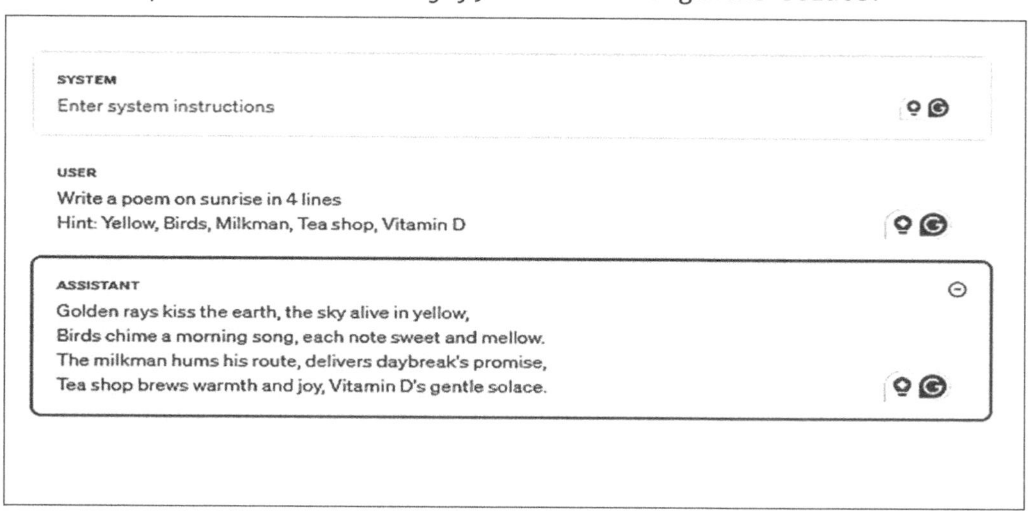

***Figure 4.25**: Directional Stimulus Prompting*

Generated Knowledge Prompting (GKP): This technique involves LLM generating valuable insights and information relating to a specific task; ultimately, it enhances the LLM's performance on a given task(s). It includes two stages, such as Knowledge Generation (KG) and Knowledge Integration (KI).

- **Knowledge Generation (KG)**: In this stage, a few-shot prompt technique is used to generate question-related knowledge statements from an LLM.
- **Knowledge Integration (KI)**: Once the question related to the knowledge statement is completed, LLM picks up these statements and makes a list of predictions with each knowledge statement generated in the previous stage.

Then, the system will select the highest-confidence prediction from the list.

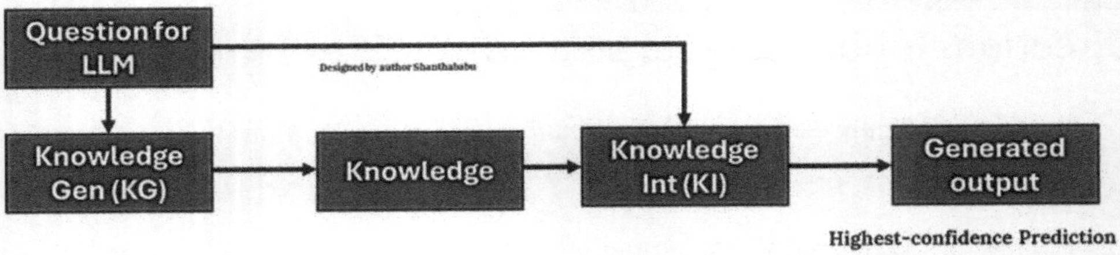

Figure 4.26: *Generated Knowledge Prompting*

In our example, we are providing knowledge of different liquids such as Water, Olive oil, Acetone, Ethanol, and Mercury. We are also finding that the density of water is greater than that of olive oil, acetone, and ethanol, along with the measures, as shown in *Figure* 4.27.

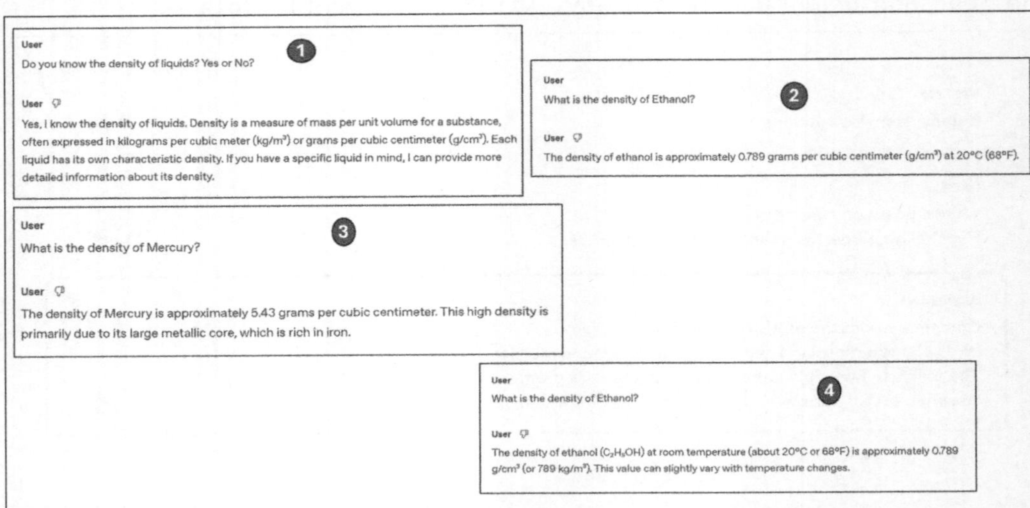

Figure 4.27: *Generated Knowledge Prompting (Steps 1-4)*

Input: `Is water density greater than Olive oil and Ethanol, as shown in` *`Figure 4.28.`*

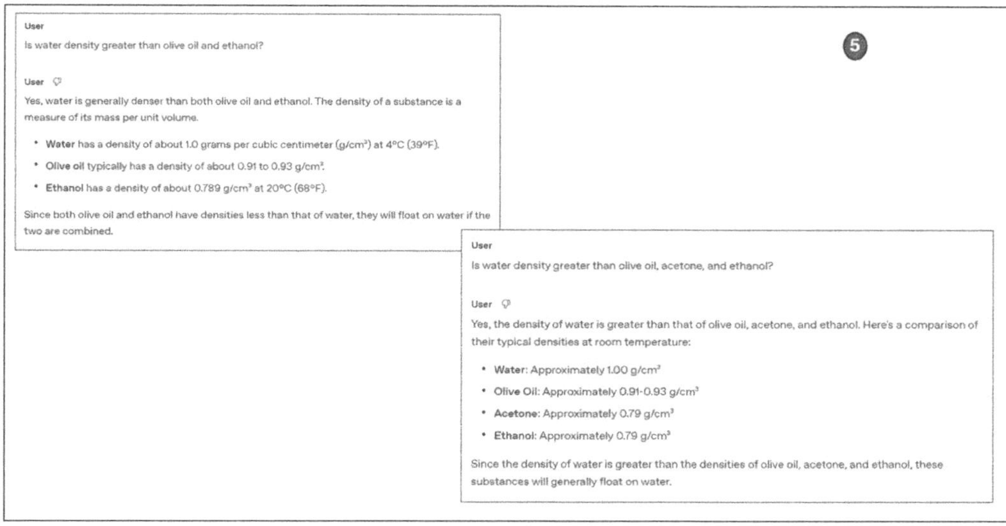

***Figure 4.28**: Generated Knowledge Prompting (Step 5)*

Chain-of-Table Prompting: So far, we have discussed various promptings for LLMs to build various use cases and provide sufficient input for them to train and excel with the nuances of the unstructured data.

LLMs are highly capable of doing all these analyses with semi-structured and unstructured data and generating human-like text with ease. It is also capable of writing stories and poems.

Then there might be the question of how we would enhance LLMs' capabilities for analyzing and understanding tabular data, playing with multiple questions or queries, and getting the results. The answer is yes! We can.

Let us explore the same. In this situation, we can use the following approach in simple terms.

Approach: Insert the table into the prompt along with the question and allow LLMs in-context learning to take over the subsequent actions. This approach explicitly uses tabular data in the chain of reasoning for a bunch of questions. It lets the LLM use the knowledge on the table and answer the questions.

Internally, this approach includes a cycle of two steps:

1. **Dynamic Planning:** In this step, typically, the LLM is involved in operation chain mode; the next operation from pools is executed based on input and the history of previous learning experiences. As you know, LLM training is based on earlier experiences.

2. **Generation of Output:** LLM generates the output based on the previous step operations and outcomes in this step. This would involve new column names, row values, and certain conditions as well as create the corresponding output in the form of a table for the end user's requirements.

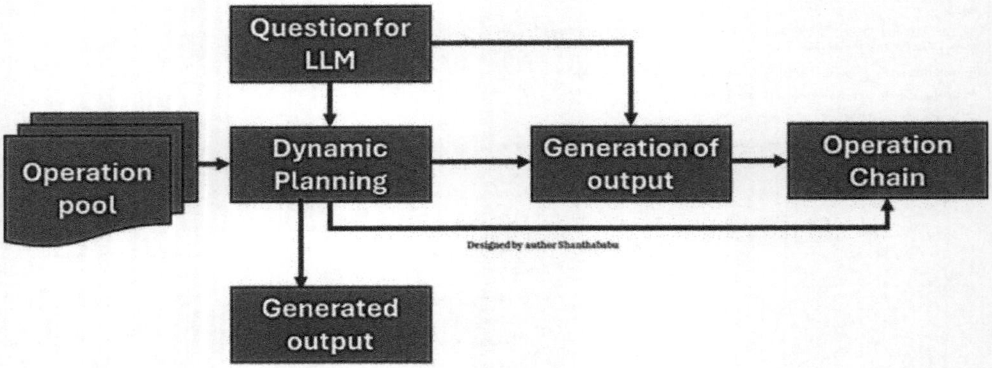

***Figure 4.29**: Chain-of-Table Prompting Workflow*

Let us try now.

Name	Age	Gender	Blood Type	Medical Condition
Bobby JacksOn	30	Male	B-	Cancer
LesLie TErRy	62	Male	A+	Obesity
DaNnY sMitH	76	Female	A-	Obesity
andrEw waTtS	28	Female	O+	Diabetes
adrIENNE bEll	43	Female	AB+	Cancer
EMILY JOHNSOn	36	Male	A+	Asthma
edwArD EDWaRDs	21	Female	AB-	Diabetes
CHrisTInA MARtinez	20	Female	A+	Cancer
JASmINe aGullaR	82	Male	AB+	Asthma

***Figure 4.30**: Chain-of-Table Prompting (Table for Demo)*

After adding the table, we will get the following output.

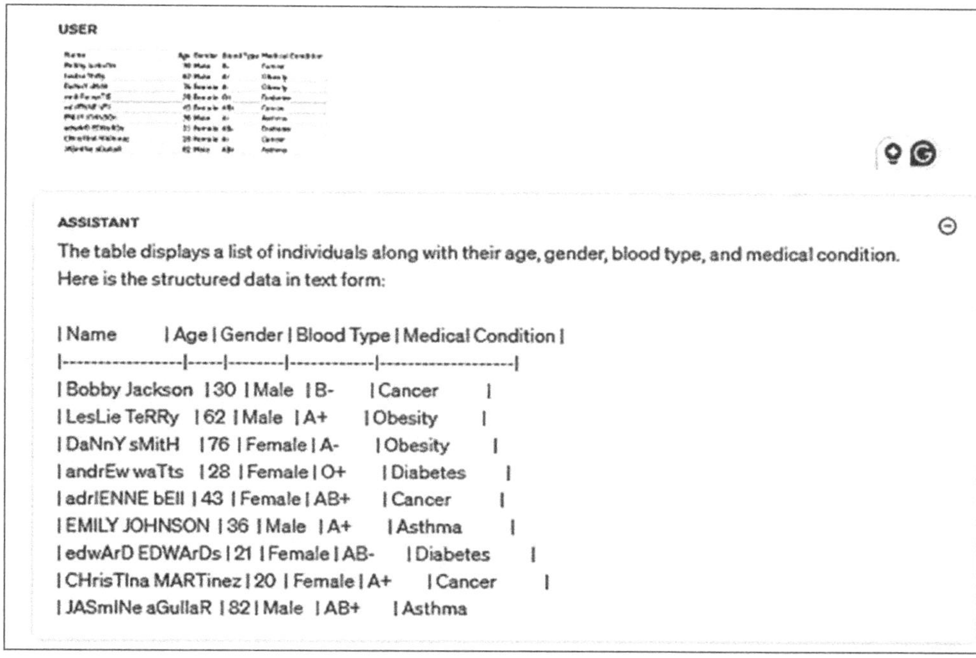

Figure 4.31: *Chain-of-Table Prompting (Table Uploaded for Analysis)*

```
Q1: What are the different medical conditions in the given table?
Q2: Who is the senior person at this table? Give their name and other details.
Q3: What blood types are in the given table?
Q4: Which medical condition is most on the table?
```

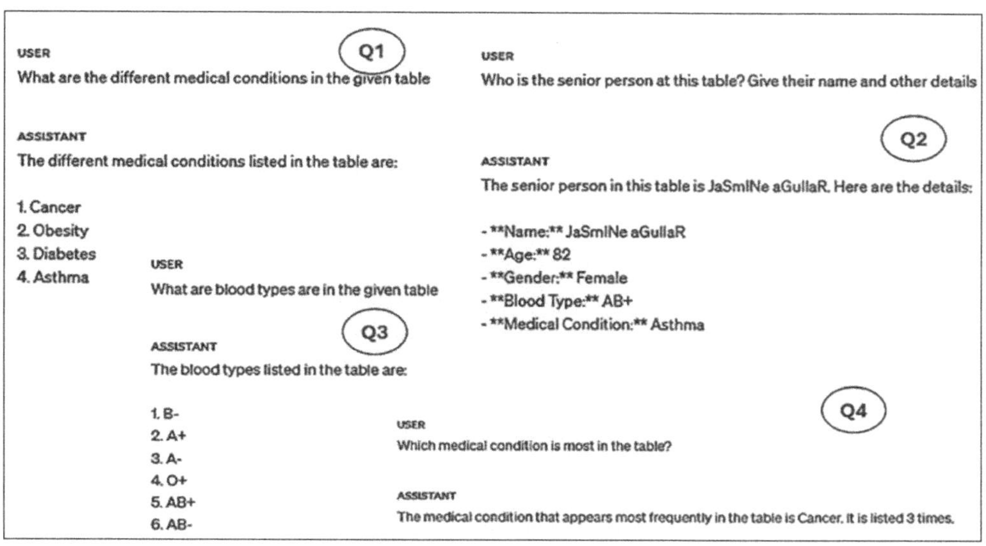

Figure 4.32: *Chain-of-Table Prompting – Query 1-4 Input and Output*

```
Q5: Add the following columns to the table: Doctor and Hospital.
Q6: Update the column Doctor name Maria for Medical condition is Diabetes and Asthma.
Q7: Remove the row which does not have values in columns.
Q8: Update the column Hospital name KGPMS for Medical condition is Diabetes and Asthma.
```

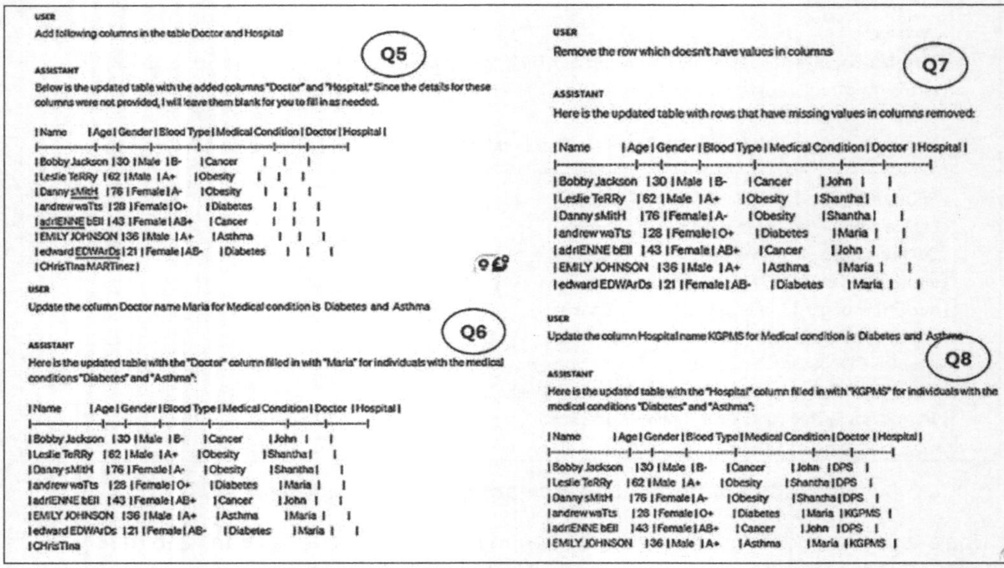

Figure 4.33: *Chain-of-Table Prompting (Query 5-8 Input and Output)*

Tree of Thoughts (ToTs): Prompting techniques are inspired by the human mind's approach to solving complex problem statements and reasoning tasks through trial and error. As complexity increases, thoughts expand as much as possible to solve the problem intelligently. The ToT technique guides the LLM in exploring all possible ideas and re-iterating as well as re-examining when needed to provide the ideal solution.

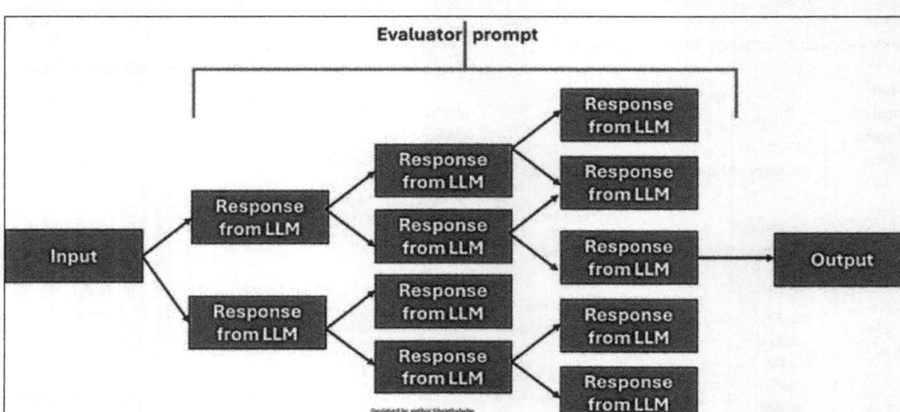

Figure 4.34: *Tree of Thoughts Workflow*

Try the following short story and find the conclusion.

Input:

User

```
John went back home from his office by car.
He entered his living room.
He was very thirsty, so he walked to the kitchen, opened the fridge,
and took a drink.
He puts a key in his shirt pocket and drinks the cold water.
He changed his shirt and wore the T-shirt.
He checks the shirt and walks to the backyard.
He put his shirt on for washing.
He took his badminton and walked to the car park.
Where is the car key?
Think through each step logically.
Imagine two different experts answering this question.
They will brainstorm the answer step by step, reasoning carefully.
They should be taking all facts into consideration.
All experts will write down 1 step of their thinking and share it with
the group.
They will each critique their response.
They will check their answer in a logical way.
Each expert will assign a likelihood of their current assertion being
correct.
Continue until experts agree on the single most likely location.
Give the conclusion.
```

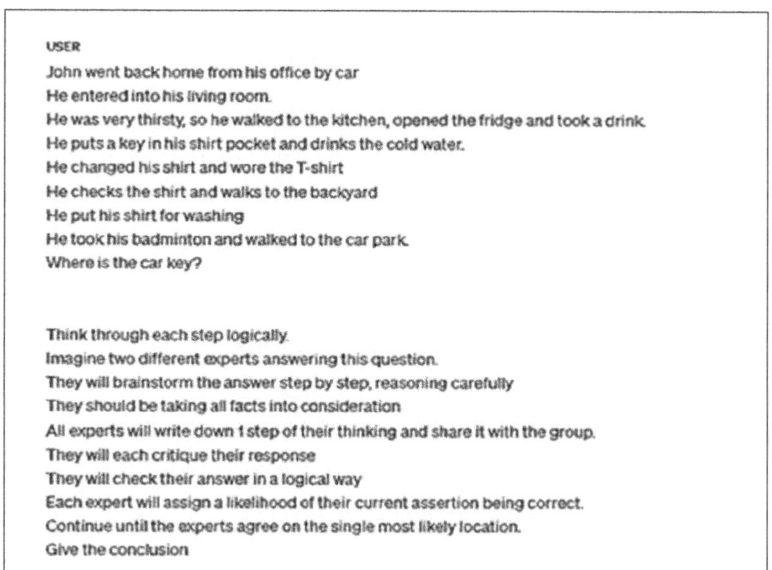
USER
John went back home from his office by car
He entered into his living room.
He was very thirsty, so he walked to the kitchen, opened the fridge and took a drink.
He puts a key in his shirt pocket and drinks the cold water.
He changed his shirt and wore the T-shirt
He checks the shirt and walks to the backyard
He put his shirt for washing
He took his badminton and walked to the car park.
Where is the car key?

Think through each step logically.
Imagine two different experts answering this question.
They will brainstorm the answer step by step, reasoning carefully
They should be taking all facts into consideration
All experts will write down 1 step of their thinking and share it with the group.
They will each critique their response
They will check their answer in a logical way
Each expert will assign a likelihood of their current assertion being correct.
Continue until the experts agree on the single most likely location.
Give the conclusion

Figure 4.35: *Tree of Thoughts – Input Story*

Output:

Assistance

```
### Expert 1 Step-by-Step Analysis:
**Step 1: Observing John's Actions at Home**
- John entered his home and immediately walked to the kitchen, then to
the fridge to get a drink because he was very thirsty.
**Step 2: Identifying the Key Placement**
- After getting the drink, John put the key in his shirt pocket and then
drank the water.
**Step 3: Changing the Shirt**
- John changed his shirt. The key was in the shirt pocket and there's no
mention of him moving it, so the key stayed in the pocket as he took off
the shirt.
### Expert 2 Step-by-Step Analysis:
**Step 1: Initial Placement Verification**
- The key was mentioned as being placed in the shirt pocket right after
John took a drink.
**Step 2: Shirt Change Implication**
- When John changed his shirt, there's no indication he transferred the
key to his new T-shirt or elsewhere, implying it stayed in the original
shirt's pocket.
**Step 3: Action Post-Changing**
- John checked the shirt (presumably to make sure nothing is left), and
then proceeded to the backyard and put the shirt for washing, indicating
the key likely remained in the shirt.
### Combined Expert Conclusion Likelihood:
**Step 1: Initial Key Placement (Likelihood: 100%)**
- The key was definitely placed in the shirt pocket.
**Step 2: Key Retention During Shirt Change (Likelihood: 95%)**
- It's highly likely the key stayed in the shirt because John didn't
indicate he moved it elsewhere.
**Step 3: Shirt Handling and Washing (Likelihood: 90%)**
- Since John checked the shirt and then put it in for washing, it's very
likely the key is still in the shirt unless he checked precisely for the
key and moved it, which isn't noted.
### Final Conclusion:
**Most Likely Location**: The key is in the pocket of the shirt that
John put into the washing.

By re-examining and logically following each detailed step provided,
both experts agree that the key was most likely not moved after being
placed in the shirt pocket. Since the last place the shirt was mentioned
is in the washing area, we conclude with a high likelihood:
**Conclusion**: The car key is most likely in the pocket of the shirt
that John put into the washing machine.
```

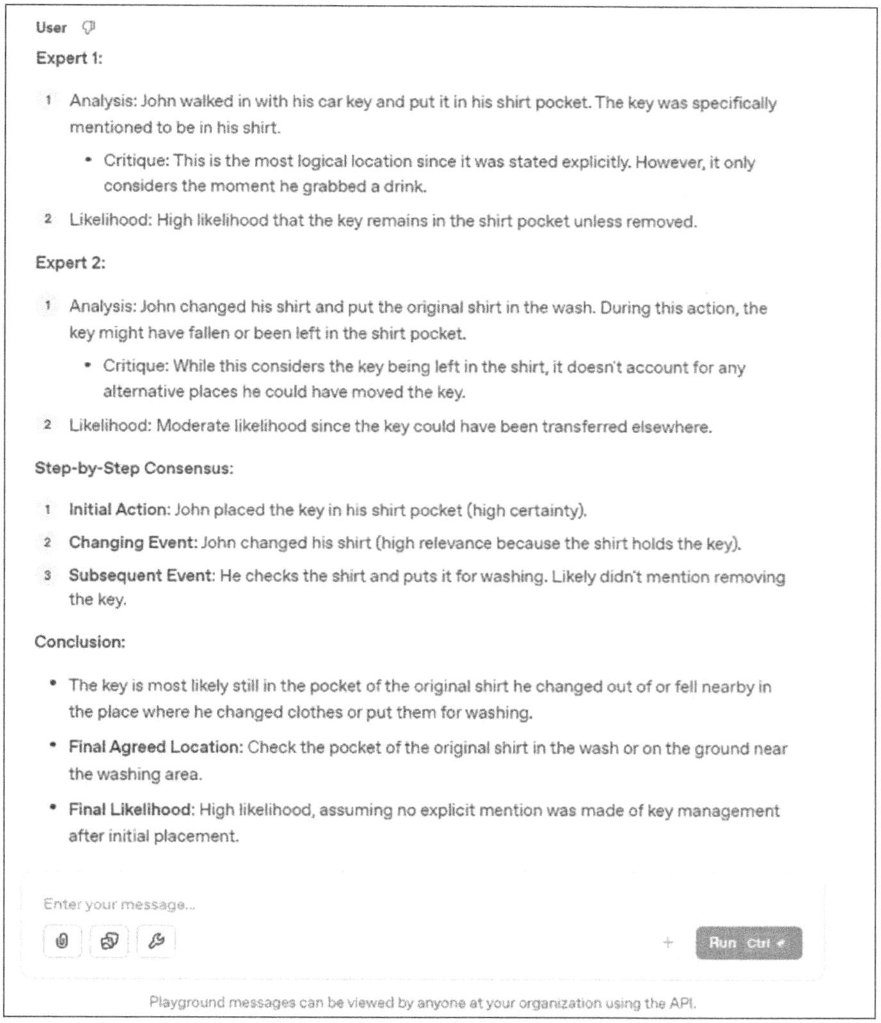

***Figure 4.36**: Tree of Thoughts – Output*

Least-to-Most Prompting (L-to-M Prompting): This technique helps to add multiple steps and lets the LMM decide on splitting the problem statements into multiple subproblems.

ReAct: The objective of the ReAct prompting is to help LLM generate reasoning traces and task-based actions as well as ensure that both are interrelated approaches.

It can be denoted as follows: **Reason + Action = ReAct**

The reasoning trace helps the model convince, track, and update plans and can handle exceptions. The task-based action step(s) gather information from external sources, such as repositories or situations, and allow the building of the interface or framework.

This framework allows LLMs to interact with external tools, such as knowledge repositories, or databases, to retrieve additional information and generate more dependable and accurate responses as output from the LLM. This helps with decision-making tasks and improves LLMs' interpretability and responsibility.

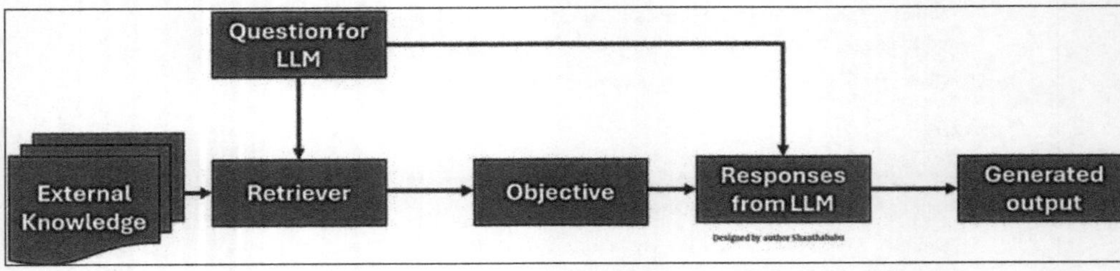

***Figure 4.37**: ReAct Architecture and Workflow*

We can combine ReAct with the Chain-of-Thoughts (CoTs) to enhance the LLM's output. Combining both these techniques helps utilize external information and internal knowledge obtained during the reasoning process.

The implementation of ReAct will be explained in detail in the next chapter.

Multimodal CoT: This technique is much more advanced than other promptings we have discussed. In it, text and vision are the input and the output in a two-stage framework format, such as rationale and answer for the input question.

Stage 1: Will generate rationale generation involved in the given input.

Stage 2: Inference answer, which influences the information generated from stage 1 (that is, rationales).

Input

```
Question: Which properties are common to these two objects?
Context: Select which one is best for drawing pictures. (with pictures)
```

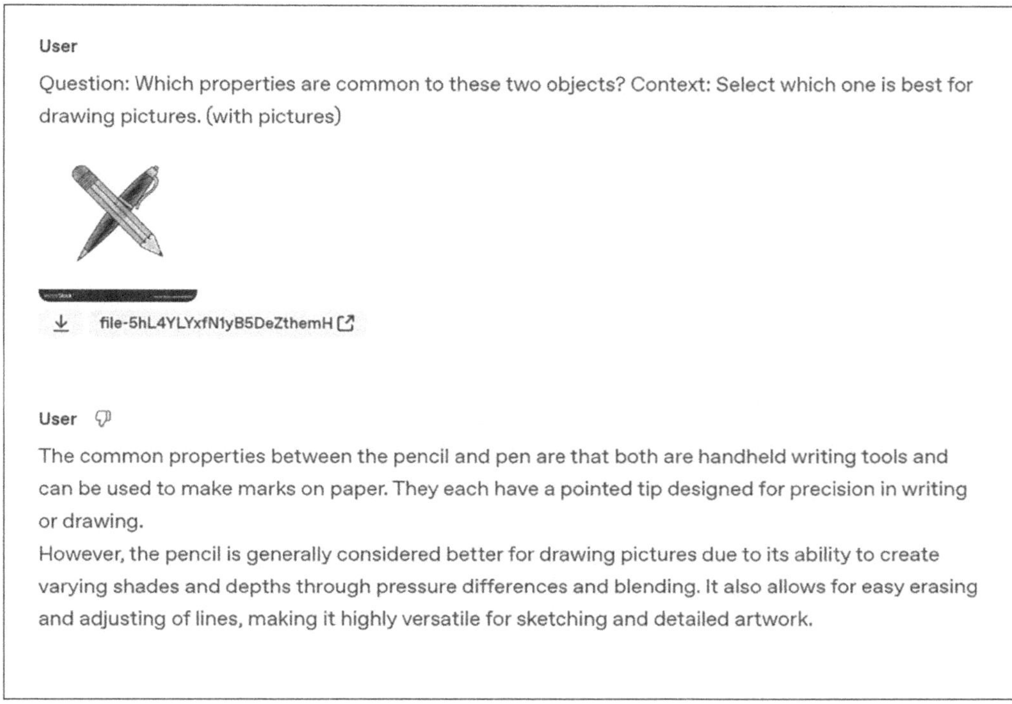

***Figure 4.38**: ReAct (Exercise)*

Graph-of-Thought Prompting (GoT): This technique is much more advanced than other promptings we have discussed and has a slight variation from Multimodal CoT prompting. It also uses text and visual inputs in addition to a "Thought Graph."

- **Text**: Normal textual input.
- **Image**: This is optional, specifically for the reasoning task.
- **Thought Graph**: Explores the relationships between the entities in the graph.

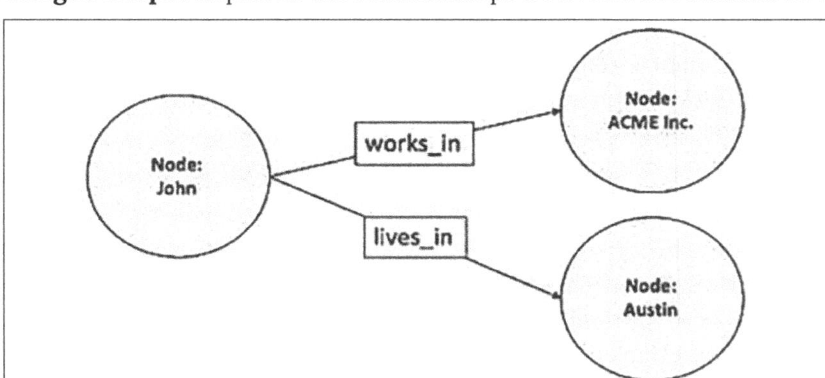

***Figure 4.39**: Graph for Exercise*

- **Question**: Explain the given graph.
- Who lives in Austin?

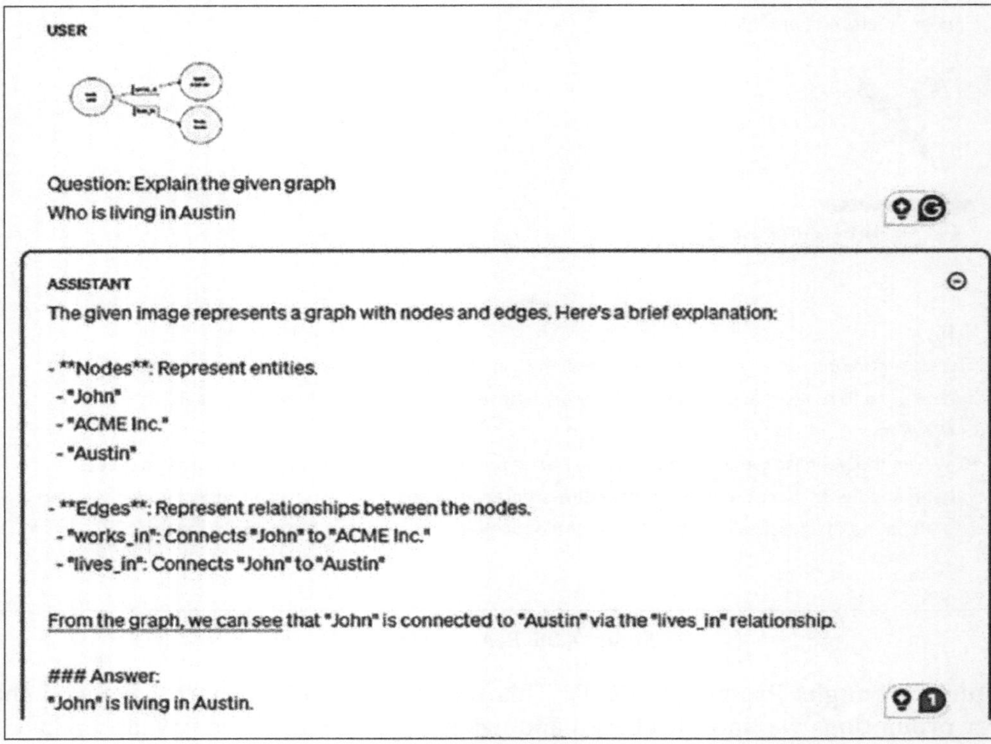

Figure 4.40: *Graph-of-Thought Prompting Exercise*

Prompt Architecture

Prompt architecture is similar to the software architectural approach. However, the components' functionality will differ based on the Gen AI model requirements. Of course, this should be aligned with ethics and consistency. Prompt architecture mainly refers to designing a framework and execution methodology for developing optimized, modular, consistent, concrete, and ethical prompting systems to enhance interactions and close associations with LLMs. It derives from a variety of techniques and specific requirements.

We should understand that prompt architecture is not an evolution of prompt engineering but a different technique. It helps us know what is inside and outside the LLM, and how to improve its practice for complex requirements and reasoning standpoints.

To distinguish between prompt engineering and architecture, the preceding is a single inference; the succeeding one involves multiple inferences and logical steps to accomplish the complex requirements. Ultimately, both extract the new LLMs' capabilities from the overall Gen AI architecture.

We have already discussed a few prompt architectures regarding prompting techniques, such as least-to-most, self-consistency, ToT, Chain-of-Table, and ReAct prompt architecture.

Step-back prompting: Chain-of-Verification (CoVe) prompt architecture is a model that is further enhanced than other prompts.

Step-Back Prompting Architecture: This technique is further enhanced from Zero. CoT prompts techniques to further develop the idea of solving the given problem by slicing and dicing it into sub-problems as the intermediate steps. This approach helps to improve the reasoning capabilities by having the model take a step back to formulate a theoretical answer and reasoning of the question before proposing to answer it.

Step 1: Step-back prompting first asks the LLM a more general question and understands the base ideas.

Step 2: The core facts and concepts come out as output from LLM.

Step 3: With this knowledge, the LLM then uses the initial to give the final response to the user.

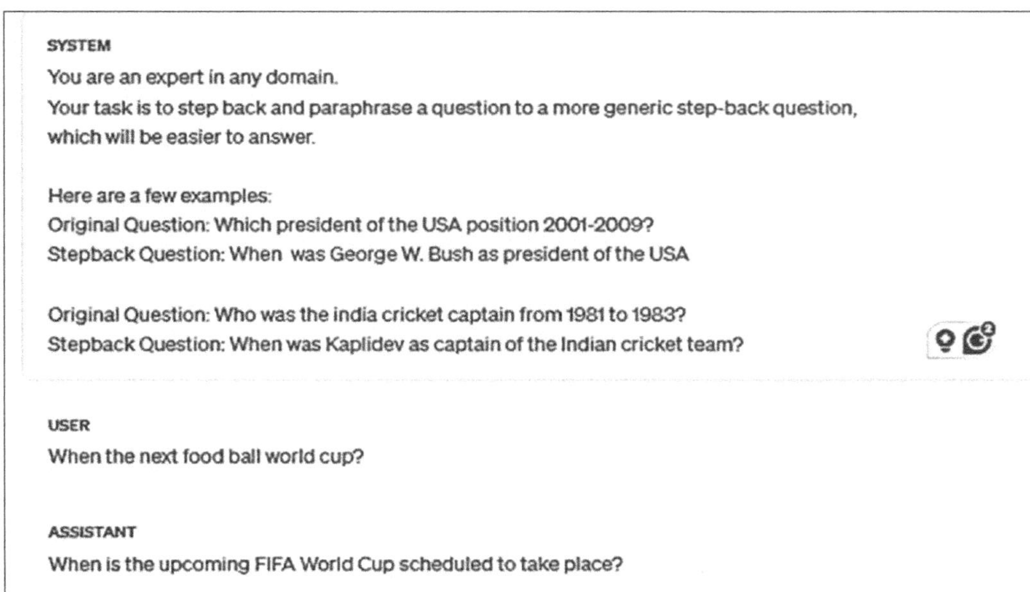

Figure 4.41: *Step-Back Prompting Architecture Exercise*

Chain-of-Verification (CoVe) Architecture: This architecture is unique among other prompt architectures since it seeks to reduce **hallucinations** in LLMs.

Step 1: Generate an initial response to a query that may contain hallucinations.

Step 2: We prompt the LLM to create a set of verification questions to check the facts and errors in its initial response (Step 1).

Step 3: The LLM will give the answers to these verification questions individually and independently, without considering an initial response.

Step 4: Incorporate the verification Q and A pairs to fix any variations with the initial response. The ultimate goal is to generate verified and validated responses.

The implementation of CoVe will be explained in detail in the next chapter.

Best Practices for Building Effective Prompts

So far, we have discussed the various components, elements, prompt techniques, and architecture. However, adopting best practices will make the entire system stable and consistent. Let us go through the list of best practices and their benefits.

Prompt engineering is the art of language and typical science. While designing the prompt, we must work on awareness, concision, clarity, compliance, logical thinking, and ethics to ensure a seamless interaction with the LLM and back-and-forth as well as utilize the available tokens within budget and other parameters.

As part of scientific searches, we have to constantly refine our approach, monitor the output, evaluate the feedback frequently, and adapt to the tones to build the best results.

- **Brief and Transparent Prompts:** While crafting the prompts, they should be brief and transparent. They should convey the necessary information and minimize redundant verbiage.
- **Fine-Tuned Prompting:** Depending on the situation, a prompt engineer must precisely determine the length of the prompt. Based on the scenario, prompt engineers can break down the directions to the LLM into as many minor and sequential prompts as possible.
- **Controlled Economy:** The prompt should be within the boundaries of the economy of language and effectively utilize the resources.
- **Quick Perception:** Prompt engineers should be conscious of the potential truncation of input and output by considering the token limits given to the LLM and working with it.
- **Delimiter Adaptation**: There should be clarity and adaptation for the uniform delimiters.
- **Structured Output:** Based on the requirements, prompt engineers should highlight the model output and pattern, such as bulleted lists, JSON, CSV, and

HTML. This helps us integrate the output with other applications' usage or process points of view.

Conclusion

In this chapter, we have discussed prompt engineering and the significance of Gen AI in every detail. We understood that prompt engineering is the process of designing and improving the input prompt(s) for LLMs and instructing the vector database to get the desired outputs for Gen AI, such as Chatbots, Agents, and more.

We have discussed and understood the facts about prompt engineering. Prompt engineers bridge the gap between Gen AI product users and LLM. They identify scripts and templates for users to customize and complete to receive the best results from the LLMs.

We explored the prompt's elements, such as instruction, context, input data, output data, output indicator, placeholder, constraints, style, and tone.

We understood the importance of role prompting and how "Role" or "Persona" explicitly defines the system's role to act like that persona, guiding the LLM to generate contextually appropriate, accurate, and relevant responses based on the nature of the role given in the prompt along with the input. We explored different prompting roles, such as professional, expert, fictional, guiding, and collaborative roles.

We understood the prompt architecture and advanced versions, such as step-back prompting, CoVe, and best practices for building effective prompts.

In the next chapter, we will explore various Azure Storage and integrate this strategy with Azure Search Services for the Azure OpenAI implementation.

CHAPTER 5
Azure Storage for Azure OpenAI Implementations

Introduction

In the previous chapter, we explored prompt engineering and its importance in Generative AI, component prompts, and categories. We discussed various prompt engineering techniques such as N-shot prompting, Chain-of-Thought (CoT) prompting, Directional Stimulus Prompting (DSP), React prompting, Multimodal CoT prompting, and Graph prompting. We also explored prompt engineering aspects such as Q and A, text summarization, chatbot responses, document classification, and named entity recognition, along with the best practices and guidelines for writing prompts while building strategic models.

This chapter will explore various Azure Storage and Integration strategies along with Azure Search Services for Azure OpenAI implementation. How can we enhance the functionality and performance of AI applications by providing efficient data storage, retrieval, and search capabilities? Blob Storage/ADLS: Azure Blob/ADLS Storage offers capabilities for storing unstructured data such as text, images, audio, and video files. How can these files be accessed directly by Azure OpenAI models for training, inference, and other processing tasks? Azure Storage provides scalable, secure, and highly available storage solutions for various data types and workloads. Azure Storage Architectural design and approaches for Azure OpenAI as well as its best practices will also be discussed.

Structure

In this chapter, we will discuss the following topics:

- Introduction to Azure and Its Environment
  - Understanding Microsoft Azure (PaaS, SaaS, DaaS, and IaaS)

- Azure Active Directory and Azure Resource Group
- Azure Resource Management
  - Management Groups
  - Subscriptions
  - Resource Groups
  - Resources
- Azure Storage Account and Storage Services
  - Blob Storage
  - ADLS Storage
- Azure Storage Services Best Practices
- Azure Storage Design and Approaches
  - Creating Azure Resource Group
  - Creating an Azure Storage Account for Blob and ADLS

Introduction to Azure and Its Environment

Before we explore a detailed understanding of Azure storage and integrate the strategy with Azure Search Services for Azure OpenAI implementation, we should understand the Azure environment, Azure Resource Group, Azure Active Directory (ADD), and others.

Understanding Microsoft Azure

Microsoft Azure is a public cloud computing platform that helps developers build, deploy, and manage data and applications. It comes with multiple solutions, such as Platform as a Service (PaaS), Software as a Service (SaaS), Data as a Service (DaaS), and Infrastructure as a Service (IaaS). All of these services help to build different platforms for customers based on requirements and business enhancements to sustain in the market, including analytics, advanced analytics, machine learning solutions, AI and Gen AI solutions, modern data warehouses and data storage, hosting applications, building secure networking, and much more. It can also replace or supplement your on-premises servers.

In high-level technical terms, it adopts virtualization technology, which helps to build the abstraction layer called a **HYPERVISOR.** This means there is a split-up blending between the hardware and the operating system. This is nothing but the traditional model, which is called on-premises.

In Microsoft Azure, **HYPERVISOR (Hyper -V)** is a software that allows multiple Virtual Machines (VMs) to run on one physical server. It also efficiently manages resources such as CPU and memory, making Azure great for safely running apps and workloads. It delivers fast, secure, and reliable performance. Additionally, it keeps each VM separate to protect the users' data.

Azure Active Directory (AAD): It is Microsoft's enterprise cloud-based Identity and Access Management (IAM) service that can synchronize with the on-premises Active Directory. Generally, AAD will connect with organization-level IDs, such as email IDs. You can connect to and access external and internal resources using this AAD for the following sources.

- External resources: Azure Portal and Microsoft Office 365
- Internal resources: Corporate-level network and Intranet

AAD has a comprehensive Role-Based Access Control (RBAC) system and several built-in roles, which the administrator configures according to the guidelines provided by the organization hierarchy and privileges.

Azure Resource Management

There are always guidelines for managing resources for secure and effective utilization. When we start working with the Azure environment, the first and foremost thing is to know how to organize and use our cloud-based resources to be highly secure and manageable, monitor them regularly, and track the cost aspects as well as other critical areas related to our workloads on a day-to-day (and even hourly) basis. This process is called Azure Resource Management.

There is a standard and recommended way to build the management group hierarchy considering naming convention and resource tagging.

Let us focus on management levels and hierarchy.

Azure provides the following four levels of management:

- Management Groups
- Subscriptions
- Resource Groups
- Resources

Figure 5.1 shows the relationship between all these levels.

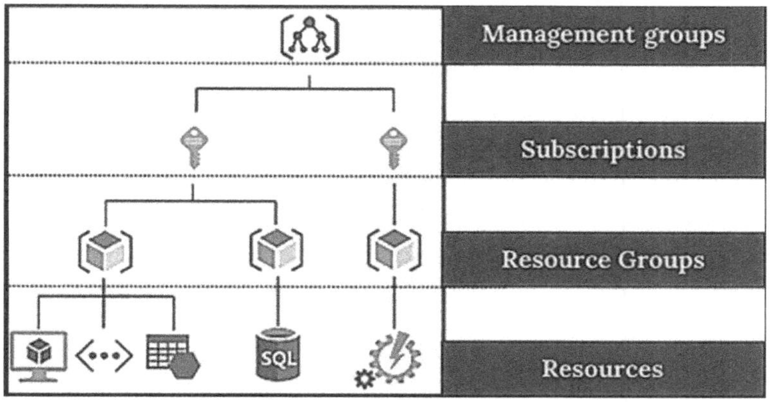

Figure 5.1: *Azure Management Levels and Hierarchy*

Management Groups: We have to manage each group in the subscriptions and efficiently apply the manage access policies and compliance for those subscriptions. These management groups provide a set of governance scopes for the preceding subscriptions. Ultimately, the governance policies and conditions we have defined would be cascaded and inherited by all associated subscriptions under this specific management group. All subscriptions will share this same Entra ID tenant within a single management group.

Features of Management Groups:

- Under a single directory, 10,000 management groups can be connected.
- Management groups can support six levels of depth, but this limit does not include the subscription level.
- One parent for each management group and subscription; simultaneously, we can have many children under each management group.
- All management groups and subscriptions are within a single hierarchy in each directory.

Subscriptions: As mentioned earlier, the subscriptions are connected to the management group. This agreement allows a specific set of users to access Azure resources such as Azure Functions, Azure Data Factory, Azure SQL Server, Azure Data Lake, Data Bricks, and so on.

This is a logical unit of Azure services linked to an Azure account to take advantage of and control Azure's cloud-based services.

Understanding the importance of well-configured access permissions in Azure Active Directory is crucial. These permissions are defined by the associated users or groups, and it is essential to remember that each subscription has limitations and usage quotas on individual resources. This is based on policies and access permissions created and used for project-specific purposes.

Effective subscription management is key to controlling costs and the resources created by the project team. By managing subscriptions appropriately, we can ensure that the resources are used efficiently for project requirements.

Azure offers four distinct tiers of subscriptions: free, basic, standard, and storage optimized. Each tier comes with its own set of features and capabilities, catering to different user needs and project requirements.

- Free and Basic tiers have very minimal configuration and capacities.
- Standard and Storage Optimized tiers have several configurations and capacities.

Resource Groups (RGs): RGs are similar to containers that hold related resources for an Azure solution for a specific product or project requirement based on the architectural demand. These are all the resources that we want to manage as a group under a subscription. This container helps us manage and deploy those resources across multiple project environments such as: development, testing, pre-production, and production.

The resources are Azure Functions, Azure Data Factory, Azure SQL Server, Azure Data Lake, Data Bricks, and others.

There are different Azure services available. Since the objective is focused on ADLS/Blob, let us go through the data perspective services since the rest is outside the scope of this book.

Azure Data Storage Resources: Microsoft's Azure data storage platform is a modern cloud storage solution for various data objects. This service offers high availability, scalability, durability, and provisioning of secured storage for data stored in the cloud. The data can be accessed from various approaches, such as linked service, FTP, HTTP, and HTTPS, even if we enable using REST API calls. We can bring the data into this storage using Azure Data Factory, Data Brick, or Synapse Analytics.

Multiple storages are available in Azure based on functionalities and usage, including Blob, Queue, File, Elastic SAN, Tables, SQL Server, Data Lake Store, and Delta Lake, as well as backup, monitoring, logging, and site recovery features.

In Azure, the data storage resources are connected to the storage account. Under each storage account, we can add any number of Azure storage resources, such as Blob, Queue, File, Elastic SAN, Tables, and Data Lake Store.

Azure Storage Account: This is a specific account for the data storage services available in the Azure environment. There is a container setup that groups Azure storage services under this account. Whenever you create any Azure data storage services, they must be tagged into one of the storage accounts. This is a unique namespace. The data services include Blob, Queue, Table, File, Disk Image, Data Lake Store, and Delta Lake.

Azure Blob Storage and Azure Data Lake Storage (ADLS) are widely used storage solutions within the Azure ecosystem. Each storage solution is designed to handle specific data types and process requirements for data analytics and advanced data analytics.

Azure Blob Storage is specifically for large object storage solutions. Its primary objective is to store and manage unstructured data such as text, documents, images, videos, and other file formats.

Capabilities:

- **Scalability**: This is highly scalable and can handle massive amounts of data.
- **Data Redundancy**: Provides multiple redundancy options to ensure data durability.
  - Locally Redundant Storage (LRS),
  - Geo-Redundant Storage (GRS), and more
- **Access Control**: Integrate with Azure Active Directory (AAD) and Shared Access Signatures (SAS) for secure data access.
- **Blob Indexer**: It supports indexing for metadata; this capability enables faster searches, which would help us while building the AI-based RAG models.

Limitations:

- **File System**: It does not support hierarchical namespaces or provide fine-grained access control at the file and directory levels.
- **Analytics and Processing**: There are shortages in built-in analytics capabilities; data processing requires external services such as Azure Databricks.

Azure Data Lake Storage (ADLS): It is a highly scalable and secure data storage service designed for data and advanced analytics services and solutions. It supports hierarchical namespace concepts to implement a hierarchical directory structure and well-organized access control to manage and analyze vast volumes of data. ADLS can manage both structured and unstructured data.

Capabilities:

- **Hierarchical Namespace**: This supports a hierarchical namespace and is similar to traditional file systems. It enables directory and file-level operations and access permissions.
- **Integration with Big Data Services**: This is compactable with big data analytics workloads and integrates with Azure Data Factory, Azure Databricks, and Azure Synapse Analytics.
- **Data Management**: AAD supports advanced data management through Access Control Lists (ACLs) and Role-Based Access Control (RBAC).

Limitations:

- **Cost**: It is generally more expensive than standard blob storage. However, this option can be used whenever we require a directory/file system pattern, such as hierarchical namespaces.
- **Complexity**: Since it supports hierarchical namespaces, setting up and managing it is challenging and complex compared to blob storage.

Both storage options allow data to be stored at three different tier levels, such as the Hot storage tier and the Cold storage tier.

- **Hot Storage**: Data objects are accessed frequently.
- **Cool Storage**: This tier level is less expensive than hot storage as the requirement for accessing the data is infrequent.
- **Achieve Storage**: This tire level is mainly used for archiving or backup data purposes, and it is comparatively the least expensive of the other tier levels of service.

There are other Azure storage services such as Azure Files, Azure Queues, Azure Tables, and Azure Container Storage.

When implementing Azure Storage services, we must follow the best practices to ensure optimal performance, security, and cost-efficient solutions.

Best Practices for Azure Storage

Follow the mentioned best practices for Azure Storage to maximize cost-effectiveness, security, and performance:

- **Storage Options:** We must understand the different options for storage services.
  - Blob Storage for unstructured data
  - ADLS for big data analytics
- **Right Access Tiers:** We must choose access tiers based on demand and review access tiers based on access patterns and necessity.
- **Security Best Practices:** Use appropriate access control based on architectural requirements.
  - Azure Active Directory (AAD) for authentication
  - Role-Based Access Control (RBAC)
- **Secure Data:** Depending on the scenario, we must enable encryption at rest and in transit and provide Shared Access Signatures (SAS) for delegated access.
- **Performance:** To track performance and detect anomalies, we must enable

monitoring and optimizing features such as Azure Monitor and Azure Storage metrics, as well as diagnostic logging to troubleshoot issues with data and access.

- **Data Redundancy and Backup:** Based on your data durability and availability requirements, choose the appropriate redundancy option (LRS, ZRS, GRS, or RA-GRS).

  Implement a regular backup plan and use automated backup solutions.

Creating Azure Resource Group

As discussed, the Resource Manager is the deployment and management service for all Azure components. The Azure storage account also belongs to the Azure Resource Manager resources, a group of logical containers.

Whenever we create an Azure storage account, we can create a new resource group or use an existing one.

Let us create a new resource group.

Step 1: Log into the Azure portal. Right-click on the resource group icon to get a small pop up window. Click on the **`Create`** Plus icon, as shown in *Figure* 5.2.

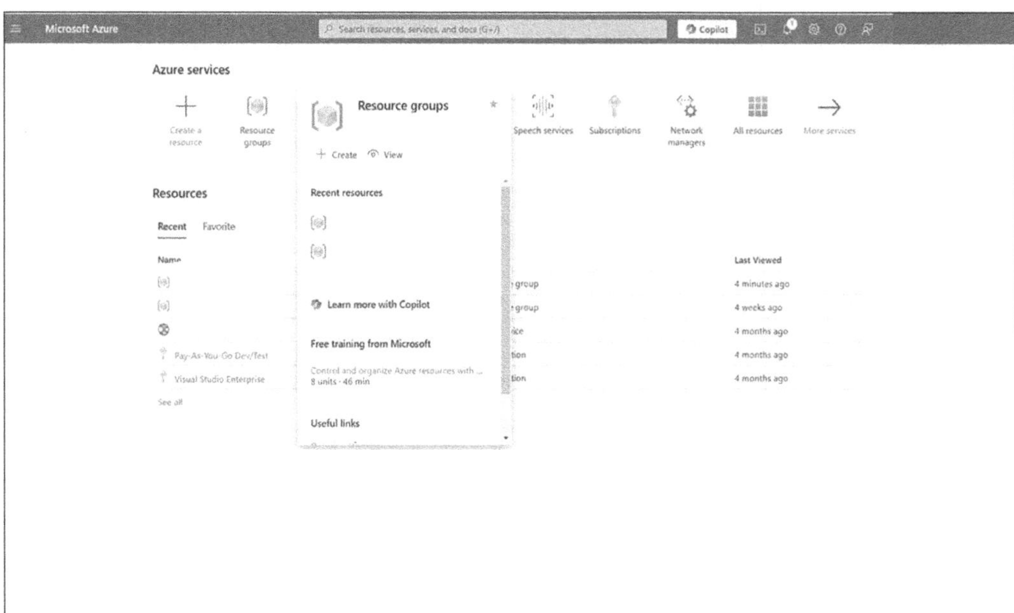

***Figure* 5.2:** *Azure Portal (Creating Resource Group)*

Step 2: Once you click on the plus icon, the application will take you to the following screen, as shown in *Figure* 5.3. Here, you need to provide the following details:

- **Subscription Type**: Free/Pay as you go (name).
- **Resource Group**: Provide a valid resource group name (it should be lowercase, and no exceptional cases are allowed).
- **Region**: Select your appropriate region.

Once the aforementioned details are provided, we must click the "`Review and Create`" button.

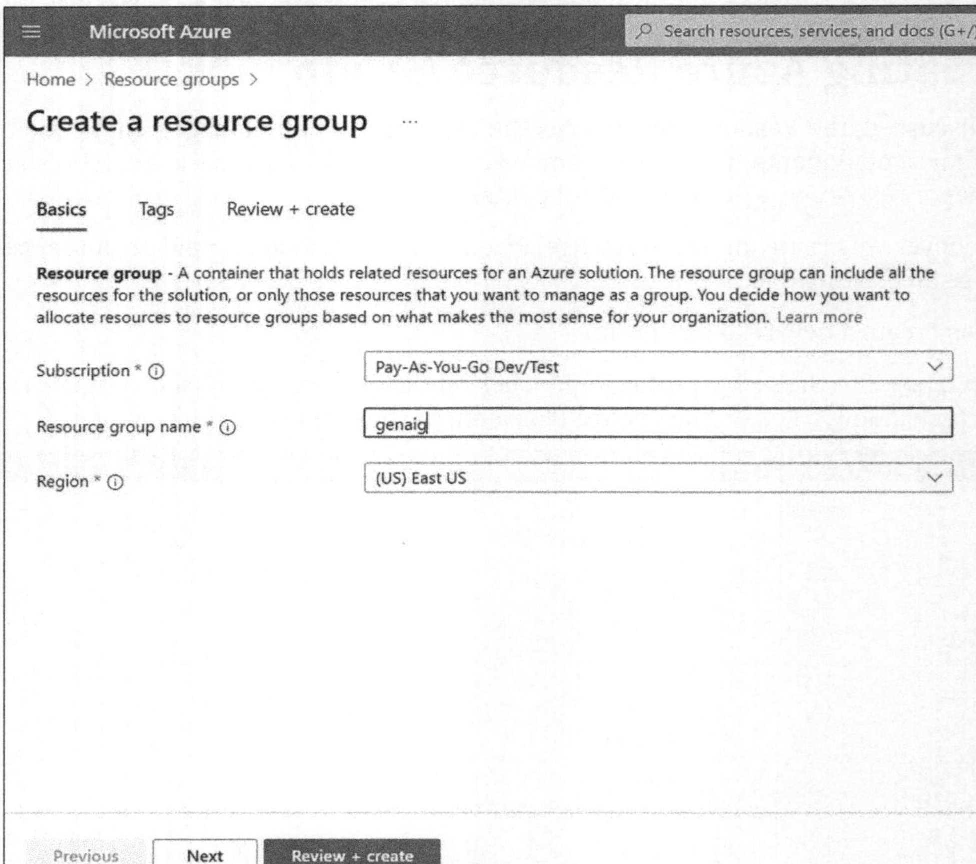

Figure 5.3: *Azure Portal (Creating Resource Group)*

Step 3: Once the details are validated, click the `Create` button.

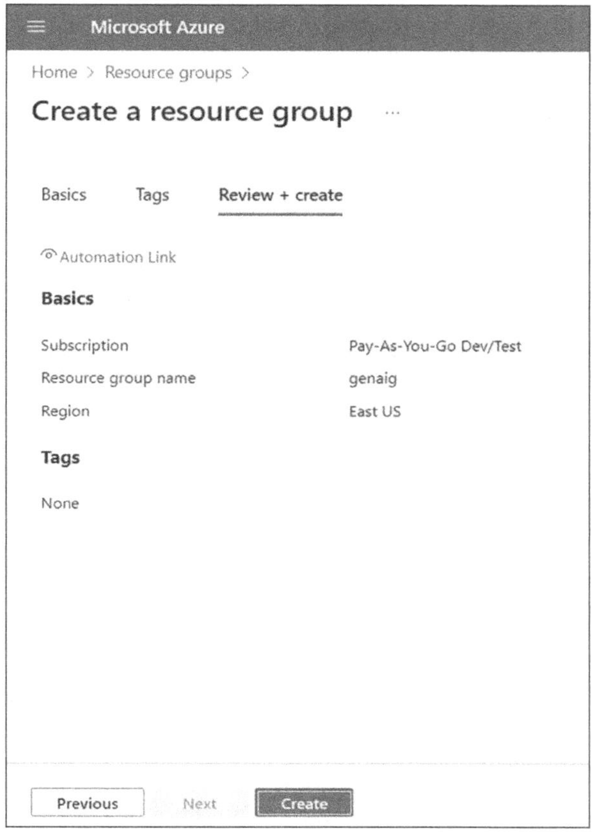

Figure 5.4: *Azure Portal (Creating Resource Group)*

Resource group preparation is in progress.

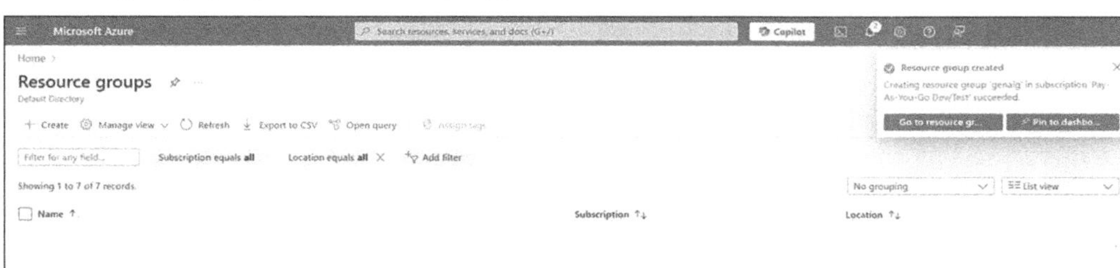

Figure 5.5: *Azure Portal (Resource Group Preparation in Progress)*

The resource group is ready to use.

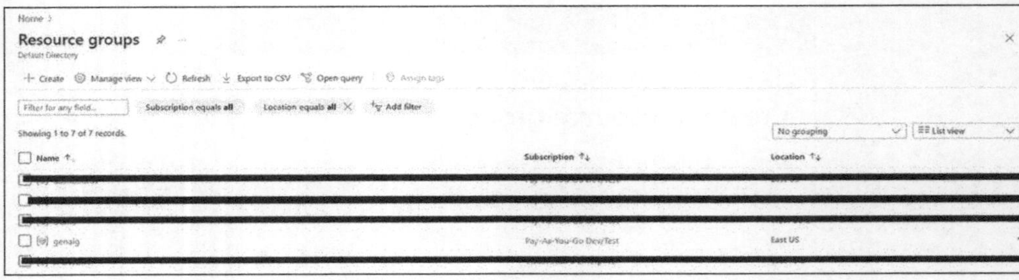

Figure 5.6: *Azure Portal (Resource Groups under the AAD)*

Once the resource group is ready, we can now start adding the components under this resource group.

Creating an Azure Storage Account for Blob

Let us create an Azure Storage account for Blob storage.

Step 1: Right-click on Storage accounts and then click on the **`(+) Create`**.

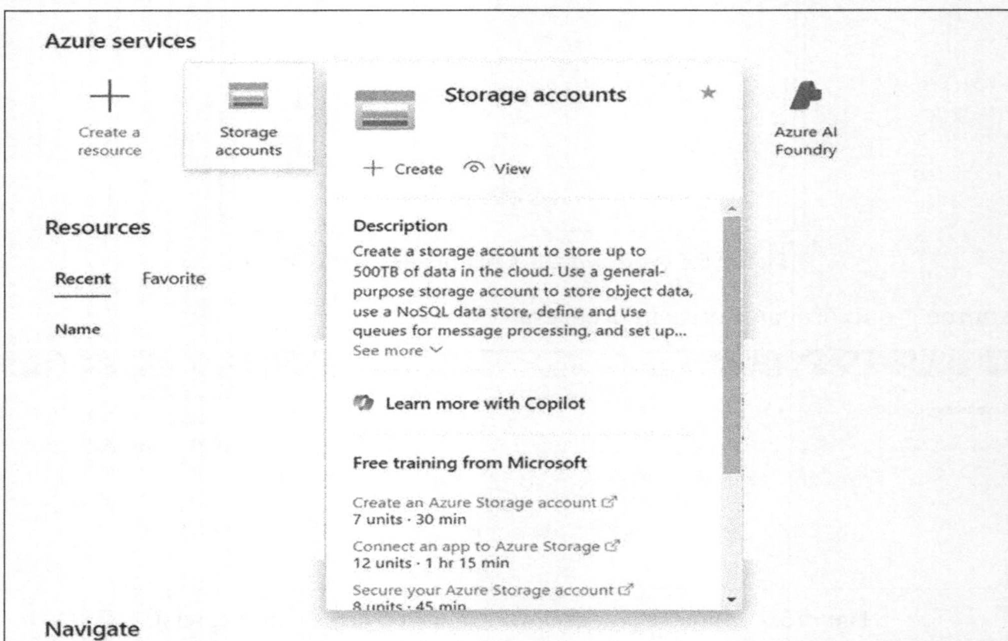

Figure 5.7: *Azure Portal (Creating Storage Accounts)*

Step 2: Once you click on the plus icon, the application will take you to the following screen, as shown in *Figure* 5.8.

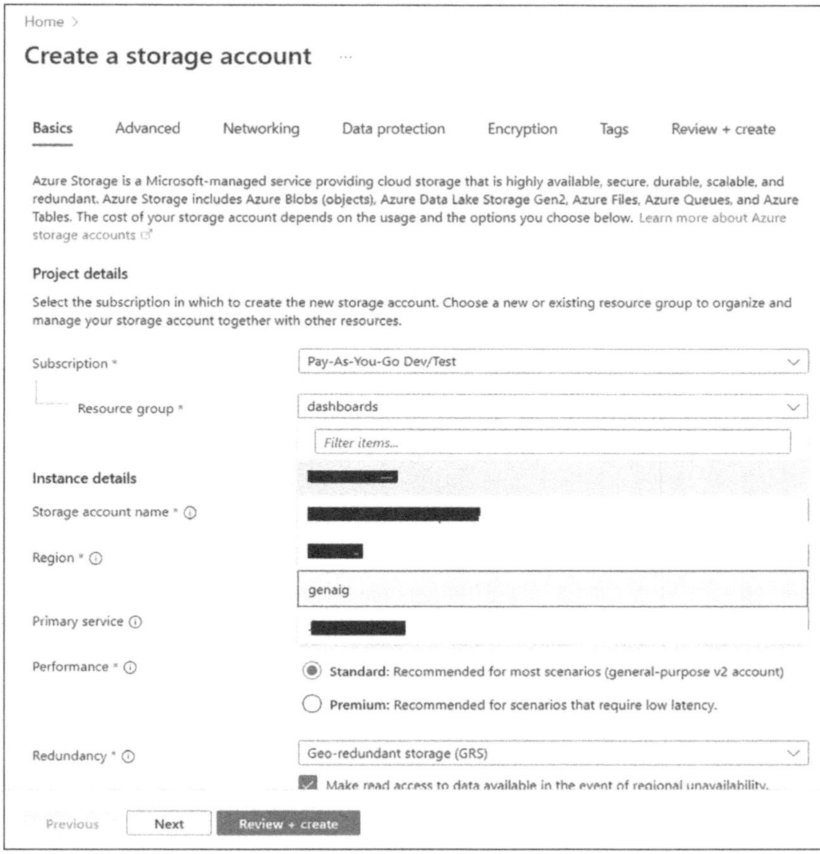

Figure 5.8: *Azure Portal (Creating Storage Accounts)*

Here, you need to provide the following details, as shown in *Figure* 5.9:

Basic Configuration:

- **Subscription Type**: Free/Pay as you go (Subscription name).
- **Resource Group**: Select the resource group from the list.
- **Storage Account Name**: Enter a valid storage name (It should be lowercase, and no exceptional cases are allowed).
- **Region**: Select your appropriate region.
- **Redundancy**: Select your replication strategy.
- **Performance**: `Standard` (or) `Premium`.

Advance Configuration:

- **Enable hierarchical namespace**: Uncheck (For blob).

Figure 5.9: *Azure Portal (Creating Storage Accounts; Basic Configuration)*

Once the aforementioned details are provided, you must click the "**`Review and Create`**" button, as shown in *Figure* 5.9. The application will take you to the screen, as shown in *Figure* 5.10. Here, you have to click on the "**`Create`**" button.

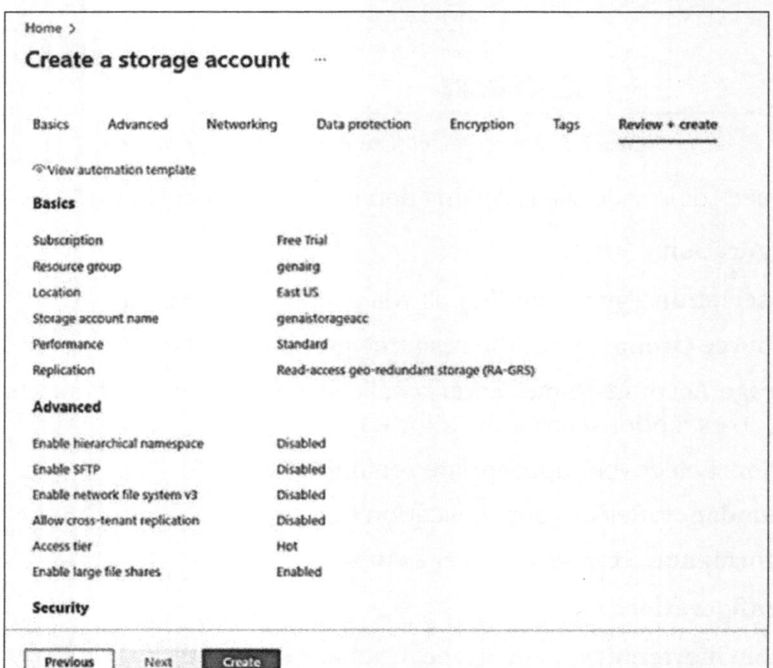

Figure 5.10: *Azure Portal (Creating Storage Accounts; Review Completed)*

Step 3: Once you click the "**`Create`**" button, the application will initiate the deployment, as shown in *Figure 5.11*.

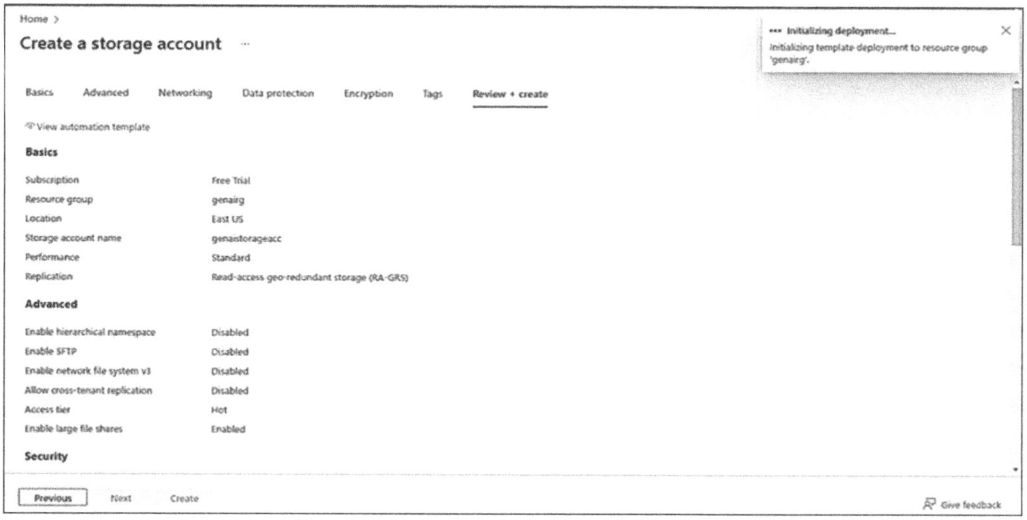

Figure 5.11: *Azure Portal (Creating Storage Accounts; Initializing Deployment In-Process)*

Step 4: After deployment completion, the following screen will display; click on the "**`Go to resource`**" button, as shown in *Figure 5.12*.

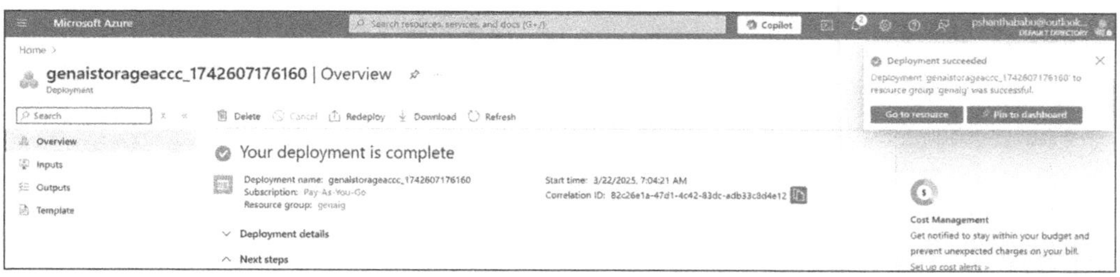

Figure 5.12: *Azure Portal (Creating Storage Accounts Resource is Ready)*

Step 5: After clicking the **`Go to resource`**, the application takes you to the following screen, as shown in *Figure 5.13*.

We have not selected "**`Enable hierarchical namespace`**." Unchecked, we have the following data storage options:

- Container
- File shares

- Queues
- Tables

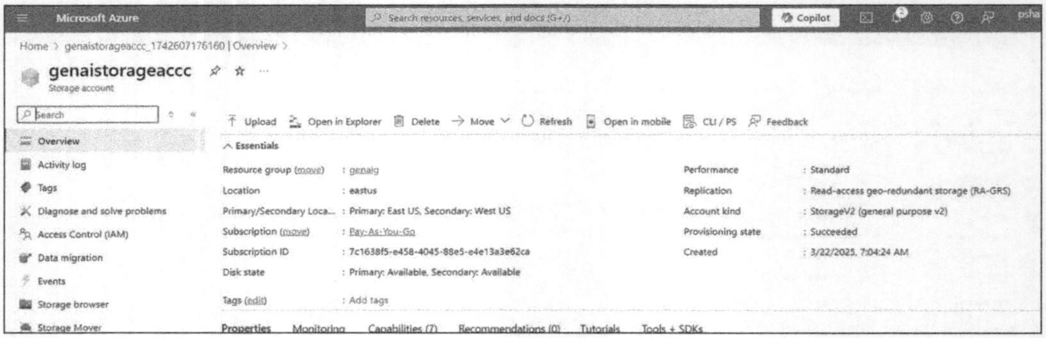

Figure 5.13: *Azure Portal (Storage Accounts Ready to Add Data Storage)*

In the Azure environment, the following storage capabilities are available such as Blob, Table, File, and Queue; based on the requirements, we can create the resources and use them appropriately.

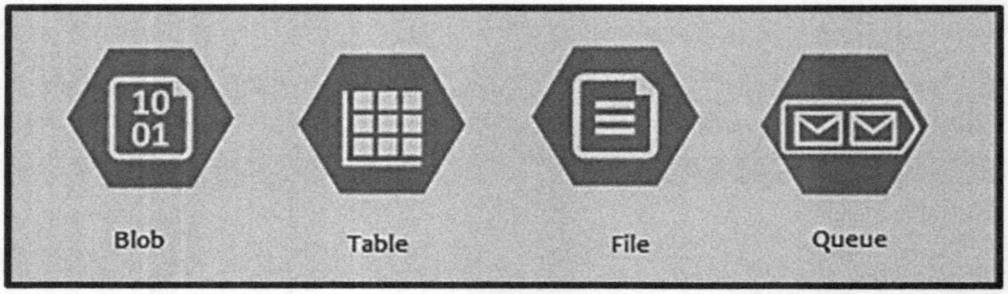

Figure 5.14: *Azure Storage (Blob, Table, File, and Queue)*

Create a Blob Container

Let us create a blob container under `genaistorageacc` (Storage account). Click on the container icon from the data storage list on the left panel.

You will get a panel to create a container(s) on the right side (highlighted).

Step 1: Click on `(+) Container` in the right panel menu, as highlighted in *Figure* 5.15.

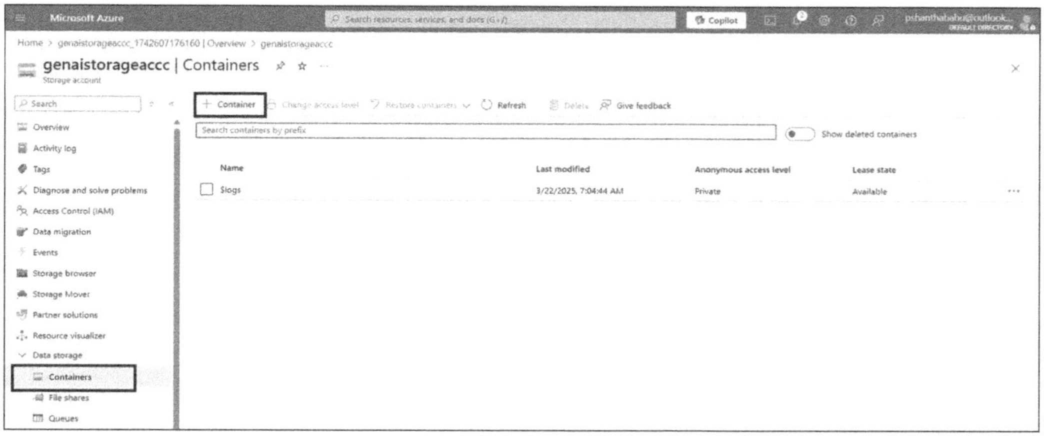

Figure 5.15: *Azure Portal (Container Creation)*

Step 2:

Here, you need to provide the following details:

- Name: name (should be lowercase, and no special cases are allowed).
- Leave the rest.

Once the preceding details are provided, we have to click on the "**`Create`**" button.

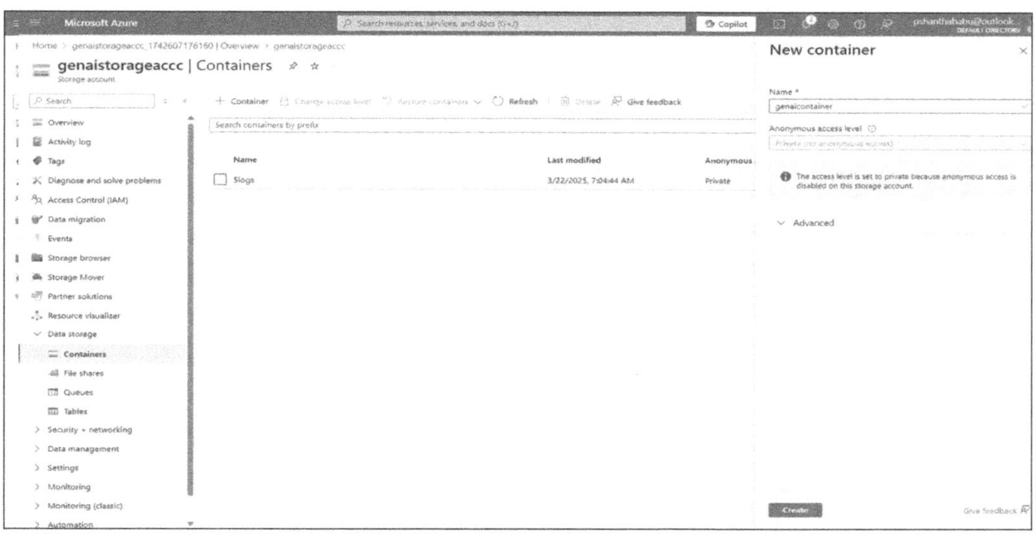

Figure 5.16: *Azure Portal (Container Creation)*

Step 3:

Once the **`Create`** button is clicked, a new container is available for usage.

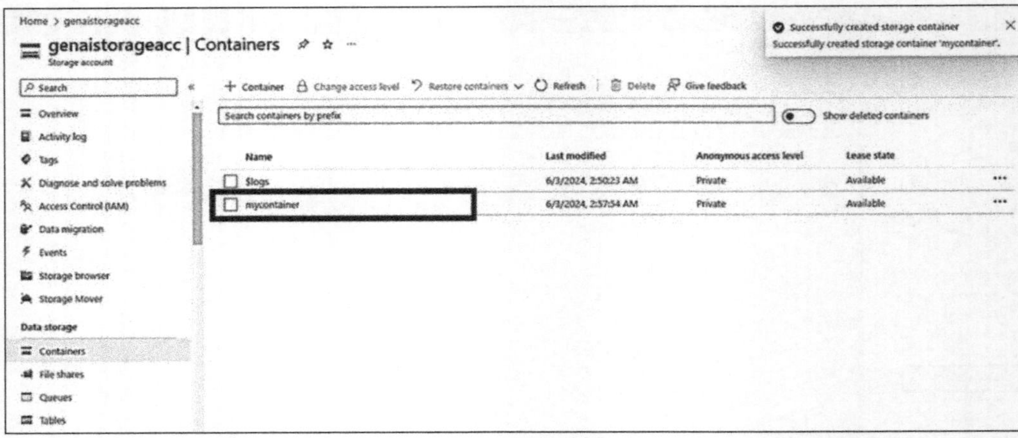

Figure 5.17: Azure Portal (*Container Creation; Container is Ready*)

Step 4: Once the container is ready, click on the right panel, as highlighted in *Figure* 5.17. You will then be taken inside the container, as shown in *Figure* 5.18.

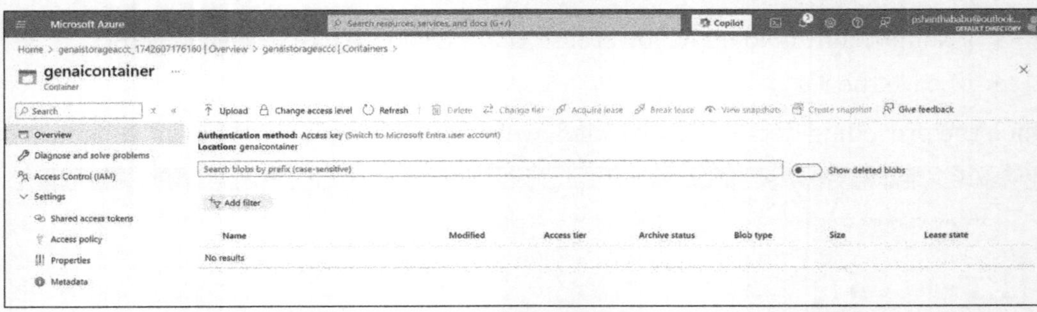

Figure 5.18: Azure Portal (*Container Creation; Inside the Container*)

We will now add the file to the container **(`mycontainer`)**.

Step 5: Click the **`Upload`** menu on the right menu. The application will bring the pop up, as shown in *Figure* 5.19.

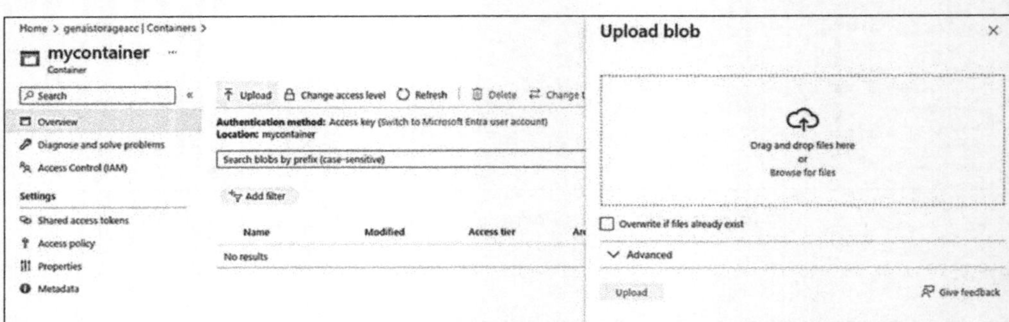

Figure 5.19: Azure Portal (*Adding Document into the Container*)

Step 6: You can browse or drag and drop the document into the highlighted space, as shown in *Figure* 5.20.

Figure 5.20: *Azure Portal (Uploading the Document into the Container)*

Step 7: Once the document is dropped on the highlighted space and ready to upload, click the **`Upload`** button, as shown in *Figure* 5.21.

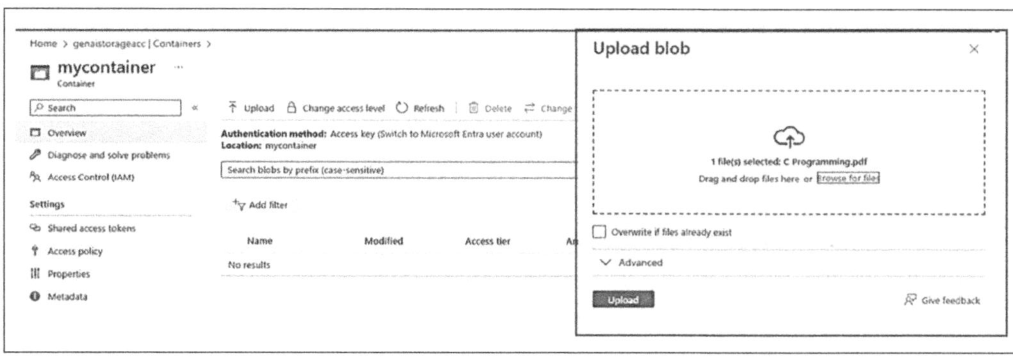

Figure 5.21: *Azure Portal (Uploading the Document into the Container Initiated)*

Step 8: The document is now available inside the container (C programming.pdf) along with details such as the date it was modified, its size, and more, as shown in *Figure* 5.22.

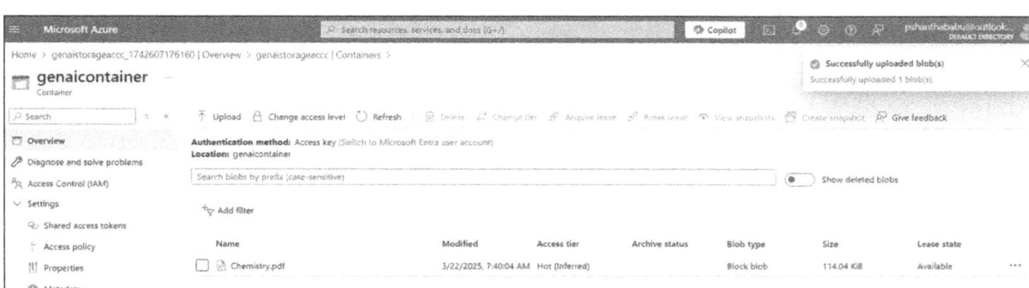

Figure 5.22: *Azure Portal (Document Saved into the Container)*

Step 9: You can view the document details by double-clicking on the file name in the preceding image. The details are shown in *Figure* 5.23.

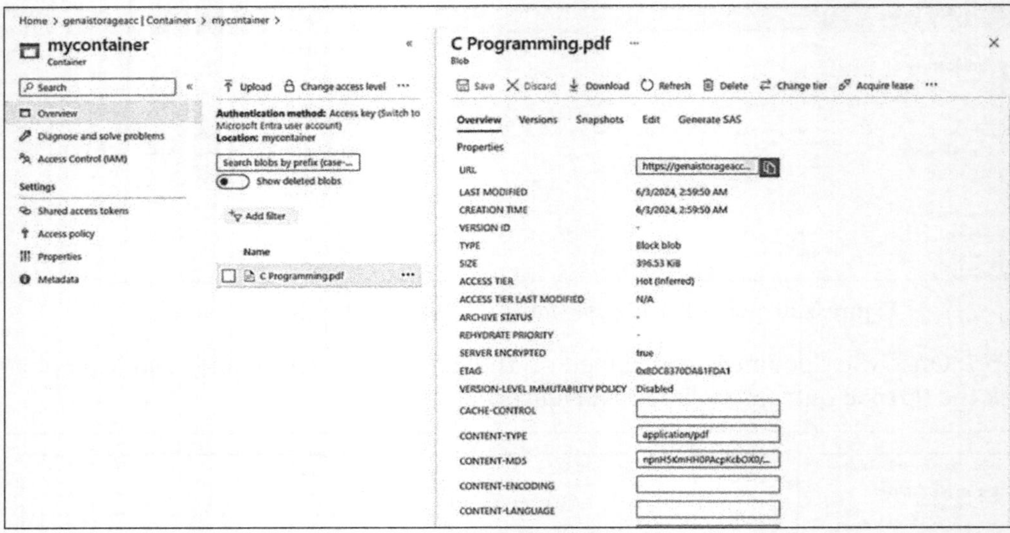

***Figure* 5.23:** *Azure Portal (Document Details)*

Step 10: Delete the document from the container.

Select the check box on the left side of the file name and click **`Delete`** on the top menu (highlighted), as shown in *Figure* 5.24.

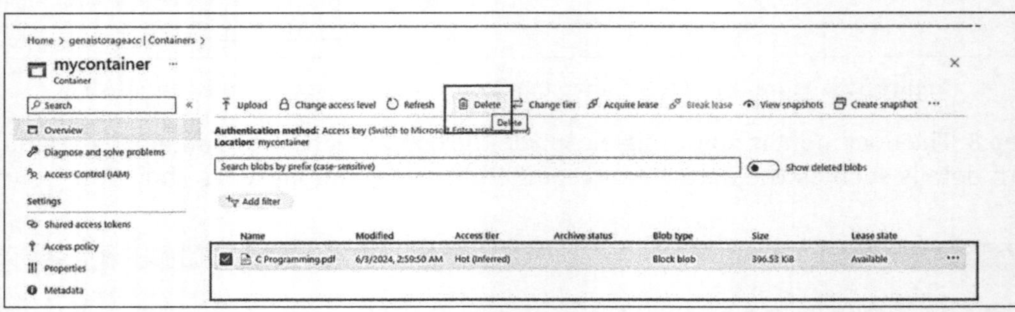

***Figure* 5.24:** *Azure Portal – Deleting the Document from the Container* (*Step* 10)

Step 11: The application will ask for confirmation, once you click on the delete menu, as shown in *Figure* 5.25.

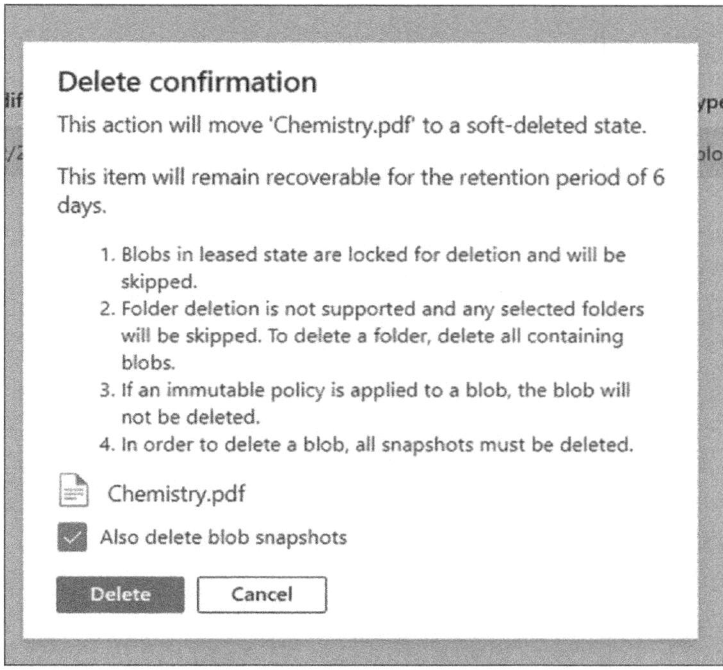

Figure 5.25: *Azure Portal (Delete Confirmation)*

Once you click on the "`OK`" button, the document will be successfully deleted, as shown in *Figure* 5.26.

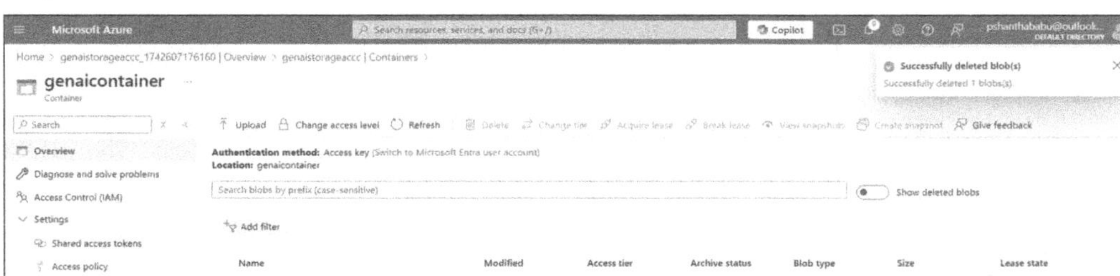

Figure 5.26: *Azure Portal (Document Deleted Successfully)*

Step 12: Delete the container.

In *Figure* 5.27, select the check box on the left side of the container name and click delete from the top menu (highlighted).

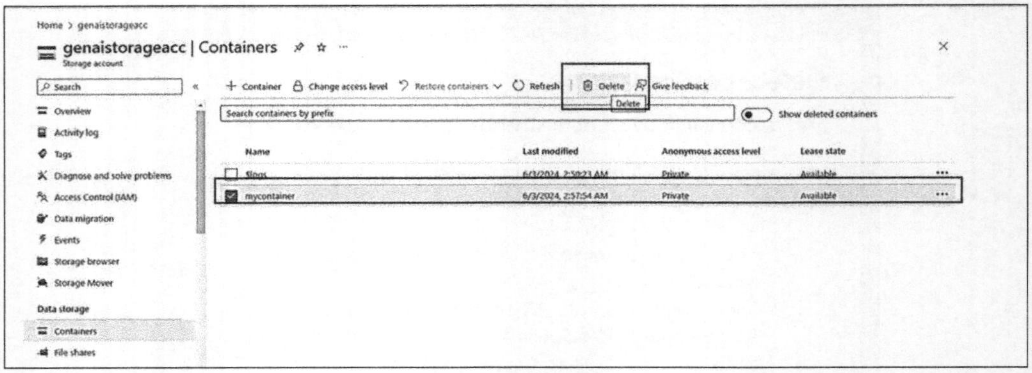

Figure 5.27: Azure Portal (Deleting the Container)

Step 13: Delete the container.

Once you click on the delete menu, the application will pop up on the screen, as shown in *Figure* 5.28 (highlighted).

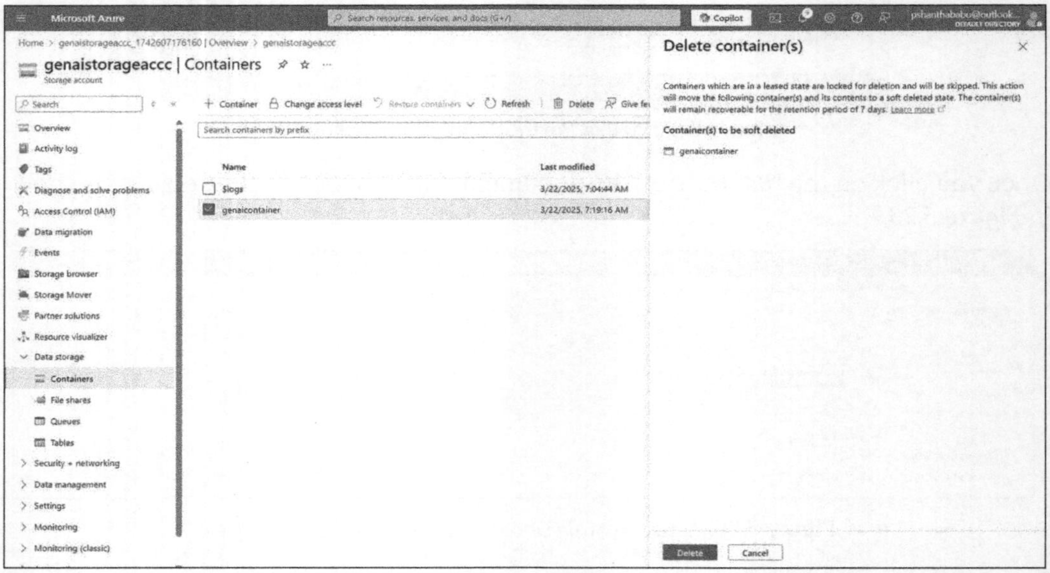

Figure 5.28: Azure Portal (Deleting the Container)

Step 14: Click on the "`Delete`" button, and the application will ask for confirmation, as shown in *Figure* 5.29. Click the "`Confirm delete`" button.

Figure 5.29: *Azure Portal (Deleting the Container Confirmation)*

After the successful deletion, the container list is empty (except $logs), as shown in *Figure 5.30*.

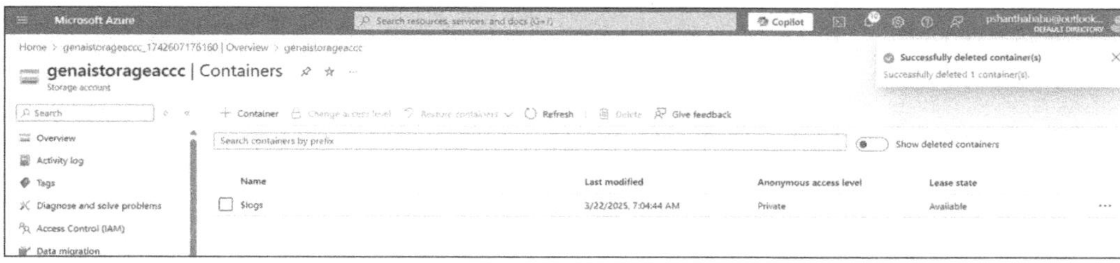

Figure 5.30: *Azure Portal Empty Container (except $logs)*

Step 15: Delete the storage account.

Go back to the home page, select and right-click the storage account, as shown in *Figure 5.31*.

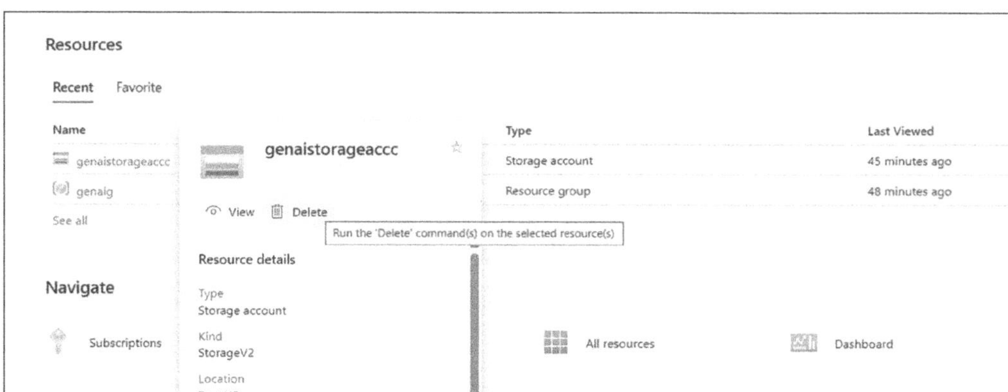

Figure 5.31: *Azure Portal (Deleting the Storage Account)*

Step 16: Delete the container.

Once you click delete, the application will pop up on the screen, as shown in *Figure 5.32* (highlighted).

Enter the text in the textbox as **`delete`** to "delete" the selected storage account and click the Delete button.

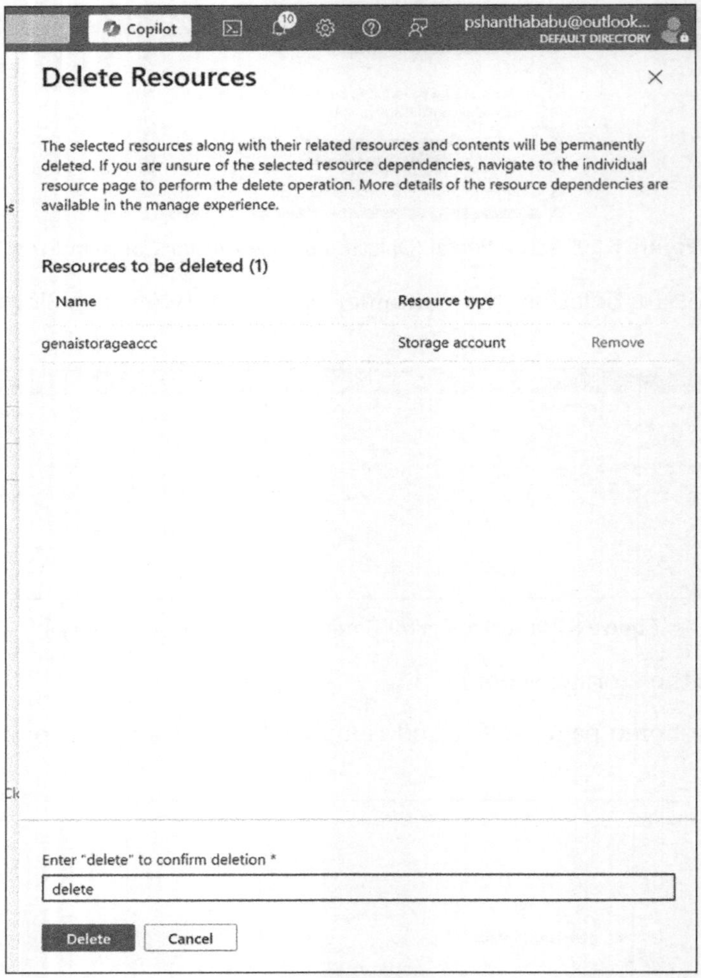

Figure 5.32: *Azure Portal (Deleting the Storage Account)*

Step 17: Delete the container.

After you enter the text in the textbox as "**`delete`**" and click the "**`Delete`**" button, you will get the confirmation dialogue box.

Click the "**`Delete`**" button to confirm your options.

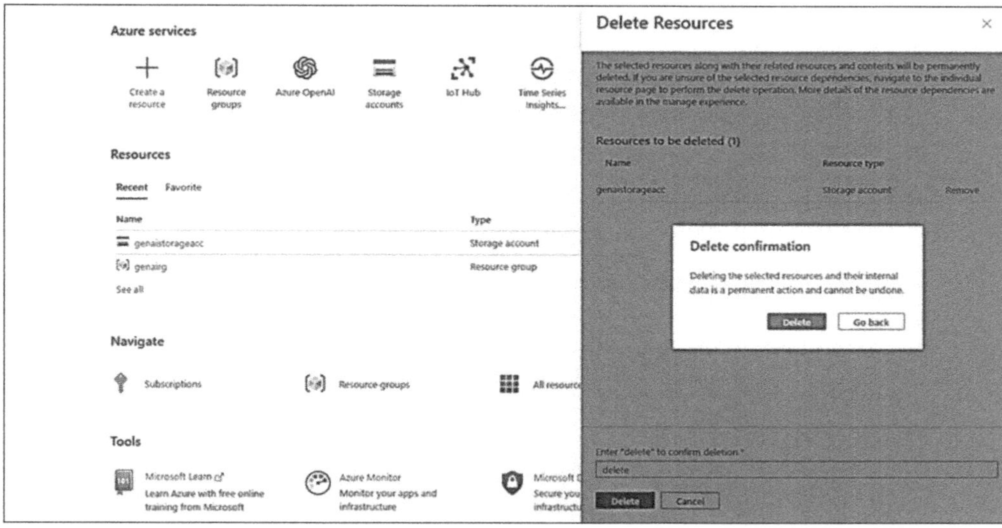

Figure 5.33: *Azure Portal (Deleting the Storage Account Confirmation)*

The storage account was successfully deleted, and now, as shown in *Figure* 5.34, we only have resource groups in the resources list.

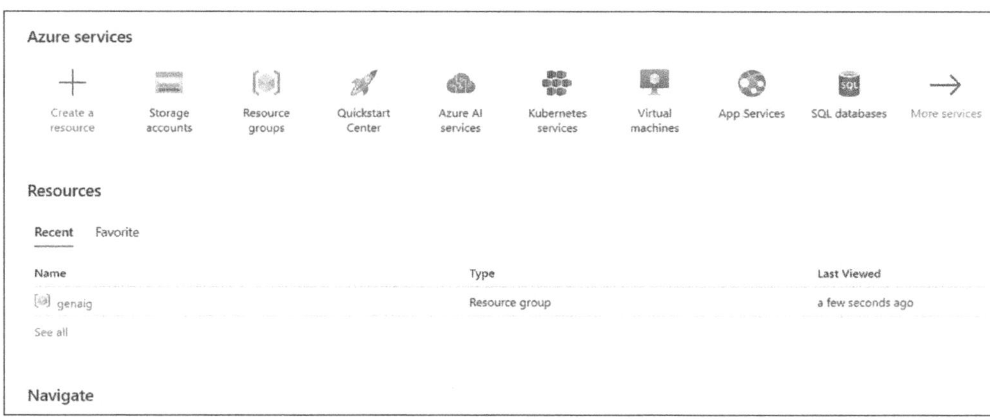

Figure 5.34: *Azure Portal (Resource List after Storage Account Deleted)*

Creating a Storage Account and ADLS Gen2

Let us create a storage account for ADLS Gen2.

Step 1: Click on the `(+) Create`, as shown in *Figure* 5.35.

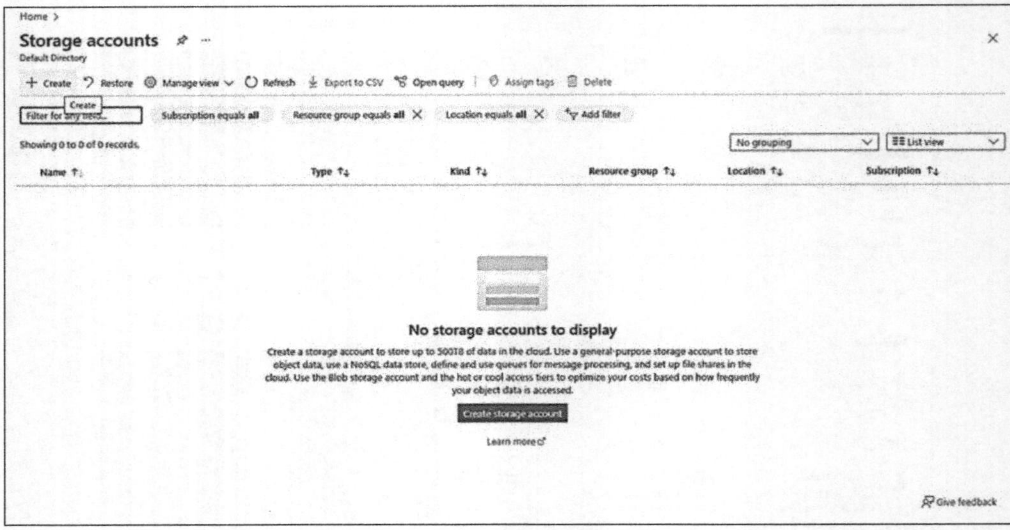

***Figure* 5.35:** *Azure Portal (Storage Account)*

Step 2: Once you click on the plus icon, the application will take you to the following screen, as shown in *Figure* 5.36.

Here, you need to provide the following details:

Basic Configuration

- **Subscription Type**: Free/Pay as you go (Subscription name).
- **Resource Group**: Select the resource group from the list.
- **Storage Account Name**: Enter a valid storage name (should be lowercase and no exceptional cases are allowed).
- **Region**: Select your appropriate region.
- **Redundancy**: Select your replication strategy.
- **Performance**: `Standard` (or) `Premium`.

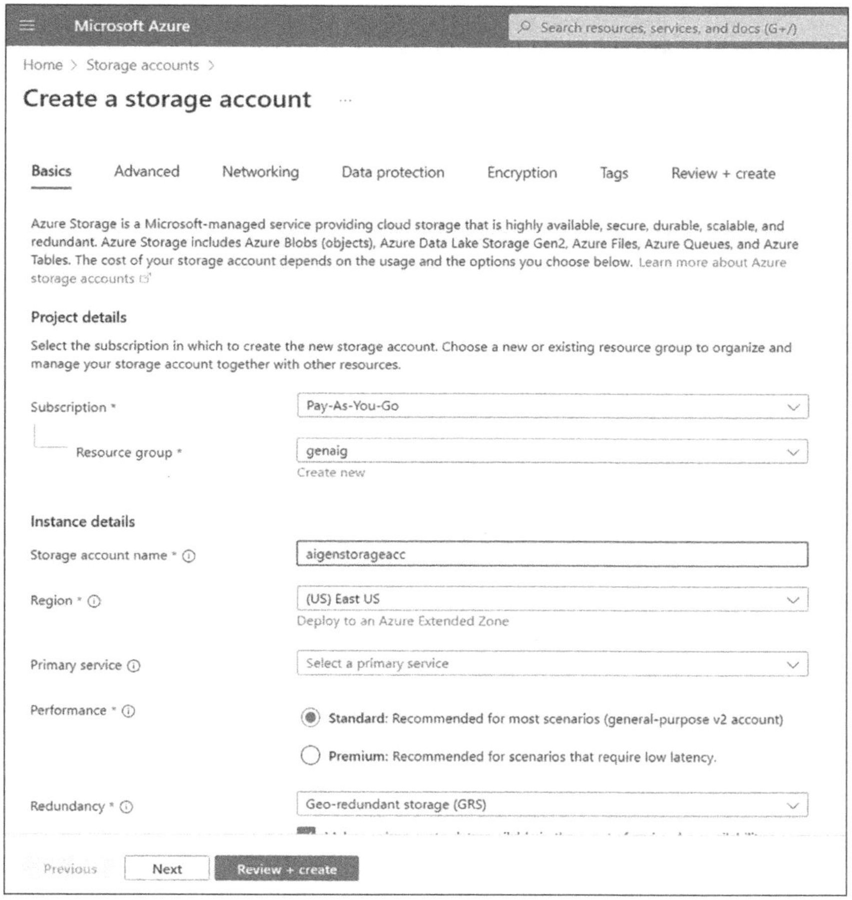

Figure 5.36: *Azure Portal (Storage Account)*

Based on your requirements, you can configure the Advanced tab.

Advance Configuration

- Enable hierarchical namespace; check (for ADLS Gen 2) *Figure* 5.37.

Once the preceding details are provided, we must click the "**`Review and Create`**" button.

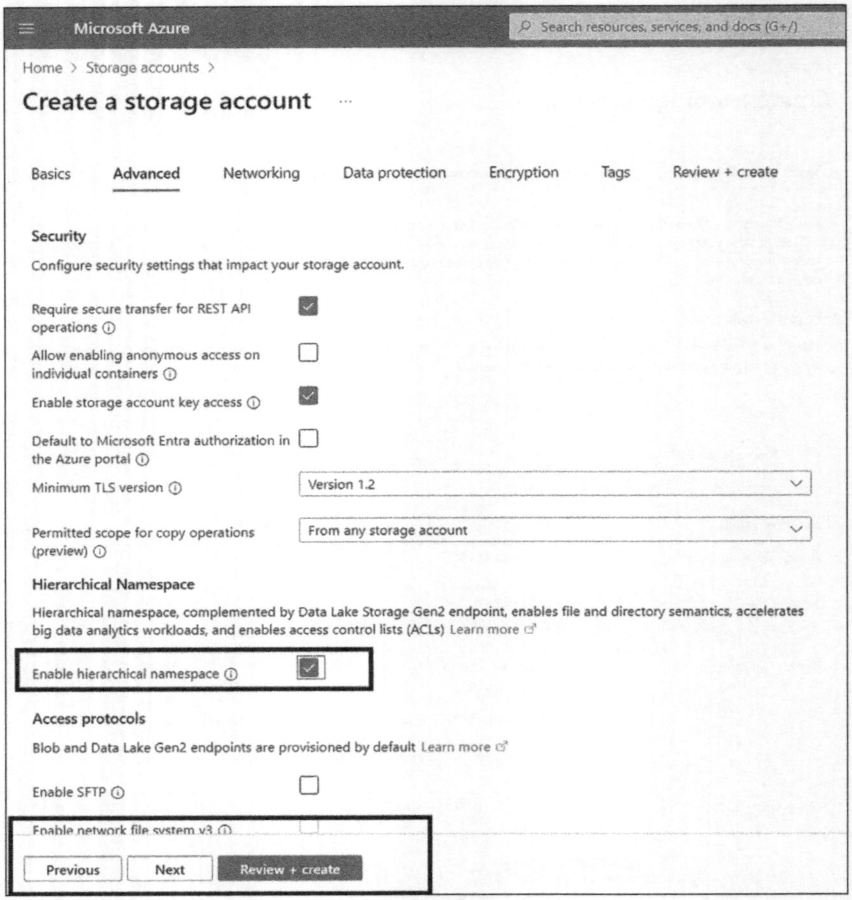

Figure 5.37: *Azure Portal (Storage Account; ADSL Gen 2-Hierarchical)*

Once the "**`Review and Create`**" button is clicked, the application starts the deployment.

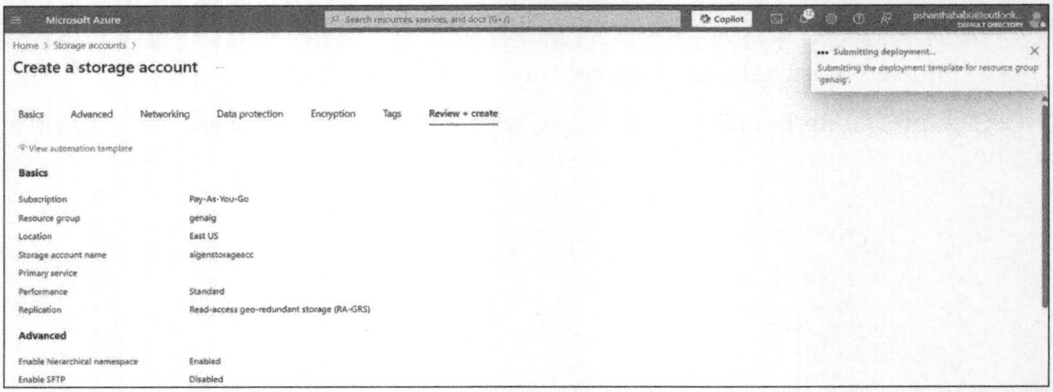

Figure 5.38: *Azure Portal (Storage Account); (ADSL Gen 2-Hierarchical) Deployment In-Process*

Figure 5.39 shows that the deployment is successfully completed, and the resource is ready to use.

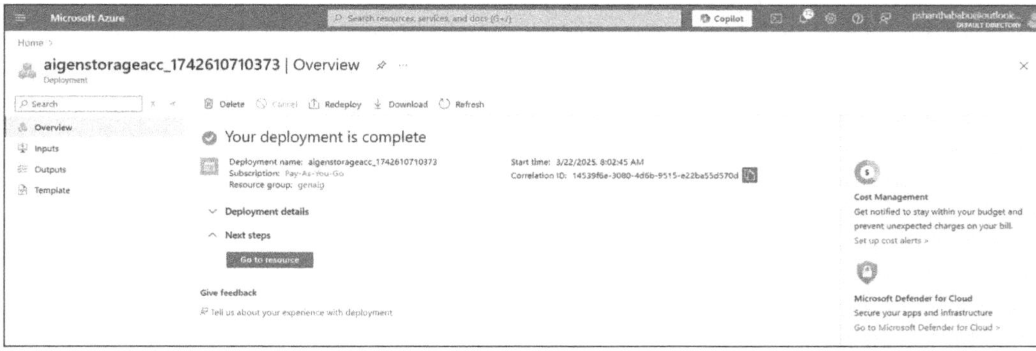

***Figure* 5.39:** *Azure Portal (Storage Account); (ADSL Gen 2-Hierarchical) Deployment Succeeded*

`genaistorageacc` (for ADLS Get 2) is now ready to add directory/directories and files.

Since we have selected "**`Enable hierarchical namespace`**" (checked), we can use the following data storage options.

- Container (look at the symbol, and you can see the difference)
- File Shares
- Queues
- Tables

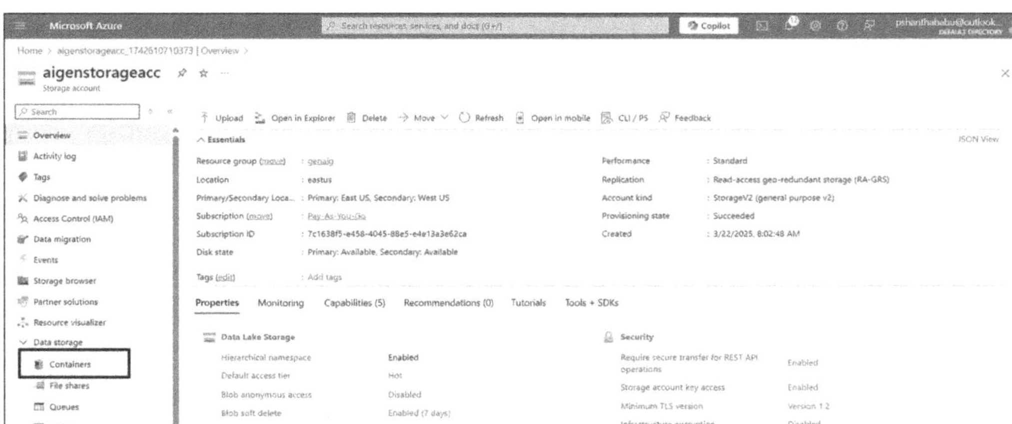

***Figure* 5.40:** *Azure Portal (Storage Account for ADSL Gen 2 is Ready to Use)*

Let us create an ADLS Gen 2 container under **`genaistorageacc`** (Storage account).

Click on the container icon from the data storage list on the left panel, and you will get the panel to create a container(s) on the right side (highlighted), as shown in *Figure 5.41.*

Step 1: Click on **`(+) Container`** in the right panel menu.

Figure 5.41: *Azure Portal (Storage Account for ADSL Gen 2; Creating Container)*

Step 2: Here, you need to provide the mentioned details:

- Name: name (should be lowercase, and no special cases are allowed).
- Leave the rest.

Once the preceding details are provided, we have to click on the "**`Create`**" button.

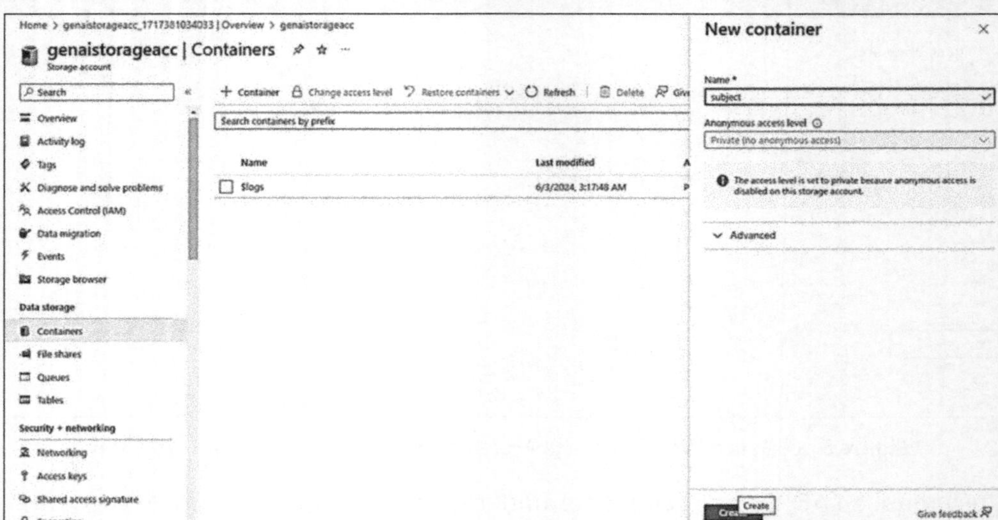

Figure 5.42: *Azure Portal (Storage Account for ADSL Gen 2; Creating Container)*

Once you click on the "**Create**" button, the application starts adding the directories, as shown in *Figure* 5.43.

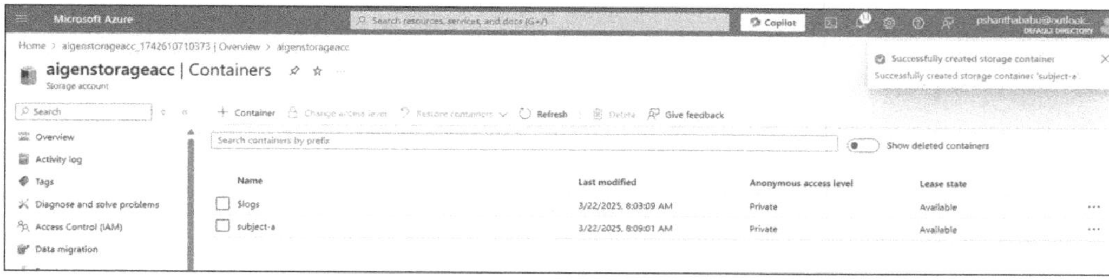

Figure 5.43: Azure Portal (*Storage Account for ADSL Gen 2; Creating Container Created Successfully*)

Step 3: Repeat the steps 1 and 2 with as many required directories for your project purpose.

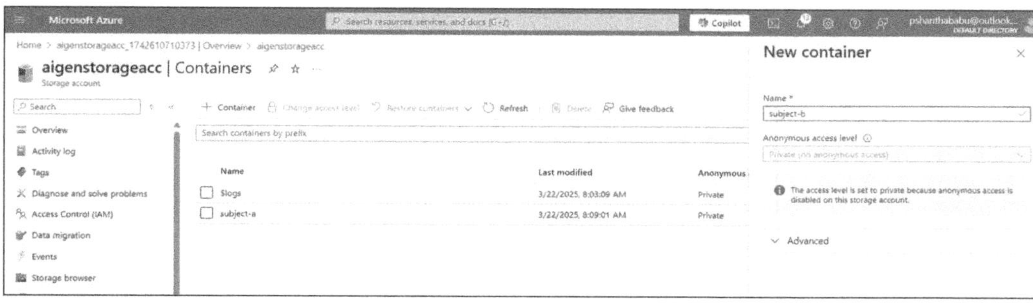

Figure 5.44: Azure Portal (*Storage Account for ADSL Gen 2; Creating Container Multiple Directories*)

After the preceding steps, the final directory structure is shown in *Figure* 5.45.

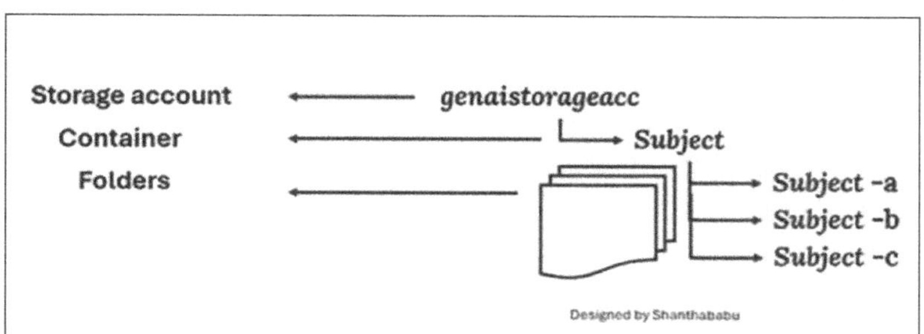

Figure 5.45: *Final Outcome: Storage Account/Container/Directories*

All three directories are added to the ADLS successfully, as shown in *Figure* 5.46.

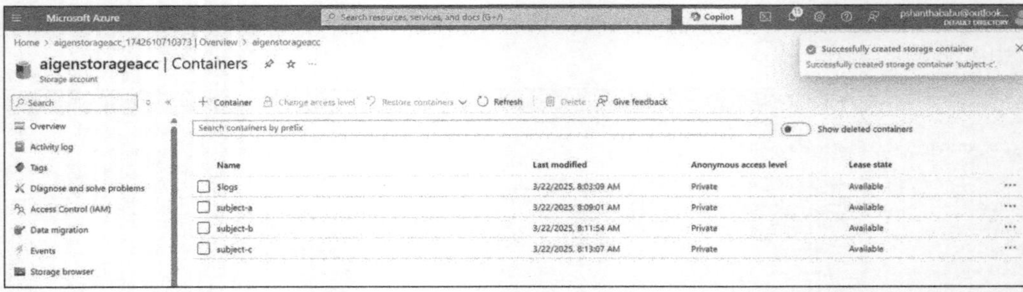

Figure 5.46: *Azure Portal (Storage Account for ADSL Gen 2 with Multiple Directory Structures)*

Let us add the document in the "`subject-a`" directory.

Step 1: Double-click the directory **`subject-a`**.

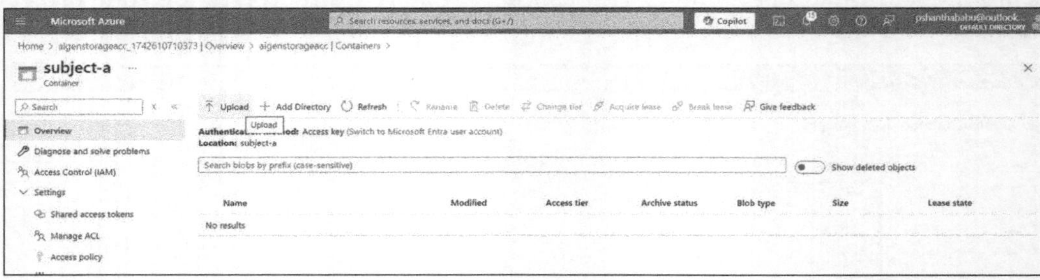

Figure 5.47: *Azure Portal (Adding the Document to the subject-a Directory)*

Step 2: Click the `Upload` menu on the right, as shown in *Figure* 5.47. The application will bring up the pop up, as shown in *Figure* 5.48.

Step 3: You can browse or drag and drop the document into the highlighted space, as shown in *Figure* 5.48.

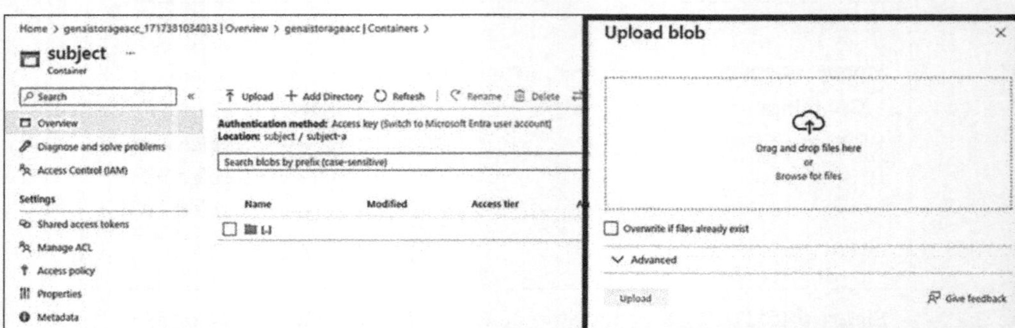

Figure 5.48: *Azure Portal (Uploading the Document into the subject-a Directory)*

Step 4: Once the document is dropped into the highlighted space (*Figure* 5.48) and is ready to upload, click the `Upload` button.

Step 5: Once the `Upload` button is clicked, the document will be successfully uploaded and displayed as shown in *Figure* 5.49.

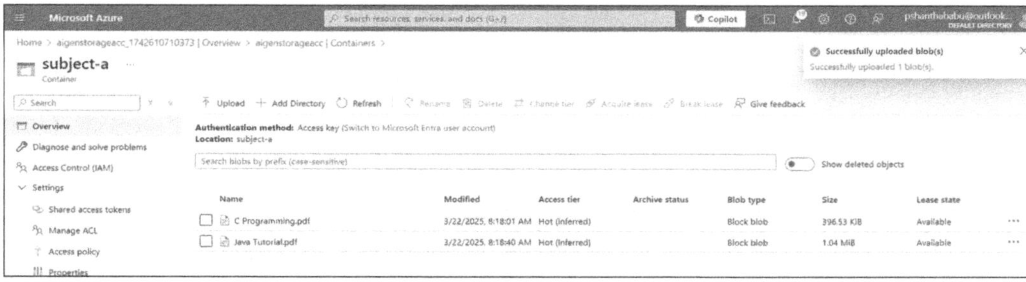

Figure 5.49: *Azure Portal (Uploading the Document into the subject-a Directory)*

All three documents are uploaded under the subject-a directory, as shown in *Figure* 5.50.

Figure 5.50: *Azure Portal (Uploaded the Document into the subject-a Directory)*

Similarly, we can upload the document(s) to the rest of the directory.

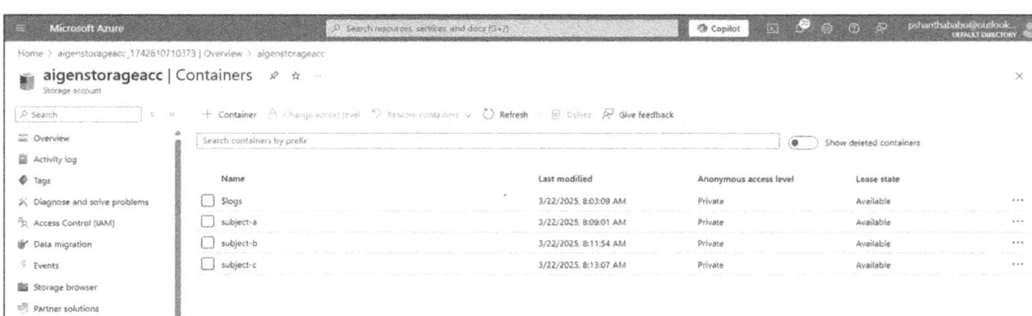

Figure 5.51: *Azure Portal (Documents are Uploaded into all the Directories)*

Step 6: You can view the file content in the directory shown in *Figure* 5.52.

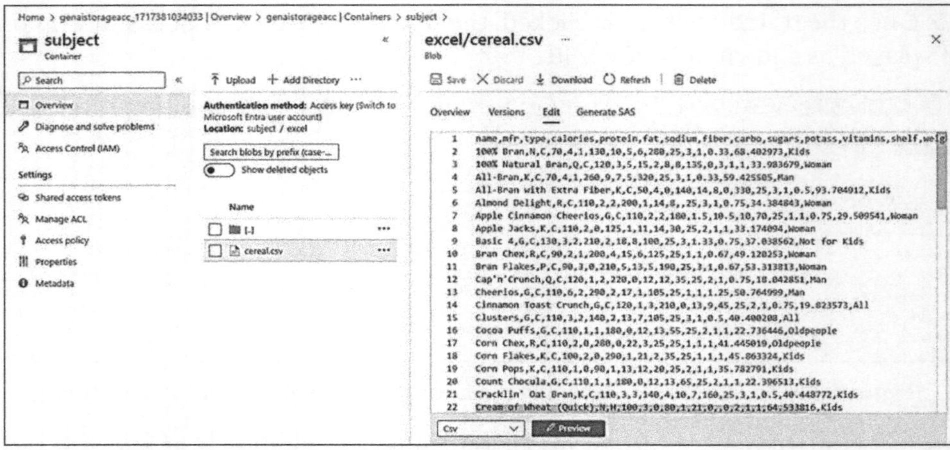

Figure 5.52: *Azure Portal (View the File Content from the Selected Directory)*

Step 6: To delete the directory from the container, select the check box on the left side of the directory name and click delete in the top menu (highlighted). Then, view.

To delete the directory from the container, select the check box near the directory name (subject-c) and click delete in the top menu (highlighted). You will get the pop up message and click the "**Yes**" button, as shown in *Figure* 5.53.

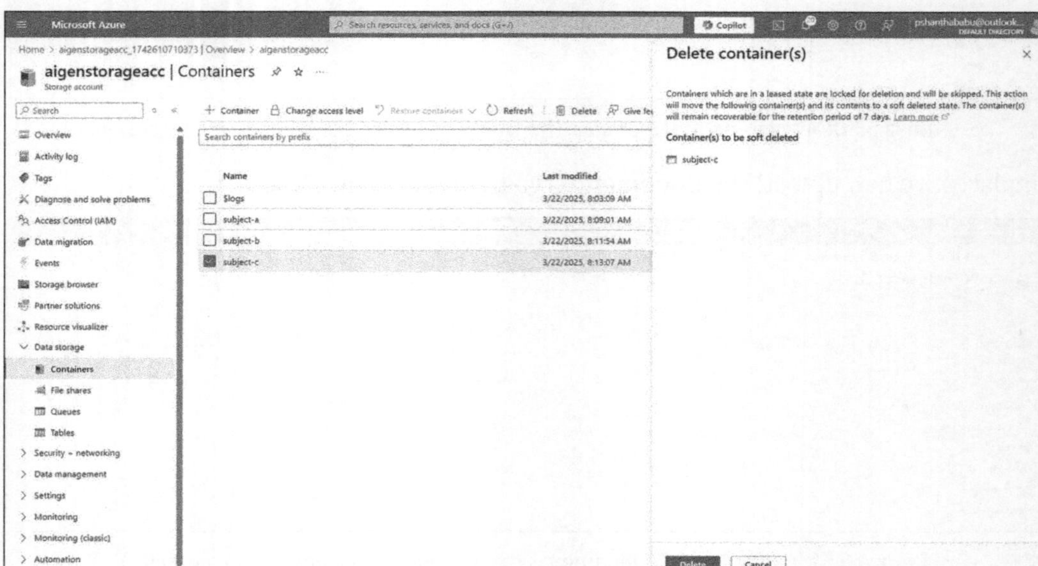

Figure 5.53: *Azure Portal (Deleting the Directory from the Container)*

The selected directory subject-c has been successfully deleted, as shown in *Figure* 5.54. We can also delete the files inside the directory(s).

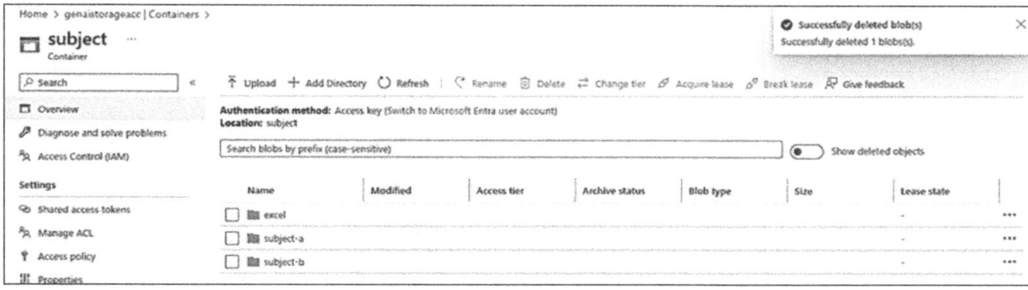

Figure 5.54: Azure Portal (*Directory Deleted Successfully; subject-c*)

Step 7: Delete the container.

Select the check box near the container name (subject), and you will get the panel on the right side to delete the container. You click the "**`Delete`**" button there, as shown in *Figure* 5.55 (highlighted).

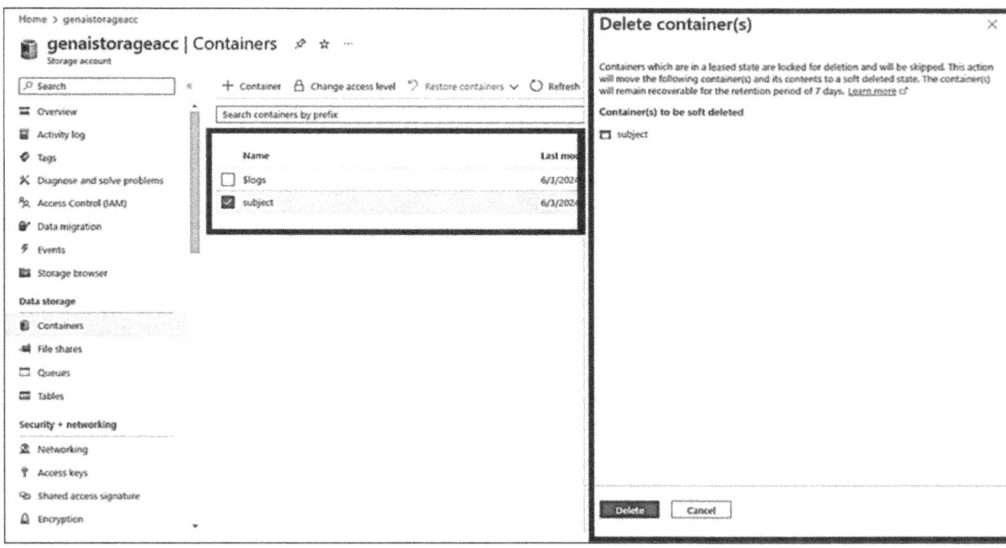

Figure 5.55: Azure Portal (*Deleting the Container*)

Step 8: Click on the **`Delete`** button, as shown in *Figure* 5.55. The application will ask for confirmation, as shown in *Figure* 5.56. Once you click "**`Confirm Delete`**," the container will be deleted from the account.

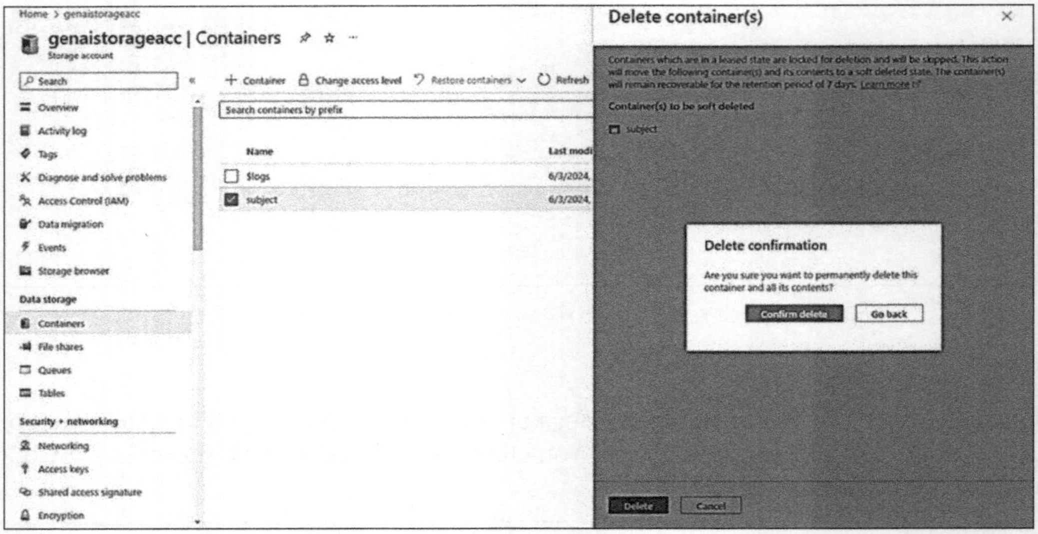

Figure 5.56: *Azure Portal (Deleting the Container Confirmation)*

Deleting the Storage Account

Step 1: Go back to the home page, select and right-click the storage account, as shown in *Figure* 5.57.

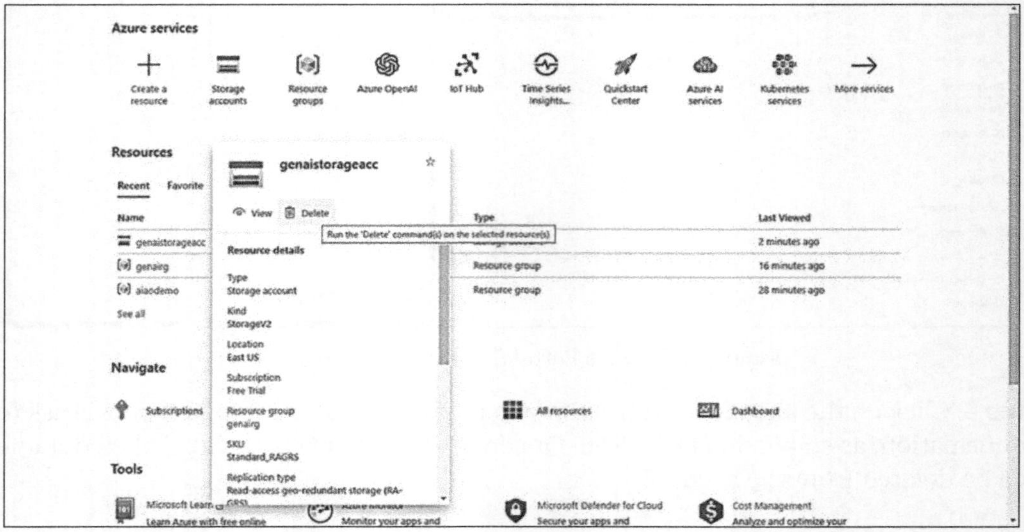

Figure 5.57: *Azure Portal (Deleting the Storage Account)*

Step 2: Delete the container.

Once you click delete, an application will pop up on the screen, as shown in *Figure* 5.58 (highlighted).

Enter the text in the textbox as "**`delete`**" to "**`Delete`**" the selected storage account and click the "**`Delete`**" button.

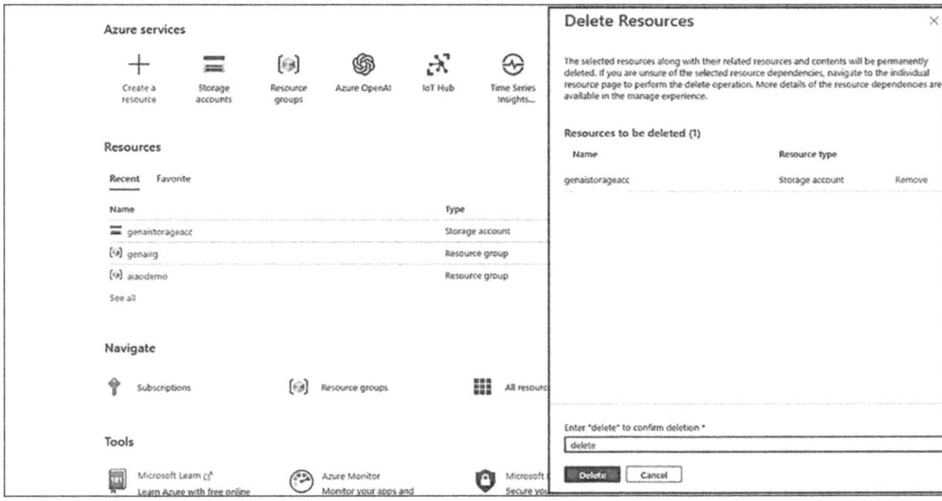

Figure 5.58: *Azure Portal (Deleting the Storage Account)*

Step 3: Delete the container.

After you enter the text in the textbox as "**`delete`**" and click the "**`Delete`**" button, you will get the confirmation dialogue box. Click the "**`Delete`**" button to confirm your options.

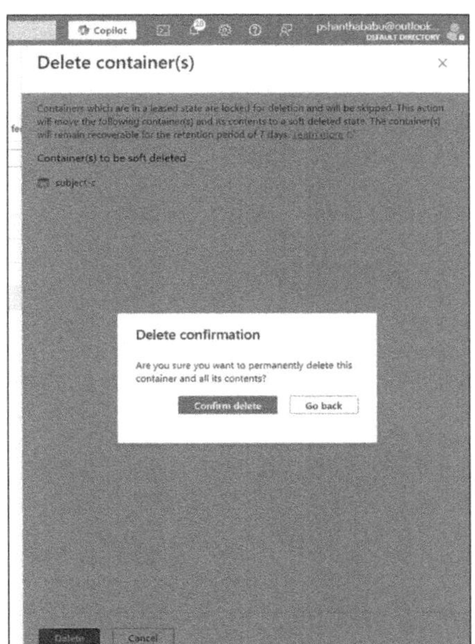

Figure 5.59: *Azure Portal (Deleting the Storage Account Confirmation)*

The storage account was successfully deleted, and now, as shown in *Figure* 5.60, the resources list only includes resource groups.

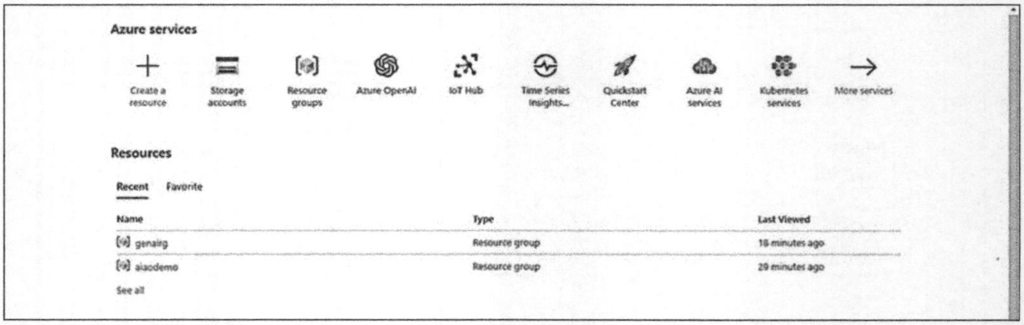

Figure 5.60: *Azure Portal (After the Storage Account is Successfully Deleted from the Group)*

Conclusion

This chapter discussed the Azure environment, Azure Resource Group, Azure Active Directory (ADD), and other related topics. Followed by this, we discovered how Microsoft Azure is a public cloud computing platform that helps developers develop, build, deploy, and manage data.

We explored Azure Active Directory, and conducted a detailed study of management groups, subscriptions, resource groups, resources and features of management groups.

We understood Azure data storage resources and their capabilities as a modern cloud storage solution for various data objects. We explored what different services offer with storage, such as high availability, scalability, durability, and provisioning of secured storage for data stored in the cloud.

We practically experimented with creating an Azure resource group, Azure storage account, blob storage, and ADLS Gen 2.

The next chapter will explore and overview Azure search services and their significance. We will conduct a detailed study of indexes, indexers, and data sources, including how to implement Azure search. Following this, we will explore the services we use to build solutions.

CHAPTER 6
Azure AI Search Services for Azure OpenAI Implementations

Introduction

In the previous chapter, we discovered how Microsoft Azure is a public cloud computing platform. We explored Azure Active Directory, its significance, and how it acts as Microsoft's enterprise cloud-based identity and access management service, along with Azure resource management, its key characteristics, and its hierarchy, including a detailed study of management groups, subscriptions, resource groups, and resources features of management groups.

We investigated what an Azure storage account is and how to set up the container under the Azure storage services group. We understood Azure Blob Storage and its characteristics and studied the different storage tiers, such as hot, cool, and archivestorage.

We practically experimented by creating an Azure resource group, Azure storage account, blob storage, and ADLS Gen 2.

This chapter will explore and overview Azure AI search services and their significance. It will also include a detailed study of indexes, indexers, and data sources and how to implement Azure search. Following this, we will explore the services we use to build solutions.

We will investigate mechanisms for indexing data, such as how Azure Search Services are helping to index and organize the data stored in Azure storage. We will also examine how scalability and performance are handled in Azure Search with large volumes of data and user queries to ensure a fast and responsive search experience for users of AI applications and the best practices in implementing Azure Search Services.

Structure

In this chapter, we will discuss the following topics:

- Overview of Azure AI Search Services and Its Significance
- Capabilities of Azure AI Search Services
    - Full-Text Search
    - AI-Driven Search
    - Data Source Integration
    - Scalability and Performance
    - Security and Compliance
    - Real-Time Monitoring and Analytics
    - Global Availability
- Azure AI Search Services: An AI Requirement
- Exploring Azure AI Search services
    - Language, Speech, Vision, and Document Intelligence
- Azure Storage and AI Search Services Integration

Overview of Azure AI Search Services

Azure AI Search, formerly known as "**Azure Cognitive Search**," is a fully managed SaaS solution provided by Microsoft Azure. The service's major objective is to provide secure information retrieval at a larger scale over user-owned data content stored in the Azure Storage Service (what we have discussed in *Chapter 5, Azure Storage for Azure OpenAI Implementations*) in traditional and conversational search applications such as chatbots, agents, or virtual assistant applications or products.

Azure AI search services can integrate complex search capabilities to enable powerful search operations and implement high-demand functionalities specific to industry use cases for various Gen AI solutions with data stored in their Azure environment.

Azure AI Search is vital in developing and implementing Gen AI products. The ability to promptly find relevant data is necessary for the end-user experience and in required formats such as text, summary, Q and A, and others to be results. Along with the prompt and LLMs, Azure AI Search uses critical functionality that helps Gen AI applications work more like humans and make suggestions that go beyond a broad keyword search and precise matching.

Azure AI Search is a powerful and flexible search solution that influences the cloud's scalability and AI's intelligence to deliver insightful, relevant, and fast search results experiences. It is tightly integrated with the Azure ecosystem, and its extensive customization options make it a valuable resource for businesses looking to enhance customer experience, productivity, and actionable insights from their own data in easy ways.

Figure 6.1 shows the basic workflow of Azure AI search services integrated with Azure storage and OpenAI parts (LLM, prompt, and others).

Figure 6.1: *Basic Azure AI Search Workflow*

Capabilities of Azure AI Search Services

Azure AI Search Services is an AI-enhanced, search-as-a-service offering from Microsoft Azure designed to deliver rich, powerful, and compelling search experiences. Following are the key capabilities of Azure AI Search Services:

- **Full-Text Search**: This is a unique capability for AI search. It supports full-text search with a vast range of linguistic analysis, including word breaking, sentences, summary, stemming, and lemmatization to understand and process natural language processing queries. The search mode is simple, with full search functionality to balance precision and recall.
    - **Rich Query Syntax**: It can support complex query constructs with wildcards, fuzzy searches, and proximity searches, enabling advanced search scenarios.
- **AI-Driven Search**: It integrates AI capabilities such as text, image, audio and video analysis, text extraction, language detection, entity recognition, and sentiment analysis through built-in **cognitive skills** and **custom skills**.
    - Custom Cognitive Skills are integrated to extend the service's data enrichment pipeline, enabling tailored AI processing.
    - **Natural Language Processing (NLP)**: Enhances search significance and understanding using NLP features such as entity recognition and language detection.
- **Data Source Integration:** AI search services are capable of integrating with data storage to enhance AI products using their own data.

- **Multiple Data Sources**: It supports indexing from various Azure data sources, such as Azure Blob Storage, Azure SQL Database, Cosmos DB, and more.
- **Data Enrichment**: Enriches data with cognitive skills during indexing, transforming the raw content into searchable information.

***Figure 6.2:** Capabilities of Azure AI Search Services*

- **Scalability and Performance:** These parameters are always focused on any component. Autoscaling helps to automatically adjust resources based on demand, ensuring high availability and performance. Additionally, factors such as indexing, partitioning, and replication enhance performance.
  - **Indexing Performance**: Capable of handling large volumes of data with efficient indexing and query execution during the operation.
  - **Partitioning and Replication**: It supports partitioning for large data sets and replication for high availability as well as fault tolerance.

  All the aforementioned factors certainly help improve the performance of the Gen AI systems.
- **Security and Compliance:** While dealing with data, we must consider these two factors to align with the perspectives of data security and governance principles. As part of this engagement, we have to adopt the following:
  - **Data Encryption**: Ensures data encryption is at rest and in transit for storage and search.
  - **Role-Based Access Control (RBAC)**: Data storage should be integrated

with Azure Active Directory (AAD) to secure access control and enable access management.

  - **Compliance**: Governance policies should adhere to various industry standards and regulatory requirements, ensuring secure and compliant data handling across the industry based on the roles and responsibilities described in the rule book.

- **Real-Time Monitoring and Analytics:** Enabling real-time monitoring and analytics is always helpful for understanding the performance of components. Precisely for this search service, we have to consider the following:
  - **Search Traffic Analytics**: It provides insights into search behavior and usage patterns, enabling optimization of search performance, relevance, and user experience so that we can design prompt engineering in an enhanced way. This will help identify traffic bandwidth so that we can plan to increase or decrease the network bandwidth.
  - **Operational Monitoring**: In the Azure environment, all the resources have this capability. This search service provides monitoring and logging capabilities to track the performance and health of search services. This capability helps to understand the AI tool's performance when several concurrent users interact with the data.
- **Global Availability:** Resource availability is critical in a cloud environment. When creating resources in Azure, we must provide attributes for resource accessibility.
  - **Regional Availability**: We assign regional availability locations across multiple regions, providing global reach and ensuring low latency for users who use AI products.
  - **Multi-Language Support**: Concerns about Gen AI–multilingual is a significant feature, so our services support multiple languages, offering global and multilingual-based AI applications, which is a highly required capability.

Azure AI Search Services: An AI Requirement

Azure AI Search Services, in the architecture of AI implementation, promptly enhance performance and efficiency due to the capabilities we discussed earlier. The following points show how AI Search services enhance AI applications and products.

- Improves operational efficiencies by reducing human intervention and various workflows through process automation and related activities.

- Improves customer experience by automating complex services that require immense effort and validation from human involvement.
- This service is compatible with traditional and next-generation searching mechanisms such as **FULL-TEXT** and **VECTOR SIMILARITY**. This has high potential for unlocking and building Gen AI applications with RAG-based products that leverage the strengths of keyword and similarity searches to retrieve the most relevant results.
- Basically, it has an excellent search capability, and this service is the best fit for significant tuning and enhanced performance, high navigation, excellent filters, absolute synonym mapping, quick autocomplete, and geospatial search capabilities.
- It can transform large homogeneous text or image file collections into chunks stored in Azure storage, with indexer and index features.
- It supports linguistic analysis and can handle non-English text to understand accents as well as preserve document string patterns.

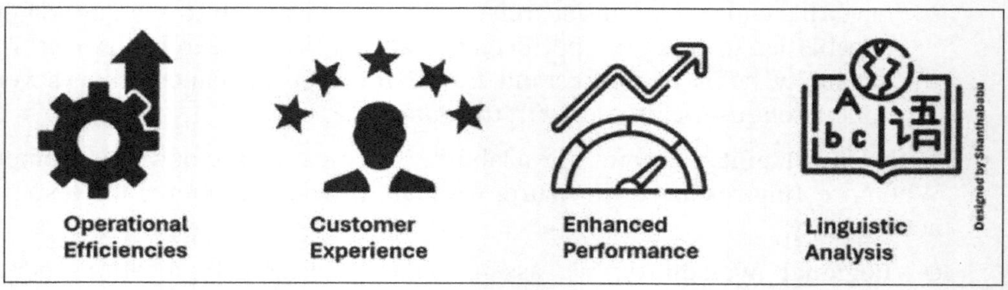

Figure 6.3: *Azure AI Search Services: An AI Requirement*

Exploring Azure AI Search Services

In Azure AI Search services, there are many services available, of which the following are predominantly used for various AI-based applications and products.

- **Language:** This service allows us to explore natural language patterns in text and analysis and provides an understanding of the context of the text. It can also build a Question-and-Answer (Q and A) chatbot. Based on the current scenario, these AI tools are in high demand for various industries to make the job easier, such as healthcare, pharma, legal, and education domains. Along with this service, it also helps with language translation.
- **Speech**: This service allows us to help a user understand speech with high-quality translation capabilities; it can build applications such as identifying a speaker, converting text to speech, and vice versa.
- **Vision**: This service helps analyze images in more detail, and we can build, deploy, and improve our own image classification and identifier models. An

image identifier or classification model helps label images according to their visual attributes. Each label represents the classification of the image.

- Azure AI Search services offer innovative computer vision capabilities, including prebuilt text extraction with Optical Character Recognition (OCR), tagging, and facial recognition.
- **Document Intelligence:** Azure AI services also encompass a document intelligence service used to build data processing from documents using data-driven strategies. It is even capable of extracting data from images and PDF files. This helps extract key/value pairs, text, and tables from documents. We can configure the output file format to be JSON.

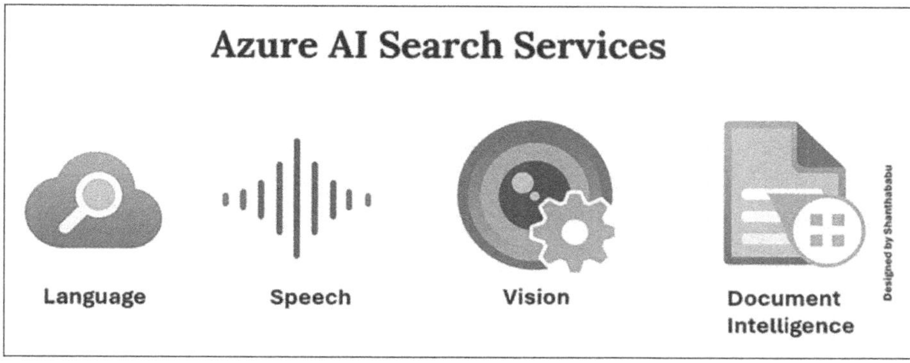

Figure 6.4: *Azure AI Search Services*

Azure Storage and AI Search Services Integration

One of the primary objectives of this book is to build the integration of storage and AI search services for blind Gen AI applications for their own data (private). The following figure shows the representation of this integration. The data is loaded into the blob or ADLS with ETL/ELT load or direct load into the storage for operational aspects. Following this, we will connect the storage with AI Search services and index the documents later. This will expose you to OpenAI services for building AI applications. We will discuss this in *Chapter 7, Getting Started with Generative AI Using Azure OpenAI Services.*

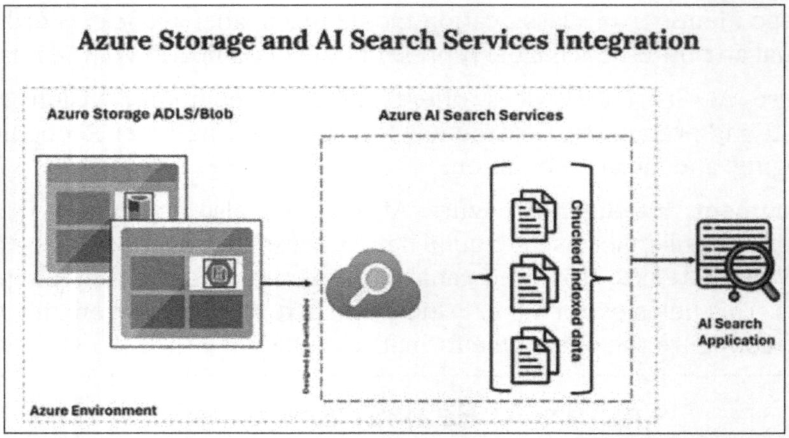

Figure 6.5: *Azure Storage and AI Search Services Integration*

Let us build the storage and AI Search integration.

Creating an Azure Storage Account for Blob

Let us create an Azure Storage account for Blob storage.

Step 1: Right-click on Storage accounts and then click on the `(+) Create`.

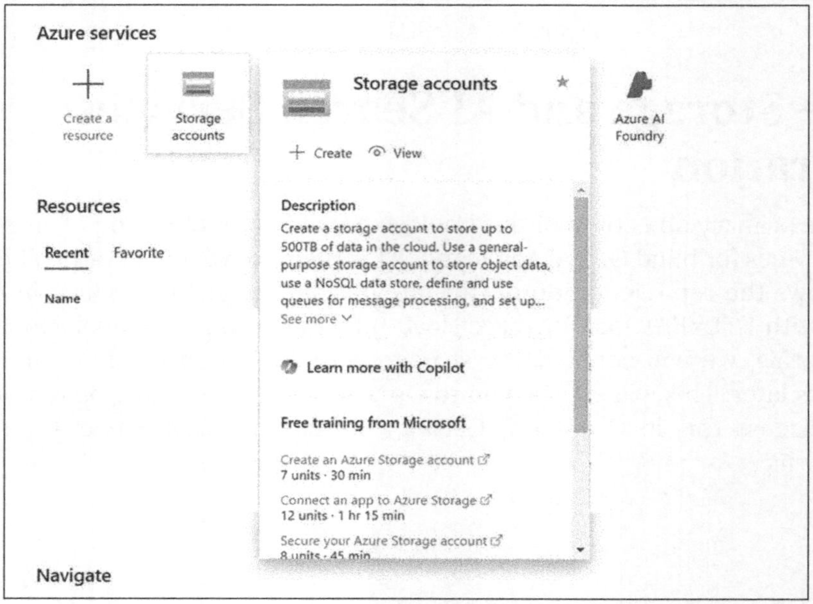

Figure 6.6: *Azure Portal (Creating Storage Accounts)*

Step 2: Once you click on the plus icon, the application will take you to the following screen, as shown in *Figure* 6.7.

Here, you need to provide the following details:

Basic Configuration:

- **Subscription Type**: Free/Pay as you go (Subscription name).
- **Resource Group**: Select the resource group from the list.
- **Storage Account Name**: Enter a valid storage name (it should be lowercase, and no special characters are allowed).
- **Region**: Select your appropriate region.
- **Redundancy**: Select your replication strategy.
- **Performance**: Standard (or) Premium.

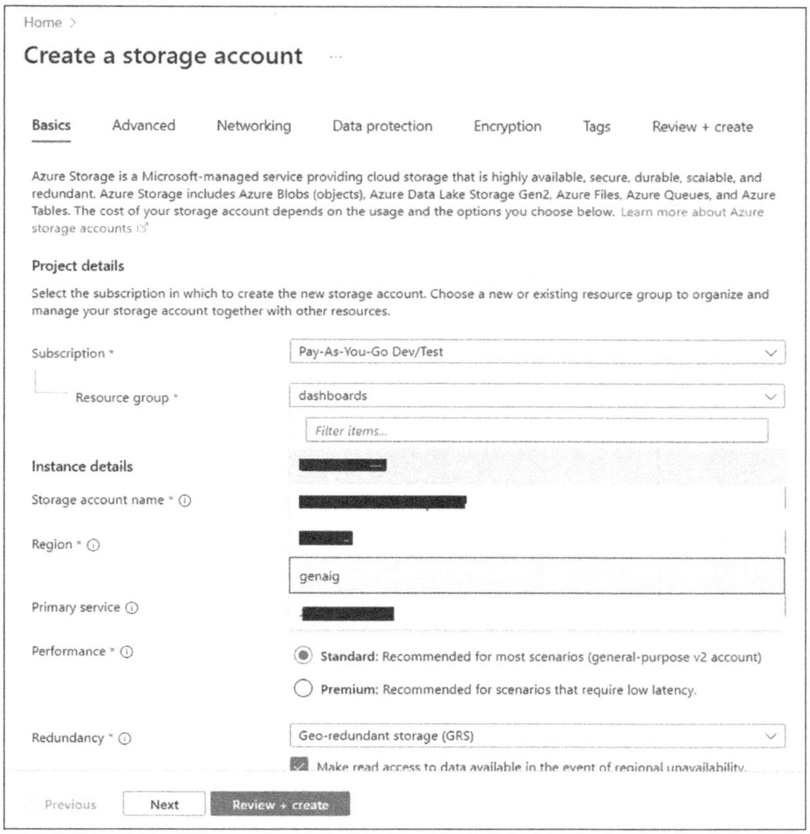

***Figure 6.7:** Azure Portal (Creating Storage Accounts)*

Advance Configuration:

- **Enable hierarchical namespace**: Uncheck (for blob).

Once the aforementioned details are provided, we must click the "`Review and Create`" button.

Figure 6.8: *Azure Portal (Creating Storage Accounts; Storage Account Name)*

Once all the mandatory fields have been filled, the portal will validate and be ready to create the resources.

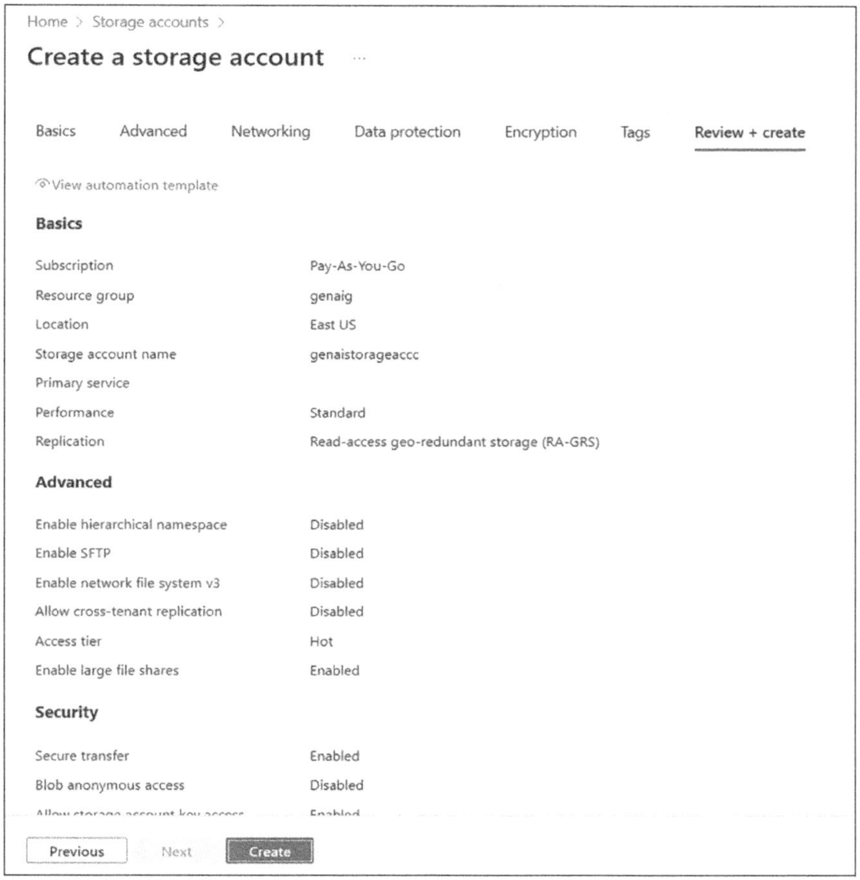

Figure 6.9: *Azure Portal (Creating Storage Accounts; Review Completed)*

Step 3: Review completed, and component deployment initiated.

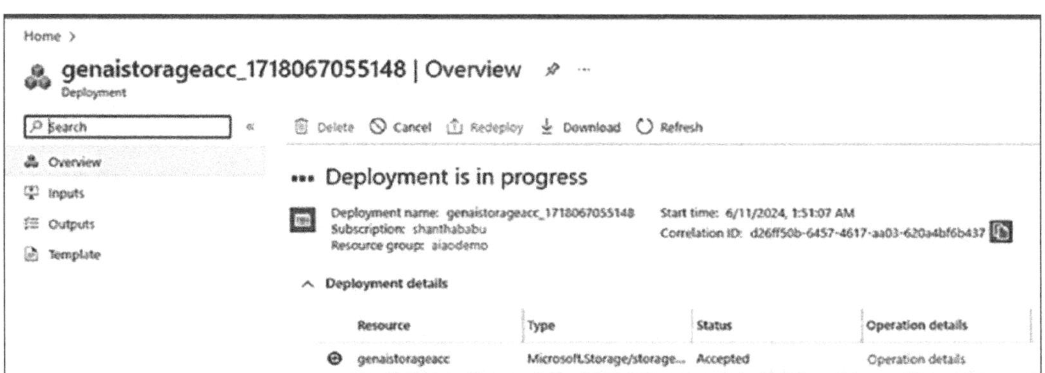

Figure 6.10: *Azure Portal (Creating Storage Accounts; Review Completed and Initializing Deployment In-Process)*

Step 4: After deployment completion, the following screen will display. Click on the **`Go to resource`** button, as shown in *Figure 6.11.*

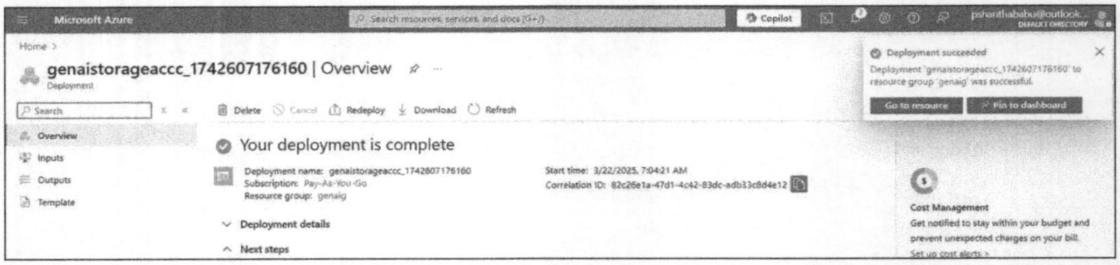

Figure 6.11: *Azure Portal (Creating Storage Accounts; Resource is Ready)*

Step 5: After clicking the **`Go to resource`**, the application takes you to the following screen.

We have not selected "**`Enable hierarchical namespace`**." Unchecked, we have the following data storage options:

- Container
- File Shares
- Queues
- Tables

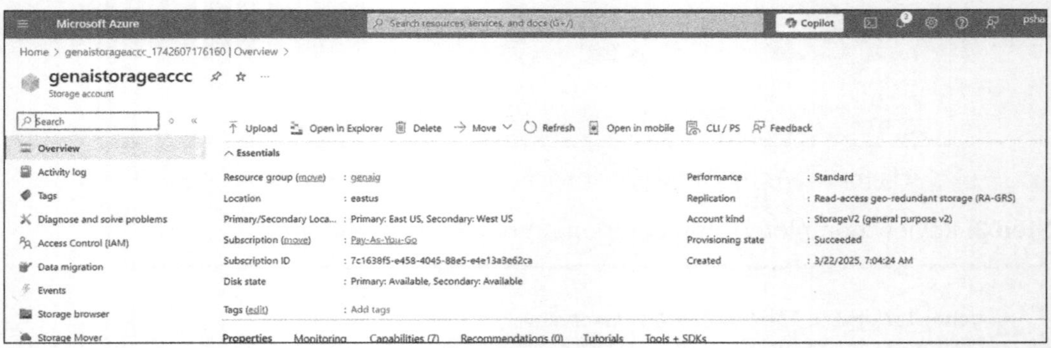

Figure 6.12: *Azure Portal (Storage Accounts Ready to Add Data Storage)*

In the Azure environment, the following storage capabilities are available such as Blob, Table, File, and Queue. Thus, based on the requirements, we can create the resources and use them appropriately.

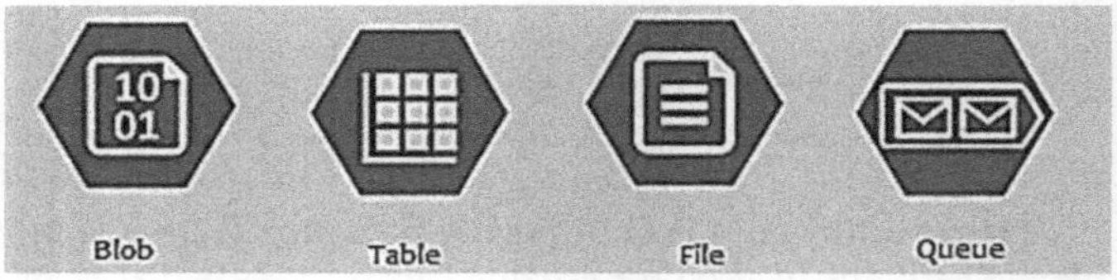

Figure 6.13: *Azure Storage (Blob, Table, File, and Queue)*

Let us create a blob container under **genaistorageacc** (Storage account). Click on the container icon from the data storage list on the left panel.

You will get a panel to create a container(s) on the right side (highlighted)

Step 1: Click on **(+) Container** in the right panel menu.

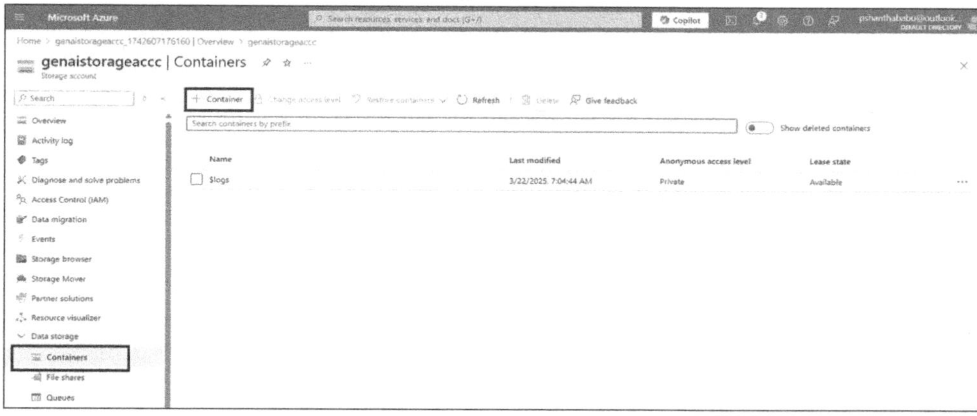

Figure 6.14: *Azure Portal (Container Creation)*

Step 2:

Here, you need to provide the following details:

- Name: name (should be lowercase, and no special characters are allowed).
- Leave the rest.

Once the preceding details are provided, we have to click on the "**Create**" button.

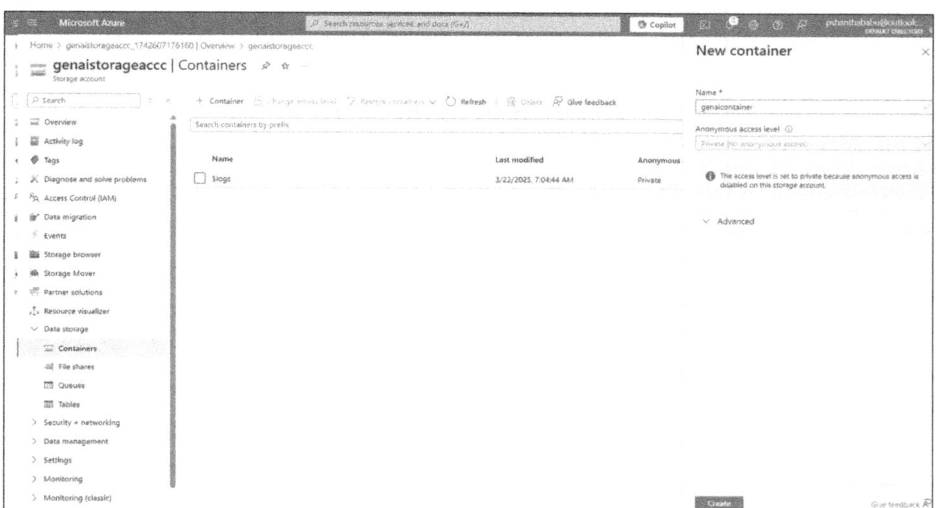

Figure 6.15: *Azure Portal (Container Creation)*

Step 3:

Once the create button is clicked, a new container will be available for use.

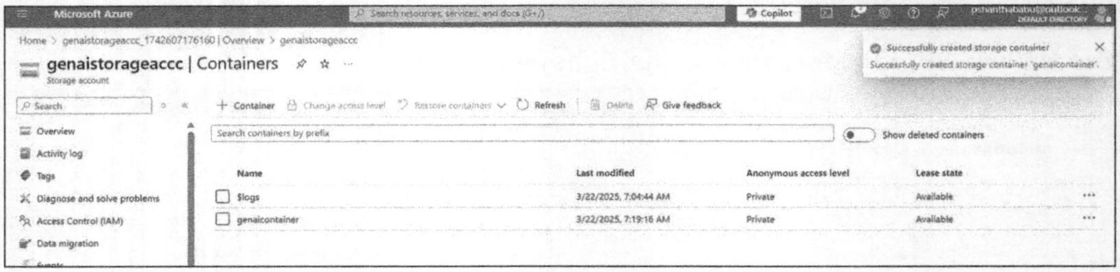

Figure 6.16: *Azure Portal (Container Creation)*

Step 4: Once the container is ready, click on the container in the right panel; then you will be taken inside the container, as shown in *Figure* 6.17.

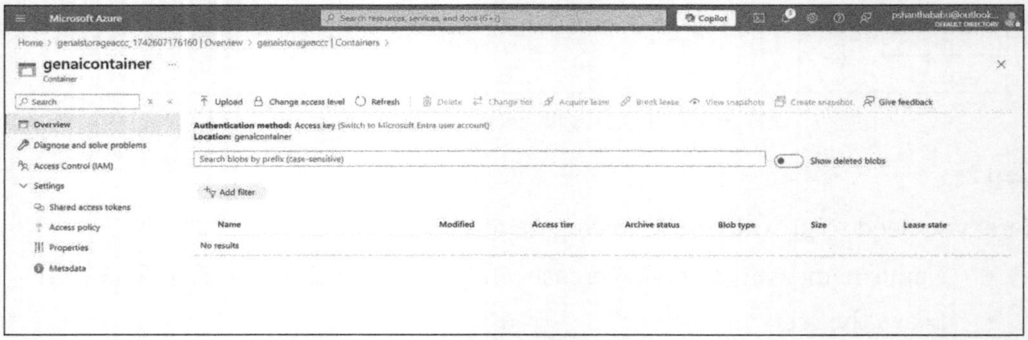

Figure 6.17: *Azure Portal (Container Creation)*

We will now add the file to the container **`genaicontainer`**.

Step 5: Click the **`Upload`** menu on the right. The application will bring up a pop up, as shown in *Figure* 6.18.

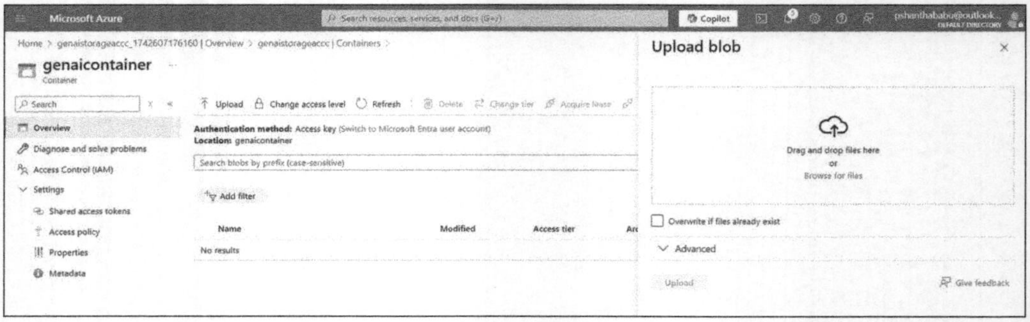

Figure 6.18: *Azure Portal (Adding Document into the Container)*

Step 6: You can browse or drag and drop the document into the highlighted space, as shown in *Figure 6.19*.

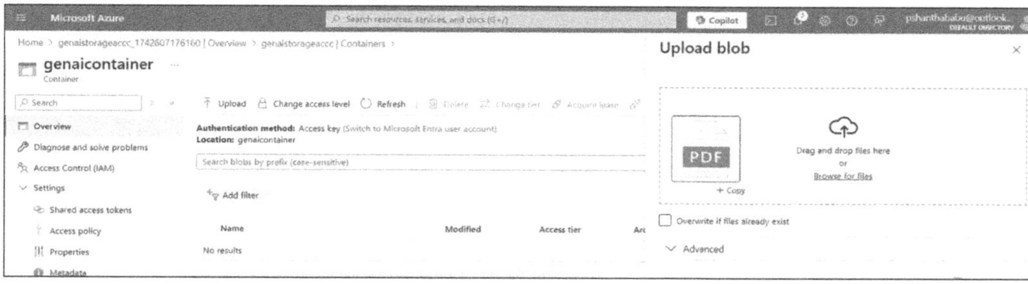

Figure 6.19: *Azure Portal – Uploading the Document into the Container (Step 6)*

Step 7: After selecting or dragging and dropping the document, you can click on the **`Upload`** button, as shown in *Figure 6.20*.

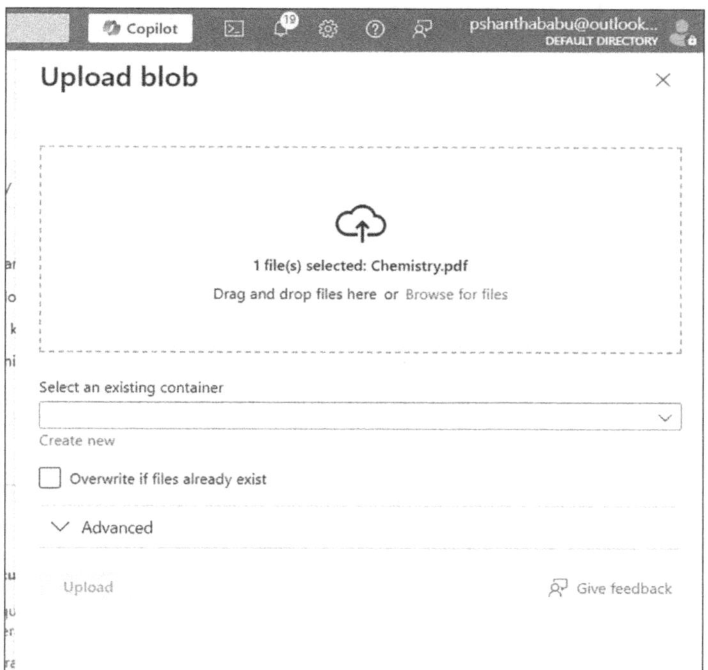

Figure 6.20: *Azure Portal (Uploading the Document into the Container)*

Step 8: The document is now available inside the container (**`Chemistry.pdf`**) along with the date modified, size, and others, as shown in *Figure 6.21*.

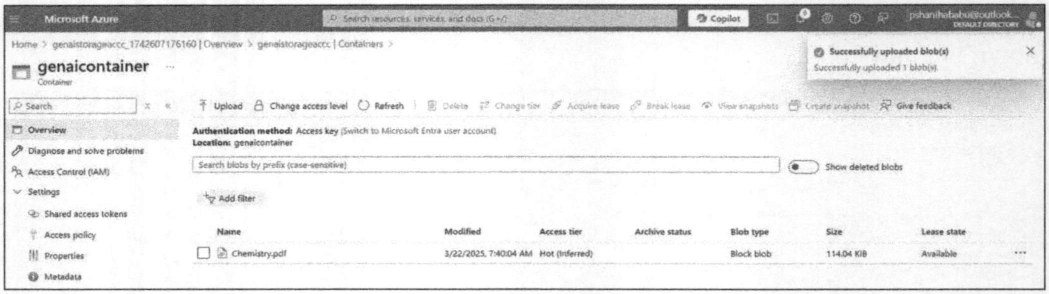

Figure 6.21: Azure Portal (Document Saved into the Container)

The document is ready to search for content; we have to configure the AI search services before that. Let us create an Azure AI Service to integrate and perform search operations.

Creating Azure AI Services

Let us create an Azure AI Service.

Step 1: Click on the Azure AI Services icon, as shown in *Figure* 6.22.

Figure 6.22: Azure Portal (Azure AI Search Services)

Step 2: Once you click on the icon, the application will take you to the following screen shown in *Figure 6.23*.

You can see the following services on the left menu:

- AI Search
- Computer/Custom Vision Search
- Speech Service
- Language Services

Various services are also mentioned.

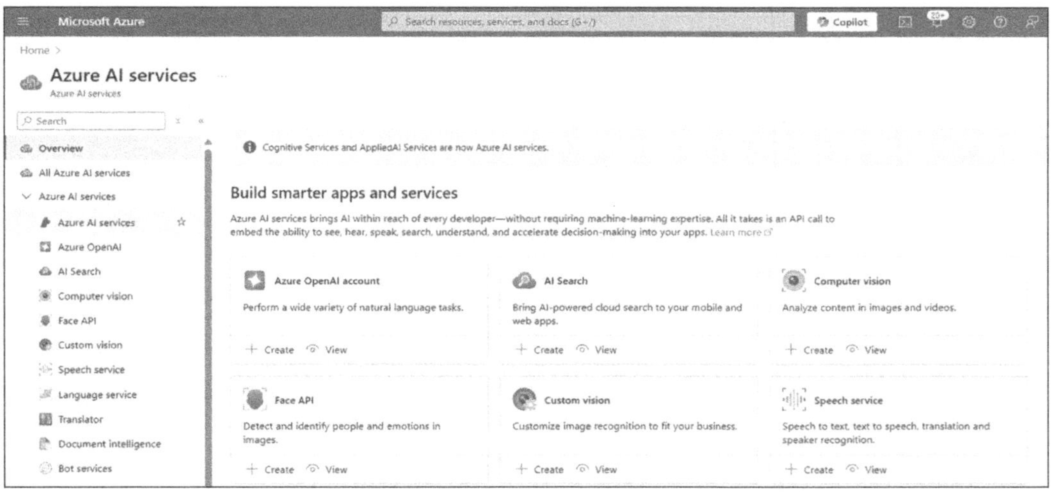

Figure 6.23: *Azure Portal (Azure AI Search Services)*

Step 3: Click the AI Search from the left menu. The application will take you to the following screen shown in *Figure 6.24*.

Click on the `(+) Create` in the right menu, as highlighted in *Figure 6.24*.

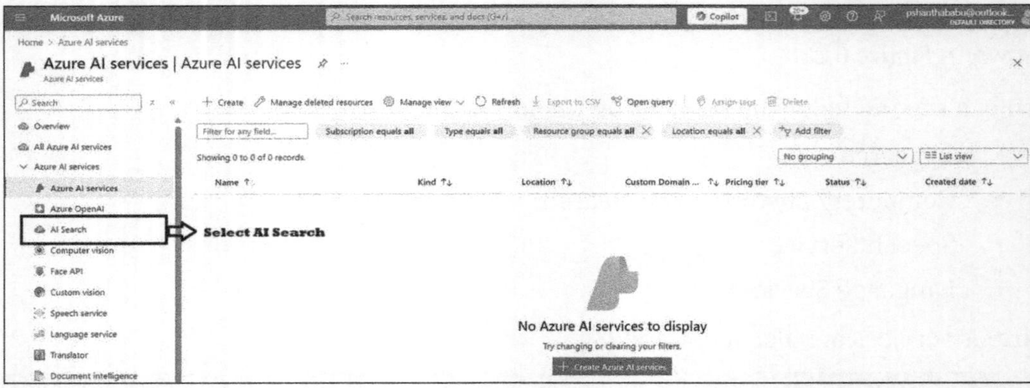

Figure 6.24: *Azure Portal (Azure AI Search Services)*

Step 4: Once you click on the plus icon, the application will take you to the following screen shown in *Figure* 6.25.

Here, you need to provide the following details:

Basic Configuration:

- **Subscription Type**: Free/Pay as you go (Subscription name).
- **Resource Group**: Select the resource group from the list.

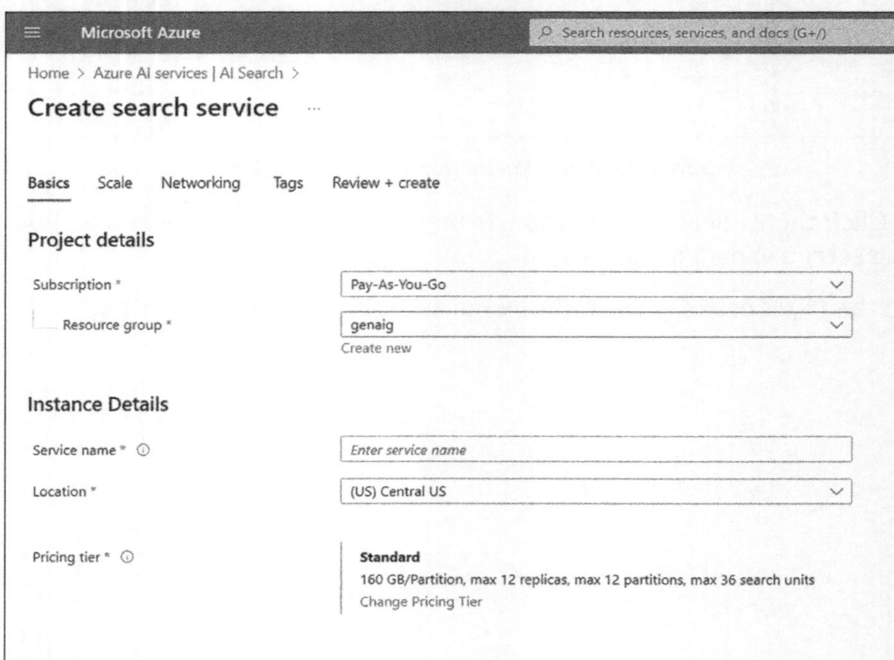

Figure 6.25: *Azure Portal (Azure AI Search Services)*

- **Service Name**: Enter a valid name (it should be lowercase, and no special characters are allowed).
- **Region**: Select your appropriate region.

Once the aforementioned details are provided, we must click the "Review and Create" button.

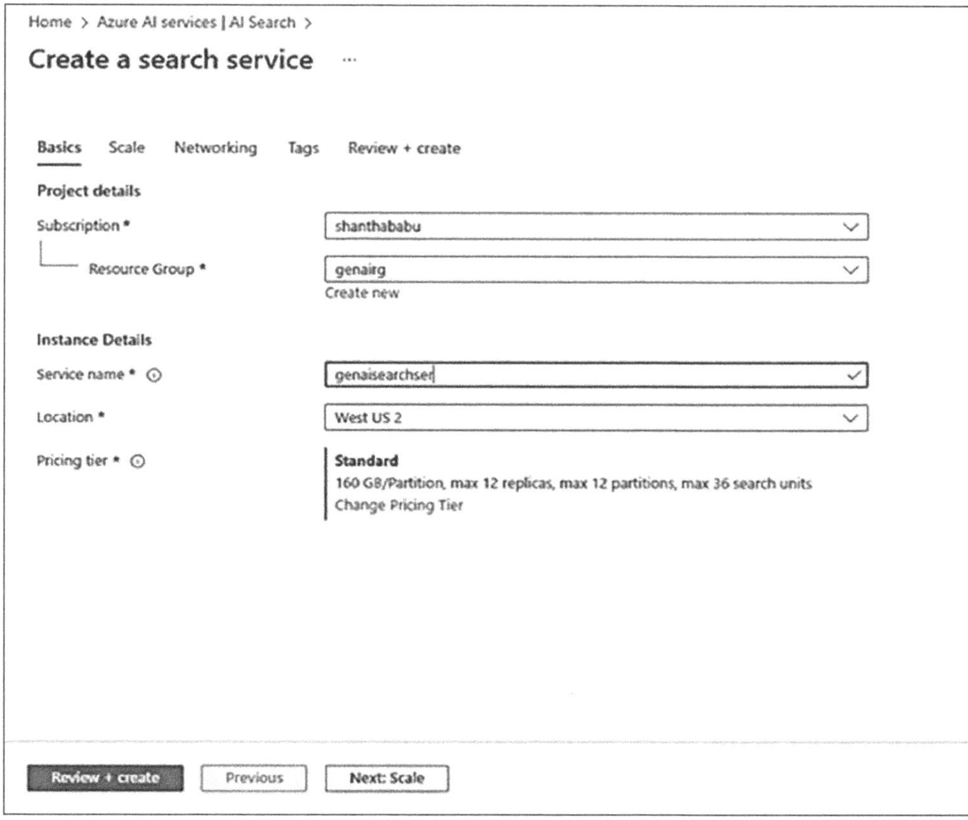

Figure 6.26: *Azure Portal (Azure AI Search Services; Configuration)*

Step 5: Validation completed, and now click on the `Create` button.

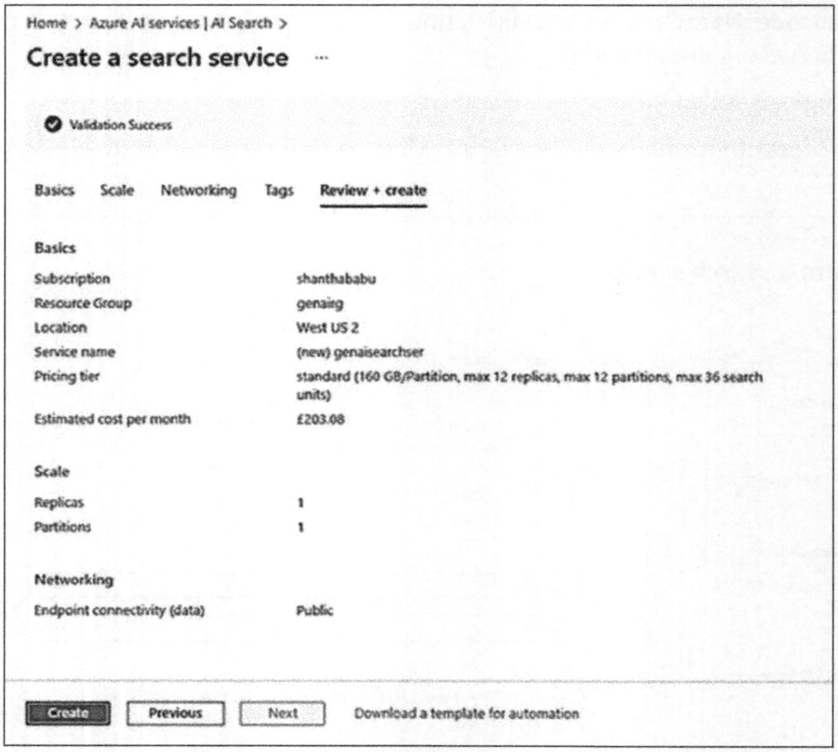

Figure 6.27: Azure Portal (*Azure AI Search Services; Validation Completed and Create*)

Initialization deployment in progress.

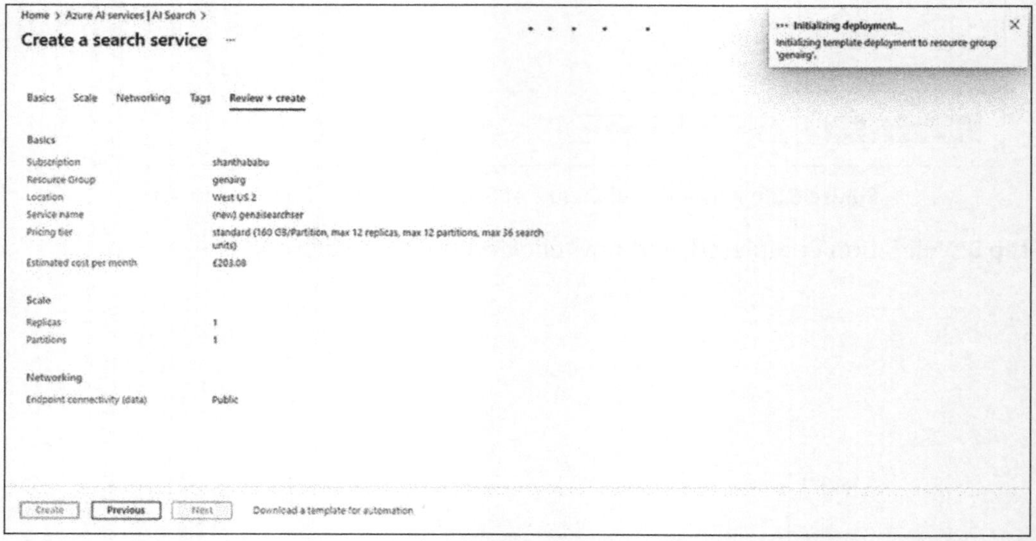

Figure 6.28: Azure Portal (*Azure AI Search Services; Initialization Deployment in Progress*)

Deployment in progress.

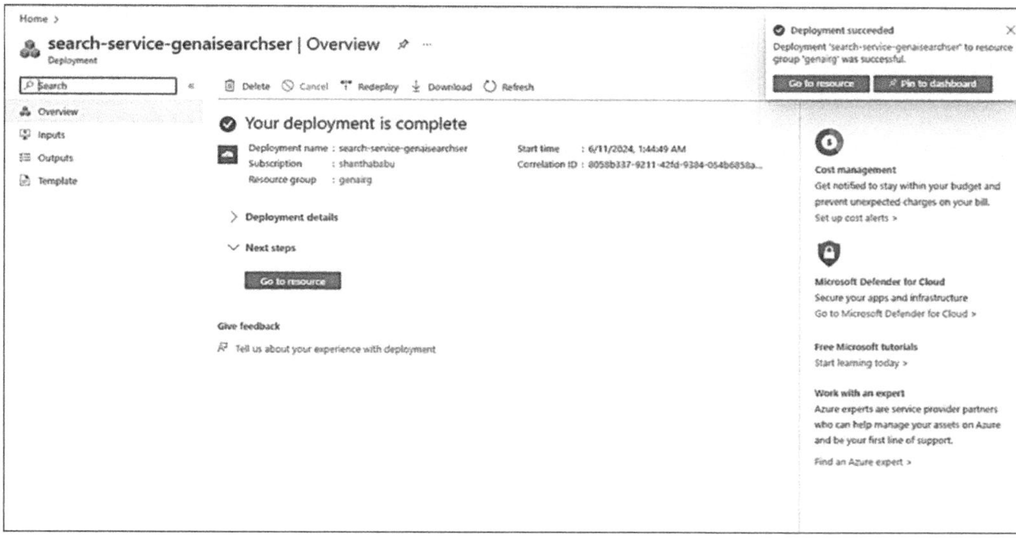

Figure 6.29: *Azure Portal (Azure AI Search Services Deployment in Progress)*

Step 6: **`genaisearchser`** is ready to use.

Let us import the data from storage.

Click on the "**`import data`**" menu in the right menu.

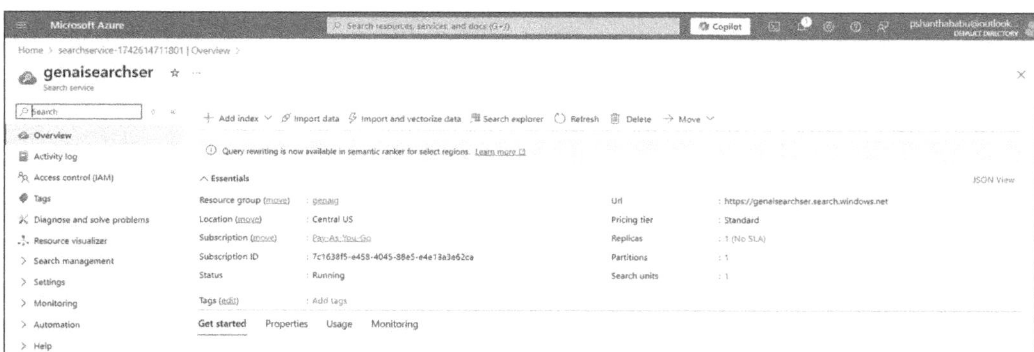

Figure 6.30: *Azure Portal (Azure AI Search Services; Import Data)*

Step 7: Once you click on the import data menu, the application will take you to the following screen shown in *Figure* 6.31.

Select **`Data Source`** from the drop-down menu, as shown in *Figure* 6.31.

For our demo, let us select **`Blob Storage`**.

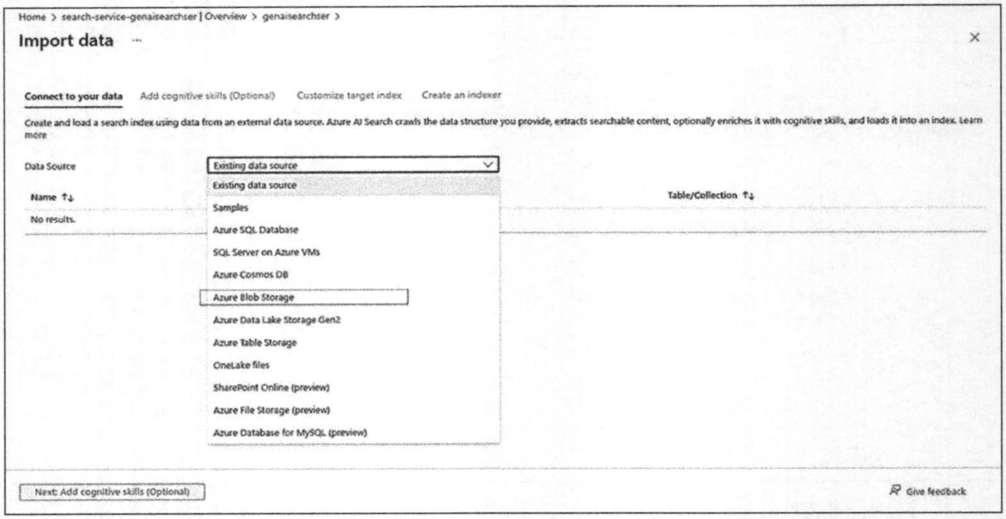

Figure 6.31: *Azure Portal (Azure AI Search Services; Data Source)*

Step 8: Once you select a data source, the application will show the following fields to configure your data source (*Figure* 6.32).

Here, you need to provide the following details:

Basic Configuration:

- **Data Source Name**: Enter a valid storage name (should be lowercase, and no special characters are allowed).
- **Subscription Type**: Free/Pay as you go (Subscription name).
- **Connection String**: Click on **`Choose an existing connection`**.

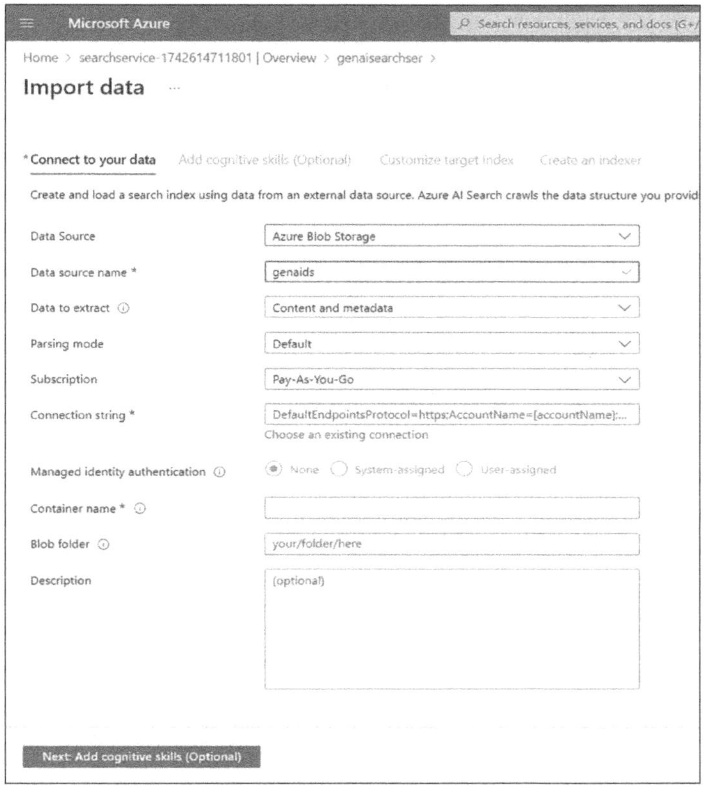

Figure 6.32: Azure Portal (Azure AI Search Services; Data Source)

Step 9: Once you click on the **`Choose an existing connection`**, the application takes you to the screen shown in *Figure* 6.33.

You can find the **`genaistorageacc`** storage, which we created in the previous demonstration, and select the same.

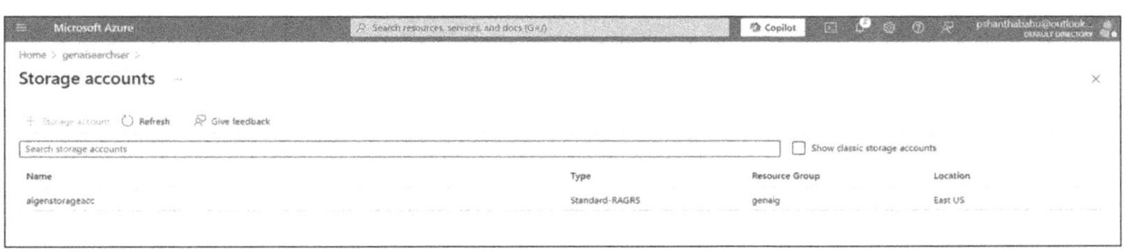

Figure 6.33: Azure Portal (Azure AI Search Services; Data Source)

Step 10: Once you choose **`genaistorageacc`** storage, the application takes you to the screen shown in *Figure* 6.34.

You can find the **`genaistorageacc`** storage, which we created in the previous demonstration, and select it.

Step 11: Once you choose your **`genaistorageacc`** storage, the application takes you to the screen shown in *Figure* 6.34. There, you can select the container inside the storage, and click the select button at the bottom of the page.

Please refer to *Figure* 6.34.

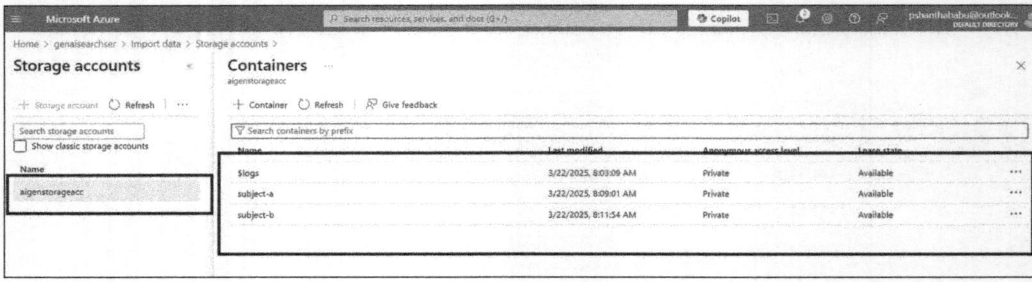

Figure 6.34: *Azure Portal (Azure AI Search Services; Data Storage; Container Selection)*

Step 12: Once you choose your container, the application returns to the screen shown in *Figure* 6.35. To follow this, click on the **`Next: Add Cognitive Skills`** button.

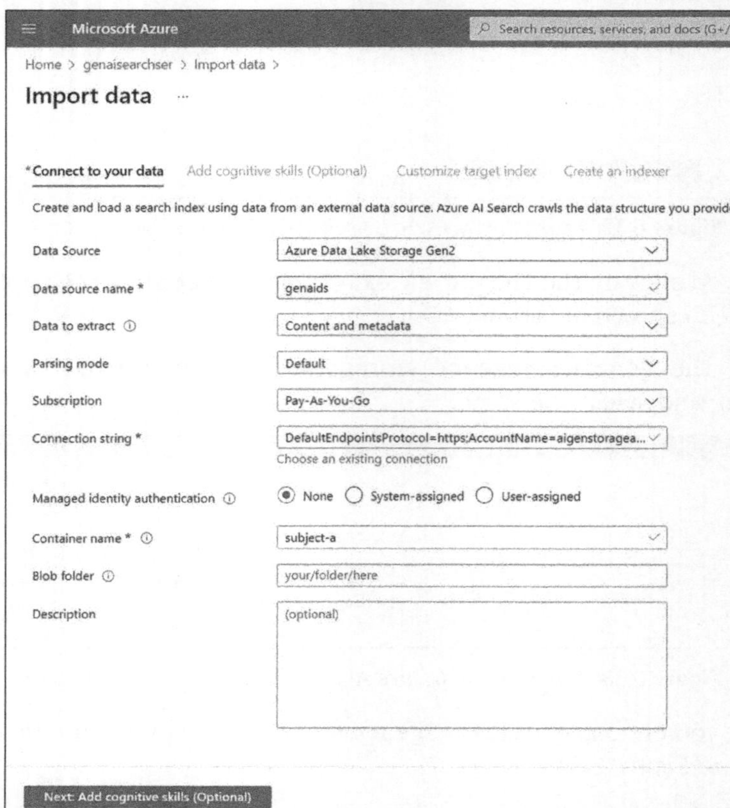

Figure 6.35: *Azure Portal (Azure AI Search Services; Configuration)*

Step 13: Once you click the "**`Next: Add Cognitive Skills`**" button, the application takes you to the screen shown in *Figure* 6.36. Following this, click on the "**`Enable OCR and merge all text into the merged_content field`**" and "**`Enable the incremental enrichment`**" options if required. If you select these options, **"`Skip to: Customize target index`"** will change to "**`Next: Customize target index`**."

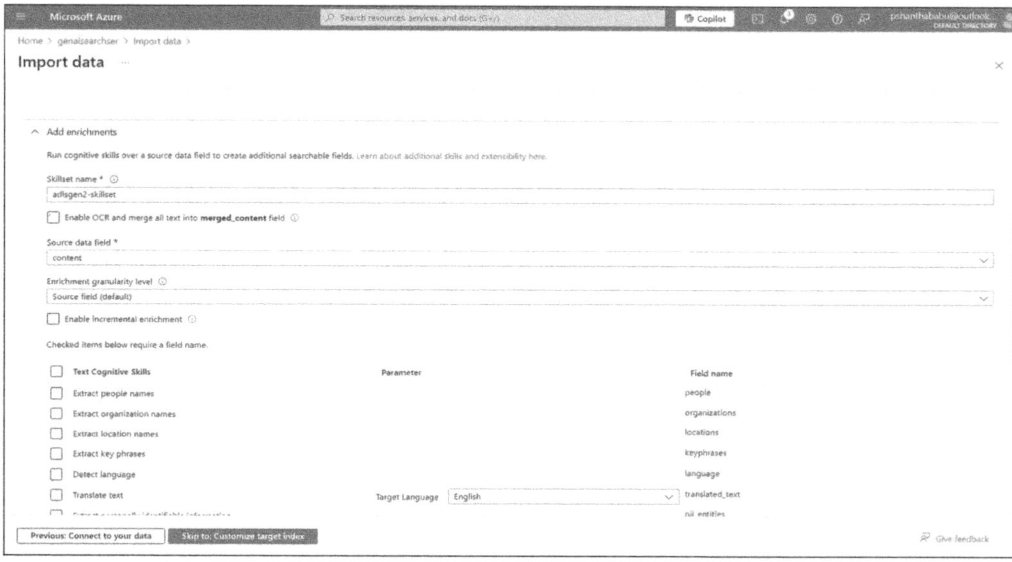

Figure 6.36: *Azure Portal (Azure AI Search Services; Configuration)*

Step 14: Once the required option is enabled, click on the **`Next: Customize target index`** button, as shown in *Figure* 6.37.

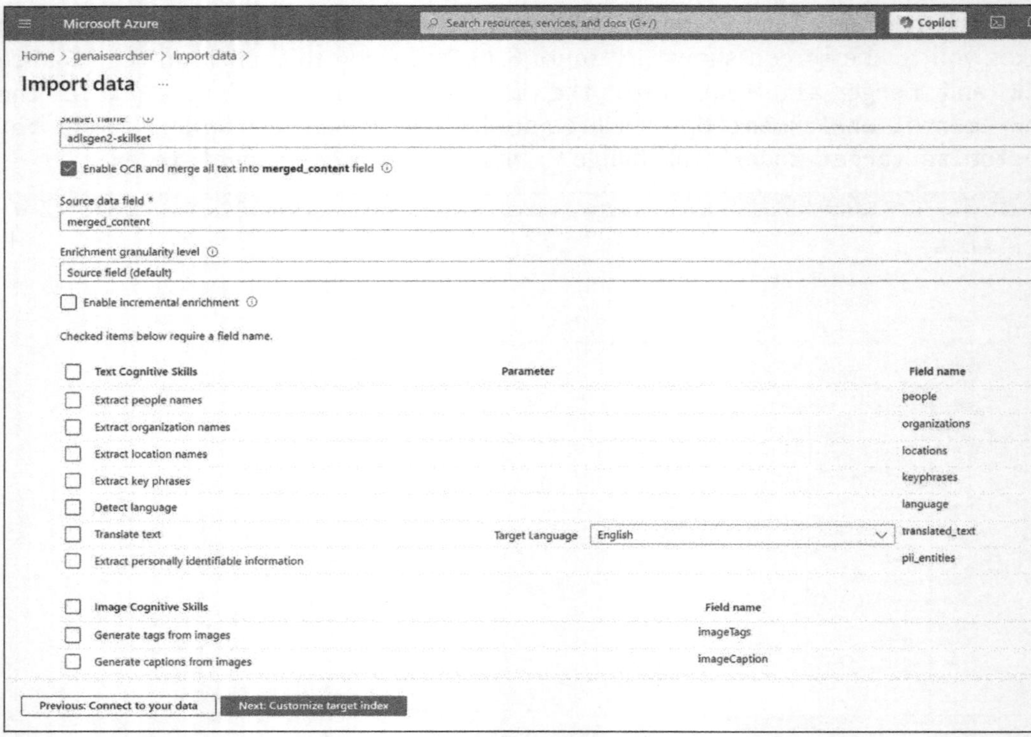

Figure 6.37: *Azure Portal (Azure AI Search Services; Configuration)*

Step 15: Once you click on the "**`Next: Customize target index`**" button, the application takes you to the following screen to configure the index name (it should be lowercase, and no special characters are allowed), followed by clicking on the **"`Next: Create Indexer`"** button.

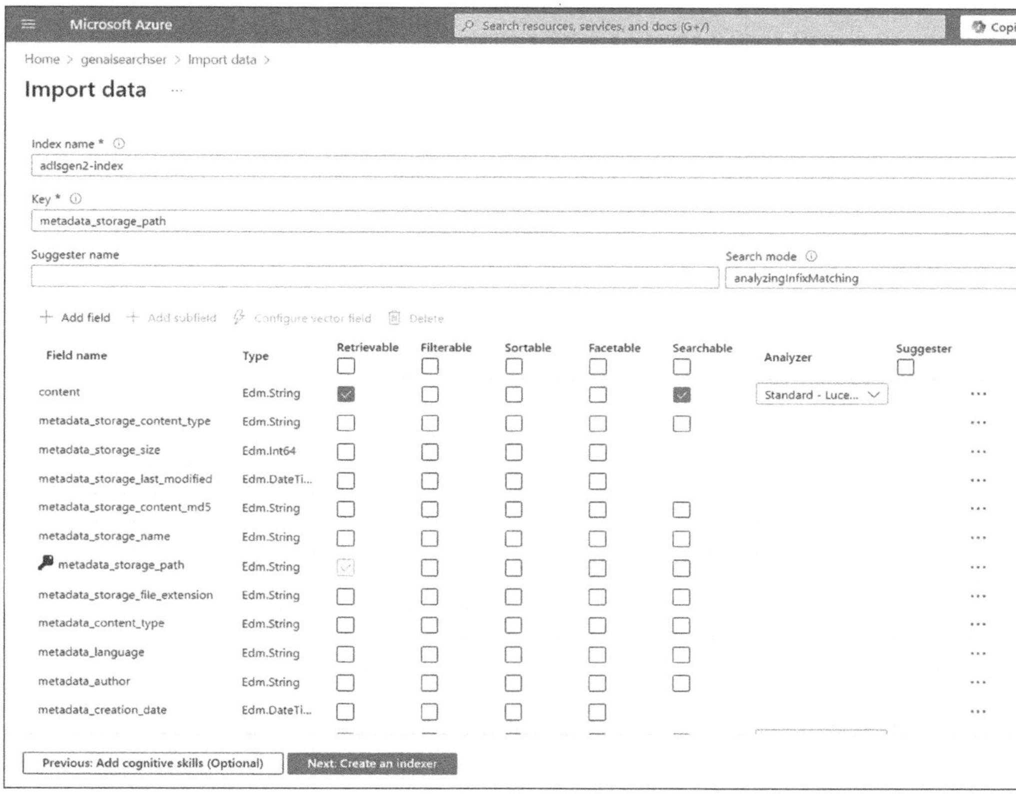

Figure 6.38: *Azure Portal (Azure AI Search Services; Configuration)*

Step 16: Once you click the **"`Next: Create Indexer`"** button, the application will validate the configuration details.

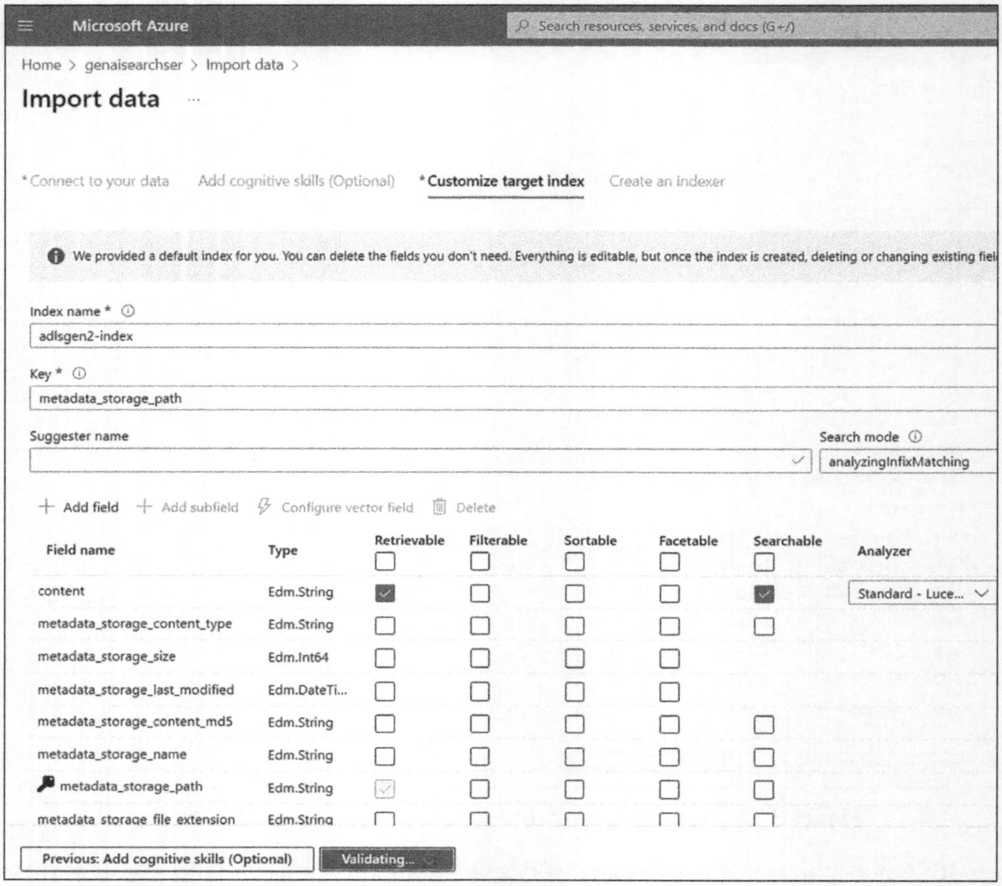

***Figure 6.39**: Azure Portal (Azure AI Search Services; Configuration Validation)*

Step 17: After validation, the application takes you to the screen, as shown in *Figure* 6.40, to configure the indexer name (it should be lowercase, and no special characters are allowed), followed by this click on the **"`Submit`"** button.

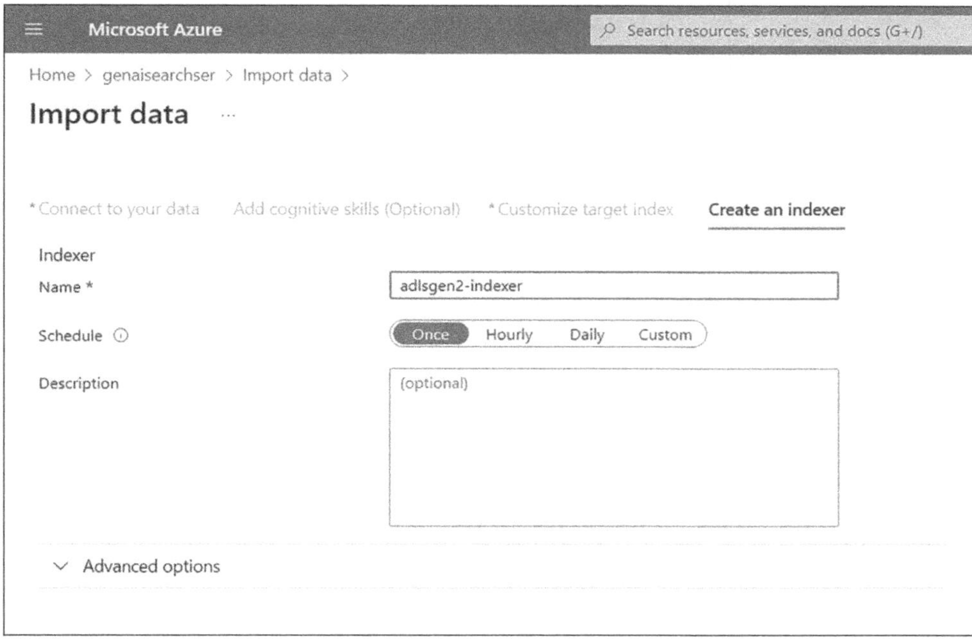

Figure 6.40: *Azure Portal (Azure AI Search Services; Submission)*

Step 18: Once you click the **"Submit"** button, the application will take you to the following screen for scheduling the index.

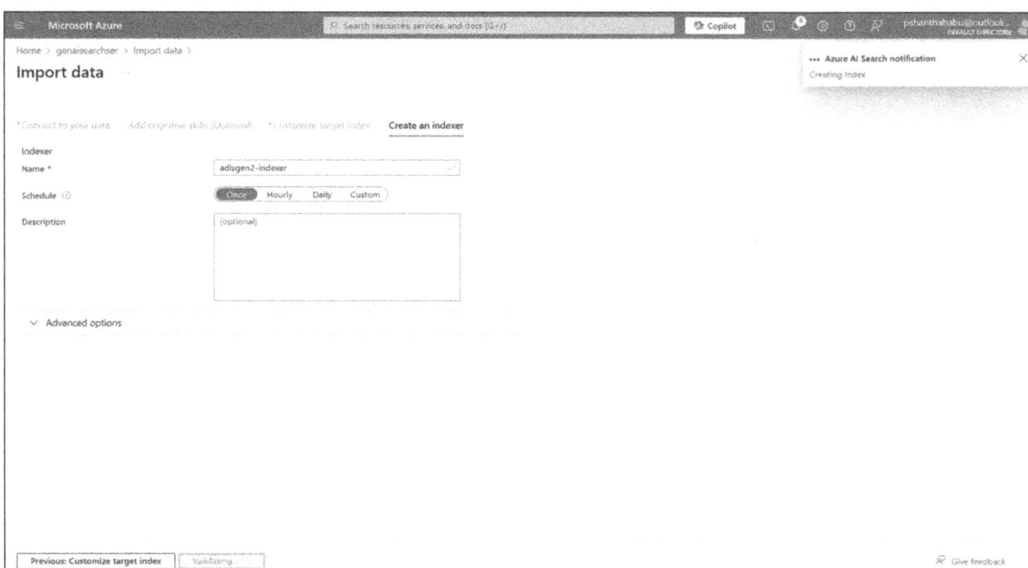

Figure 6.41: *Azure Portal (Azure AI Search Services; Configuration Index Scheduling)*

Step 19: Once you click the **"`Submit`"** button, the application is successfully configured and ready for search.

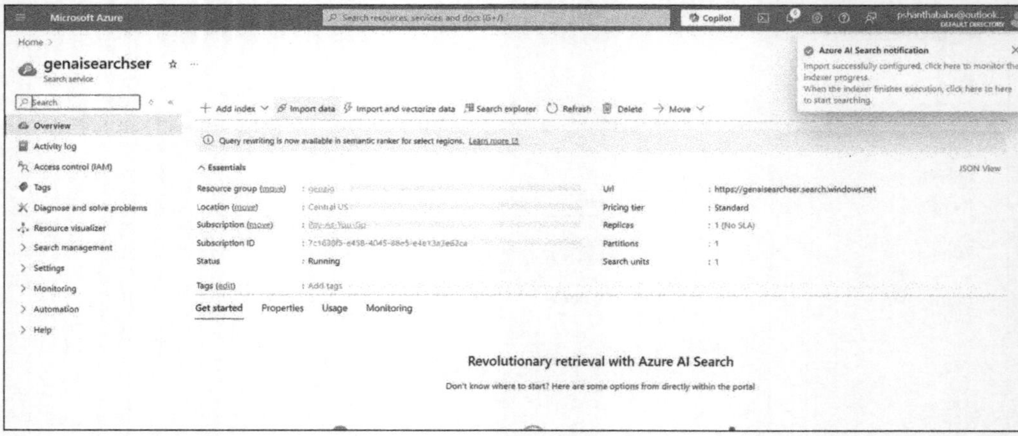

Figure 6.42: Azure Portal (Azure AI Search Services; Ready to Search)

Figure 6.43 shows the indexer details along with a number of successful documents.

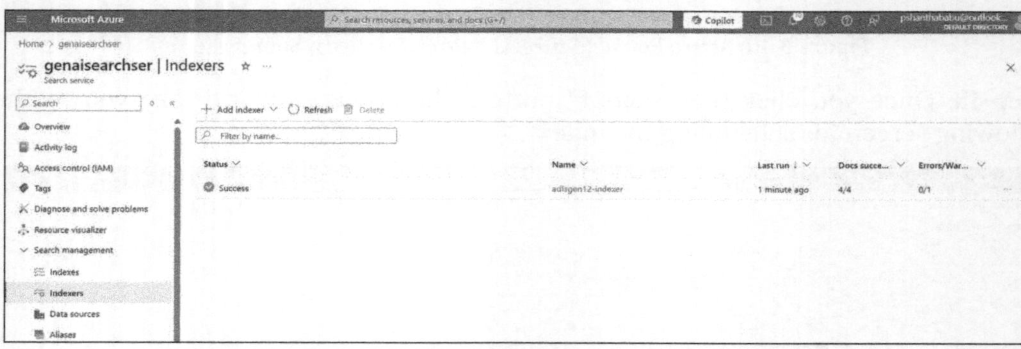

Figure 6.43: Azure Portal (Azure AI Search Services; Indexer)

Figure 6.44 shows the index details along with the number of documents indexed.

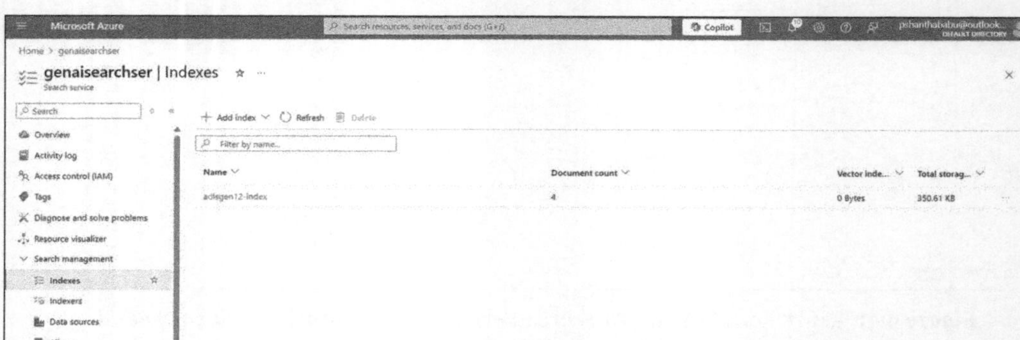

Figure 6.44: Azure Portal (Azure AI Search Services; Indexer)

Step 20: Searching window.

When you double-click on the index name, the application will take you to the screen, as shown in *Figure* 6.45.

***Figure* 6.45:** *Azure Portal (Azure AI Search Services; Search Window)*

Step 21: Searching window, and searching "**`ionic bonding`**" in the search text box, as highlighted in *Figure* 6.46.

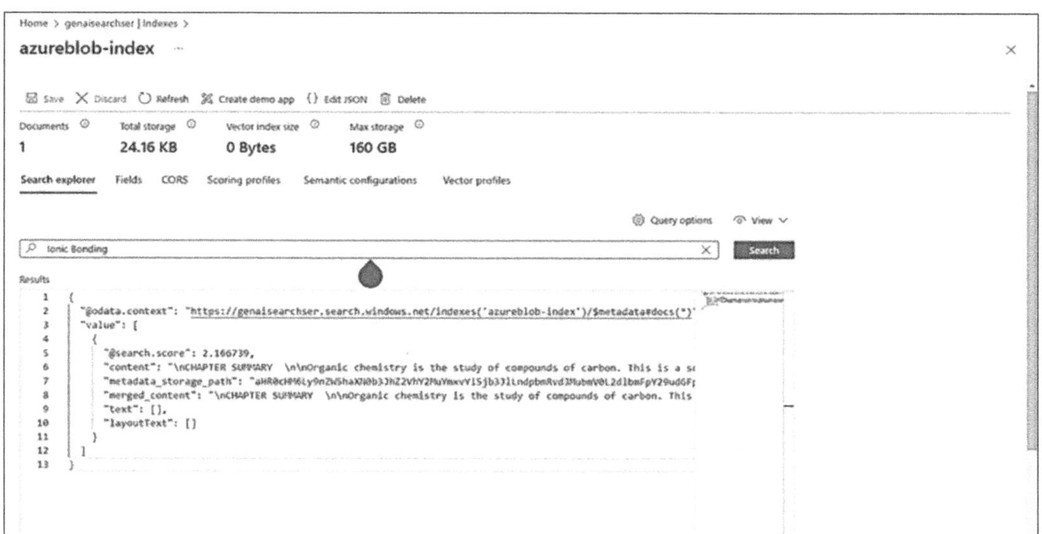

***Figure* 6.46:** *Azure Portal (Azure AI Search Services; Search Operations)*

View option: In the search window, we have two modes:

- `Query view` (Default)
- `JSON view`

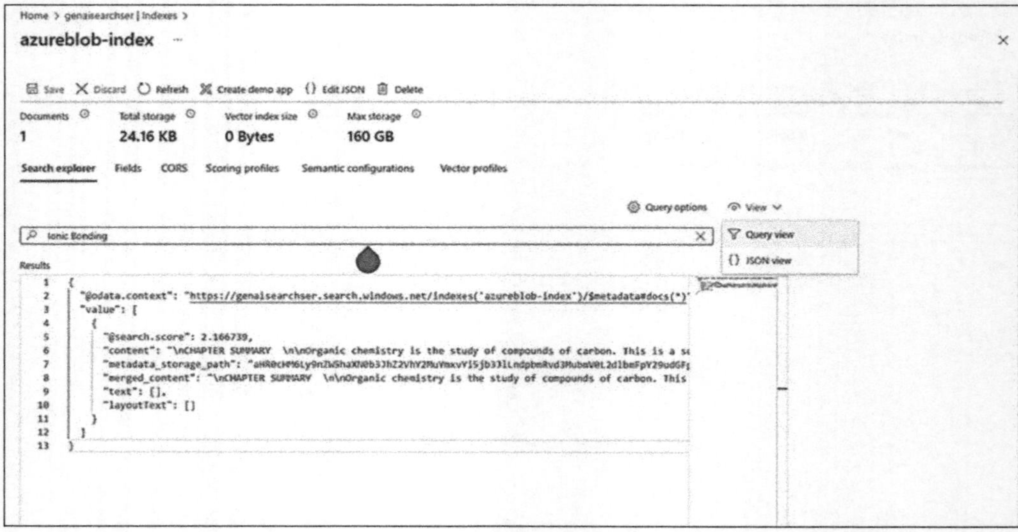

Figure 6.47: *Azure Portal (Azure AI Search Services; View Options)*

Search window: `JSON view`.

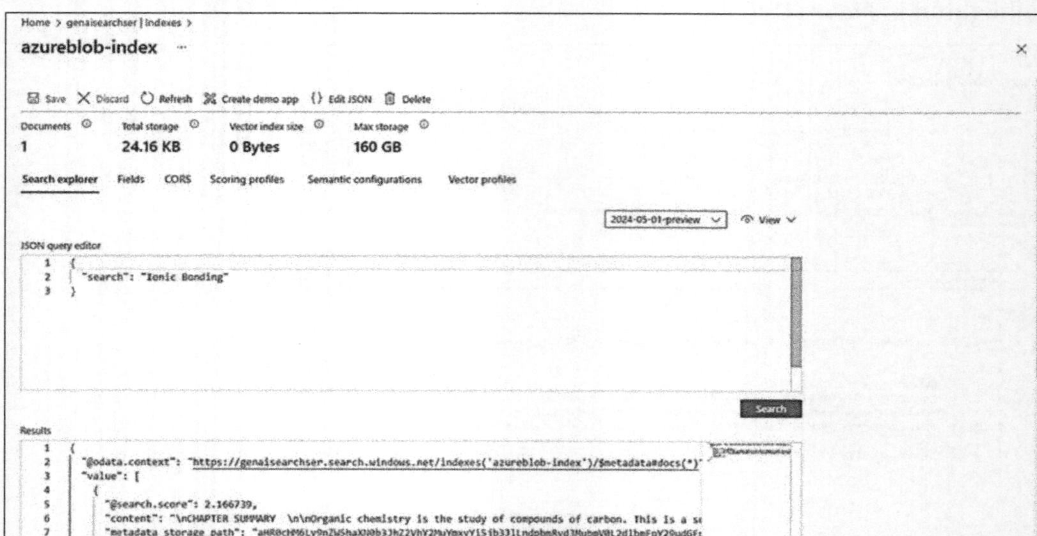

Figure 6.48: *Azure Portal (Azure AI Search Services; JSON View)*

Step 22: Delete the indexer; select the (**`azureblob-indexer`** on the left side of the panel and click **`Delete`** on the top menu). A pop up window will appear on the right side of the panel.

Under this indexer, you can select the index, data source, and skillset, and click the **`Delete`** (red) button.

Figure 6.49: *Azure Portal: (Azure AI Search Services; Deleting Indexer and Components)*

It is ready to delete the index, data source, and skillset under the indexer.

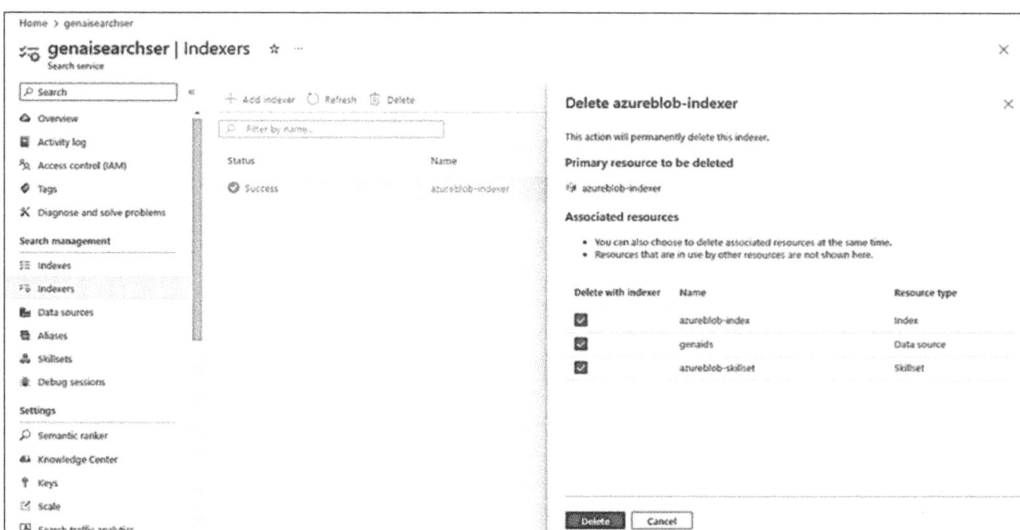

Figure 6.50: *Azure Portal (Azure AI Search Services; Deleting Indexer in Progress)*

Step 23: After successful deletion, click on the **`Refresh`** menu at the top. The indexer panel is now empty.

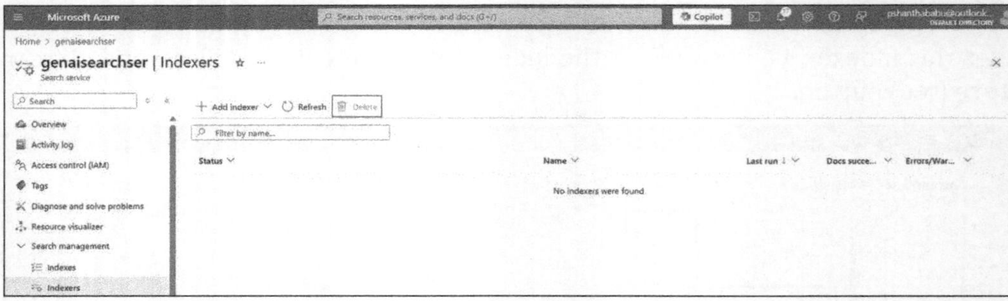

Figure 6.51: *Azure Portal (Azure AI Search Services; Indexer Deleting Process Completed)*

Step 24: Delete the AI Search service. Go to the home page, select your AI Search (**`genaisearchser`**), and right-click. You will get a popup window, as shown in *Figure* 6.52.

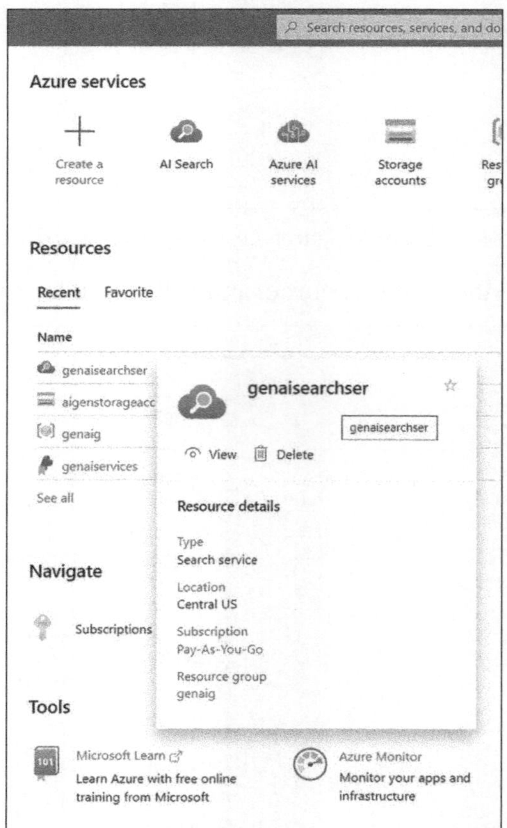

Figure 6.52: *Azure Portal (Azure AI Search Services; Deleting Process)*

Step 25: Delete the AI Search services.

Once you click delete, the application will pop up on the screen, as shown in *Figure 6.53* (highlighted). Enter the text in the textbox as **`delete`** to "**Delete**" the selected storage account, and click the "**`Delete`**" button

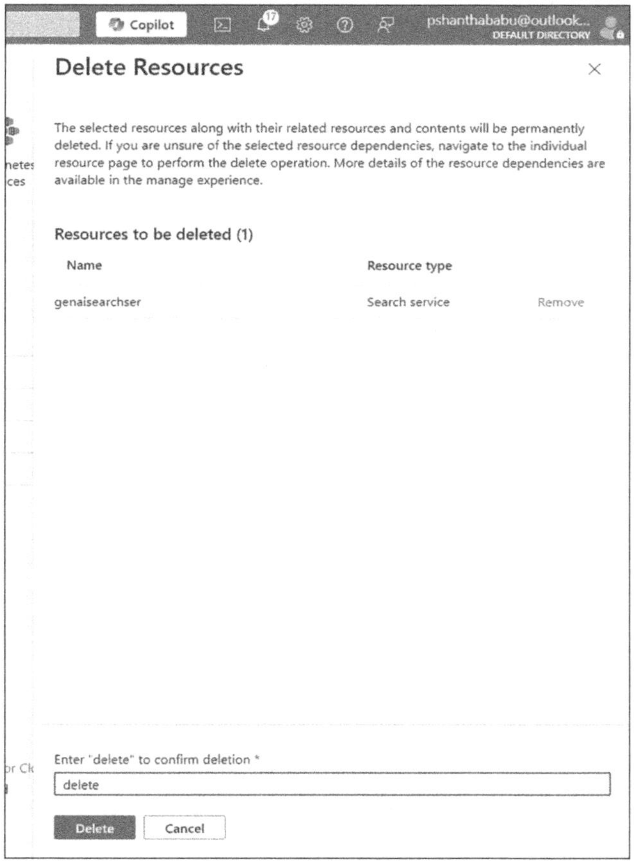

Figure 6.53: *Azure Portal (Azure AI Search Services; Deleting Process)*

Step 26: After you enter the text in the textbox as "**`delete`**" and click the **`Delete`** button, you will get the confirmation dialogue box. Click the **`Delete`** button to confirm your options.

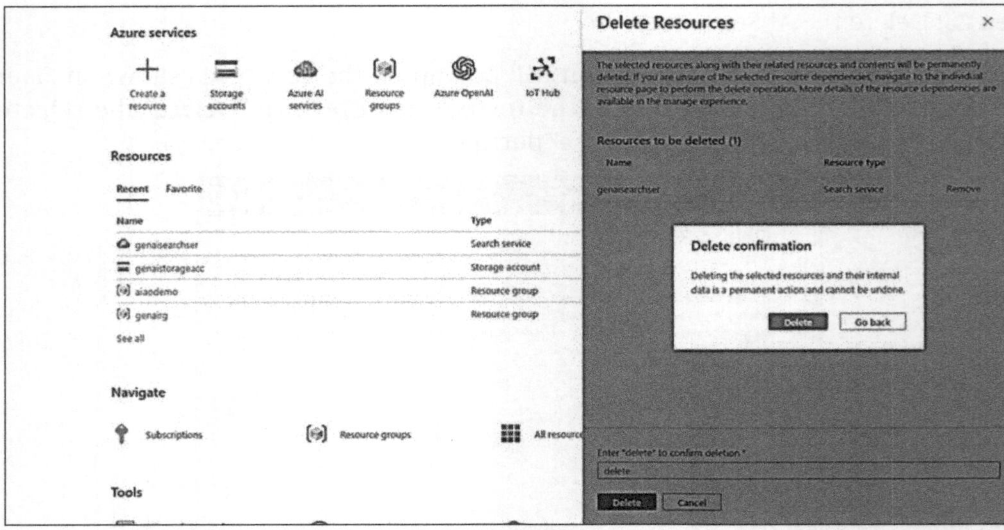

Figure 6.54: *Azure Portal (Azure AI Search Services; Deleting Confirmation)*

The AI Search Service was successfully deleted. As shown in *Figure* 6.55, the resources list only includes resource groups.

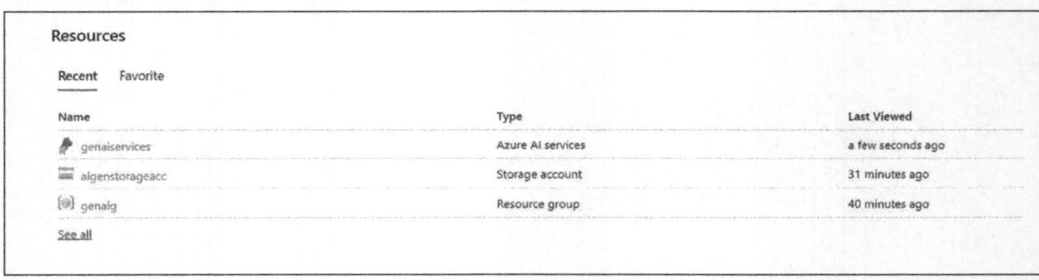

Figure 6.55: *Azure Portal (Resource Group)*

Conclusion

This chapter discussed the Azure AI Search and Storage Service environment in detail, along with its capabilities, its necessity in AI, various Azure AI Search services, Azure Storage and AI Search Services Integration with a detailed demonstration.

We explored Azure AI Search Service capabilities in terms of Full-Text Search, rich query syntax, AI-driven search, Custom cognitive skills, Natural Language Processing (NLP), Data Source Integration, Multiple Data Sources, Scalability and Performance, Indexing Performance, Partitioning, and Replication. We also investigated what Azure AI Search services such as Language, Speech, Vision, and Document Intelligence are.

We practically experimented with creating an Azure storage account specifically for AI search services, learning how to add files inside the container. We then explored how to build AI search services, integrate them with blob storage and index documents, and perform simple search operations.

The next chapter will provide an overview of Azure OpenAI Services and how they can be utilized. We will explore the Azure OpenAI Studio environment, Playground, Chat, assistant, and chat playground.

CHAPTER 7

Getting Started with Generative AI Using Azure OpenAI Services

Introduction

The previous chapter provided a detailed overview of Azure AI Search Services, mentioning their significance, capabilities, and integration with Azure Storage. We explored features such as Full-Text Search, AI-driven search, Natural Language Processing (NLP), custom cognitive skills, and scalability, demonstrating their role in delivering fast, relevant, and insightful search experiences. A step-by-step approach guided us through creating an Azure storage account, building AI search services, integrating with blob storage, indexing documents, and performing simple search operations, ensuring a clear understanding of these concepts.

This chapter offers a comprehensive overview of Azure OpenAI Services and their practical utilization. You will explore the Azure OpenAI Studio environment that includes the Playground, Chat Playground, and Assistant Playground. We will learn how to set up prompts, configuration parameters, exports, and imports with your own data. We will also understand the OpenAI deployment process, including building models and deployments by providing endpoints to Azure OpenAI-based models. We will dive into Azure OpenAI in the LangChain solution and approach. We will discover how to fine-tune models configured with settings to meet our needs, including content moderation models, version handling, and deployment sizes. We will even build a model with public and private data and deploy an AI app as a web application and copilot, integrating it with MS Teams and other components.

Structure

In this chapter, we will delve into the following topics:

- Understanding OpenAI
  - Essential Concepts in OpenAI
- Significance of AOAI Services in Gen AI
  - Enhanced Innovation Tools
  - Microsoft AOAI Capabilities
  - Exploring AOAI
  - Understanding the AOAI Architecture Workflow
- Concepts in Azure OpenAI Studio
  - Creating an Azure Storage Account for Blob
  - Creating Azure AI Services
- Azure OpenAI Studio: Add your data and Configuration
- Deployment: Chatbot
- Playground: Completions
- Understanding the Environment
- DALL-E Playground

Understanding OpenAI

Before we explore Azure OpenAI (AOAI), let us understand OpenAI and its capabilities.

OpenAI is an organization focused on artificial intelligence research, aiming to develop Artificial General Intelligence (AGI) that benefits humanity. It emphasizes creating safe and useful AI products while advancing AI research responsibly.

OpenAI was founded in December 2015 by Elon Musk, Sam Altman, Greg Brockman, Ilya Sutskever, John Schulman, and Wojciech Zaremba. Its goal is to conduct cutting-edge research and promote as well as develop friendly AI that aligns with human values and interests.

OpenAI is known for its significant contributions to AI research, particularly in natural language processing. Some of its notable models include:

- **Generative Pre-trained Transformer (GPT) Series**: These are language models designed to understand and generate human-like text. GPT-3 and 4o are among the most well-known models. They have 175 billion parameters and can perform various language tasks. We discussed this in *Chapter 1, Introduction to Generative AI*.

- **DALL-E**: An AI system that can generate images from textual descriptions from the prompt with or without image reference, showcasing the capability of AI in understanding and creating visual content from text.
- **Codex**: An AI model capable of writing code in any language. This powerful tool, such as GitHub Copilot, helps programmers generate code snippets based on natural language prompts as input based on the requirements.

One of its most significant partnerships is with Microsoft, which has invested in OpenAI and integrates its technologies into products such as Azure AI. This is the so-called Azure OpenAI (AOAI).

Essential Concepts in OpenAI

The following are the essential concepts in OpenAI:

- **Text Generation Models:** In general, OpenAI helps us to generate text using text generation models that we often refer to as "Generative Pre-Trained Transformers" or, in short, "GPT-x." We discussed its history in *Chapter 1, Introduction to Generative* AI. GPT-3.5 and GPT-4.0 (recent version) have been trained to understand natural and formal language. The inputs for these models are also referred to as "*prompts*." We discussed various prompt techniques in *Chapter 4, Prompt Engineering and Its Significance*. We understood how the prompt is essential for giving the appropriate input and providing instructions with or without examples of how to complete a task successfully. This includes various tasks, including content generation, summarization, conversation, innovative and creative writing, and so on.
- **Assistants:** These assistants operate based on the instructions provided within the context window of the model. They also usually have access to tools, which allows them to perform more complex tasks such as running code or retrieving information from a file. Read more about assistants in our Assistants API Overview.
- **Embeddings:** An embedding is a vector representation of a piece of data stored in vector space. We discussed them in detail in *Chapter 3, Vector Database and Embedding Techniques*. In this case, similar data tends to have embeddings closer together than unrelated data in the vector space. OpenAI offers text embedding models that take text as input and output. This helps systems with search, clustering, classification, recommendations, anomaly detection, and much more.
- **Tokens**: Tokens commonly represent a sequence of characters. This is a bunch of text divided in chunks and processed by the models. As we write sentences with words separated by spaces, similarly, the token of each word typically starts with a space character. As a rule of thumb, one token is approximately four characters or 0.75 words in English text.

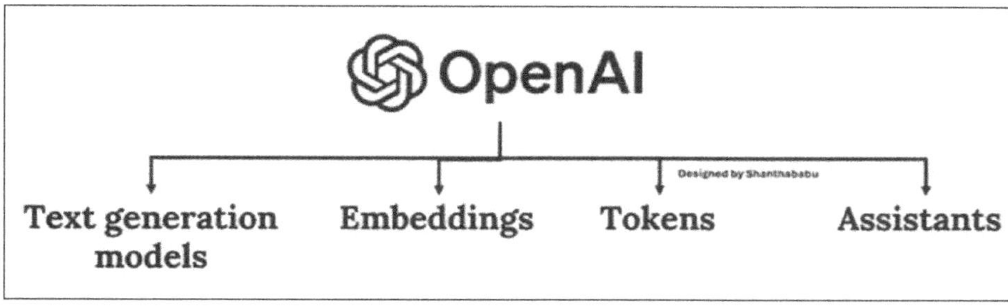

Figure 7.1: *OpenAI Services – Key Concepts*

Significance of AOAI Services in Gen AI

Azure OpenAI Services, a collaboration between Microsoft and OpenAI, provides significant advancements in deploying and utilizing Gen AI across various industries. Microsoft Azure OpenAI Services is pivotal in advancing AI technology by providing the necessary infrastructure, tools, and ethical frameworks. AOAI's integration with other Microsoft ecosystems, commitment to security and compliance, and focus on ethical AI deployment make it a basis for developing and applying Gen AI technologies based on market demand.

This extraordinary collaboration synergy between Azure and OpenAI is reshaping technology to an astonishing level. This engagement leads to a powerful transformation, and leverages Artificial Intelligence (AI) in the cloud computing space.

Microsoft Azure OpenAI is an influential AI service that allows industries to create multiple use cases and deploy AI models on the Azure platform. This enables lots of things to be automated, processing large amounts of data, and interacting with end customers, and it opens new potential for various businesses looking to leverage Gen AI solutions for their various levels of operations.

Here is a detailed exploration of their significance:

- **Scalable AI Infrastructure:** AOAI Services offers a robust and scalable infrastructure that allows organizations to develop, test, and deploy AI models efficiently. It can handle large datasets, processing, and analyzing massive amounts of data quickly and effectively. It supports extensive workloads and enables the deployment of AI applications across different regions and scales.
- **Integration with Microsoft Ecosystem:** These services are seamlessly integrated with Microsoft's suite of products and cloud services, such as storage, computing power, and security features that support AI development, testing, and deployment. They can also integrate with Word, Excel, and Outlook with AI capabilities.
- **Advanced Language Models:** AOAI Services leverage advanced language models such as GPT-3.5 turbo and GPT-4; they provide Natural Language

Processing (NLP) capabilities and enable sophisticated text understanding, generation, and translation. Most of the use cases are around conversational AI, which powers chatbots and virtual assistants to engage in human-like conversations, and provide personalized support for various industry-specific use cases.

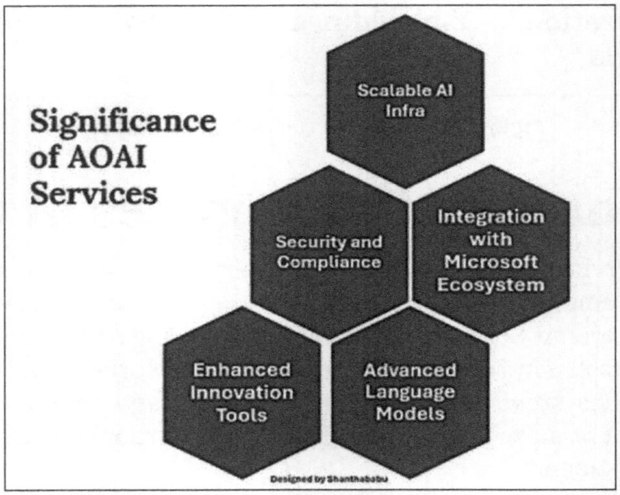

***Figure** 7.2: Significance of AOAI Services*

Enhanced Innovation Tools

AOAI Services offers enhanced innovation in various fields such as healthcare, finance, retail, and manufacturing.

- **Healthcare**: Supporting medical research, diagnostics, and patient care through AI-driven insights and automation.
- **Finance**: Enhancing fraud detection, risk assessment, and customer service with intelligent AI solutions.
- **Retail**: Improving customer experience through personalized recommendations, inventory management, and demand forecasting.
- **Manufacturing**: Improving product manufacturing quality and performance through personalized recommendations, inventory management, and demand forecasting.
- **Security and Compliance:** Microsoft Azure provides robust security and compliance features that ensure the implementation of best security practices to safeguard AI applications, infrastructure, and data privacy by protecting the sensitive data and adhering to global privacy regulations such as GDPR and HIPAA.

Microsoft AOAI Capabilities

Microsoft has emphasized various AI capabilities of AOAI, such as:

- Content/Text generation
- Summarization
- Semantic search
- Code generation

Note: *Chapter 10, Generative AI Use Cases for Industries-I, and Chapter 11, Gen AI Implementation Use Case with Azure OpenAI-II, discuss the extensive AOAI capabilities and use cases.*

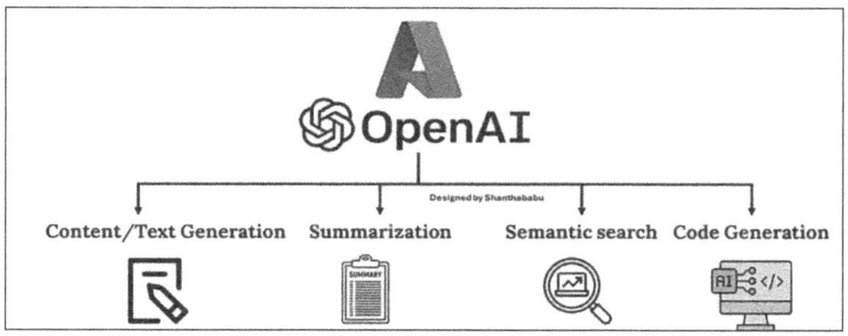

Figure 7.3: *Microsoft AOAI Capabilities*

Exploring AOAI

To explore AOAI, let us log into the Azure portal and demonstrate its various features and capabilities.

AOAI Studio is a trusted cloud platform that enables AI developers to drive innovation and reshape the future with AI, along with high security and responsibility. This comprehensive platform helps and accelerates production-ready AI tools to support enterprise-level chatbots, crucial content generation products, robust data analysis tools, high-speed ML solutions, and more.

AI developers can expose and consume endpoints to utilize and explore APIs and models for their use cases. They can also seamlessly build and test solutions with a collaborative Azure ecosystem and responsible AI tools for industry-specific use cases.

Understanding the AOAI Architecture Work-flow

Figure 7.4 shows the AOAI architecture workflow.

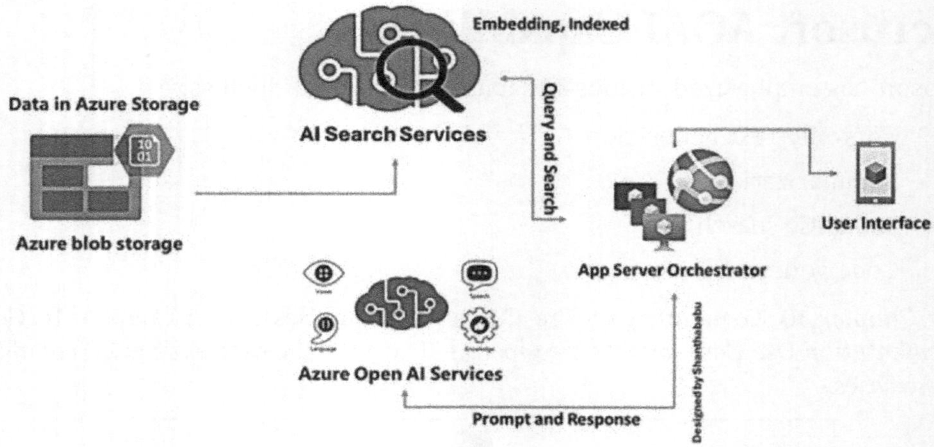

Figure 7.4: *AOAI Architecture Workflow*

1. Create a Storage Account (ADLS/Blob) and load the document.
2. Create an AI Search Service connecting storage accounts and documents as well as create indexing.
3. Create OpenAI Services and connect AI Search Services.
4. Deploy OpenAI Services as a web app and copilot.

Let us create an AOAI resource, and then we will explore various concepts in Azure Open AI Studio.

AOAI Resource Creation

Let us do an exercise on how to create Azure OpenAI resources for our demonstrations.

Step 1:

Log into the Azure portal and create the resources as we have done in *Chapter* 5, *Azure Storage for Azure OpenAI Implementations.*

To create an Azure OpenAI resource, search the textbox highlighted in the following figure or the list of resources.

Once you locate the service, select **`Create`**.

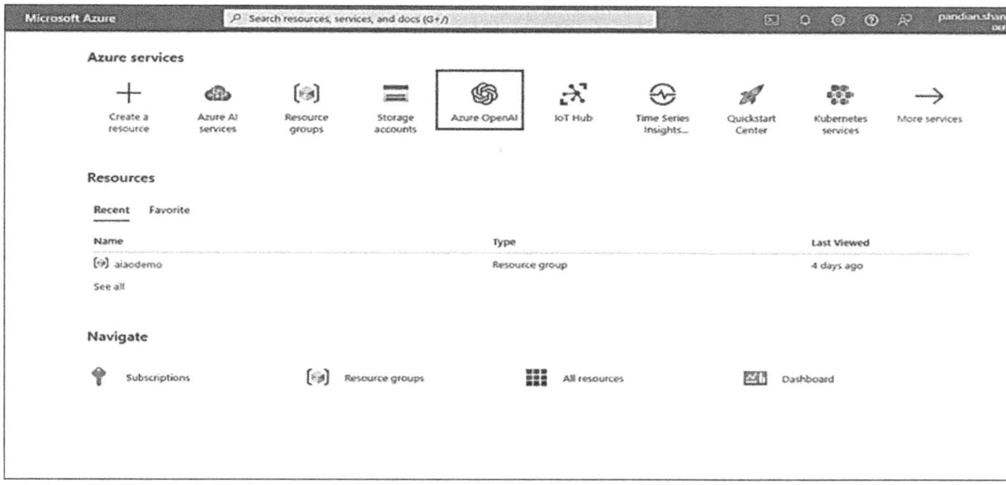

Figure 7.5: Microsoft (*AOAI Resource Creation Step 1; Search*)

Step 2: Click on the AOAI icon. A pop up window will appear, and you will see the **`(+) Create`** icon.

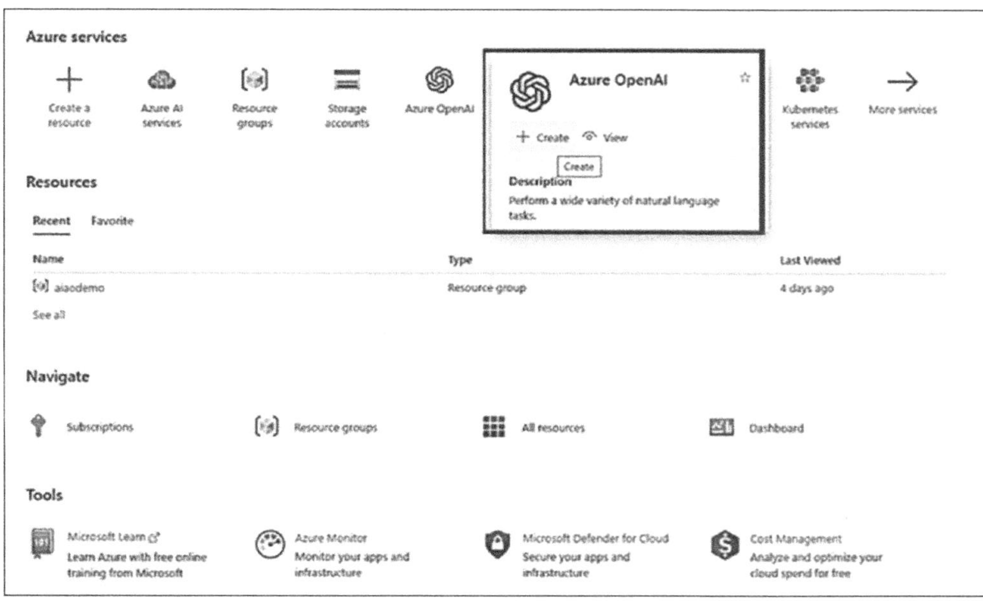

Figure 7.6: Microsoft (*AOAI Resource Creation Step 2; Create*)

Step 3: Once you click on the **`Create (+)`** icon, the application takes you to *Figure 7.7*.

Basic Configuration:

a. **Subscription Type**: Free/Pay as you go (Subscription name).

b. **Resource Group**: Select the resource group from the list.

c. **Region**: Select your appropriate region.

d. **Name**: Enter a valid storage name (it should be lowercase with no special characters).

e. **Pricing Tier**: We can go with the Standard tier, and for more info on pricing, visit the Azure OpenAI pricing page. Then, click the "`Next`" button.

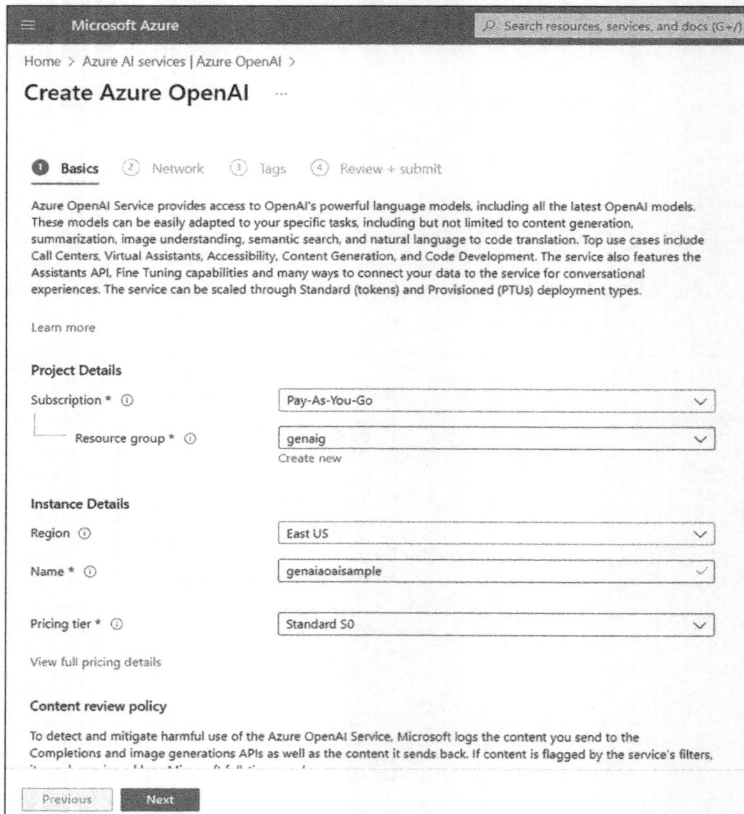

Figure 7.7: *Microsoft (AOAI Resource Creations Step 3; Configuration)*

Step 4: Once you click on the "`Next`" button, the application takes you to the network security configuration, and there are three options for the security type:

- **Option 1**: All networks, including the internet, can access this resource.
- **Option 2**: Select networks and configure network security for your Azure AI services resource.
- **Option 3**: Disabled; no network can access this resource. You can configure private endpoint connections, the exclusive way to access this resource.

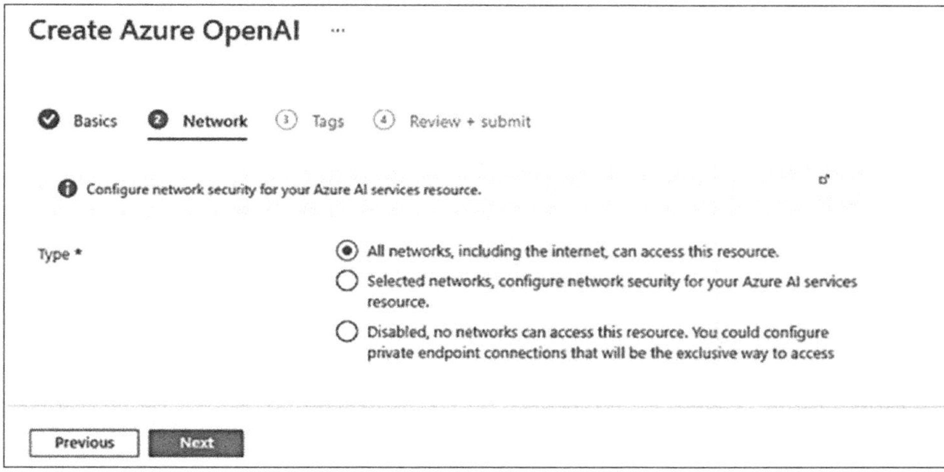

Figure 7.8: *Microsoft (AOAI Resource Creation Step 4; Configuration)*

Step 5: After network configuration, click the "**`Next`**" button and configure any Tags for your resources, as desired.

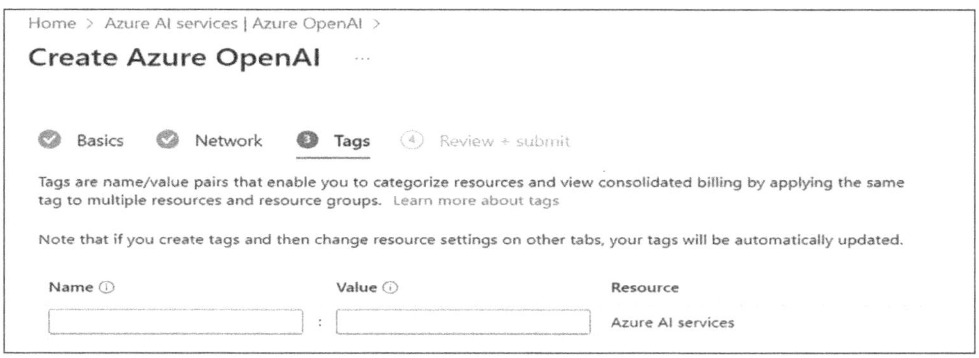

Figure 7.9: *Microsoft (AOAI Resource Creations Step 5; Configuration)*

Step 6: Followed by Tags, click on the "**`Next`**" button to move to the final stage in the process; click "**`Review + submit`**." The initializing deployment will start, as shown in *Figure 7.10*.

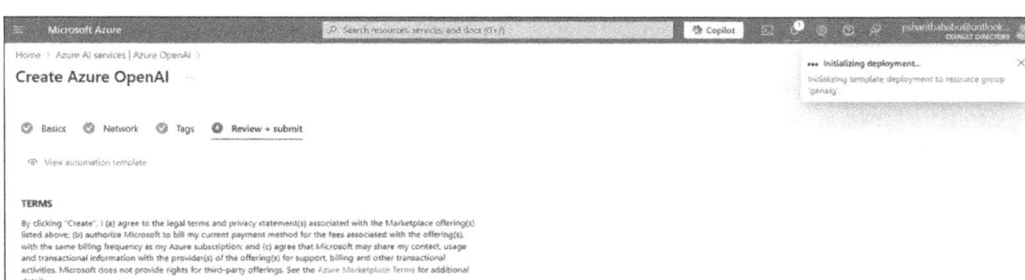

Figure 7.10: *Microsoft (AOAI Resource Creations Step 5; Iinitialization)*

Once the initialization process is completed, the system will take care of the deployment in progress, as shown in *Figure 7.11*:

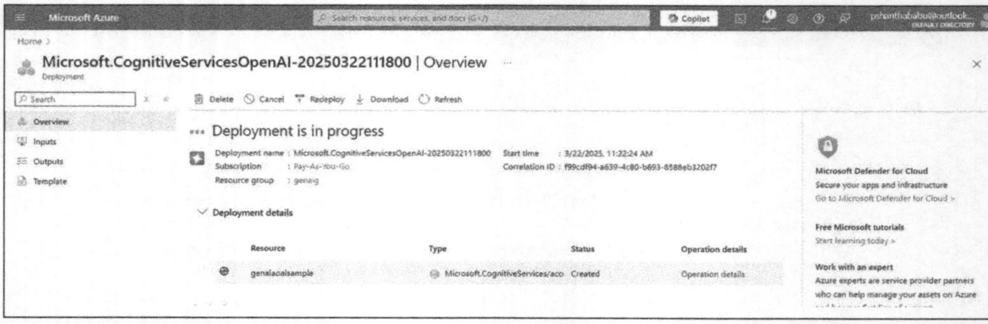

Figure 7.11: *Microsoft (AOAI Resource Creation Step 6; Deployment is in Progress)*

Step 7: After the deployment process is completed, the application will take you to the following page, where *Figure 7.12* shows that the new resource is available. Click on "**`Go to resource`**."

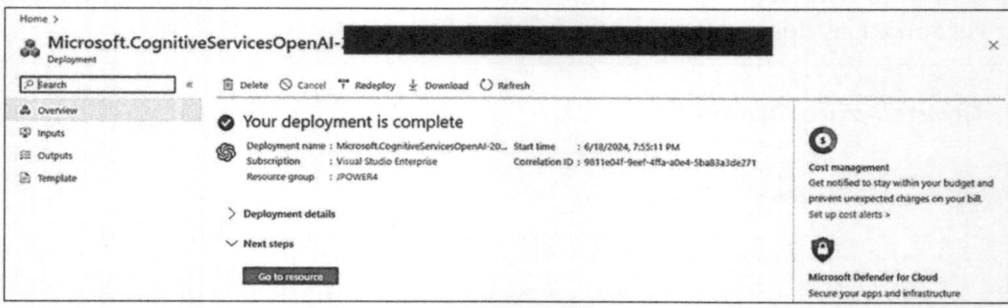

Figure 7.12: *Microsoft (AOAI Resource Creations Step 7; Resource is Ready)*

Step 8: Once you click the "**`Go to resource`**" button, the application takes you to the screen shown in *Figure 7.13*.

The key points from this page are as follows:

- Resource Group
- Subscription ID
- Keys and Endpoints

Once you notice the preceding key points, click on the "**`Go to Azure OpenAI Studio`**" menu highlighted in *Figure 7.13*:

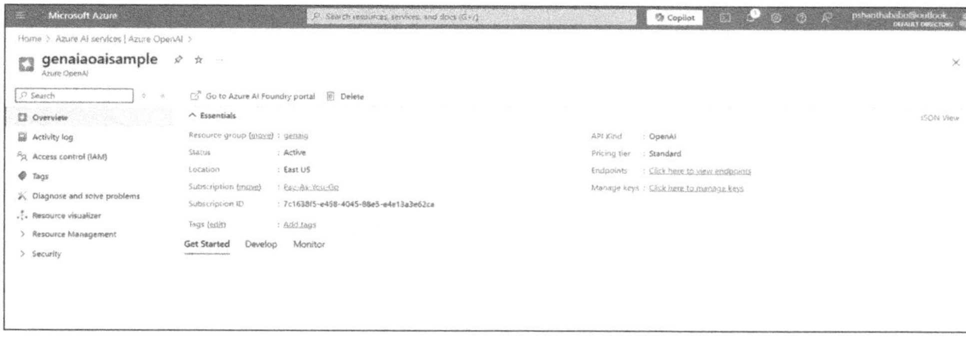

Figure 7.13: *Microsoft* (AOAI Resource is Ready)

Step 9: Once you click on the "**`Go to Azure OpenAI Studio`**" menu highlighted in *Figure* 7.13, the application will take you to the AOAI Studio, as shown in *Figure* 7.14:

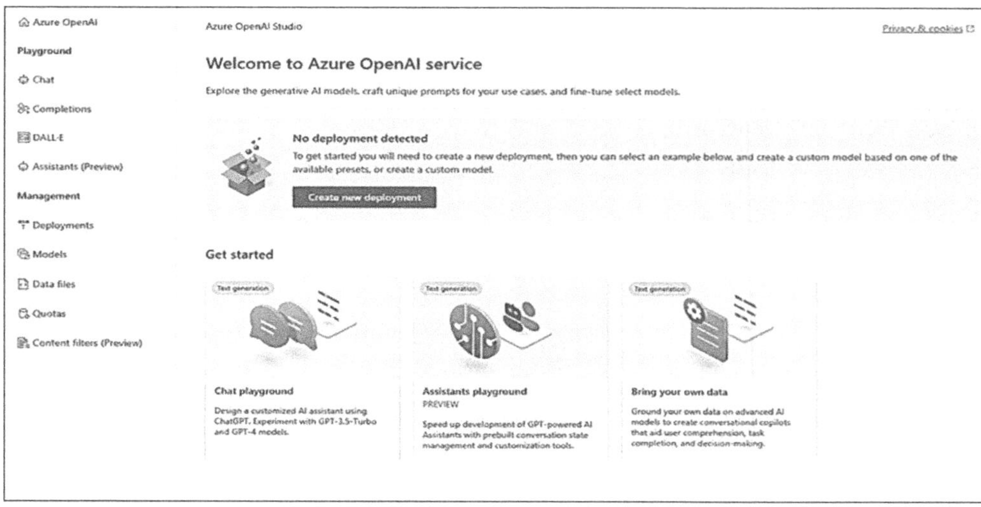

Figure 7.14: *Microsoft* (AOAI Studio)

Concepts in Azure Open AI Studio

Let us explore the concepts in the AOAI Studio. Here in the studio, we have significant blocks, as shown in *Figure* 7.14, such as:

- Chat Playground
- Compilation Playground
- Bring Your Own Data
- DALL-E Playground

The following concepts and components from Azure Open AI Studio are observed in the left panel, as shown in *Figure* 7.14:

- Playground
  - Chat
  - Completions
  - DALL-E
- Management
  - Deployments
  - Models
  - Data Files
  - Quotas
  - Content filters

Playground Chat: This specific component is an absolutely no-code approach through various versions of the GPT-x.x. It consists of a simple text box where you can submit a prompt to generate a completion, as we discussed various prompt techniques in *Chapter 4, Prompt Engineering and Its Significance*. This is typically the same OpenAI playground (https://platform.openai.com/playground/chat?models=gpt-4o), but this feature resides inside the Azure environment.

In the Playground, you can start testing your deployments with different prompts. A list of examples of what you can achieve with available models is already available, or you can create your own prompt and test it on the playground.

Step 1: *Figure* 7.15 shows the Chat playground environment. This page will initially have no deployed models and will be blank. When you click on the "`Create new deployment`" button, the application will take you to something similar to *Figure* 7.16.

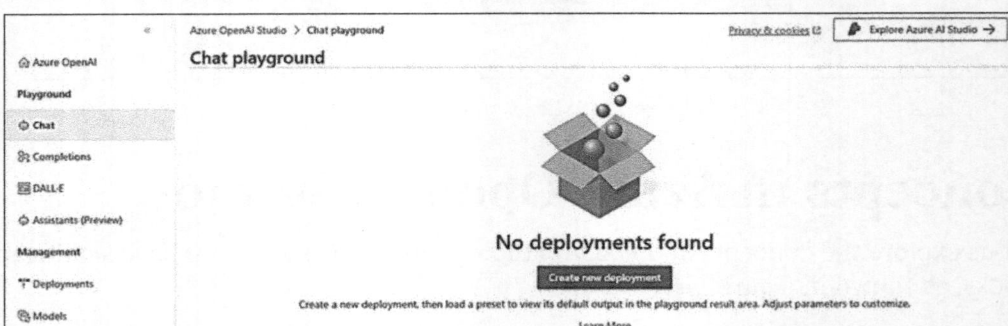

Figure 7.15: *Microsoft (AOAI Studio; Chat Playground Environment)*

Step 2: Here, you have to select the model from the list, as shown in *Figure 7.16*:

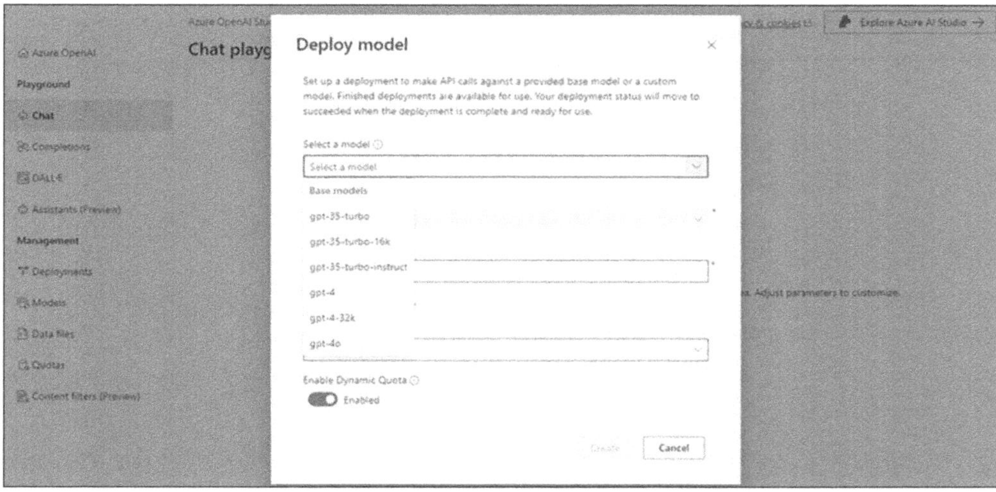

Figure 7.16: *Microsoft (AOAI Studio; Model Creation)*

Step 3: Deploy model configuration:

a. **Select a Model**: Choose your OpenAI model.

b. **Model Version**: Go with auto-update to default.

c. **Deployment Type**: Your desired type (Standard).

d. **Deployment Name**: Enter a valid storage name (it should be lowercase with no special characters).

e. **Content Filter**: Default.

f. **Token**: Based on your needs (cost involved).

Once you have configured it, click on the "`Create`" button.

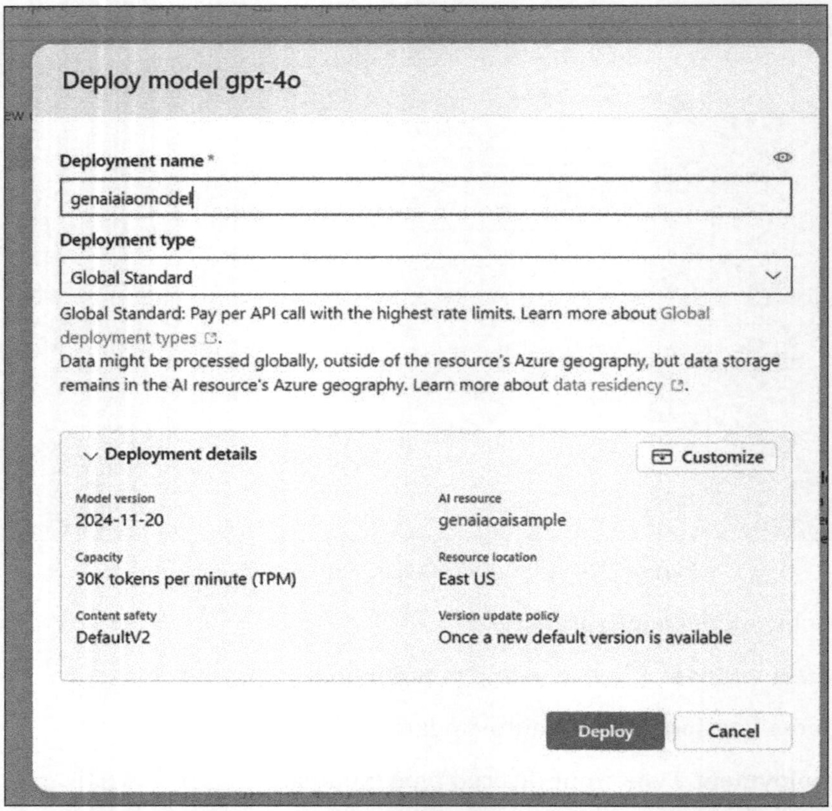

Figure 7.17: *Microsoft (AOAI Studio; Model Configuration)*

Once you click the create button, the application will take you to *Figure* 7.18, where you can find the following panels: Set up, Configuration, and Playground.

Set up: Under this configuration, you will find two menu options: Prompt and Your Own Data.

- **Prompt**: Under the Prompt, you can find the default system message and list of templates.
- **Your own data**: You can add your own data and prompts to that content (we will explore this later in the chapter).

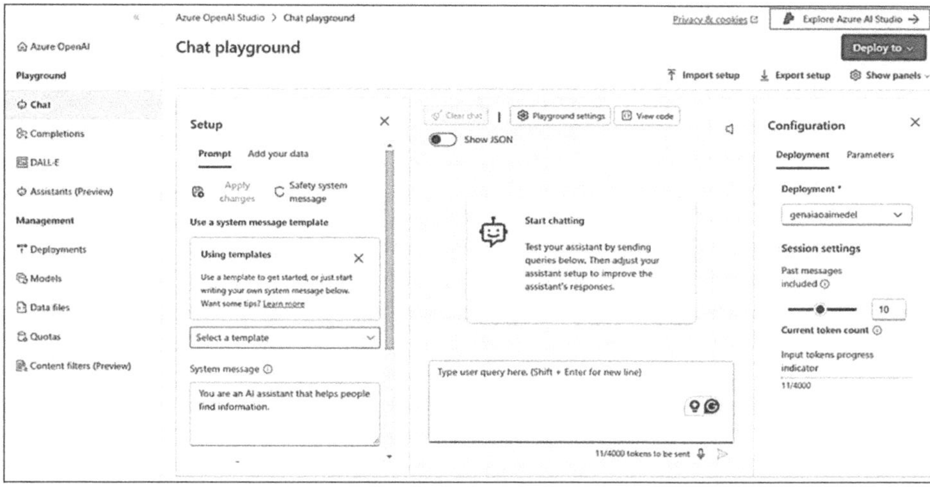

Figure 7.18: *Microsoft (AOAI Studio; Model Configuration)*

Step 4: When you click on Select a template, you can see the available template, as shown in *Figure* 7.18, or write your own template based on your use cases and click on **`Apply changes`** to incorporate the prompt assistance you are looking for in your requirements.

Step 5: To test the playground, in the chat window, the question is posted as "**`Explain C Programming`**," and you can see the output from the publicly available data, as shown in *Figure* 7.19:

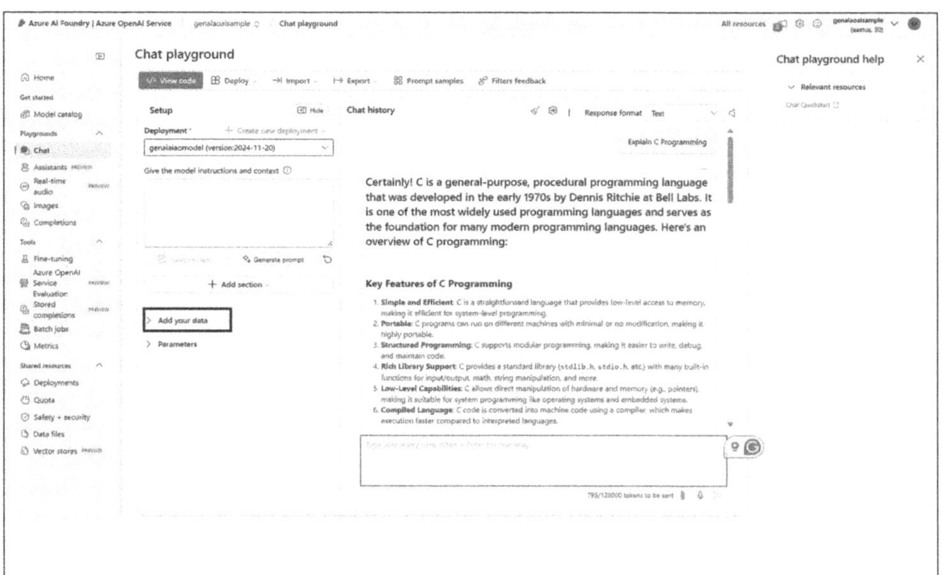

Figure 7.19: *Microsoft (AOAI Studio; Testing with Public Data)*

Play with your own data: To work with your own data, click "**`Add your data`**" in *Figure 7.19*. The application will guide you to a pop up screen, as shown in *Figure 7.20*. We can select the appropriate data source from the list.

Before selecting a data source, you must create your data storage using ADLS Gen2 or Azure Blob Storage and indexing using Azure AI Search. This indexing process uses powerful Azure AI Search Services, an essential function discussed in *Chapter 5, Azure Storage for Azure OpenAI Implementations*, and *Chapter 6, Azure AI Search Services for Azure OpenAI Implementations.*

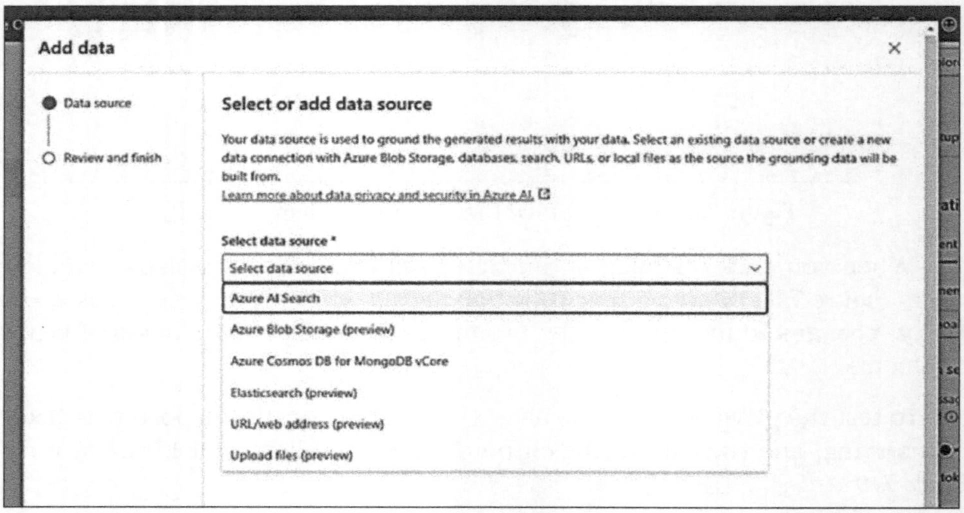

Figure 7.20: *Microsoft (AOAI Studio; Add Your Data Source Configuration)*

Creating an Azure Storage Account for Blob

Let us do an exercise on how to create an Azure Storage Account for Blob for our demonstrations.

Step 1: Creating a storage account is straightforward, as detailed in *Chapter 5, Azure Storage for Azure OpenAI Implementations*. Let us create a blob container under **`genaistorageacc`** (Storage account). Click on the container icon from the data storage list on the left panel, as shown in *Figure 7.21*:

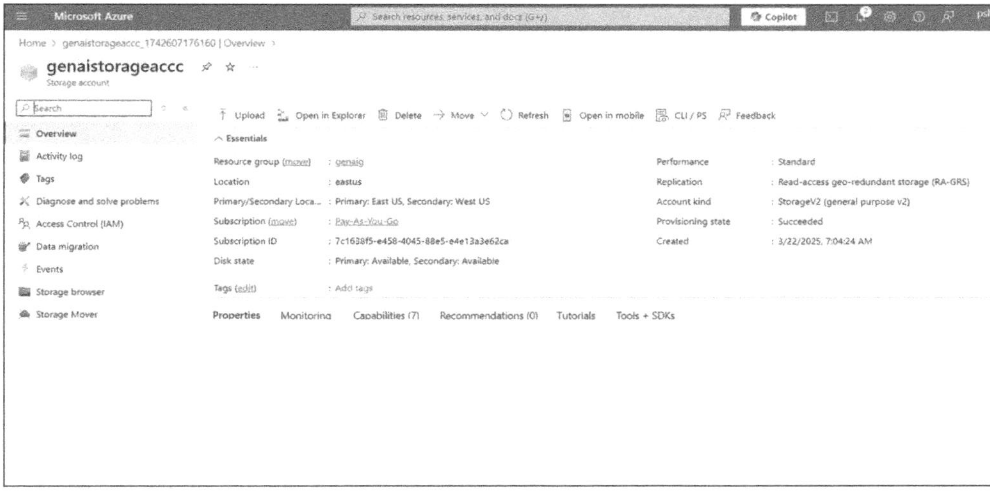

Figure 7.21: *Microsoft (Azure Storage Account Configuration)*

Step 2: On the right side, you will see a panel to create a container(s) (highlighted). Click on **`(+) Container`** in the right panel menu, as shown in *Figure* 7.22.

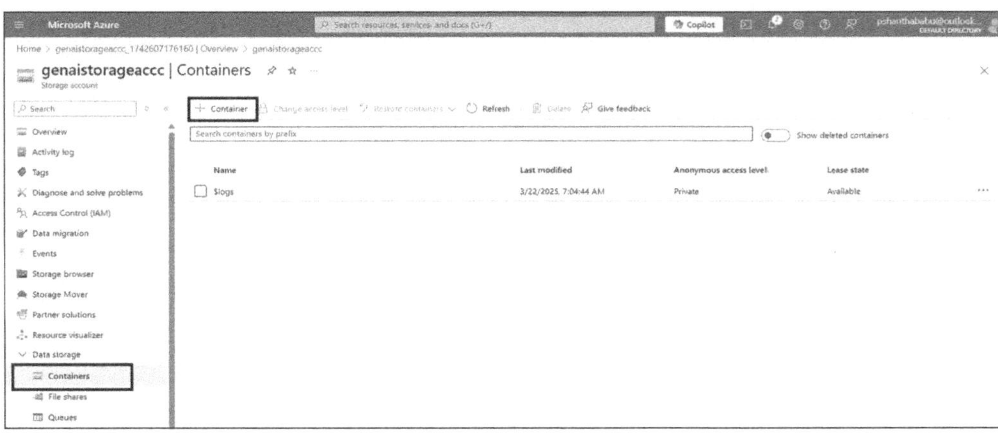

Figure 7.22: *Microsoft (Azure Storage Account Configuration)*

Step 3:

Here, you need to provide the following details:

a. Name: name (should be lowercase with no special cases.)

b. Leave the rest.

Once the preceding details are provided, we must click the "**`Create`**" button.

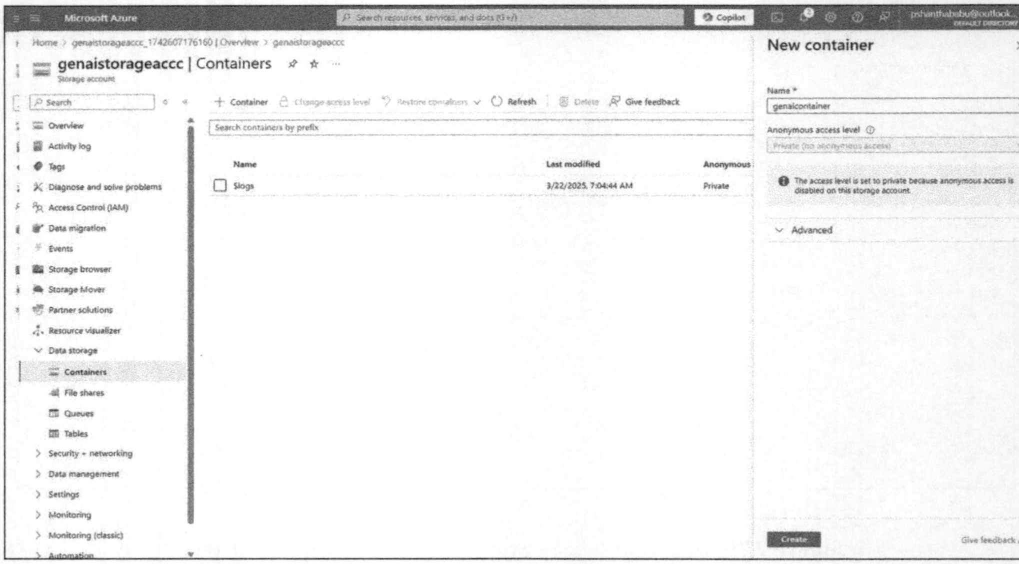

Figure 7.23: *Microsoft (Azure Storage Account Configuration)*

Step 4: A new container will be available once the create button is clicked.

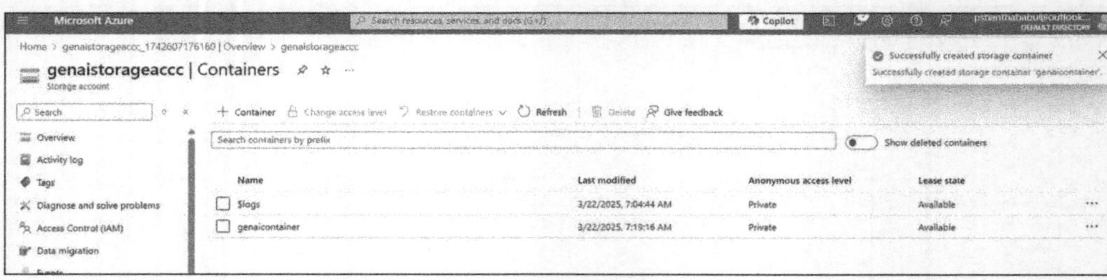

Figure 7.24: *Microsoft (Azure Storage Account Configuration)*

Step 5: Once the container is ready, click on the container in the right panel; then you will be taken inside the container, as shown in *Figure 7.25*.

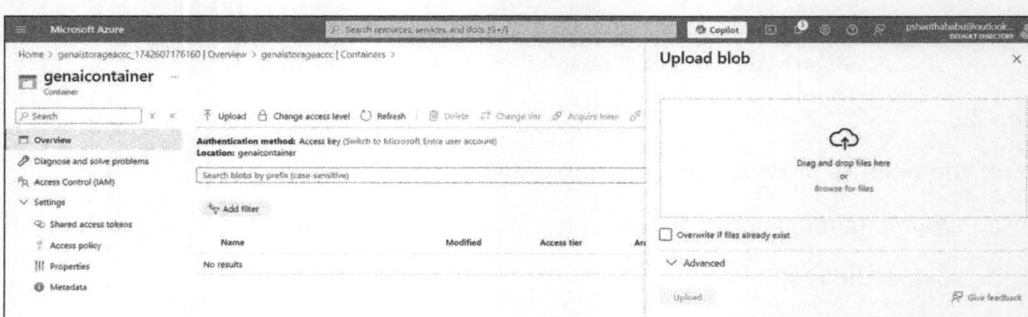

Figure 7.25: *Microsoft (Azure Storage Account Configuration)*

Step 6: You can browse or drag and drop the document in the highlighted space, as shown in *Figure 7.26*:

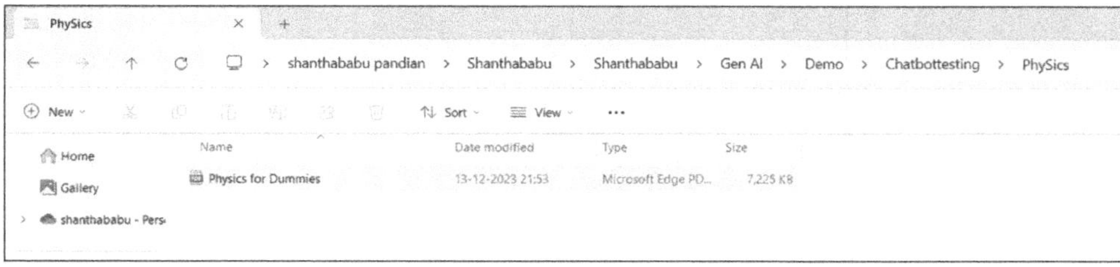

***Figure 7.26:** Microsoft (Azure Storage Account Configuration)*

Step 7: Drop the selected document, as shown in *Figure 7.27*:

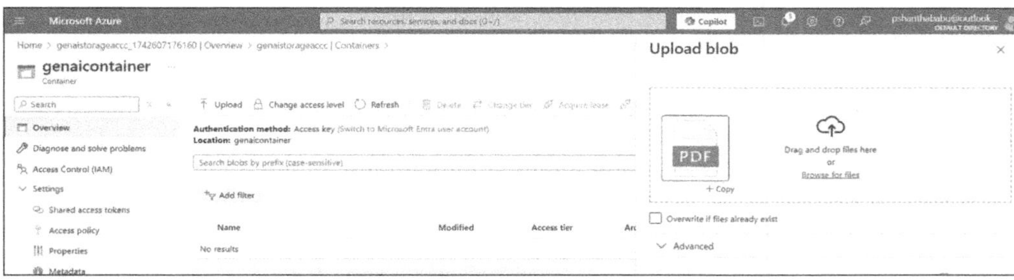

***Figure 7.27:** Microsoft (Azure Storage Account Configuration)*

Step 8: Once the document is dropped in the highlighted space and is ready to upload, click the **`Upload`** button, as shown in *Figure 7.28*:

***Figure 7.28:** Microsoft (Azure Storage Account Configuration)*

Once you click "**`Upload`**," the file will be successfully uploaded to the container. You can see the file, as shown in *Figure 7.29*:

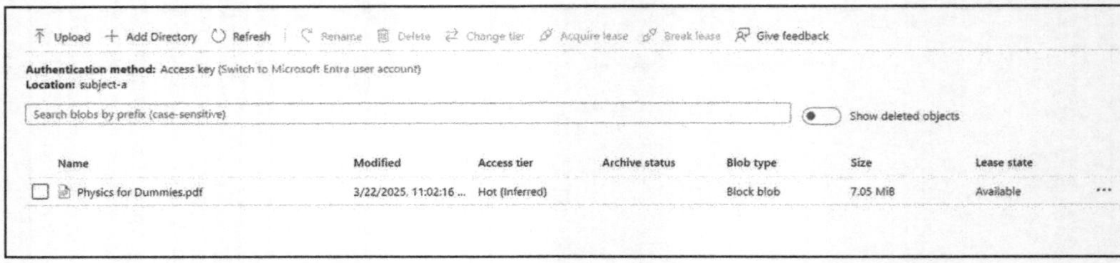

Figure 7.29: *Microsoft (Azure Storage Account Configuration)*

Creating Azure AI Services

Let us create an Azure AI Service.

Step 1: Click on the Azure AI Services icon in *Figure 7.30*:

Figure 7.30: *Azure Portal (Azure AI Search Services)*

Let us create an Azure AI Search. Please refer to *Chapter 6, Azure AI Search Services for Azure OpenAI Implementations*. Here, we will create Azure AI Search Services and connect storage directly.

Step 2: Click on AI Search from the left menu, as shown in *Figure* 7.30. The application will take you to the following screen shown in *Figure* 7.31:

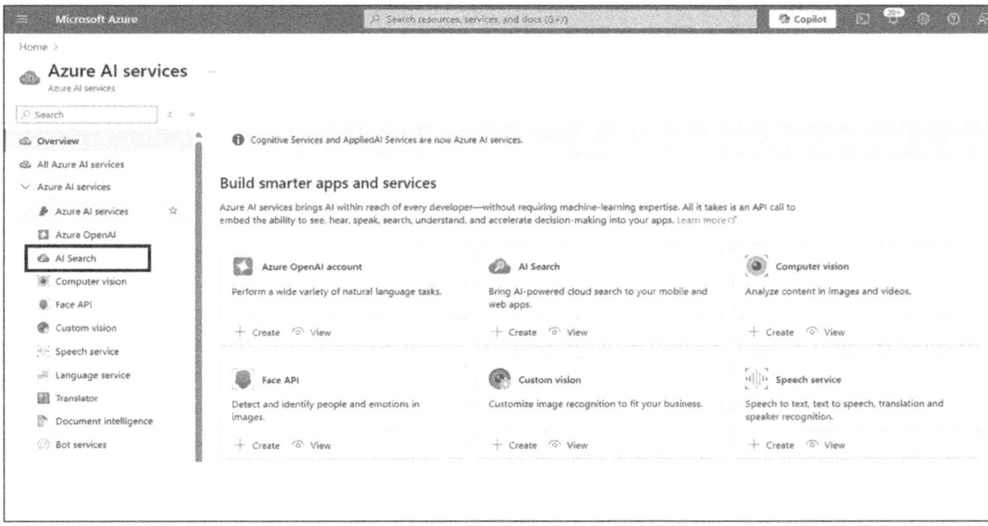

Figure 7.31: *Azure Portal (Azure AI Search Services)*

Step 3: Once you click on the plus icon highlighted in *Figure* 7.32, the application will take you to the screen shown in *Figure* 7.33:

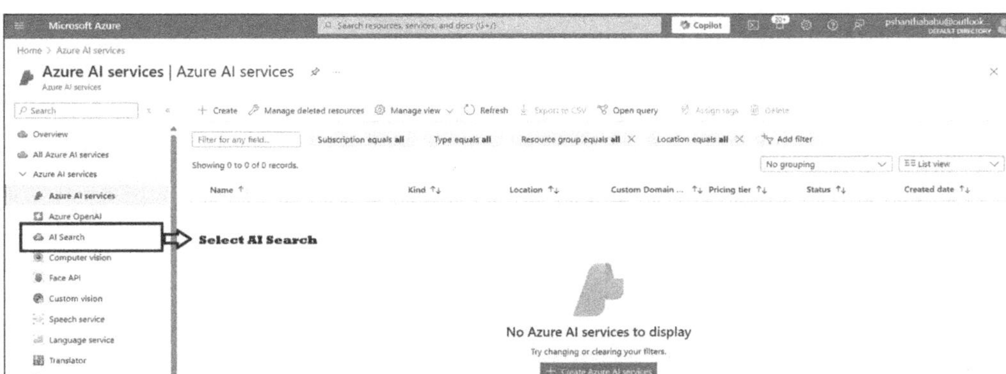

Figure 7.32: *Azure Portal (Azure AI Search Services)*

Step 4: Once you click on the `(+) Create` in the top menu, as highlighted in *Figure* 7.32, the application will take you to *Figure* 7.33.

Here, you need to provide the following details:

Basic Configuration:

- **Subscription Type**: Free/Pay as you go (Subscription name).
- **Resource Group**: Select the resource group from the list.
- **Service Name**: Enter a valid name (it should be lowercase with no special characters).
- **Region**: Select your appropriate region.

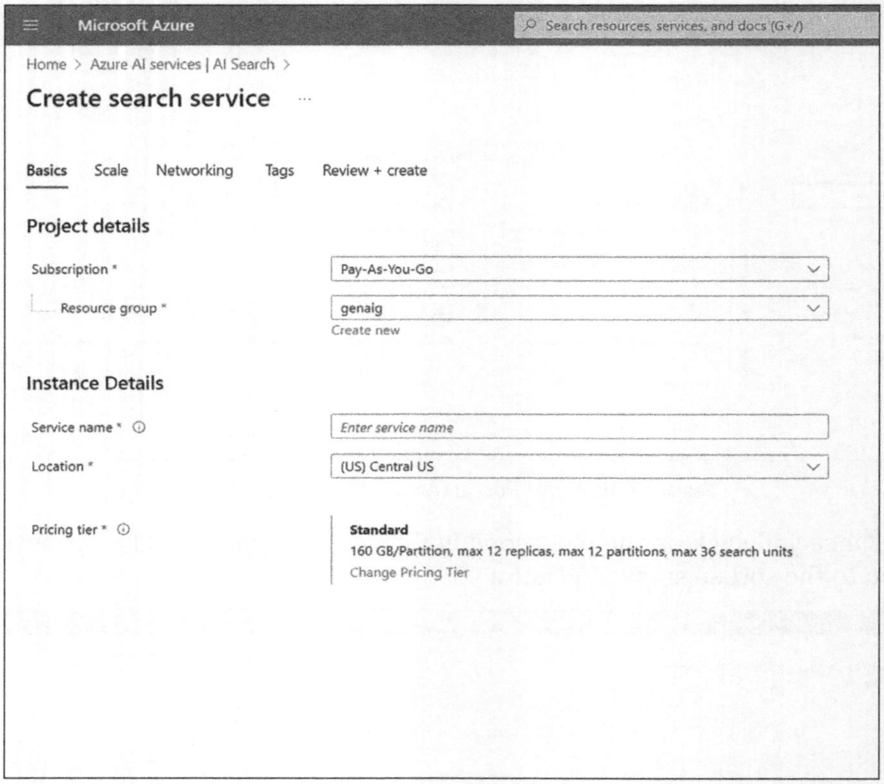

Figure 7.33: *Azure Portal (Azure AI Search Services)*

Once the aforementioned details are provided, we must click the "`Review and Create`" button to proceed with completing the validation and click on the "`Create`" button. After deployment is in progress, click on the "`Go To Resource`" button, and the application will take you to the screen shown in *Figure* 7.34:

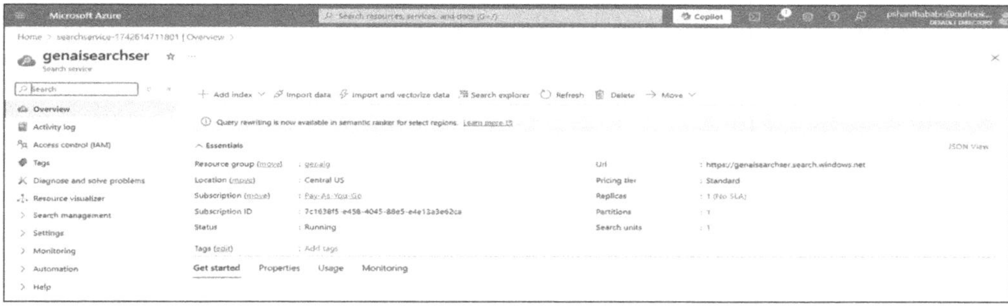

Figure 7.34: *Azure Portal (Azure AI Search Services; Ready to Configure Import Data)*

Step 5: Azure AI Search Services are ready to be configured with data storage. To import data from the storage, click on the import data menu highlighted in *Figure* 7.35.

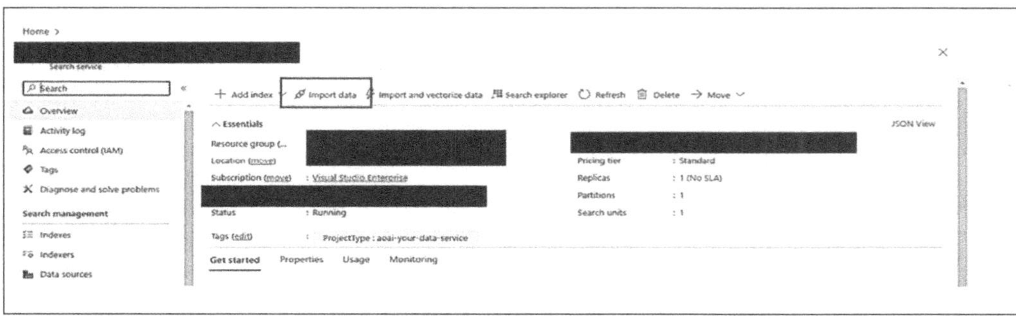

Figure 7.35: *Azure Portal (Azure AI Search Services; Import Data)*

Step 6: The application will take you to the following screen once you click the import menu. As a first step, we have to select the Data Source from the list shown in *Figure* 7.36.

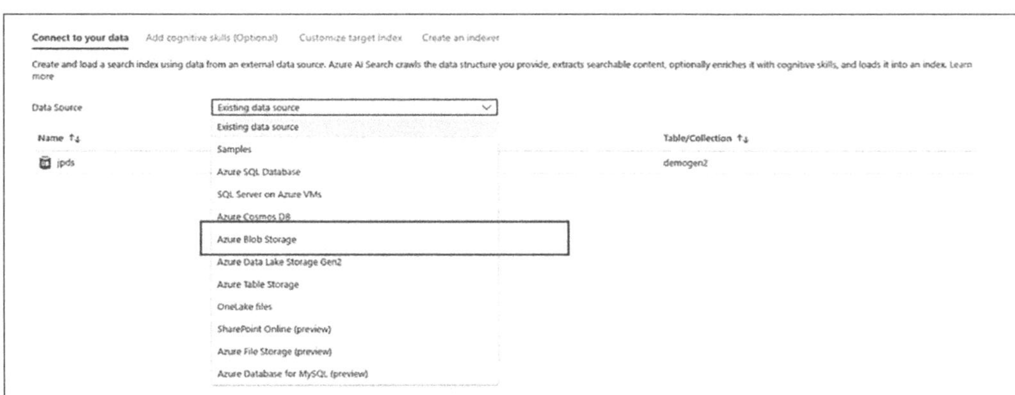

Figure 7.36: *Azure Portal (Azure AI Search Services; Import Data)*

Since we have already created the blob storage and stored the file, we will select Azure Blob storage from the list shown in *Figure* 7.36. This will take you to the list of storage accounts, as shown in *Figure* 7.37.

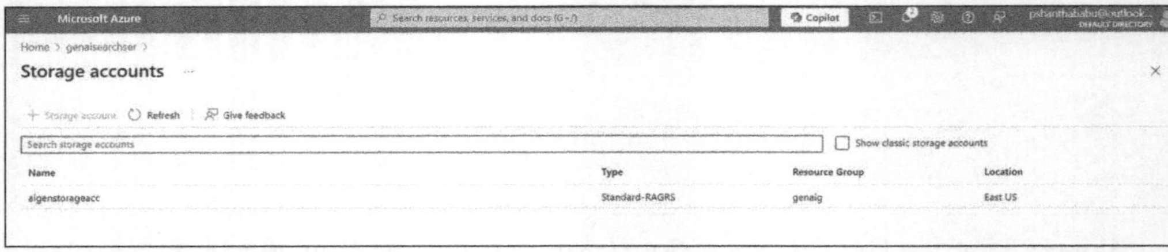

Figure 7.37: Azure Portal (*Azure AI Search Services; Storage Account Selection*)

Step 7: We must select the highlighted storage, as shown in *Figure* 7.37. The application will then take us to the following screen, as shown in *Figure* 7.38. Select the container **`demogen2`**.

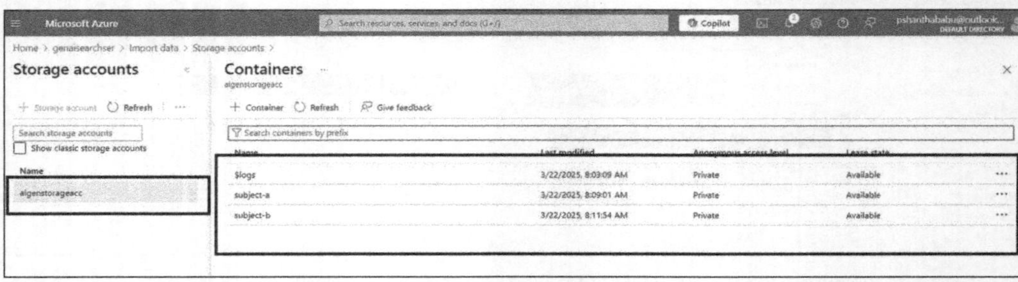

Figure 7.38: Azure Portal (*Azure AI Search Services; Storage Account-Container Selection*)

Step 8: Once we select the container, the application will take you to the following screen; we must configure the following:

a. **Data Source**: Completed in the earlier steps.

b. **Data Source Name**: Enter a valid name (it should be lowercase with no special characters).

c. **Pricing Mode**: Default

d. **Subscription**: Select your subscription.

e. **Connection String and Container Name**: Selected from the blob storage and container in the earlier steps.

Follow the appropriate configurations and click on the "**`Next`**" button, as shown in *Figure* 7.39.

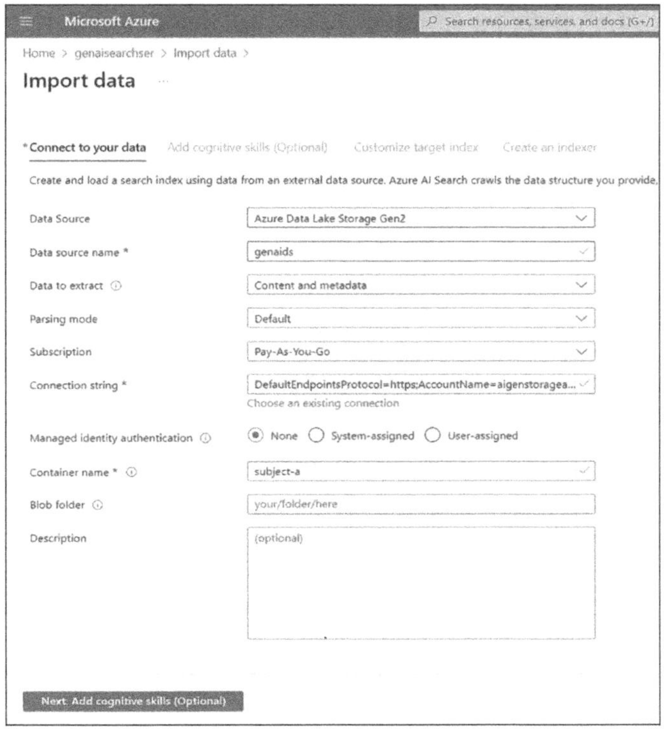

Figure 7.39: *Azure Portal (Azure AI Search Services; Configuration)*

Step 9: We have to provide the index name and other required configurations, as shown in *Figure* 7.40, followed by clicking on "**`Create an Indexer`**."

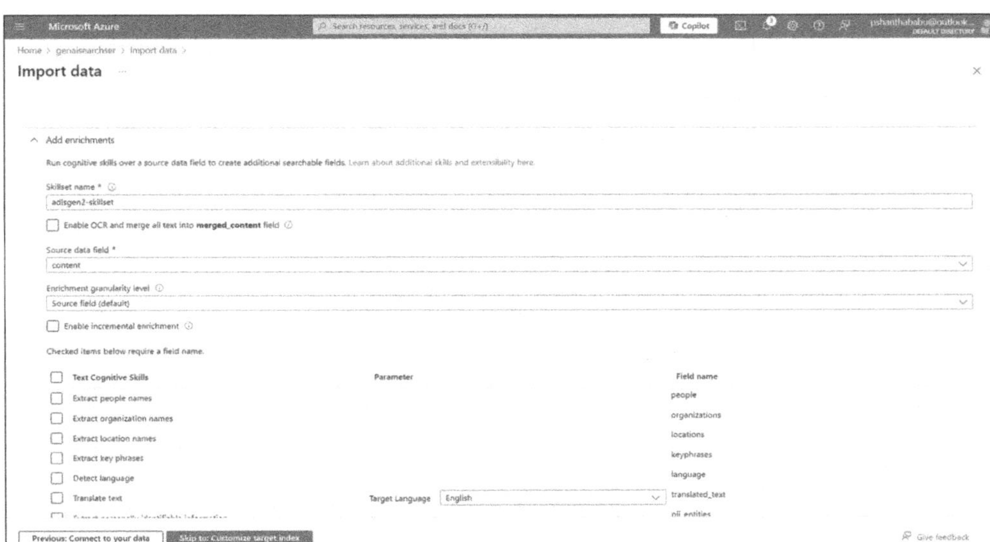

Figure 7.40: *Azure Portal (Azure AI Search Services; Configuration)*

Step 10: We have to provide the **`Indexer Name`** and **`Schedule`** for reindexing purposes (**`Once`**, **`Hourly`**, **`Daily`**, and **`Custom`**) and other required configurations, as shown in *Figure* 7.41, followed by clicking on "**`Create an Index`**."

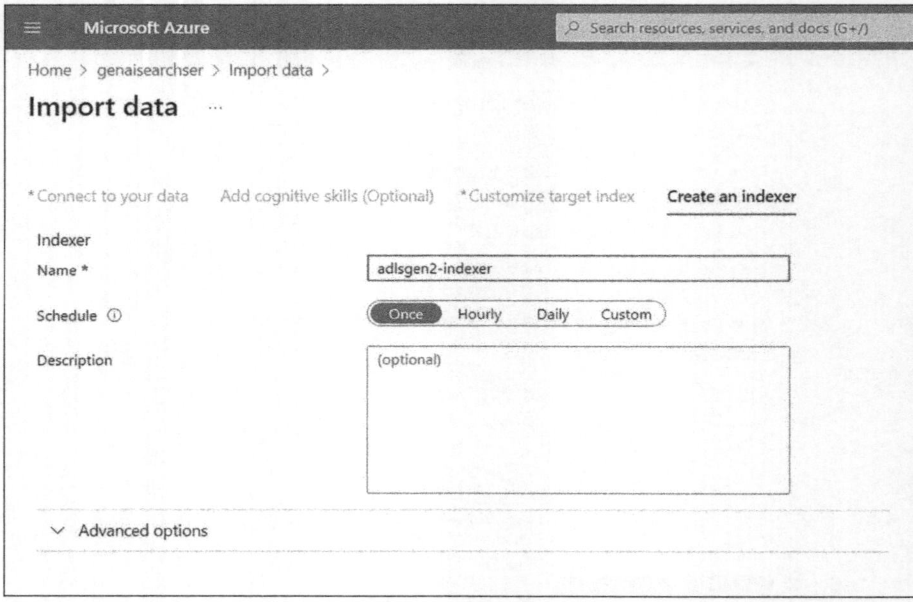

Figure 7.41: *Azure Portal (Azure AI Search Services; Configuration)*

After successfully creating the index, the application takes you back to the Azure AI Search screen, as shown in *Figure* 7.42. We can observe the number of documents indexed for us to search using Azure AI Search. (For demo purposes, we uploaded one document, and that index was successful for us.)

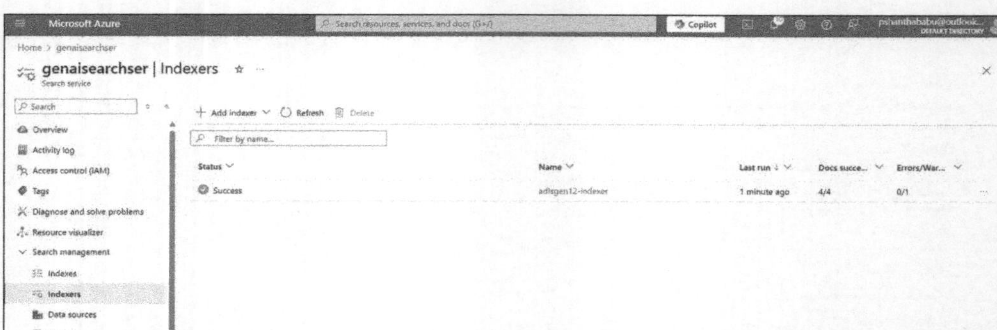

Figure 7.42: *Azure Portal (Azure AI Search Services; Indexer Page)*

Figure 7.43 shows the Index page, the number of documents, and storage size.

Figure 7.43: Azure Portal (*Azure AI Search Services; Index Page*)

Let us search for text in the indexed document in Azure AI Search Services; double-clicking on the index will take you to the following screen, as shown in *Figure* 7.44. Here, we search for "**`Hang time`**" in the document and results in the results window.

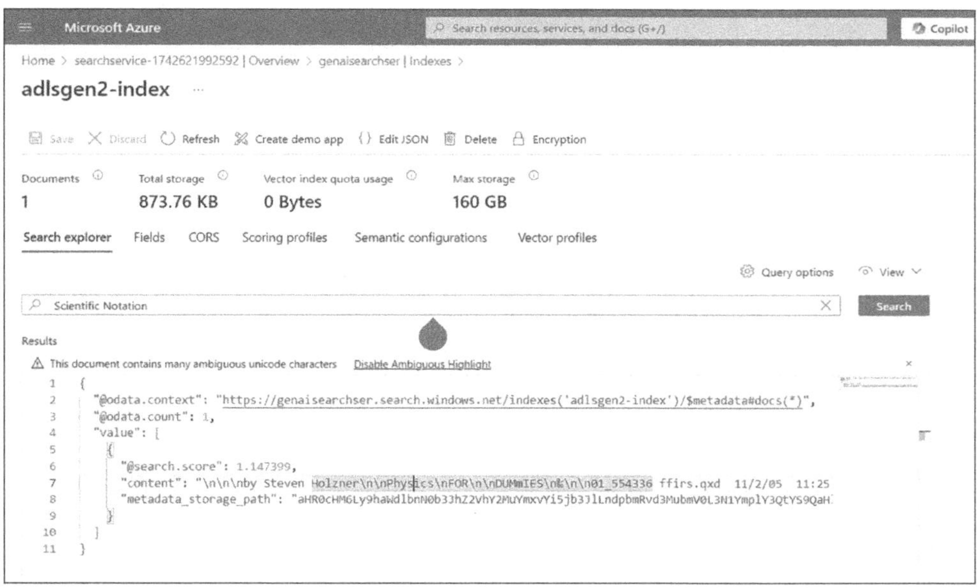

Figure 7.44: Azure Portal (*Azure AI Search Services; Index Page*)

The Azure AI Search Services configuration has been completed.

Azure OpenAI Studio: Add Your Data and Configuration

Step 1: Return to Azure OpenAI Studio and create "Add your data using Azure AI Search service." Click on "**`Add your data`**." This is highlighted in *Figure* 7.45:

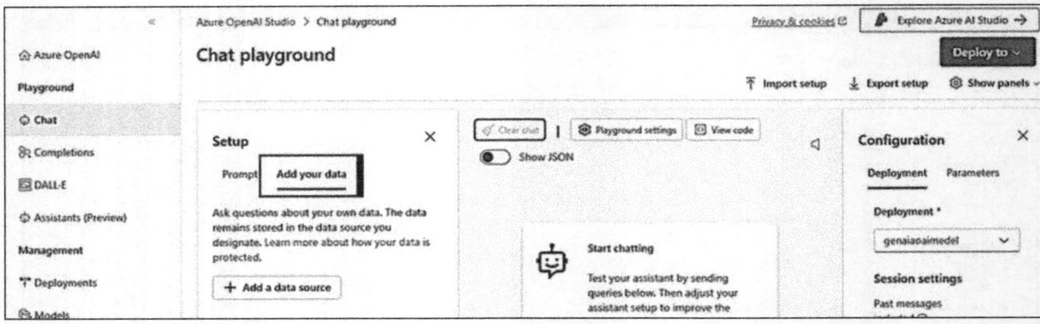

Figure 7.45: *Azure Portal (Azure OpenAI Studio)*

Step 2: Once you click "**`Add your data`**," the application will pop up the following, as shown in *Figure* 7.46, where we have to select the data source from the list. You should choose **`AI Azure Search`**.

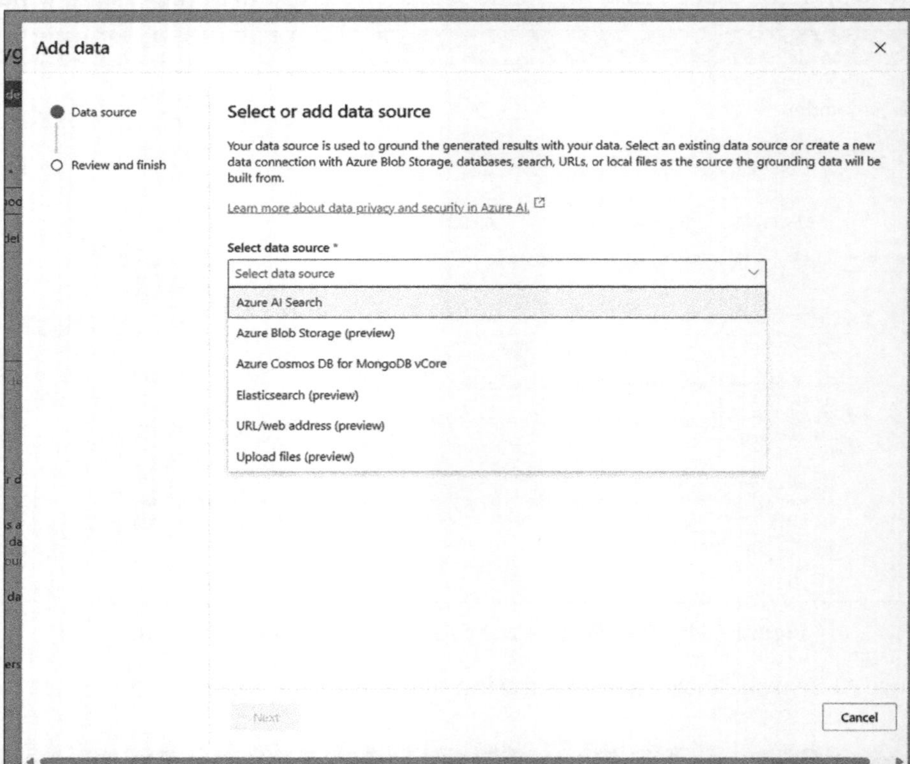

Figure 7.46: *Azure Portal (Azure OpenAI Studio; Select Data Source)*

Step 3: Once you select the data source, we have to configure the following:

- Subscription
- Azure AI Services and Index: We created the earlier steps.

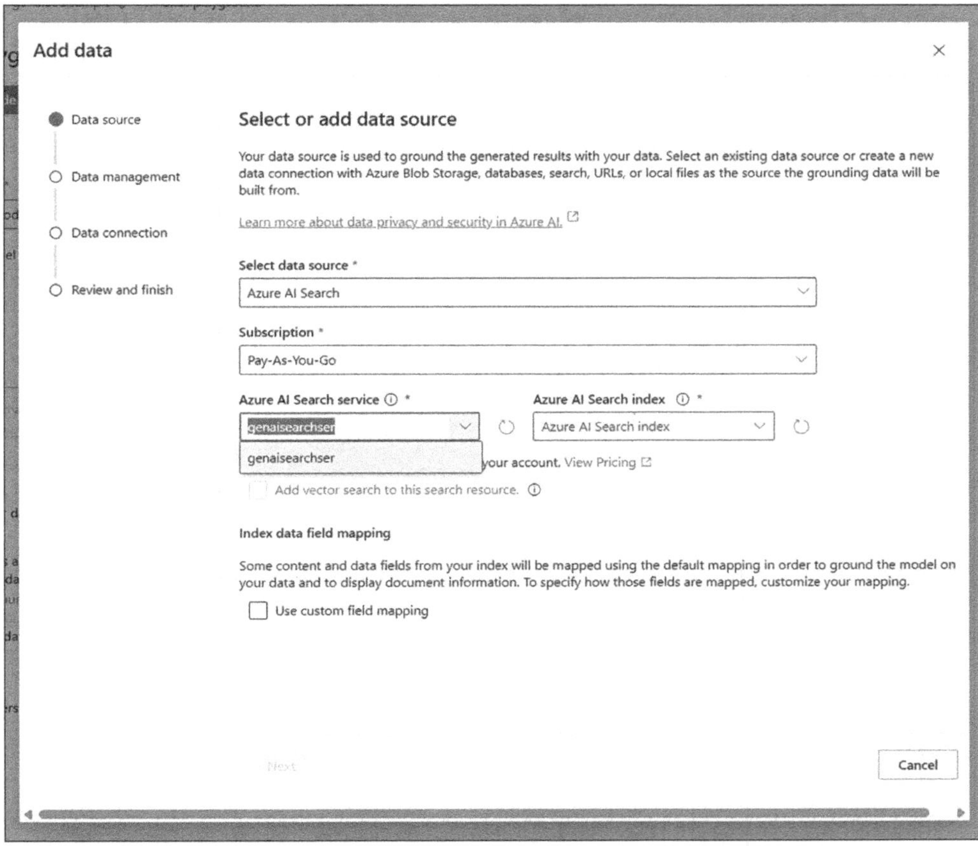

Figure 7.47: *Azure Portal (Azure OpenAI Studio; AI Search Service Selection)*

Step 4: Once you select Azure AI Search, you will see the relevant index in the index list, as shown in *Figure* 7.48.

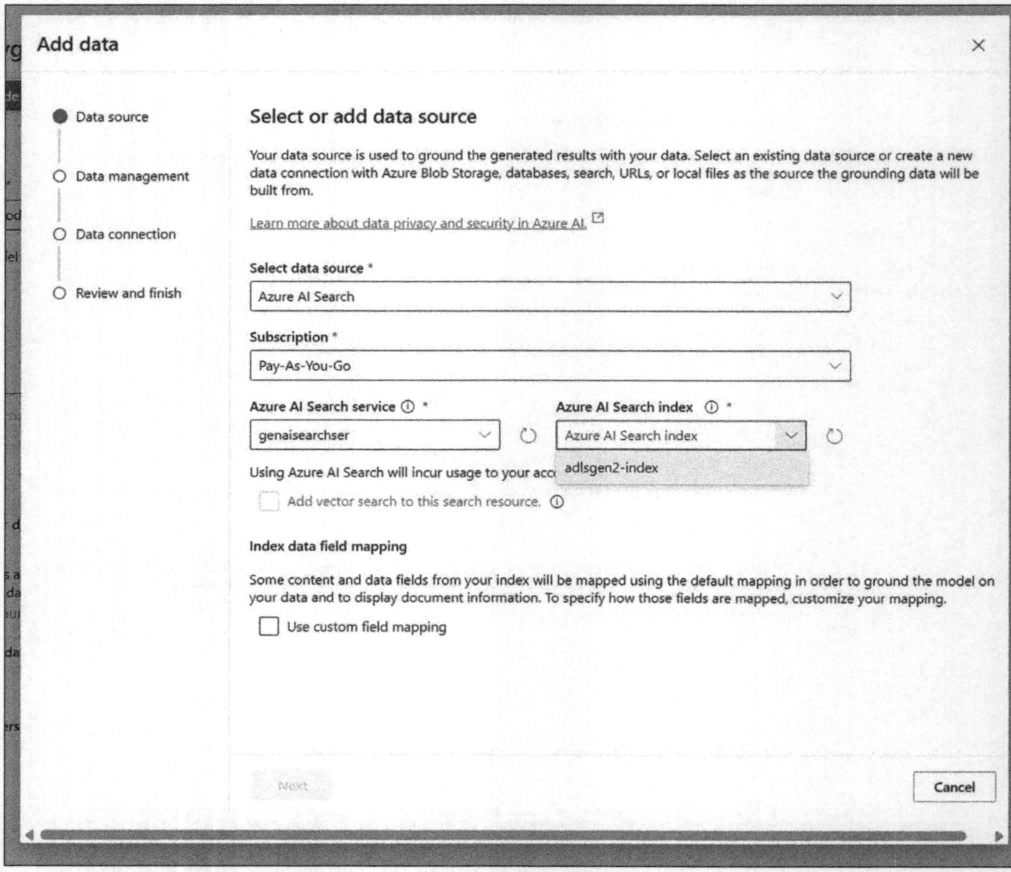

Figure 7.48: *Azure Portal (Azure OpenAI Studio; AI Search Service Index Selection)*

Step 5: Once Azure AI Search Services and Indexes are selected, click the "**Next**" button.

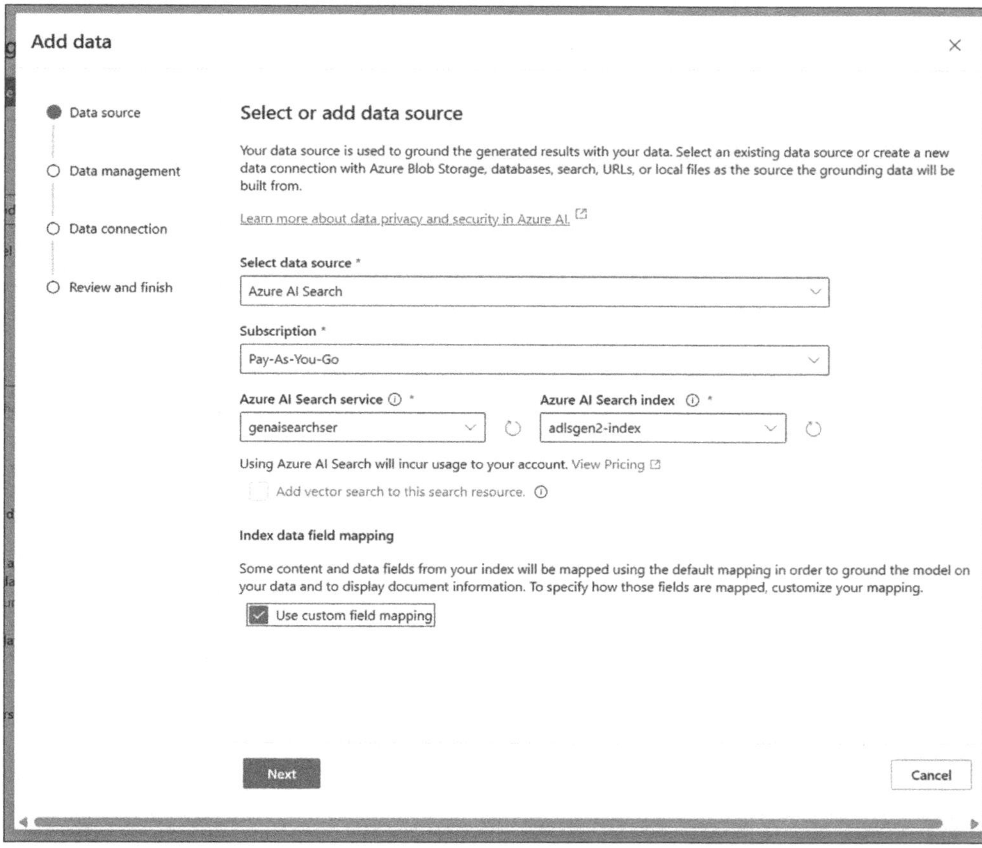

Figure 7.49: *Azure Portal (Azure OpenAI Studio; AI Search Service and Index)*

Step 6: Configure the index data field mapping based on your requirement, as shown in *Figure* 7.50. Following this mapping, click the "**`Next`**" button, as shown in *Figure* 7.50.

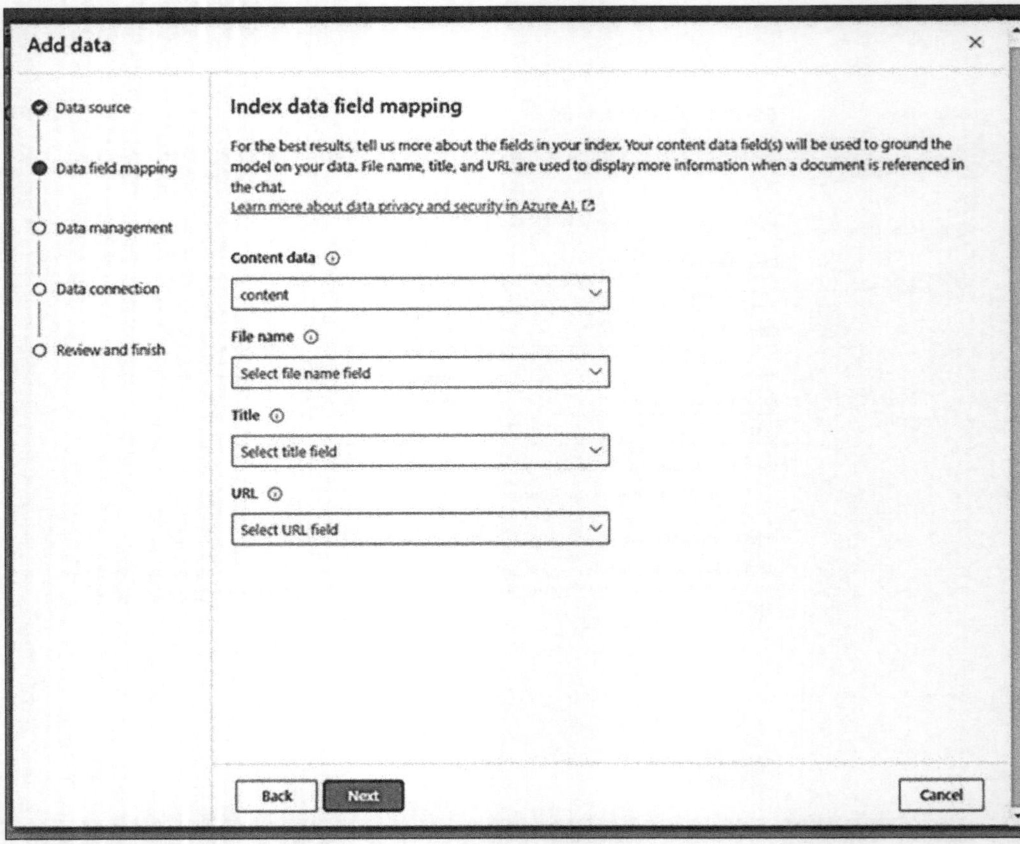

Figure 7.50: *Azure Portal (Azure OpenAI Studio; Index Data Field Mapping)*

Step 7: Configure the data management based on your requirements, as shown in *Figure* 7.51, and follow it by clicking on the "**`Next`**" button.

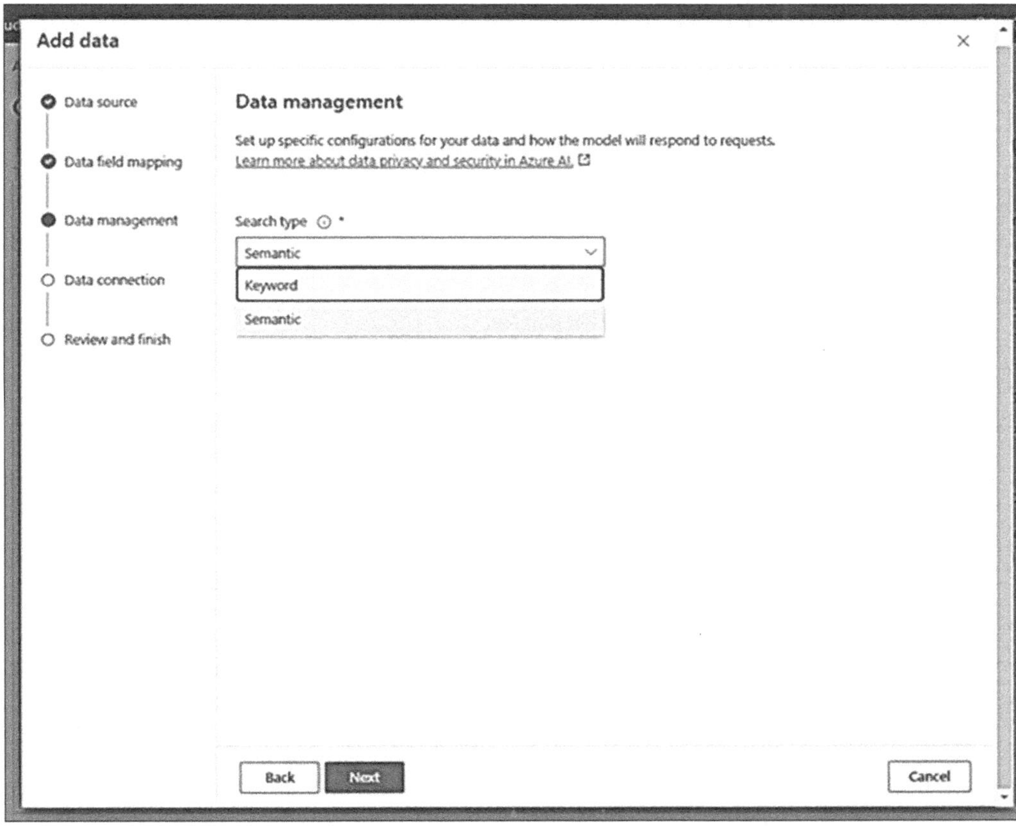

Figure 7.51: *Azure Portal (Azure OpenAI Studio; Data Management)*

Step 8: Configure the data connection based on your requirements, as shown in *Figure* 7.52, and follow it by clicking on the "**`Next`**" button.

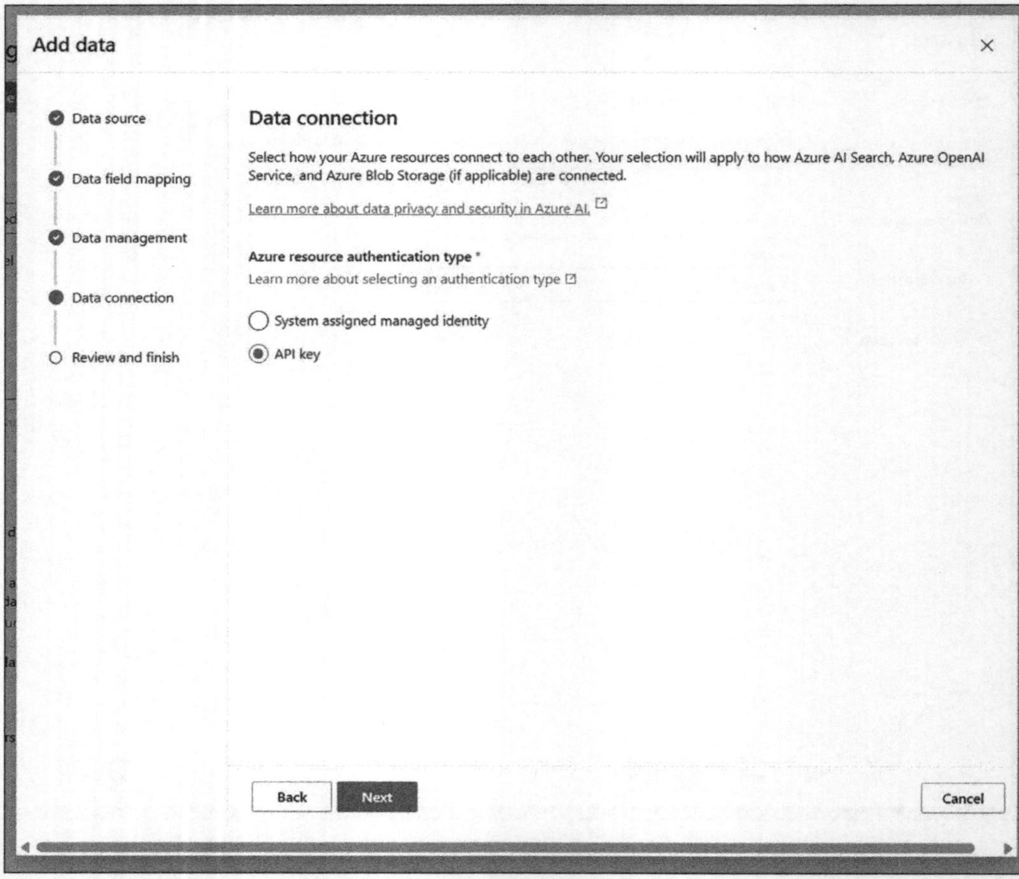

Figure 7.52: *Azure Portal (Azure OpenAI Studio; Data Connection)*

Step 9: Review and Finish. Verify that your requirements are configured appropriately, as shown in *Figure* 7.53, and follow it by clicking on the "**`Save and Close`**" button.

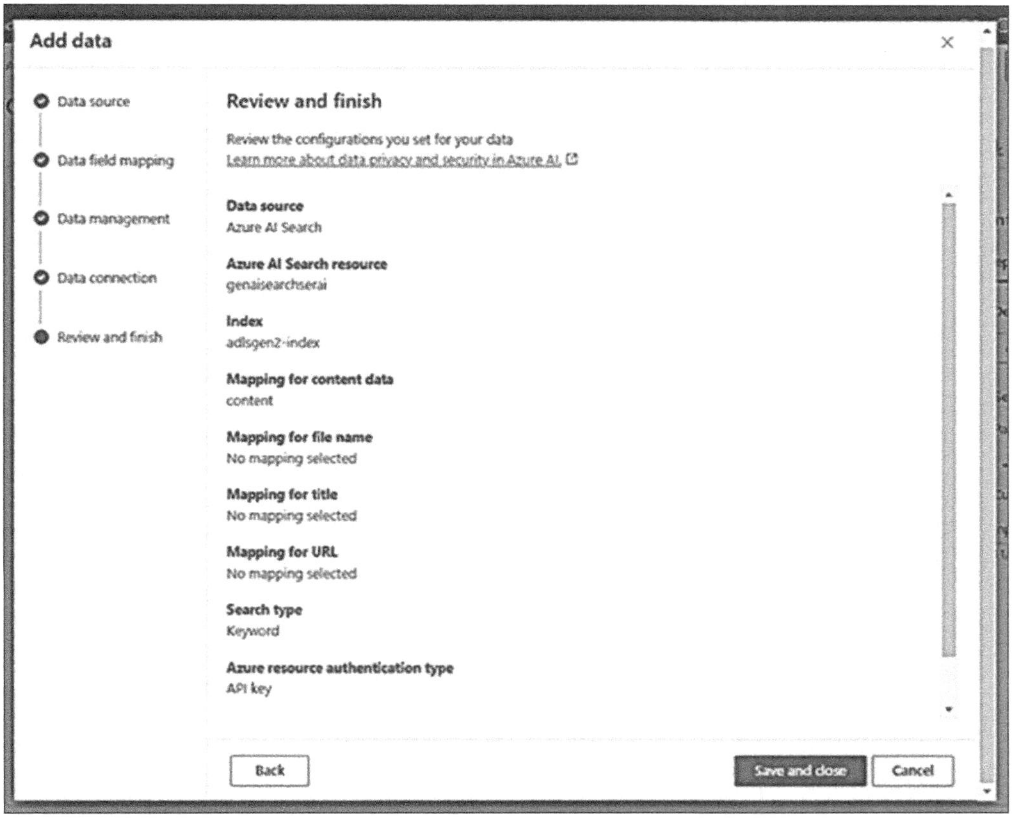

Figure 7.53: *Azure Portal (Azure OpenAI Studio; Review and Finish)*

Now, **`Chat playground`** is ready to play with added data residing in the Azure Storage Service and indexed in the Azure AI Search Service.

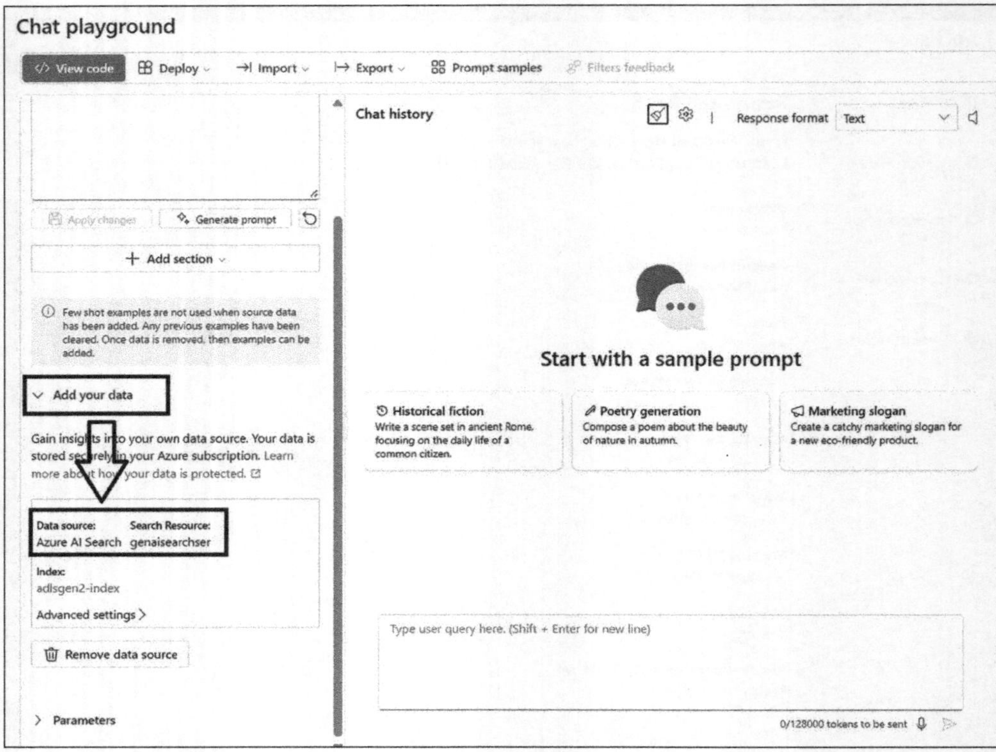

Figure 7.54: *Azure Portal (Azure OpenAI Studio; Chat Playground)*

The following document is stored in Azure Storage Services and indexed in Azure AI Search Services.

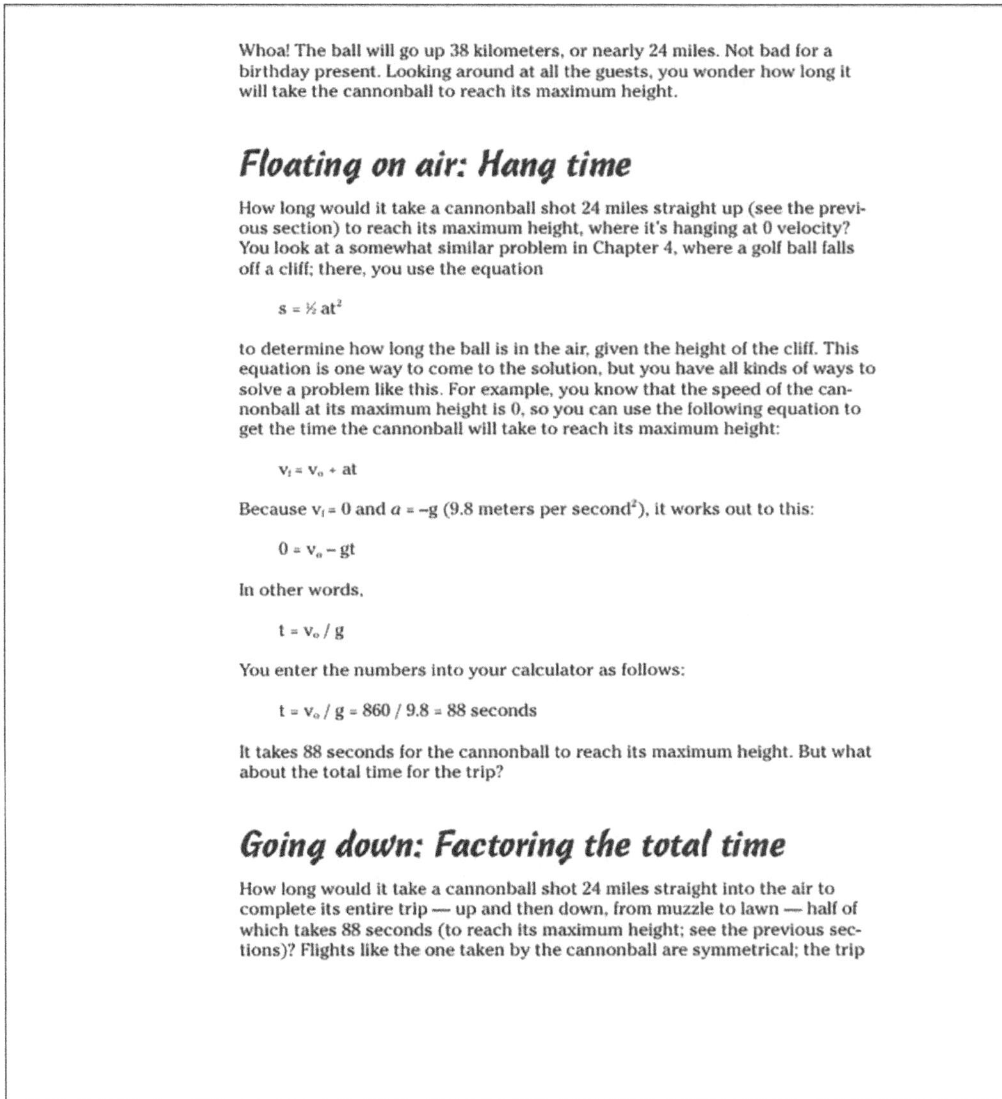

Whoa! The ball will go up 38 kilometers, or nearly 24 miles. Not bad for a birthday present. Looking around at all the guests, you wonder how long it will take the cannonball to reach its maximum height.

Floating on air: Hang time

How long would it take a cannonball shot 24 miles straight up (see the previous section) to reach its maximum height, where it's hanging at 0 velocity? You look at a somewhat similar problem in Chapter 4, where a golf ball falls off a cliff; there, you use the equation

$$s = \frac{1}{2} at^2$$

to determine how long the ball is in the air, given the height of the cliff. This equation is one way to come to the solution, but you have all kinds of ways to solve a problem like this. For example, you know that the speed of the cannonball at its maximum height is 0, so you can use the following equation to get the time the cannonball will take to reach its maximum height:

$$v_f = v_o + at$$

Because $v_f = 0$ and $a = -g$ (9.8 meters per second^2), it works out to this:

$$0 = v_o - gt$$

In other words,

$$t = v_o / g$$

You enter the numbers into your calculator as follows:

$$t = v_o / g = 860 / 9.8 = 88 \text{ seconds}$$

It takes 88 seconds for the cannonball to reach its maximum height. But what about the total time for the trip?

Going down: Factoring the total time

How long would it take a cannonball shot 24 miles straight into the air to complete its entire trip — up and then down, from muzzle to lawn — half of which takes 88 seconds (to reach its maximum height; see the previous sections)? Flights like the one taken by the cannonball are symmetrical; the trip

Figure 7.55: *Sample Document*

Now, we can discuss the question with a chatbot through the window: "`What is Hang time`?" We observed the chatbot's response along with the citations highlighted in *Figure 7.56*.

You can try multiple questions and get the answers and respective citations.

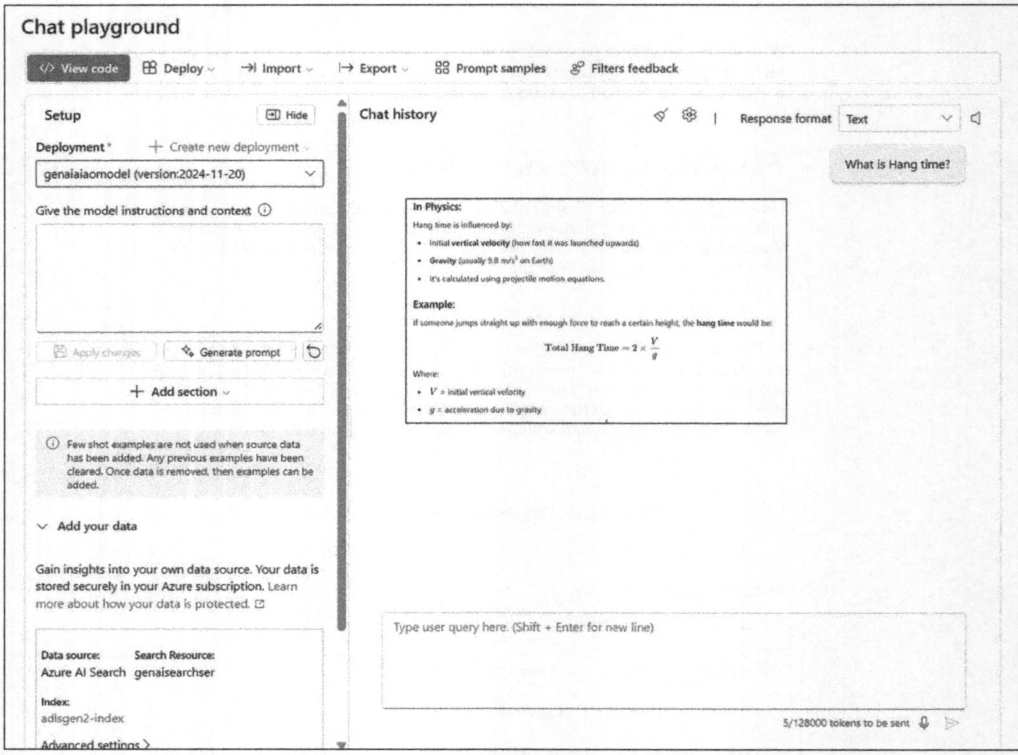

Figure 7.56: *Azure OpenAI Studio; Chat Playground*

Deployment: Chatbot

We can deploy the chatbot as Webapp or Copilot.

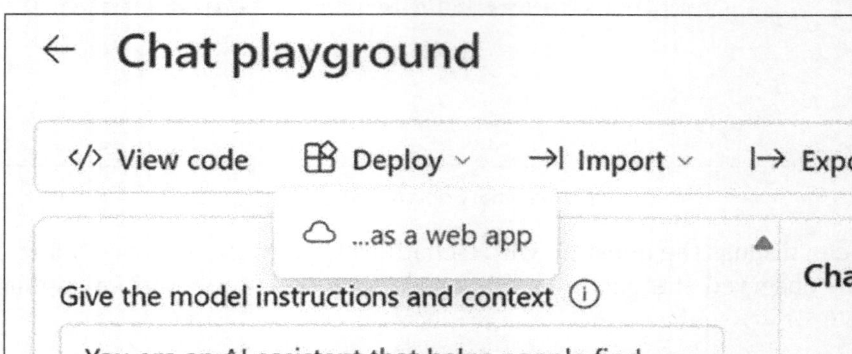

Figure 7.57: *Azure OpenAI Studio (Chat Playground; Deployment Options)*

Step 1: Once you click on the web app option in the "`Deploy to`" the menu at the top, the application will pop up in the window, as shown in *Figure* 7.58.

We need to configure the following items:

- **Name**: Enter a valid name (it should be lowercase with no special characters).
- **Subscription**: Select your subscription.
- **Resource Group**: Select the appropriate resource group.
- **Location**: Desired location.
- **Price Plan**: Desired price plan.

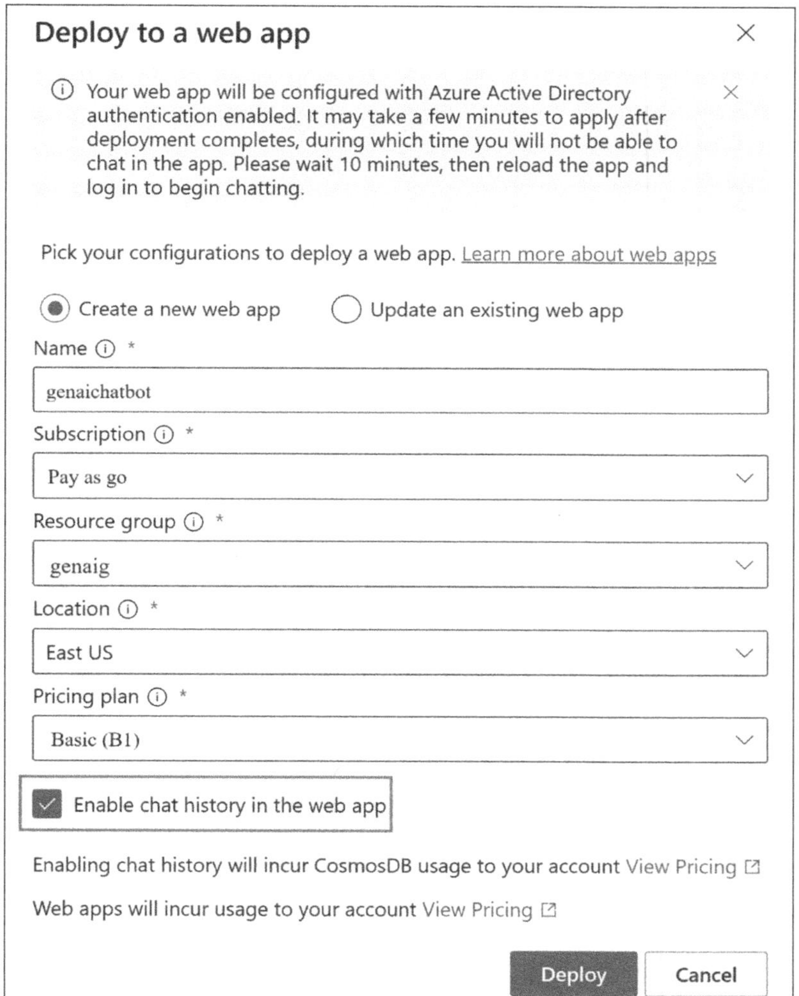

Figure 7.58: *Azure OpenAI Studio (Chat Playground; Deployment; Web App)*

Step 2: Once all configurations are completed, click the "**`Deploy`**" button.

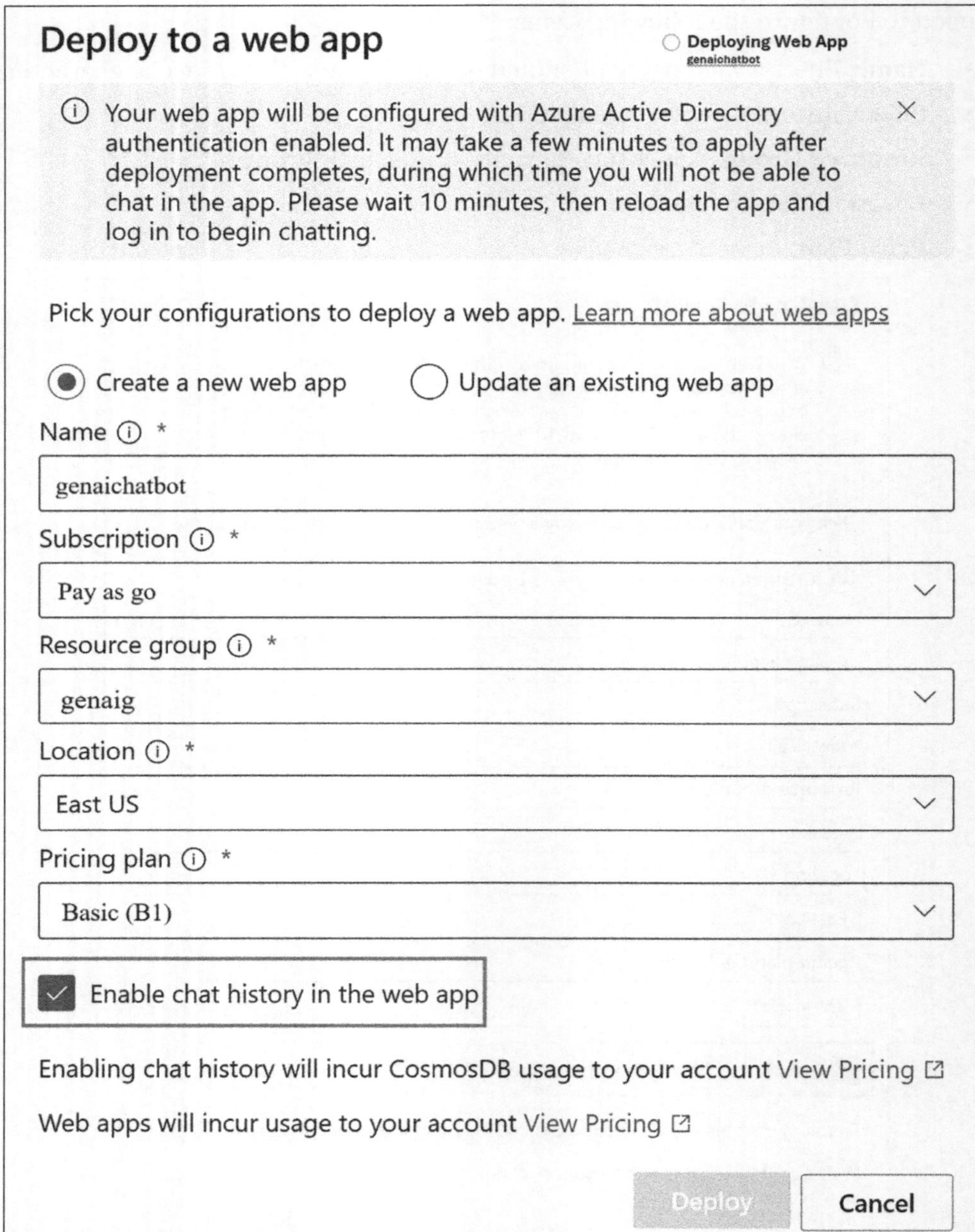

Figure 7.59: *Azure OpenAI Studio (Chat Playground; Web App Deployment in Progress)*

Step 3: Once the deployment is completed successfully, the web app can be found in the resource list, as shown in *Figure* 7.60, and the highlighted app service.

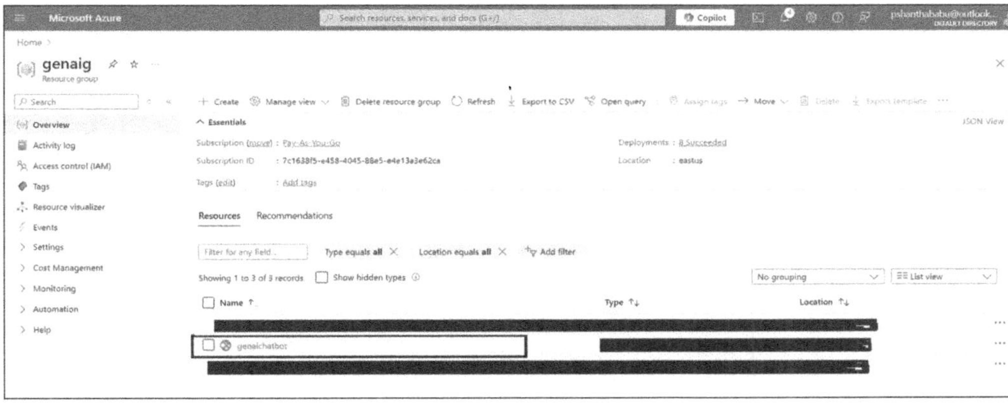

Figure 7.60: *Azure Web App*

Step 4: Double-click on your web app from the resource list. The application will take you to the screen shown in *Figure* 7.61. You can find the highlighted URL (default domain) by clicking, copying, and pasting it into the browser.

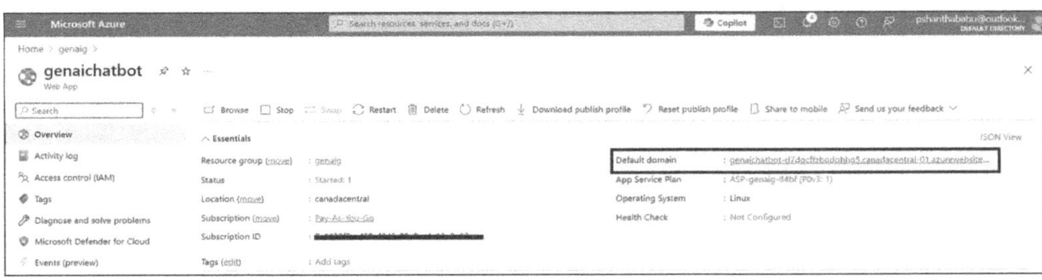

Figure 7.61: *Azure Web App Properties (URL)*

Step 5: Once you click on the highlighted URL (default domain) in *Figure* 7.61, your web application will launch, as shown in *Figure* 7.62 (we can open it through the browser also).

Figure 7.62: *Azure WebApp; Ready to Use*

Now, we can discuss the question with a chatbot through the window: "`Explain Centripetal Force`?" We observed the chatbot's response and the citations highlighted in *Figure* 7.63. You can try multiple questions and get the answers with respective citations. Click on the citation link to get the details on the right side of the window.

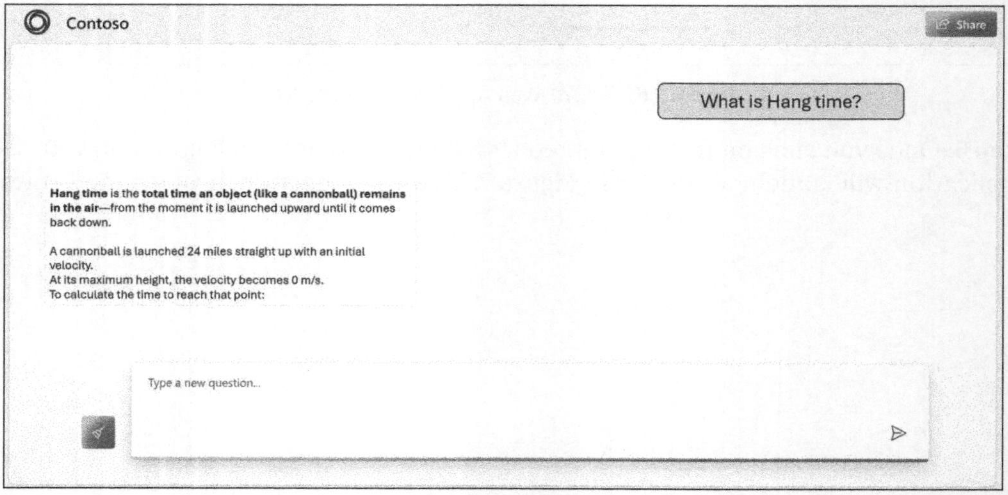

Figure 7.63: *Azure WebApp; Exploring the Data*

The following document is stored in Azure Storage Services and indexed in Azure AI Search Services. We can compare *Figure* 7.64 and *Figure* 7.65.

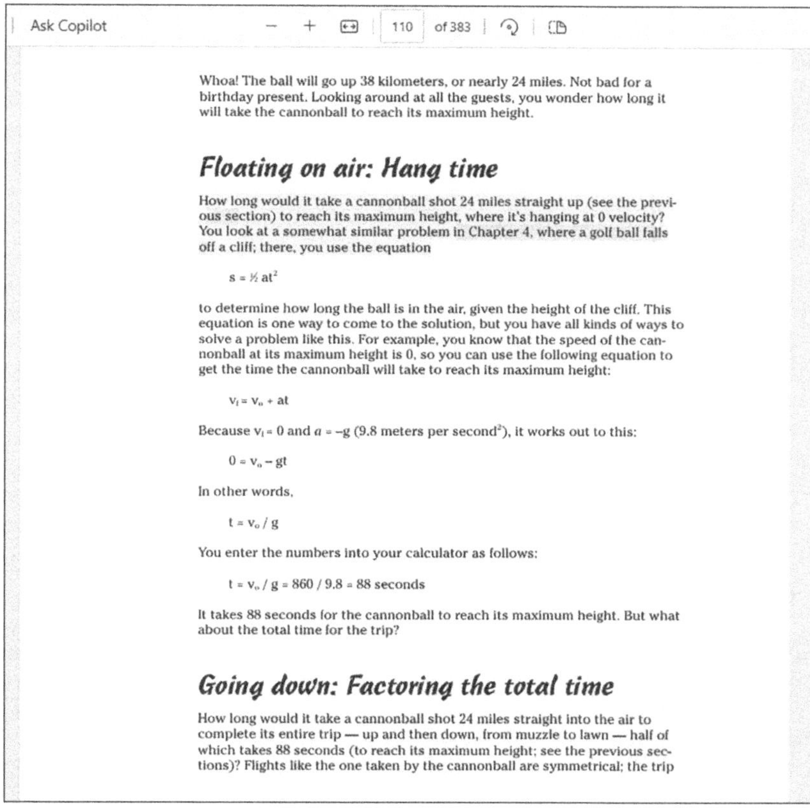

Whoa! The ball will go up 38 kilometers, or nearly 24 miles. Not bad for a birthday present. Looking around at all the guests, you wonder how long it will take the cannonball to reach its maximum height.

Floating on air: Hang time

How long would it take a cannonball shot 24 miles straight up (see the previous section) to reach its maximum height, where it's hanging at 0 velocity? You look at a somewhat similar problem in Chapter 4, where a golf ball falls off a cliff; there, you use the equation

$$s = ½ at^2$$

to determine how long the ball is in the air, given the height of the cliff. This equation is one way to come to the solution, but you have all kinds of ways to solve a problem like this. For example, you know that the speed of the cannonball at its maximum height is 0, so you can use the following equation to get the time the cannonball will take to reach its maximum height:

$$v_f = v_o + at$$

Because $v_f = 0$ and $a = -g$ (9.8 meters per second^2), it works out to this:

$$0 = v_o - gt$$

In other words,

$$t = v_o / g$$

You enter the numbers into your calculator as follows:

$$t = v_o / g = 860 / 9.8 = 88 \text{ seconds}$$

It takes 88 seconds for the cannonball to reach its maximum height. But what about the total time for the trip?

Going down: Factoring the total time

How long would it take a cannonball shot 24 miles straight into the air to complete its entire trip — up and then down, from muzzle to lawn — half of which takes 88 seconds (to reach its maximum height; see the previous sections)? Flights like the one taken by the cannonball are symmetrical; the trip

Figure 7.64: *Sample Data*

Step 6: Now, we can deploy the chatbot as Copilot, "**`A new copilot in Copilot Studio`**" submenu, as shown in *Figure 7.65*:

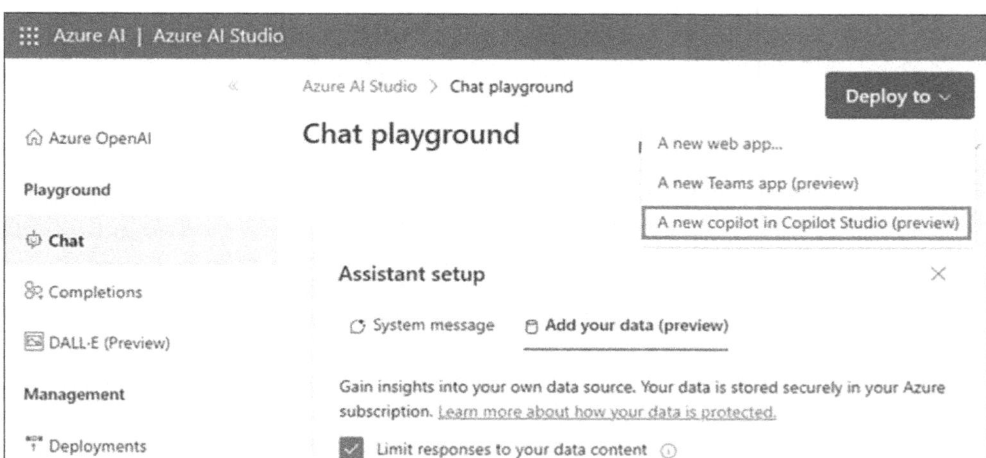

Figure 7.65: *Azure OpenAI Studio; Deploying into Copilot*

Step 7: Once you click on the "**`A new copilot in Copilot Studio`**" submenu, as shown in *Figure* 7.65, the application will pop up on the screen, as shown in *Figure* 7.66:

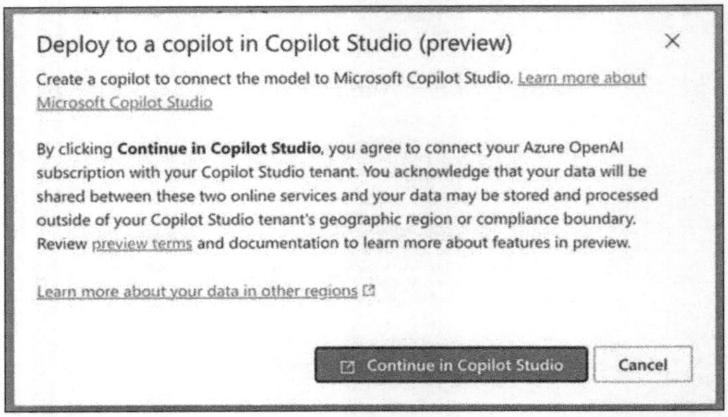

Figure 7.66: *Azure OpenAI Studio; Deploying into Copilot Studio*

Step 8: Once we click on the "**`Continue in Copilot Studio`**," the application will take us to the **`Copilot Studio`**, as shown in *Figure* 7.67:

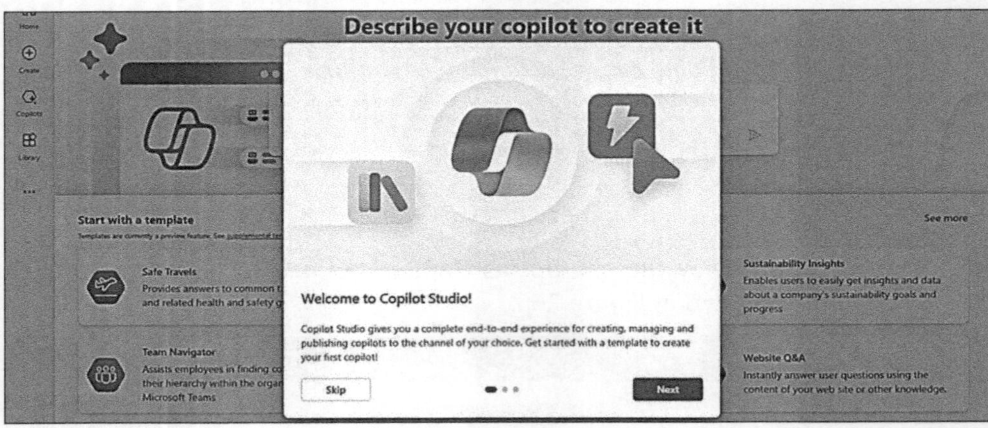

Figure 7.67: *Deploying into Copilot Studio*

Your Copilot is ready. We can connect this with MS Teams and will discuss it more in the upcoming chapters.

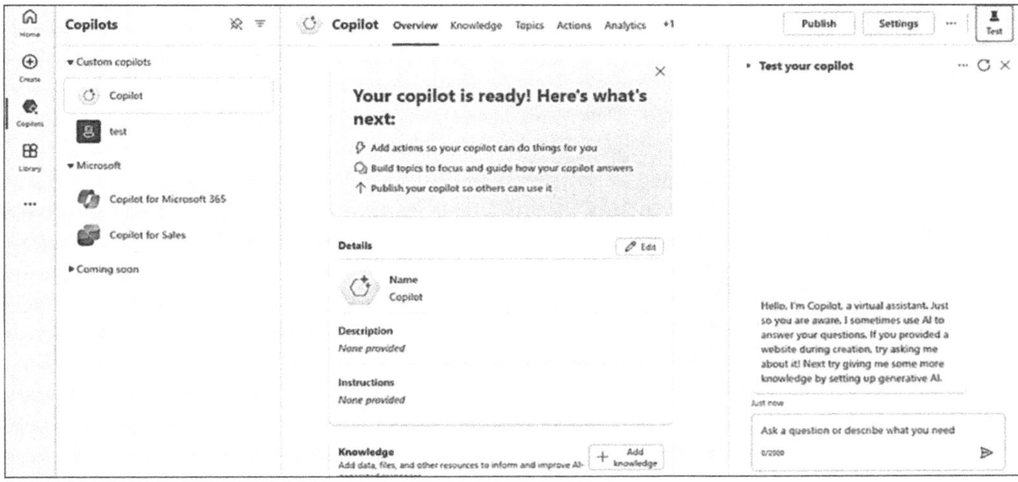

Figure 7.68: *Copilot Studio; Chatbot is Ready*

Playground: Completions

Step 1: We can create the new model as we created earlier. Click on "`Create a new deployment`."

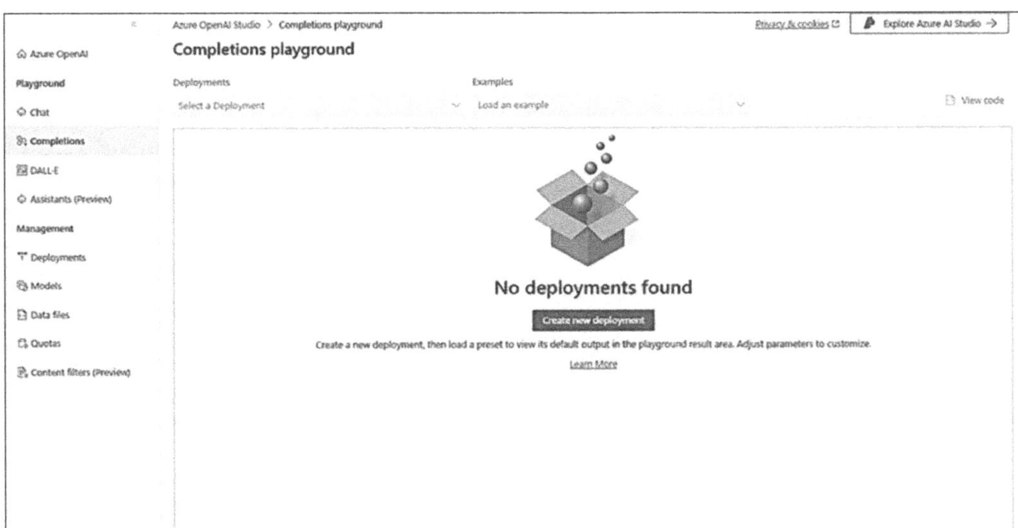

Figure 7.69: *Playground; Completions*

Step 2: Once we click "`Create new deployment`," the application will take you to the following configuration screen; we have to configure the following items:

a. **Model**: Select your required model.

b. **Deployment Type**: Your desired type (Standard).

c. **Deployment Name**: Enter a valid storage name (it should be lowercase, and no special characters are allowed).

d. Token per minute rate limit.

Once all the aforementioned configurations are completed, click the "`Create`" button.

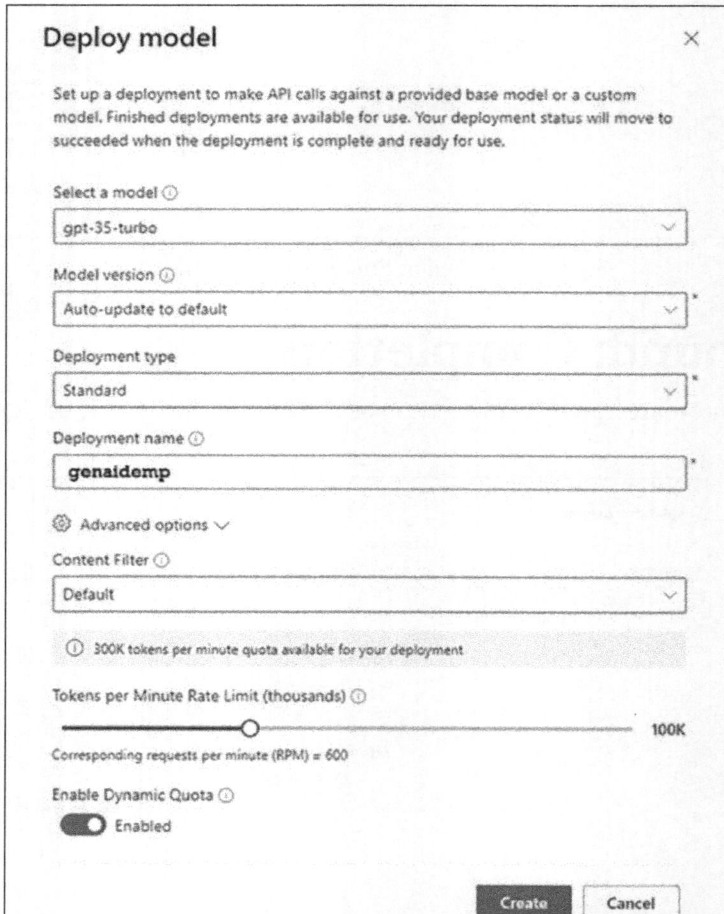

Figure 7.70: *Playground; Completions*

Step 3: Once the completions component is created, the application will take you to the screen shown in *Figure 7.71*:

Figure 7.71: *Playground; Completions*

Understanding the Environment

On the right-side menu, we have vital parameters to configure your completions effectively; let us discuss:

- **Temperature**: It ranges from 0 to 1 and dramatically controls the results' randomness. A lower temperature value will get more deterministic in its responses as output. So, the optimized value will generate reasonable answers.
- **Max Length:** Ranges from 0–2048; based on the range, the lengths of the model's response will generate.
- **Stop Sequences:** These help make responses stop at a desired point, such as the end of a sentence or list.
- **Top Probabilities**: It ranges from 0 to 1 and dramatically controls the tokens of the model. Setting this to 0.9 will be considered the top 90% of all possible tokens and will factor them in when generating a response for the input from the completions.
- **Frequency Penalty:** This ranges from 0 to 1 and dramatically controls the repetition of the same tokens in the generated response by the completions. The penalty is indirectly proportional to probabilities. So, the higher the penalty, the lower the probability.
- **Presence Penalty:** It ranges from 0–2, and it helps reduce the chance of repeating any token that appears in the output text. It also increases the likelihood of introducing new topics in response to the input text.
- **Pre-Response Text:** Insert text after the user's input and before the model's response. This can help prepare the model for a response.

- **Post-Response Text:** Insert text after the model's generated response to encourage further user input, as when modeling a conversation.

By default, we have many examples of the completions we can select and demonstrate.

Select "`Generate an email`," and you will get the text shown in *Figure* 7.72.

***Figure* 7.72:** *Playground; Completions (Experimental)*

Once you click on the "`Generate`" button, you will get the auto-generated solution, as shown in *Figure* 7.73:

***Figure* 7.73:** *Playground (Completions; Experimental Output)*

DALL-E Playground

DALL-E Playground is an interactive application in the Azure OpenAI Studio that allows users to create creative images from textual descriptions as a prompt using DALL-E; it provides a user-friendly interface for generating, editing, and experimenting with AI-generated images creatively. The setting is fundamental and straightforward.

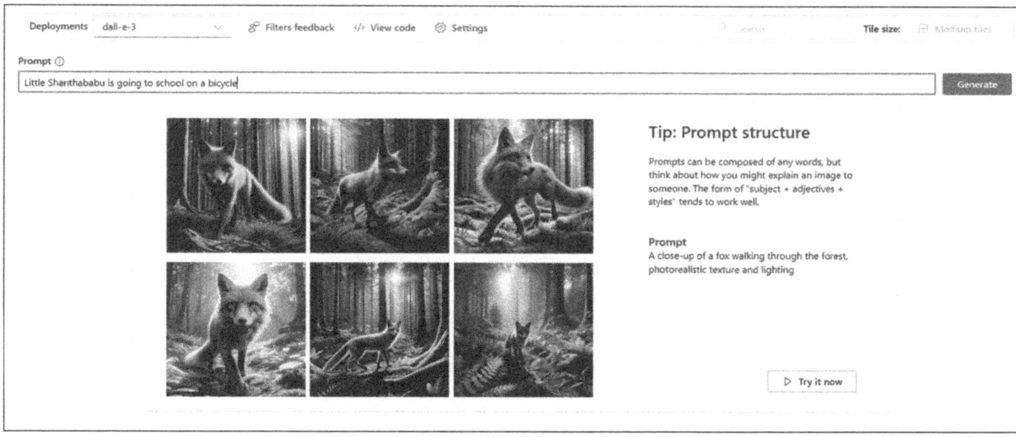

Figure 7.74: *DALL-E Playground Environment*

In the prompt text, you can see the outcome as shown in *Figure* 7.75 and *Figure* 7.76.

- Little boy and girl going to school and eating chocolates.
- Little Shanthababu going to school on a bicycle.

Sample 1 Output:

Figure 7.75: *DALL-E Playground (Experimental Sample Output-1)*

Sample 2 Output:

Figure 7.76: *DALL-E Playground (Experimental Sample Output-2)*

Assistants Playground (Preview)

This component is still in the preview status in the playground. The platform allows users to interact with AI assistants, including OpenAI models such as ChatGPT. It enables users to explore different capabilities, test interactions, and experiment with AI in a controlled environment. We have done many exercises in *Chapter 4*, *Prompt Engineering and Its Significance.*

Step 1: Click the "`Create new deployment`" button, as shown in *Figure 7.77*.

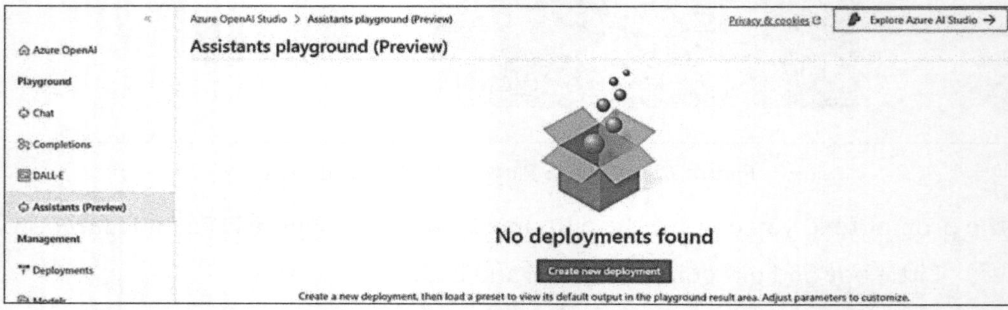

***Figure** 7.77: Assistants Playground (Preview)*

Step 2: Once we click "`Create new deployment`", the application will take you to the succeeding configuration screen; we have to configure the following items:

a. **Model**: Select your required model.

b. **Deployment Type**: Your desired type (Standard).

c. **Deployment Name**: Enter a valid storage name (it should be lowercase, and no special characters are allowed).

d. Token per minute rate limit.

Once all the preceding configurations are completed, click the "`Create`" button.

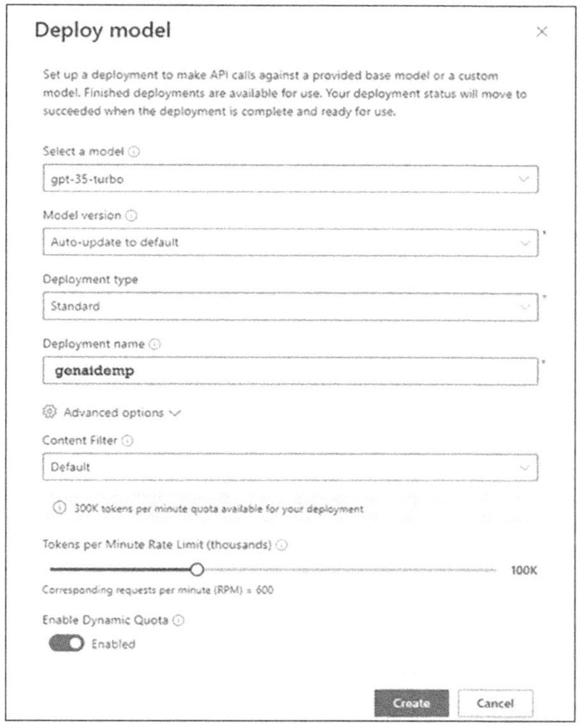

Figure 7.78: *Assistants Playground Configuration*

Figure 7.79 shows the Assistants playground environment for reference.

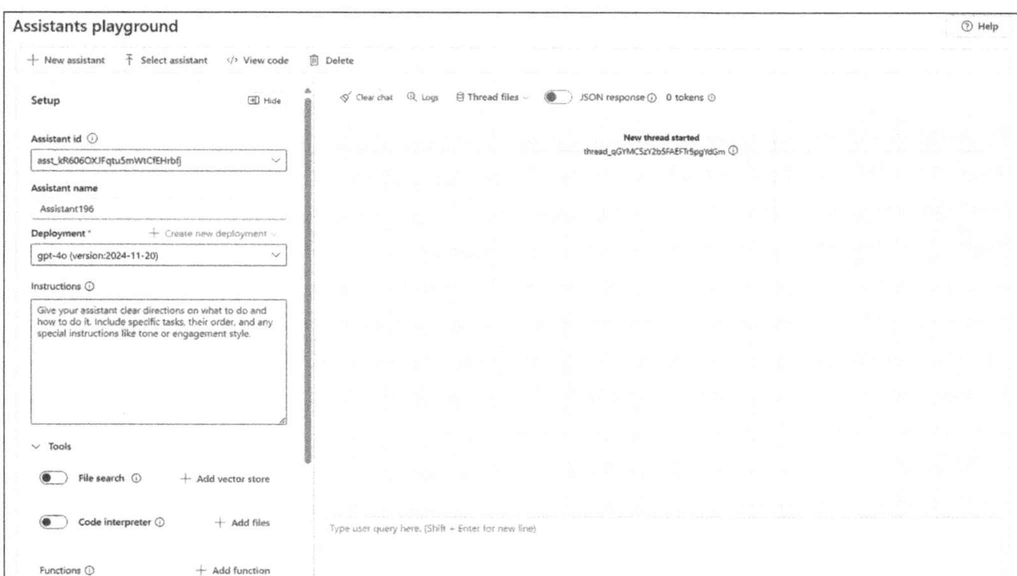

Figure 7.79: *Assistants Playground Environment*

Conclusion

This chapter discussed Azure OpenAI Services and how to precisely connect with the Azure AI Search and Storage Service environment. We explored OpenAI and its capabilities. We also learned about its background and how an artificial intelligence research organization developed in the space of AI.

We understood that OpenAI is an organization that focuses on artificial intelligence research, aiming to develop Artificial General Intelligence (AGI) that benefits humanity. It emphasizes creating safe and functional AI products while advancing AI research responsibly.

We discussed the AOAI architecture workflow and demonstrated the following concepts with clear steps and screenshots: Chat Playground, Compilation Playground, Bring Your Own Data, and DALL-E Playground.

The next chapter will provide a way for Azure AI Studio to lead in a new era of Gen AI development and empower developers to explore, build, test, and deploy AI products. We will explore models, capabilities, responsible AI and prompts to see how Azure AI Studio provides the necessary support to build the solution.

CHAPTER 8
Advanced Azure AI Studio-I

Introduction

In the previous chapter, we provided a comprehensive overview of Azure OpenAI Services and their practical utilization, ensuring that you are well-prepared to delve into the Azure OpenAI Studio environment, Playground, Chat, Assistant, and Chat Playground. We created models with endpoints for Azure OpenAI-based solutions, comprehended the OpenAI deployment procedure, and configured prompts, configuration parameters, and data imports/exports. In addition, we explored the LangChain methodology, adjusted models using unique parameters, and dealt with deployment sizes, version control, and content moderation. Lastly, we developed and implemented an AI application that integrated with MS Teams and other components, using both public and private data.

This chapter is a gateway to how Azure AI Studio is leading in a new era of Gen AI development, empowering developers to confidently explore, build, test, and deploy AI products. We will delve into models, capabilities, responsible AI, and prompts to showcase how Azure AI Studio provides the necessary support for building solutions. We will explore a unified platform and how it enables us to build tailor-made AI products, integrate pre-built services and models, and understand how prompt orchestration and evaluation work (prompt flow). We will also discuss content safety and mechanisms and how responsible AI tools can be used for privacy, security, and compliance, providing developers with the tools required to navigate the complexities of Gen AI with confidence and ethical considerations.

Structure

In this chapter, you will delve into the following topics:

- Azure AI Studio Invents a New Era of Gen AI Development
- Core Capabilities of Azure AI Studio for Gen AI

- Azure AI Studio Empowerments
    - Azure AI Studio Architecture
- Azure AI Studio and its Environment
- Understanding Responsible AI Using Azure AI Studio
- Prompt Flow: Architecture and Components
- Building Prompt Workflow
- Azure AI Content Safety

Azure AI Studio Invents a New Era of Gen AI Development

In Microsoft Azure, the Azure AI Studio is a tightly coupled Integrated Development Environment (IDE) that helps us design and streamline AI models' creation, deployment, and management, particularly in Gen AI under the Azure ecosystem. It serves as a hub for developers, data scientists, and enterprises to build, test, and implement Gen AI models with powerful computing and data management capabilities. It transforms customer experiences and automates complex workflows.

Azure AI Studio is revolutionizing the development of Gen AI applications. It enables business opportunities by building more innovative, faster, and efficient solutions for its problem statements and sustaining the business within the market and competitors. Azure provides robust infrastructure, high computation, privacy controls, and seamless LLM integration.

With Azure AI Studio, we can shape the future of AI-driven innovative solutions. The possibilities for Gen AI development with Azure are vast.

With Azure AI Studio, you can leverage pre-built AI services, customize models, and use Azure's cloud infrastructure to effectively upscale AI solutions and maximize their benefits for business problems.

Azure AI Studio is indeed at the forefront of a new era of Gen AI development, providing advanced tools and platforms.

Here is how Azure AI Studio is leading this new era:

Key Features of Azure AI Studio:

- **Azure OpenAI Service:** Azure AI Studio allows perfect integration with OpenAI. It has powerful generative models such as GPT-3.0, 3.5 (turbo), and GPT-4o. It helps businesses leverage advanced Natural Language Processing (NLP) capabilities for text generation, summarization, translation, and other tasks.
- **No-Code/Low-Code Interface**: Microsoft Azure allows businesses to innovate

faster, reduce costs, and improve decision-making with minimal technical support. This environment is for non-technical and technical users. This interface represents a significant advancement in AI toolmaking by providing intuitive and innovative tools using different AI models for various purposes. This opens up new opportunities for organizations to connect with AI's power to solve complex business problems efficiently.

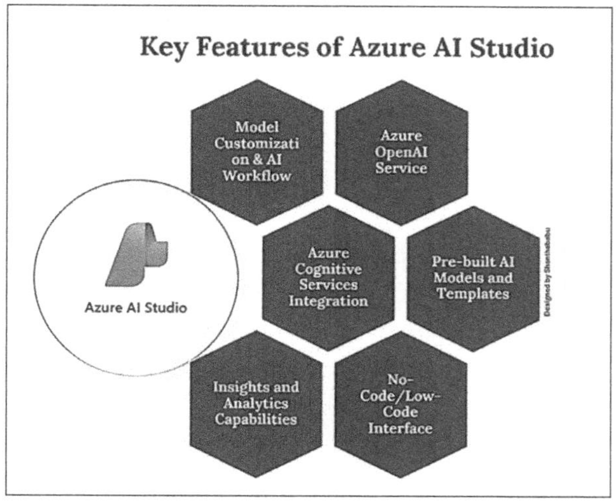

Figure 8.1: *Key Features of Azure AI Studio*

- **Pre-built AI Models and Templates**: Azure AI Studio provides access to a library of pre-built models and templates that allow users to start their AI projects quickly. From text generation to object detection, these templates can accelerate development, saving time and effort.
    - Text Analysis and Generation
    - Image Analysis and Speech Services
    - Predictive Analytics and Anomaly Detection
    - Recommendation Systems
    - Code Generation
- **Azure Cognitive Services Integration**: Azure AI Studio can connect directly with Azure Cognitive Services, which includes powerful AI capabilities such as text analytics, speech recognition, image analysis, and more. These services complement generative AI models, enabling developers to create multi-modal applications. This integration service enhances the development of AI-powered applications that handle complex tasks such as ***vision***, ***speech***, ***language***, and ***decision-making***. This leads to incorporating advanced AI functionalities into solutions and reduces the need for significant coding or model development from scratch.

Critical Areas of Integration are as follows:

- Vision Services
  - Computer Vision
  - Optical Character Recognition (OCR)
- Speech Services
  - Speech-to-Text
  - Text-to-Speech
  - Speech Translation
- Language Services
  - Text Analytics
  - Language Understanding (LUIS)
  - Translator
- Decision Services
  - Personalizer
- Form Recognizer
- **Model Customization and AI Workflow**: It has the capabilities for specific use cases to customize and fine-tune models. AI developers can adapt models to an industry and train them using their own data, adjusting parameters to obtain results for specific needs such as healthcare, banking, finance, or supply chain management. Azure AI Studio supports the entire lifecycle of AI development, from data ingestion, preparation, indexing, model building, training the model, deploying, and monitoring. Workflow, as a whole, simplifies the transition from development to production and integrates Large Language Model Operations (LLMOps); it ensures continuous model monitoring, performance optimization, and deployment automation, which is essential for maintaining generative AI applications at a larger scale.
- **Insights and Analytics Capabilities**: Azure AI Studio offers robust data-driven analysis and insights from your AI models. It provides real-time analytics so businesses can perform model exercises, monitor model performance, extract and understand trends, and make data-driven decisions to optimize AI applications, enhance performance, and get the maximum benefits. Along with enterprise-grade security and data privacy, it also offers compliance with global standards such as GDPR, CCPA, and PII.

Core Capabilities of Azure AI Studio for Gen AI

Azure AI Studio for Gen AI has a massive core set of capabilities. It empowers businesses and AI developers to connect with high-end, cutting-edge AI technologies to design, build, customize, deploy, and maintain a wide range of industry-specific AI-driven solutions.

We explored how Azure AI Studio simplifies the development of complex generative AI-powered applications by integrating with Azure Cognitive Services, AI Workflow, Azure OpenAI Service, No-Code/Low-Code Interface, LLMs, computer vision, and various other AI services. This simplification is a significant relief for developers, as it reduces the burden of dealing with multiple tools and services. Following are the core capabilities of Azure AI Studio in the context of Gen AI:

- **Text Generation**: This is the base for Gen AI's minimum purpose and building applications for creative writing, content creation, or well-formatted customer communication with LLM models. LLMs enable developers to generate human-like text based on user input using models such as OpenAI's GPT. It can be used for various industries' content creation, document drafting, chatbots, email drafting, customer service bots, text summarization, and question-answer systems.
- **Chatbots and Conversational AI**: Azure AI Studio leverages powerful language models, enabling businesses to develop intelligent interaction tools for business development, such as creating sophisticated and context-aware conversational agents that can be developed and deployed across various platforms to enhance the performance of the business and production unit. Following are the core capabilities and features that Azure AI Studio offers for chatbots and conversational AI development:
  - Pre-Built Language Models
  - Natural Language Understanding (NLU)
  - Multilingual Capabilities
  - Sentiment Analysis and Emotion Detection
  - Voice-Enabled Conversational AI
- **Code Generation**: It helps automate code writing for software development, reducing development time spent on repetitive coding tasks and speeding up development cycles. It can generate code using natural language instructions, assist developers with automated code snippets, debug help, and even complete function writing.
  - Automatic Code Suggestion
  - Code Summarization
  - Automating Routine Coding Tasks
  - Writing Boilerplate Code

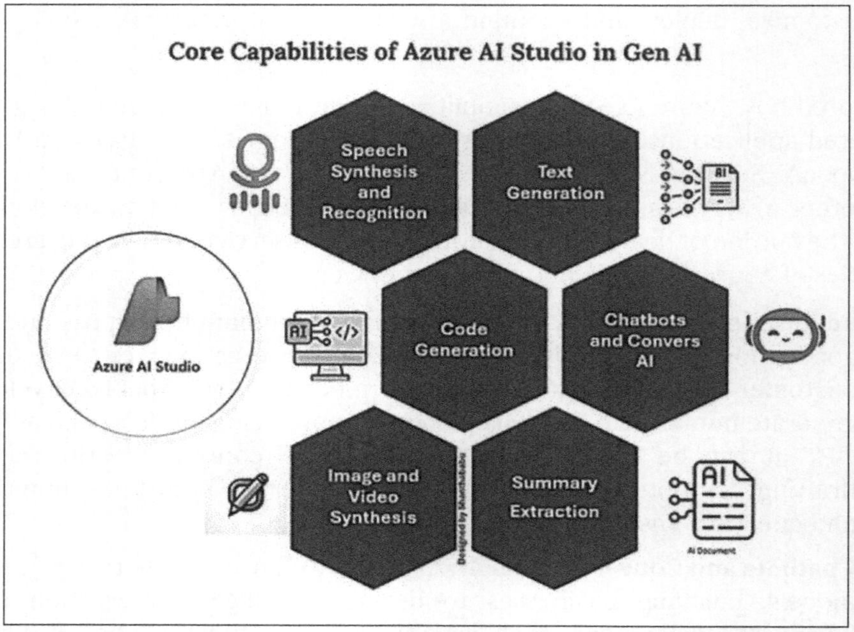

Figure 8.2: *Key Features of Azure AI Studio*

- **Summarization and Extraction**: Using LLM capabilities, we summarize and extract critical information from the most extended documents from large datasets. This feature enables businesses to efficiently process large volumes of text, extract necessary information, or generate concise summaries without losing context or meaning. These features allow businesses to streamline processes such as document management, improve decision-making, and extract data into actionable insights.
    - **Text Summarization**: Generate consolidated versions of long documents, reports, or articles.
    - **Information Extraction**: Using pre-built models, the identification and extraction of essential entities such as dates, names, and key phrases from unstructured data.
    - **Multilingual Support**: It supports multi-language extraction and summarization, making it useful for global enterprises that deal with content in various languages.
- **Image and Video Synthesis**: Azure AI Studio offers robust image and video synthesis capabilities, which allow businesses to create, manipulate, and enhance visual content using Gen AI technology. It simplifies generating and transforming images and videos for various applications and multiple needs.
    - Image Generation and Manipulation
    - Text-to-Image Synthesis

  - Image Enhancement
  - Video Synthesis and Editing
- **Speech Synthesis and Recognition:** Azure AI Studio offers powerful tools for speech synthesis and recognition for various use cases specific to the industry, enabling applications that can interact with users through natural languages. Azure AI Studio integrates Azure Cognitive Services for speech synthesis and speech-to-text capabilities for various sectors, such as customer service, education, healthcare, and more.

Azure AI Studio Empowerment

Azure AI Studio empowers users to build, deploy, and manage AI solutions seamlessly for AI developers with its user-friendly interface, and it integrates powerful AI tools such as machine learning, natural language processing, and computer vision in this entire journey. Further, this helps us to develop robust AI solutions using simplified AI Studio architecture and its environmental components, such as API and model choice, model benchmarks, and prompt catalog. We will discuss them in detail in this session.

Azure AI Studio Architecture

As we discussed, AI Studio provides a unified experience for AI developers to build, evaluate, and deploy AI models through a web portal, SDK, or CLI. AI Studio is built on capabilities and services provided by other Azure services.

The top-level AI Studio has primary layers such as **AI hub resources** and **AI projects**, which are on **Azure Machine Learning**.

AI Services: This primary layer is connected to **Azure Services** as connected resources, such as Azure OpenAI, Azure AI services, and Azure AI Search, which are used by the hub and projects referenced in top layers and blocks, as shown in *Figure* 8.3:

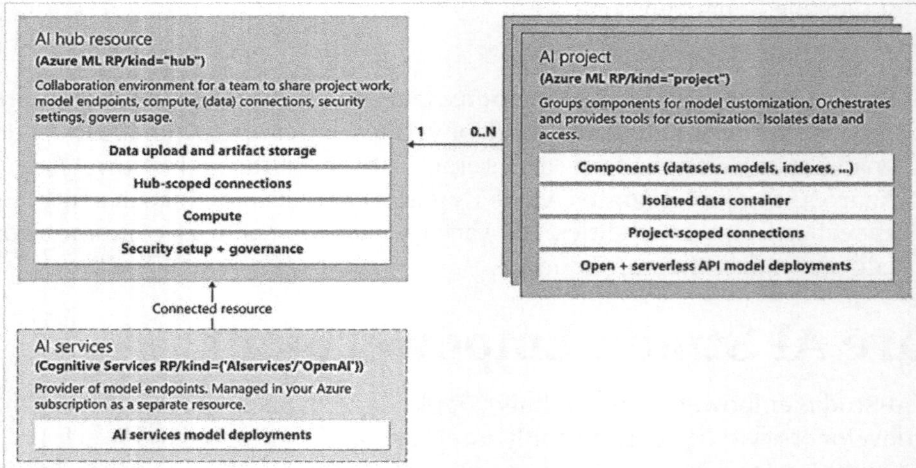

Figure 8.3: *Azure AI Studio Architecture*

Source: https://learn.microsoft.com/en-us/azure/ai-studio/concepts/architecture

- **AI Studio Hub**: The hub is the top-level resource in the AI Studio architecture. It provides the following features to establish the hub layer, consisting of multiple child projects. This is mainly for a collaboration environment for the development team to share the project tasks, endpoints, compute, data connections, and security and governance:
  - **Security and Governance:** This layer starts with the security configuration, which is mandatory for managing the network, establishing the limits for projects and model endpoints, and building the governance for the architecture.
  - **Compute**: The compute resources are on top of the security and governance layers. The primary objective for interactive development is fine-tuning the performance, incorporating the open source, and building serverless models and deployments. The significant results for computing are better resource utilization and cost optimizations. Ultimately, it offers high application availability and performance through built-in capabilities such as load balancing, monitoring, and auto-scaling based on the compute demand.
  - **Hub-Scoped Connections**: These help establish connections to other Azure services, such as Azure OpenAI, Azure AI services, and Azure AI Search. Projects created from the hub share these features.
  - **Data Upload and Storage:** This architecture uses an Azure storage account for data upload and an integrated platform for artifacts storage.
- **AI Studio Project:** This block shows that the Azure resource provider for the

project is Microsoft Machine Learning Services and Workspaces. Each project is a child resource of the hub; we can observe the connecting points 1...0...N in *Figure* 8.3; this block provides the following features, which consist of a group of components for model and tool customization:

- **Components:** It consists of reusable components, including datasets, models, and indexes for various applications.
- **Isolated Data Container:** Here, the data container is isolated and used for uploading the data to and from within the storage and is inherited from the hub.
- **Project-Scoped Connections**: This helps project members' private access control to data stored in an Azure Storage account without giving that same access to other projects.
- **Open Source and API**: Mainly for model deployments from the catalogue and fine-tuned model endpoints.

- **Azure Monitor:** In this architecture, the **Azure Monitor** and **Azure Log Analytics** monitor and log the resources used by Azure AI Studio, which we discussed previously.
- **Encryption Features:** Azure AI Studio uses encryption techniques to protect data **at Rest** and **In Transit**. The Microsoft-managed keys are used for encryption and enable this feature by default. However, we can use your own encryption keys to strengthen the data security policies.

Table 8.1 lists the dependent Azure resources and their respective resource providers in Azure Studio Architecture:

Azure Resources	**Purpose**
Azure AI Search	• Provides search capabilities for your AI-Projects.
Azure Storage account	• It stores artifacts for your projects, such as flows and evaluations. • Data is secured using Azure ABAC for the project identity.
Azure Key Vault	• It stores secrets, such as connection strings, for your resource connections.
Azure Container Registry	• This store stores docker images created using a custom runtime for prompt flow.
Azure Application Insights and Log Analytics Workspace	• For log storage, when you opt for application-level logging for your deployed prompt flows.

Table 8.1: *Dependent Azure Resources*

Best features of the platform include:

- You can interact with the project **Code-First** directly from the studio via **the Visual Studio Code** environment.
- AI Studio is the most trusted environment for AI developers to build innovative AI products. It provides a seamless effort to **explore, design, build, test, deploy**, and **manage** using cutting-edge AI technologies and robust ML models.
- The AI Studio hub layer provides enterprise security and a highly collaborative environment with secure, shared **file systems, data governance, pre-trained models**, and **computing power**.
- It adopts required AI practices such as **responsible, secure, and safe**. The state and association help to save the product along this product drive.

Note:

Azure AI Studio uses RBAC and ABAC to secure the shared storage account.

- ***Role-Based Access Control (RBAC):*** *AI Studio provides a control plane proxy that allows developers to perform operations on connected Azure AI services and reduces the complexity of RBAC management in the environment by performing the operations on these resources with the required Azure RBAC permissions on the hub.*
- ***Attribute-Based Access Control (ABAC):*** *Each Azure hub we created has a default storage account. Each child project of an Azure hub inherits the hub's storage account.*

Azure AI Studio and its Environment

Let us understand Azure AI Studio. The platform empowers AI architects and developers to design and develop AI-driven innovative products that will shape the future of AI with safe, secure, and responsible products and tools for business enhancements and sustainability.

This well-built, comprehensive platform accelerates the development of AI products with production-ready copilots to support safe, secure enterprise chatbots or assistance, content generation tools, data analysis and decision-making tools, and more.

AI developers can explore multiple APIs and models for their use cases based on the demand to build and test solutions with highly collaborative and responsible in-house AI tools, safeguard data privacy and security, adopt best practices, and deploy AI-driven innovative solutions in the form of websites, applications, and other production environments based on industry requirements. It supports the development team in managing solutions by continuously monitoring and implementing industry-specific governance policies in production with other Azure components and services precisely.

AI Studio is designed for architects and developers to design, develop, and deploy solutions. We can evaluate the model responses with the prompt flow for better performance for the AI tools we are designing and ready to deploy into production.

This platform enables excellent scalability features for quickly transforming the minimum viable product (MVP) into a full-fledged, production-suitable product, along with continuous monitoring and enhancement support for the product's long-term success in the market trend and business improvements.

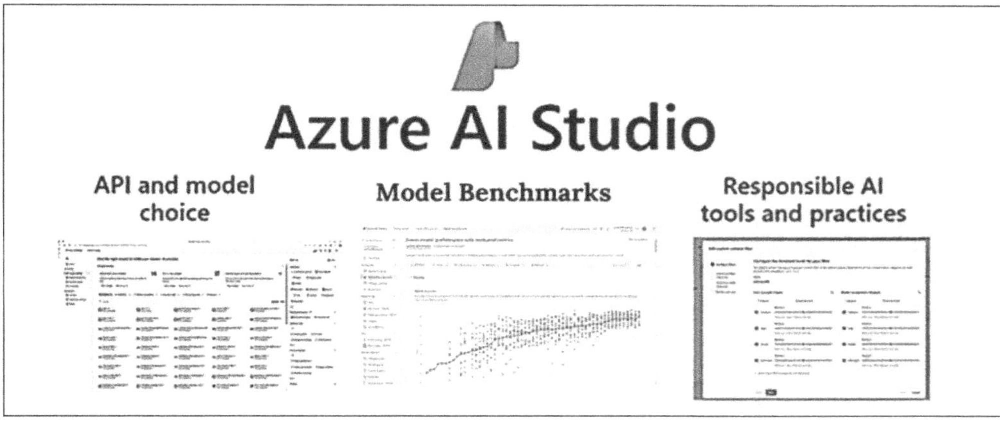

Figure 8.4: *Azure AI Studio High-Level Components*

Azure AI Studio Project: Projects help you organize your AI assets and save "state" across different tools, data connections, and more. You can create a project.

Step 1: Click "**`New project`**" to provide the project hub details, as shown in *Figure* 8.5:

Figure 8.5: *Azure AI Studio (New Project Creation)*

Step 2: Select the hub from the Hub list or create a new one. If you click "**`Create a new hub`**," the application takes you to the configuration page, as shown in *Figure* 8.6:

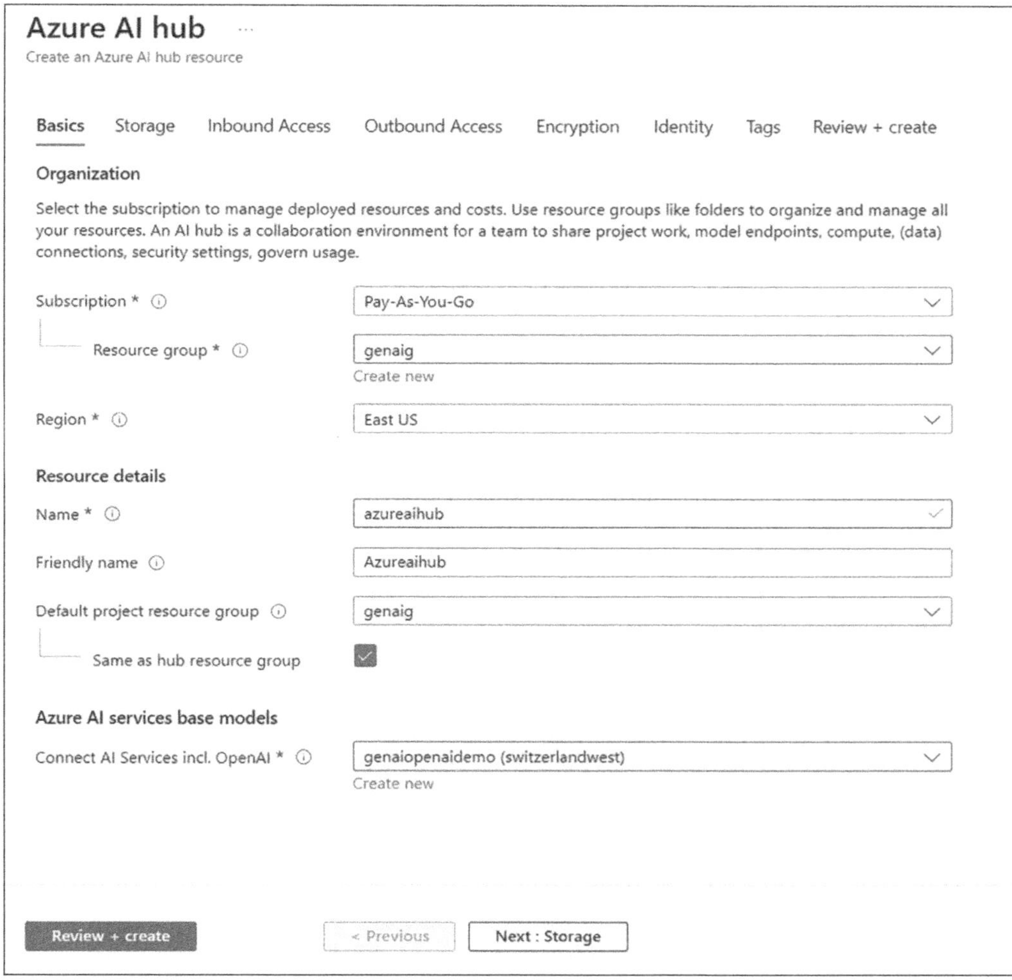

Figure 8.6: *Azure AI Studio (New Project Creation)*

Step 3: As shown in *Figure* 8.7, we must provide all the mentioned mandatory fields and click the **`Next`** button.

- Subscription
- Resource Group
- Location
- Connect to Azure AI Services/Azure OpenAI
- Connect to Azure AI Search

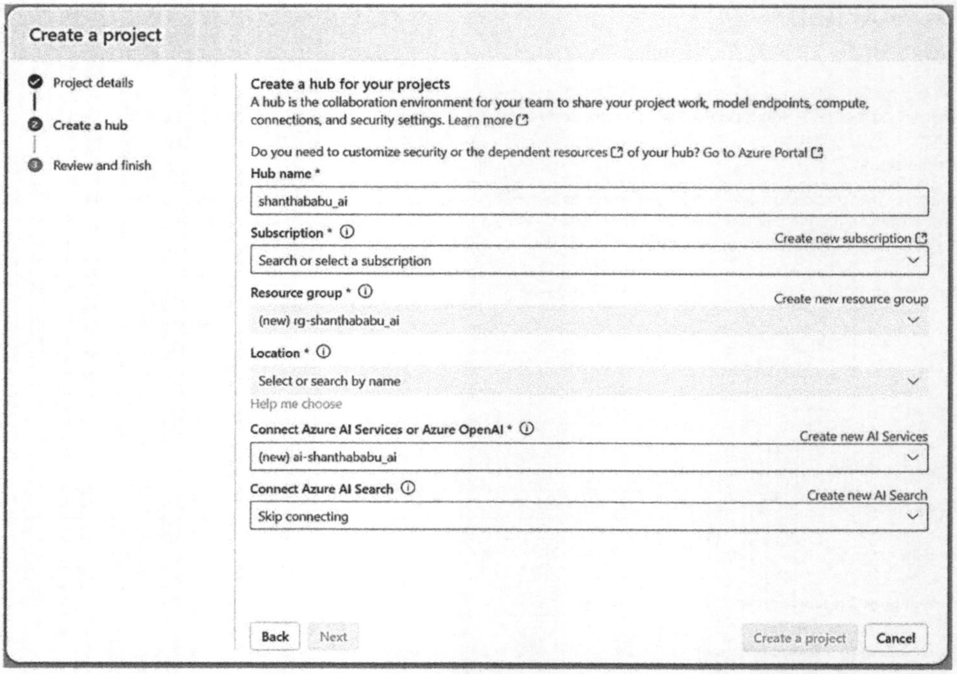

Figure 8.7: *Azure AI Studio (Hub Configuration)*

Step 4: Review the configuration and click "`Create a project`."

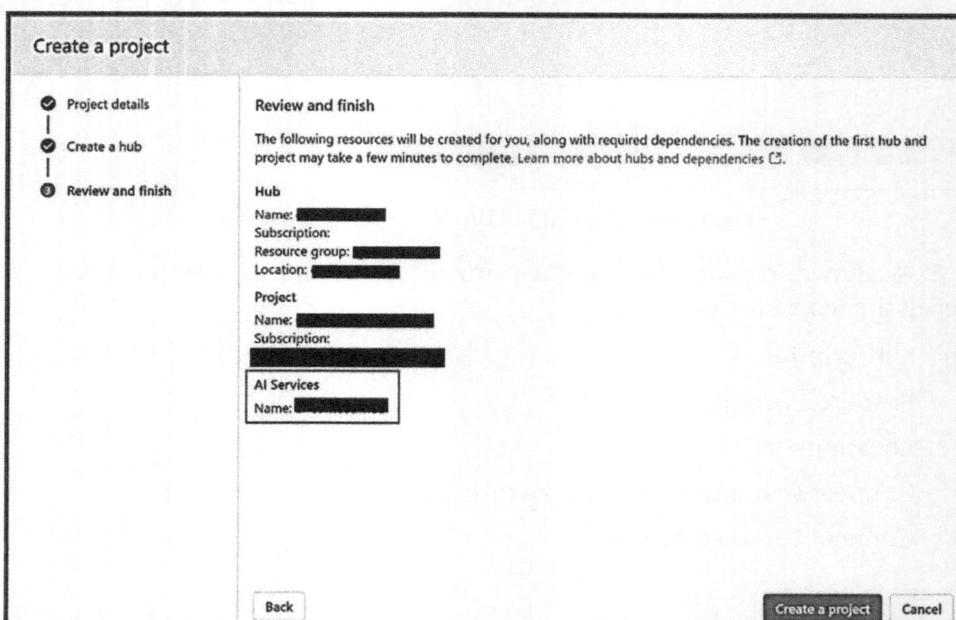

Figure 8.8: *Azure AI Studio (Review and Finish)*

Step 5: Creating the project resources.

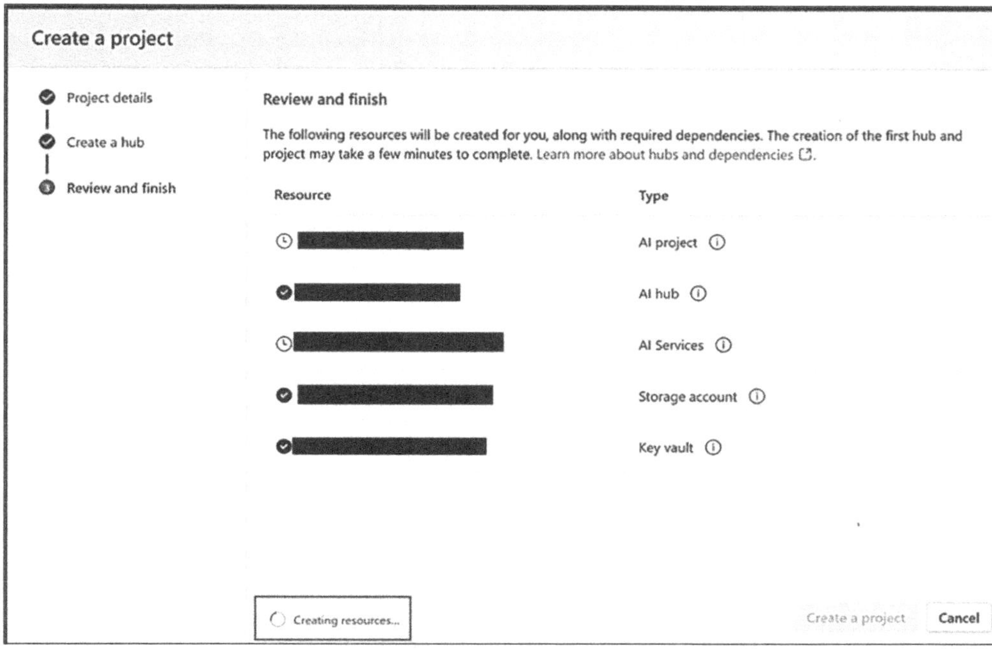

***Figure 8.9**: Azure AI Studio (Creating the Project Resources)*

Step 6: Once all is done, review the project settings:

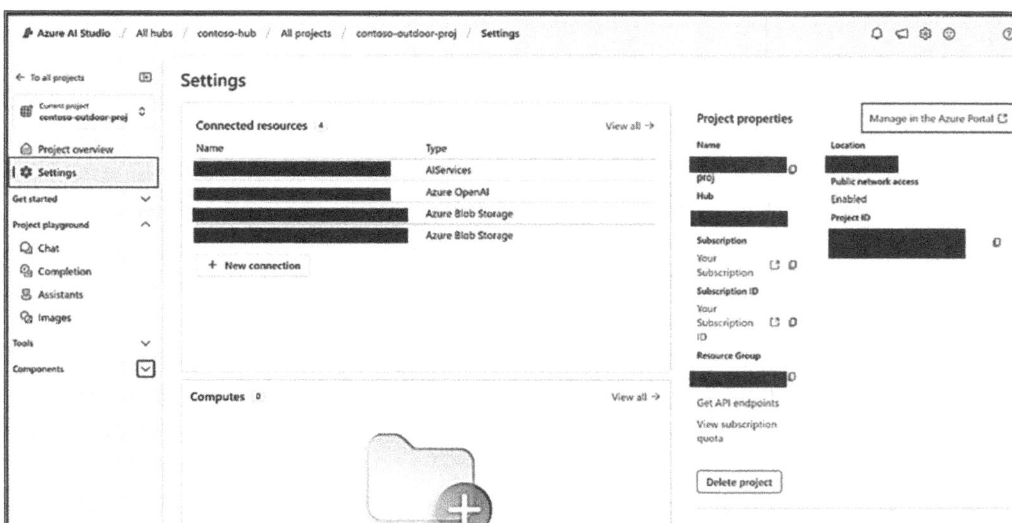

***Figure 8.10**: Azure AI Studio (View Project Settings)*

API and Model Choice

Azure AI Studio is a comprehensive platform providing developers with the tools, models, and infrastructure to **explore**, **build**, **test**, and **deploy** AI-driven solutions for multiple use cases with flexibility.

It integrates with powerful **AI models**, extensive **capabilities**, and a strong emphasis on **Responsible AI,** focusing on accessibility and scalability while streamlining **prompt orchestration and evaluation** processes. It empowers developers with AI-powered product development at each stage of the lifecycle of AI development:

- **Model Catalog:** Azure AI Studio offers access to compelling **1780+ pre-trained models.** It helps developers integrate AI functionalities into their applications without starting from scratch by configuring, getting services, and building useful AI tools. *Figure* 8.11 shows the Azure AI Studio's model catalogue, where developers can find a suitable model to develop their custom AI solution.

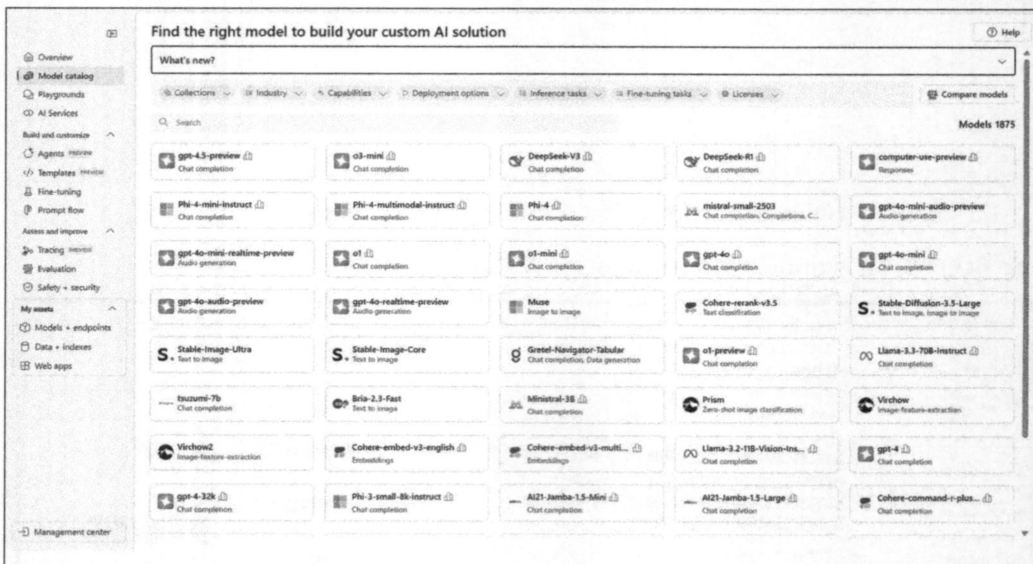

Figure 8.11: *Model Catalog View in Azure AI Studio*

- **Language Models**: Azure AI Studio curates multiple models, such as GPT-4x, Llama, Hugging Face, and so on, for natural language processing (NLP), allowing developers to build chatbots, content generators, and automated customer service systems.
    - Model selection: `gpt-4o`

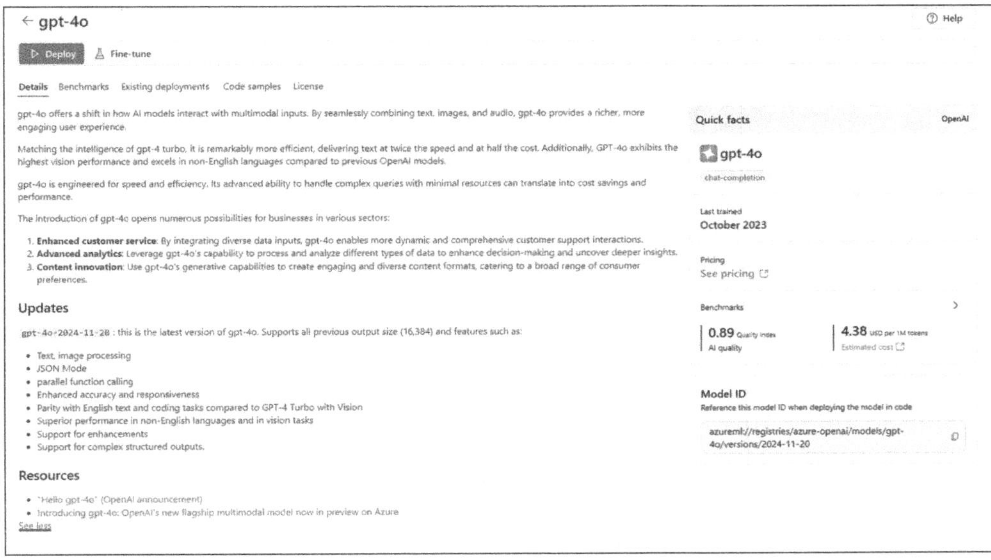

Figure 8.12: *Model Selection: gpt-4o from Model Catalog*

- Model (**`gpt-4o`**) configuration and deployment.

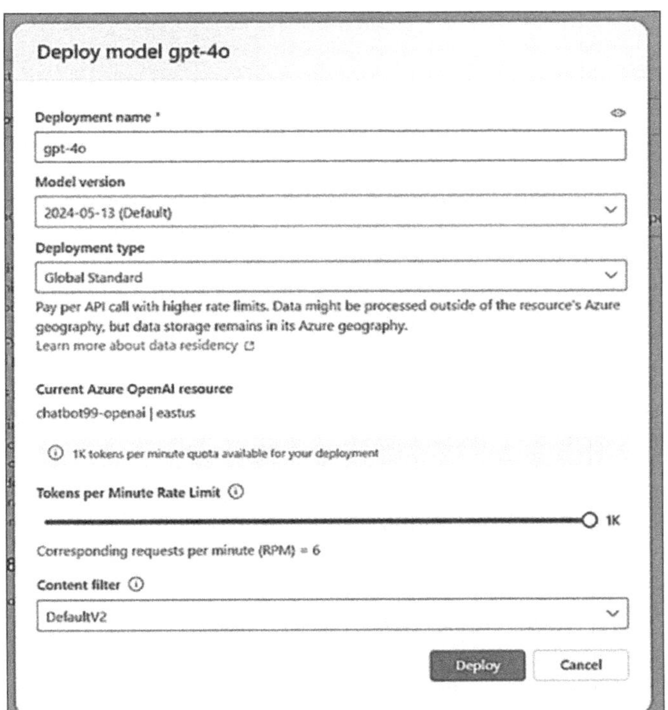

Figure 8.13: *Model (gpt-4o) Configuration and Deployment*

- **Vision and Image Models:** Azure AI Studio provides specialized vision and image processing and analysis models, such as DALL·E HuggingFace. AI developers can use models to generate images from text prompts provided by the user, while **Azure Cognitive Services** offers powerful tools for image classification, object detection, and facial recognition. This feature in AI Studio is robust and similar to this, it is available in Azure Open AI, as we covered in *Chapter 7, Getting Started with Generative AI Using Azure OpenAI Service.*
    - Model Selection from the list (`dall-e-3`).

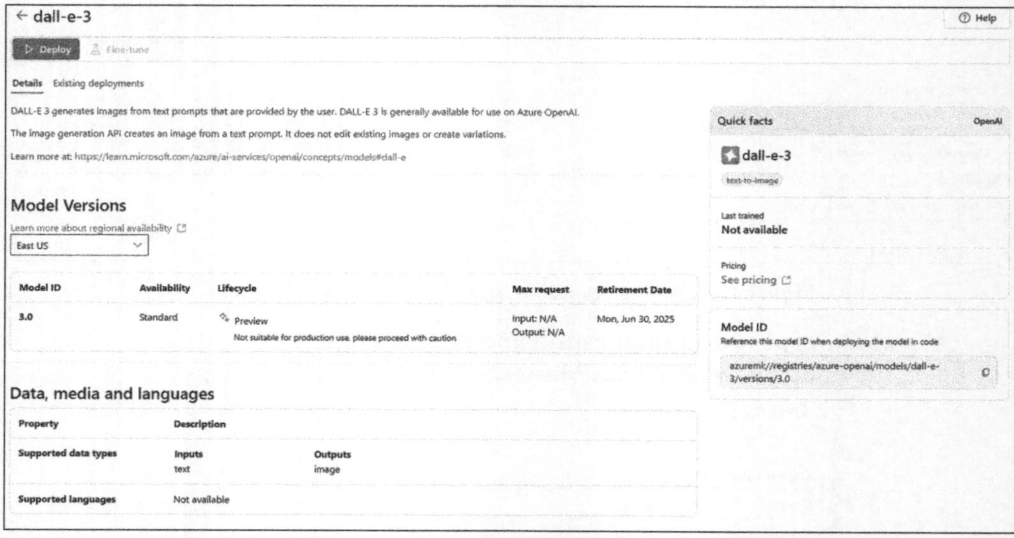

Figure 8.14: *Model Selection from the List (dall-e-3)*

- Model (`dall-e-3`) configuration and deployment.

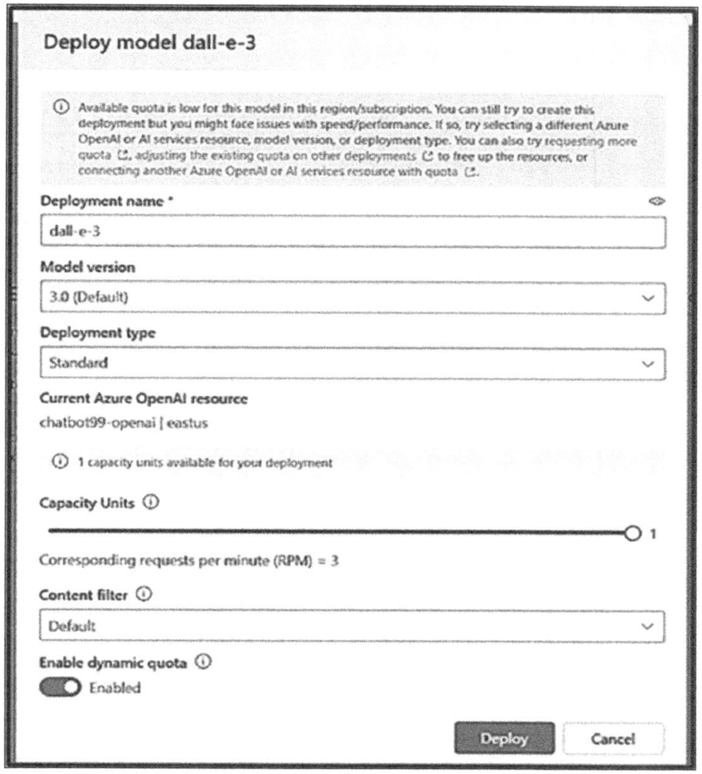

Figure 8.15: *Model (dall-e-3) Configuration and Deployment*

It consists of a vast collection so that AI architects can decide on the model from different providers.

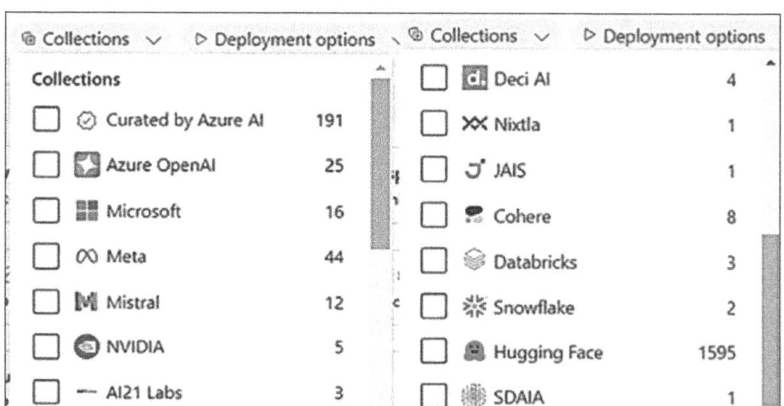

Figure 8.16: *Model Providers*

It consists of a vast collection of **inference tasks**, which AI architects can choose based on their use cases.

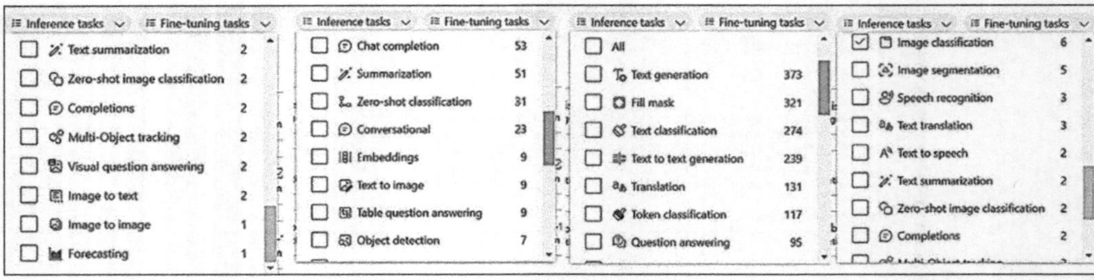

Figure 8.17: *Inference Tasks*

Model Benchmarks: This feature allows AI developers to compare AI models' performance across industry-standard datasets, helping them determine where specific models perform effectively and selecting the best models from the list.

This helps evaluate the models using the following factors:

- Accuracy
- Coherence
- Fluency
- GPT similarity metrics

Accuracy: Accuracy scores are presented at the dataset and the model levels.

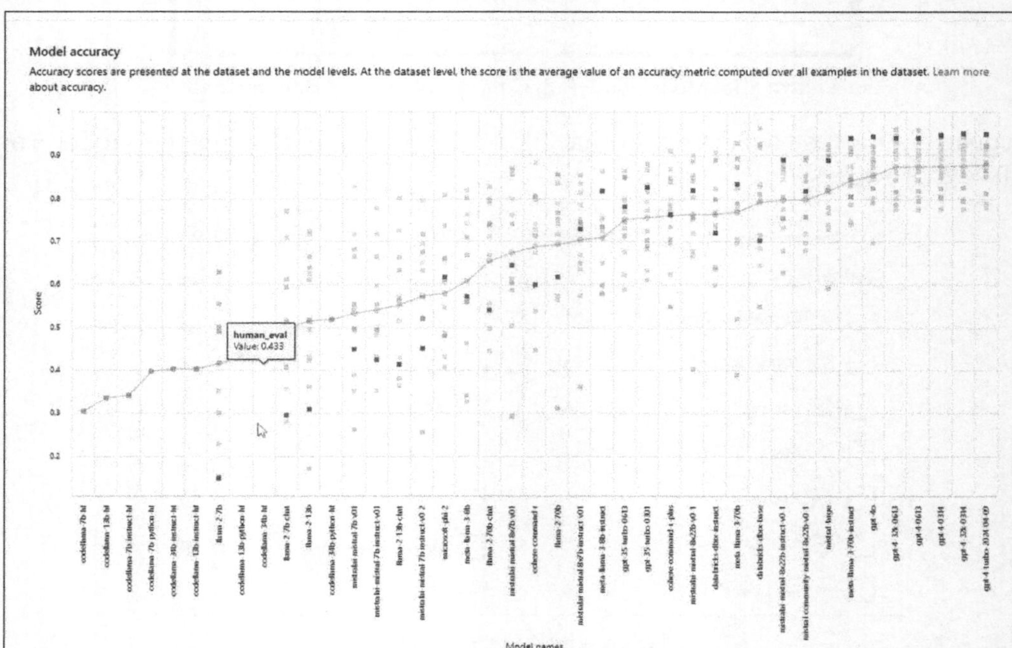

Figure 8.18: *Azure AI Studio Model Benchmarks: Accuracy*

Coherence: It evaluates how well the language model can produce output that flows efficiently and resembles human-like language.

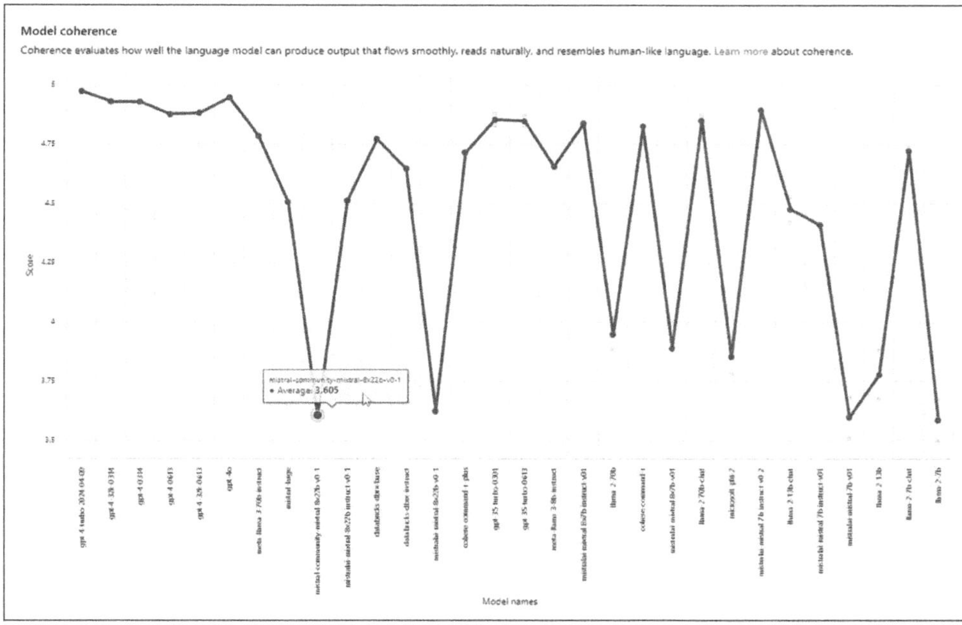

Figure 8.19: *Azure AI Studio Model Benchmarks: Coherence*

Fluency: This measures the language expertise of a Gen AI's predicted answer(s).

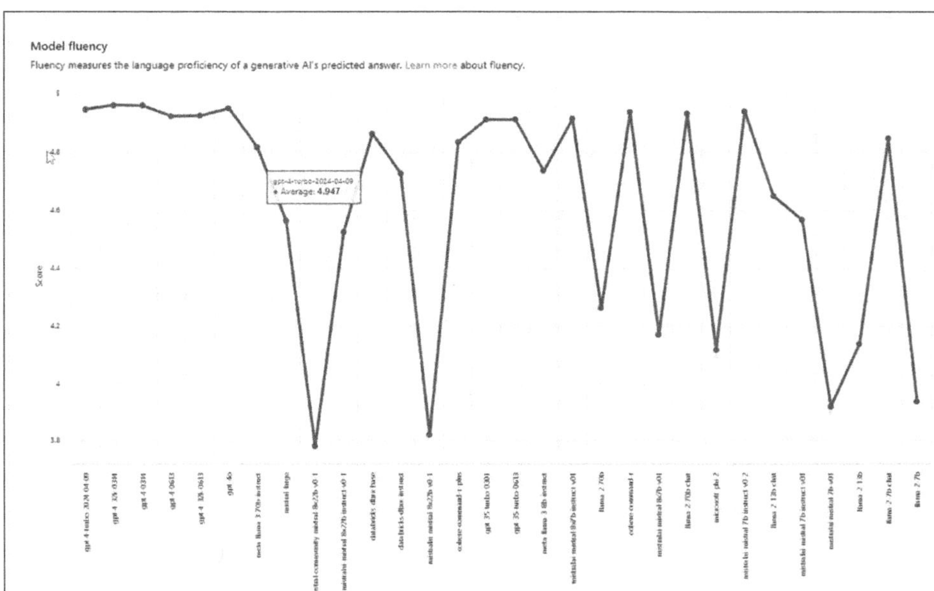

Figure 8.20: *Azure AI Studio Model Benchmarks: Fluency*

Similarity: It measures the similarity between the source data and the generated response(s) by a GPT-based AI model.

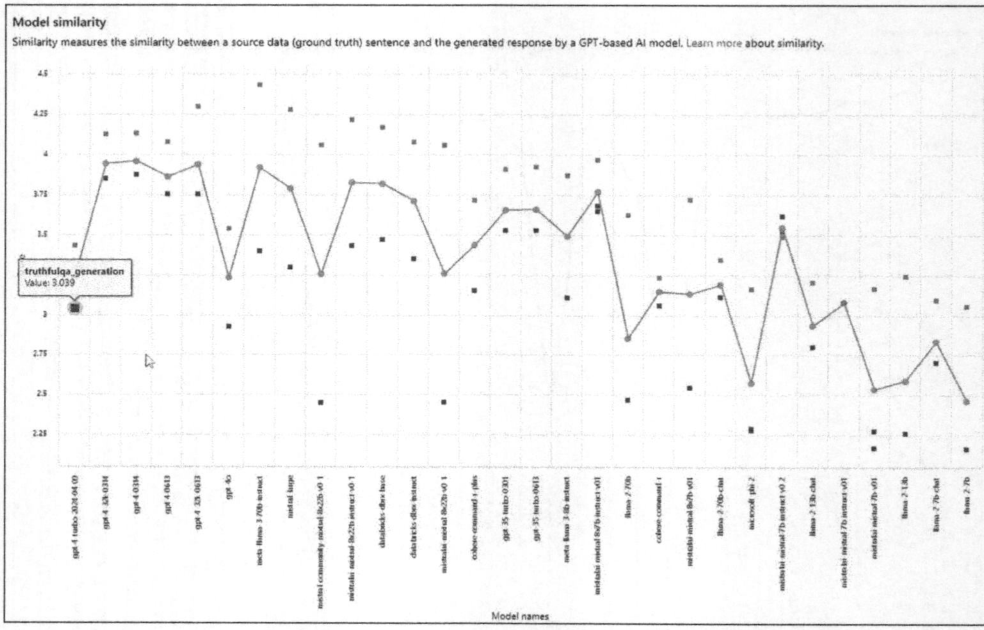

Figure 8.21: *Azure AI Studio Model Benchmarks: Similarity*

Comparison: It displays the average metric calculations.

Comparison

All numbers displayed in overview are average metric calculations. If models have multiple tasks that they support, the number displayed is an average across all tasks. If you would like to see individual calculations, please switch to list view.

Model	Accuracy ↓	Coherence	Groundedness	Fluency	Relevance	GPTSimilarity
gpt-4-turbo-2024-04-09	0.877	4.974	--	4.947	4.039	3.235
gpt-4-32k-0314	0.875	4.93	4.202	4.962	4.104	3.942
gpt-4-0314	0.874	4.929	4.254	4.96	4.08	3.959
gpt-4-0613	0.874	4.877	4.296	4.924	4.334	3.862
gpt-4-32k-0613	0.873	4.881	4.139	4.925	4.381	3.936
gpt-4o	0.854	4.947	4.09	4.951	4.19	3.232
meta-llama-3-70b-instruct	0.842	4.785	3.911	4.818	3.346	3.917
mistral-large	0.817	4.506	3.892	4.564	3.63	3.79
mistral-community-mixtral-8x22b	0.797	3.605	3.285	3.78	3.235	3.252
mistralai-mixtral-8x22b-instruct-v	0.797	4.513	4.115	4.526	4.146	3.825
databricks-dbrx-base	0.792	4.771	3.786	4.864	3.585	3.819
meta-llama-3-70b	0.769	--	--	--	--	--
databricks-dbrx-instruct	0.764	4.647	4.002	4.729	4.011	3.713

Figure 8.22: *Azure AI Studio Model Benchmarks: Comparison*

Prompt Catalog

We discussed Prompt Engineering in *Chapter 4, Prompt Engineering and Its Significance*, in various aspects when working with Gen AI models, as it gives users greater control over the content generation, high customization of the output, and influence on the outputs for end users.

Dexterously designed prompts can generate the desired content, address specific business requirements and appropriate answers, and serve various applications from different domains with the support of generative AI models.

Azure AI Studio provides the prompt catalog feature, which contains many prompts for common use cases such as generating text or images. You can filter the prompts by following the options and sub-options.

- Modality
  - Chat, Image, Video, and Completions
- Industry
  - Retail and Education
- Task
  - Summarization, Chat Completion, Content Creation, and others

The following figure shows the features of the Prompt Catalog:

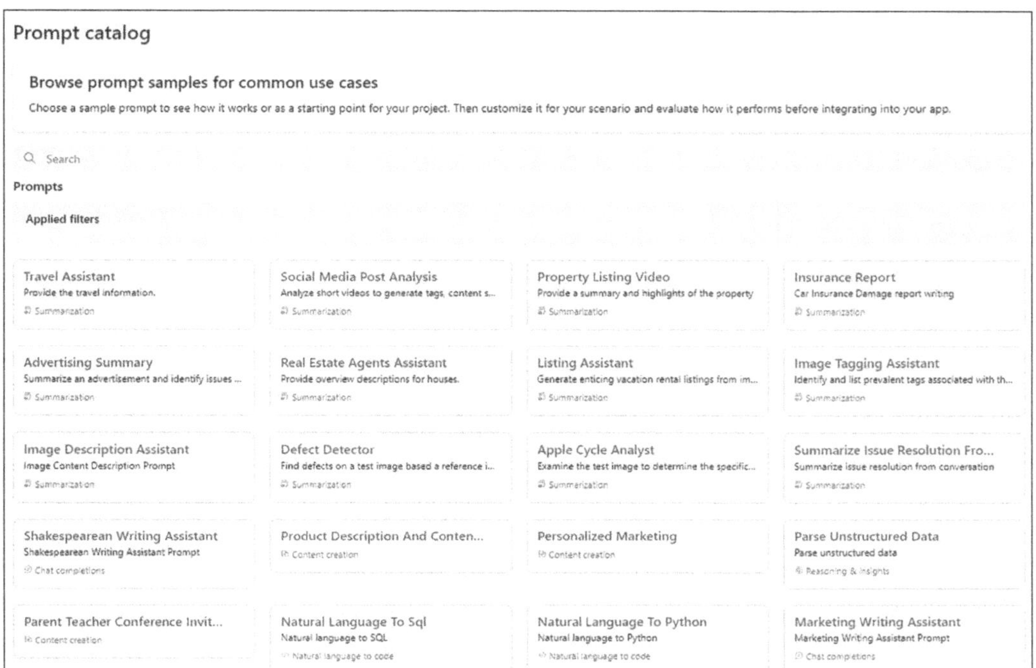

Figure 8.23: *Azure AI Studio Prompt Catalog*

Figure 8.24 (**`Advertising Summary`**, **`Product Description`**, **`Content Creation`**, and **`Image Description Assistant`**) provides a few samples.

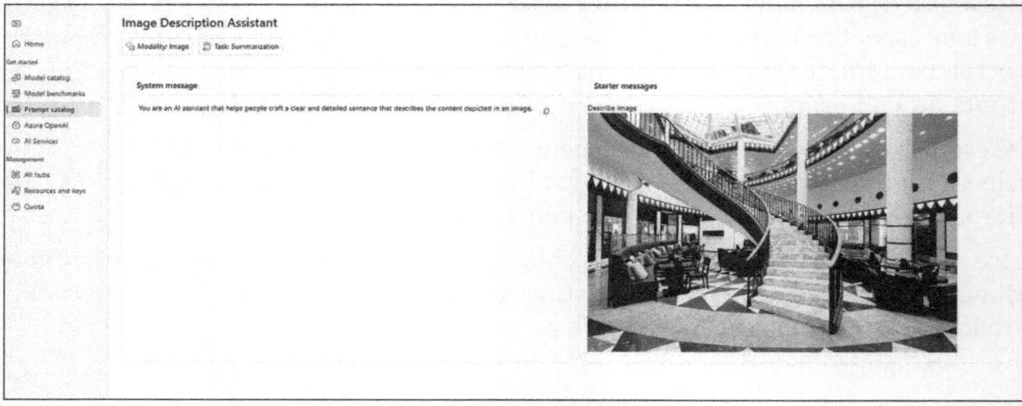

Figure 8.24: *Azure AI Studio Prompt Catalog Samples*

AI Services and Playgrounds will be discussed in *Chapter* 9, *Advanced Azure AI Studio-II*.

Responsible AI Initiatives

Before we start discussing Responsible AI in Azure AI Studio, let us go through some major technology providers that offer responsible AI platforms that embed these mechanisms into the AI development lifecycle:

- **Microsoft's Responsible AI** framework tightly integrates privacy, security, and ethical standards. It offers developers tools such as **Fairlearn**, **InterpretML**, and **Differential Privacy** for safer AI deployment and deployment for an AI development team.
- **Google's AI Principles** focus on designing and developing AI with fairness, accountability, and built-in end-user safety. They leverage tools such as the **What-If Tool** for bias detection. The tool helps practitioners test performance in hypothetical situations, analyze the importance of different data and features, and build the envisaged model behavior across multiple reasonable models and subsets of proper input while aligning to ML fairness metrics.
- **IBM's AI Fairness 360** and **AI Explainability 360** help developers reduce bias, enhance model transparency at a 360-degree range, and control the AI tools from various serious considerations while building AI-driven tools.

By using these safety mechanisms and responsible AI tools from their respective technology providers, developers can confidently create generative AI-driven systems that comply with regulatory standards and are safe for extensive use in specific domains.

Understand Responsible AI using Azure AI Studio

Responsible AI principles ensure that AI solutions are designed, developed, and deployed ethically, transparently, and fairly since this technology digests all data and generates different outcomes such as text, images, and video.

Azure AI Studio provides a compelling, unified platform for developers to explore, design, build, test, and deploy AI solutions based on requirements. It offers access to advanced Gen AI models and extensive development features and capabilities.

Built-in Responsible AI principles enable a structured approach, along with prompt orchestration and assessment, to empower developers to create high-quality, ethical, and scalable AI products for sensitive decision-making tools. Data plays a significant role in those solutions.

Azure AI Studio ensures sensitive text generation models align with Microsoft's Responsible AI principles. This includes monitoring and controlling AI products' outputs to avoid harmful or biased content under any circumstance and providing high clarity in how text is generated by considering the following factors.

- Ethical AI
- Bias Mitigation
- Explainability
- Compliance and Security

Let us discuss the significant factors contributing to building responsible AI solutions using Azure AI Studio.

- **Ethical AI Use**: The Responsible AI framework ensures that developers and businesses use AI technology to promote accountability in product outcomes as fair, justify the functional aspects, and ensure the end user's privacy. Moreover, Microsoft also provides guidelines and tools for developers to avoid harmful use cases, such as generating fraudulent content or interfering with user privacy concerns.

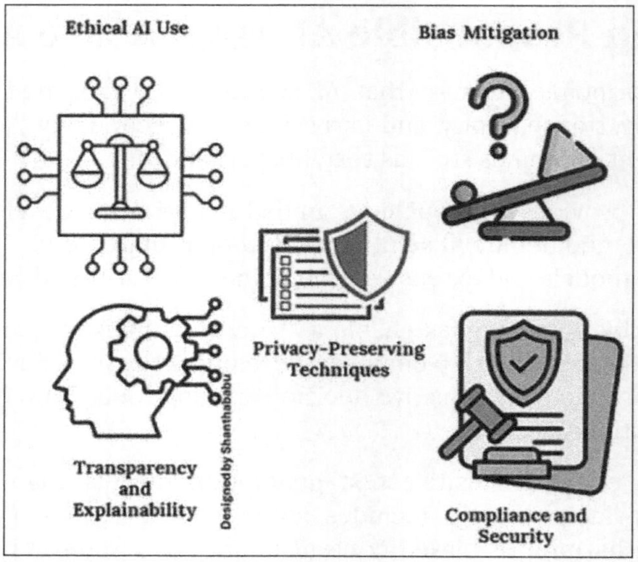

Figure 8.25: *Responsible AI Framework Promises for AI Studio*

- **Bias Mitigation**: Azure AI Studio provides tools for detecting and mitigating biases in AI models and ensures that AI-driven decisions are rational and unbiased, especially in sensitive applications such as hiring, healthcare, banking, law forums, financial services, and so on.
- **Transparency and Explainability**: Responsible AI frameworks ensure transparency and accountability through explainable AI (XAI) tools, which provide insights into how models make decisions. Azure AI Studio provides a platform that supports explainable AI, including features that help developers understand how AI models make decisions internally and clear explanations that help AI-solutions architect to aid customers in comprehending the output from the AI products. This enables appropriate trust, particularly in high-stakes industries such as healthcare, finance, and law forums.
- **Compliance and Security**: The Azure AI Studio platform ensures compliance with regulatory standards such as **GDPR**, **HIPAA**, **PII,** and **ISO**. It also ensures that Gen AI models and data practices adhere to regional data privacy regulations, making it suitable for developing AI-driven solutions in industries that handle sensitive data, such as healthcare or finance.

  Regarding security aspects, encrypting data at **REST** and in **TRANSIT** ensures that sensitive information is not exposed during AI processing and data movements from an access control point of view. **Role-based** and **Attribute-Based** access control mechanisms must be ensured, and only authorized personnel can access AI models and datasets.
- **Privacy-Preserving Techniques**: The Azure AI Studio platform ensures

differential privacy and federated learning. This ensures that individual data points cannot be reverse engineered from a model's output; instead, it adds noise to the data while maintaining accuracy. Moreover, the models are trained across decentralized data sets without raw data leaving their source, ensuring adherence to privacy compliance and maintaining data integrity and security.

Prompt Flow

Prompt flow is a remarkable feature in Azure AI Studio. It is a development tool designed to streamline the entire development cycle. This includes designing, evaluating, and refining prompts to achieve the desired model output using an excellent user interface to develop AI applications powered by Large Language Models (LLMs). In other words, it provides a complete solution that streamlines the process of prototyping, designing, iterating, and deploying AI applications.

Prompt Flow Architecture

Prompt flow architecture consists of five layers or pillars, as shown in *Figure* 8.26, such as:

- **Data Source**: As we know, the data source for Gen AI can be structured, semi-structured, or unstructured.
- **Prompt Flow Building**: We can build the prompt flow using Azure Machine Learning Studio or Azure AI Studio, which will be discussed in the following section.
- **Experiment:** Once the prompt flow is ready, we will test it to observe that it exhibits the expected output, which will be discussed in the following section.
- **Evaluation:** After completing the prompt flow building and experiments, we should evaluate them for various aspects, such as Model and Prompt flow, Dataset and Prompt flow, using the Azure AI Studio Evaluation feature, which will be discussed in the following section.

  The internal processes of the experiment and evaluation are self-explanatory in *Figure* 8.26.
- **Deployment**: After all the earlier layers are completed, we can deploy the prompt flow, monitor it, and log each step for further enhancements.

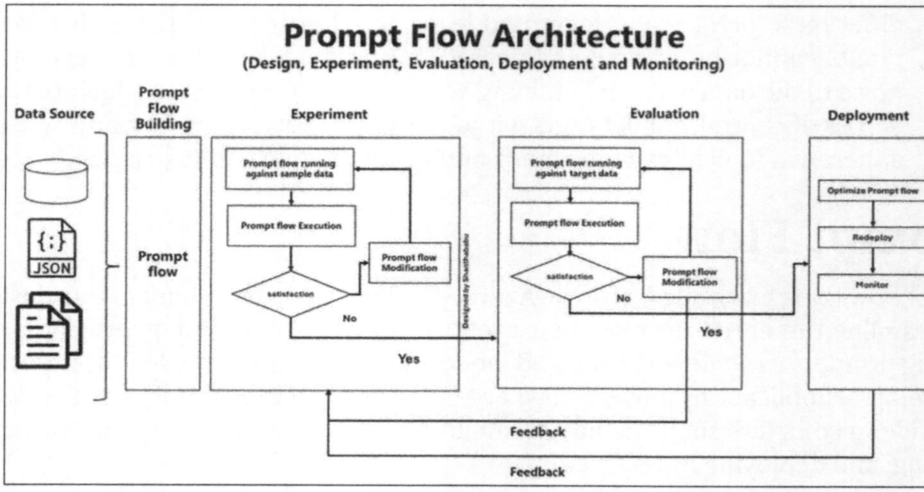

Figure 8.26: *Responsible AI Framework Promises for AI Studio*

In Azure AI Studio, prompt orchestration allows AI architects and developers to create complex workflows that coordinate tasks with various models based on business needs.

- **Multi-Step Prompts**: Developers can chain together prompts to create dynamic, multi-step workflows. For example, we can first generate a response from a model such as GPT-4 and then pass that output to a Machine Learning sentiment analysis or text summarization model for further analysis of the given dataset.
- **Decision-Making Based on Prompts**: In some scenarios, two or more conditional logic can be applied to model outputs to determine the next step in a workflow and move forward. For example, if the sentiment analysis reveals a negative tone, the system could escalate the query to a customer service representative. In **Chapter 4, Prompt Engineering and Its Significance,** we have discussed various types of prompts along with decision-making capabilities.
- **Cross-Model Orchestration**: Azure AI Studio allows prompt orchestration across different models. A single workflow can use multiple models based on the situation, such as GPT-4 for text generation, Azure Speech for voice synthesis, and Azure AI Services for sentiment analysis, creating a unified AI experience with all these capabilities.

We can create **Prompt flows** either in Azure AI Studio or Azure Machine Learning Studio.

- **Interactive Prompt Design**: Azure Machine Learning Studio provides AI developers with the features to design, evaluate, and refine prompts to achieve the desired model output. The prompt flow interface allows us to create prompts for various perspectives, such as **flows, runs, connections, runtime, and vector indexes**, and **refine prompts** to ensure they generate the desired outputs. The prompt flow interface allows users to provide input, view model responses, and adjust them in real time.

Step 1: Go to the Azure home page, search for Azure Machine Learning, and click the resource.

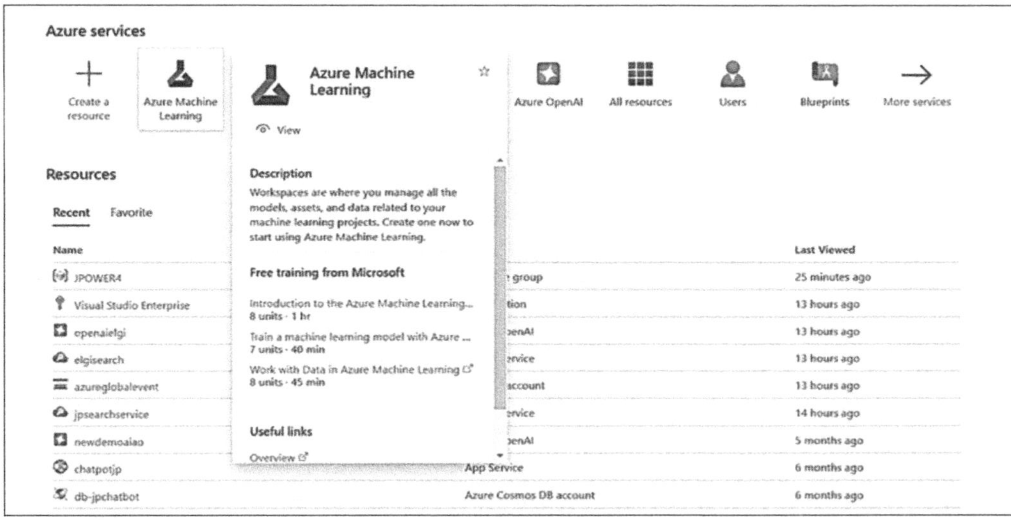

Figure 8.27: *Searching for Azure Machine Learning Studio on the Azure Home Page*

Step 2: The Azure portal takes you to the `Azure Machine Learning` page, where you can create a new workspace for your purpose and then click the "`New workspace`" button.

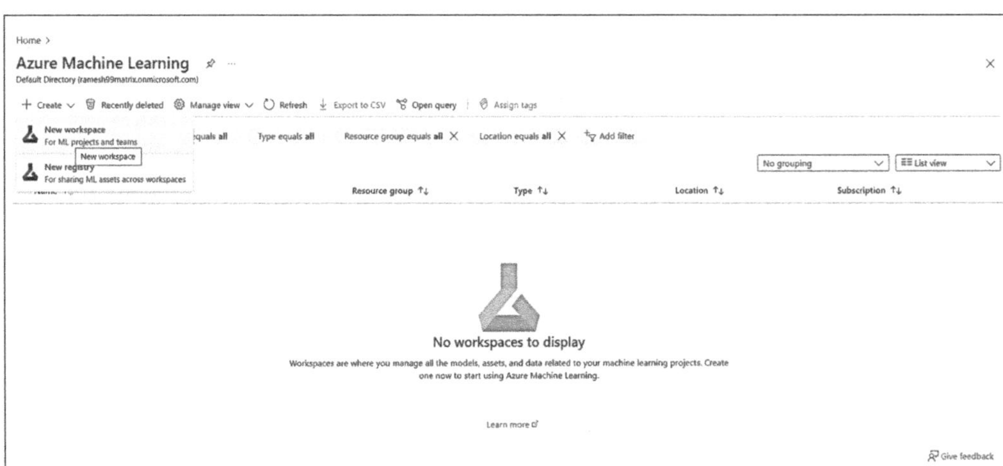

Figure 8.28: *Azure Machine Learning Studio; Workspace Collection Page*

Step 3: The Azure portal takes you to the **`Azure Machine Learning`** new workspace page, where we have to configure the workspace, as shown in *Figure* 8.29:

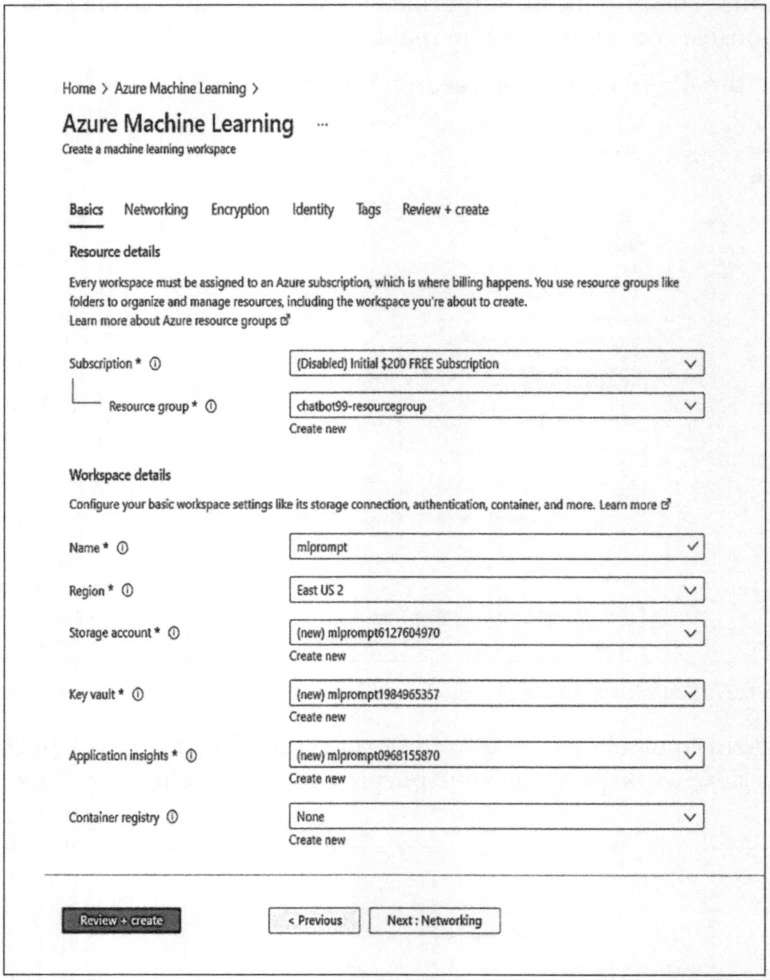

Figure 8.29: *Azure Machine Learning Studio; New Workspace Configuration*

Step 4: After the Azure Machine Learning new workspace page configuration, click the "**`Review + Create`**" button; the portal will take us to the following page, as shown in *Figure* 8.30, and then click "**`Create`**."

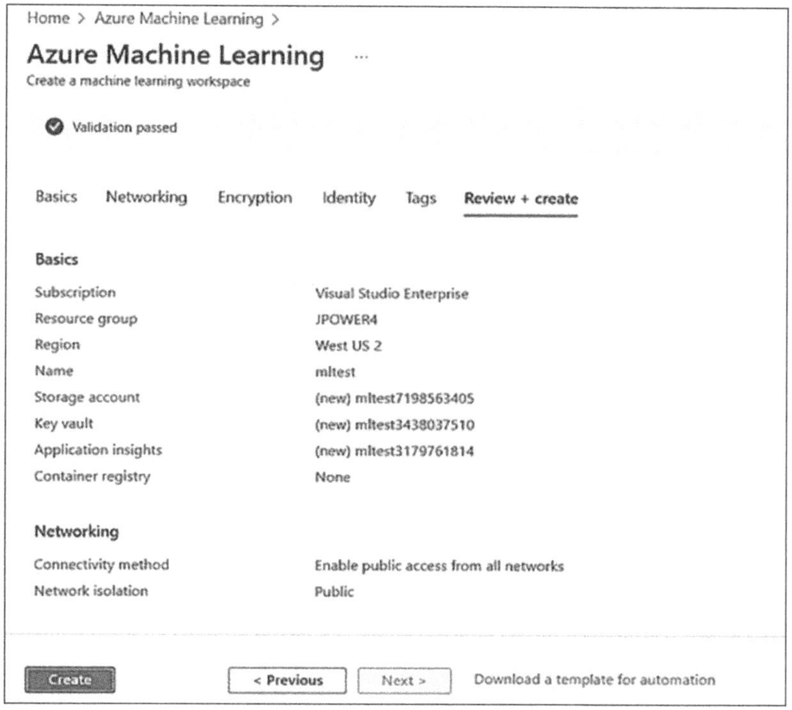

Figure 8.30: *Azure Machine Learning Studio; New Workspace Configuration in Progress*

Step 5: The portal will take you to the workspace page, as shown in *Figure* 8.31, and then click "`Lunch Studio`."

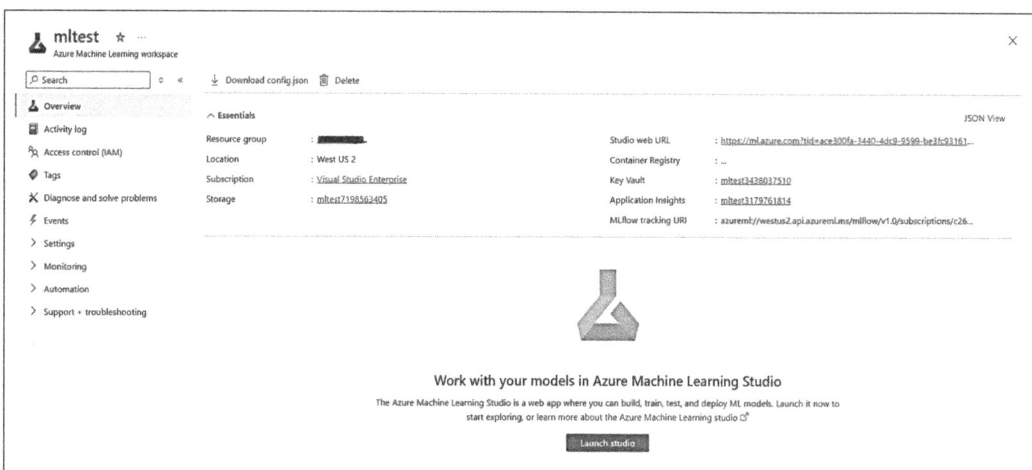

Figure 8.31: *Azure Machine Learning Studio -New Workspace is Ready to Launch*

Step 6: The portal will take us to the `Machine Learning Studio` page, as shown in *Figure* 8.32. On the left menu, we can see the Prompt flow.

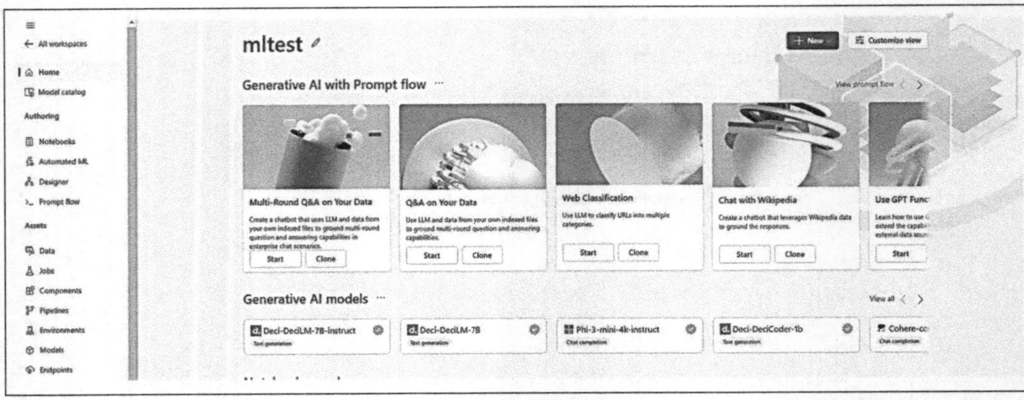

Figure 8.32: *Azure Machine Learning Studio; New Workspace is Ready to Use*

Step 7: Click Prompt flow in the left menu. The portal will see different types of flows, as shown in *Figure* 8.33. Click the "`Click`" button in the standard flow highlighted.

Figure 8.33: *Azure Machine Learning Studio; Prompt Flow*

Step 8: If you want, you can change the folder name. Then, click the "`Create`" button, as shown in *Figure* 8.34.

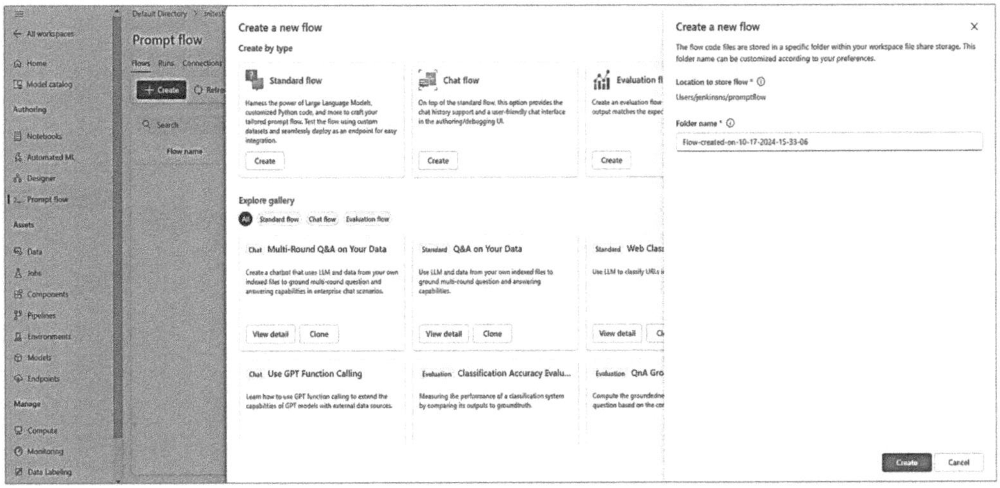

Figure 8.34: *Azure Machine Learning Studio; Prompt Flow (Standard Flow)*

Step 9: The Azure portal will take us to the prompt interface, as shown in *Figure* 8.35.

Prompt Flow: Component

- **Creating Flow:** This menu helps us to create the flow for our requirements.
- **Runs**: Displays the runs of the flow which we created.
- **Connections**: This helps us to develop connections between remote APIs and the data sources.
- **Runtime**: Specifically, to associate the compute for our runtime.
- **Vector Index:** Add vector database or store.

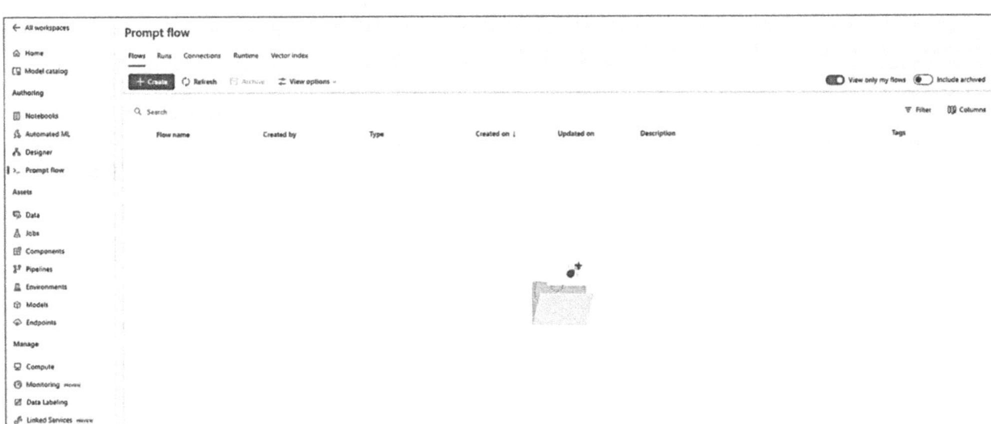

Figure 8.35: *Azure Machine Learning Studio; Prompt Flow Interface*

Building Prompt Workflow

Step 1: As a first step, we have to create the connection; click the "**`+Create`**" menu, and a list of connection options will appear. For our convenience, we are building the Azure OpenAI resource (please refer to the detailed steps explained in *Chapter* 7, *Getting Started with Generative* AI *Using Azure OpenAI Service*).

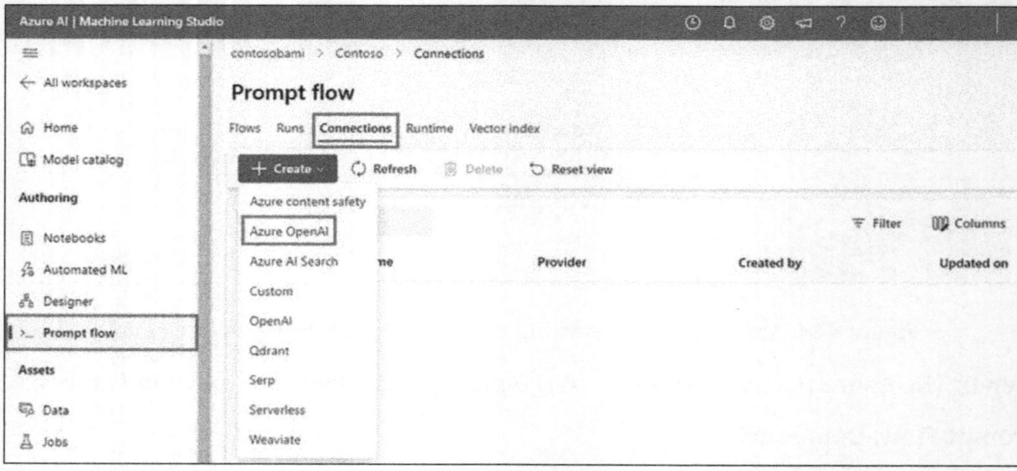

Figure 8.36: *Azure Machine Learning Studio (Prompt Flow; Connection Options)*

Step 2: Click "**`Azure Open AI`**." The Azure portal will take you to the connection configuration window, as shown in *Figure* 8.37. Once all the details are provided, click the "**`Save`**" button.

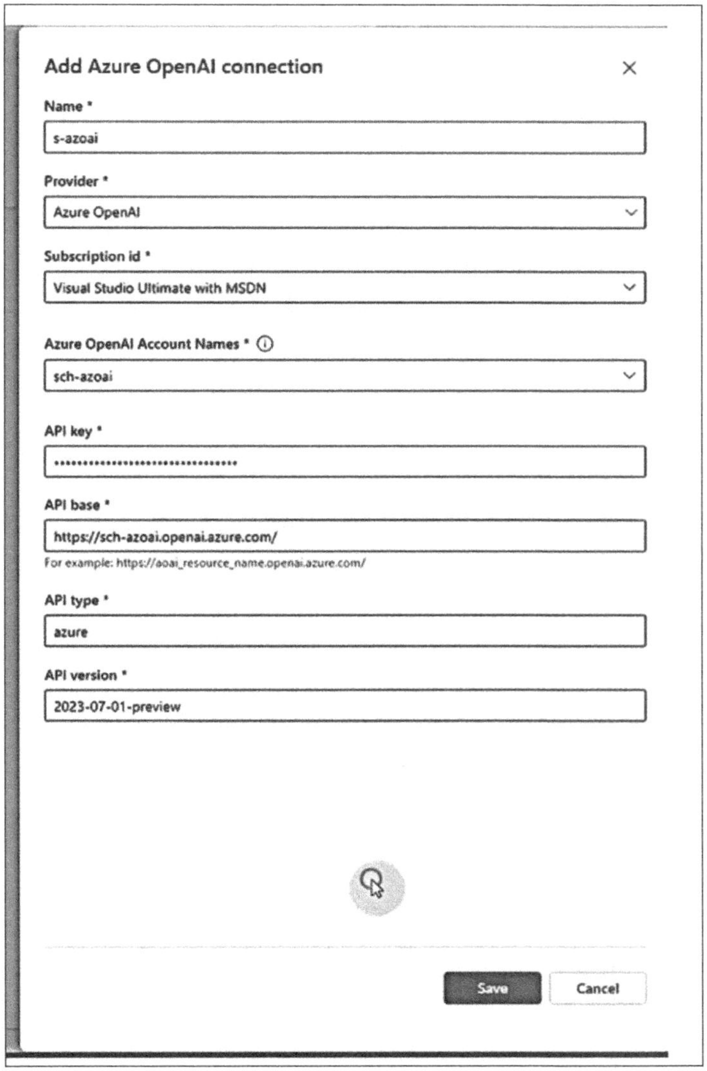

Figure 8.37: *Azure Machine Learning Studio (Prompt Flow; Creating a Connection)*

Step 3: Once the "**Save**" button is clicked, the connection is available for us to use for further assistance in creating prompt flows.

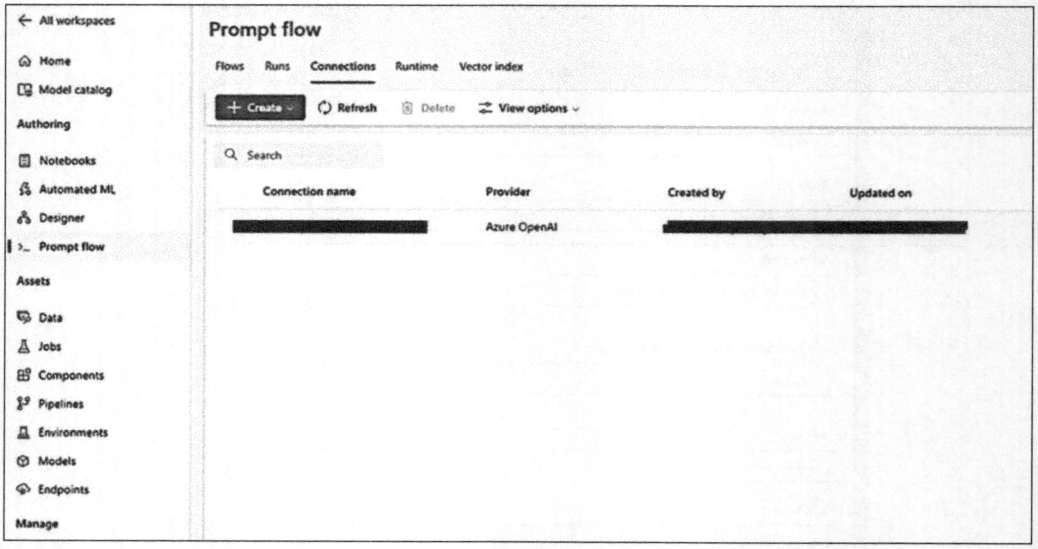

Figure 8.38: *Azure Machine Learning Studio (Prompt Flow; Creating a Connection)*

Step 4: The compute instance is mandatory for the Runtime, so we should create the compute instance and refer to the **Runtime** configuration before creating the runtime.

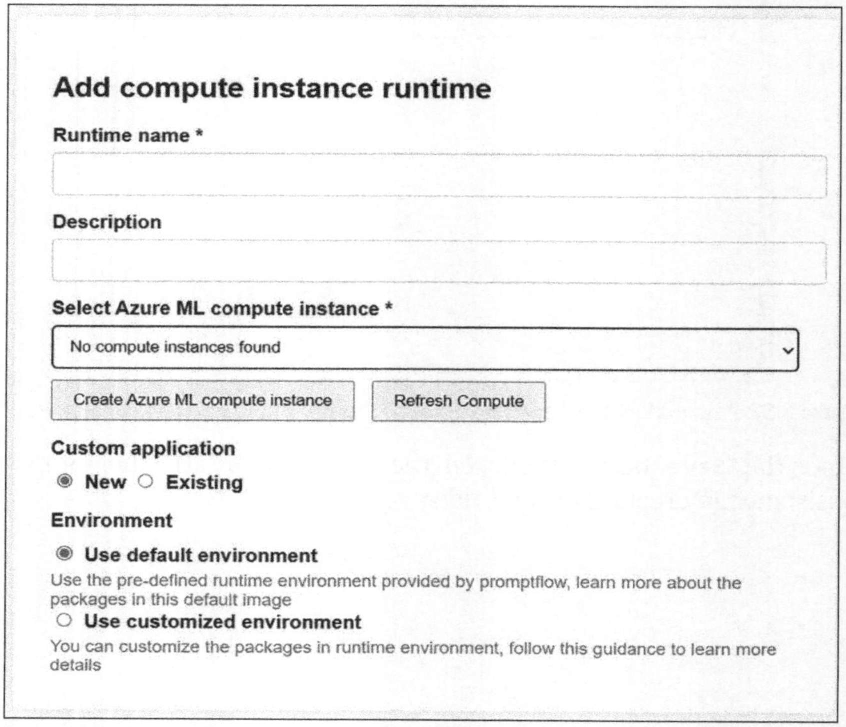

Figure 8.39: *Azure Machine Learning Studio (Prompt Flow; Creating Runtime-Compute)*

Step 5: Create a new compute instance by clicking "**`+ Create`**" at the top. You can select the compute from the left menu highlighted in *Figure* 8.40:

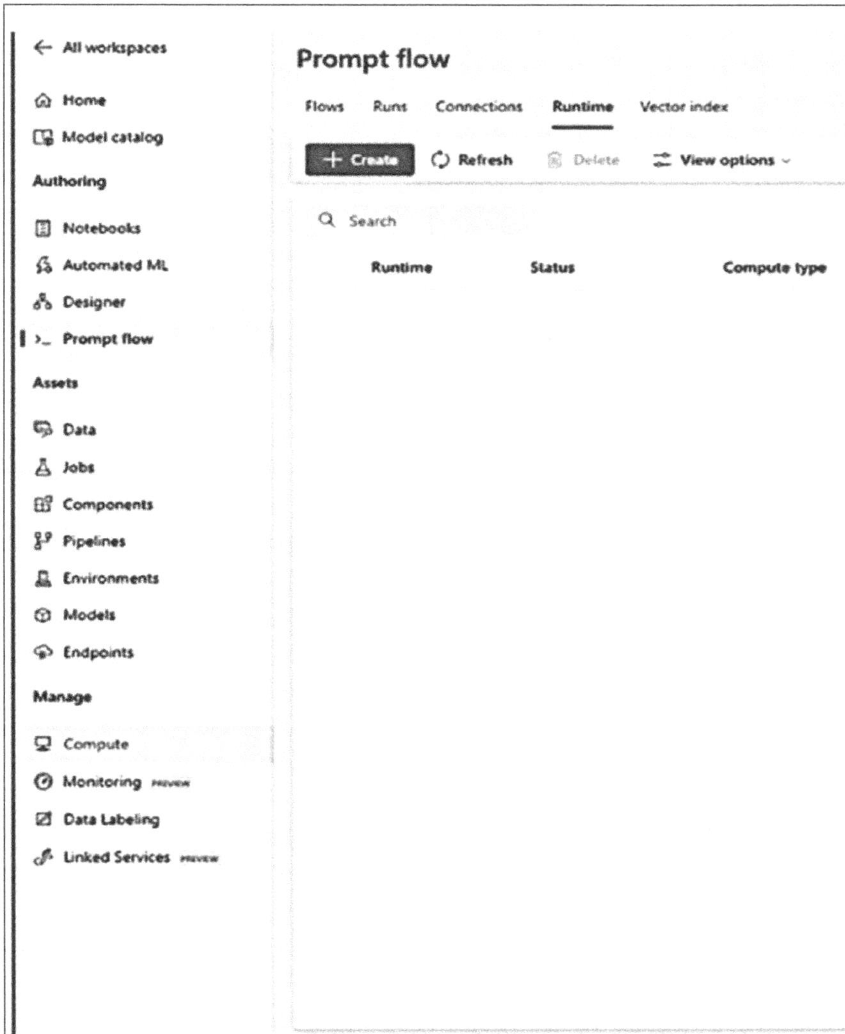

Figure 8.40*: Azure Machine Learning Studio (Creating a Compute Instance)*

Step 6: Once we select **`Compute`** from the left menu, the Azure portal will take us to the compute configuration screen, as shown in *Figure* 8.42. Based on the requirements, we can choose CPU/GPU and VM size. Then, click "**`Review and Create`**".

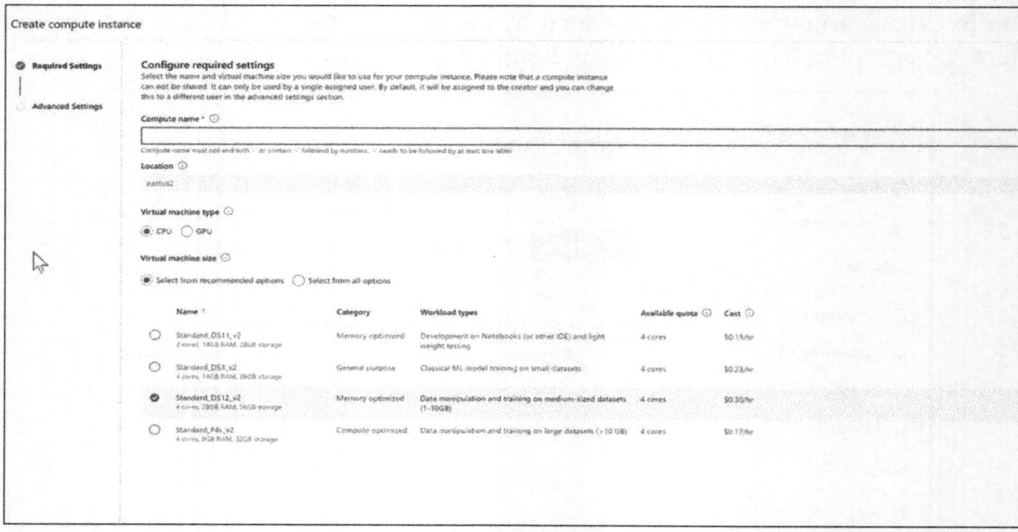

Figure 8.41: *Azure Machine Learning Studio (Creating a Compute Instance in Progress)*

Step 7: The Azure portal will review the VM details and be ready to create, as shown in *Figure 8.42*. Click "**`Create`**" to create a new compute for us.

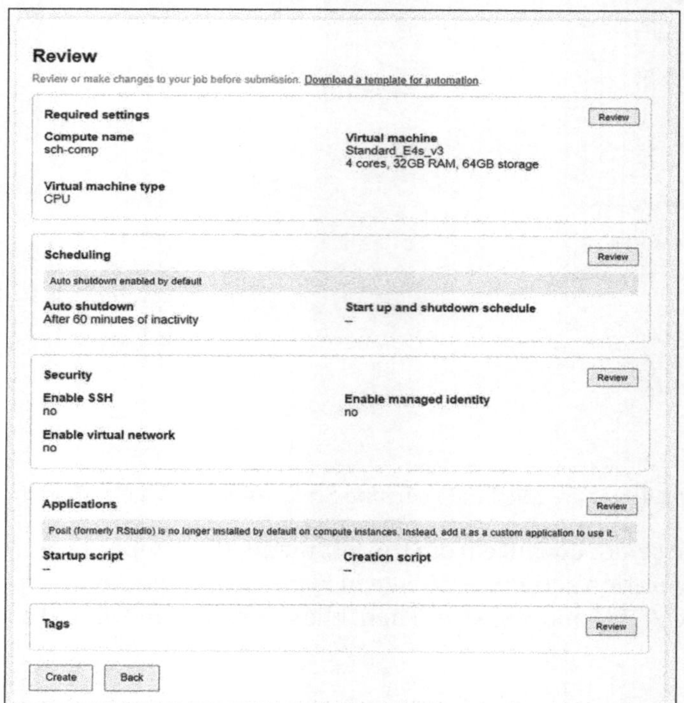

Figure 8.42: *Azure Machine Learning Studio (Creating Compute Instance in Progress; Review Done)*

Step 8: The Azure portal will create the compute successfully, as shown in *Figure* 8.43.

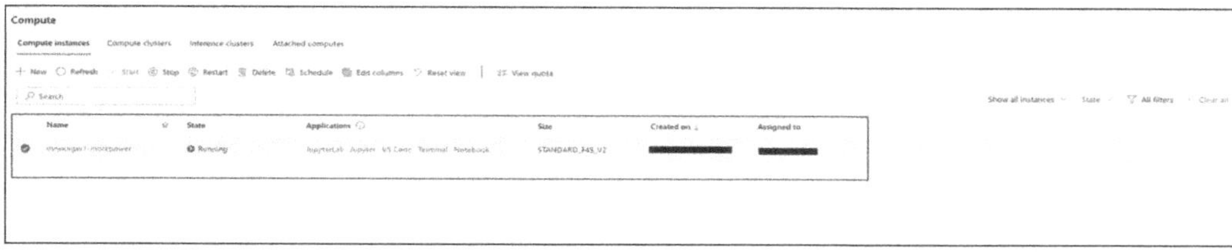

Figure 8.43: *Azure Machine Learning Studio; Compute Instance Created Successfully*

Step 9: Go to Step 4, select the compute instance from the compute ML Instance, and click it, as shown in *Figure* 8.44.

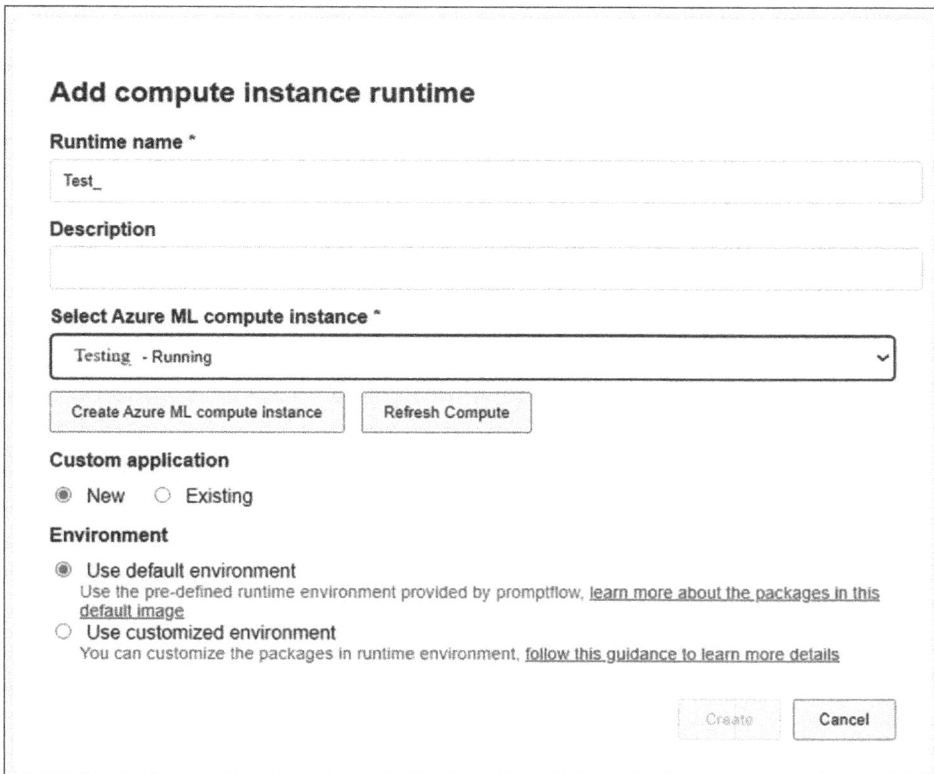

Figure 8.44: *Azure Machine Learning Studio; Compute Instance Adding to Runtime*

Step 10: The Azure portal will ask to restart the compute instance, as shown in *Figure* 8.44. Restart the compute and compute instance in the list, as shown in *Figure* 8.45.

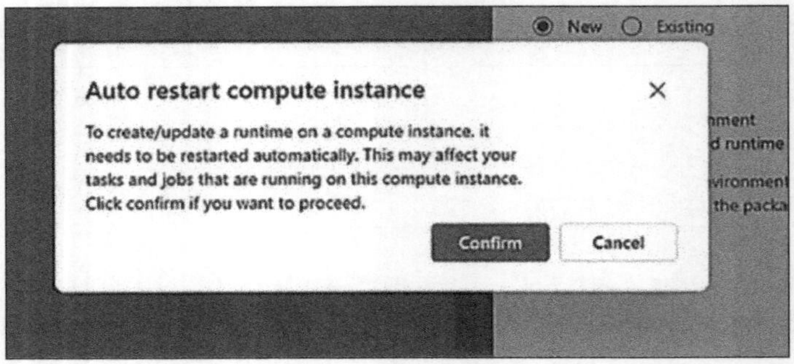

Figure 8.45: *Auto Restart Compute Instance*

Compute Instance for the Runtime

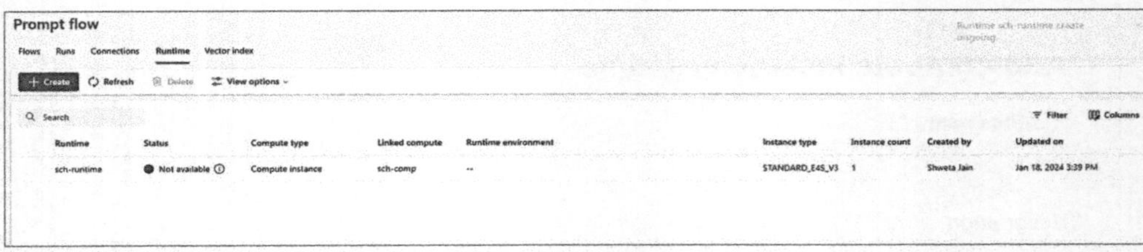

Figure 8.46: *Compute Instance Added Successfully under the Runtime*

Step 11: Creating Prompt flow.

Click "**`+ Create`**" in the top menu, as shown in *Figure* 8.46.

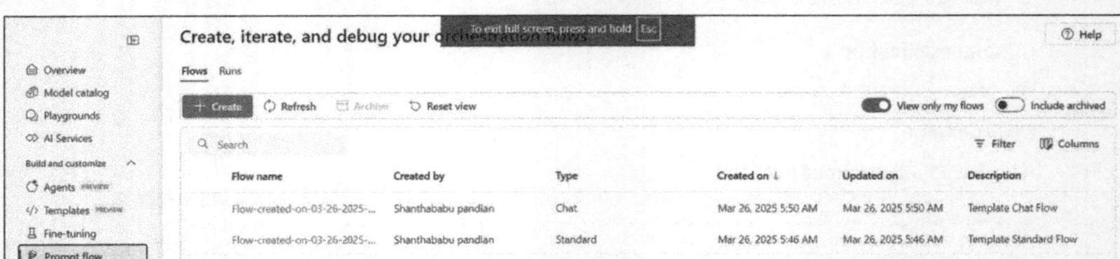

Figure 8.47: *Azure Machine Learning Studio; Prompt Flow*

Step 12: Once we click "**`+ Create`**" menu, the Azure portal takes us to the screen shown in *Figure* 8.48. There, we can observe the types of flow and choose based on the project requirements.

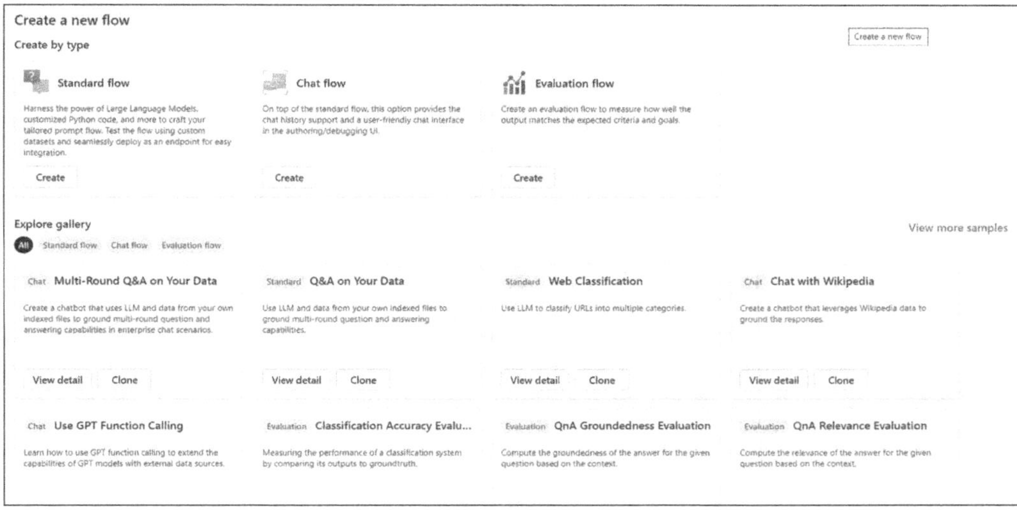

Figure 8.48: *Azure Machine Learning Studio; Prompt Flow; Types*

Step 13: Click **`Standard flow`**. The Azure portal will pop up a window asking us to name the prompt folder, as shown in *Figure* 8.49. Click "**`Create`**".

Figure 8.49: *Azure Machine Learning Studio; Creating Prompt Flow (Standard)*

Prompt Flow Tools: The fundamental tools/building blocks of a flow are LLM, Prompt, Python, and more. All these simple blocks of tools in the prompt flow are tightly integrated to execute the set of actions as a chain process.

- **LLM Tool**: The prompt flow LLM tool uses Large Language Models for natural language processing.

- **Prompt Tool**: The prompt flow Prompt tool offers a collection of textual templates based on the **Jinja** template engine. It facilitates the definition of prompts and is helpful when prompt tuning is required before the prompts are fed into the LLM in the prompt flow.
- **Python Tool**: The prompt flow Python tool offers customized code. It allows us to quickly create Python tools, edit code, and verify results.

Step 14: A default flow will be created for us to demonstrate along with a graph with predefined steps (inputs ➔ joke ➔ echo ➔ outputs), as shown in *Figure* 8.50.

Each flow should have at least one **NODE(S)** (for example, joke), connecting the nodes to form the chain known as flow. By connecting nodes, we establish a seamless chain of operations that guides data flow and business process functionalities through your application.

In the defined flow, the node(s) take center stage and represent specific tools with unique capabilities. These nodes can handle data processing, business-specific task execution, and algorithmic operations with inputs and outputs at both ends.

A Directed Acyclic Graph (DAG) graph visually represents the workflow structure. This graph showcases the connectivity and dependencies between nodes, providing a clear overview of the entire workflow, as shown in *Figure* 8.50.

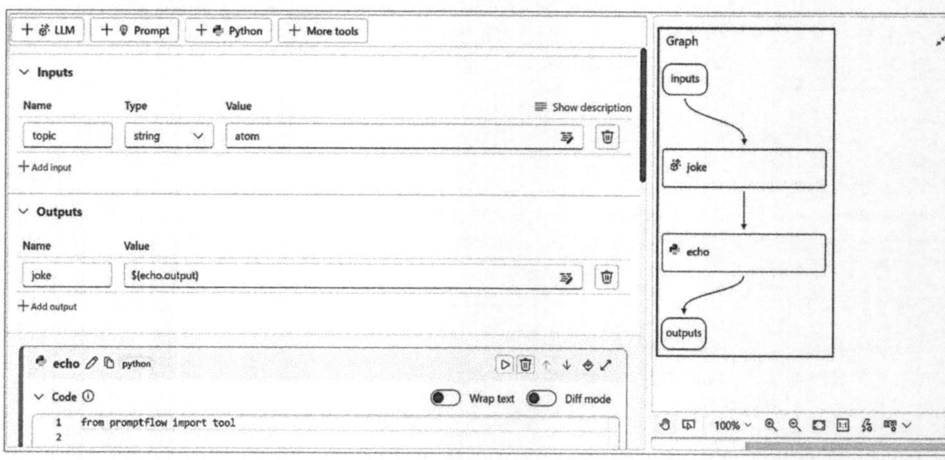

***Figure* 8.50:** *Azure Machine Learning Studio; Prompt Flow Component Configuration (Standard)*

The flow provides a comprehensive framework for managing data flow and processing data within your application, helping you develop your LLM-based AI application.

- **Flow Configuration:**
  - Input from the user and inputs.
  - Input to Outputs from echo.

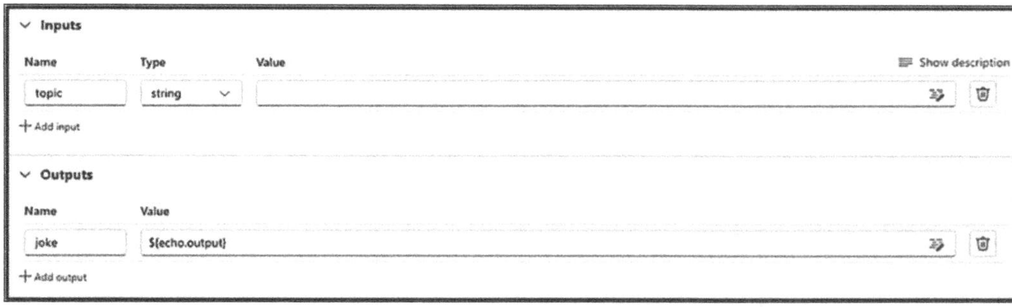

Figure 8.51: *Prompt Flow I/P Component Configuration (Standard)*

- **Node Configuration:**
    - The node will be executed by configuring the inputs (topics).
    - We can change the system message based on our requirements.

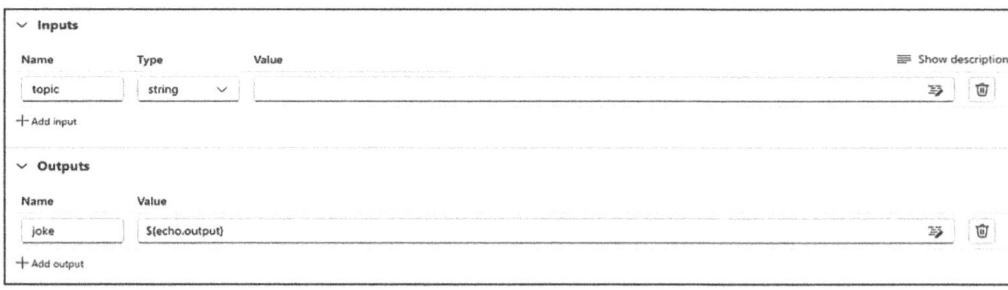

Figure 8.52: *Prompt Flow Node Component Configuration (Standard)*

- **Node Configuration for LLM**: If you want to execute the node with LLM, you must configure it by changing the connection to the Azure OpenAI resource from the drop-down box.

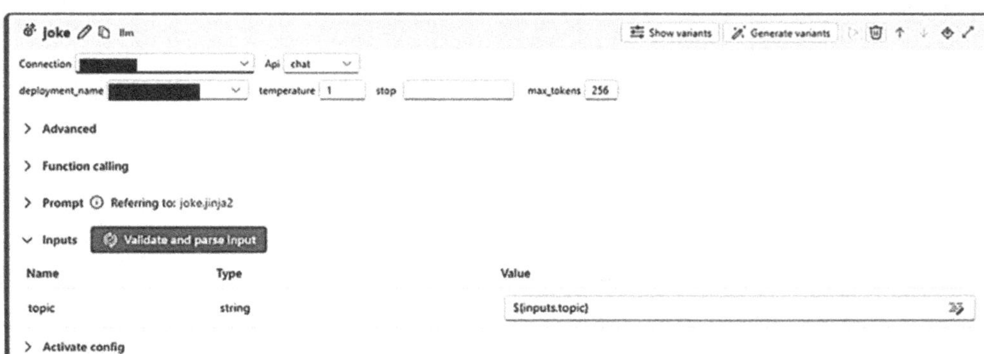

Figure 8.53: *Prompt Flow; Node with LLM Component Configuration (Standard)*

- **Echo configuration**
  - Input for echo is output from Node (joke).

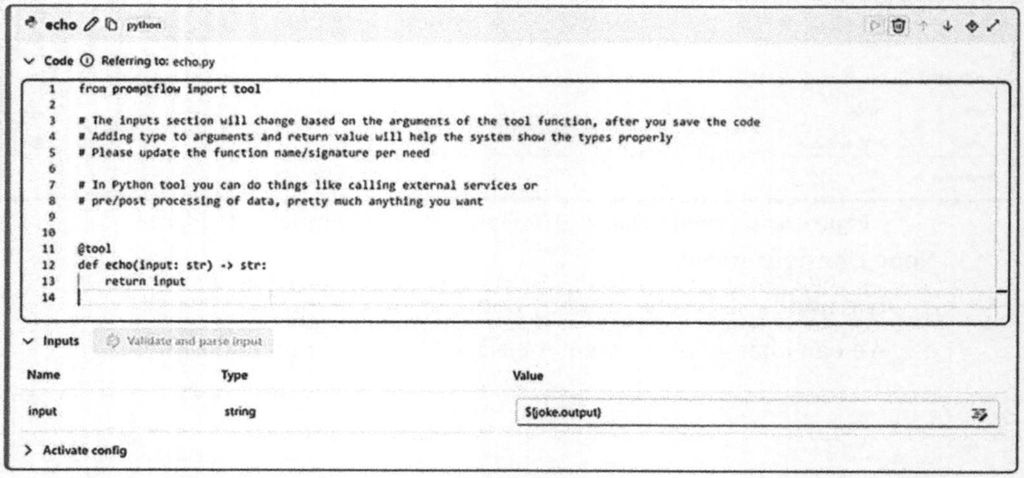

Figure 8.54: *Prompt Flow; Echo Component Configuration (Standard)*

After we provide the input, we must hit the "**Run**" button, as shown in *Figure* 8.55. We can observe that each block will be executed one by one, and graphical representation blocks will turn green with a check mark.

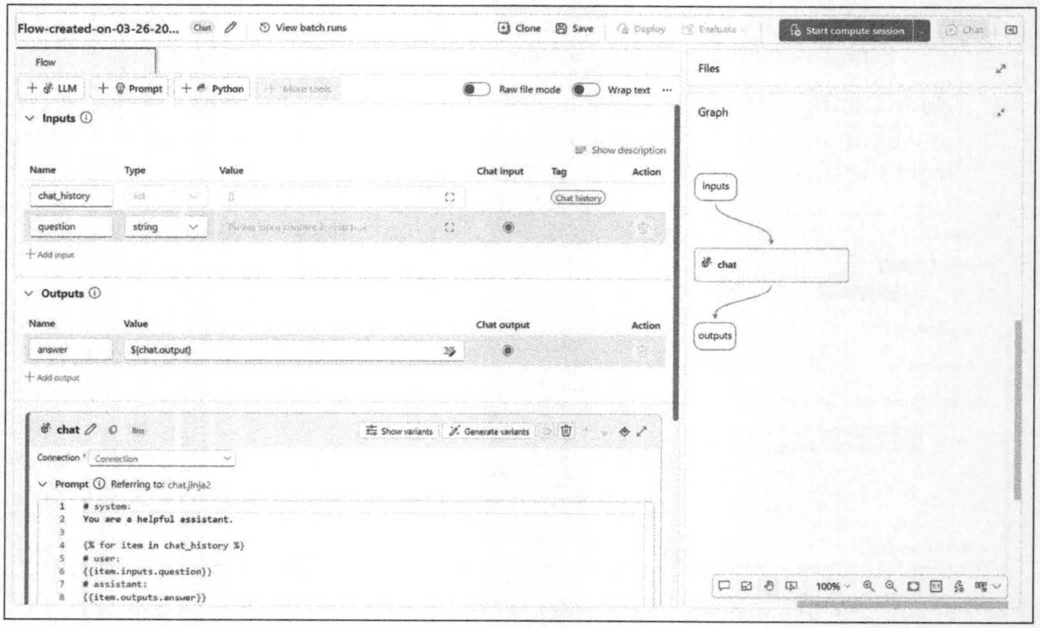

Figure 8.55: *Prompt Flow; Echo Component Configuration (Standard)*

Outputs

- **Output**: Status of the flow.

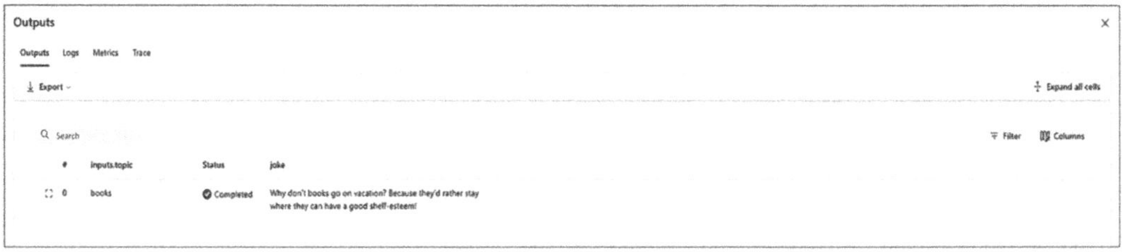

Figure 8.56: *Prompt Flow; Outputs Evaluation (Output)*

- **Logs**: Flow logs for each stage.

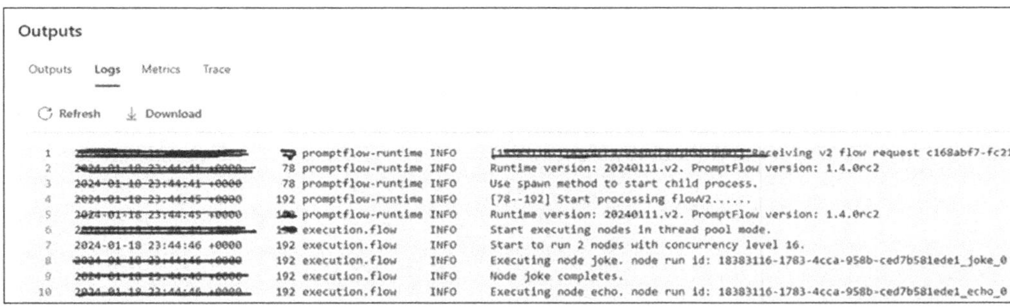

Figure 8.57: *Prompt Flow; Outputs Evaluation (Logs)*

- **Metrics**: On each stage.

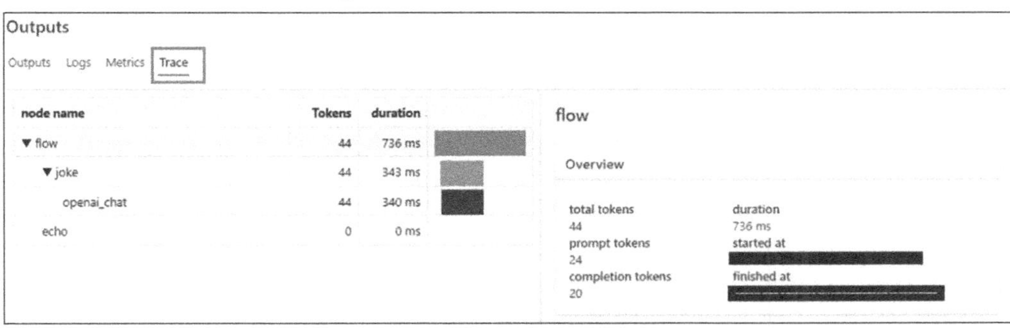

Figure 8.58: *Prompt Flow; Outputs Evaluation (Trace)*

Prompt Evaluation and Scoring: Azure AI Studio offers tools to evaluate the quality of prompt-generated outputs. Models can be scored based on accuracy, relevance, coherence, and sentiment, and the dataset that we will use for AI product development. This will effectively support AI developers, and architects can use this feedback to adjust their prompts and data to improve the model's performance.

Step 1: Select Evaluate from the left menu and click "**`Automated evaluation`**" from the top right menu, as shown in *Figure* 8.59.

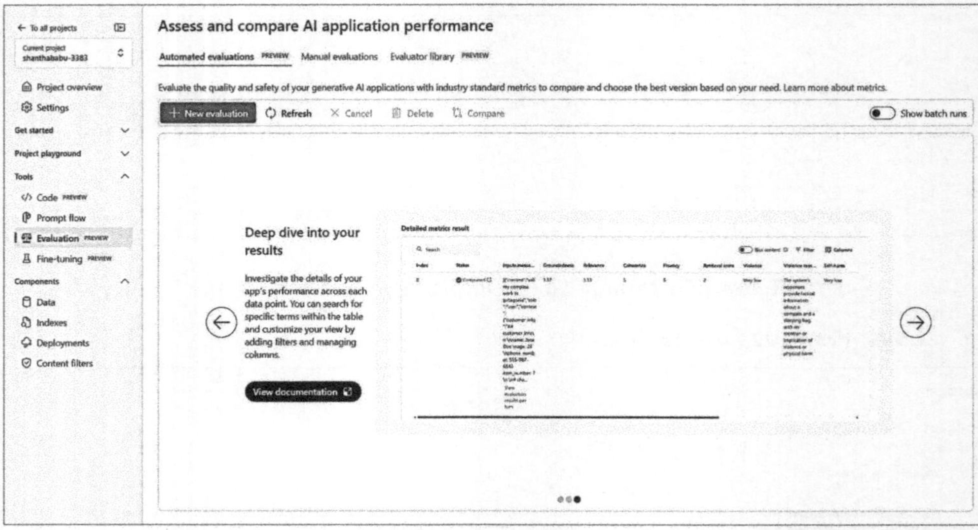

Figure 8.59: *Azure AI Studio; Evaluation*

Step 2: We can select from the options that are Model, Dataset, or Prompt flow, as shown in *Figure* 8.60.

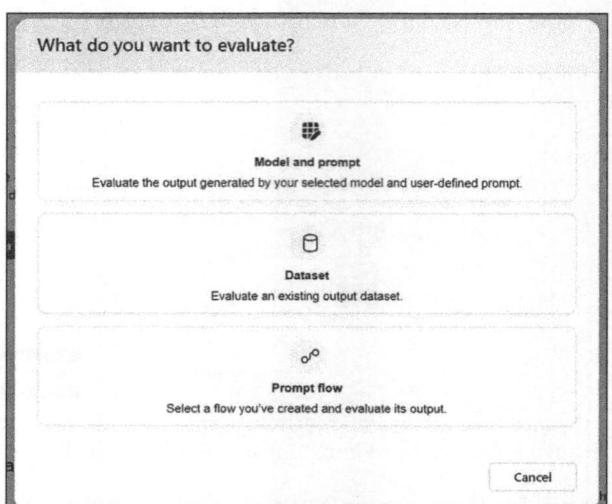

Figure 8.60: *Azure AI Studio; Evaluation (Model-Dataset-Prompt flow)*

Step 3: Let us try with the Evaluate Dataset.

Select Dataset: The Azure portal will take us to create a new evaluation page, configure it based on the requirements, and click "**`Next`**."

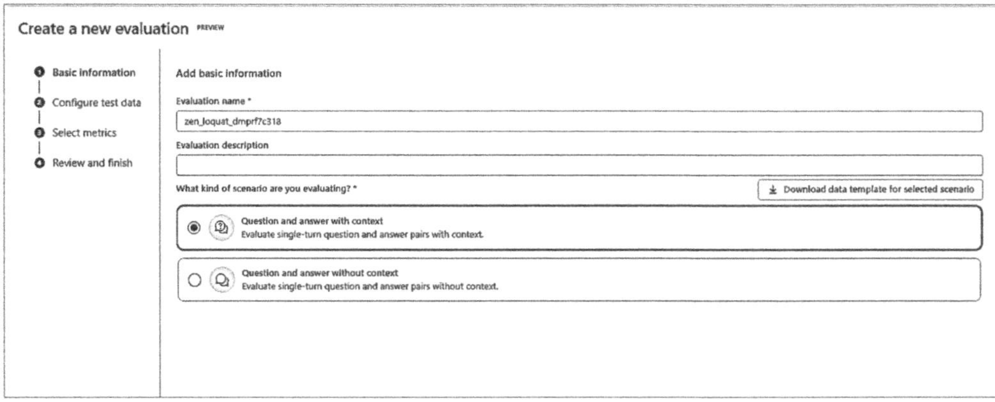

Figure 8.61: *Azure AI Studio; Dataset Evaluation (Stage 1)*

Step 4: Configure the data; we can add an existing dataset or create a new one, and then click "**`Next`**."

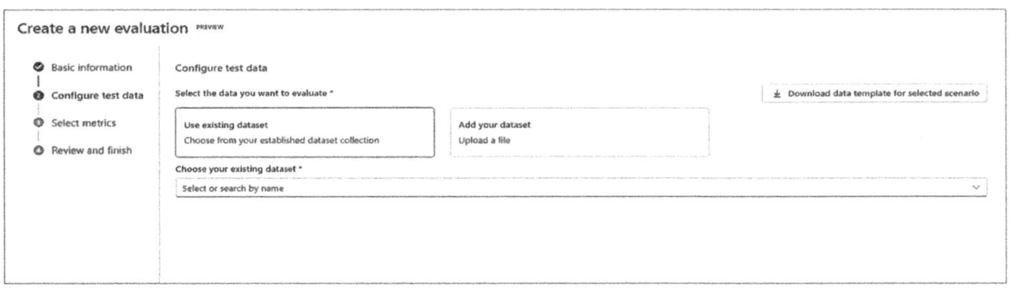

Figure 8.62: *Azure AI Studio; Dataset Evaluation (Stage 2)*

Step 5: Select the dataset from your local drive, as shown in *Figure* 8.63.

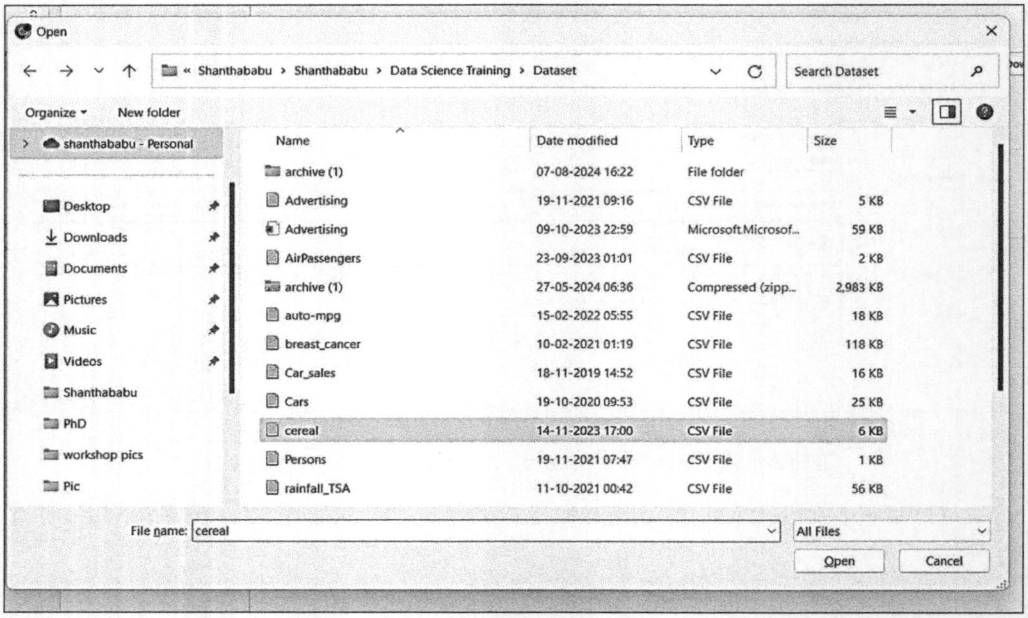

Figure 8.63: *Azure AI Studio; Dataset Evaluation (Stage 3)*

Step 6: Once the dataset is uploaded, we can see its preview in *Figure* 8.64 and click "**Next**."

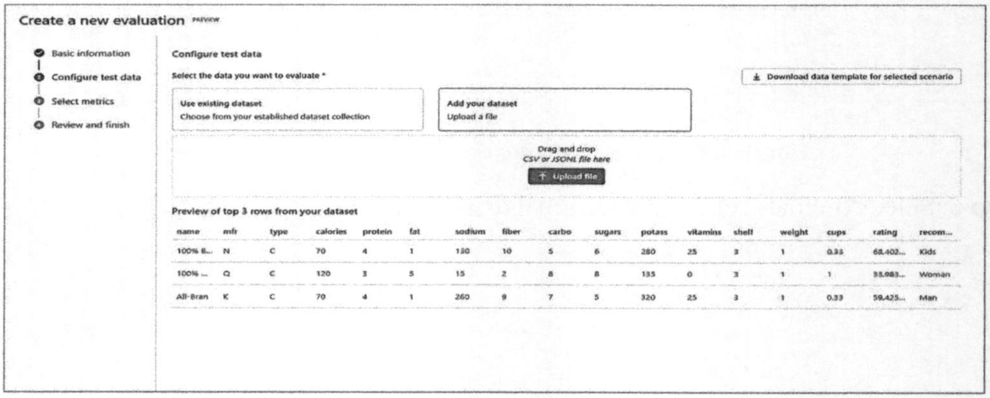

Figure 8.64: *Azure AI Studio; Dataset Evaluation (Stage 4)*

Step 7: Following the uploaded dataset, we have to select the metrics for our evaluation purpose and click "**Next**."

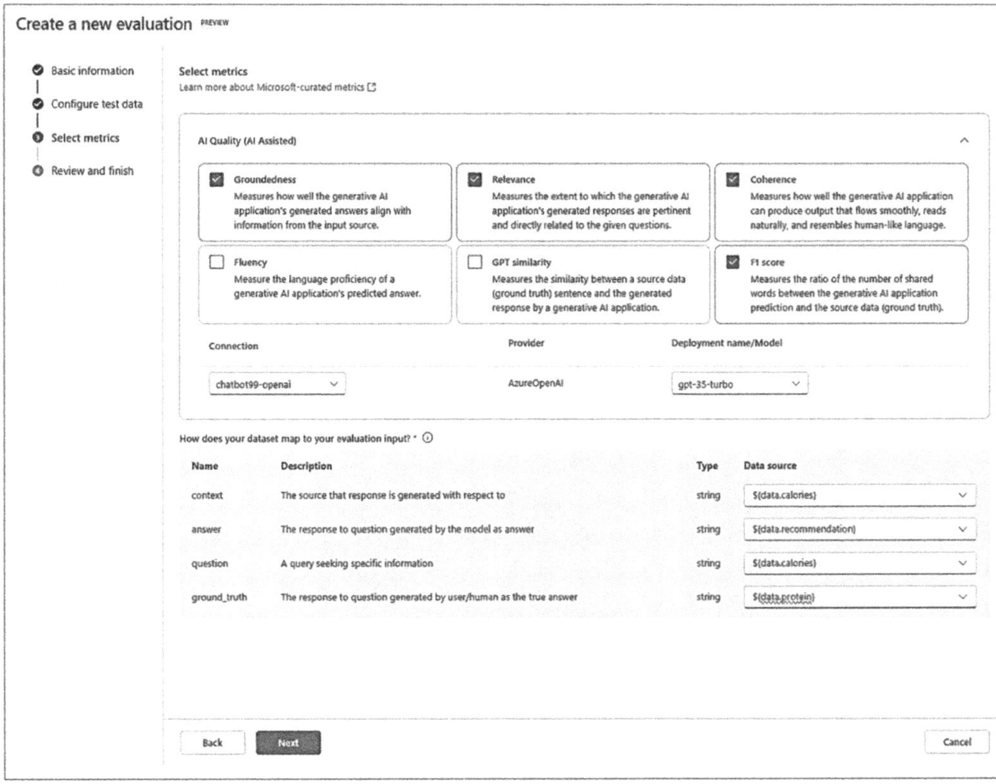

Figure 8.65: *Azure AI Studio; Dataset Evaluation (Stage 5)*

Step 8: Following the metrics selection process, the system will review and process the evaluation metrics; once it is done, click "**`Submit`**."

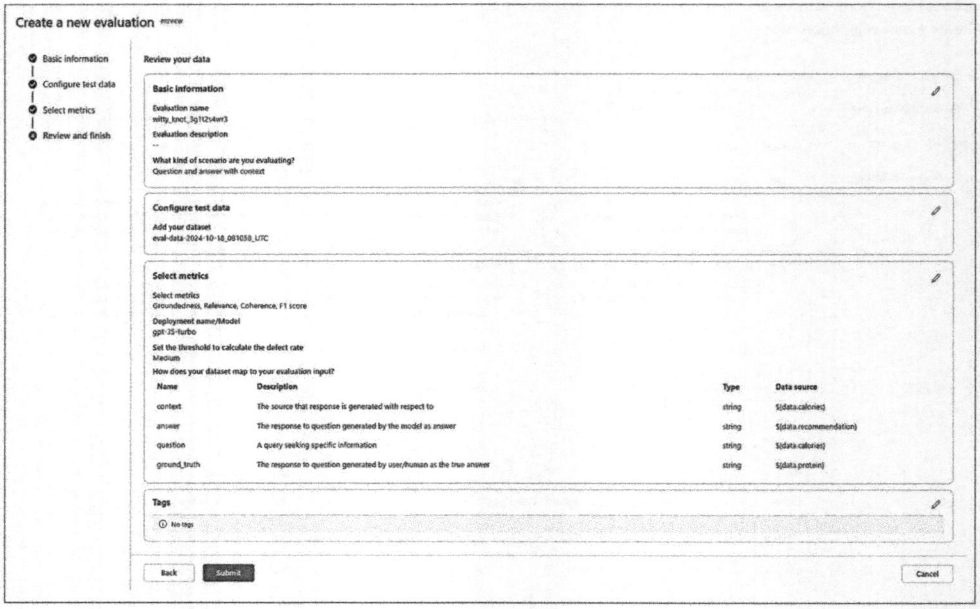

Figure 8.66: Azure AI Studio; *Dataset Evaluation (Stage 6)*

Step 9: *Figure* 8.67 shows the processed evaluation for a given dataset.

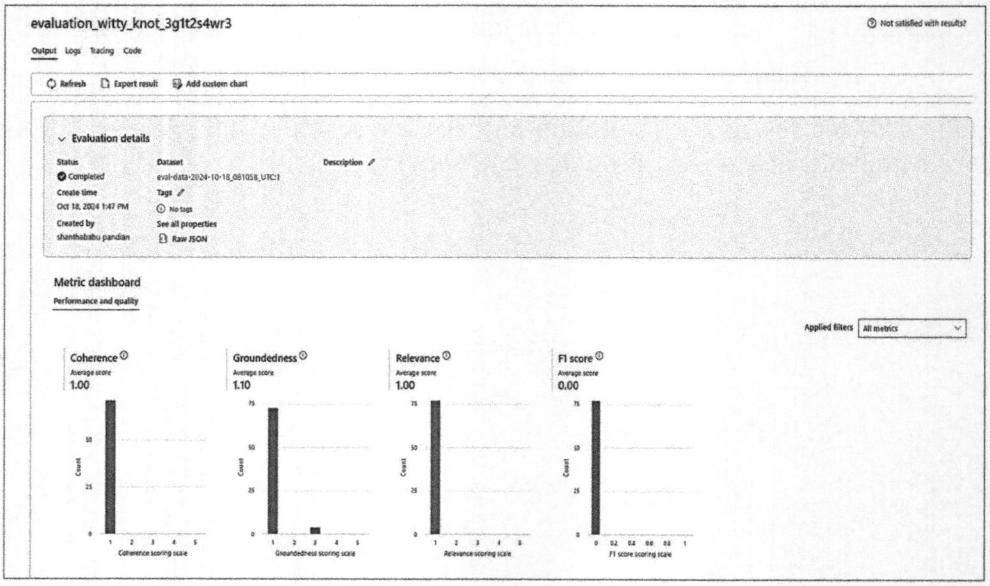

Figure 8.67: Azure AI Studio; *Dataset Evaluation Metrics (Stage 5)*

We can also generate the customer metrics, as shown in *Figure* 8.68.

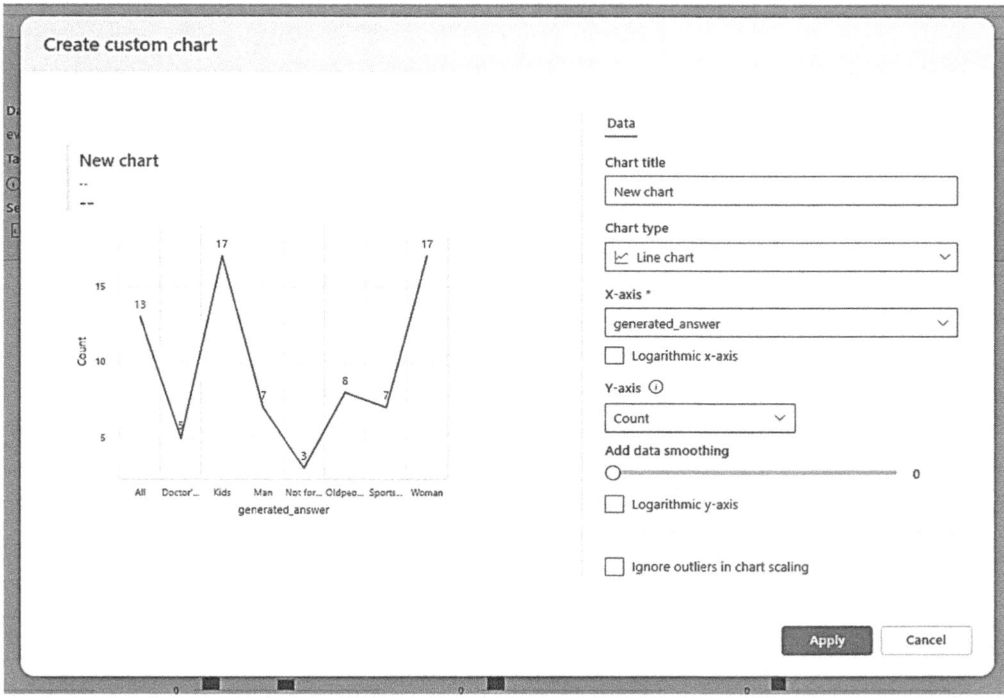

Figure 8.68: *Azure AI Studio; Dataset Evaluation Custom Metrics*

Evaluation Dashboard, as shown in *Figure* 8.69.

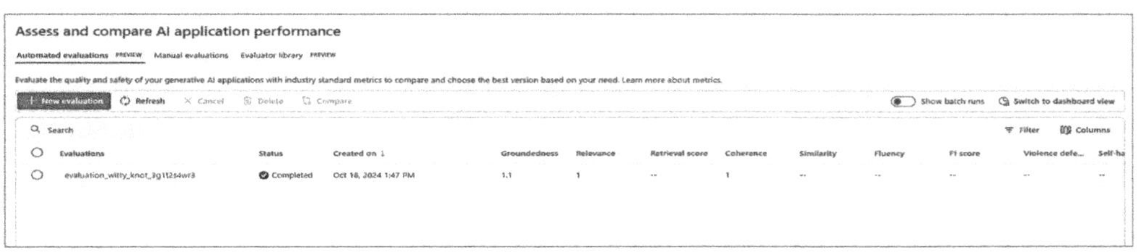

Figure 8.69: *Azure AI Studio; Evaluation Dashboard*

Model and Prompt: In the earlier exercise, we created a dataset evaluation in Step 2. If we select the Model and Prompt option, the Azure portal will take you to the page similar to *Figure* 8.70. Once the basic configurations are provided, it will create the evaluation and generate the results based on our selection.

- Language
  - Coherence
  - Fluency

- Safety
  - Self-harm-related content
  - Hateful and unfair content
  - Sexual content

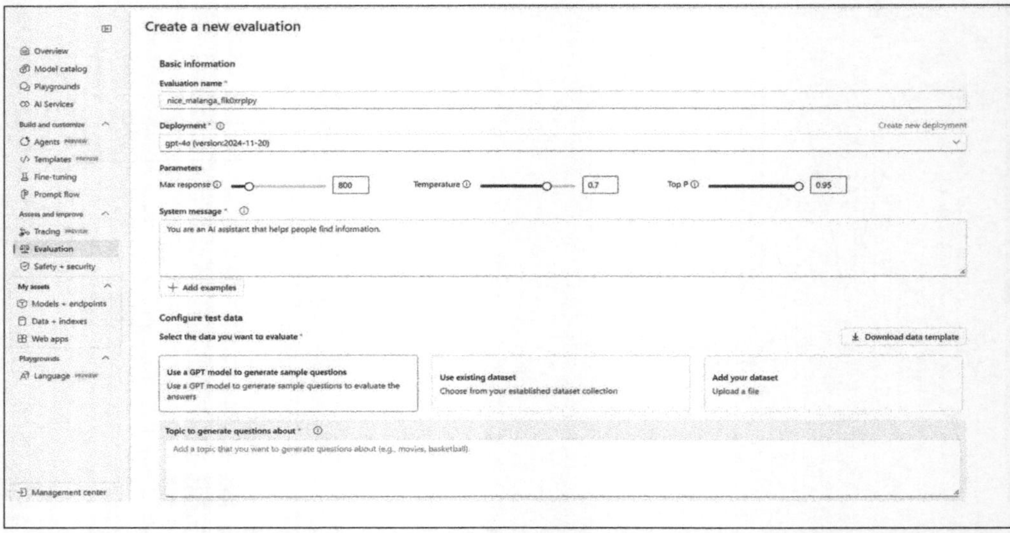

Figure 8.70: *Azure AI Studio; Evaluation Model and Prompt*

Prompt flow evaluation is very similar to dataset evaluation; instead of the dataset, we have to select the existing flow and add the test data to generate output for evaluation. It is important to note that within a flow, we might have multiple nodes, each of which could have its own set of variants. In such cases, we must specify the node and the variants we wish to assess during the evaluation process.

- **Reusable Prompt Templates:** Once an optimized prompt flow has been designed, it can be saved as a template and reused across projects. This practice benefits businesses that need to scale their AI solutions across different departments and customize them based on demand.
- **Contextual Learning and Memory:** In conversational AI-driven solutions, prompt flows can include memory, allowing the AI to recall previous interactions or context within a session. This improves the capability of AI-driven solutions to handle multi-turn conversations and creates more human-like interactions in the production environment.
- **Deployment and Scaling:** Once the solution is built and tested, Azure AI Studio simplifies deployment and scaling:
  - **One-Click Deployment**: After building and testing AI models, developers can deploy them as APIs with minimal effort. Azure AI Studio supports **Azure Kubernetes Service (AKS)** and **Azure App Service** for deploying

scalable AI solutions.

- **Global Availability and Scaling**: Azure's global infrastructure ensures that AI solutions built in Azure AI Studio can scale to meet the demands of global enterprises, handling large datasets and real-time requests without performance degradation.
- **Monitoring and Maintenance**: Azure AI Studio provides monitoring tools that track model performance in production environments. Developers can monitor metrics such as response times, error rates, and user interactions, enabling continuous optimization and troubleshooting.

Azure AI Content Safety

Content safety, privacy, security, and compliance are essential considerations in any domain; after the development of Gen AI, these responsibilities are now on the shoulders of AI-driven product development and deployment, along with the responsibility for those AI tools that support the following industries: education, finance, banking, healthcare, and law forums.

Apply various mechanisms and industry best practices to ensure that AI systems operate safely, securely, and adeptly.

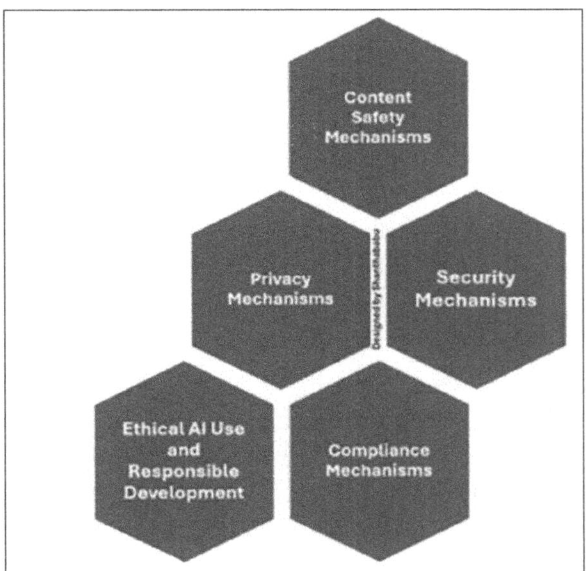

Figure 8.71: *AI-based Safety and Security Mechanisms*

Here is an overview of these elements:

Content Safety Mechanisms: As a social responsibility, the AI development team must take responsibility while designing, developing, and deploying the systems into production, primarily those systems used for content generation or conversation, such as social media platforms or conversational AI from an industry perspective. These systems require mechanisms to protect end users from harmful, hateful, unfair, and sexual content. Some critical approaches include:

- **Content Filtering and Moderation:** The AI architect and development team must select and train AI models that automatically flag and remove harmful content, such as hate speech, violence-triggering content, or inappropriate language.
- **Warning Mechanisms:** AI systems can alert users of the content they are about to post without knowing the community guidelines, nudging them to reconsider automatically and save them from violating the guidelines.
- **Bias and Fairness Auditing**: Regular audits should be conducted to detect and mitigate any biases and unfair content generated. They must be tested to ensure they do not discriminate based on race, gender, or other protected characteristics.

Privacy Mechanisms: Since AI tools use massive amounts of data, especially personal data, they must handle them with strict safeguards to comply with global, country, and region-level privacy regulations such as General Data Protection Regulation (GDPR) and California Consumer Privacy Act (CCPA).

Some privacy-focused mechanisms include:

- **Data Minimization**: Collect only the minimum amount of data necessary for a task and avoid unnecessarily storing sensitive data.
- **Anonymization**: Introducing an anonymization process to strip off personal data by carefully identifying the details to make it harder to trace back to individuals. This protects privacy even if data leaks occur.
- **Differential Privacy**: Differential privacy techniques can also add noise to private data and ensure that individual users' data cannot be reverse engineered while allowing useful insights to be derived from datasets.
- **Federated Learning**: Implementing federated learning techniques to train AI models directly on users' devices instead of sending data to a central server for AI training. This approach will ensure that data stays local and private and only shares model updates.

Compliance Mechanisms are similar to Privacy Mechanisms with a few additional AI Governance Frameworks.

Security Mechanisms: Along with content and privacy, data security is critical to protect AI systems and the data they handle from unauthorized users. These mechanisms include the following techniques:

- **End-to-end Encryption**: Encryption can protect communications between users and AI systems and ensure that third parties cannot intercept and read data.

- **Access Controls and Authentication**: Only authorized users and systems can access sensitive AI features or datasets.
- **Adversarial Testing**: AI models can be tested against adversarial attacks, which attempt to trick them into making incorrect predictions.
- **AI Model Protection**: AI models must be protected from tampering, theft, or reverse engineering, which can expose vulnerabilities or intellectual property.

Azure provides the AI Content Safety Studio, which is an AI service. The interactive studio allows us to view, explore, and try out sample code for detecting harmful content across different modalities that detect harmful or unfair content in user-generated and AI-generated content from AI-driven applications and services. This content includes text, summaries, conversation text, audio, images, and video.

Get started with Content Safety Studio.

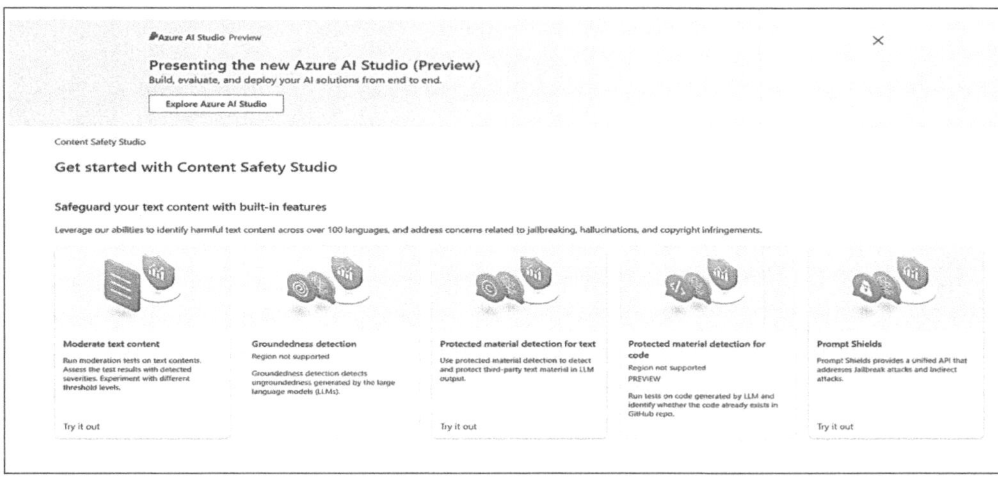

Figure 8.72: *Azure AI Content Safety*

Let us discuss the Azure Content Safety Studio features.

The following Azure AI Content Safety features are available in the Content Safety features:

- **Moderate Text Content:** The text moderation tool allows us to run tests on text content quickly and facilitates testing a single sentence or an entire dataset based on the demand with a user-friendly interface that lets you assess the test results directly in the portal. It can export the code; we can implement the tool directly in our application, streamlining our workflow and saving time to analyze the content safety, privacy, security, and compliance parameters.

Step 1: Select the Moderate text content option from the list, as shown in *Figure* 8.73:

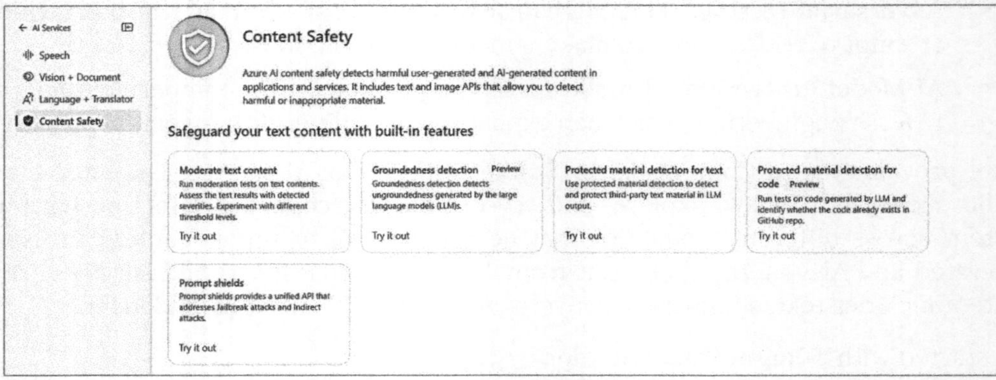

Figure 8.73: *Azure AI Content Safety*

Step 2: Choose an Azure AI service and select a sample (for example, Safe content).

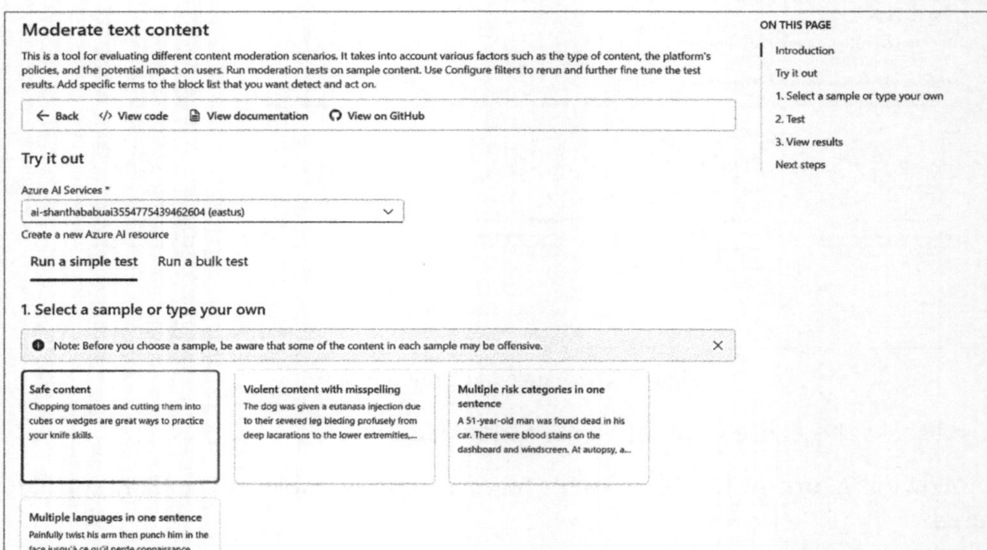

Figure 8.74: *Azure AI Content Safety; Moderate Text Content*

Step 3: Configure Filters (Violence, Self-harm, Sexual, and Hate) and Submit the chosen text to Azure AI Content Safety Studio:

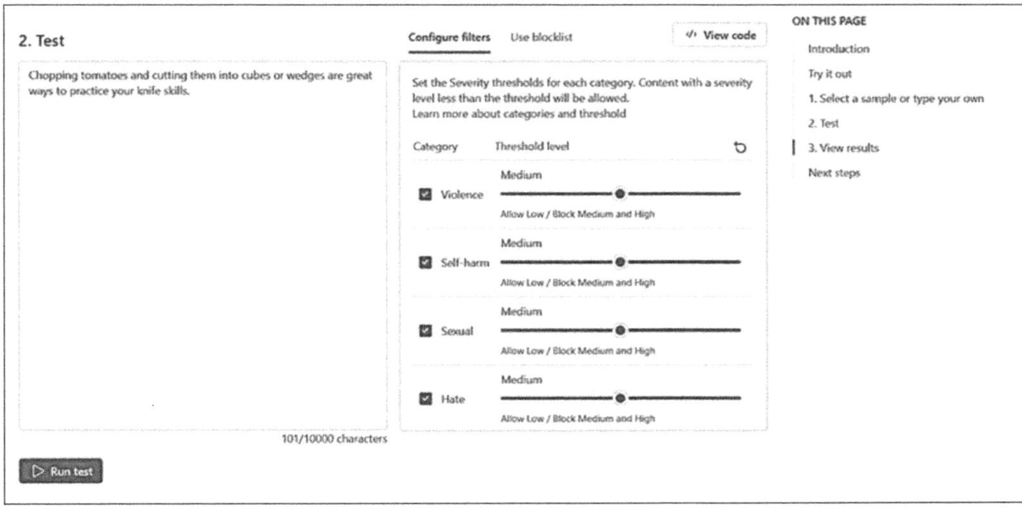

Figure 8.75: *Azure AI Content Safety; Moderate Text Content*

After the above configuration, you will get the following Azure AI Content Safety:

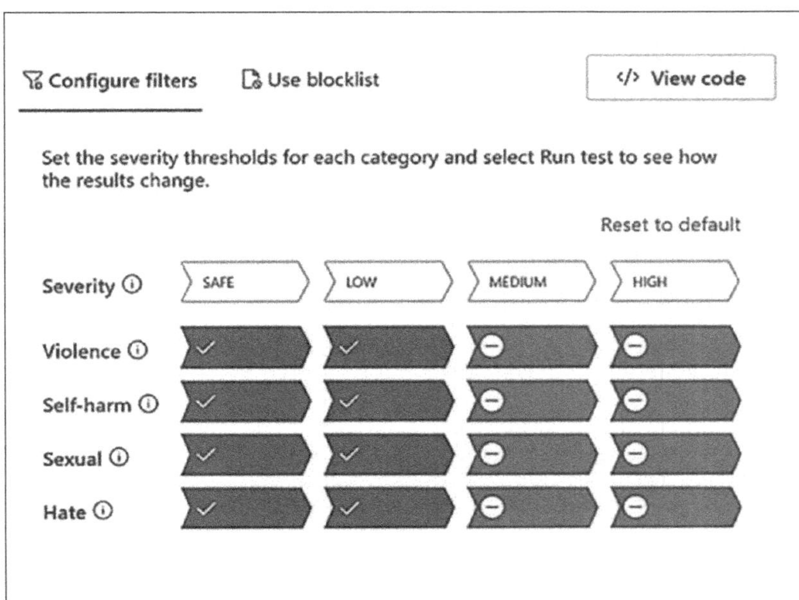

Figure 8.76: *Azure AI Content Safety; Moderate Text Content (Validating the Configuration)*

Step 4: Review the moderation results:

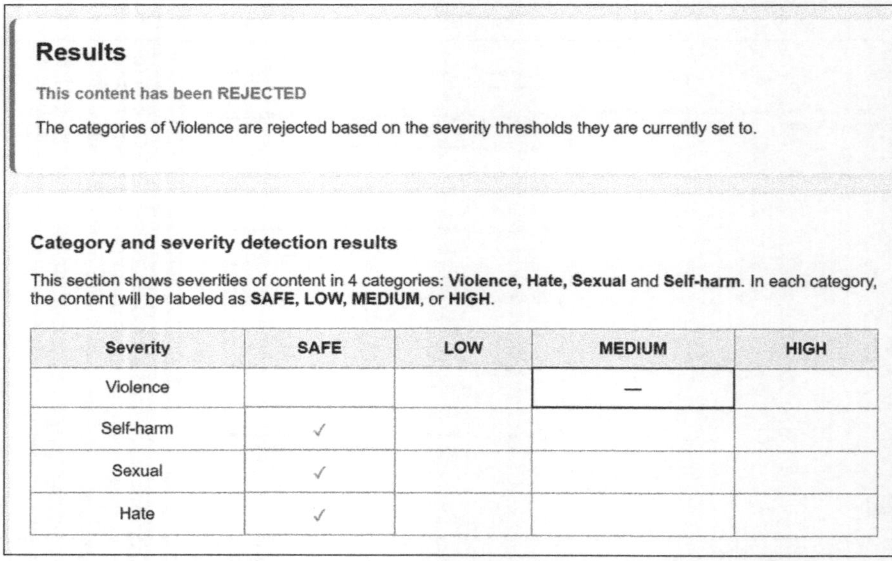

Severity	SAFE	LOW	MEDIUM	HIGH
Violence			—	
Self-harm	✓			
Sexual	✓			
Hate	✓			

Figure 8.77: *Azure AI Content Safety; Moderate Text Content (Results)*

- **Moderate Image Content:** Of course, the image moderation tool also analyzes the level of content safety, privacy, security, and compliance. This will allow us to efficiently run tests on images to ensure they meet our standards and rules within the aforementioned parameters. Again, this tool is typically similar to the **Moderate Text Content** tool.

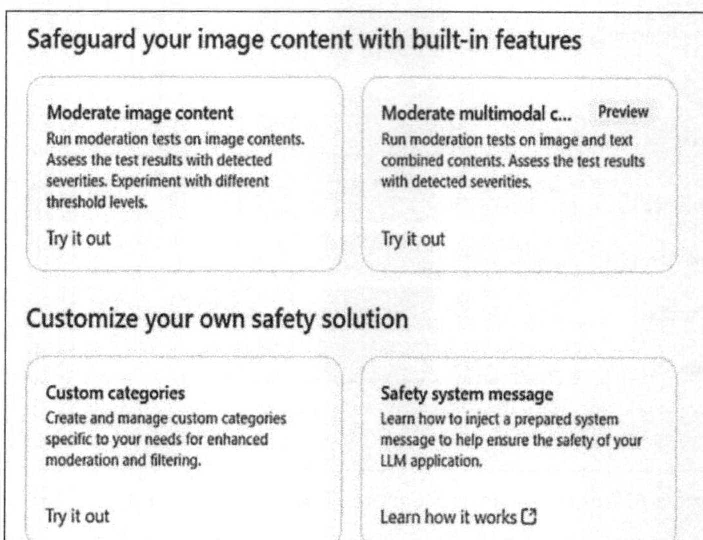

Figure 8.78: *Azure AI Content Safety; Moderate Image Content*

- **Customized:**
    - Custom categories: It helps to create and manage custom categories specific to your needs for enhanced moderation and filtering.
    - Safety system message: It learns how to inject a prepared system message to help ensure the safety of your LLM application.
- **Monitor Online Activity:** The powerful monitoring page lets us easily track our moderation API usage and trends across the modalities previously discussed. This feature enables you to access detailed response information as listed:
    - Category
    - Severity distribution
    - Latency
    - Error
    - Blocklist detection.

  It provides a complete overview of our content/image moderation performance. It allows AI developers to optimize workflows and ensure that content aligns with AI-based safety and security mechanisms, ranking content moderation performance and achieving your content goals.

Conclusion

This chapter delved into Azure AI Studio's role in advancing generative AI, highlighting its robust, integrated environment for developing, deploying, and managing AI models within the Azure ecosystem.

The chapter covered Azure AI Studio's extensive capabilities for building industry-specific AI solutions. It also examined the platform's architecture, which supports model evaluation and deployment through a unified interface, SDK, and CLI.

Furthermore, the chapter emphasized Azure AI Studio's Responsible AI features, covering content safety, ethical AI practices, and mechanisms for monitoring and controlling AI outputs to mitigate any bias and ensure compliance. An in-depth look at the prompt flow architecture demonstrated Azure AI Studio's flexibility in data integration, model experimentation, and evaluation, reinforcing its value for scalable, ethical AI development.

The next chapter explores Azure's Language, Speech, Vision Studio and their tools. We will learn how to start projects with or without code, leverage client libraries, REST APIs, and incorporate conversation and vision features, such as OCR and facial recognition, into our applications effortlessly.

Chapter 9
Advanced Azure AI Studio–II

Introduction

In the previous chapter, we provided a gateway to how Azure AI Studio is leading a new era of Gen AI development, empowering developers to confidently explore, build, test, and deploy AI products. In order to illustrate how Azure AI Studio facilitates solution design, the chapter examined models, capabilities, responsible AI, and prompts. We investigated its single platform. In order to prepare developers to handle the intricacies of Gen AI with assurance and ethical considerations, we also covered content safety measures and the application of responsible AI technologies for privacy, security, and compliance.

This chapter explores Speech, Language, and Vision Studio. We will take a deep dive into Azure AI-Speech Studio and the Language Studio platform service features to showcase how it provides you with an easy-to-use experience in creating custom projects and models to work on your data. We will get started with No code and Code with your application's available client libraries and REST APIs. We will learn how to use Speech Studio with your own text and how to build solutions for text-to-speech voice. We will also learn how Azure AI Vision is a unified service that offers innovative computer vision capabilities and allows apps to analyze images, read text, and detect faces with prebuilt image tagging, text extraction with optical character recognition (OCR), and responsible facial recognition. We will also understand how to incorporate vision features into our projects without requiring machine-learning expertise.

Structure

In this chapter, you will delve into the following topics:

- Deep Dive into Azure Speech Studio
    - Azure Speech Studio: Features
    - Azure Speech SDK: Speech-to-text and Text-to-Speech

    - Significance of Azure AI Speech
- Deep Dive into Azure Vision Studio
    - Azure Vision Studio: Features
    - Azure Vision SDK Image Analytics Implementation
- Deep Dive into Azure Language Studio
    - Azure Language Studio: Features
    - Azure Language SDK Image Analytics Implementation
    - Critical Capabilities of Spatial Analysis
- Microsoft Visual Studio Code
    - VS Code Environment Study
    - Best Practices for VS Code Environment
    - Significance of VS Code as Azure AI SDK
    - Comparative Study of VS Code with Other SDKs
- Azure AI Foundry

Deep Dive into Azure Speech Studio

Azure Speech Studio provides speech-to-text and text-to-speech functionality. Log in to the Azure portal, search “**`Azure Speech Studio`**”, and click it, as shown in *Figure 9.1*. Click **`"AI Services"`** in the left menu (highlighted in the following figure), which is integrated with generative AI.

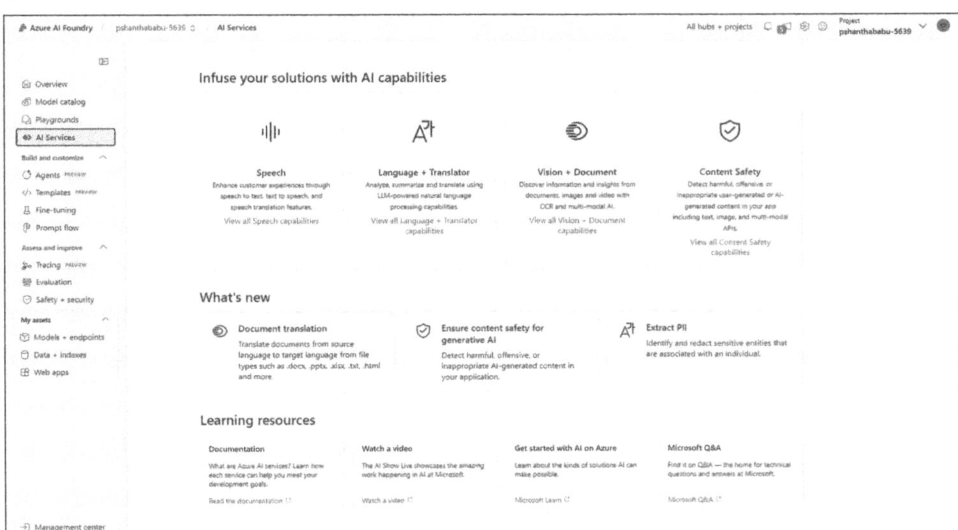

Figure 9.1: *Azure AI Studio Service*

If you click "**Speech**", as shown in *Figure* 9.2, the portal will take you to the screen shown in *Figure* 9.3. This screen allows you to quickly test your audio on a speech recognition endpoint without writing any code.

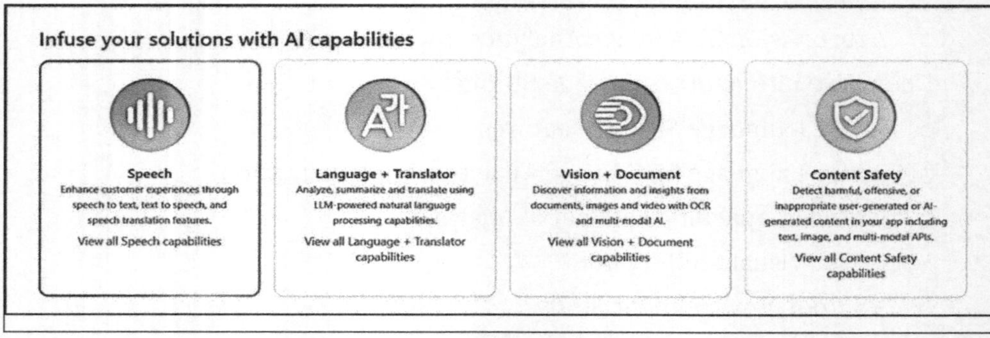

Figure 9.2: *Azure AI Studio Service*

Speech gives your apps the ability to hear, understand, and even talk to your customers with features such as speech-to-text and text-to-speech.

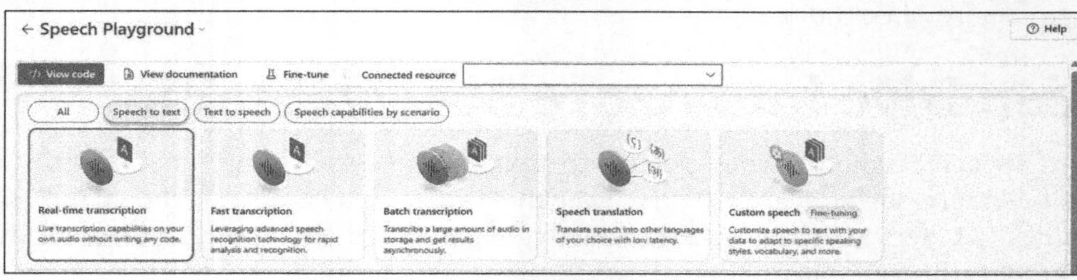

Figure 9.3: *Azure AI Studio; Speech*

Select Real-time Speech-to-Text from the list of choices, as shown in *Figure* 9.3. You will then be taken to the screen shown in *Figure* 9.4.

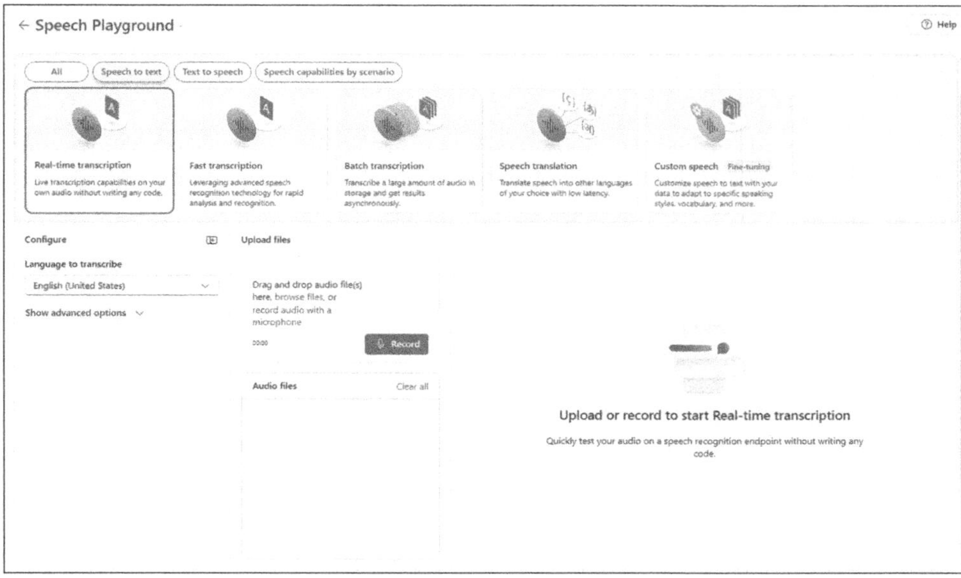

Figure 9.4: Azure AI Studio; *Real-time speech-to-text*

We have to configure the following parameters for demonstration:

- **Connected Azure AI Services**: Connect to or create an Azure AI Services resource, as shown in *Figure* 9.4.
- **Language to transcribe**: You can select the preferred language from the list, as shown in *Figure* 9.5.

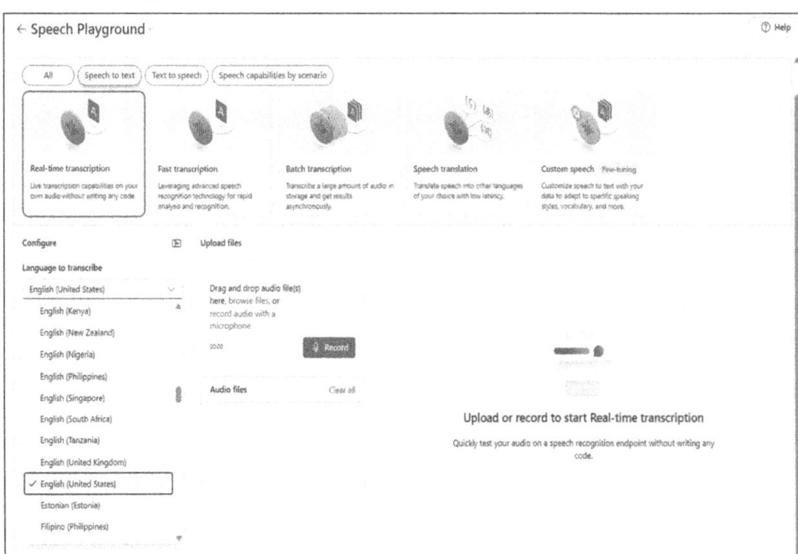

Figure 9.5: Azure AI Studio; *Real-time Speech-to-Text (Language to transcribe)*

The following are advanced options to enhance the performance of the speech-to-text process, as shown in *Figure* 9.6:

- **Language identification**: On or Off.

  It is used to identify the language spoken in the audio when compared against a list of supported languages. We can select the language from the list.

  - **At-start**: Identifies the language once within the first few seconds of audio.
  - **At-start**: Identifies the language duration of the audio.
- **Speaker diarization:** On or Off.

  It helps to separate the speakers' audio data from the multiple speakers. When enabled, the number of speakers is automatically detected and labeled in the transaction results and restricted to 20 speakers at a time.
- **Custom endpoint:** This is a user-configured API endpoint tailored for specific AI tasks and requirements. To improve recognition accuracy, use a deployed model from custom speech.
- **Output format:** We have two options: simple and detailed output formats.
  - **Simple output**: Includes display format and timestamps.
  - **Detailed output:** Includes more formats (such as display, lexical, Inverse Text Normalization (ITN), and masked ITN), timestamps, and N-best lists.
- **Phrase list**: It helps improve transcription and accuracy by providing a list of known phrases, such as names of people or specific locations (for example, John, Smith, Robin, London, Chennai, and New York). Each phrase is separated by commas or semicolons.

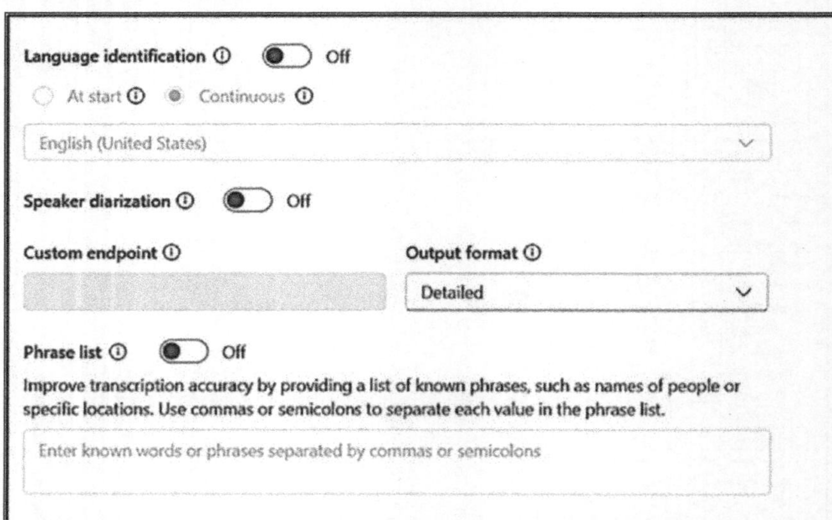

Figure 9.6: *Azure AI Studio; Real-time Speech-to-Text (Advanced Options)*

After completing all the configurations discussed in the previous step, you can record the audio directly by clicking the microphone icon or uploading it locally, as shown in *Figure* 9.7. Once the recording is completed or uploaded, we can see the files in the audio files container.

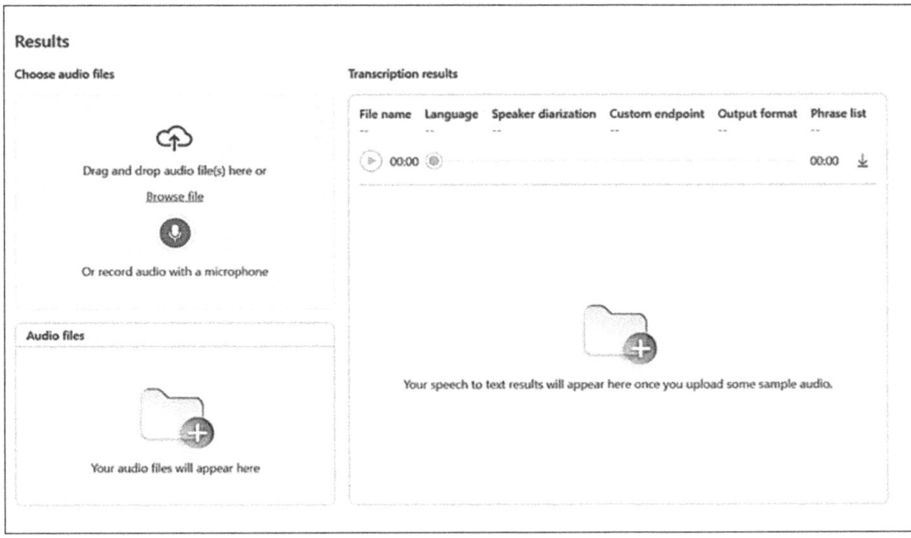

Figure 9.7: *Azure AI Studio; Real-time Speech-to-Text (Recording or Uploading)*

Select the file from the audio files list and click **RUN** icon in the transcription results container; the audio from the file will be converted to text, as shown in *Figure* 9.8.

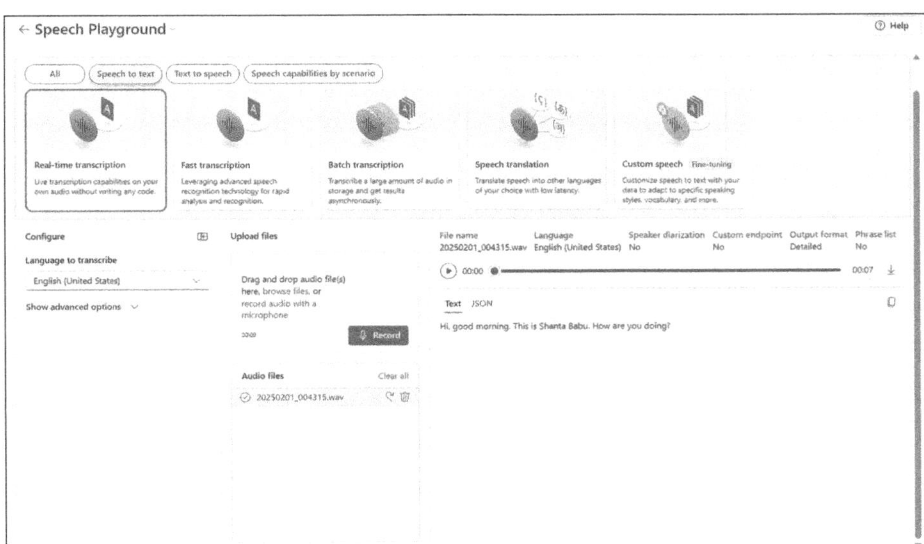

Figure 9.8: *Azure AI Studio; Real-time Speech-to-Text (Transcription Results)*

Azure Speech SDK

This SDK exposes many speech service capabilities so you can develop speech-enabled applications. It is available in many programming languages and across platforms such as Python, C, C++, C#, and Java. Speech SDK is ideal for batch processing and real-time scenarios using local devices such as microphones, recorders, files, and Azure Blob Storage. If you cannot use the Speech SDK directly by installing it, in those scenarios, you can use REST APIs to access the Speech service, or you can install the SDK in the Python environment as follows:

Install the Speech SDK for Python:

Before you install the Speech SDK for Python, satisfy the following platform requirements.

Install a version of Python from 3.8 or later.

- To check your installation, open a terminal and run the following command:

  Input: `python --version`.

  Output: `Python 3.8.10`.

  If you get a response like the preceding one, you are fine to go.
- If you are using macOS or Linux, you might need to run the command:

  Input: `python3 --version instead`.

  Output: `Python 3.8.10`

Steps to Install PyPI:

To install the **Speech SDK for Python**, run the following command in a console window.

```
pip install azure-cognitiveservices-speech
```

```
!pip install azure-cognitiveservices-speech

Collecting azure-cognitiveservices-speech
  Downloading azure_cognitiveservices_speech-1.41.1-py3-none-win_amd64.whl.metadata (1.5 kB)
Downloading azure_cognitiveservices_speech-1.41.1-py3-none-win_amd64.whl (2.4 MB)
   ---------------------------------------- 0.0/2.4 MB ? eta -:--:--
   ---------------------------------------- 0.0/2.4 MB 682.7 kB/s eta 0:00:04
   -- ------------------------------------- 0.1/2.4 MB 1.8 MB/s eta 0:00:02
   ---------- ----------------------------- 0.6/2.4 MB 5.5 MB/s eta 0:00:01
   ------------------------ --------------- 1.5/2.4 MB 9.4 MB/s eta 0:00:01
   ---------------------------------------  2.4/2.4 MB 11.7 MB/s eta 0:00:01
   ---------------------------------------- 2.4/2.4 MB 10.9 MB/s eta 0:00:00
Installing collected packages: azure-cognitiveservices-speech
Successfully installed azure-cognitiveservices-speech-1.41.1
```

Figure 9.9: *Speech SDK Installation for Python*

Run this command in a console window to upgrade to the latest Speech SDK.

```
pip install --upgrade azure-cognitiveservices-speech
```

You can check the installed SDK using the following command. You will get the Azure-cognitive services-**speech.__version__** variable, as shown in *Figure* 9.10.

```
pip list
```

```
!pip list

Automat                           20.2.0
autopep8                          2.0.4
azure-cognitiveservices-speech    1.41.1
```

***Figure* 9.10**: *Speech SDK Installation Confirmation*

Following this, you can start using this SDK by importing the library.

```
import azure.cognitiveservices.speech as speechsdk
```

Speech-to-Text Implementation Using Azure Speech SDK Python

To call the Speech service inside the Python code using the Speech SDK, we must create a **SpeechConfig** instance in the Azure portal and get the Speech resource key and region, such as your speech key, associated region, and endpoint.

Step 1: In the Azure portal, search for the Azure Speech Service, and you will get the service, as shown in *Figure* 9.11. Once you click "**Speech service**", the portal will take you to the page, as shown in *Figure* 9.12.

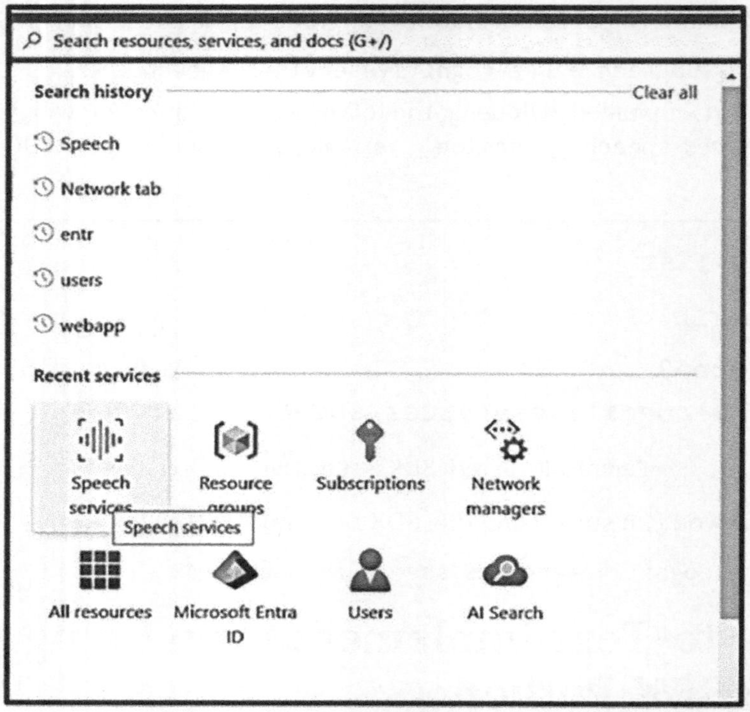

Figure 9.11: *Speech Service in Azure Portal*

Step 2: Click "**`Create Speech service`**", as shown in *Figure* 9.12.

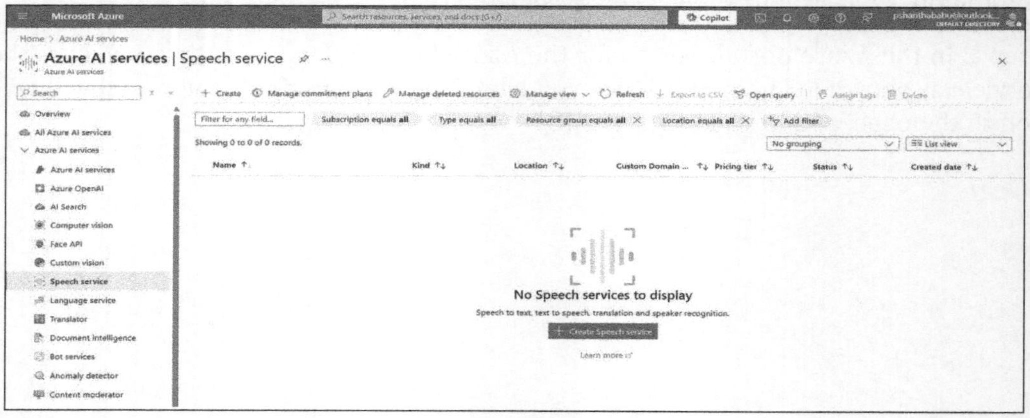

Figure 9.12: *Azure Speech Service Page*

Step 3: The portal will take you to the configuration page, as shown in *Figure* 9.13. We need to provide the following details and click **`Review + Create`**.

- Subscription
- Resource Group

- Region
- Name
- Pricing Tier

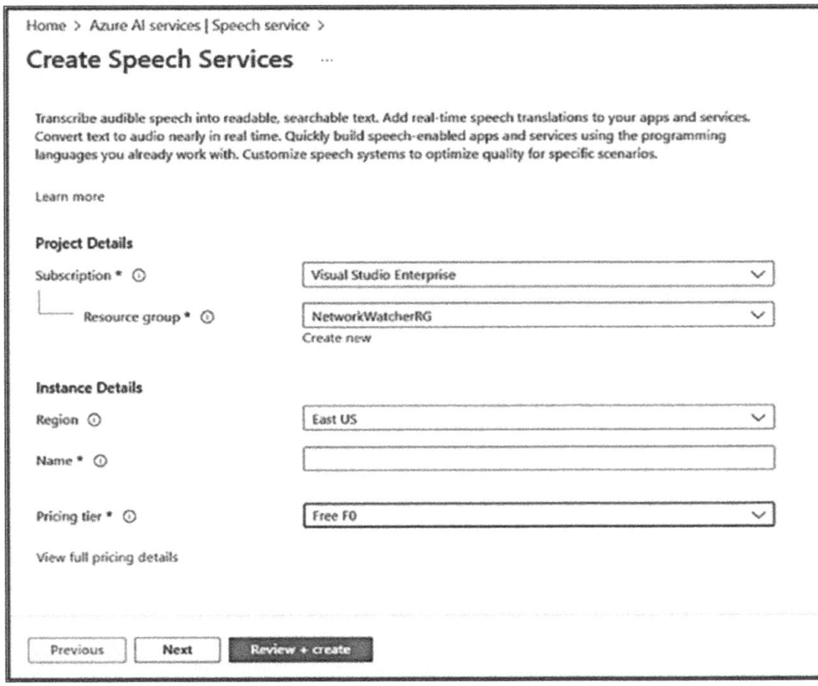

Figure 9.13: *Azure Speech Service Configuration*

Step 4: Once the resource is created successfully, we must go to the key and end point, copy, and save it for implementation.

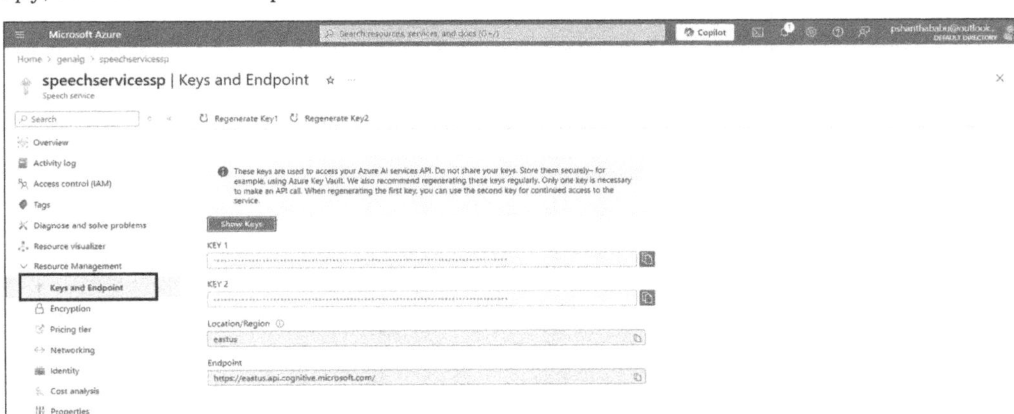

Figure 9.14: *Azure Speech Service Keys and Region*

Now that we have Speech SDK installed and the Key and Endpoint ready, we can start writing the code and call the appropriate service along with the key and endpoint.

Real-time Speech is recognized from a microphone.

```
import os
import azure.cognitiveservices.speech as speechsdk

def real_time_speech_to_text():
    ##########################
    # Speech Configuration
    ###########################
    speech_config = speechsdk.SpeechConfig(subscription=os.environ.
get('XXXX'), region=os.environ.get('XXXX'))
    speech_config.speech_recognition_language="en-US"

    ##############################################################
    # Audio Configuration - setting laptop or desktop as default_
microphone
   ###############################################################
    audio_config = speechsdk.audio.AudioConfig(use_default_micro-
phone=True)
    speech_recognizer =speechsdk.SpeechRecognizer(speech_config=speech_
config, audio_config=audio_config)

   print("########################")
   print("Please turn on your microphone and speak")
   print("#########################")

  ##################################
  # Get the audio from the mic
  ##################################
  speech_recognition_result = speech_recognizer.recognize_once_async().
get()


   ####################
   # Audio analysis
    ####################

    # 1. Recognized the Speech
    if speech_recognition_result.reason == speechsdk.ResultReason.
RecognizedSpeech:
        print("Recognized: {}".format(speech_recognition_result.text))
    # 2. Speech not recognized
    elif speech_recognition_result.reason == speechsdk.ResultReason.
NoMatch:
```

```
        print("No speech could be recognized: {}".format(speech_recogni-
tion_result.no_match_details))
    # 3. Speech canceled
    elif speech_recognition_result.reason == speechsdk.ResultReason.
Canceled:
        cancellation_details = speech_recognition_result.cancellation_
details
        print("Speech Recognition cancelled: {}".format(cancellation_
details.reason))
        if cancellation_details.reason == speechsdk.CancellationReason.
Error:
            print("Error details: {}".format(cancellation_details.error_
details))
            print("Did you set the speech resource key and region val-
ues?")
# Calling the function
real_time_speech_to_text()
```

Output

```
########################
Please turn on your microphone and speak
########################
RECOGNIZED: Text=Welcome to the real-time speech to text world
```

Speech recognizes from a stored file locally.

```
import os
import azure.cognitiveservices.speech as speechsdk

def real_time_speech_to_text():
    #########################
    # Speech Configuration
    ##########################
    speech_config = speechsdk.SpeechConfig(subscription=os.environ.
get('XXXX'), region=os.environ.get('XXXX'))
    speech_config.speech_recognition_language="en-US"

    ############################################################
    # Audio Configuration - setting laptop or desktop as default_micro-
phone
   #############################################################
   audio_config = speechsdk.audio.AudioConfig(filename="C:\xxxxx\xxxxx\abc.
wav")
   speech_recognizer =speechsdk.SpeechRecognizer(speech_config=speech_
config, audio_config=audio_config)

   print("######################")
   print(" Start Listening to the audio from the file.")
```

```
   print("########################")

  ##################################
  # Get the audio from the mic
  ##################################
  speech_recognition_result = speech_recognizer.recognize_once_async().
get()


   ####################
   # Audio analysis
    ####################

    # 1. Recognized the Speech from an audio file
    if speech_recognition_result.reason == speechsdk.ResultReason.
RecognizedSpeech:
        print("Recognized: {}".format(speech_recognition_result.text))
    # 2. Speech not recognized from an audio file
    elif speech_recognition_result.reason == speechsdk.ResultReason.
NoMatch:
        print("No speech could be recognized: {}".format(speech_
recognition_result.no_match_details))
    # 3. Speech canceled due to audio file disturbance
    elif speech_recognition_result.reason == speechsdk.ResultReason.
Canceled:
        cancellation_details = speech_recognition_result.cancellation_
details
        print("Speech Recognition cancelled: {}".format(cancellation_
details.reason))
        if cancellation_details.reason == speechsdk.CancellationReason.
Error:
            print("Error details: {}".format(cancellation_details.
error_details))
            print("Did you set the speech resource key and region
values?")
# Calling the function
real_time_speech_to_text()
```

Output

```
########################
 Start Listening to the audio from the file.
########################
RECOGNIZED: The magic of thinking BIG, so think big
```

Features of Azure AI Speech Studio (Text-to-Speech)

Here are the primary key features of Azure AI Speech Studio:

- **Real-time Speech-to-Text:** It helps quickly check the speech-to-text by dragging audio files or recording without using any code.
- **Batch Speech-to-Text:** This feature is integral to industry-specific solutions. It helps to quickly check batch transcription capabilities to transcribe large amounts of audio from Azure storage and generate text results in asynchronous mode.
- **Customized Speech:** It can create speech recognition models well-tailored to a set of vocabulary and accents.
- **Pronunciation Assessment**: This feature evaluates speech pronunciation and measures the speaker's accuracy and fluency in the language spoken. These features are mainly used for learning new languages and precisely assessing the speaker's proficiency in that language.
- **Speech Translation**: It helps quickly check and translate speech into other preferred languages with low latency.
- **Audio Content Creation**: We can build highly natural audio content for various applications, such as news broadcasts and video narrations, as well as building audiobooks.

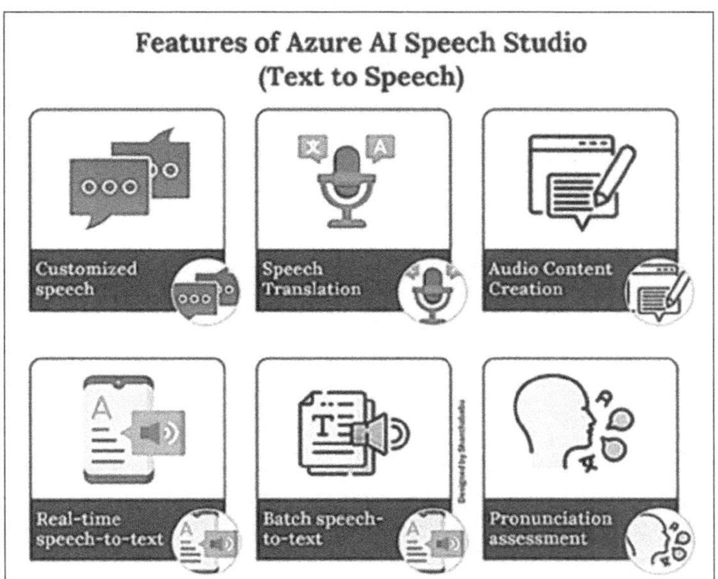

Figure 9.15: *Features of Azure AI Speech Studio*

Speech-To-Text

We have discussed speech-to-text and will now focus on text-to-speech. This capability enables our applications and devices to convert text into human-like synthesized speech in the required language. This process is known as **SPEECH SYNTHESIS**. It can create human-like prebuilt neural voices or a custom neural voice unique to our product or brand in the market demand to reach the customer quickly.

Real-time Convert Text-to-Speech Implementation:

This is similar to a speech-to-text process, but the input is text, and the speech SDK feature will help convert it into speech.

```
import os
import azure.cognitiveservices.speech as speechsdk

#########################
# Speech Configuration
##########################
my_speech_config = speechsdk.SpeechConfig(subscription=os.environ.
get('XX'), region=os.environ.get('XX'))

######################################
# Mentioning audio output configuration
#####################################
my_audio_config = speechsdk.audio.AudioOutputConfig(use_default_
speaker=True)

#########################################
# Make the application understand the input text of different languages
#########################################
my_speech_config.speech_synthesis_voice_name='en-US-AvaMultilingual
Neural'
my_speech_synthesizer=speechsdk.SpeechSynthesizer(speech_config=my_
speech_config, my_audio_config=audio_config)

print("###################")
print("Please enter the text that you want to speak <...>")
print("###################")
text = input()

my_speech_synthesis_result = my_speech_synthesizer.speak_text_async
(text).get()

###################
# Text analysis
###################
```

```
    # 1. Recognized the Speech
if my_speech_synthesis_result.reason == speechsdk.ResultReason.
SynthesizingAudioCompleted:
    print("Speech synthesized for text [{}]".format(text))
    # 2. Speech canceled
elif my_speech_synthesis_result.reason == speechsdk.ResultReason.
Canceled:
    cancellation_details = my_speech_synthesis_result.cancellation_
details
    print("Speech synthesis canceled: {}".format(cancellation_details.
reason))
    if cancellation_details.reason == speechsdk.CancellationReason.Error:
        if cancellation_details.error_details:
            print("Error details: {}".format(cancellation_details.error_
details))
            print("Did you set the speech resource key and region val-
ues?")
```

Input:

```
Please enter the text that you want to speak <...>
I'm the best, and I can deliver
```

Significance of Azure AI Speech

Azure AI Speech is a powerful service that offers advanced speech-to-text, text-to-speech, and speech-to-text translation capabilities. It enables natural and efficient communication between humans and systems. Let us discuss its key features.

- **Enhanced Accessibility:**
  - It can convert spoken language into written text for accessibility and documentation purposes. Additionally, it supports individuals with visual impairments or those requiring auditory-based interactions.
- **Multilingual Support:**
  - It can recognize and synthesize speech in multiple languages, enabling global applications. It also supports real-time translation, promoting communication across different linguistic barriers.
- **Customization and Personalization:**
  - It offers personalized speech synthesis with natural rhythmic patterns and accents for realistic communication.
- **Scalability and Integration:**
  - It can be easily integrated with other Azure services, such as Azure Bot Service and Azure Cognitive Services, for various use cases.

- **Real-Time and Offline Capabilities**:
    - It supports real-time speech recognition for live interactions and offline functionality by storing prerecorded audio files.
- **Security and Compliance**:
    - It provides security and ensures compliance with global standards such as GDPR and HIPAA.
- **Versatile Applications**:
    - Powers applications such as voice assistants, automated customer service, transcription services, and real-time language translation.
    - Enhances user engagement with voice-enabled interfaces.
- **Innovation and AI Advancements:**
    - It leverages state-of-the-art AI to deliver accurate and context-aware speech processing. It supports the development of innovative applications such as voice recognition, pattern matching, cloning, and emotional speech synthesis.

Significance in Business and Technology:

- **Productivity**: It helps automate tasks such as transcription at the stop and reduces manual involvement, effort, and errors.
- **Global Reach**: It enables businesses to connect with multilingual audiences seamlessly with less effort and build healthier relationships.
- **Inclusivity**: It promotes accessibility and inclusivity, ensuring services are available to all individuals, regardless of disabilities or language barriers.
- **Customer Experience**: It enhances customer interactions through voice-enabled interface applications, reducing wait times and improving satisfaction.

Real-Time Applications with Azure AI Speech

Azure AI Speech offers robust, real-time speech-to-text, text-to-speech, and speech translation capabilities, enabling transformative applications across various industries. Here are some real-world examples:

- **Customer Support and Virtual Assistants:** Interactive voice response (IVR) systems powered by Azure AI Speech provide natural conversational experiences.
- **Real-Time Transcription for Meetings and Events:** Helping during the meeting transcription for live transcription.
- **Language Translation in Multilingual Communication:** Quick real-time speech translation in applications.

- **Education and Training:** Live captioning for online classes and lectures, such as providing real-time subtitles for virtual classrooms, helping students with hearing impairments or language differences follow lessons effectively. It provides real-time language practice and learning.
- **Healthcare and Telemedicine:** Voice-enabled medical transcription systems convert doctor-patient conversations into accurate medical records in real-time, improving telemedicine and patient care efficiency.

Azure AI Speech's real-time applications empower businesses to build intelligent, voice-enabled solutions that enhance user experience, productivity, and accessibility.

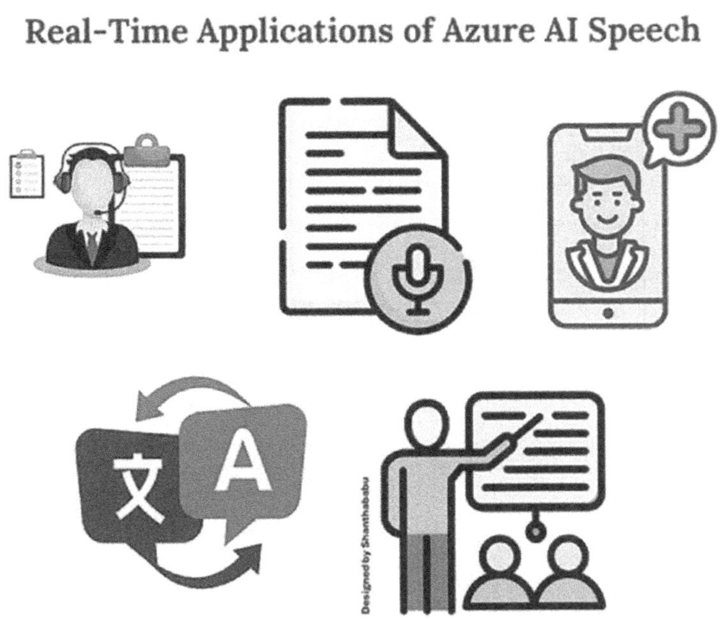

Figure 9.16: *Real-Time Applications of Azure AI Speech*

Speech Studio exclusively provides various capabilities and scenarios to play around with quickly, as shown in *Figure* 9.17, such as:

- Captioning with speech-to-text
- Post-call transcription and analytics
- Live chat avatar
- Language learning

This is similar to the Azure Open AI playground discussed in *Chapter 7: Getting Started with Generative AI Using Azure OpenAI Services.*

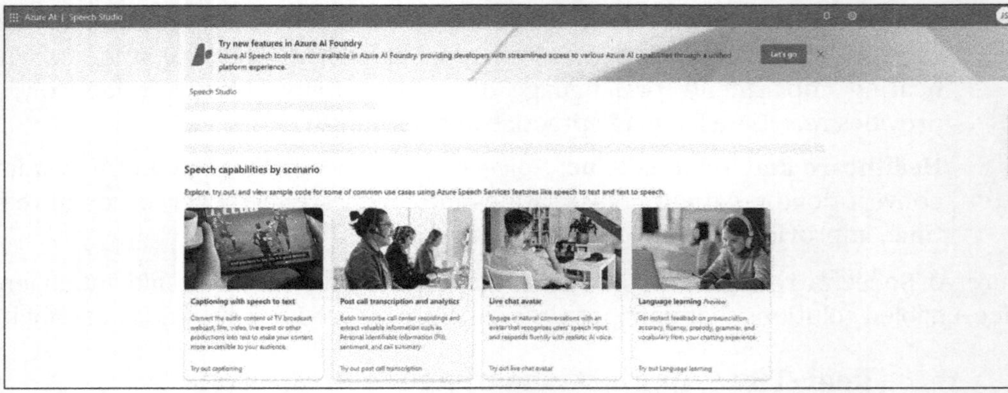

Figure 9.17: *Azure AI Speech Capabilities*

In the preceding list of capabilities, "**Post-call transcription and analytics**" is highly recommended and plays a vital role in many industries. It analyzes customer support executive' performance and customer behavior and drives insights through summarization and sentiment analysis.

It can analyze transcribed audio files and classify sensitive personally identifiable information (PII) into pre-defined classes using **Conversation PII Preview** and sentence-level sentiment scores. As shown in *Figure* 9.18, we can switch the PII on and off option during the analysis to prevent data leakage and ensure GDPR or PII compliance.

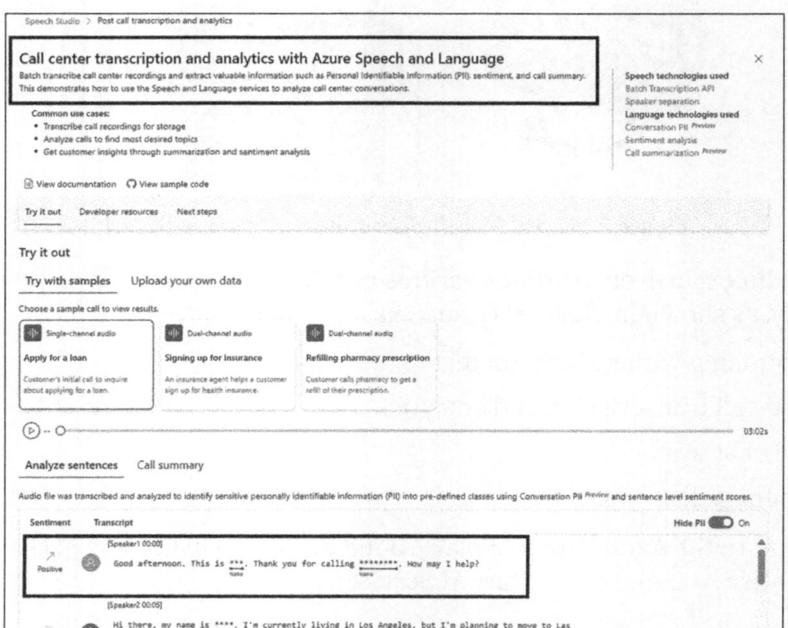

Figure 9.18: *Azure AI Speech Capabilities; Post-call Transcription and Analytics*

In terms of **speech-to-text conversion**, the following options are available and ready to play with input as text and audio to convert speech to text and vice versa, as shown in *Figure* 9.19.

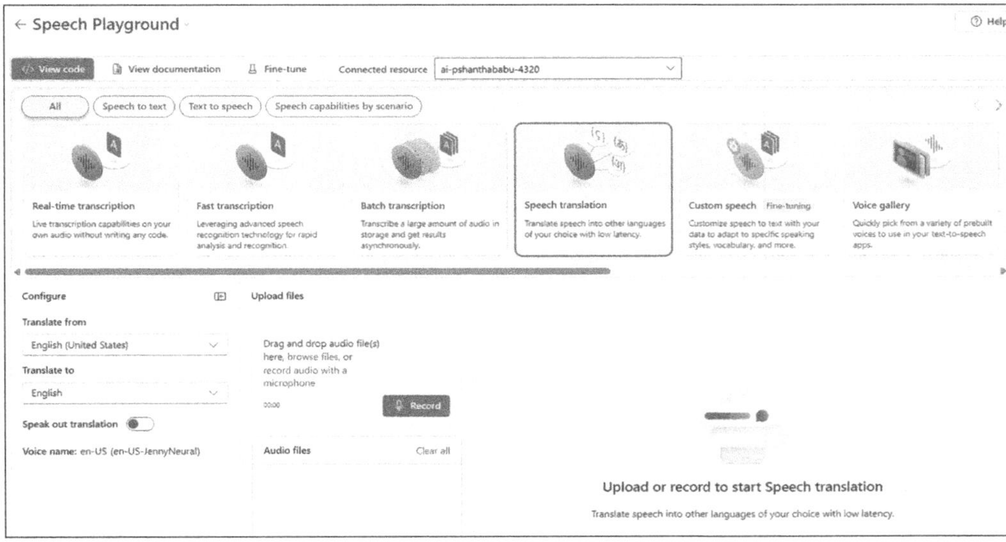

***Figure* 9.19:** *Azure AI Speech Studio; Speech-to-Text Conversion*

- **Real-time Speech-to-Text:** This helps us quickly test our audio for speech recognition without endpoint references or code.
- **Whisper Model on Azure OpenAI Service:** The OpenAI Whisper v2-large model helps to enable quick and efficient transcription and translation of audio content from fifty-seven languages into English without any disfluencies with transcribing and translating, prompts, or temperature options. It also provides better output in terms of capitalization frequency, perfect sentences, and punctuation.
- **Batch Speech-to-Text:** As the name implies, batch speech-to-text enables us to transcribe a large volume of audio stored in the ADLS storage by enabling a shared access signature (SAS) URI and asynchronously receive transcription results from the model.
- **Custom Speech:** It helps improve speech-to-text recognition accuracy for our target scenarios. Custom Speech provides five types of improvement: terminology, sentence structure, pronunciation, acoustic variance, and output format. It consists of five steps: Evaluate, Define targets, Prepare your data, Train a model, and Integrate.
- **Pronunciation Assessment with Speech-to-Text:** This feature evaluates speech pronunciation and gives feedback on its accuracy and fluency. It helps improve speakers' pronunciation so they can speak and present confidently.

- **Speech Translation:** This exciting feature allows us to translate speech into other languages of our choice with low latency. Figure 9.20 shows the translation from English to Tamil.

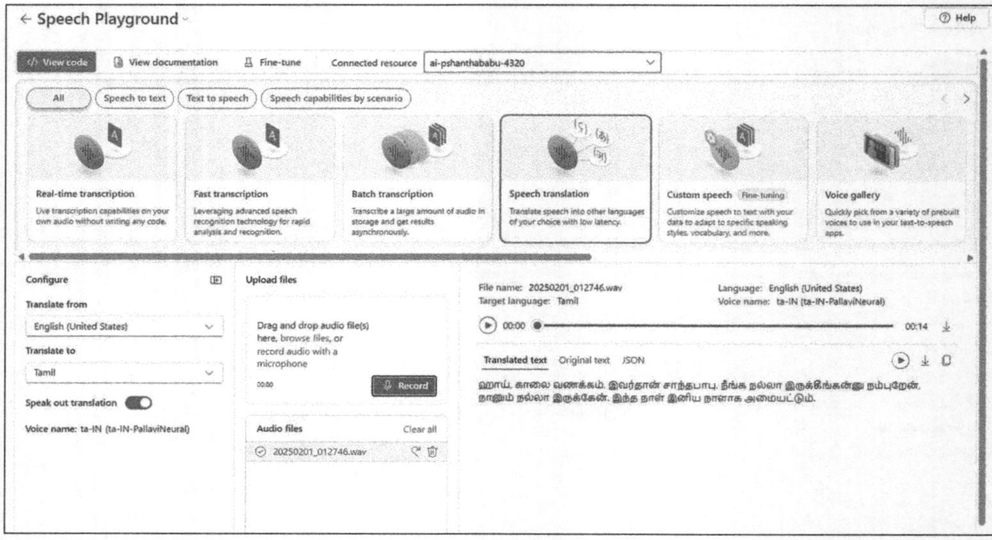

Figure 9.20: *Azure AI Speech-to-Text; Translation from English to Tamil*

In terms of **Text-to-speech conversion**, the following options are available and ready to use, allowing input as text and audio to convert speech-to-text and vice versa, as shown in *Figure* 9.21.

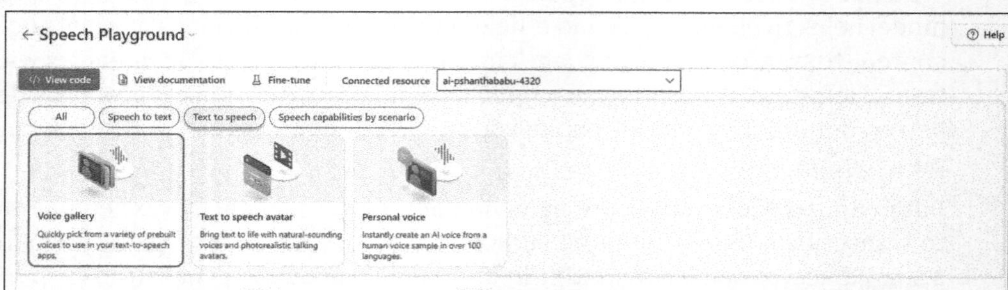

Figure 9.21: *Azure AI Speech Studio; Text-to-Speech Conversion*

Voice Gallery: Build apps and services that speak naturally, choosing from 564 voices across 154 languages and variants. Bring your scenarios to life with highly expressive and human-like neural voices.

Custom Neural Voice: Custom Neural Voice (CNV) lets you create a natural-sounding synthetic voice trained on human voice recordings. Your custom voice can adapt across languages and speaking styles and is perfect for adding a one-of-a-kind voice to your text-to-speech solutions.

Personal Voice: Create an AI voice from human voice samples, giving users a personalized voice experience across 100 languages.

Speech Synthesis Markup Language (SSML)

SSML is a standard XML-based markup language that enhances the control over text-to-speech (TTS) systems. It allows developers to define how speech synthesis engines interpret text to generate speech, providing customization options for tone, pitch, pronunciation, speaking rate, volume, emphasis, and pauses. It gives you more control and flexibility than plain text input.

Key Features of SSML:

- **Voice Customization**: It controls the speech's pitch, rate, and volume to generate the desired voice characteristics, which are used to build the AI-powered tool based on the requirements.
- **Pronunciation and Emphasis Control**: It adjusts the pronunciation of words or phonemes to suit the specific application context or locale to adapt the expected pronunciation. It helps to specify the level of emphasis on particular words, sentences, or phrases to convey meaning, importance, or significance.
- **Pauses and Breaks**: When building TTS tools, we should introduce the appropriate pauses or adjust the timing between words for natural-sounding speech.
- **Language Switching**: It dynamically switches between multiple languages in a single speech synthesis output and modifies rhythm and intonation for better alignment with natural speech. It also incorporates effects such as whispering or specific voice styles.

Here is an example demonstrating SSML:

- **Controlling Speech Rate and Pitch**

```
<speak xmlns="xxxxxxx" version="1.0">
    <voice name="en-US-AriaNeural">
        <prosody rate="slow" pitch="high">Welcome to our er-
vice!</prosody>
        <prosody rate="fast" pitch="low">We are here to assist
you.</prosody>
    </voice>
</speak>
```

Output: The first sentence is spoken slowly with a high pitch, while the second is spoken quickly with a low pitch.

- **Pausing between Words**

```
<speak xmlns="xxxxxxxx" version="1.0">
    <voice name="en-US-GuyNeural">
        Welcome to our <break time="500ms"/> service.
        Your satisfaction is our <break time="1s"/> priority.
    </voice>
</speak>
```

Output: Introduces pauses of 500 milliseconds and 1 second between sentences for a more natural flow.

- **Emphasizing Words**

```
<speak xmlns="xxxxxxxxxxxxxxxxxxxxx" version="1.0">
    <voice name="en-US-JennyNeural">
        Please <emphasis level="moderate">review</emphasis> the
terms carefully.
        <emphasis level="strong">Thank you</emphasis> for your
attention!
    </voice>
</speak>
```

Output: Places moderate emphasis on "review" and a strong emphasis on "thank you."

- **Pronunciation with Phonemes**

```
<speak xmlns="xxxxxxxxxxxxxxxxxxxxxxx" version="1.0">
    <voice name="en-GB-RyanNeural">
        The correct pronunciation of "data" is <phoneme
alphabet="ipa" ph="deɪtə">data</phoneme>.
    </voice>
</speak>
```

Output: Ensures the word "data" is pronounced as "day-tuh" using IPA phonetic notation.

- **Language Switching**

```
<speak xmlns="http://www.w3.org/2001/10/synthesis" version="1.0">
    <voice name="en-US-AriaNeural">
        Hello! <lang xml:lang="es-ES">¿Cómo estás?</lang>
    </voice>
</speak>
```

Output: Switches from English to Spanish for the phrase "¿Cómo estás?" ensuring accurate pronunciation.

- **Adjusting Volume**

```
<speak xmlns="xxxxxxxxx" version="1.0">
    <voice name="en-US-AriaNeural">
        <prosody volume="x-loud">Emergency alert!</prosody>
```

```
        <prosody volume="x-soft">This is a test.</prosody>
    </voice>
</speak>
```

Output: The first sentence is spoken loudly, while the second is spoken softly.

Deep Dive into Azure Vision Studio

Azure Vision Studio is designed to simplify the exploration, prototyping, and deployment of Computer Vision (CV) capabilities within the **Azure AI Vision** service. It offers intuitive tools for CV developers and non-technical users to experiment with vision-based AI solutions without extensive coding knowledge.

It empowers businesses to leverage cutting-edge AI Vision capabilities quickly and efficiently to build, test, and deploy a fully operational AI model into production. Vision Studio provides the tools and flexibility needed to accelerate innovation in computer vision.

It can follow aspects and build innovative tools in the CV domain for various industries such as retail, healthcare, manufacturing, media, and entertainment.

Image Analysis:

- Image Analysis is a computer vision technique that extracts valuable insights from images on the spot or in storage. It involves object recognition, pattern detection, feature extraction, and data interpretation.
- Image analysis has revolutionized various industries with enhanced automation, efficiency, and decision-making capabilities. It can detect objects, people, landmarks, the nature of the disease, and text. Then, generate metadata such as tags, categories, and descriptions from the images.
- In healthcare, it plays a critical role in medical imaging and surgical assistance to detect diseases or abnormalities and help the early detection of illnesses such as cancer, fractures, or heart conditions.

Optical Character Recognition (OCR):

- Extracts text from images, including handwriting and printed text, from photocopies in the manufacturing, agriculture, and processing industries. It supports multiple languages to meet the global demand.
- Identifies and locates objects within images that are specifically useful for applications such as tracking stock levels using object detection and OCR on product labels, inventory management, and safety monitoring. It extracts information from medical forms or analyzes medical imaging for patterns.

Face Recognition:

- This technology enhances security, reduces fraud risks, improves operational efficiency and customer experience, and reduces manual effort in identity verification and monitoring processes.

- Detect and analyze faces, including emotions, age, and facial landmarks, and compare the faces for authentication or identification purposes in security and surveillance-based applications.
- Authentication and identity verification in banking and financial services, personalized shopping, recognizing repeat customers, and offering personalized recommendations or promotions.

Video Analysis:

- It leverages AI and computer vision to extract meaningful insights from video footage that could be streaming or storage. This technology is widely used across industries for security, monitoring, automation, and analytics.
- It analyzes video content for objects, actions, and speech and generates insights from live or recorded video feeds.
- Typically, security and surveillance are used for object detection and tracking, followed by identifying video feeds. This use case will enhance public safety by detecting unauthorized access or suspicious activity.

Azure Vision Studio: Features

Azure Vision Studio provides many features from the point of view of vision, so let us discuss them here.

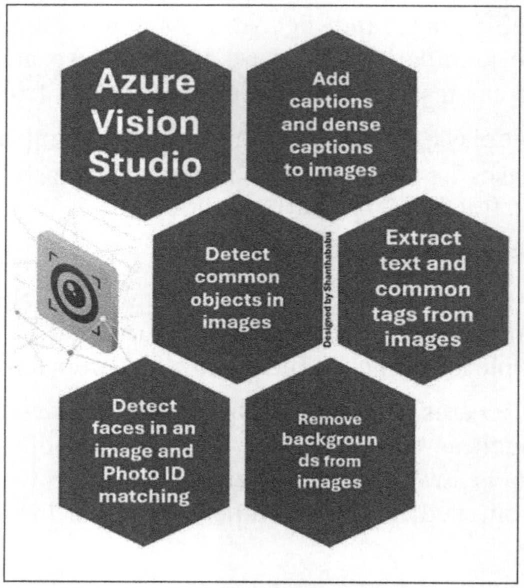

***Figure* 9.22:** *Azure Vision Studio Features*

Add Captions and Dense Captions to Images: This is a no-code feature in Vision Studio; it can generate human-readable captions for all important objects detected in the given image. The dense caption feature helps describe an image's content.

The following steps will help you do this exercise.

Step 1: Click the "**`Add captions to images`**" feature on the Vision Studio page; the portal will take you to the page shown in *Figure* 9.23.

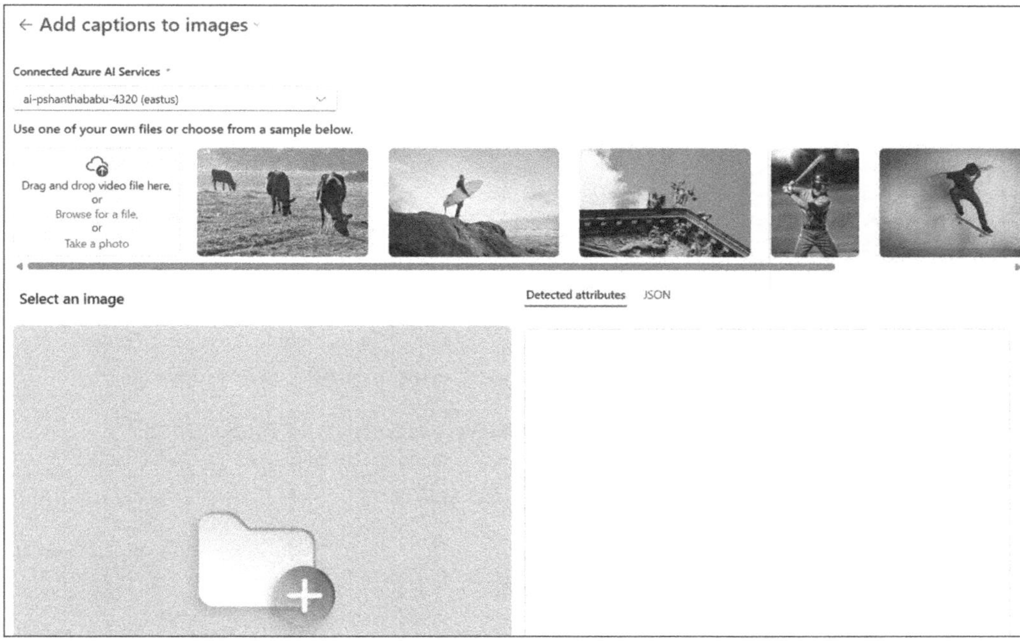

***Figure* 9.23:** *Azure Vision Studio Features; Add Captions in Progress*

Step 2: Select the available image from the list of images; we can observe the "**`A sandwich cut in half`**" in the right-side textbox, as shown in *Figure* 9.24.

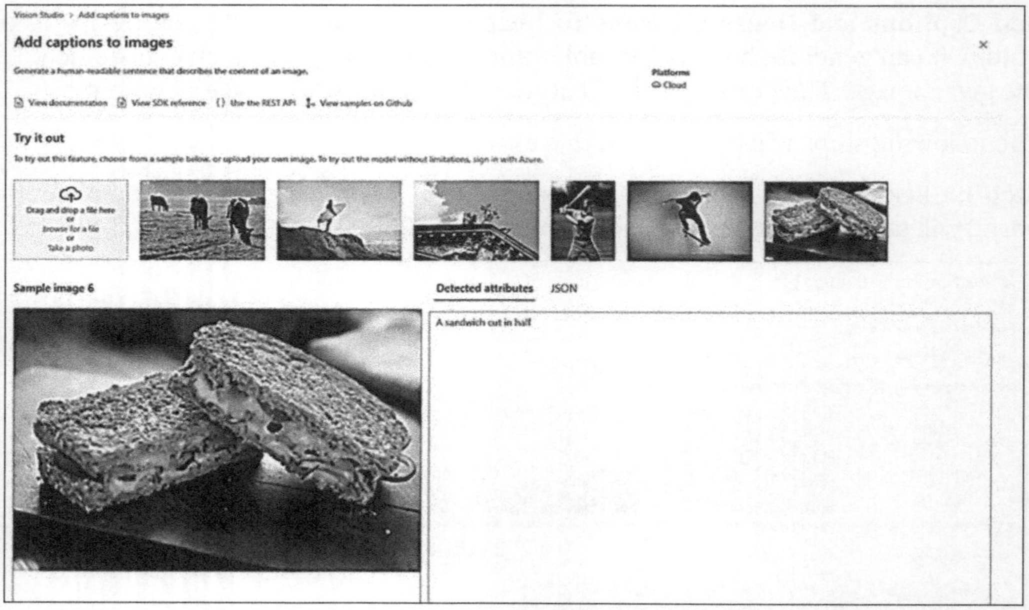

Figure 9.24: *Azure Vision Studio Features; Caption for the Selected Image*

Step 3: Browse the image from your local folder, select it, and click "**`Open`**."

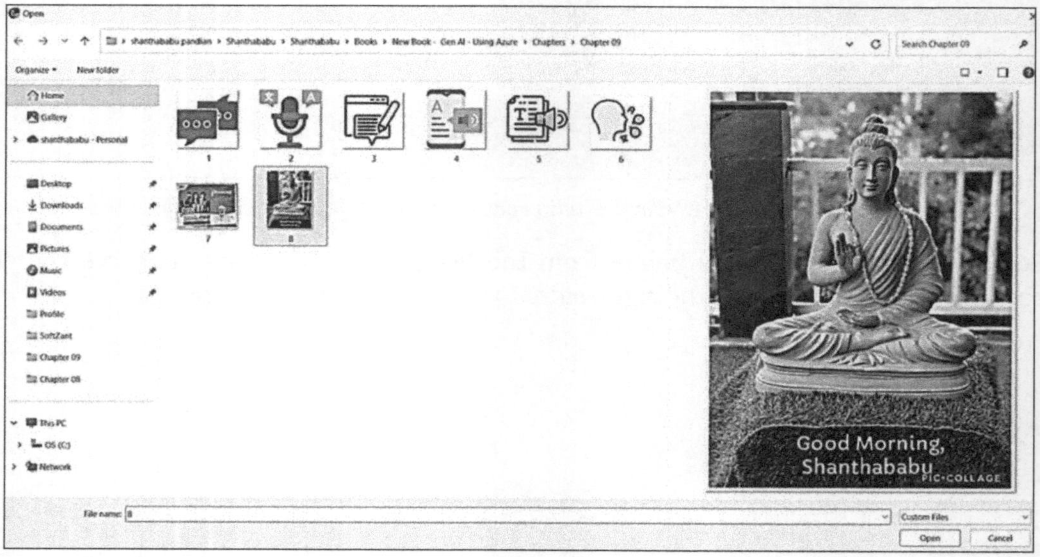

Figure 9.25: *Image from the Local Folder*

Step 4: Select the image loaded in the appropriate place. In the right-side textbox, we can observe "**`A statue of a man sitting on grass`**" [Buddha Status], as shown in *Figure 9.26*.

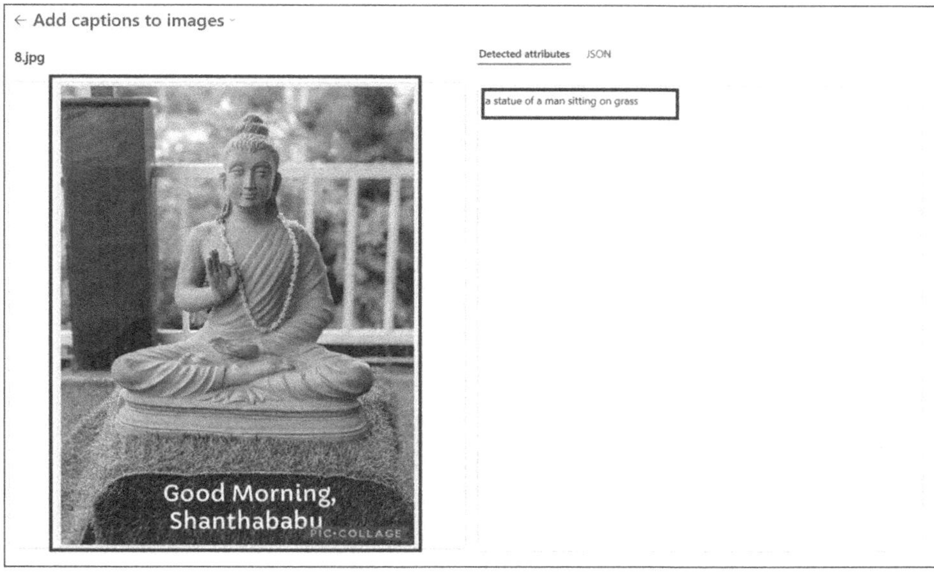

Figure 9.26: *Azure Vision Studio Features; Caption for the Selected Image*

Add Dense Captions to Images: We can add captions to the given images; they are human-readable captions for all important objects detected in the given image.

Click the "`Add dense captions to images`" feature on the Vision Studio page; the portal will take you to the page, and select the image from the given list. You will observe that, as shown in *Figure* 9.27, the captions for all the important objects detected in the given image are displayed.

Figure 9.27: *Azure AI Vision Studio; Add Dense Captions to Images*

Extract Text and Common Tags from Images: This feature helps extract printed and handwritten text in supported languages from images, PDFs, and TIFF files. The optical character recognition (OCR) capability supports pictures and documents with mixed languages and does not require the language to be specified. We can also extract tags based on thousands of recognizable objects, living beings, scenery, and actions.

Click the "`Extract text from images`" feature on the Vision Studio page. The portal will take you to page (1). Select the image from the given list. The extracted text (2) will appear in the right-side textbox, as shown in *Figure* 9.28.

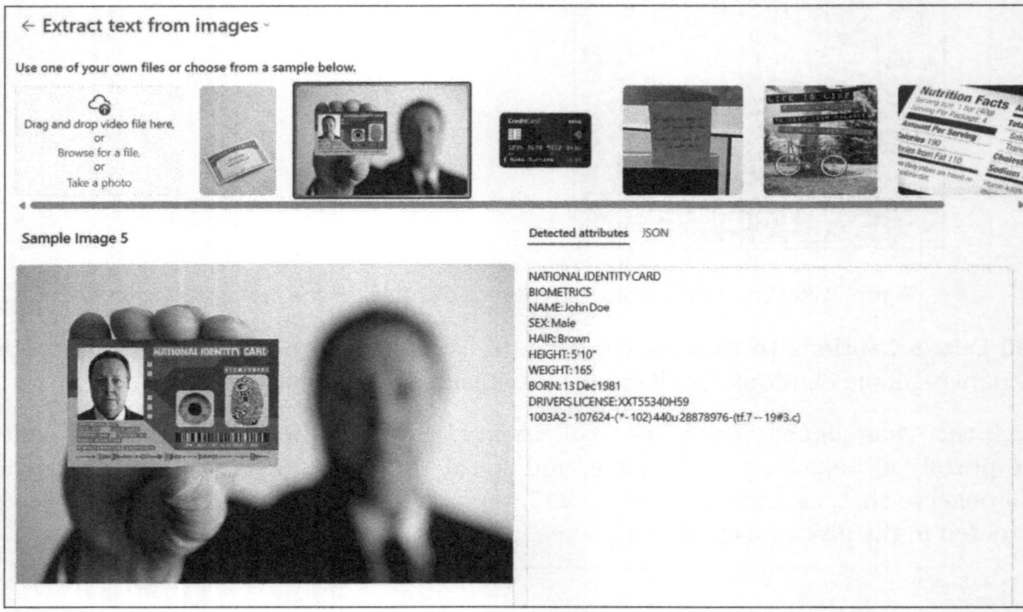

Figure 9.28: *Azure AI Vision Studio; Extract Text from Images*

Extract Common Tags from Images

Click the "`Extract common tags from images`" feature on the Vision Studio page. The portal will take you to the page. Select the image from the list. The extracted common tags from the image will appear in the right-side textbox, as shown in *Figure* 9.29.

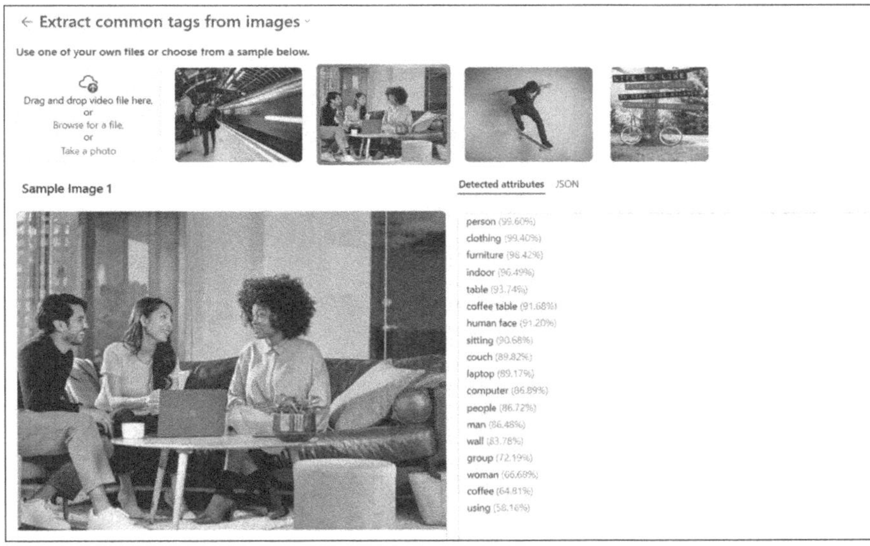

Figure 9.29: *Azure AI Vision Studio – Common Tags from Images*

Detect Common Objects in Images: This feature detects and extracts bounding boxes based on thousands of recognizable objects and living beings. It helps detect as many objects as possible from the given picture.

Click the "`Detect common objects in images`" feature on the Vision Studio page. The portal will take you to the page. Select the image from the list. The detected common objects in the images, along with the percentage of the object in the image in brackets, will appear in the right-side textbox, as shown in *Figure* 9.30.

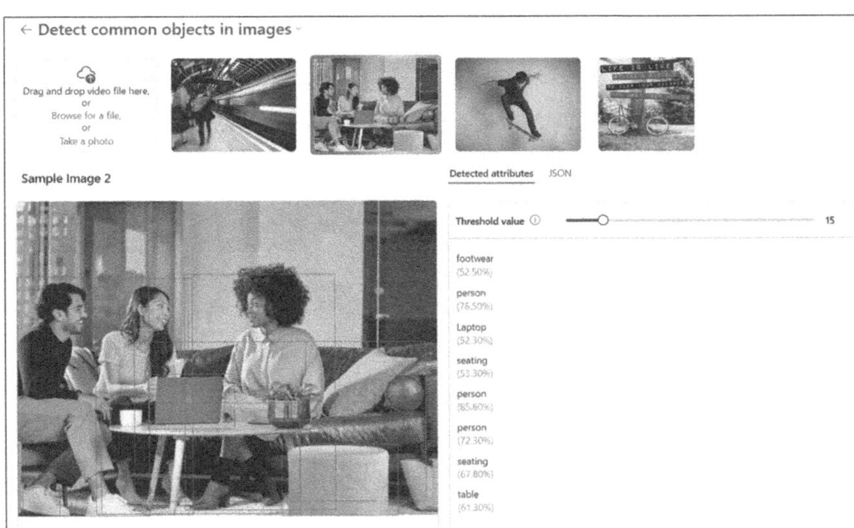

Figure 9.30: *Azure AI Vision Studio; Detect Common Objects in Images*

Recognize and Analyze Shelf Products: Find specific objects within a single image for use cases, such as locating products on shelves, merchandise on a store display, or items on an assembly line.

Click the "`Recognize and analyze shelf products`" feature on the Vision Studio page. The portal will take you to the page. Select the image from the list. Recognize and analyze shelf products appearing in the right-side textbox, as shown in *Figure* 9.31.

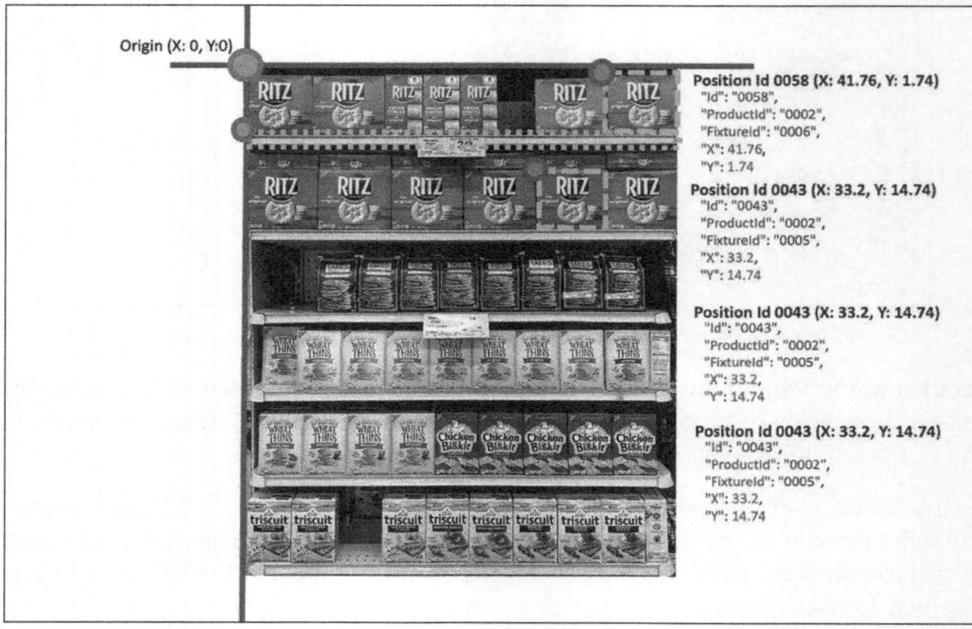

***Figure* 9.31:** *Azure AI Vision Studio; Recognize and Analyze Shelf Products*

Similarly, we have the following features and can play around with them in the same way discussed earlier.

- **Remove Backgrounds from Images:** Easily remove the background and preserve the foreground elements of your image.
- **Search Photos with Image Retrieval:** Retrieve specific moments within your photo album. For example, you can query your university graduation day pictures to find your friends or relatives and search for images based on their content rather than relying solely on manually assigned keywords or tags.
- **Detect Faces in an Image and Photo ID Matching:** This feature will detect the location of one or more human faces in an image, along with attributes such as pose, whether they are wearing a face mask or not, and facial landmarks. It will also match a photo of a person to a photo ID to verify their identity, among other functionalities.

Spatial Analysis

Spatial Analysis in Azure Vision Studio is an advanced feature that leverages computer vision to extract and analyze spatial data from video feeds. It helps understand and interpret the movement and interactions of people or objects within a defined space, enabling intelligent decision-making and operational improvements across various domains.

Azure Vision Studio's Spatial Analysis transforms video feeds into actionable insights, driving efficiency and innovation in security, retail, healthcare, and more. *Figure* 9.32 shows the Azure Vision Studio features.

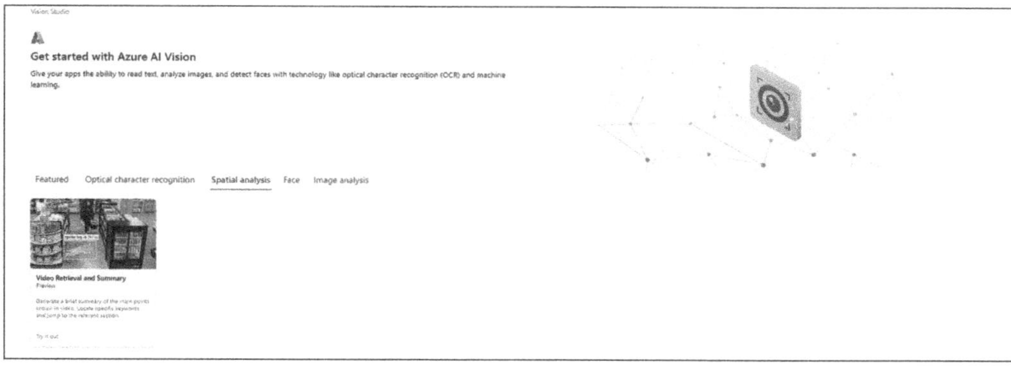

***Figure* 9.32:** *Azure AI Vision Studio; Spatial Analysis*

Critical Capabilities of Spatial Analysis:

- **People Counting**: It helps detect and count the number of people in a designated area. It is specifically used to monitor foot traffic in retail stores, public spaces, or highly secured areas; monitor the people and employees in the manufacturing processes lane; and align safety measures.
- **Distance Measurement**: It helps to measure the distance between people or objects (equipment and lab instruments). This plays a significant role in enforcing social distancing in the manufacturing industry, workplaces, airports, and healthcare facilities.
- **Queue Management and Heatmaps**: These help to analyze the queue lengths and waiting times, provide guidance and visualize high-traffic areas using spatial data. To optimize service efficiency in banks, airports, or retail checkouts.
- **Activity Detection and Zone Monitoring**: It helps to identify movements or actions within a space, such as sitting, standing, or walking, and tracks when people enter or exit predefined zones. This helps to monitor employee activity or customer behavior and enhance security by detecting unauthorized access to restricted areas.

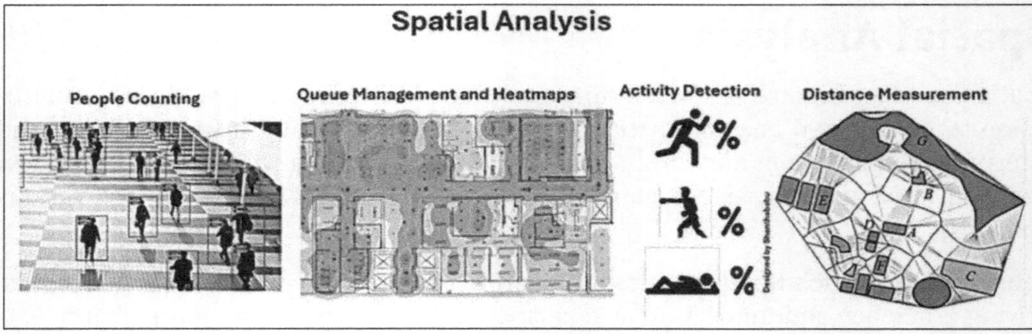

Figure 9.33: *Azure AI Vision Studio; Spatial Analysis*

Azure Image Analysis SDK

The Azure Image Analysis SDK is a development toolkit that enables AI developers to integrate advanced image analysis capabilities into their applications using Azure AI Vision Services. This SDK allows seamless interaction with Azure's image processing features, such as object detection, facial recognition, and OCR. It is a typical code-based development and exposes many vision service capabilities so you can develop computer vision-enabled applications. It is available in many programming languages and across platforms such as Python, C, C++, C#, and Java.

Critical Capabilities of Azure Image Analysis SDK are: Object Detection and Recognition, Optical Character Recognition (OCR), Image Classification, Facial Recognition, Spatial Analysis, Scene Understanding, and Content Moderation.

You can install the SDK in the Python environment by following the steps mentioned previously in the section "Azure Speech SDK" of "Deep Dive into Azure Speech Studio."

Steps to Install PyPI:

To install the **Speech SDK for Python**, run the following command in a console window:

```
pip install azure-ai-vision-imageanalysis
```

```
[8]: !pip install azure-ai-vision-imageanalysis
     Requirement already satisfied: azure-ai-vision-imageanalysis in c:\users\pandi\anaconda3\lib\site-packages (1.0.0)
     Requirement already satisfied: isodate>=0.6.1 in c:\users\pandi\anaconda3\lib\site-packages (from azure-ai-vision-imageanalysis) (0.7.2)
     Requirement already satisfied: azure-core>=1.30.0 in c:\users\pandi\anaconda3\lib\site-packages (from azure-ai-vision-imageanalysis) (1.32.0)
     Requirement already satisfied: typing-extensions>=4.6.0 in c:\users\pandi\anaconda3\lib\site-packages (from azure-ai-vision-imageanalysis) (4.12.2)
     Requirement already satisfied: requests>=2.21.0 in c:\users\pandi\anaconda3\lib\site-packages (from azure-core>=1.30.0->azure-ai-vision-imageanalysis) (2.3
     2.2)
     Requirement already satisfied: six>=1.11.0 in c:\users\pandi\anaconda3\lib\site-packages (from azure-core>=1.30.0->azure-ai-vision-imageanalysis) (1.16.0)
     Requirement already satisfied: charset-normalizer<4,>=2 in c:\users\pandi\anaconda3\lib\site-packages (from requests>=2.21.0->azure-core>=1.30.0->azure-ai-
     vision-imageanalysis) (2.0.4)
     Requirement already satisfied: idna<4,>=2.5 in c:\users\pandi\anaconda3\lib\site-packages (from requests>=2.21.0->azure-core>=1.30.0->azure-ai-vision-image
     analysis) (3.7)
     Requirement already satisfied: urllib3<3,>=1.21.1 in c:\users\pandi\anaconda3\lib\site-packages (from requests>=2.21.0->azure-core>=1.30.0->azure-ai-vision
     -imageanalysis) (2.2.2)
     Requirement already satisfied: certifi>=2017.4.17 in c:\users\pandi\anaconda3\lib\site-packages (from requests>=2.21.0->azure-core>=1.30.0->azure-ai-vision
     -imageanalysis) (2024.7.4)
```

Figure 9.34: *Vision SDK Installation for Python*

Image Analysis: Implementation Using Azure Vision SDK Python

To call the vision service inside the Python code using the vision SDK, we must create a **Vision Config** instance in the Azure portal and get the vision resource key and region, such as your speech key and associated region and endpoint.

Step 1: In the Azure portal, search for Azure vision service. We will get the service shown in *Figure* 9.35. Once you click the vision service, the portal will take you to the page shown in *Figure* 9.36.

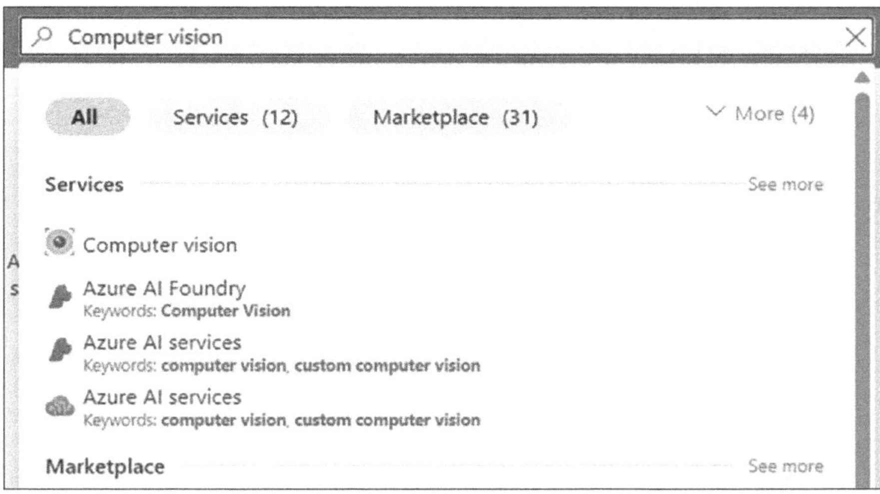

***Figure* 9.35:** *Computer Vision Services in the Azure Portal*

Step 2: Click "`Create Computer vision`", as shown in *Figure* 9.36.

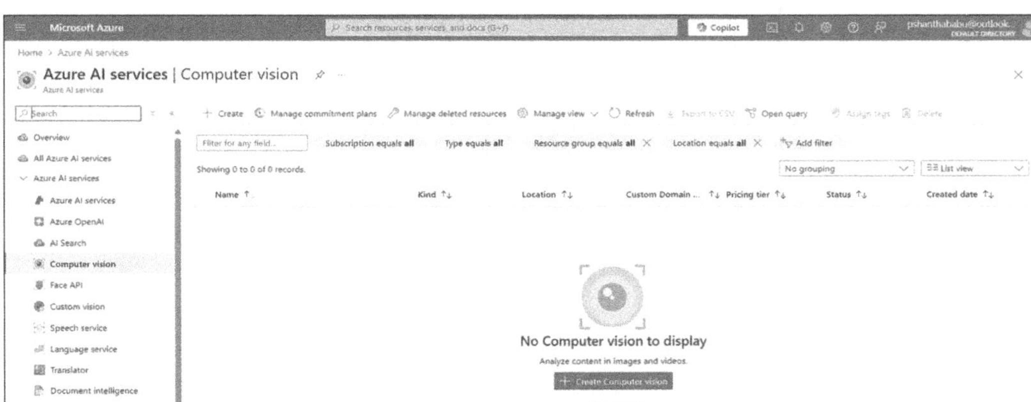

***Figure* 9.36:** *Azure Computer Vision Service Page*

Step 3: The portal will take you to the configuration page, as shown in *Figure* 9.37. You need to provide the following details and "**`Review and Create`**":

- Subscription
- Resource Group
- Region
- Name
- Pricing Tier

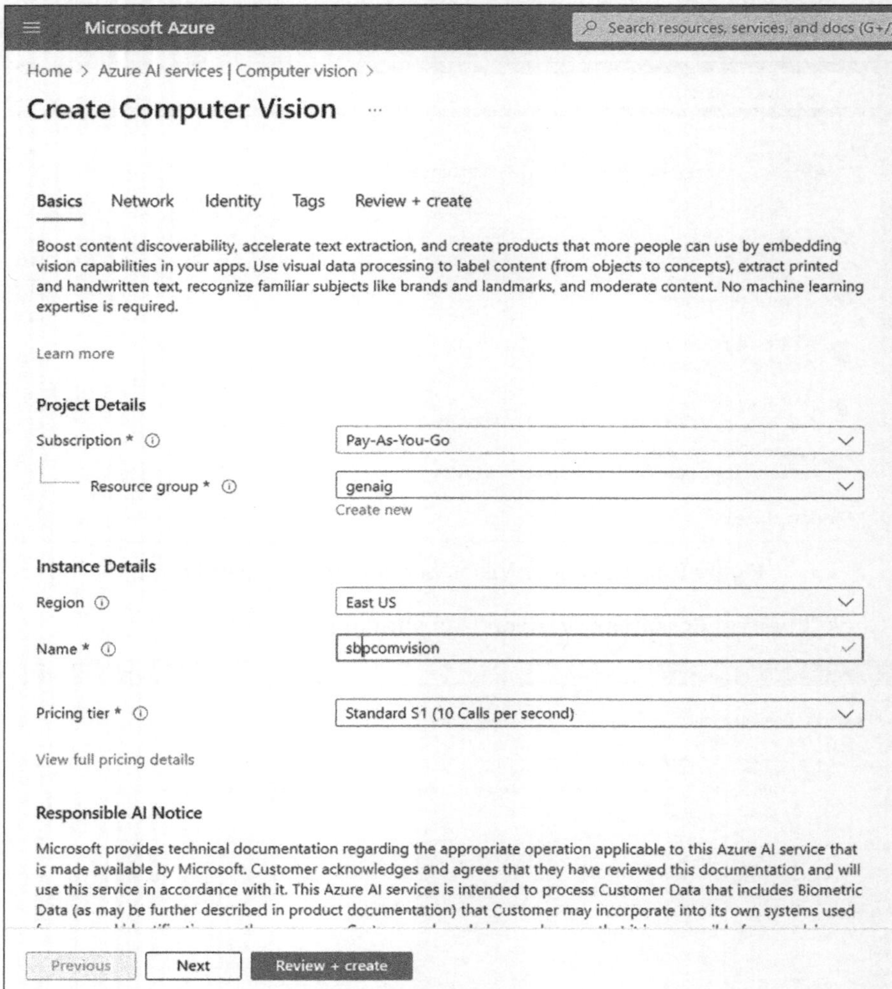

Figure 9.37: *Azure Computer Vision Service Configuration*

Step 4: Once the resource is created successfully, we must go to the key and end point, copy, and save it for implementation.

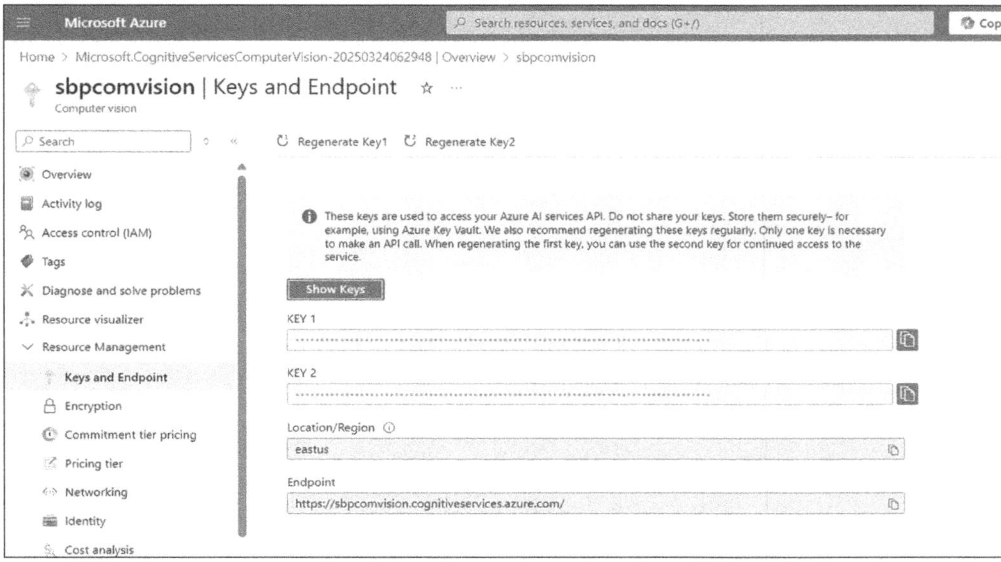

Figure 9.38: *Azure Speech Service Keys and Region*

Now that we have the Speech SDK installed and the Key and Endpoint ready, we can start writing the code and calling the appropriate service along with the key and endpoint.

Real-time speech is recognized from a microphone:

```
print("##################")
print("Import libraries")
print("###############")
import os
from azure.ai.vision.image analysis import ImageAnalysisClient
from azure.ai.vision.imageanalysis.models import VisualFeatures
from the azure. Core.credentials import AzureKeyCredential

# Vision Configuration
try:
    endpoint = os.environ["VISION_ENDPOINT"]
    key = os.environ["VISION_KEY"]
except KeyError:
    print("Mandatory fields are missing 'VISION_ENDPOINT' or 'VISION_KEY
'")
    exit()

# Create an Image Analysis client
client = ImageAnalysisClient(
    endpoint=endpoint,
    credential=AzureKeyCredential(key)
```

```
)

print("#################################")
print("# Get a caption for the image.")
print("#################################")


result = client.analyze_from_url(
    image_url="XXXXXXXXXXXXX",visual_features=[VisualFeatures.CAPTION, VisualFeatures.READ],
    gender_neutral_caption=True,  # Optional (default is False))

print("#################################")
print("Azure Vision - Image analysis:")
print("#################################")

print(" Caption For the given image is:")
if the result. Caption is not None:
    print(f"   '{result.caption.text}', Confidence {result.caption.confidence:.4f}")

print("#################################")
print(" OCR analysis results:")
print("#################################")

print(" Read:")
if the result. Read is not None:
    for line in result.read.blocks[0].lines:
            print(f"     Word: '{word.text}', Bounding polygon {word.bounding_polygon}, Confidence {word.confidence:.4f}")
```

Input:

Figure 9.39: *Input Image for Analysis*

Output:

```
Caption for the given image is a newspaper advertisement with people on
it (90%)

OCR analysis results:
text (100.00%)
human face (99.58%)
clothing (99.01%)
man (98.54%)
smile (93.86%)
advertising (87.00%)
poster (86.92%)
glasses (84.50%)
person (83.22%)
```

Deep Dive into Azure Language Studio

Azure Language Studio is a web-based interface that simplifies the exploring, testing, and deploying of natural language processing (NLP) features offered by Azure AI-Language. It provides a no-code and low-code environment for developers, data scientists, and business users to leverage the power of AI for text analysis, understanding, and generation.

Azure Vision Studio is designed to simplify the exploration, prototyping, and deployment of Computer Vision (CV) capabilities within the **Azure AI Vision** service. It offers intuitive tools for CV developers and non-technical users to experiment with vision-based AI solutions without extensive coding knowledge.

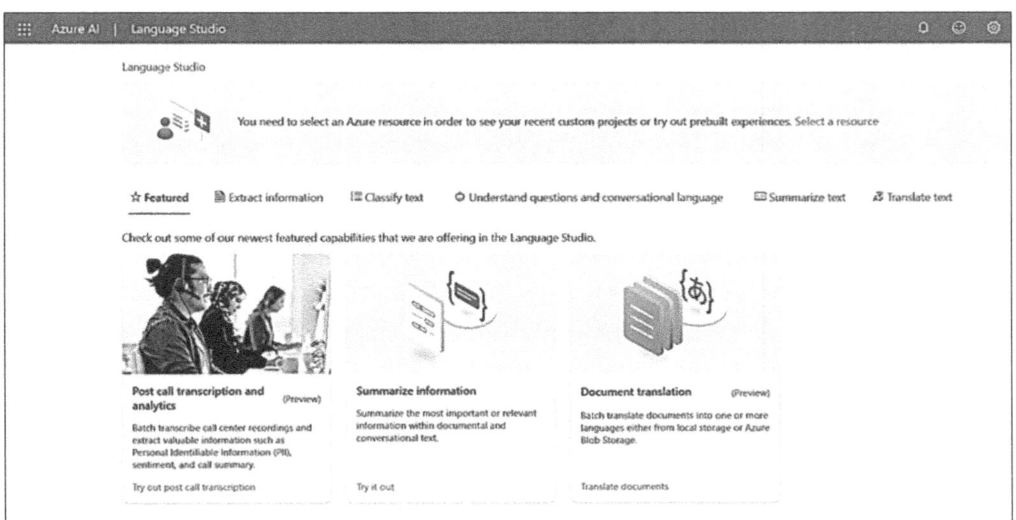

Figure 9.40: Azure Language Studio

Key Features of Azure Language Studio

Here are the primary key features of Azure Language Studio:

- **Text Analytics**: It helps to extract key phrases, named entities, and sentiments from the given text input. It can also identify personally identifiable information (PII) for privacy compliance, leading to the identification of themes and sentiments.
- **Custom Text Classification**: You can create and deploy models to classify text into custom categories and help categorize support tickets or emails for efficient routing. Example: Email classification and storing in appropriate folders.
- **Conversational Language Understanding (CLU)**: It is powerful in building conversational AI models that understand intents and extract entities. It allows us to create virtual assistants and chatbots with domain-specific conversation flows for various industry-specific use cases.
- **Document Summarization**: This capability plays a vital role in many industries, such as law firms, healthcare, and education, where it is used to summarize long documents into concise overviews based on demand.
- **Multilingual Support**: This feature is highly recommended and required at global level business communications to process text in multiple languages for international applications. It translates customer feedback from various regions into actionable insights.

Azure Language Studio is exclusively used for the following operations in various analytics:

Extract Information:

- **Extract PII**: This prebuilt capability uses Named Entity Recognition (NER) to identify sensitive personally identifiable information (PII) in text and categorize it into pre-defined classes or types, such as person, address, email, phone number, passport number, bank account number, and so on.
- **Extract Critical Phrases**: The Key Phrase Extraction API evaluates unstructured text and returns a list of key phrases for each JSON document. This capability is functional if you need to identify the main points from your text quickly.
- **Extract Named Entities**: This prebuilt capability uses NER to identify entities in text and categorize them into pre-defined classes or types such as person, location, event, product, and organization.

Classify Text:

- **Analyze Sentiment and Opinions**: This helps with text analytics for the API's Sentiment Analysis feature and provides sentiment labels such as negative, neutral, and positive.

- **Detect Language**: This feature evaluates text input for each document and returns language identifiers with a score that indicates the strength of the analysis.
- Other features include understanding questions and conversational language, summarizing, and translating text.

Microsoft Visual Studio Code

Microsoft offers a diversity of packages you can use to build Gen AI applications with the help of various packages (for example, Python: Pandas, NumPy, PyPDF2, OpenAI, Vector DB–FAISS, Pinecone, LangChain framework, and others) to manage the implementation work, along with multiple Azure services such as Azure Identity, Storage, Azure OpenAI, Azure Cognitive Search, and more that provide AI functionality to build the solution.

To build generative AI applications, use the following Azure AI SDKs for Python:

Azure Cognitive Services SDKs:

- **Text Analytics**: `azure-ai-textanalytics`, perform sentiment analysis, key phrase extraction, named entity recognition, and more.
- **Vision:** azure-ai-vision performs image analysis, OCR, object detection, and more.
- **Speech**: `azure-cognitiveservices-speech`; it performs Speech-to-text, text-to-speech, and real-time translation.
- **Custom Vision**: `azure-cognitiveservices-vision-customvision` trains and deploys custom image classification and object detection models.

By using Azure's AI services through SDKs within a code editor such as Visual Studio Code (VS Code), developers can quickly implement a wide range of AI capabilities–such as natural language processing, computer vision, anomaly detection, and more–without needing to develop AI models from scratch.

The Azure AI SDK within VS Code allows developers to integrate advanced AI capabilities into applications easily. The SDK supports various Azure cognitive services, enabling sentiment analysis and image recognition tasks. With VS Code's debugging and development environment, you can quickly build, test, and deploy robust AI solutions that leverage Azure's cloud infrastructure.

By following best practices, leveraging VS Code's tools, and exploring Azure's various cognitive offerings, we can efficiently develop AI-driven applications suited for multiple domains, including natural language processing, computer vision, and predictive analytics.

Here is an overview of the Azure AI SDK within the VS Code environment study:

- **Install Azure Extensions**: To work with Azure AI SDK in VS Code, you must install several Azure extensions. The most important ones are **Azure Account**, **Azure AI Tools**, and **Azure CLI**. These extensions allow you to log into Azure, manage resources, and integrate Azure AI capabilities directly within the VS Code environment.
- **Install Azure AI SDK Libraries**: Azure SDKs for different AI services are available for various programming languages (for example, Python, JavaScript, and C#).

  For example, we can install libraries such as azure-ai-text analytics, azure-ai-form recognizer, azure-cognitive services-vision, and others depending on the specific AI service we need. (Discussed earlier)

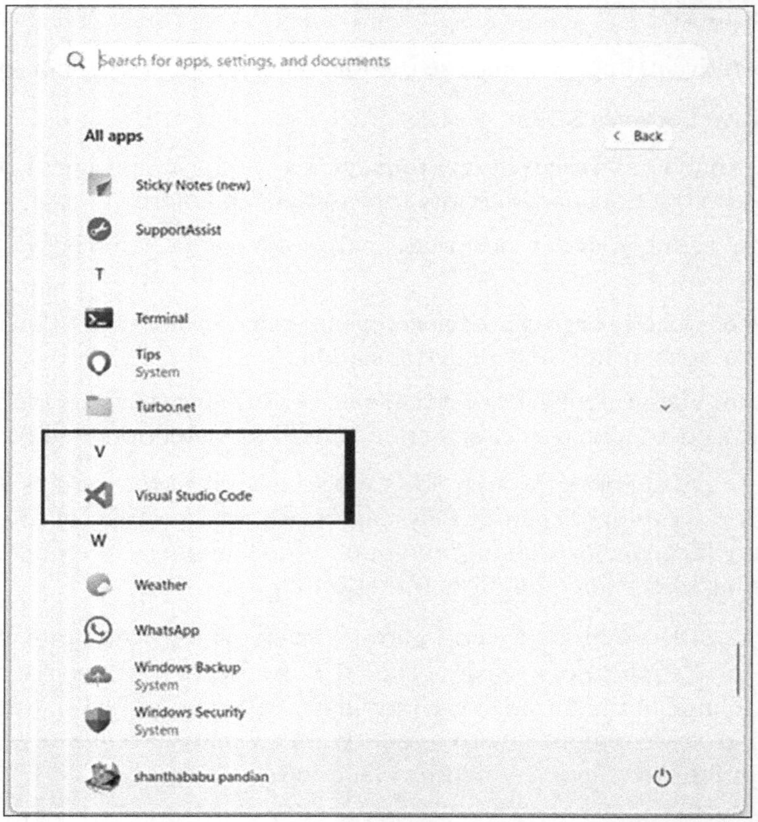

Figure 9.41: *VS Code for Azure Studio Implementation*

Figure 9.42 shows the VS code environment.

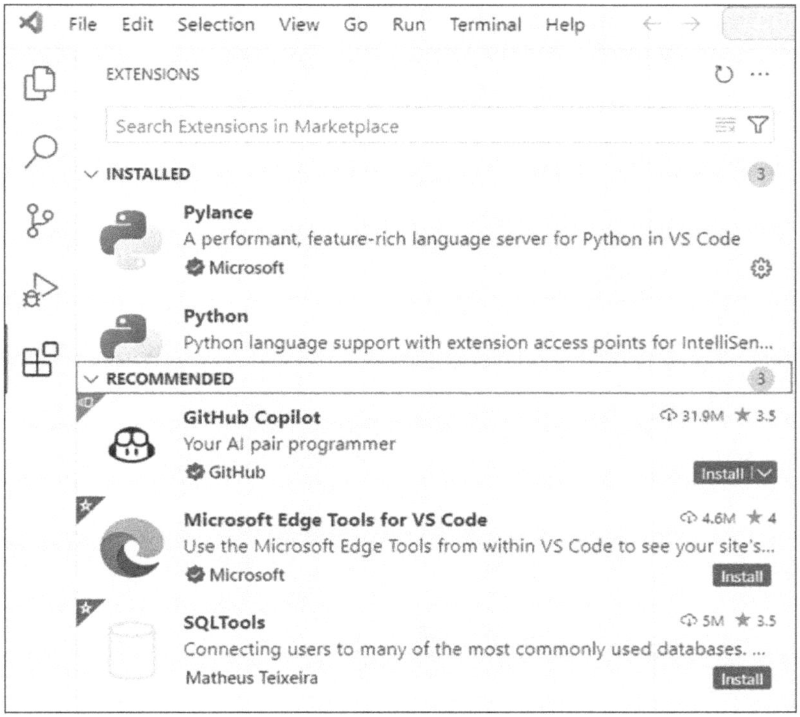

Figure 9.42: *VS Code Environment*

With the SDK and extensions set up in VS Code, we can:

- **Authenticate with Azure**: Use the Azure Account extension to authenticate and connect to your Azure resources. We can sign in to your Azure account directly from VS Code, which enables the SDK to access your cognitive services.
- **Create and Manage Resources**: You can create, manage, and configure AI resources, such as Cognitive Services and Language Services, within the Azure portal or CLI, which can be accessed via the SDK.
- **Code and Test AI Features**: Write code in your preferred language (Python, JavaScript, C#, and so on) and make API calls directly within VS Code. Use the SDK to send data to Azure AI services and receive results. For instance, you might pass a string to the Text Analytics API to determine sentiment or provide an image to the Computer Vision API for object detection.
- **Debugging and Output**: VS Code provides tools to test, debug, and adjust the AI model integrations. Output and error messages from the API calls will help you refine the integration.
- **Error Handling**: Azure AI SDKs provide error messages for failed API requests. Use VS Code's debugging tools to capture these errors and troubleshoot issues such as incorrect authentication, network issues, or API usage.

- **Environment Configuration**: VS Code's environment configuration allows you to manage environment variables and secrets. This helps secure sensitive information such as API keys and endpoint URLs.

Best Practices for VS Code Environment

Streamline your workflow with best practices for VS Code:

- **Use Azure Key Vault**: Store and manage secrets such as API keys and connection strings in Azure Key Vault and access them securely within VS Code.
- **Apply Rate Limiting**: Many cognitive services have rate limits. Apply rate limiting and error handling to avoid exceeding API call limits.
- **Log API Calls**: Maintain logs of API responses to monitor usage and understand the AI's decision-making, which can help debug and optimize the AI model's integration.
- **Optimize Data Input**: Preprocess your data before sending it to Azure AI services to ensure cleaner results and reduce unnecessary API costs.

Significance of VS Code as Azure AI SDK

For several reasons, integrating Azure AI SDK with Visual Studio Code (VS Code) is significant for AI developers and data scientists. It combines the power of Azure's AI services with the efficiency of a more widespread, versatile development environment than any other environment.

Visual Studio Code and Azure AI SDK provide a robust and efficient development environment that streamlines the end-to-end process of building, testing, and deploying AI models on Azure.

VS Code's robust integration with Azure services, flexibility, debugging capabilities, and collaborative features make it an ideal platform for developing AI applications.

VS Code significantly enhances the productivity and capabilities of developers and data scientists working with Azure AI.

Here is why VS Code is particularly valuable when working with the Azure AI SDK:

- **Seamless Integration with Azure Services:** VS Code, with its **Azure extensions**, allows developers to connect directly to Azure resources, making it easier to manage Azure Cognitive Services, Machine Learning, and other AI capabilities.
- **Intelligent Code Suggestions**: VS Code provides intelligent code completion, syntax highlighting, and AI-driven code suggestions, improving productivity and reducing errors when working with Azure SDKs.

- **Debugging Tools**: VS Code offers powerful debugging tools that allow developers to trace issues in real-time. This is particularly useful when fine-tuning AI models and working with complex code.
- **Integrated Terminal and Git Support**: With an integrated terminal and Git support, VS Code enables efficient version control and command-line operations, making it easier to manage development workflows.
- **Language and Library Flexibility:** VS Code supports multiple programming languages, making it flexible for using Azure AI SDKs with Python, JavaScript, C#, and more.
- **Jupyter Notebook Integration**: VS Code supports Jupyter Notebooks, allowing users to write, test, and visualize code interactively. This is especially valuable for machine learning and data exploration with Azure AI services.
- **Efficient Collaboration and Sharing**: VS Code enhances collaboration among team members working on Azure AI projects through GitHub integration and the ability to share code.
- **Cost and Resource Management:** VS Code allows developers to monitor and manage their Azure usage directly within the editor, helping them keep track of costs associated with Azure Cognitive Services, storage, and other resources.

Comparative Study of VS Code with Other SDKs

Following is an analysis comparing VS Code's features with other popular Software Development Kits (SDKs).

Features	VS Code with Azure AI SDK	Google Colab	PyCharm with ML/Cloud Extensions	AWS CLI / GCP SDK
Cloud Integration	Directly integrated with Azure for cloud resource control	Limited to Google services, web-only	Limited cloud integrations and extra setup required	Command-line only, limited IDE support
Multi-Language Support	High support (Python, C#, JavaScript, R, and more)	Primarily Python	Primarily Python, some R, and Java support	Language agnostic, CLI-driven
Extension Marketplace	Extensive (Azure, AI, ML, Data Science extensions)	Limited to Colab add-ons	Limited, fewer cloud AI extensions available	No extensions, CLI only

Collaboration	Excellent (Live Share and GitHub integration)	Limited (commenting only)	Limited; extra setup needed for real-time collab	None (command-line)
Debugging	Comprehensive debugging tools	Minimal debugging support	Strong Python debugging	None, command-line
Jupyter Notebook Support	Native, in-editor support	Yes, browser-based only	Supported but less integrated	None
Cost Management	Real-time tracking via Azure extension	None	No integrated cost management	Requires AWS/GCP Console
CI/CD Support	Integrated with GitHub Actions and Azure DevOps	Limited (requires exporting to GitHub)	Supports Jenkins/ GitLab but requires configuration	CLI-based, limited to cloud-native CI/CD

***Table 9.1**: Comparative Study of VS Code with Other SDKs*

Azure AI Foundry

Azure AI Foundry is a comprehensive suite of tools, services, and frameworks provided by Microsoft Azure to accelerate the design, development, deployment, and management of AI and ML solutions. It is designed to help organizations leverage the power of AI to drive innovation, enhance operational efficiency, and solve complex business problems.

Key Features:

- **Integrated AI Ecosystem**: It combines pre-built AI models, customizable AI services, and development frameworks for seamless AI solution creation.
- **AI Model Development**: It provides tools for building, training, and deploying custom AI models using Azure Machine Learning and Azure OpenAI.
- **No-Code and Low-Code Capabilities**: It features tools such as Azure AI Studio for users with minimal coding expertise, enabling quick prototyping and implementation.
- **Pre-Built AI Models**: It offers a library of pre-trained models for NLP, computer vision, and predictive analytics.
- **Scalable Infrastructure**: It is highly powered by Azure's robust cloud infrastructure, ensuring scalability for AI workloads of any size.
- **Responsible AI Practices**: These include tools and frameworks to ensure

ethical AI usage, address bias, maintain transparency, and build responsible AI practices.

- **Integration with Azure Services**: It seamlessly integrates with other Azure services such as Azure Data Factory, Power BI, and Azure Cognitive Services.

Azure AI Foundry Architecture

AI Foundry provides a unified experience for AI architects, developers, and data scientists to build, evaluate, and deploy AI models through a web portal, SDK, or CLI. It is built on capabilities and services provided by other Azure services, as shown in *Figure* 9.43.

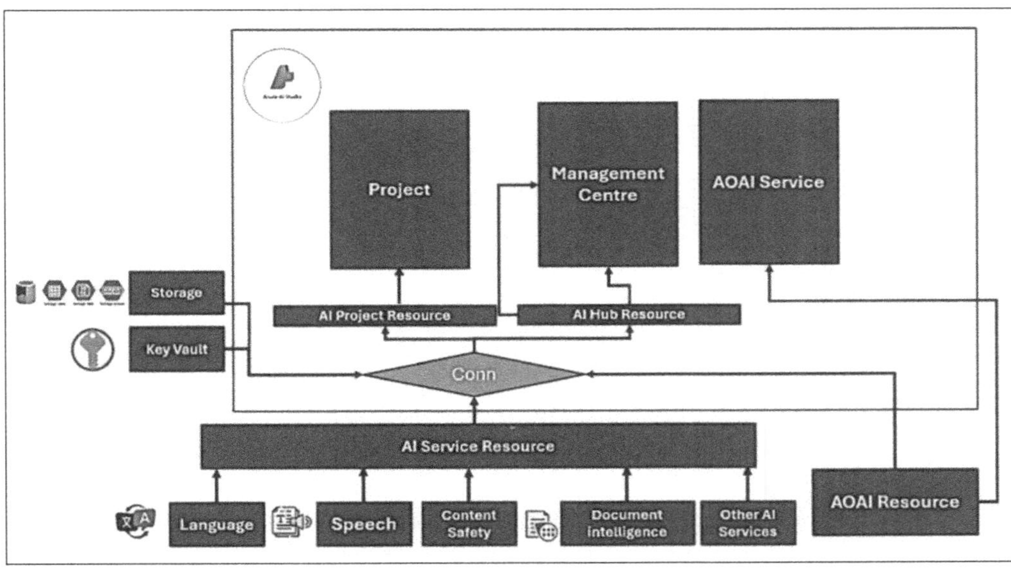

Figure 9.43: *Azure AI Foundry Architecture*

Azure AI Foundry provides access to the following resources in the given architecture:

- **Azure OpenAI**: Provides access to the latest OpenAI models. It enables the creation of secure deployments, playgrounds, fine-tuned models, and batch jobs. A significant advantage is that when using the Azure AI Foundry portal, you can work directly with Azure OpenAI without an Azure Studio project.
- **Management Center:** It enables streamlining the governance and management of AI Foundry resources such as hubs, projects, connected resources, and deployments.
- **AI Foundry Hub**: This is the top-level resource in the AI Foundry portal and is based on the Azure Machine Learning service. The features it provides are security computing resources, project management configuration, and an Azure storage account for data upload and artifact storage.

AI Foundry Project: This is same as the Azure AI Studio Architecture discussed in *Chapter 8, Advanced Azure AI Studio–I.*

Azure portal launches the page, as shown in *Figure* 9.44.

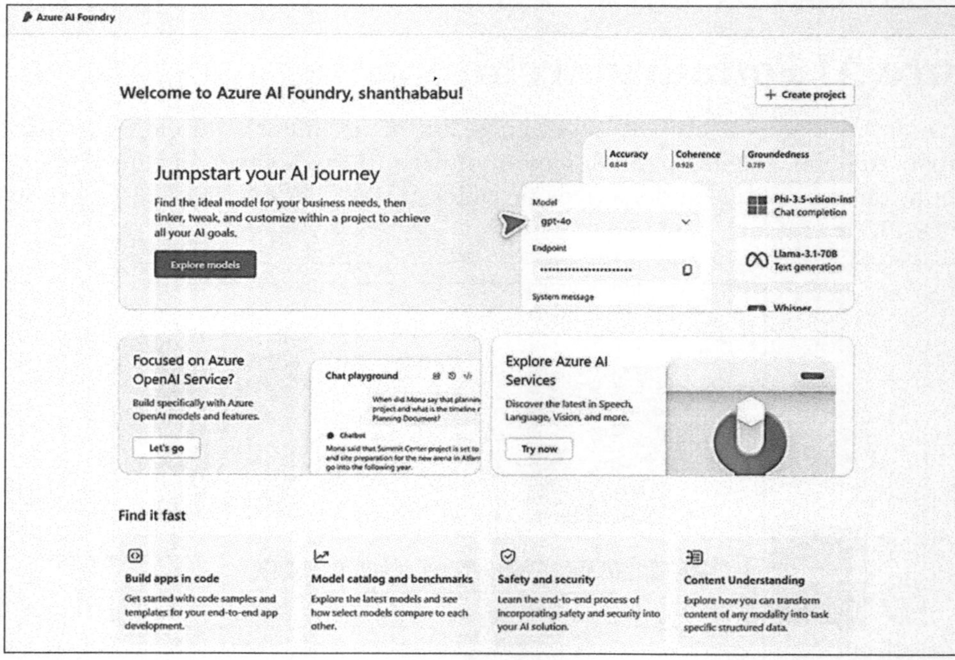

Figure 9.44: *Azure AI Foundry*

Click Explore models; the portal takes you to the page shown in *Figure* 9.45; it provides GPT, Whisper, TTS, DALL-E, LLaMA, Phi, Hugging Face, and many more models.

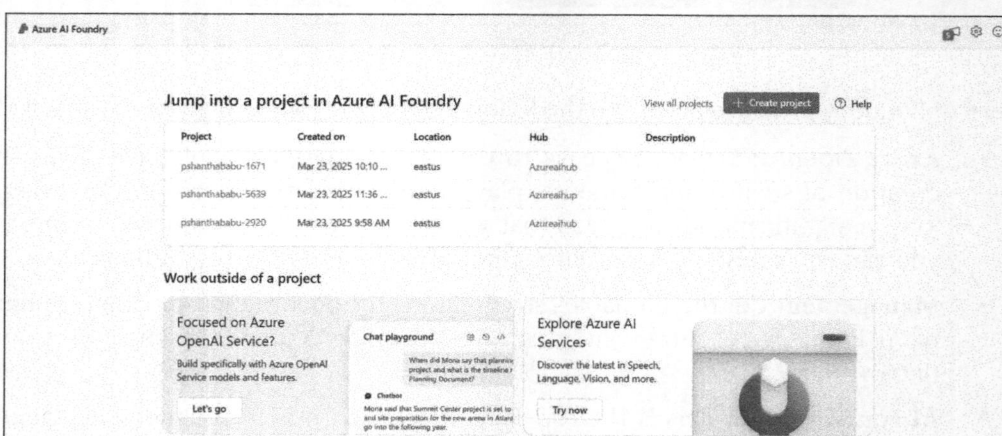

Figure 9.45: *Azure AI Foundry; Models*

Azure AI Foundry Project

It provides the environment for the development of the work. You can work on your project in the Azure AI Foundry development environment. You can also connect to projects from your code, similar to other Azure studio components. Once you are ready to build, customize, test, and operationalize, a project is where you will want to be, and you can choose a model to deploy or work with any of the AI Services.

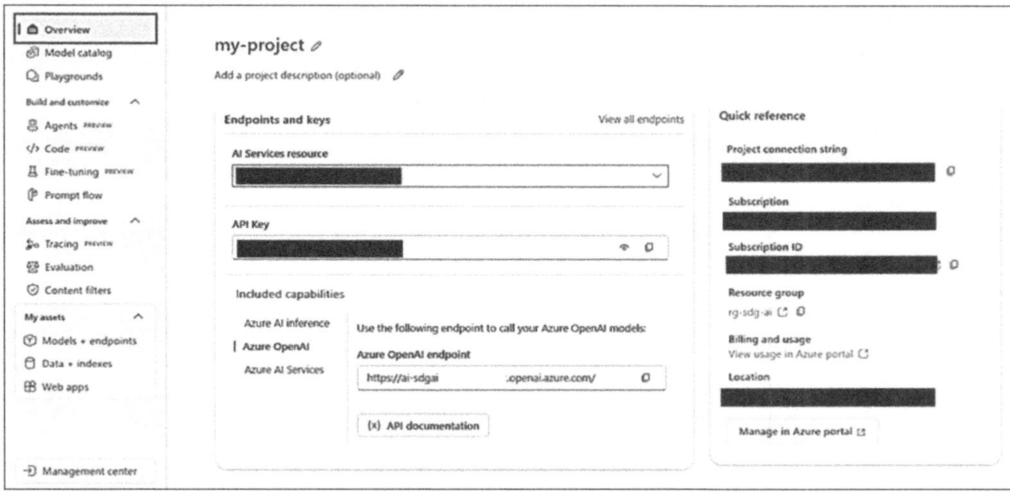

Figure 9.46: *Azure AI Foundry; Project*

The rest of the features are similar to Azure Studio we discussed in *Chapter* 8, *Advanced Azure AI Studio–I*.

Conclusion

This chapter exclusively discusses Azure AI Speech Studio, Vision, and Language, along with No-code and Code implementation using Python with respective SDKs.We have understood how Azure AI Studio and tools like Azure Speech SDK, Vision Studio, and Language Studio provide a comprehensive ecosystem for developing AI-powered solutions.

We deep-dived into the Visual Studio Code environment, its significance, and how it empowers development. We have how it further enhances productivity by providing a reliable development environment that is compatible with and supports Azure AI SDKs.

This deep dive into Azure's advanced AI tools underscores their significance in modern business and technology. Their real-time applications, critical spatial analysis capabilities, and emphasis on best practices set a benchmark for AI innovation, making Azure a leader in transforming industries with intelligent solutions. We discussed the Azure AI Foundry architecture and project overviews.

In the next chapter, we will explore the various use cases of Generative AI and its impact as well as significance on business development, user benefits, and ease of life, including healthcare, finance, and banking. We will also learn about the potential implications of AI in the above industry, how we can bring ethical considerations when using genetic AI, and how AI ensures good security.

CHAPTER 10
Generative AI Use Cases for Industries-I

Introduction

In the previous chapter, we explored Azure AI Studio's features from the aspects of Language, Speech, and Vision. We explored Azure AI Language Studio, which provides a user-friendly environment for developing unique projects and models. We used client libraries and REST APIs to test both code-based and no-code methods. Additionally, we tested Language Studio's chat features using legitimate formats and custom text. Furthermore, we looked at Azure Speech Service and discovered how to use Azure OpenAI Service to create solutions using these voices. We also discussed how SSML elements are supported by OpenAI text-to-speech voices in Azure Speech. We examined Azure AI Vision's unified vision capabilities, including prebuilt models for facial recognition, text extraction with OCR, and image analysis. Lastly, we showed that vision characteristics might be incorporated into applications without the need for machine learning knowledge.

In this chapter, we will explore the various use cases of Generative AI and the different aspects of its impact and significance on business development, user benefits, and the quality of life, which includes healthcare and medicine, by exploring how Generative AI revolutionizes healthcare by assisting in medical report analysis, drug discovery, personalized medicine, and patient care. We will also investigate the role of generative AI in financial forecasting, fraud detection, and customer service within the banking and finance sector. Furthermore, we will study the involvement of Gen AI in the entertainment and media industry for content generation, including the production of music, art, literature, and virtual influencers. We will go beyond to cover how manufacturing is adopting Industry 4.0 to investigate the role of Generative AI in smart manufacturing production lines, predictive maintenance, quality control, and supply chain optimization; how agriculture and food processing systems adapt to Gen AI; and explore applications in precision agriculture, crop monitoring, pest detection, and food supply chain management. Lastly, we will go through the potential implications of AI in the mentioned industries, ways to bring ethical considerations when using genetic AI, and evaluate whether AI offers good security.

Structure

In this chapter, you will delve into the following topics:

- Necessities of Gen AI in Various Industries
    - Banking and Financial Industry
    - Healthcare, Entertainment, and Media
    - Manufacturing and Industry 4.0
    - Agriculture and Food
- Ethical Consideration in Gen AI in Different Industries
- Discussion on Security Aspects of Gen AI

Necessities of Gen AI in Various Industries

Generative AI offers enormous potential to transform any industry by enhancing innovation, optimizing processes, incorporating personalized experiences, and driving modernization from an industry perspective. Every industry has a vast amount of historical data. Gen AI, with its ability to generate new solutions in terms of developing content, text, images, audio, and video for various issues and challenges dependent on the industry needs. Gen AI addresses complex challenges and unlocks new opportunities across all sectors that we will be discussing in this chapter extensively.

Gen AI is necessary in various industries because it can automate, optimize, and innovate processes that traditionally require significant human effort and time. Here are the necessities for Generative AI across different sectors.

Multiple parameters determine the necessity of Gen AI across different domains, as shown in the following list:

- **Innovative**: Creatively execute the task to generate new ideas and solutions, leading to users being driven by creative and innovative thoughts regarding product design, sales and marketing, decision-making, business content creation, and image, audio, and video generation based on the business domain needs.
- **Accelerating Innovation**: It helps speed up the agile way of developing and deploying new technologies, products, and services in terms of innovation.
- **Automation**: Automating routine tasks will improve efficiency and effectiveness and reduce manual effort, cost, and time.
- **Inaccuracy Reduction**: Automation obsessively minimizes human errors by providing accurate and consistent outputs based on data patterns from historical data and models.

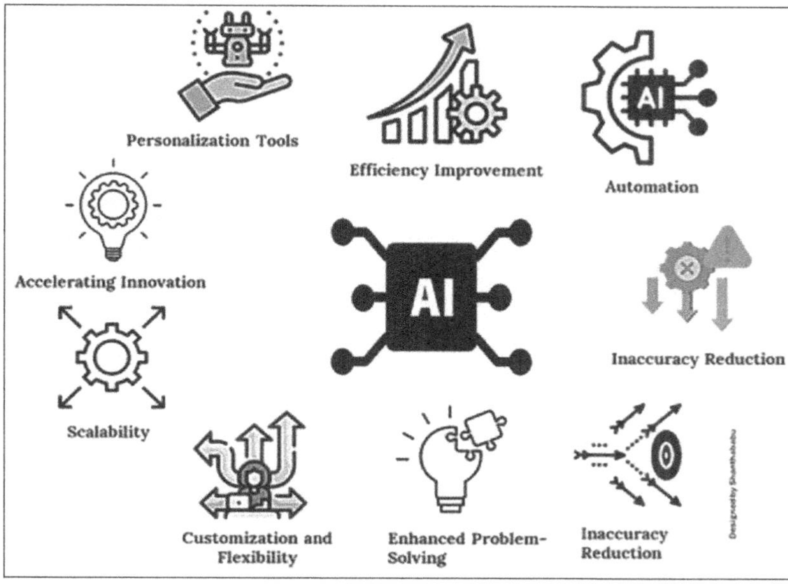

***Figure 10.1**: Necessities of Gen AI in Various Industries*

- **Efficiency Improvement**: Once automation is in place, it helps streamline processes and operations, which leads to optimized resource sharing, cost savings, and quicker execution.
- **Enhanced Problem-Solving**: Innovative solutions provide advanced AI tools and techniques for solving complex problems and addressing challenges across various industries.
- **Personalization Tools**: AI tools help to create customized solutions and tailored versions for individual needs and preferences, and at the same time to enhance user engagement and satisfaction at different levels (for example, AI tools: Google Assistant, Amazon Alexa, and Siri).
- **Scalability**: It facilitates the creation of scalable solutions based on the demand and volume that can handle small, medium, and large volumes of data and adapt to the growing needs.
- **Customization and Flexibility**: Customization and flexibility should always be available, adapted to different requirements and scenarios, and offer resourceful applications across multiple industries (Finance, Banking, Entertainment and Media, Manufacturing, and Agriculture and Food Systems).

Let us review the necessities of different domains at a high level.

Healthcare: Gen AI has a broad and transformative scope in the healthcare industry. Its ability to process and analyze vast amounts of data and generate actionable insights makes it a unique tool for healthcare providers, researchers, and the patient community. Here are the key areas where it is making a significant impact:

- Drug Discovery and Development
- Medical Imaging and Diagnostics
- Personalized Medicine
- Virtual Health Assistants and Chatbots

Gen AI can revolutionize the industry by enhancing efficiency in various aspects, from personalizing patient care to accelerating research and development and improving overall health outcomes.

Banking: Gen AI offers potential transformative opportunities in banking, which is a highly critical and essential domain for interconnection with all other domains in the industry. Hence, this domain is responsible for enhancing the services and support listed.

- Customer service
- Fraud detection
- Risk management optimization
- Banking Operations

These are vital requirements and always fulfil the demands. Its ability to analyze vast amounts of data and generate valuable insights helps lead to more informed decision-making, improve customer experiences, and increase operational efficiency and effectiveness in day-to-day activities.

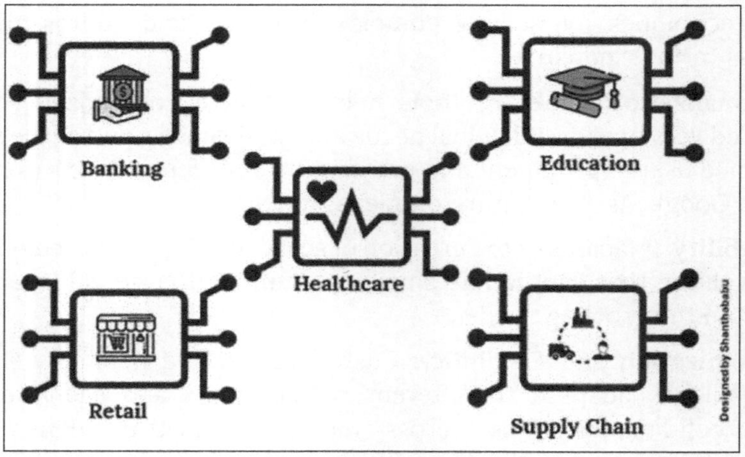

Figure 10.2: *Gen AI in Various Industries*

Retail and Supply Chain: Gen AI in the retail and supply chain industry offers various applications and significantly enhances the following aspects. By leveraging the power of Gen AI, retailers and supply chain management can gain a competitive edge, drive innovative solutions, and meet their customers' evolving demands.

- Customer experience
- Optimize inventory
- Supply Chain Management
- Personalize marketing efforts
- Operational efficiency

Our primary objective is to provide personalized shopping experiences and product recommendations. The company optimizes inventory management strategies to prevent stockouts and overstock situations and enhances visual merchandising for online and in-store display options.

Education: Gen AI in education offers transformative potential benefits in many ways. These include personalizing learning experiences for students and research scholars and innovative tools as resources for students, teachers, and professors. Its incredible ability to generate tailored content precisely for student communities to understand the perspective of exam preparation, provide real-time support, and enhance learning outcomes educational quality and equity.

- Personalized Learning
- Content Creation
- Tutoring and Support
- Assessment and Evaluation

So far, we have discussed the influence of Gen AI on different domains. Let us examine individual industries and learn more about them.

Gen AI in the Banking and Financial Industry

As we know, the banking and financial industries are different entities with slim liners in between, but they have a mutual connection. Generally, banks are used to managing and enabling the customers' deposits and transactions and providing safety for their savings and considerable interest on money and fixed deposits. At the same time, finance broadly comprehends the management of huge volumes of funds, whether for individuals, corporations, or governments, and financing for multiple purposes such as business development, housing, infrastructure enhancements, industry, education, and others

Let us focus on banking and understand the benefits of Gen AI, followed by financial services, and later connect with them.

Gen AI has a significant scope in the banking industry, namely, other IT services, such as supporting applications, database management, and reporting services. Gen AI offers numerous opportunities to enhance services, improve efficiency, and create value with innovative solutions. Here are some key areas where Generative AI can be applied:

There are two broader categories:

- Customer-focused
- Bankers-focused

Customer-focused Gen AI Scope and Opportunity

Customer Service and Support: In every industry, the end customer service and their satisfaction are critical factors to success in the business and instrumental for sustainability; banking is not an exceptional case here.

Gen AI-based tools help assist in the form of chatbots and virtual assistants across 365-degree support, such as:

- 24/7 Customer inquiry
- Support for common banking tasks
    - Account related inquiries
    - Transaction history queries
    - Loan application inquiries and status

They innovatively analyze and generate visualizations, provide personalized banking experiences for individual customers, and provide personalized financial advice and product recommendations for their financial benefits.

Enhanced Customer Support: AI-powered chatbots are used to provide 24/7 support. These chatbots can handle inquiries, resolve issues, and guide customers through processes with human-like interactions so customer queries and clarifications are sorted out on time at the maximum rate and gain customer satisfaction quickly along with the feedback process via the chatbot. This virtual assistant offers real-time, personalized assistance, helping customers navigate products, services, or websites more effectively without any other human assistance. So, the vast amount of time and cost are gradually reduced for the banking sector.

Automated and Faster Response Times: AI automates routine customer service tasks, such as account inquiries and order tracking, and ensures quick and accurate responses among customers. AI-powered chatbots offer fast response times. Instant query resolution using AI reduces wait times and improves customer experience.

Credit Scoring Assessments: Gen AI tools proactively involve risk management assessment in terms of credit scoring by analyzing customer data, calculating the credit score using "**Credit Scoring Models**," and helping banks improve accuracy in assessing creditworthiness. Along with predictive analytics strategies forecasting potential risks in investments and loans, customers and Qantas, and Gen AI tools help banks mitigate potential losses, evaluate customer repayment capacity, and assess genuineness in the market.

Dynamic Pricing and Offers: AI can analyze market trends and customer behavior to offer real-time discounts, dynamic pricing, and personalized promotions, providing customers with the best value. Furthermore, it delivers personalized incentives and loyalty rewards based on customer preferences and purchasing patterns. In all this, we need to build a better product and service design focused on customer-driven, innovative products so that Gen AI can analyze customer feedback and preferences to generate new product ideas or service improvements, leading to offerings that better meet customer needs.

Data Security and Operational Efficiency: Gen AI assistance helps with "Threat Detection"–identifying and mitigating cybersecurity threats by analyzing network traffic and user behavior. It also ensures compliance with data privacy regulations by generating policies and processes that protect customer data. Based on data analysis, Gen AI assists decision-makers with actionable insights and recommendations.

Accessibility and Inclusion: This factor plays a vital role in any industry, specifically in banking real-time language translation services. It makes products and services accessible to a global audience that can adopt any language and attract customers using their native language-based interactions. It supports language translation, provides **"Assistive Technologies,"** and AI-driven tools for customers with disabilities, such as voice recognition, text-to-speech, or personalized learning tools. On top of that, businesses can use AI to ensure fair and unbiased customer interactions, promoting ethical practices in customer engagement in terms of **Ethical AI Use and Sustainable Recommendations**.

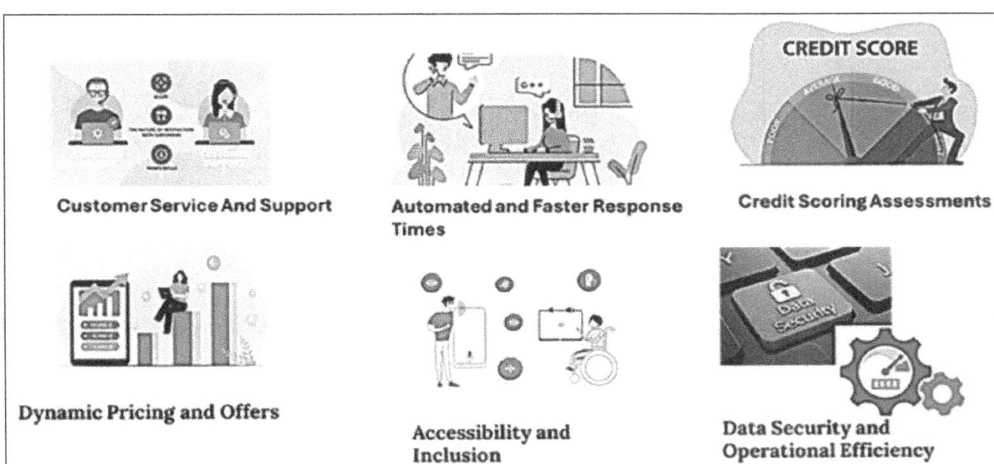

Figure 10.3: *Customer-focused Gen AI Scope and Opportunity*

Bankers-focused Gen AI Scope and Opportunity

Gen AI-based tools are common platforms for both sides of the industry, such as customer and banker-specific. Let us discuss such an application.

Fraud Detection and Prevention: In any domain, preventing fraud is an inevitable consideration to stabilize the process and credibility of customer service. The banking industry is a high-potential fraud detection and prevention target in that scenario. Gen AI is helping the banking industry build anomaly detection-based tools to track transactions, identify unusual patterns in a sequence of transactions, and alter and provide guidance for preventive measures.

- Anomaly Detection
- Real-Time Monitoring

Loan and Mortgage Underwriting: Gen AI is highly capable of generating standard content and evaluating the given data based on industry requirements. This specific tool is essential to effectively enhance the service at both ends. This is achieved by building the documentation based on the instructions from bankers and helping customers fill it out to streamline the loan approval process by automating the evaluation of customers' applications by considering the risk assessment model and making the decision quickly to reduce overall processing time.

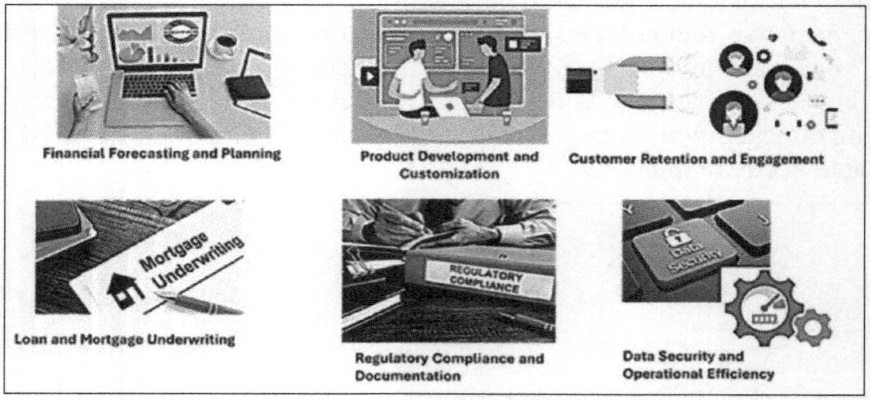

Figure 10.4: *Banker-focused Gen AI Scope and Opportunity*

Regulatory Compliance and Documentation: Gen AI has the capability to automate compliance checks, build reporting, and support the bank's adherence to regulatory requirements, auto-audit compliance documents, and regulatory submissions.

Financial Forecasting and Planning: Investment bankers' budget and forecast annually based on historical conditions and market situations. The tool helps generate accurate financial forecasts and budgets by analyzing historical data and market conditions. Aids in long-term strategic planning by predicting future economic trends and market shifts.

Product Development and Customization: Bankers always consider new product designs to enhance or add new features to their customer benefits and attract more customers to expand their market. They use AI to generate ideas for new financial products and services tailored to customer needs and personalize existing products and services to meet individual customer preferences better; in recent years, Gen AI roles have become unavoidable in strengthening the new product development perspective.

Customer Retention and Engagement: Bankers consider enhancing their products, services, and methods to assess customer retention exercises. They use the "Churn Prediction" methodology to identify customers at risk of leaving and generate strategies to retain them. They also create personalized marketing campaigns based on user behavior and preferences to maintain customers and attract more.

Gen AI in the Healthcare Industry

Generative AI in the healthcare industry claims high potential and revolutionizes use cases, ultimately enhancing the efficiency of existing processes in terms of drug design and development, personalizing patient care, accelerating research and development, and improving overall health domain outcomes. The ability to process and analyze vast amounts of data and generate actionable insights makes it an invaluable tool for healthcare providers, researchers, and patients by providing decision-making tools and generating documents. Apparently, Generative AI has a broad and transformative scope in the healthcare industry, as do other industries and the most demanding perspectives.

Let us discuss the areas where they are making a significant impact using Gen AI:

Drug Discovery and Development: Gen AI-based drug discovery and development are recently revolutionizing the pharmaceutical industry by accelerating the identification process and developing new drugs and enhancing existing ones in terms of effectiveness in treatment, customer credibility, reducing the time-consuming of going to market, reducing manufacturing costs, and increasing the overall success rate.

In this specific use case, the following factors are majorly influencing:

- **Molecule Generation**: Drug discovery and development require careful consideration and detailing during the molecule generation; in the earlier days, this was taken care of by experts' involvement in every stage and back-and-forth method based on the experts' opinion. Using Gen AI, we can design new drug molecules with historical data and appropriate inputs from experts and considerable review and improvements in molecule generation; this approach is eventually speeding up the discovery process and significantly improving it in terms of standards and objectives in a lesser duration than the traditional method. It helps to enhance the following activities in drug discovery and development in the following aspects:

- Accelerated Drug Discovery
- Enhanced Drug Design
- Precision Medicine
- Improved Safety and Efficacy

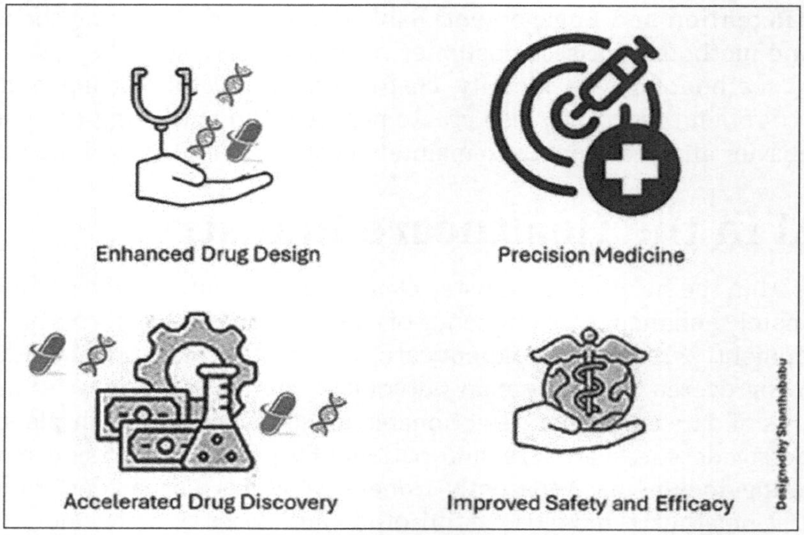

Figure 10.5: *Gen AI in Drug Discovery and Development*

Data Integration and Management in the Healthcare Industry: As part of the Data Science process, data integration and management are critical factors. They involve streamlining the process of combining data from various data sources into a composite assessment, enhancing operational efficiency, and enabling informed decision-making across healthcare systems to help doctors, administrators, and patients. This approach supports real-time data analysis and encourages a complete understanding of doctors' and patients' needs and service delivery metrics as expected criteria.

- **Multi-Omics Integration (MoI):** AI integrates data from various sources, such as genomics, proteomics, and metabolomics, to provide a comprehensive view of disease mechanisms and drug interactions. With this MoI, AI can process and analyze biomedical data and extract meaningful insights that can significantly help drive drug discovery and development.

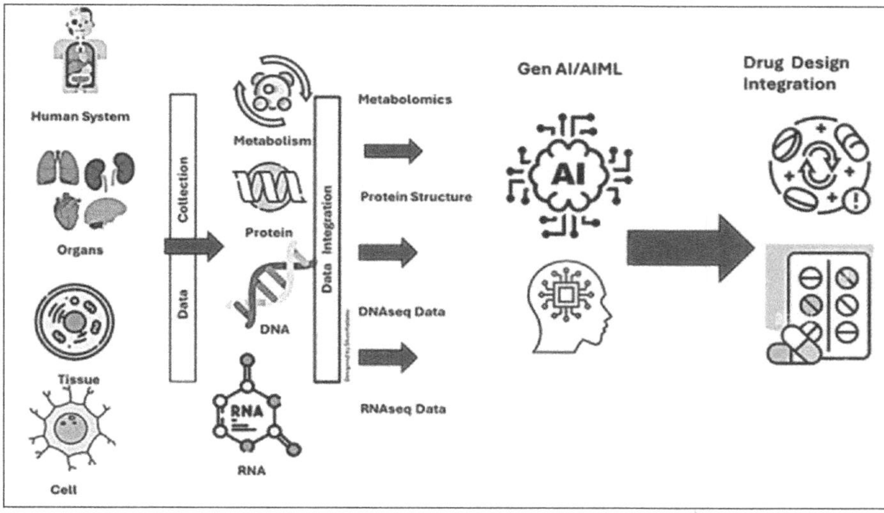

Figure 10.6: *Gen AI Solutions for Multi-Omics Integration*

Collaboration and Innovation Program: Collaboration and innovation ideas consistently help industries at different levels. Specific AI-pharma company partnerships and collaborations are becoming increasingly common and have high potential outcomes and benefits for society. These partnerships combine expertise in data science and drug development to accelerate innovation in drug design and development as well as accelerate faster than earlier.

This collaboration can be achieved through open-source platforms driven by AI that allow researchers and scientists to share their data and collaborate on drug design, discovery research, and development projects. These projects nurture innovative ideas and implementation, speed development, and significantly reduce individual investment and timeframe.

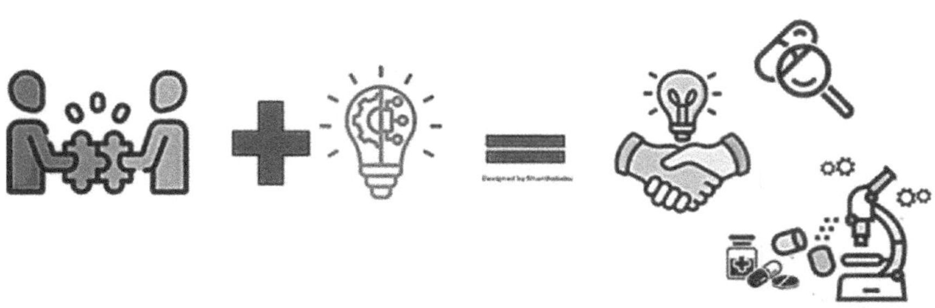

Figure 10.7: *Gen AI Solutions for Collaboration and Innovation in Drug Design and Development*

AI-Powered Medical Imaging and Diagnostics: Medical Imaging and Diagnostics are major practices in the healthcare industry. They involve leveraging advanced tools and technologies, such as MRI and CT scans, along with AI-powered tools, to provide precise, expedited, and rapid diagnostic insights, facilitate early detection, generate reports faster, and provide personalized treatment plans for patients. This AI-powered medical imaging and diagnostics integration improves accuracy and enhances medical experts' and patients' experience at different levels of outcomes by enabling more targeted interventions and actions.

- **AI-based Image Enhancement**: Gen AI certainly improves the quality of medical images right from the start and maximizes the outcomes in great milestones in this industry, such as MRIs, CT scans, X-ray processing, and reporting aspects.
- **AI-based diagnosis:** It assists radiologists at a higher level in identifying anomalies and diagnosing patients' conditions and reports with accurate data and image form diagnosis.
- **AI-powered 3D Modeling:** AI-powered 3D modeling creates very detailed medical images, which improves visualization, treatment planning, and high-level benchmarking.

Personalized Medicine: Gen AI can tailor medical treatment to individual patients based on medical reports and ongoing health conditions and compare the genetic influence of the profiles. With all these analyses, AI-driven systems analyze datasets. They can enhance the efficacy of therapies by predicting treatment outcomes, optimizing drug prescriptions, and customizing healthcare strategy plans. This can eventually lead to improved patient care, reduced treatment times and medical expenses, and optimal support for the healthcare division.

- **Patient Monitoring and Management:** This digital technology continuously monitors and manages patient health in real-time using Generative AI technologies, greatly influencing the prediction of health events, adjusting treatments dynamically based on the patient's health condition using advanced algorithms and strategies, and providing healthcare professionals with actionable insights, predictive analyses, and solutions actively, thus enhancing patient care, follow-up, and optimizing clinical workflows with less manual intervention, and so on. Indeed, this mode of operation helps make cost-effective and time-consuming processes on both sides.
- **Predictive Analytics:** With AI capabilities, doctors and clinical assistants can forecast disease progression, respond to treatments based on patient data, and find insights and solutions using AI assistance.
- **Customized Treatment Plans**: Each patient's unique medical history, data, health conditions, and treatment would vary based on severity. AI assistants can design personalized treatment plans, provide personalized patient recommendations and involvements, and manage chronic diseases.
- **IoT-enabled Patient Alert Systems:** IoT-enabled and integrated with AI, these systems generate alerts for healthcare providers in case of any critical challenges in patient conditions and provide immediate attentive solutions to the clinic and patient's health.

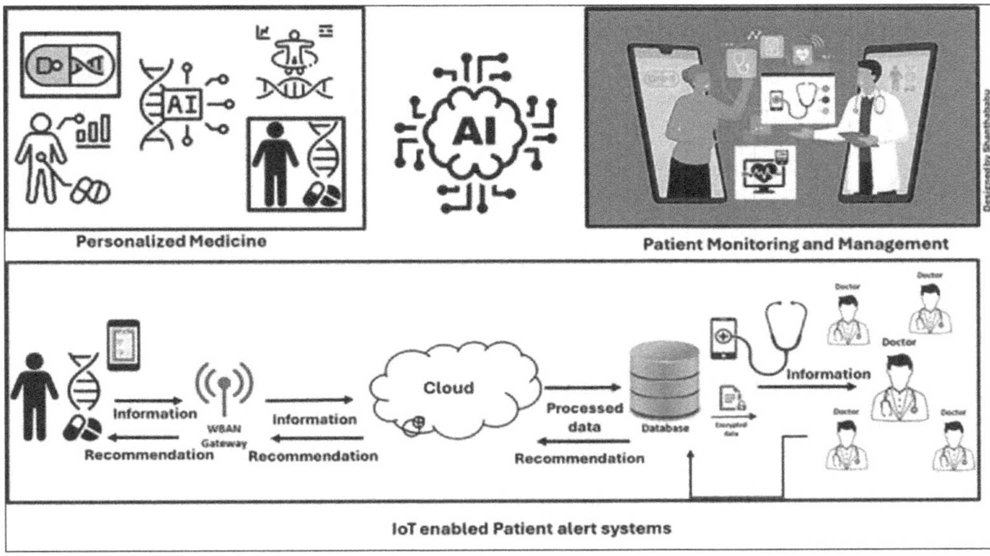

***Figure 10.8**: Gen AI Solutions for Personalized Medicine*

Healthcare Operations and Management: Healthcare operations and management incorporate various activities and strategies to ensure that healthcare facilities operate efficiently while providing high-quality IN/OUT patient care. This involves everything from day-to-day administrative tasks to strategic planning and implementation regarding quality, safety, and security.

By integrating Generative AI in healthcare operations and management activities, we can revolutionize the industry by improving service efficiency, personalizing patient care, quality of treatment, patient safety, security of facility operations, and enhancing decision-making processes effectively and efficiently. Here is an indication of how Gen AI can be utilized effectively within healthcare operations and management practices.

- **Virtual Health Assistants and Chatbots:** Patients can interact with AI-driven chatbots for 24/7 support, immediate assistance from nearby clinics, and virtual doctor consultations.
- **Streamlined Administrative Processes:** Gen AI is capable of automating documentation by creating and managing it accurately, reducing the burden on healthcare staff's time and effort, and minimizing errors and costs.
- **Scheduling and Staff Allocation**: In healthcare facilities, various sectors that contribute to clinical and non-clinical operations are considered. Involvement of a list of staff such as Clinical, Administrative, Support, and Ancillary Services.

  Scheduling staff allocation is a tedious job; with the help of AI algorithms, we can optimize the scheduling by predicting various peak time frames, managing staff rosters, and allocating resources efficiently to reduce wait times, improve patient flow, optimize cost, plan the resource needs effectively, and arrest revenue leakage.

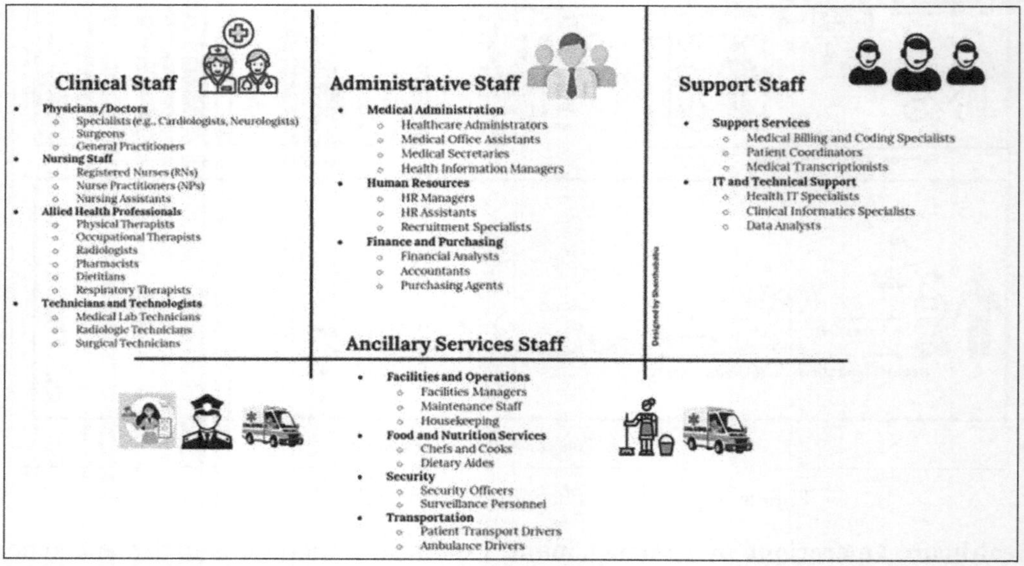

Figure 10.9: *Healthcare Operations and Management Optimization*

Gen AI in the Entertainment and Media Industry

The entertainment and media industry incorporates many sectors and activities to provide content and experiences for delight and intelligence. This industry includes traditional forms such as film, television, radio, and digital media, such as streaming platforms, video games, social media, and so on. Without question, the integration of Generative AI in this industry is transforming a lot.

Gen AI technologies such as natural language processing, image generation, and predictive analytics features enable more personalized and interactive experiences with global audiences or customers from various cultural backgrounds.

Let us discuss the impact of Gen AI across various segments of the industry:

Content Creation: Innovative idea creation and implementation are mandatory actions in every industry, especially content creation in the entertainment and media industry, which has high expectations and is a crucial factor in sustaining and keeping customers/audiences. Generally, it involves a multi-faceted process of producing quality and ethical material to entertain and engage all types of audiences. This process is crucial for various forms of the media industry, such as filmmaking, television content for day-to-day programs and schedules, online platforms, web series and OTT services, digital publishing, and more. Let us discuss a few cases in which Gen AI can be applied in this industry.

- **Film and Video Production**: In film and video production, the following significant tasks, such as scriptwriting, dialogue, and manually building the effects, are traditionally followed by experts. They develop these from their experience over days, months, or years, based on the complexity of the storyline proposed by the directors and the producer's interest. However, as discussed before, Gen AI can assist in scriptwriting, generating dialogue, or creating realistic CGI effects that are less resource-intensive than traditional methods uses algorithms and learned from a vast dataset in the domain. AI tools, such as GPT and DALL-E, are used to generate story ideas and visual effects, respectively, with maximum updating of the outcome and a shorter timeline until everyone is satisfied.
- **Music Composition**: In the film-making industry, music plays a significant role in most situations, determining the success of movies or dramas. Gen AI and specialized algorithms can create music by learning from a vast dataset of genres, styles, cultures, and regions, providing artists with new tools for inspiration, collaboration, and attracting the audience. AI systems, such as OpenAI's Jukebox, can generate music in various styles, with lyrics based on the inputs.
- **Game Development**: The gaming industry is continuously developing at different levels. AI can help generate dynamic gaming environments, characters, situations, and interactions between non-player characters. It can even complete game levels and gain points to attract players. Obviously, it enhances the gaming experience with greater variability and complexity and connects AR and VR technology.
- **Automated Editing**: The outcome of films, video production, and music composition should be edited, with pacing and transitions adjusted based on predefined styles. The specialized AI-powered systems help in significantly reducing the production times and costs during the audio and video content editing process.
- **Interactive Storytelling**: Gen AI and specialized algorithms can create stories by learning from a vast dataset. This enables highly interactive narrative stories based on the requested input as a story outline and base that adapts to choices made by viewers or players, offering a personalized story experience that can vary significantly with each interaction.

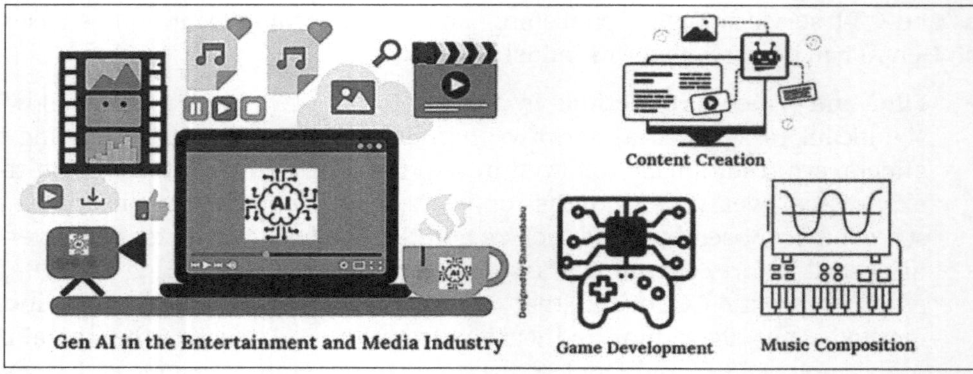

Figure 10.10: *Gen AI in Content Creation*

- **Audience Engagement and Analytics:** In this digital world, audience engagement and analytics tools play pivotal roles in the media and entertainment industries. This drives strategic decisions, improves user experience, and helps the industry build new content creators, marketers, and ideation platform managers to understand audience behavior, inclinations, and patterns through data-driven insights by collecting vast amounts of data.

Personalization and Recommendation Systems: These systems are highly recommended in the entertainment and media industry. They enhance audience engagement by tailoring content to individual preferences using data extracted from user interaction, demographics, devices, and context data collection. This is followed by data analysis, processing, and recommendation generation using ranking algorithms and context-aware recommendations. Indeed, continuous learning and A/B testing methods are added to the feedback loop.

These systems use sophisticated algorithms to analyze user behavior and data, providing personalized content suggestions and experiences.

- **Streaming Platforms**: Gen AI algorithms analyze capable user behavior and recommend personalized movie(s), TV channels, music(s), albums, and so on. In recent years, OTT platforms such as Netflix and Spotify have used AI to understand individual preferences and optimize their suggestions, improving user engagement and recommending movies and songs appropriately.
- **Advertising**: Based on market analysis, AI-driven tools can analyze and create targeted advertisements, enhance the effectiveness of products and campaigns, and predict consumer tastes, behavior, and preferences, allowing them to deliver high-quality and personalized advertising content.

Gen AI in the Manufacturing and Industry 4.0

Industry 4.0, also known as the fourth industrial revolution, fundamentally transforms the manufacturing landscape through the integration of digital technologies. This era is defined by the seamless incorporation of the Internet of Things (**IoT**), **big data analytics**, **cloud computing**, **artificial intelligence,** and sophisticated **automation systems** into industrial processes. These technologies converge to create smart factories that are more consistent, efficient, adaptable, and approachable. At the heart of this transformative wave is Artificial Intelligence (**AI**), which enhances decision-making, optimizes manufacturing operations, improves supply chain management, promotes innovative business models, and increases sustainability efforts.

Further, the adoption of AI within manufacturing not only paves the way for innovative business models but also accelerates the prioritized shift towards digital transformation. It promotes customization, personalization, and sustainability across various manufacturing industry sectors, irrespective of product manufacturing at the plant level. AI-driven solutions empower industries to produce higher-quality goods more efficiently, manage resources effectively, reduce waste materials, plan shifts effectively, train employees for current manufacturing standards, build health and safety, and raise a more sustainable manufacturing environment. This capability to design and produce customized products that meet specific customer needs with acceptable quality enhances effectiveness and stabilizes the global market.

Generative AI plays a vital transformative role in the manufacturing industry, especially as part of the broader movement towards Industry 4.0. This integration significantly shifts towards more self-directed, competent, and customizable manufacturing designs and processes. Here is how Generative AI is reshaping these industry-specific areas.

Product Design and Development: Product design and development in every manufacturing unit is a critical process involving the conception, design, and realization of new products and improvements to existing products based on feedback from reliable customers. This phase is essential for industries to stay in a competitive market. Here is a breakdown of the stages and key elements involved in product design and development within the manufacturing industry:

- **Idea Generation and Screening:** This is the initial stage, which involves brainstorming and gathering ideas from various sources, including customer needs, competitor strengths, internal team capabilities, and market analyses and research data points. Following the idea generation, they evaluate them against specific criteria, such as feasibility, market potential, facilities available in-house, employees' capabilities, alignment with business goals and budget, and alignment with profit and loss projections. This practice helps to narrow down the options to the most viable ones. With the help of Gen AI tools such as chatbots and AI assistance, we could help us create innovative ideas for the proposed use cases.
- **Concept Development:** Once the idea is developed and frozen, the proposed concepts must be considered for the conceptual design stage. This stage

involves developing digital concepts of the selected ideas using AI-integrated Computer-Aided Design (CAD) tools to create precise 3D models.

- **Prototyping**: Following the concept development, the rapid prototyping stage, such as 3D printing, is used to create physical or virtual product models. This helps operators finalize design, and stakeholders begin testing the product as a pilot version to assess the concept's practicality and advise the engineering team on making necessary adjustments and improvements. Of course, AI can help provide precise steps to build the prototype and suggest improvements.
- **Feasibility Analysis:** The engineering team must perform a technical feasibility analysis once the prototyping is completed and the stakeholders have provided positive feedback. The financial team must perform an economic feasibility analysis by integrating with Gen AI. This will ensure that the product can be manufactured within current capabilities and technologies while considering the cost implication factors of manufacturing and launching the product in the market, including ROI estimates and break-even analysis. Gen AI-integrated feasibility analysis components will expedite the analysis and generate insights to better understand the visibility of the product that will be sustained in the competitive market.

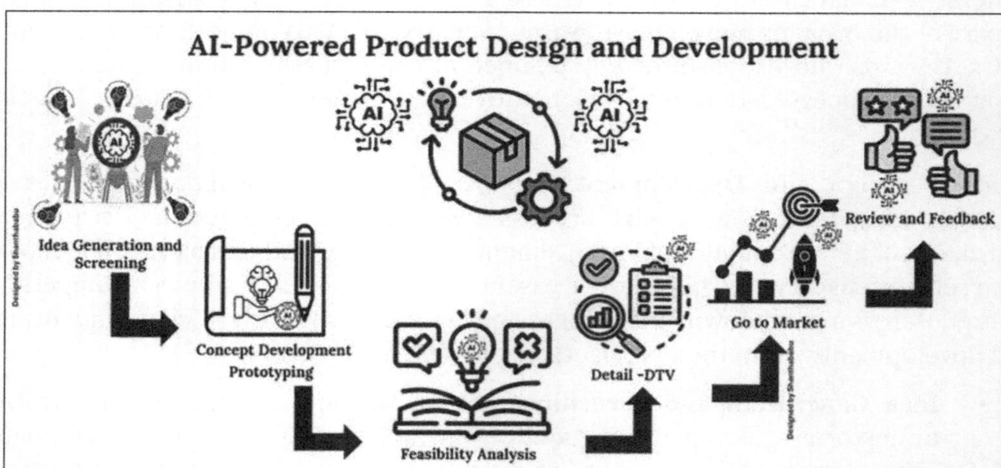

Figure 10.11: *AI-Powered Product Design and Development*

- **Detailed Design, Testing, and Validation (Detail-DTV):** Once the aforementioned stages are completed, we must work on component design, developing detailed specifications for each product component, whether they are materials, semi-finished, or fully finished sub-products such as electronics, electrical, or mechanical components that are assembled and integrated with open-source software. After all, testing and validation (functional, system, and user level) must be followed, and outcomes must be recorded to ensure the product is on point. AI can evaluate and predict product performance, quality, and improvement recommendations.

- **Production Planning and Go-to-Market:** Once the detail DTV is completed, the industry must plan production and supply chain management to deliver the product to the customer. Gen AI can prepare and schedule production and supply chain plans and ensure a reliable supply chain, timelines, and resource allocation, while developing a marketing strategy to promote the new product effectively.
- **Post-Launch Review and Feedback:** After the product launch, the mandatory activity is collecting customer feedback and reviews. We can handle this using an AI chatbot or assistance, collect data, and perform market analyses for product features, quality, and sales assessments. This will lead to continuous improvement of the product and process enhancement based on market feedback for the future version of the same product or similar product.

Optimization of Manufacturing Processes: The following factors are helping in optimizing the manufacturing processes effectively:

- **Predictive Maintenance and Quality Assurance**: Predictive maintenance is essential for equipments such as Milling Machines, Sealing Machines, Air Compressors, Generators, and Heating and Cooling Systems. Gen AI algorithms can analyze data from sensors and machines to predict when the equipment will require maintenance or replacement, thus minimizing downtime and extending the machinery's lifespan.

  AI models can automatically inspect and analyze the final products from each production line, identifying defects or quality deviations more accurately than human inspectors.

  AI-driven systems analyze products during and after production via visual inspection techniques, such as IoT-enabled systems, and consistently ensure quality standards are met.
- **Process Optimization**: Process optimization in manufacturing is a critical strategy similar to predictive maintenance. This process enhances the efficiency and effectiveness of production processes and optimization in terms of costs, productivity, and product quality and gains a competitive edge in the market. We can use Gen AI to simulate and optimize manufacturing processes, and models can propose adjustments to machine settings such as temperature, pressure, viscosity level, workflows, and material composition inputs. This maximizes efficiency, reduces waste and cost, and increases quality and utilization of the equipment at optimized levels and performance monitoring and maintaining.

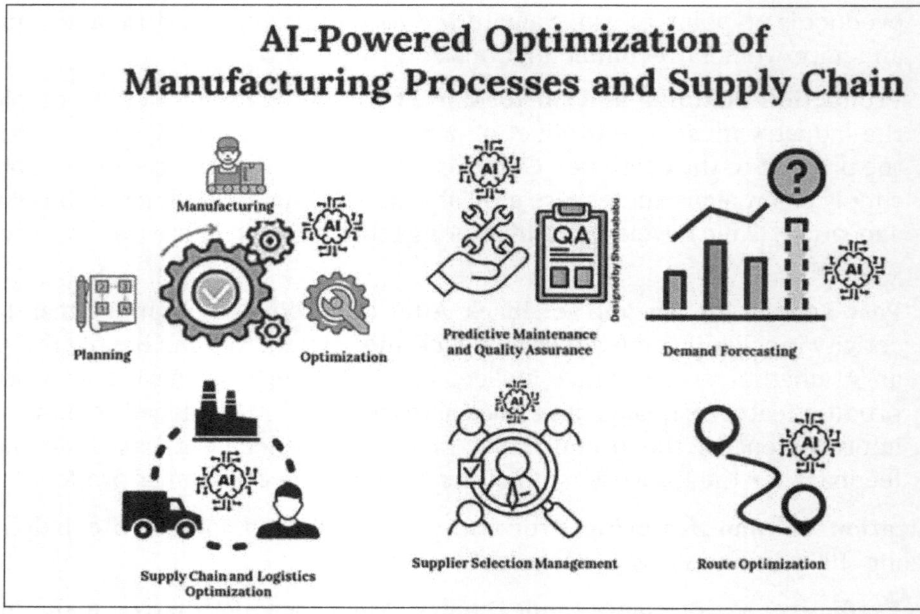

***Figure 10.12**: AI-Powered Product Design and Development*

Optimization of Processes and Supply Chain: Gen AI introduces innovative solutions that can adapt and learn from data, offering dynamic optimization in real-time data and solutions. In recent years, optimization of manufacturing processes and supply chain logistics through Generative AI represents a significant advancement in the manufacturing industry. It drives efficiency, reduces costs and manual efforts, enhances productivity, and dispatches goods as planned ETA to customer locations.

- **Demand Forecasting**: Demand forecasting is a crucial aspect of business planning that predicts future customer demand for products or services. Gen AI can accurately predict future product demand by analyzing historical data such as sales, market trends, consumer behavior, competitive landscape, supply chain actors, and other external factors such as weather or global economic indicators. This helps in effectively planning production volumes and inventory levels.
- **Supply Chain and Logistics Optimization:** Optimizing supply chain and logistics operations is essential for the manufacturing industry after the product arrives at the customer's location. Concerning the manufacturing industry, we must strengthen supply chain management by effectively managing inventory, delivery systems, and customer satisfaction, as well as improving coordination and communication across the supply chain.
- **Supplier Selection and Inventory Management**: Supplier selection and inventory management are critical functions within supply chain management that directly affect production quality, supplier reliability, and efficiency in

delivering the materials to the warehouse on time without disturbing the production line for ongoing orders. At the same time, understanding the flow of goods—raw materials from other sub-manufacturers to warehouse inventory—is essential to satisfying current and near-future orders in the pipeline.

Gen AI can analyze supplier performance data from historical datasets; this analysis will help procurement teams make data-driven decisions about which supplier is best in terms of quality, cost, on-time delivery reliability, and risk level.

Manage inventory levels, track status, and communicate with floor managers to plan production schedules and plans with chatbots and AI assistants, and simultaneously predict fluctuations in demand and supply chain interferences. This helps to maintain the optimal stock levels of raw materials and semi-furnished components in the inventory for the production line, minimize the risk of stockouts or overstock situations, and reduce holding costs and inventory stock maintenance difficulty.

- **Route Optimization**: Route optimization in supply chain management is a critical component for cost-effective transportation and delivering the product to the customer's location on time as per the scheduled date and time. AI algorithms can determine the various factors and routes for delivery products based on historical data, extract live traffic and weather conditions, and derive the optimized route and delivery of the product, considerably minimizing delivery times and fuel consumption of the vehicle and providing appropriate rest time for drivers' health and safety.

Collaborative AI: Gen AI can act as the center point to facilitate better collaboration across different departments, such as predictive maintenance, process optimization, demand forecasting, supplier selection, inventory, planning and scheduling, quality assessment, packing and dispatches, energy usage optimization, safety enhancements and workplace monitoring, training and augmentation, and risk assessment.

Gen AI in the Agriculture and Food Industry

This sector is critical to any industry in the global economy in terms of ensuring food security for the country, providing employment across different levels, and contributing significantly to national GDPs. It encompasses a broad range of activities related to the cultivation of crops, raising livestock such as cows, sheep, chickens, and pigs, and producing food products such as grain, wheat, rye, oats, corn, and rice.

We might have a question about how Gen AI is helping to transform the industry; of course, this is rapidly becoming a transformative force in the agriculture and food industry by introducing new efficiencies and capabilities that significantly impact how food is grown, processed, and distributed. Let us understand how Generative AI is being used in this sector:

Crop and Livestock Management: There is no doubt that crop and livestock management are foundational aspects of agricultural practices in any country. Both play a critical role in ensuring the quality and quantity of food in terms of the economic viability of farms in secure ways. Effective management practices are essential to maximize the productivity of food products, enhance self-obtained animal welfare, minimize environmental impacts, and provide employment opportunities. Gen AI can support the factors we have discussed so far.

- **AI-based Predictive Analytics for Crop Health**: Crop health is a vital aspect of agricultural management, influencing the harvest's yield and quality. Crop health management involves monitoring, preventing, and controlling factors that can harm plants, including diseases, pests, and nutrient deficiencies.

  To build effective crop health, Gen AI models use data collected through drones, satellites, and IoT sensors to predict crop health conditions, issues, and pest infestations. This exercise allows for timely interventions and actions that can prevent crop losses and provide solutions for recovery from the disease. This will be a continuous monitoring process and control activities in this domain.

  This can help improve the following management activities: crop monitoring and diagnostics, various crop diseases, pest management, nutrient enhancement and management, water, climate and environmental management, and plant stress management.

- **AI-Powered Genetic Improvement**: Genetic improvement research and development practices in agriculture are phenomenally growing across the global agriculture and food industry. As we know, the primary objective of this R&D and implementation is to modify the selected plants and animals' genetics to enhance their characteristics such as yield, disease resistance, climate adaptation, drought tolerance, nutritional content, nutritional enhancements, and adaptability to various environmental conditions. This genetic improvement is a powerful tool in **MODERN AGRICULTURE**. It is driving significant advancements in the productivity and sustainability of plants and animals by judiciously following ethical and regulatory boundaries and guidelines based on individual countries. Ultimately, this increases agricultural productivity, enhances food safety and security, and develops sustainable farming best practices.

  To derive the strategies, AI-driven genetic algorithms generate simulations to predict the outcomes of crossbreeding in crops and livestock and aim to enhance the desirable traits mentioned above.

Precision Agriculture Management: Precision agriculture is a farming management concept that uses information technology and a wide range of factors, such as control systems, sensors (IoT), robotics, drones, autonomous vehicles, automated hardware,

GPS guidance, and software, to enhance crop production efficiency, quality, disease-free crops, high profitability, minimum waste, environmental impact assessment, and so on. Let us discuss how Gen AI is intervening in this precision agriculture management.

- **AI-Based Planting and Harvesting**: Automated planting and harvesting are regular activities in agriculture, and AI certainly enables the development of autonomous tractors and harvesters to plant and harvest crops with minimal human intervention, optimizing planting patterns by analyzing the historical dataset discussing the crops and soil conditions and helping to harvest at peak ripeness based on machine-learned algorithms and understanding training datasets.
- **AI-Enabled Soil and Crop Monitoring**: Soil and crop monitoring are fundamental aspects of precision agriculture management, which we also discussed in the previous section. This optimization helps farmers optimize the use of resources, enhance crop yields, and reduce environmental impacts such as disease resistance, climate adaptation, drought tolerance, and many more factors that are to be monitored effectively and rely on AI technologies and strategies to gather and analyze data regarding soil conditions and crop health.

  With the help of AI, we can collect data through drones, satellites, and IoT sensors in the form of images to assess soil conditions, health, crop status, and any impacts, providing recommendations for fertilizer and water management customized to individual field conditions. AI can also simultaneously predict crop health conditions, issues, and pest infestations. It can build notes in text and reports and provide recommendations to enhance crop growth in all possible ways.

Food Processing and Safety: Food processing and safety are crucial aspects of the food industry, involving various techniques and best practices incorporated to transform raw ingredients into finished products by considering all health and safety aspects. Effective management of these processes is essential to maintaining food quality, extending shelf life in a safer mode of natural preservatives, and promoting consumer health regulations. These advancements in technology not only enhance the efficiency of food production but also significantly improve food safety, how to reduce waste, and direction to ensure compliance with health regulations.

AI-powered food processing and safety technologies are revolutionizing how food is produced, processed, and monitored for quality and safety, with available data in the form of documents, images, audio, and video references, converting them into ease of access, expediting the process, and providing the appropriate guidance for the food processing industry.

- **AI-Powered Recipe Development**: Before processing food, the food industry has a recipe development process that is crucial for ensuring the consumer's taste and needs for their daily consumption, satisfaction, and alignment with demands and supply to strengthen supply-chain management. AI models can generate new recipes and food combinations by analyzing consumer flavor preferences, existing food databases, and feedback from social media, shopping malls, and restaurants, often creating unique and innovative food pairings and products in the market to compete with peer food manufacturers.

- **AI-Enabled Resource Management**: AI helps optimize resource utilization, such as water consumption, fertilizer needs, and pesticides, reducing waste and environmental impact with the help of available data, documents, and images, building the guidelines, and sharing the best practices for food processing units. They monitor the same and revert them in terms of reports and reward recommendations to top management and make sure that the food industry utilize the resources effectively and efficiently by considering the greenhouse effect and sustainable process industry.
- **AI-Enabled Food Quality Control**: AI-driven systems perform visual inspections of food items on production lines using IoT and digital cameras and weight machines to identify defects, quantity, quality, and contamination issues and ensure consistent product quality and safety from the processing unit to the dispatching unit and prepare reports, evidence, and recording for various analysis and improvement perspectives.

Ethical Consideration in Gen AI

Before we understand the ethical considerations in Gen AI, there are several ethical considerations in different fields depending on the nature of the domains.

Let us explore the four main principles of ethics:

- Autonomy
- Beneficence
- Justice
- Non-maleficence
- Respect
- Competence
- Responsibility
- Integrity

Autonomy: It refers to the right of individuals or groups to make decisions about their own lives and actions without compulsion. It emphasizes respecting people's independence, sensitivity, and views and ensuring informed consent before making decisions.

Beneficence: It refers to acting in the best interest of individuals. It promotes the well-being of others in industries such as Healthcare, Banking, Consumer Goods, and others by providing beneficial care and working to maximize positive outcomes.

Justice: It focuses on fairness, equality, and ensuring that individuals and groups are treated equitably. It enables and enforces a fair distribution of resources and opportunities, without discrimination, in major industries such as legal, healthcare, or organizational contexts.

Non-Maleficence: Non-maleficence means "**NOT HARM**." As it implies, it emphasizes avoiding actions that could cause harm to others, specifically in industries like healthcare and legal, where minimizing risks and inhibiting harm is a key ethical responsibility.

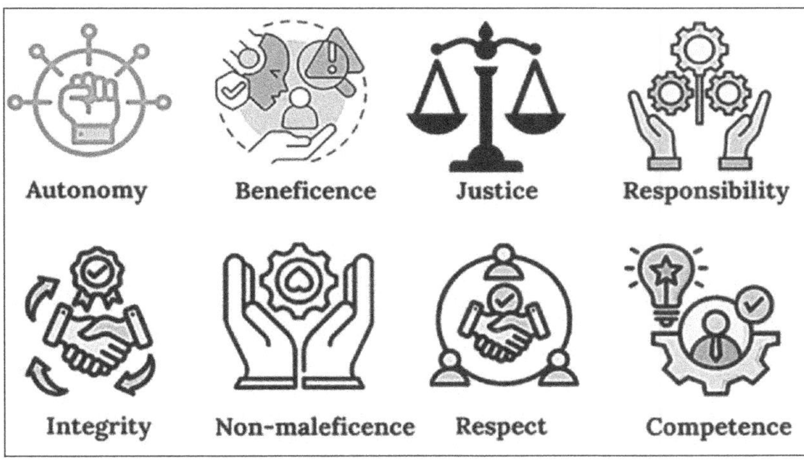

***Figure 10.13**: Principles of Ethics to Considerations*

Respect: As we know, it means treating individuals courteously, valuing their perspectives, and celebrating their contributions, regardless of differences. Some of them are dignity, rights, and views of others.

Competence: In any industry, individuals must perform their roles effectively and continuously improve to meet ethical and professional standards. For this, they must maintain and demonstrate the necessary skills, knowledge, and abilities required in their profession to sustain themselves in the domain and move up the organization ladder.

Responsibility: It emphasizes accountability for one's actions and decisions in a highly critical position in the organization. It involves being answerable to stakeholders, fulfilling professional requirements, and transparently taking ownership of successes and failures.

Integrity: Integrity is a significant factor in any thriving industry. It involves factors that should adhere to moral and ethical principles that are maintaining honesty and consistency in every action and making the right decision. Integrity promotes trust and reliability by ensuring that personal and professional conduct aligns with ethical values in the groups.

Even though we have multiple ethical considerations, we consider four ethical considerations in the Gen AI environment: autonomy, beneficence, justice, and non-maleficence.

Ethical considerations in Generative AI are essential activities that communicate and promise the end users that the system strongly supports social and industrial ethics and that any vulnerabilities are brought up along with the AI systems across various industries. Ensuring that AI tools and technology are responsible, fair, secure, personal data, and are beneficial to all stakeholders is always crucial.

Let us discuss the industries we discussed earlier in this chapter and what ethical parameters are incorporated into AI-powered systems in buildings without deviating from the legal aspects, rules and regulations specific to an industry, country, or region and without any hesitation for the public and organizations to use.

Ethical Consideration in Banking and Financial Industry

We have discussed various tools that help the banking and financial industry, such as fraud detection and prevention, loan and mortgage underwriting, regulatory compliance and documentation, financial forecasting and planning, product development and customization, and customer retention and engagement.

Adopting Generative AI in the banking and financial industry brings forth a range of ethical considerations. While it offers immense potential in automating services, improving customer experience, and detecting fraud, it also poses significant ethical challenges that financial institutions must address.

Key Ethical Considerations:

- **Bias and Fairness:**
    - **Bias in AI Models**: Since we use historical data, it often reflects societal biases, and if AI learns from biased data, it can reproduce prejudiced lending or investment recommendation practices. Leading to biased decisions in areas such as loan approvals, credit scoring, or fraud detection.
    - **Fairness in Decision-Making**: Unfair decisions due to biased AI could lead to loss of trust and legal challenges under anti-discrimination laws and order. This is why ensuring fairness and transparency in decision-making is crucial.

- **Privacy and Data Security:**
    - **Regulatory Compliance**: Regulators such as the **General Data Protection Regulation (GDPR)** in Europe, **California Consumer Privacy Act (CCPA) and Personally Identifiable Information (PII)** in the United States of America, **Health Insurance Portability and Accountability Act (HIPAA)**, and many compliances across the globe are mandated a "right to explanation" for automated decisions. Financial institutions must ensure that Gen AI decisions are interpretable and justifiable based on rules and regulations. Ensuring that customer data is used in compliance with these regulations while training AI models is critical to avoid breaches and penalties as part of **Data Protection Regulations.**
    - **Sensitive Financial Data**: Gen AI systems can raise significant privacy concerns, especially if data is mishandled, used without masking, or used without explicit consent for the customer's highly sensitive data, such as transaction histories, account information, and personal identifiers (name, DOB, phone number, and so on).
- **Autonomy and Accountability:**
    - **Automated Decision-Making**: Financial institutions must clearly define accountability and the right direction while building AI-driven decisions because AI is increasingly taking over decision-making processes in risk assessment and investment strategies.
    - **Human Oversight**: Financial institutions should implement "***human-in-the-loop***" systems to monitor and, if needed, override AI decisions. IA should maintain human oversight in critical decision-making areas wherever necessary.
- **Job Displacement and Workforce Impact:**
    - **Job Automation**: Financial institutions must consider how they can retrain or support displaced workers through cross-technology training or upskilling them and work alongside AI expertise, data science, and machine learning engineering. Since Gen AI can potentially automate roles in customer service, investment management, and fraud detection, in this situation, the higher management should take appropriate action during job displacement.
- **Trust and Public Perception:**
    - **Ethical Trust in AI:** Financial institutions should prioritize ethical AI practices such as ensuring fairness, transparency, and privacy, which can enhance their brand's reputation and build stronger customer relationships and trust.
    - **Trust Destruction**: There might be a situation in which the customers may feel that AI decisions are unfair, biased, and impersonal, and they may

lose trust in the financial institution and their AI products so that they might move into different banks or financial institutions. This destruction should maintain transparency, fairness, and human empathy in customer interactions, and appropriately handling and preserving customer relationships are essential aspects of AI tools.

Ethical Consideration in the Healthcare Industry

We have discussed various Gen AI tools that help enhance the healthcare industry's operations and performance. Ethical considerations in this industry are much more sensitive than in other industries since they deal with highly confident data.

Ethical considerations in the healthcare industry ensure that patient rights, dignity, and safety data are protected at a high level without leaking data. It should balance autonomy, beneficence, non-maleficence, and justice that are essential for providing high-quality care while maintaining trust and equity in healthcare-promised deliveries.

- **Autonomy:** As we discussed earlier, what is "Autonomy," and what is emphasized here? Let us understand how this is correlated with the healthcare industry. Here, they must respect patient autonomy by ensuring that they are fully informed about the risks, benefits, and alternatives of their treatment options and make sure to align with respect for patient choices and interests and a critical aspect of autonomy, where patients should give their voluntary consent after they understood the proposed medical interventions and treatment, and at the same time, the patient's data should be protected.
- **Beneficence:** Healthcare constantly promotes and promises well-being by being ethically obligated to act in the patient's best interests, providing treatments that benefit them efficiently, and enhancing the patient's overall quality of life by balancing risks and benefits while ensuring that actions are taken to maximize positive outcomes in their services.
- **Non-Maleficence:** A significant part of humanity is "Do No Harm," and healthcare professionals must avoid causing harm to patients under any circumstances. They must exercise caution and care during treatments and procedures for all patients and ensure no unnecessary harm is inflicted.
- **Justice:** Fair and equitable access resources are distributed fairly, ensuring equal access to medical care regardless of gender, race, socioeconomic status, or other factors. It must work to reduce inequalities, ensuring that the vulnerable populations are not mistreated and neglected at all costs.
- **Confidentiality and Privacy:** In healthcare, confidentiality and privacy are significant factors in retaining the patient's details as protected information

and maintaining confidentiality requirements based on GDPR and HIPAA regulations to ensure privacy. Here, we have established trust between the patient and the provider. Confidentiality fosters trust, allowing patients to disclose personal health information to healthcare providers, and they must promise and take necessary care without fear of disclosure.

- **Resource Allocation:** This factor is crucial in dealing with the internal challenges of ensuring fair distribution during crises or resource scarcity. This includes allocating resources such as ventilators, ICU beds, and medications. Prioritizing the care of resources maximizes benefits without unfairly disadvantaging any individuals or group.
- **Cultural Competence:** Healthcare professionals must respect a patient's gender, language, cultural, religious, and personal beliefs in their treatment plans. Providing culturally relevant care addresses all mentioned barriers and delivers ethical and practical healthcare.

Gen AI should understand and align with all the aforementioned parameters, guidelines, and requirements to satisfy end customers and serve the purpose's objectives.

Ethical Consideration in the Entertainment and Media Industry

The entertainment and media industry profoundly impacts society, shaping public opinion, culture, and behavior. While dealing with all these aspects, the influence of ethical consideration comes with significant ethical responsibilities to safeguard society in many ways. Ethical considerations in the entertainment and media industry revolve around truth, privacy, and the effects of media on individual and societal issues and challenges.

- **Truth and Accuracy:** Truth and accuracy are crucial in the entertainment and media industry. Entertainment has an ethical obligation to present information honestly and accurately. To this end, media and entertainment experts should distinguish fact from fiction and clarify the importance of differentiating between fiction and reality so the public is not misled. AI should take care of the content, which should be true and accurate and have appropriate references and justification points to withstand originality.
- **Children and Vulnerable Audiences:** Media and entertainment are highly sensitive to their audience, especially children and vulnerable adults. They have a responsibility to protect vulnerable groups. Media content creators are responsible for protecting children and other vulnerable audiences from harmful content, and they should build it according to guidance and reasonable practices. This includes dangerous behavior, violence, sexual content, and hurting particular groups of people by language, religion, and country. All of this would negatively influence impressionable viewers.

- **Intellectual Property**: Intellectual property is a significant concern in the media and entertainment industry. The use of AI to generate creative content raises questions about ownership and rights over AI-created materials such as music, articles, or videos.

So, the Gen AI tool should consider all these guidelines and keep up the promise to serve the media and entertainment industry.

Ethical Consideration in Manufacturing and Industry 4.0

Ethical considerations in manufacturing and Industry 4.0 involve balancing technological advancements such as IoT, AI, and Digital twins with social, environmental, and economic responsibilities. As AI and data-driven processes become more established, manufacturers must respect worker rights, protect privacy, and foster fair competition.

- **Job Displacement and Workforce Impact:** Industry 4.0 integrates automation and artificial intelligence, enabling the most sophisticated manufacturing industry. All departments in the units are well-connected. It strengthens supply chain management, which may lead to job displacement for workers in the manufacturing plant doing manual or repetitive tasks. Manufacturers must ethically address this by investing in reskilling their workforce and preparing employees for new, high-demand roles and responsibilities created by advanced technologies. This ensures that workers are not left behind as the industry evolves; this would be a win-win situation for the industry and employers.
- **Worker Safety and Well-being:** Industries are responsible for workers' safety and well-being, especially when workers interact with robots. Ethical manufacturing practices must ensure that automated systems are designed and monitored continuously to minimize the risk of accidents and harm to human workers during product manufacturing operations and maintenance.
- **Data Privacy and Security:** Industry 4.0 involves gathering large amounts of data from various sources, such as employees, machines, and processes. Manufacturers must consider employee data and privacy, handle it securely, and use it responsibly. Ethical considerations are required in manufacturing industries, and they must invest in robust cybersecurity measures to protect sensitive manufacturing processing data, including intellectual property of products, employee information, personal details, and other supply chain management data.
- **Transparency and Accountability:** Industry 4.0 enhances supply chain visibility significantly through real-time data collection, tracking, and data analytics,

and it establishes significant improvements. Ethically, manufacturers must ensure data transparency regarding sourcing materials, the flow of operations, the regions employees come from, and the human rights issues in the specific region or country. Manufacturing industries are accountable for the entire lifecycle of their products, from raw materials to final disposal.

- **Product Safety and Quality:** Ethical concerns arise around product safety, which is also an essential factor in the manufacturing industry's data privacy and the long-term reliability of these interconnected products. Since Industry 4.0 products integrate IoT devices that continuously collect data and interact with other systems, data security and privacy are essential to meet the highest safety and quality standards to protect consumers and end-users from harm.
- **Energy Consumption and Climate Change:** Ethics is essential to data security and privacy. It also involves actively adopting energy-efficient processes contributing to the fight against climate change. Industry 4.0 technologies can help reduce energy consumption through automation, smart grids, and predictive analytics to bring "**Green Manufacturing**." Every industry is responsible for adopting greener manufacturing methods, such as reducing emissions and adopting low-impact materials and renewable energy sources, contributing to achieving global sustainability goals.

Ensuring that Artificial Intelligence systems are built and used in the manufacturing industry is essential. They should be free from biases that could result in unfair worker treatment and skewed business decisions.

Ethical Consideration in the Agriculture and Food Industry

As the global population grows and the demand for food increases rapidly, this industry is the backbone of the globe and a growing economic icon for any country. It prioritizes relevant ethical practices that promote sustainability, fairness, and public health while addressing the challenges of climate change, biodiversity loss, and food security. These challenges include environmental sustainability, food safety, animal welfare, labor practices, and social justice.

- **Food Safety and Public Health:** As mentioned earlier, this industry is responsible for adapting its ethics regarding safe food production. Ethical farming practices limit the excessive use of pesticides, herbicides, and antibiotics in food production. These practices involve maintaining high standards in essential ingredients, food production methodology, processing techniques, quality checks, and packaging to prevent contamination and foodborne illnesses, and using harmless additives to preserve the food.
- **Reducing Food Loss:** Food waste is a significant global problem, with large quantities of food being lost during production, storage, quality checks,

transport, and discarded at the consumer level. Ethical practices also aim to reduce food waste through efficient plans such as proper storage supply chains, collecting the wastage at all stages, and providing guidelines to reduce the same through continuous monitoring. At the consumer level, food waste should be brought to appropriate places such as **food banks; donations from grocery stores, food processing units,** and restaurants can help address hunger while reducing waste.

- **Reasonable Labor Practices:** The agriculture industry often relies on seasonal work, so the following ethical considerations require that all workers receive fair wages, safe working environments, and access to healthcare. Due to other challenges, child labor has to be prevalent in agriculture. In ethical farming practices, we must ensure that children are not exploited and that education and the well-being of young workers are prioritized.
- **Ethical Treatment of Livestock**: Ethical considerations in livestock farming include humane treatment of animals, adequate space, food, and water; regular medical check-ups; and ensuring they are free from unnecessary woes and disease-free environments. Establish sustainable livestock practices by implementing free-range systems and pasture-raised environments.
- **Biodiversity and Conservation:** Ethical considerations include preserving genetic diversity and growing crops using heirloom or indigenous seeds. It should avoid practices that destroy natural habitats, such as converting forests or wetlands into farmland. This helps protect wildlife corridors.

AI in the agriculture and food industry raises ethical questions across all departments and layers, enhances the industry's overall strength, and provides the right direction for following ethics and high standards.

Based on the aforementioned discussion, implementing ethical guidelines and standards for deploying Gen AI is vital. This involves adherence to legal standards, proactive engagement with stakeholders, ethical audits, and continuous monitoring to ensure that AI technologies improve human well-being without causing harm or inequity.

Discussion on Security Aspects of Gen AI

Data is crucial and highly sensitive when implementing Gen AI across different industries. Each industry faces unique challenges and requires specific security measures to protect data against threats and ensure data integrity and security.

Here is a detailed discussion of the security aspects of Gen AI in various industries:

- **Banking and Financial Industry**
    - **Data Security and Privacy**: Data is susceptible in the banking and financial

industry and protecting it from unauthorized access is a significant task. Data should be encrypted during transit, and secure data storage solutions and implementing robust access controls are essential. The industry should keep customer information, savings, and transactions private.

- **Fraud Detection**: This activity is a significant backbone for this industry. Gen AI can detect patterns that are indicative of fraud. However, these systems must be safeguarded against manipulation and exploitation by highly advanced cyber-attacks.
- **Regulatory Compliance**: AI systems should ensure compliance with global financial regulations such as GDPR, CCPA, and PII. To maintain compliance, AI systems should be regularly audited and updated.

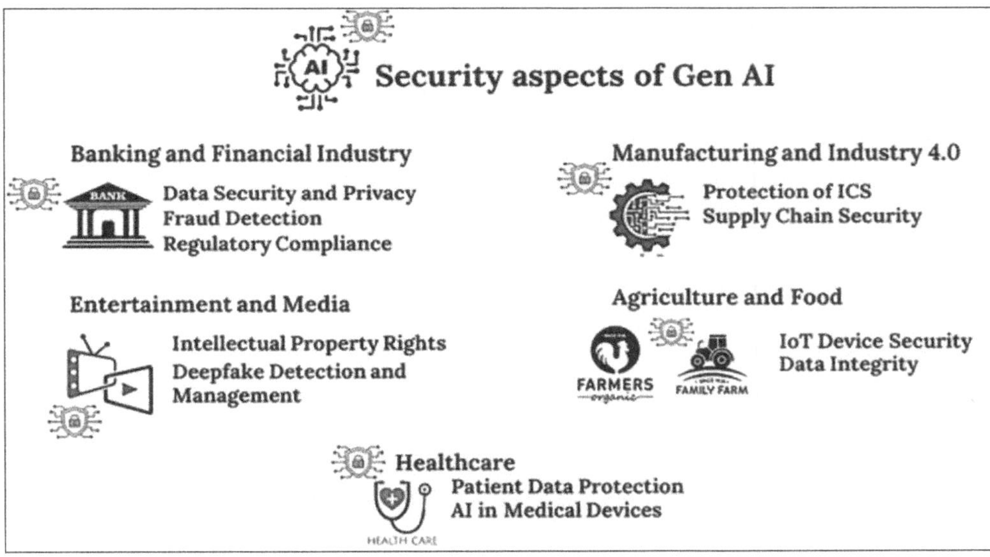

Figure 10.14: *Security Aspects of Gen AI in Various Industries*

- **Healthcare Industry**:
  - **Patient Data Protection**: Healthcare data requires heavy security, which is crucial for both parties if it gets leaked in the public. In developed countries such as the USA, the UK, and Europe, it is protected under laws such as GDPR and HIPAA. AI systems should be architected to handle GDPR, HIPAA, PHI, and PII. They must include encryption and strict authentication mechanisms across the system.
  - **AI in Medical Devices**: In recent years, advanced and much more sophisticated medical devices have been tightly integrated with AI systems and IoT-enabled features. So, their enterprise architecture response is to secure the data transferred from source to destination and utilize it by the AI systems. Ensuring their security from cyber threats is crucial. This

includes implementing firmware updates and intrusion detection systems to prevent hacks and secure the entire system.

- **Entertainment and Media:**
  - **Intellectual Property Rights**: When designing content using an AI system in the entertainment and media industry, we must consider the importance of protecting content and the IP rights of digital content utilizing as base input or generated output. Controlling **Digital Rights Management (DRM)** and watermarking are necessary to safeguard content and follow IP guidelines and best practices.
  - **Deepfake Detection and Management**: AI's ability to create realistic fake videos and images is based on input, and there might be no control over it. This leads to significant security and privacy risks. To control this, we have to build the features of AI systems to detect and flag deep fake content, which is essential.
- **Manufacturing and Industry 4.0:**
  - **Protection of Industrial Control Systems (ICS)**: Securing ICS systems in manufacturing plants is crucial since they often use ICS systems that are vulnerable to cyber-attacks; these systems rely on AI-driven continuous monitoring to detect any anomalies in data and potential threats and flag them for appropriate action.
  - **Supply Chain Security**: AI can continuously monitor supply chain integrity. As manufacturing demand increases and global supply chains expand to meet demand, it is crucial to have secure networks to protect against disruptions caused by cyber threats. This ensures that AI systems themselves are not susceptible to tampering.
- **Agriculture and Food:**
  - **IoT Device Security**: Agriculture increasingly uses IoT devices, so data is transferred from source to destination and utilized by AI systems for various assessments. Here, the entire system requires secure protocols and regular updates to ensure it is safe from cyber threats.
  - **Data Integrity**: Data integrity used in AI-driven agricultural decisions must be maintained at high security to ensure that outputs, such as crop yield predictions and soil health assessments, are accurate. Ensuring that only authorized personnel can access AI systems and the data they generate is crucial to prevent malicious activities.

A layered security approach that includes physical, network, application, and data security measures is the ideal architecture in all these sectors. Continuous monitoring, regular security audits and assessments, and staying updated with the latest cybersecurity trends and details are a few ways.

Conclusion

This chapter discusses the necessity of Gen AI in various industries and how it can automate, optimize, and innovate processes that traditionally require significant human effort and time for different sectors. Understanding the multiple parameters determines the necessity of Gen AI across different domains, as shown in the following list: innovative, Accelerating Innovation, Automation and Inaccuracy Reduction, Efficiency Improvement, etc., We reviewed the different domains' necessities at a high level and explored the list of domains in detail below. We analyzed Healthcare, Banking and Financial, Entertainment and Media, Manufacturing and Industry 4.0, and Agriculture and Food Industries. How Gen AI offers transformative potential opportunities in banking and how this is a highly critical and essential domain for interconnection with all other domains in the industry. Explored the services and support as following customer service, optimized risk management, and streamlined operations.

The next chapter will discuss how the OpenAI solution benefits your business, takes your business to the next level, and what Azure OpenAI can offer you.

Chapter 11
Gen AI Implementation Use Case with Azure OpenAI–II

Introduction

In the previous chapter, we explored the various use cases of Generative AI in great detail. We explored the role of Generative AI in various fields such as healthcare, finance, entertainment and the media industry, manufacturing, and agriculture and food processing. We also studied the potential implications of AI in these industries, discussed how to address ethical considerations when using Generative AI, and examined how AI enhances security.

In this chapter, we will examine how the OpenAI solution benefits businesses and how it can take your business to the next level.

This chapter focuses on Azure OpenAI and its applications in telehealth, where it analyzes call center data, in manufacturing for automating processes and predicting failures, in banking and financial services for advisor support, and in education, detailing its workflow and implementation.

Structure

In this chapter, you will delve into the following topics:

- Azure OpenAI Solutions for Business Advantage
- Industry-Centric Benefits of AOAI Solutions
- Architectural Design and Development for Specific Industries

- Healthcare
- Manufacturing Sector
- Banking and Financial Services
- Education

Azure OpenAI Solutions for Business Advantage

In *Chapter 7, Getting Started with Generative AI Using Azure OpenAI Services*, we discussed how OpenAI and its essential concepts are crucial for effectively leveraging Gen AI. We evaluated how Azure OpenAI Services (AOAI) significantly enhance innovative thinking and offer advanced tools for building intelligent applications in various industries.

Microsoft's AOAI capabilities seamlessly integrate with Azure's ecosystem, enabling businesses to explore generative AI solutions in greater detail. The Azure OpenAI Studio facilitates easy model design, development, testing, and deployment while adhering to a robust architectural workflow. Key concepts include creating Azure Storage accounts for Blob data management, setting up Azure AI Services, and leading them to support Azure OpenAI for AI-driven solutions. These tools empower AI architects and developers to harness the full potential of Generative AI for transformative business and technological applications.

AOAI transforms business operations by enabling personalization, enhancing decision-making, forecasting, predicting, and providing insights into data. It also drives innovative solutions within a secure, scalable, and integrated Azure ecosystem. The platform offers comprehensive tools for real-time applications, automation, and global scalability while ensuring enterprise-grade security and seamless integration.

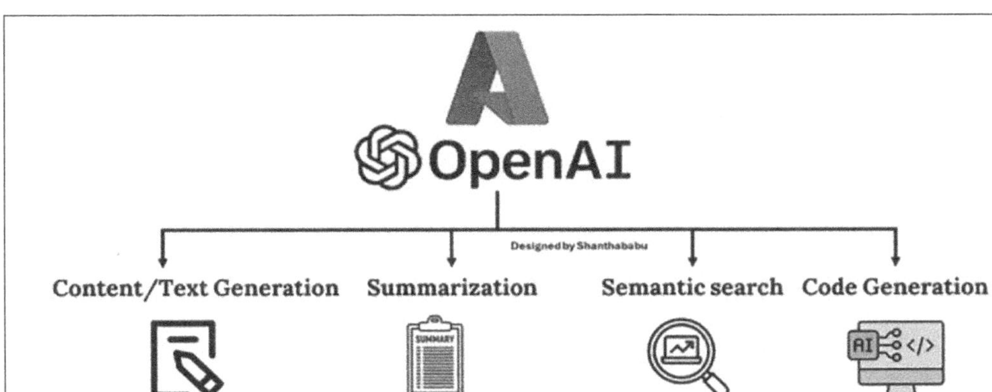

Figure 11.1: *Microsoft AOAI Capabilities*

Thus, it provides a future-ready platform for leveraging the power of Gen AI in diverse applications across industries such as retail, healthcare, finance, education, manufacturing, media and entertainment, logistics and transportation, energy and utilities, legal and compliance, smart cities, and agriculture.

AOAI empowers various industries by providing advanced Gen AI solutions that enhance efficiency. These solutions are data-driven and innovative, improving decision-making within stipulated timeframes and supporting industries. By leveraging models such as GPT, Codex, and DALL-E within Azure's secure and scalable ecosystem, businesses can create tailored solutions to meet industry-specific challenges.

AOAI provides industry-specific solutions that address unique challenges while optimizing processes, enhancing customer experiences, and fostering innovation. With Azure's secure and scalable platform, industries can leverage generative AI to transform operations and achieve sustainable growth.

Industry-Centric Benefits of AOAI Solutions

Retail: The retail industry has always understood customer behavior and planning, optimizing supply chains, and creating personalized shopping experiences. AI empowers retailers to innovate and enhance operational efficiency by integrating advanced Generative AI capabilities into their processes using Azure OpenAI and Studios (Speech, Language, and Computer Vision).

- **Personalized Shopping**: AI in personalized shopping transforms the customer experience by analyzing user behavior, preferences, purchase history, and current trends and tastes to provide tailored product recommendations. It enhances engagement through dynamic content such as personalized ads, targeted promotions based on festivals, events, and seasons, and curated shopping lists that are customer-centric. AI-driven tools optimize real-time interactions by offering location-specific deals or predicting customer needs during seasonal events. By personalizing the shopping drive, businesses improve customer satisfaction and loyalty while increasing sales. AI supports planning for future production and strengthening the supply chain systems in terms of innovative approaches that help in inventory management and demand forecasting by aligning offerings with customer preferences.
- **Demand Forecasting**: AI-powered applications in demand forecasting empower businesses to predict future customer needs by analyzing historical sales data, current market trends, and external factors such as seasonality or economic changes in local and international markets. It enhances accuracy, enabling businesses to optimize inventory levels, reduce stockouts, avoid overstocking, and execute optimistic plans. AI-driven forecasts adapt quickly

to changing customer tastes and interest conditions, ensuring timely supply chain and inventory adjustments. This leads to cost savings, improved resource allocation, inventory and logistics planning, and increased customer satisfaction. Industries such as retail, manufacturing, and logistics benefit significantly from AI's precision in anticipating demand fluctuations.

AI-powered applications can also predict trends during peak seasons, such as festivals, and optimize inventory systems for Christmas, New Year, Diwali, and Ramzan.

Healthcare: The healthcare industry rapidly utilizes AI-powered tools to enhance patient care (inpatient and outpatient), diagnose diseases, optimize operations, and improve medical outcomes, which is highly beneficial for the public. These solutions leverage Azure AI services and provide innovative approaches to diagnostics, treatment planning, and administrative efficiency. AI-empowered tools help innovate and enhance operational efficiency by integrating advanced AI and Gen AI capabilities into their processes using OpenAI and Studios, which has the features and flexibility to build solutions quickly and cost-effectively and adapt to data governance guidelines.

- **Medical Documentation**: AI-powered solutions are helping to automate the transcription and summarization of patient records with precision and high accuracy. It reduces administrative burdens, saves time for healthcare professionals, and ensures accuracy in medical documentation with AI-driven insights and continuous improvements.
- **Diagnostics Support**: AI in diagnostic support revolutionizes the healthcare industry by enhancing **the** accuracy, time **efficiency**, and outcome efficiency of medical diagnoses. Advanced AI models analyze imaging patient data, such as X-rays, MRIs, and CT scan reports. They can detect anomalies such as tumors or fractures faster with high precision and minimal manual intervention. These AI-powered tools assist healthcare professionals such as doctors, nurses, and lab technicians in detecting diseases, enabling timely interventions, and starting treatment without delays. AI-powered diagnostics reduce human error, significantly shorten the time needed for analysis and ensure appropriate therapies. This improves patients' healthcare system.
- **Virtual Health Assistants**: AI in virtual health assistants enhances patient engagement by providing 24/7 support for scheduling appointments, medication reminders, and answering health-related queries, quickly monitoring the progress of live data from virtual locations, and connecting the patients' healthcare and relationship with healthcare employees. This could be in AI-powered applications or chatbots that deliver personalized guidance based on patient data, making healthcare more accessible and efficiently remotely operating. It can also monitor symptoms and provide recommendations for further care when necessary. This technology improves the overall patient experience and streamlines healthcare operations. It

reduces medical staff's workload, space constraints, travel expenses, and so on. This approach helps the industry by handling routine inquiries and triaging non-urgent cases through a virtual assistant procedure.

Finance: AI in finance is pitching high, revolutionizing by automating various processes, enhancing accuracy, and enabling data-driven decisions. It empowers predictive and forecasting analytics for stock market trends, risk assessment predictions, and fraud detection, improving financial security and operational efficiency. AI algorithms can process vast datasets to provide individualized financial advice to customers, develop investment strategies, build credit scoring for applying for loans, and enable easy approvals.

Financial-based chatbots and virtual assistants enhance the customer experience in all aspects, enabling them to interact 24/7 and guide them in the right direction without delay. These tools automate inquiries and offer AI-powered solutions, optimizing and elevating wealth management accessibility. Additionally, real-time anomaly detection systems reduce fraud and compliance risks, addressing customer safety and security concerns.

AI also streamlines regulatory report generation and validation as part of operational activity, ensuring adherence to global standards to retain the financial sector and compete in the international market. This integration transforms finance into a more intelligent, faster, and secure ecosystem.

Financial-based AI empowers tools to help build the appropriate tools using Azure storage, OpenAI, and Studio features. It also provides the flexibility to build the solution quickly and cost-effectively and adapt to data governance guidelines.

- **Fraud Detection**: AI in fraud detection empowers financial institutions to analyze real-time transactions to identify fraudulent activities through pattern analysis. By collecting data and applying AI techniques, we can identify unauthorized activity on an account and detect suspicious behavior. AI-powered products help reduce financial losses and ensure compliance and trust through robust security measures.
- **Risk Assessment**: AI-driven predictive modeling can be used for credit scoring, investment decisions, and customer advice, highlighting the risk involved in planning well ahead. Financial institutions can analyze historical data to assess customers' credit scores before they take out loans.

Education: AI is revolutionizing education in various ways by personalizing learning experiences, fostering accessibility, and enhancing administrative efficiency. AI-driven adaptive learning platforms help build tailored content specific to individual students' needs and ensure a more effective learning journey.

Azure AI-powered capabilities help build applications that enhance accessibility for students with disabilities through tools such as speech-to-text, text-to-speech, and personalized assistive technologies to improve and assess students.

Predictive analytics helps institutions identify at-risk students early, enabling timely intervention and support, guiding them to direct their efforts appropriately, and monitoring their progress.

Automated grading systems save teachers time, accurately evaluate assignments and exams, and publish the results without delay according to the planned schedule.

- **Virtual Tutors**: AI-powered chatbots and virtual assistant tutors address queries and facilitate continuous learning and support while generating e-Learning content for study materials and preparing quizzes and question papers.
- **Language Translation**: AI-powered language processing tools enable global collaboration by seamlessly translating content into multiple languages based on the user's requirements. The classical multilingual support for global accessibility in educational platforms enhances the interaction between international students and faculty members.

Manufacturing:

AI drives innovation and efficiency in the manufacturing sector by enabling process automation, enhancing quality control, optimizing operations, building smart manufacturing systems, and connecting the dots to establish Industry 4.0.

AI-powered predictive maintenance and enhanced quality control systems analyze sensor data to prevent equipment failures, thereby reducing downtime and maintenance costs. Subsequent inspections improve product consistency and reduce waste. They integrate robotics with AI, accelerate production lines, and ensure precision and scalability in manufacturing tasks.

AI-driven supply chain optimization ensures smooth operations by predicting challenges, recommending alternative solutions on the spot, and providing guidance, thus effectively reducing overall operational costs.

AI-empowered tools help innovate and enhance operational efficiency by integrating advanced AI and Gen AI capabilities into their processes using Azure Storage, OpenAI, Studios, and monitoring features. These tools offer the flexibility to build solutions quickly and cost-effectively and adapt to data governance guidelines.

- **Energy Management**: AI-powered systems improve sustainability by reducing energy consumption and optimizing resource allocation and utilization. They also facilitate generative design, allowing engineers to create innovative product designs with enhanced functionality.
- **Digital Twins**: The breakthrough is in building virtual replicas of physical assets in digital twin concepts. This enables manufacturers to simulate and optimize production processes and enhance the quality of products before implementation. It transforms manufacturing by boosting productivity, reducing costs, and fostering sustainable best practices.

Media and Entertainment:

AI is also revolutionizing the media and entertainment industry by enhancing the creation of high-quality content based on demand, such as text, audio, and video, to meet with the audience's taste. As a result, content creators can leverage the capabilities of AI tools to generate video editing, scriptwriting, and visual effects, streamlining production workflows, improving creativity, and fulfilling audience demand.

Azure-based AI-powered recommendation systems help analyze and deliver personalized content, boosting user satisfaction based on viewer preferences. These systems use Azure Storage, Monitoring, OpenAI, Studios, Machine Learning (ML), and Deep Learning (DL) capabilities.

AI-driven analytics help media companies understand trends, predict demand, and optimize ad placement for maximum impact. By integrating AI, the media and entertainment industry delivers more engaging, efficient, robust, cost-effective, and personalized experiences for audiences worldwide.

1. **Language and Visual Translation:** Real-time language translation and subtitle generation make content accessible to global audiences and bring them together on common platforms and interests. Converting text into images and videos using DALL-E can generate custom visual effects for advertisements and media campaigns.

- **Customer Sentiment Analysis**: Customer sentiment analysis helps gauge audience reactions to movies, shows, and campaigns. It tracks and analyzes audience feedback on media content, providing valuable feedback for content optimization, and assists media professionals in creating quality and high-revenue movies, shows, and more.

Logistics and Transportation:

AI is transforming the logistics and transportation industry by optimizing planning and scheduling operations, effectively reducing resources and costs, and enhancing customer satisfaction through on-time product delivery and commitment. By leveraging AI, the sector ensures sustainability, reliability, and improved efficiency across the value chain.

AI-powered route optimization systems analyze current traffic, guide truck drivers, monitor delivery stages, and monitor weather conditions along the route. These systems then plan delivery schedules to determine the most efficient paths, saving time, driver effort, and fuel.

Warehouse automation with AI-driven robotics streamlines inventory management, enabling faster order fulfillment and quick and error-free allocation. AI enhances fleet management by analyzing real-time data for tracking, scheduling, and operational efficiency.

Azure OpenAI and ML-driven chatbots provide personalized notifications about shipment stages, tracking, and delivery updates to improve customer experience and retain them.

- **Route Optimization**: AI-powered tools help predict the most efficient delivery routes, saving time and fuel costs. Ultimately, this enhances maintenance and planning tasks such as monitoring vehicle running capabilities and health, preventing breakdowns, reducing downtime, and evaluating driver capabilities.
- **Real-Time Tracking**: Monitoring shipments and forecasting delivery timelines precisely helps plan for future deliveries, gives upfront commitments, enhances the customer experience, builds good relationships, and distinguishes us from other competitors. Customer support with interactive AI assistants ensures 24/7 query resolution. This facilitates the demand forecasting models to help logistics companies optimize inventory levels, reduce overstock or shortages, and plan well ahead.

Energy and Utilities:

AI is also revolutionizing the energy and utilities sector by optimizing energy production, tracking energy utilization, providing guidance, improving grid management systems, and encouraging sustainability. These AI systems help analyze equipment performance by collecting data to detect faults, estimate repair costs early, analyze downtime, ensure grid stability, minimize power outages, and plan proper energy production and utilization schedules.

Many energy companies use Azure AI-powered tools for reservoir management systems and energy trading to predict market trends, pricing fluctuations, and plan for households and businesses to reduce energy consumption and costs. Optimizing extraction in oil and gas operations strengthens energy production systems, and optimization techniques for energy manufacturing companies will enable the balancing of supply and demand for energy across various sectors.

- **Energy Demand Forecasting**: Energy Demand Forecasting techniques are instrumental in predicting consumption patterns across households and various power-consuming sectors, building AI-powered data analytics, and optimizing energy distribution and utilization.
- **Energy Auditing and Regulations:** AI-powered tools can help the energy sector build auditing tools and provide regulatory guidance to all stakeholders to understand environmental issues, such as consuming high voltage and producing waste from individuals, and guide them in avoiding penalties and hazards. Regular audit reports will help energy-utilizing sectors keep them within the right benchmarks.

Healthcare Use Cases Using Azure OpenAI

Azure OpenAI (AIAO) offers transformative capabilities that enhance efficiency, accuracy, and innovation for the healthcare industry at a lower cost than other cloud providers by leveraging advanced Gen AI models such as Azure OpenAI GPT Models (for example, GPT-4 and GPT-3.5), Codex (OpenAI), DALL-E (OpenAI), Azure Cognitive Services Language Models, Azure Cognitive Services Vision Models, Azure Speech-to-Text and Text-to-Speech Models, and Azure Translator Models. By integrating them with Azure's secure and scalable ecosystem, healthcare providers can streamline operations, improve patient outcomes, and drive innovation.

Medical Documentation and Summarization (Med-Docs and Summary): AI-powered tools, such as Azure Cognitive Services and Azure OpenAI, can transcribe patient-physician conversations into structured notes using advanced speech-to-text models. These notes are then summarized using AI-driven natural language processing (NLP) techniques, ensuring concise and accurate medical records for further treatment. This ensures accuracy in medical documentation with AI-driven insights.

- **Use Case**: Automate the transcription and summarization of clinical notes, patient histories, and medical consultations.
- **Benefits**:
  - Integrating with Azure's secure infrastructure ensures sensitive patient data remains protected and compliant with healthcare regulations such as HIPAA.
  - Azure AI also enables multilingual capabilities, allowing documentation in multiple languages.
  - This reduces administrative burdens on healthcare providers, enhances clinical efficiency, and ensures patients' medical histories are easily accessible.
  - A streamlined documentation process improves overall healthcare delivery and decision-making.

Architectural Design and Development for (Med-Docs and Summary) Using Azure Ecosystem

High-Level Architecture Design: The architecture captures medical conversations, processes, and analyzes the data, and generates structured documentation summaries for doctors, nurses, and lab technicians, ensuring data privacy and compliance.

Architecture Layers: To attain the maximum benefits, we must maintain the minimum requirements of the following layers while constructing this proposed tool.

Table 11.1 shows the proposed implementation's different layers, describes each layer, and recommends Azure components.

Layer	Description	Azure Components
Input Layer	Captures unstructured medical data from various sources such as conversations, audio, and text.	- Azure Speech Services (Speech-to-Text)
Data Ingestion Layer	Ingest raw data (transcribed text or manual inputs) into the system for further processing.	- Azure Logic Apps - Azure Event Hubs - Azure Blob Storage
Processing Layer	Processes and cleanses the ingested data to ensure quality and prepare it for summarization.	- Azure Cognitive Services - Azure Data Factory
AI/ML Layer	Applies AI/ML models for summarization, sentiment analysis, and information extraction.	- Azure OpenAI (GPT-4 for summarization) - Azure Machine Learning - Azure Cognitive Services (Language)
Data Storage Layer	Stores structured data for long-term retention and real-time access.	- Azure SQL Database - Azure Cosmos DB - Azure Data Lake
Application Layer	Provides APIs and tools for real-time summarization and integration with external systems.	- Azure API Management - Azure Functions
Visualization Layer	Presents structured data in a user-friendly format for healthcare professionals.	- Power BI - Azure App Service (for web or mobile app interfaces)
Security and Compliance Layer	Ensures HIPAA compliance, role-based access, and secure data transmission and storage.	- Azure Active Directory - Azure Key Vault - Azure Security Centre

Table 11.1: *Architecture Layers for Med-Docs and Summary*

Figure 11.2 shows Microsoft Azure, an Architectural Design and Development Environment for the Healthcare Industry. *Table* 11.1 describes each layer's functionality, and its implementation is elaborated using Python code.

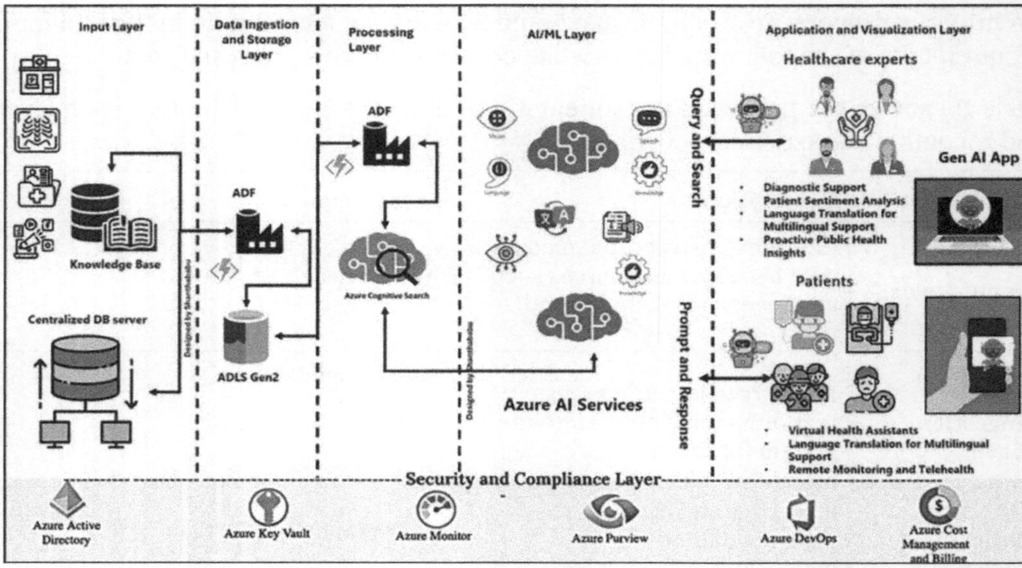

Figure 11.2: *Microsoft Azure; Architectural Design and Development Environment for the Healthcare Industry*

Python Code for Med-Docs and Summary Implementation

Let us implement the medical documentation and summarization system using the Azure ecosystem, Python libraries, and Azure SDKs for different layers.

Install all required libraries before you get started:

```
# Install required Azure SDKs
# pip install azure-cognitiveservices-speech
# pip azure-storage-blob azure-ai-textanalytics
# pip azure-mgmt-resource
#pip azure-keyvault azure-ai-openai
#!pip install langchain
#!pip install openai
#!pip install PyPDF2
#!pip install faiss-cpu
#!pip install tiktoken
#!pip install langchain-community
```

Import all the required libraries before you get started:

```
print("################")
print("Import all required libraries ")
print("################")
import os
```

```
from azure.storage.blob import BlobServiceClient
from azure.cognitiveservices.speech import SpeechConfig, SpeechRecognizer,
AudioConfig
from azure.ai.textanalytics import TextAnalyticsClient
from azure.core.credentials import AzureKeyCredential
from azure.identity import DefaultAzureCredential
from azure.ai.openai import OpenAIClient

print("######################")
print("Add all required environment variables")
print("######################")

AZURE_SPEECH_KEY = os.getenv("AZURE_SPEECH_KEY")
AZURE_SPEECH_REGION = os.getenv("AZURE_SPEECH_REGION")
AZURE_BLOB_CONNECTION_STRING = os.getenv("AZURE_BLOB_CONNECTION_STRING")
AZURE_TEXT_ANALYTICS_KEY = os.getenv("AZURE_TEXT_ANALYTICS_KEY")
AZURE_TEXT_ANALYTICS_ENDPOINT = os.getenv("AZURE_TEXT_ANALYTICS_ENDPOINT")
AZURE_OPENAI_API_KEY = os.getenv("AZURE_OPENAI_API_KEY")
AZURE_OPENAI_ENDPOINT = os.getenv("AZURE_OPENAI_ENDPOINT")

print("###################")
print("# Initialize Azure Components")
print("###################")

def init_clients():
    # Initialize Text Analytics Client
    text_analytics_client = TextAnalyticsClient(
        endpoint=AZURE_TEXT_ANALYTICS_ENDPOINT,
        credential=AzureKeyCredential(AZURE_TEXT_ANALYTICS_KEY),
    )
    # Initialize Blob Storage Client
    blob_service_client = BlobServiceClient.from_connection_
string(AZURE_BLOB_CONNECTION_STRING)

    # Initialize OpenAI Client
    openai_client = OpenAIClient(
        endpoint=AZURE_OPENAI_ENDPOINT, credential=AzureKeyCreden-
tial(AZURE_OPENAI_API_KEY)    )
    return text_analytics_client, blob_service_client, openai_client
```

The required setup is done. Now, we have to implement individual layers.

```
print("################################")
print("   Layer 1: Input Layer (Speech-to-Text Conversion)        ")
print("################################")

def speech_to_text(audio_file_path):
```

```
    speech_config = SpeechConfig(subscription=AZURE_SPEECH_KEY, region
=AZURE_SPEECH_REGION)
    audio_config = AudioConfig(filename=audio_file_path)

    recognizer = SpeechRecognizer(speech_config=speech_config, audio_
config=audio_config)
    print("Recognizing...")
    result = recognizer.recognize_once()

    if result.reason == result.Reason.RecognizedSpeech:
        print(f"Recognized text: {result.text}")
        return result.text
    else:
        print("Speech recognition failed.")
        return None


print("######################################")
print("   Layer 2: Data Ingestion Layer (Upload to Azure Blob Storage)
")
print("######################################")

def upload_to_blob(container_name, blob_name, content):
    blob_service_client = BlobServiceClient.from_connection_
string(AZURE_BLOB_CONNECTION_STRING)
    blob_client = blob_service_client.get_blob_client(container=
container_name, blob=blob_name)

    blob_client.upload_blob(content)
    print(f"Uploaded content to Blob: {blob_name}")

print("#########################")
print("   Layer 3: Processing Layer (Text Analysis)    ")
print("#########################")

 def analyze_text(text, text_analytics_client):
    result = text_analytics_client.extract_key_phrases(documents=[text])
    if not result.is_error:
        print(f"Key Phrases: {result[0].key_phrases}")
        return result[0].key_phrases
    else:
        print(f"Error in text analysis: {result[0].error}")
        return []
print("################################")
print("   Layer 4: AI/ML Layer (Summarization with Open         ")
print("################################")
```

```
def summarize_text(text, openai_client):
    response = openai_client.completions.create(
        engine="text-davinci-003",
        prompt=f"Summarize the following medical text:\n\n{text}",
        max_tokens=150,
    )
    print(f"Summary: {response.choices[0].text.strip()}")
    return response.choices[0].text.strip()

print("####################")
print("   # Main Execution Workflow        ")
print("####################")

def main():
    # Initialize Azure Clients
    text_analytics_client, blob_service_client, openai_client = init_
clients()

    # Input Layer: Convert Speech to Text
    audio_file_path = "patient_audio.wav"  # Example audio file
    recognized_text = speech_to_text(audio_file_path)

    if recognized_text:
        # Data Ingestion Layer: Upload to Blob Storage
        upload_to_blob(container_name="medical-records",blob_name="raw_
text.txt", content=recognized_text)
        # Processing Layer: Analyze Text
        key_phrases = analyze_text(recognized_text, text_analytics_client)

        # AI/ML Layer: Summarization
        summary = summarize_text(recognized_text, openai_client)
        # Final Output
        print("### Final Output ###")
        print(f"Original Text: {recognized_text}")
        print(f"Key Phrases: {key_phrases}")
        print(f"Summary: {summary}")

if __name__ == "__main__":
    main()
```

Table 11.2 shows other critical use cases and their benefits.

Use Case	Description	Benefits
Virtual Health Assistants	AI-powered chatbots can handle patient inquiries, schedule appointments, provide medication reminders, and deliver preliminary health advice.	It improves accessibility to healthcare services and reduces wait times for patients.
Diagnostic Support	Analyze medical images (X-rays, MRIs, CT scans) to detect anomalies and provide diagnostic support. Assist in identifying early signs of diseases.	It enhances diagnostic accuracy and speeds up the detection of critical conditions.
Patient Sentiment Analysis	Analyze patient feedback, reviews, and social media to gauge satisfaction and identify areas for improvement.	Enhances the quality of care and patient experience.
Language Translation for Multilingual Support	Translate medical content using AI into multiple languages, including patient instructions and documentation.	It enhances communication in diverse populations and ensures equitable access to care.
Ethical AI in Medical Research	Use AI to identify bias in clinical studies and ensure diversity in datasets.	Promotes ethical standards and inclusivity in medical research.
Proactive Public Health Insights	Analyze large-scale health data to predict and manage disease outbreaks, track vaccination progress, and optimize healthcare policies.	Improves community health management and resource planning.

Table 11.2: *Healthcare Use Cases Using Azure OpenAI*

Manufacturing Use Cases Using Azure OpenAI

Azure OpenAI is revolutionizing the manufacturing sector by offering innovative solutions for predictive maintenance, quality assurance, supply chain optimization, and more. Its integration with Azure's ecosystem provides manufacturers with the tools to enhance productivity, reduce costs, and achieve sustainable growth while staying competitive in a rapidly evolving market. With advanced generative AI models such as GPT and integration with Azure's robust ecosystem, manufacturers can address challenges, reduce costs, and enhance productivity.

Azure OpenAI (AIAO) offers transformative capabilities that enhance efficiency, accuracy, and innovation tools for the manufacturing industry while being cost-effective compared to other cloud providers by leveraging advanced Gen AI models Manufacturers can streamline operations, improve patient outcomes, and drive innovation by integrating them with Azure's secure and scalable ecosystem.

Predictive Maintenance: Predictive maintenance leverages IoT sensor data and advanced analytics to forecast equipment failures and proactively schedule maintenance activities. By analyzing real-time and historical data, businesses can detect anomalies, predict failures, and take corrective actions before breakdowns occur. IoT sensors monitor equipment parameters such as temperature, vibration, and pressure. AI models analyze this data to identify patterns signaling potential issues. Maintenance teams are alerted, allowing them to perform repairs during planned downtime, maximizing efficiency and reducing costs.

Key Benefits:

- **Reduces Downtime**: Based on the data collected from individual equipment, we can assess its health and prevent unexpected failures, ensuring continuous operations for planned production schedules.
- **Extends Equipment Life**: Continuous monitoring of the equipment's performance and early identification of issues enable timely maintenance interventions that minimize wear and tear and extend the equipment's life.
- **Lower Maintenance Costs**: Optimizes maintenance schedules, reducing unnecessary repairs and emergency interventions in advance, lowering maintenance costs, and allowing better planning for production schedules.

Architectural Design and Development for (Predictive Maintenance) Using Azure Ecosystem

High-Level Architecture:

The architecture focuses on capturing IoT sensor data, processing it for anomaly detection, leveraging AI models for predictive maintenance insights, and presenting actionable insights through a user-friendly interface.

Architecture Layers:

To attain the maximum benefits, we must maintain the minimum requirements of the following layers while constructing this proposed tool.

Table 11.3 shows the proposed implementation's different layers, describes each layer, and recommends Azure components.

Layer	Description	Azure Components
IoT Data Collection Layer	Collect real-time data from IoT sensors monitoring equipment.	- Azure IoT Hub - Azure IoT Edge
Data Ingestion Layer	Capture and store raw sensor data for processing and analysis.	- Azure Event Hubs - Azure Blob Storage
Data Processing Layer	Cleanse and preprocess data to ensure quality and readiness for AI analysis.	- Azure Stream Analytics - Azure Data Factory
AI/ML Analysis Layer	Analyze pre-processed data using AI models to detect anomalies and predict equipment failures.	- Azure OpenAI (GPT models) - Azure Machine Learning - Azure Synapse Analytics
Data Storage Layer	Store processed data, predictions, and historical records for future reference and compliance.	- Azure SQL Database - Azure Cosmos DB - Azure Data Lake
Visualization and Insights Layer	Present predictions and maintenance schedules to end-users via dashboards and notifications.	- Power BI - Azure App Service
Integration and API Layer	Provide APIs to integrate insights into existing maintenance management systems.	- Azure API Management - Azure Functions
Security and Compliance Layer	Ensure secure handling of sensitive IoT and operational data while maintaining regulatory compliance.	- Azure Active Directory - Azure Key Vault - Azure Security Centre

Table 11.3: *Architecture Layers for Predictive Maintenance*

Figure 11.3 shows Microsoft Azure, an Architectural Design and Development Environment for the Manufacturing Industry. *Table* 11.3 describes each layer's functionality, and its implementation is elaborated using Python code.

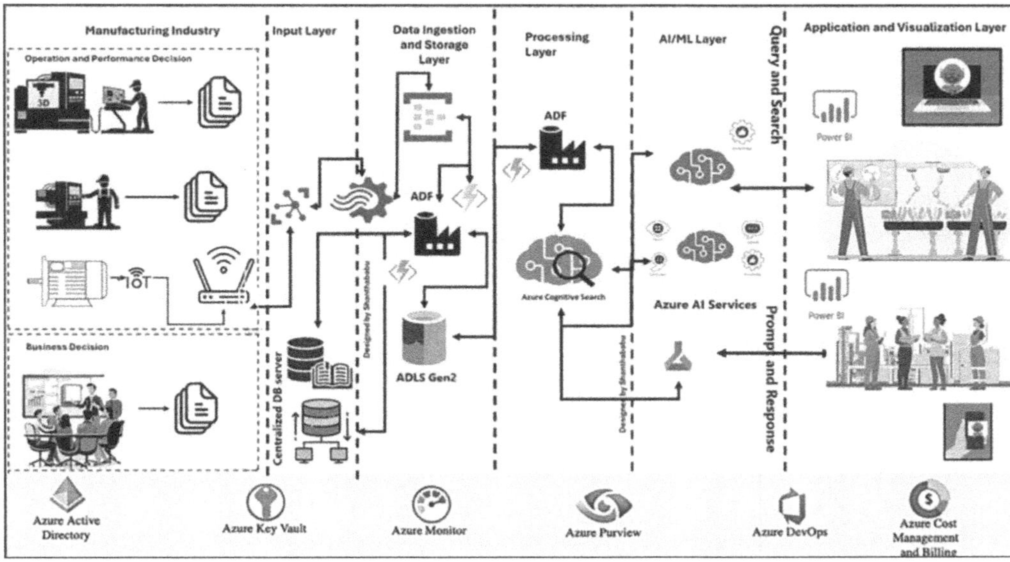

Figure 11.3: *Microsoft Azure; Architectural Design and Development Environment for Manufacturing Industry*

Python Code for Predictive Maintenance Implementation

Let us implement a predictive maintenance system using the Azure ecosystem, Python libraries, and Azure SDKs for different layers.

Install all the required libraries before you get started:

 # Install required Azure SDKs

 # !pip install azure-iot-device

#!pip azure-storage-blob

#pip azure-mgmt-resource

#pip azure-ai-machinelearning

#pip azure-eventhub

#pip azure-keyvault azure-ai-openai

Import all required libraries before you get started:

```
import os
from azure.iot.device import IoTHubDeviceClient, Message
from azure.storage.blob import BlobServiceClient
from azure.eventhub import EventHubProducerClient, EventData
```

```
from azure.ai.openai import OpenAIClient
from azure.core.credentials import AzureKeyCredential
from azure.identity import DefaultAzureCredential
from azure.ai.ml import MLClient
from azure.ai.ml.entities import Job, AmlCompute, Input

print("#####################")
print("Add all required environment variables")
print("#####################")

AZURE_IOT_HUB_CONNECTION_STRING = os.getenv("AZURE_IOT_HUB_CONNECTION_
STRING")
AZURE_BLOB_CONNECTION_STRING = os.getenv("AZURE_BLOB_CONNECTION_STRING")
AZURE_EVENT_HUB_CONNECTION_STRING = os.getenv("AZURE_EVENT_HUB_CONNEC-
TION_STRING")
AZURE_OPENAI_API_KEY = os.getenv("AZURE_OPENAI_API_KEY")
AZURE_OPENAI_ENDPOINT = os.getenv("AZURE_OPENAI_ENDPOINT")
AZURE_STORAGE_CONTAINER = "sensor-data"

print("###################")
print("  # Initialize Azure Client                 ")
print("###################")

def init_clients():
    blob_service_client = BlobServiceClient.from_connection_
string(AZURE_BLOB_CONNECTION_STRING)
    event_hub_client = EventHubProducerClient.from_connection_
string(AZURE_EVENT_HUB_CONNECTION_STRING)
    openai_client=OpenAIClient(endpoint=AZURE_OPENAI_ENDPOINT,
credential=AzureKeyCredential(AZURE_OPENAI_API_KEY))
    return blob_service_client, event_hub_client, openai_client
```

The required setup is done. Now, we have to implement individual layers.

```
print("##############################")
print("  # Layer 1: Data Collection (IoT Sensor Simulation)       ")
print("##############################")



def send_sensor_data_to_iot_hub(sensor_data):
    device_client = IoTHubDeviceClient.create_from_connection_
string(AZURE_IOT_HUB_CONNECTION_STRING)
    message = Message(sensor_data)
    device_client.send_message(message)
    print(f"Sent data to IoT Hub: {sensor_data}")

print("#####################################")
```

```
print("   Layer 2: Data Ingestion Layer (Upload to Azure Blob Storage)
")
print("######################################")


def store_data_in_blob(blob_service_client, file_name, content):
    blob_client = blob_service_client.get_blob_client(container=AZURE_
STORAGE_CONTAINER, blob=file_name)
    blob_client.upload_blob(content, overwrite=True)
    print(f"Uploaded sensor data to Blob Storage: {file_name}")

print("#########################")
print("   Layer 3: Processing Layer (Text Analysis)    ")
print("#########################")


def send_data_to_event_hub(event_hub_client, data):
    event_data = EventData(data)
    with event_hub_client as client:
        client.send_batch([event_data])
    print(f"Sent data to Event Hub: {data}")

print("####################################")
print("   Layer 4: AI/ML Analysis (Predictive Insights with OpenAI)
")
print("####################################")

def analyze_data_with_openai(openai_client, data):
    response = openai_client.completions.create(
        engine="text-davinci-003",
        prompt=f"Analyze the following IoT sensor data and predict
possible equipment failures:\n\n{data}",
        max_tokens=150
    )
    prediction = response.choices[0].text.strip()
    print(f"Prediction: {prediction}")
    return prediction

print("####################")
print("   # Main Execution Workflow        ")
print("####################")

def main():
    # Initialize Azure Clients
    blob_service_client, event_hub_client, openai_client = init_clients()

    # Simulated Sensor Data for demonstrating the flow
```

```
    sensor_data = {
        "temperature": 85.5,
        "vibration": 0.03,
        "pressure": 101.2
    }
    sensor_data_str = str(sensor_data)

print("##############################")
print("   # Calling each layer to execute the work flow      ")
print("##############################")

    # Layer 1: Send Data to IoT Hub
    send_sensor_data_to_iot_hub(sensor_data_str)

    # Layer 2: Store Data in Blob Storage
    store_data_in_blob(blob_service_client, "sensor_data.json", sensor_
data_str)

    # Layer 3: Stream Data to Event Hub
    send_data_to_event_hub(event_hub_client, sensor_data_str)

    # Layer 4: Analyze Data with OpenAI
    prediction = analyze_data_with_openai(openai_client, sensor_data_
str)

    # Final Output
    print("### Final Prediction Output ###")
    print(f"Sensor Data: {sensor_data}")
    print(f"Prediction: {prediction}")

if __name__ == "__main__":
    main()
```

Table 11.4 shows the other critical use cases and their benefits.

Category	Use Case	Benefits
Quality Control and Assurance	Use AI-powered vision systems to detect defects and generate real-time quality insights.	Enhances product quality and reduces waste by identifying issues early.
Supply Chain Optimization	Forecast demand, optimize inventory levels, predict disruptions, and suggest alternatives.	Ensures timely delivery of goods while minimizing costs.
Process Automation	Automate repetitive tasks such as report generation and workflow management using GPT.	It frees up workforce capacity for higher-value tasks and improves operational efficiency.

Production Planning and Scheduling	Optimize production schedules based on demand, resources, and delivery timelines.	Maximizes resource utilization and ensures timely order fulfilment.
Digital Twins and Simulation	Create digital twins for performance simulation and optimization.	Reduces physical testing costs and enables real-time process optimization.
Workforce Training and Support	Use generative AI to create training manuals, simulations, and step-by-step instructions.	Enhances workforce skills and accelerates the onboarding process.
Energy Management	Monitor and analyze energy consumption patterns to identify inefficiencies.	Reduces energy costs and supports sustainability goals.
Demand Forecasting	Analyze historical data, trends, and external factors to predict demand.	Improves production planning and inventory management.
Chatbots for Operations Support	Deploy AI-powered chatbots for troubleshooting, process guidance, and equipment configuration.	Reduces dependency on experts and ensures consistent support.
Safety Monitoring and Risk Mitigation	Use AI to monitor real-time video and sensor data for unsafe conditions.	It enhances workplace safety and reduces accidents.
Product Lifecycle Management (PLM)	Optimize and manage every stage of a product's lifecycle, from design to disposal.	Increases efficiency and reduces costs associated with product updates.
Multilingual Communication	Translate technical documents and training materials for global operations.	Improves communication across multinational teams and ensures clarity.

Table 11.4: *Manufacturing Use Cases Using Azure OpenAI*

Banking and Financial Services Use Cases Using Azure OpenAI

AOAI has transformative potential in the banking and financial sector and also offers numerous benefits while posing particular challenges. AOAI models help mitigate fraudulent activities by analyzing transactions based on patterns and flagging anomalies with precision and high accuracy. This allows the banking and financial sectors to reduce financial losses, foster customer trust, retain them, and bring in new customers. The platform's scalability ensures that the AI models can seamlessly handle increased workloads as transaction volumes grow regularly since the Azure environment is highly scalable and has high computational capabilities. Additionally, through advanced chatbots, AOAI improves operational efficiency by automating tasks such as credit risk analysis, regulatory compliance reporting, and customer service. It also supports language, speech, and vision-based models and studios, enabling faster processes and cost savings and sustaining recent technology implementations in various aspects.

Personalized financial services powered by AOAI enhance customer engagement by tailoring advice and recommendations to individual needs. Adopting data privacy and compliance with GDPR, PII, and CCPA regulations is critical when handling sensitive financial information. The major challenge here is the complexity of training AI models, which requires high-quality datasets and can be resource-intensive. Moreover, the dynamic nature of fraudulent tactics demands constant updates and retraining of AI models to stay ahead of threats. AOAI's capabilities in streamlining operations and enhancing security make it a game-changing tool for the banking and finance industry, provided its adoption is managed effectively.

Fraud Detection and Prevention: Fraud detection and prevention are critical components of banking and financial services to safeguard transactions and protect customer trust. AI-powered systems can analyze transaction patterns to detect anomalies indicating fraudulent activity, such as unauthorized access, unusual spending behavior, suspicious transactions, and identity theft. These systems utilize advanced machine learning models and real-time data analytics to identify irregularities and flag suspicious activity immediately.

AOAI enhances the accuracy and speed of fraud detection by processing large datasets with high computational speed, identifying complex patterns, and deriving insights. This proactive approach minimizes financial losses, mitigates risks, and strengthens overall security.

Key Benefits:

- **Enhanced Security**: It enables real-time analysis of transaction patterns, ensuring early detection of fraudulent activities, reducing risks, and protecting customer data.
- **Reduced Financial Losses**: It ensures the proactive identification of fraud and minimizes monetary losses and operational disruptions caused by unauthorized transactions and suspicious activities.
- **Improved Accuracy and Customer Trust**: AI-driven systems reduce false positives, improve fraud detection precision, and build customer confidence, strengthening trust in the institution's ability to safeguard their finances.

Architectural Design and Development for (Fraud Detection and Prevention) Using Azure Ecosystem

High-Level Architecture Design: Fraud detection and prevention in banking and financial services rely on advanced real-time analytics, AI models, and robust security layers. The Azure ecosystem offers scalable and secure components to implement a comprehensive solution.

Architecture Layers: To attain the maximum benefits, we must maintain the minimum requirements of the following layers while constructing this proposed tool.

Table 11.5 shows the proposed implementation's different layers, describes each layer, and recommends Azure components.

Layer	Description	Azure Components
Data Collection Layer	Collect real-time transaction data from banking systems, ATMs, and online platforms.	- Azure IoT Hub (for device interactions) - Azure Event Hubs
Data Ingestion Layer	Stream transaction data to ensure efficient and real-time processing.	- Azure Event Hubs - Azure Data Factory
Data Storage Layer	Store raw transaction data, historical records, and flagged anomalies for future reference and audits.	- Azure Blob Storage - Azure Data Lake Storage
Data Processing Layer	Process and normalize transaction data for analysis and anomaly detection.	- Azure Stream Analytics - Azure Databricks
AI/ML Analysis Layer	Use machine learning models and AI algorithms to detect anomalies and predict fraudulent transactions.	- Azure Machine Learning - Azure OpenAI - Azure Synapse Analytics
Decisions and Insights Layer	To notify fraud detection teams and generate actionable insights and alerts for potential fraud cases.	- Azure Cognitive Services - Azure Logic Apps
Visualization Layer	Provide dashboards for fraud monitoring, risk scoring, and trend analysis.	- Power BI - Azure Monitor
Security and Compliance Layer	Ensure data privacy, regulatory compliance, and secure access to fraud detection systems.	- Azure Active Directory - Azure Key Vault - Azure Security Centre

Table 11.5: *Architecture Layers for Fraud Detection and Prevention*

Figure 11.4 shows Microsoft Azure, an architectural design and development environment for the banking and financial industry. *Table* 11.5 describes each layer's functionality, and its implementation is elaborated using Python code.

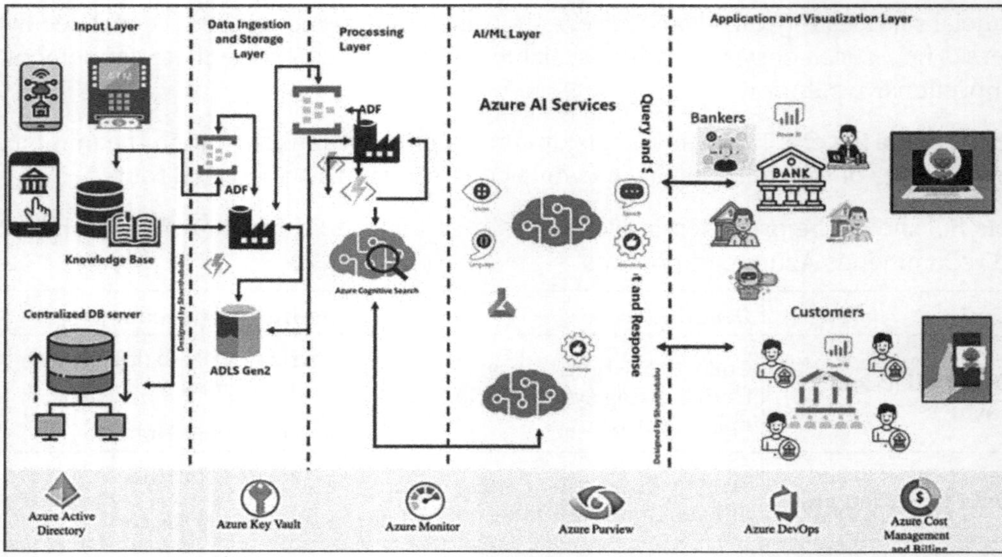

Figure 11.4: *Microsoft Azure; Architectural Design and Development Environment for Banking and Finance Industry*

Python Code for Fraud Detection and Prevention Implementation

Let us implement a fraud detection and prevention system using the Azure ecosystem, Python libraries, and Azure SDKs for different layers.

Install all the required libraries before you get started:

```
# Install necessary Azure SDKs:
pip install azure-eventhub
pip install azure-storage-blob azure-ai-ml pandas
# pip install azure-cognitiveservices-speech
# pip azure-storage-blob azure-ai-textanalytics
# pip azure-mgmt-resource
#pip azure-keyvault azure-ai-openai
#!pip install langchain
#!pip install openai
#!pip install PyPDF2
#!pip install faiss-cpu
#!pip install tiktoken
#!pip install langchain-community

print("################")
print("Import all required libraries ")
```

```
print("#################")

from azure.eventhub import EventHubProducerClient, EventData
from azure.storage.blob import BlobServiceClient
from azure.identity import DefaultAzureCredential
from azure.ai.ml import MLClient
import pandas as pd
import json
import random


print("#######################")
print("Add all required environment variables")
print("#######################")

# Configuration
EVENT_HUB_CONNECTION_STRING = "your_event_hub_connection_string"
EVENT_HUB_NAME = "your_event_hub_name"
BLOB_CONNECTION_STRING = "your_blob_storage_connection_string"
BLOB_CONTAINER_NAME = "fraud-data"
BLOB_FILE_NAME = "transactions.json"
SUBSCRIPTION_ID = "your_subscription_id"
RESOURCE_GROUP = "your_resource_group"
WORKSPACE_NAME = "your_workspace_name"

print("####################")
print("   Layer 1: Data Collection Layer     ")
print("####################")

def collect_transaction_data():
    """
    Collects real-time transaction data and sends it to Azure Event Hub 
for processing.
    """
    transactions = [
        {"transaction_id": i, "amount": random.randint(10, 5000), 
"location": random.choice(["USA", "UK", "India"]),
         "status": "pending"} for i in range(1, 101)
    ]

    # Send data to Azure Event Hub
    producer = EventHubProducerClient.from_connection_string(conn_
str=EVENT_HUB_CONNECTION_STRING, eventhub_name=EVENT_HUB_NAME)
    with producer:
        event_data_batch = [EventData(json.dumps(transaction)) for 
transaction in transactions]
```

```
        producer.send_batch(event_data_batch)
    print("Transaction data sent to Event Hub.")


print("######################")
print("   Layer 2: Data Ingestion Layer        ")
print("######################")

def ingest_data():
    """
    # It simulates streaming data from Event Hub and prepares it for
storage.
    """
    print("Ingesting data from Azure Event Hub...")
    # This function can use Azure Data Factory or Databricks to prepare
data for further layers.

print("###################")
print("   Layer 3: Data Storage Layer     ")
print("###################")

def store_data_in_blob():
    """
    Stores transaction data in Azure Blob Storage for future reference
and analysis.
    """
    blob_service_client = BlobServiceClient.from_connection_string(BLOB_
CONNECTION_STRING)
    container_client = blob_service_client.get_container_client(BLOB_
CONTAINER_NAME)
    blob_client = container_client.get_blob_client(BLOB_FILE_NAME)

    # Simulate storing transaction data
    transactions = [
        {"transaction_id": i, "amount": random.randint(10, 5000),
"location": random.choice(["USA", "UK", "India"]),
         "status": "processed"} for i in range(1, 101)
    ]

    blob_client.upload_blob(json.dumps(transactions), overwrite=True)
    print(f"Transaction data stored in Blob Storage: {BLOB_FILE_NAME}")

print("###################")
print("   Layer 4: Data Processing Layer   ")
print("###################")

def process_data():
```

```
    """
    Processes and normalizes transaction data for fraud detection.
    """
    print("Processing data with Azure Stream Analytics and Data-
bricks...")
    # Simulate data normalization and aggregation.
    # This would involve transforming data and detecting anomalies in
real use cases.

print("###################")
print("   Layer 5: AI/ML Analysis Layer    ")
print("###################")


def analyze_data_with_ai():
    """
    Applies AI/ML models to detect anomalies and flag potential fraud.
    """
    print("Analyzing data with Azure Machine Learning and OpenAI...")
    ml_client = MLClient(DefaultAzureCredential(), SUBSCRIPTION_ID,
RESOURCE_GROUP, WORKSPACE_NAME)

    # Simulated AI model scoring
    flagged_transactions = [{"transaction_id": 101, "amount": 4000,
"status": "flagged"}]
    print("Flagged Transactions for Fraud:", flagged_transactions)

print("########################")
print("     Layer 6: Decision and Insights Layer       ")
print("########################")


def generate_fraud_alerts():
    """
    Generates actionable alerts for fraud detection teams using Azure
Logic Apps.
    """
    print("Generating alerts using Azure Logic Apps and Cognitive
Services...")
    # Simulate sending alerts to fraud teams.

print("########################")
print("           Layer 7: Visualization Layer                 ")
print("########################")


def generate_dashboard():
```

```
    """
   # Generates a Power BI dashboard for fraud monitoring.
    """
    # Simulate data visualization
    transactions = pd.DataFrame([
        {"transaction_id": i, "amount": random.randint(10, 5000),
"location": random.choice(["USA", "UK", "India"]),
         "status": "processed"} for i in range(1, 101)
    ])
    print("Transaction Summary by Location:")
    print(transactions.groupby("location").amount.sum())


print("############################")
print("      Layer 8: Security and Compliance Layer         ")
print("############################")


def ensure_security_compliance():
    """
    Ensures data security, regulatory compliance, and access control.
    """
    print("Enforcing security and compliance with Azure Active Directory
and Key Vault...")
    # Implement role-based access control, secure credentials, and
compliance monitoring.


print("############")
print("       Main Workflow       ")
print("############")

def main():
    print("Starting Fraud Detection Workflow...")
    collect_transaction_data()    # Layer 1
    ingest_data()                 # Layer 2
    store_data_in_blob()          # Layer 3
    process_data()                # Layer 4
    analyze_data_with_ai()        # Layer 5
    generate_fraud_alerts()       # Layer 6
    generate_dashboard()          # Layer 7
    ensure_security_compliance()  # Layer 8
    print("Fraud Detection Workflow Completed.")

if __name__ == "__main__":
    main()
```

Table 11.6 shows other critical use cases and their benefits.

Use Case	Description	Benefits
Credit Risk Analysis	Evaluate customer data, credit history, and spending behavior to assess creditworthiness.	Provides accurate risk assessment and speeds up loan approvals.
Personalized Banking Services	Deliver tailored financial advice, investment suggestions, and product recommendations.	Improves customer engagement and cross-selling opportunities.
Customer Service Automation	AI-powered chatbots and virtual assistants to resolve customer queries and manage account requests.	Reduce operational costs and enhance customer experience with instant support.
Anti-Money Laundering (AML)	Monitor transactions for suspicious patterns to detect and prevent money laundering activities.	Ensures compliance with regulations and mitigates financial crimes.
Loan Application Assistance	Automate the loan application process by collecting data, verifying documents, and providing updates.	Accelerates the approval process and enhances the user experience.
Regulatory Compliance Reporting	Automate compliance checks and reporting processes to meet regulatory requirements.	Reduces manual effort, ensures accuracy, and avoids legal penalties.
Market Sentiment Analysis	Analyze news, social media, and market data to gauge sentiment and its impact on stock prices.	Aid in informed trading and investment decisions.
Financial Forecasting	Predict revenues, expenses, and market trends based on historical data and market analysis.	Enables strategic planning and resource allocation.
Customer Churn Prediction	Identify patterns in customer behavior to predict dissatisfaction or potential account closures.	Helps retain customers and implement proactive engagement strategies.
Chatbots for Internal Operations	AI-powered chatbots assist employees with policy clarifications, HR queries, or system troubleshooting.	It improves operational efficiency and reduces dependency on manual support.

Table 11.6: *Banking and Finance Use Cases Using Azure OpenAI*

Education Domain Use Cases Using Azure OpenAI

AOAI provides transformative capabilities that enhance learning, streamline administrative processes, and improve accessibility in education. Institutions can deliver personalized, innovative, and efficient education solutions by integrating advanced AI models with Azure's secure and scalable ecosystem.

AOAI Services bring powerful language models, such as GPT-4, GPT-3.5, Codex (OpenAI), and DALL-E (OpenAI) to the education sector, enabling innovative solutions that enhance learning experiences, streamline administrative tasks, and support educators and students alike.

AI-powered tutors and chatbots leverage Azure AI and OpenAI's capabilities to create scalable, secure, and efficient systems that cater to users' educational and support needs. They enhance user experiences by leveraging Azure AI services such as Cognitive Search, OpenAI, and Bot Service, enabling real-time responses and personalized support.

Knowledge Base and Information Retrieval Systems: These AI-driven solutions are designed to organize, manage, and retrieve information efficiently. By leveraging advanced AI models, such as Azure OpenAI and tools such as Azure Cognitive Search, they enhance user experiences with semantic understanding and natural language processing. They are widely used in educational and enterprise solutions, training, and providing instant answers. These systems also support multilingual capabilities, ensuring global accessibility and inclusivity.

Key Benefits

- **Efficient Search**: Azure Cognitive Search ensures users can quickly retrieve accurate and relevant information. Chatbots, powered by Azure Bot Service and OpenAI provide users with round-the-clock assistance.
- **Semantic Understanding**: Natural language processing via Azure OpenAI improves search accuracy by understanding context and intent.
- **Scalable Data Management**: Azure Blob Storage and Data Lake efficiently handle large volumes of structured and unstructured data, automating routine queries, freeing up educators and administrators for more complex tasks.
- **Accessibility**: Multilingual capabilities make information accessible to global audiences, and conversational interfaces improve student and user interaction with services.

Architectural Design and Development: Knowledge Base and Information Retrieval Using Azure Ecosystem

High-Level Architecture Design: The architecture includes layers such as Data Collection (Azure Blob Storage and Azure Event Hubs) for capturing raw information, Data Processing (Azure Databricks and Azure Text Analytics) for preparing data, and Knowledge Base Creation (Azure Cognitive Search) for indexing and organizing content. AI/ML Integration with Azure OpenAI and Bot Services powers natural language understanding and conversational interactions, while Visualization Layers (Power BI) provide insights. With robust security via Azure Active Directory and Key Vault, this ecosystem ensures efficient information retrieval, real-time interaction, and seamless user experiences across domains such as education, customer support, and enterprise operations.

Architecture Layers: To attain the maximum benefits, we must maintain the minimum requirements of the following layers while constructing this proposed tool.

Table 11.7 shows the different layers of the proposed implementation, describing each layer and recommending Azure components.

Layer	Description	Azure Components
Data Collection Layer	Collects FAQs, documents, and user queries from multiple sources for knowledge base creation.	- Azure Blob Storage - Azure Cognitive Search
Data Processing Layer	Processes and normalizes text for indexing and retrieval.	- Azure Databricks - Azure Text Analytics
Knowledge Base Creation	Structures and indexes data to create a searchable knowledge base.	- Azure Cognitive Search
AI/ML Model Integration	Leverages AI models for advanced natural language understanding and chatbot functionality.	- Azure OpenAI - Azure Machine Learning
Decision-Making Layer	Provides relevant answers, recommendations, and conversational responses.	- Azure Logic Apps - Azure Functions
User Interaction Layer	Enables interaction through web apps, mobile apps, or voice assistants.	- Azure Bot Service - Azure Communication Services

Visualization Layer	Offers analytics and insights on user queries and system performance.	- Power BI
Security and Compliance Layer	Ensures data security, privacy, and regulatory compliance.	- Azure Active Directory - Azure Key Vault - Azure Security Centre

Table 11.7: *Architectural Layers for Knowledge Base and Information Retrieval*

Figure 11.5 shows Microsoft Azure, an architectural design and development environment for the banking and financial industry. *Table* 11.7 describes each layer's functionality, and its implementation is elaborated using Python code.

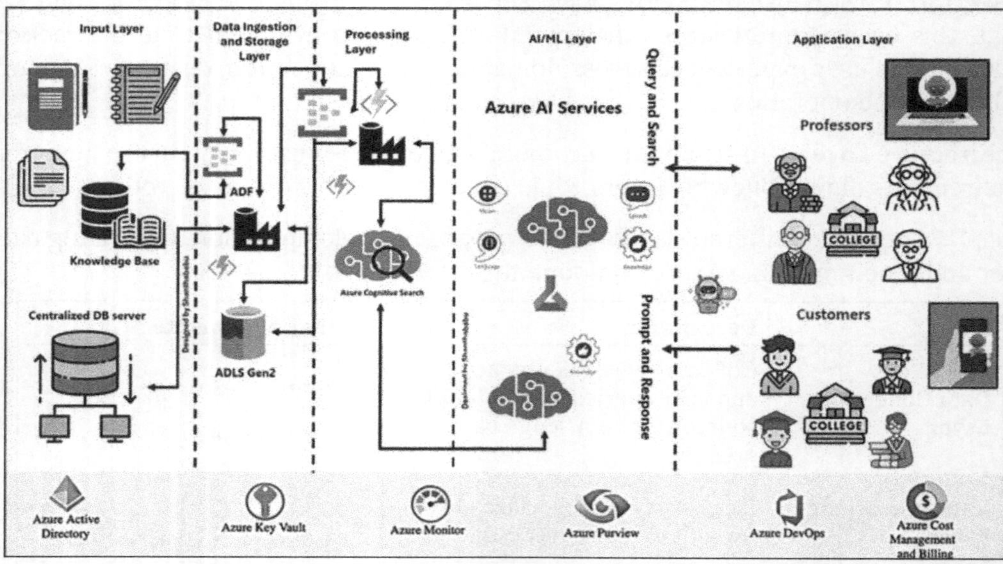

Figure 11.5: *Microsoft Azure; Architectural Design and Development Environment for Education Domain*

Python Code for Knowledge Base and Information Retrieval Implementation

Let us implement the knowledge base and information retrieval system using the Azure ecosystem, Python libraries, and Azure SDKs across different layers.

```
print("###################")
print("    Install required Azure SDKs      ")
print("###################")

#pip install azure-ai-text analytics
#pip install azure-cognitiveservices-search-knowledge
```

```
#pip install azure-eventhub
#pip install azure-storage-blob
#pip install azure-botbuilder

print("################")
print("Import all required libraries ")
print("################")

from azure.storage.blob import BlobServiceClient
from azure.ai.textanalytics import TextAnalyticsClient
from azure.cognitiveservices.search.knowledge.qnamaker import QnAMaker-
Client
from azure.core.credentials import AzureKeyCredential
from azure.eventhub import EventHubConsumerClient
from azure.ai.formrecognizer import DocumentAnalysisClient
from azure.identity import DefaultAzureCredential

import json
import random

print("######################")
print("Add all required environment variables")
print("######################")

BLOB_CONNECTION_STRING = "your_blob_connection_string"
BLOB_CONTAINER_NAME = "knowledge-base"
TEXT_ANALYTICS_ENDPOINT = "your_text_analytics_endpoint"
TEXT_ANALYTICS_KEY = "your_text_analytics_key"
QNA_ENDPOINT = "your_qna_endpoint"
QNA_KEY = "your_qna_key"
EVENT_HUB_CONNECTION_STRING = "your_event_hub_connection_string"
EVENT_HUB_NAME = "knowledge-hub"

print("###################")
print("   Layer 1: Data Collection Layer     ")
print("###################")
def upload_to_blob():
    """
    Uploads documents to Azure Blob Storage for Knowledge Base creation.
    """
    blob_service_client = BlobServiceClient.from_connection_string(BLOB_
CONNECTION_STRING)
    container_client = blob_service_client.get_container_client(BLOB_
CONTAINER_NAME)

    # Example document
    document = {
```

```
        "id": "101",
        "question": "What is AI?",
        "answer": "AI stands for Artificial Intelligence, which is the
simulation of human intelligence in machines."
    }

    blob_client = container_client.get_blob_client("knowledge_base.
json")
    blob_client.upload_blob(json.dumps(document), overwrite=True)
    print("Knowledge Base uploaded to Blob Storage.")

print("###################")
print("  # Layer 2: Data Processing Layer")
print("###################")

def process_documents():
    """
    Processes uploaded documents using Azure Text Analytics.
    """
    text_client = TextAnalyticsClient(endpoint=TEXT_ANALYTICS_ENDPOINT,
credential=AzureKeyCredential(TEXT_ANALYTICS_KEY))
    document = "Artificial Intelligence is revolutionizing industries."

    # Perform sentiment analysis
    response = text_client.analyze_sentiment(documents=[document])[0]
    print(f"Document Sentiment: {response.sentiment}")


print("######################")
print("     Layer 3: Knowledge Base Creation        ")
print("######################")

def create_knowledge_base():
    """
    Creates a searchable knowledge base using Azure QnA Maker.
    """
    qna_client = QnAMakerClient(endpoint=QNA_ENDPOINT, creden-
tials=AzureKeyCredential(QNA_KEY))
    knowledge_data = [
        {
            "id": 1,
            "questions": ["What is machine learning?", "Define ML."],
            "answer": "Machine learning is a subset of AI that enables
machines to learn from data."
        }
    ]
    print("Knowledge Base Created:", knowledge_data)
```

```
print("########################")
print("        Layer 4: AI-Powered Interaction        ")
print("########################")

def chatbot_interaction():
    """
    Simulates an AI-Powered Tutor/Chatbot using Azure Bot Service.
    """
    user_query = "What is AI?"
    # Fetch from the knowledge base (simulated for simplicity)
    knowledge_base = {
        "What is AI?": "AI stands for Artificial Intelligence, which
simulates human intelligence in machines."
    }

    response = knowledge_base.get(user_query, "Sorry, I don't have an
answer for that.")
    print(f"User Query: {user_query}")
    print(f"Chatbot Response: {response}")

print("########################")
print("            Layer 5: Visualization Layer               ")
print("########################")

def generate_dashboard():
    """
    Generates a dashboard summary (simulated).
    """
    data = [
        {"question": "What is AI?", "hits": 25},
        {"question": "What is ML?", "hits": 18},
    ]
    print("Knowledge Base Usage Dashboard:")
    for entry in data:
        print(f"Question: {entry['question']} | Hits: {entry['hits']}")

print("########################")
print("        Layer 6: Security and Compliance        ")
print("########################")

def ensure_compliance():
    """
    Ensures secure access using Azure Active Directory and Key Vault.
    """
    print("Enforcing data security with Azure AD and Key Vault...")
```

```
    # Simulated security setup
    print("Data encrypted and access restricted.")

print("###############")
print("        Main Workflow             ")
print("###############")



def main():
    print("Starting Knowledge Base and AI-Powered Tutor Workflow...")

    # Execute each layer
    upload_to_blob()            # Layer 1: Data Collection
    process_documents()         # Layer 2: Data Processing
    create_knowledge_base()     # Layer 3: Knowledge Base Creation
    chatbot_interaction()       # Layer 4: AI Interaction
    generate_dashboard()        # Layer 5: Visualization
    ensure_compliance()         # Layer 6: Security

    print("Workflow Completed.")

if __name__ == "__main__":
    main()
```

Table 11.8 shows other critical use cases and their benefits.

Use Case	Description	Benefits
Content Generation and Summarization	Generates lesson plans, lecture notes, and summarizations of articles or research papers.	- Assists in high-quality content creation. - Simplifies complex information. - Supports differentiated instruction.
Language Translation and Support	Translates educational materials and assists in foreign language learning.	- Facilitates global collaboration. - Supports bilingual programs. - Enhances cultural understanding.
Predictive Analytics for Student Performance	Predicts academic risks and suggests personalized resources for improvement.	- Enables proactive support. - Enhances decision-making. - Improves academic outcomes.

Curriculum Development	Aligns content with standards and identifies content gaps.	- Maintains relevance and rigor. - Streamlines curriculum design. - Supports continuous improvement.
Administrative Task Automation	Automate routine communications and scheduling tasks.	- Reduces administrative burden. - Increases process efficiency. - Frees educators from teaching tasks.
Plagiarism Detection and Academic Integrity	Identifies content similarities and educates on ethical research practices.	- Ensures fairness. - Protects institutional reputation. - Educated on proper citations.
Virtual Classrooms and Interactive Learning	Develops interactive modules and facilitates live Q&A sessions.	- Enhances engagement. - Supports active learning. - Provides instant clarification.
Exam Preparation and Study Aids	Creates practice tests and study guides for assessments.	- Helps students prepare effectively. - Identifies weak areas. - Reduces test anxiety.

Table 11.8: *Educational Use Cases Using Azure OpenAI*

Conclusion

This chapter provides a detailed discussion on Azure OpenAI solutions for business benefits across industries such as Retail, Healthcare, Finance, Education, Manufacturing, Media and Entertainment, Logistics and Transportation, and Energy and Utilities.

We explored specific use cases within these industries and their implementation in terms of architectural design and development using the Azure Ecosystem for healthcare, manufacturing, banking and finance, and education industries, along with Python code.

Index

P

R

S

T

V